ELUSIVE UNION

ELUSIVE UNION:

THE PROCESS OF ECONOMIC AND MONETARY UNION IN EUROPE

Kenneth Dyson

Longman
London and New York

Longman Group Limited,
Longman House, Burnt Mill,
Harlow, Essex CM20 2JE, England
and Associated Companies throughout the World.

*Published in the United States of America
by Longman Publishing, New York*

First published 1994

ISBN 0 582 25132 X CSD
ISBN 0 582 25131 1 PPR

British Library Cataloguing-in-Publication Data
A catalogue record for this book is
available from the British Library

Library of Congress Cataloging-in-Publication Data
Dyson, Kenneth H. F.
    Elusive union : the process of economic- and monetary union in
Europe / Kenneth Dyson.
      p. cm.
    Includes bibliographical references and index.
    ISBN 0-582-25132-X : £40.00. -- ISBN 0-582-25131-1 : £17.99
    1. Monetary unions--Europe. 2. Currency question--Europe.
3. Monetary policy--Europe. 4. Treaty on European Union (1992)
5. Europe--Economic integration. I. Title.
HG3942.8.D97   1994
332.4 '94--dc20

94-19952
CIP

Set by 7 in 9.5 Times
Produced by Longman Singapore Publishers (Pte) Ltd.
Printed in Singapore

For Ann, Charles and Thomas

CONTENTS

PREFACE

This is not another book about the costs and benefits of the European Monetary System (EMS) and of the transition to Economic and Monetary Union (EMU). Such books are appropriately the provenance of economists; and economists have already generated a large and impressive literature on this topic. Economists have also by no means restricted themselves to technical arguments about transaction costs, the pros and cons of devaluation, the values of external exchange-rate discipline and central bank independence in curbing inflation, and the advantages of EC-wide coordination in macro-economic policy. Policy advocacy has been a strong and persistent theme in their work, leaving the reader often unsure where the main direction of influence lies: from economic evidence to advocacy, or from advocacy to the marshalling of technical argument. The normative and empirical is impressively intertwined. Indeed, as we shall see in this book, economic belief – or rather the prevalence of certain beliefs – is crucial to any explanation of the process by which the EC was propelled towards ever closer monetary integration from the late 1970s onwards. Economists have, therefore, been far from disinterested spectators of the EMS and EMU policy process. They have been a key part of it, providing reasons to act in particular ways.

In this book we are concerned with a different type of question from that asked by the economist: with the policy process by which the movement towards closer monetary integration, and the still very uncertain objective of EMU, has been shaped and guided. How might this process be described, and how might its emergence and development be explained? Part of the explanation lies in identifying which actors have agenda-setting and veto power within this EC policy process and the kinds of bargaining relations in which they are organized. *Who* controls the writing of the 'rules of the game' in European monetary integration and unification? What are the corporate self-interests of the leading policy actors and the public interests with which they identify themselves?

But we must also focus on *why* the actors with this power chose, at a particular time, to propel the EC in the direction that they did. This question directs our attention to sources of structural power over policy, to the dynamics of change in the international political economy represented, for instance, by financial markets and by currency relationships. It also leads us to consider the beliefs that underpin policy, including those of the economists writing and talking so prolifically about the EMS and EMU – notably the power of 'sound money' ideas. In this context we need, in addition, to take account of the impact of the specific institutional characteristics of the EC, notably its 'two-level' policy process, on the values, norms and learning patterns of the policy actors involved in the EMS and EMU.

In addition to the questions of who is powerful and why, we need to ask *how* the

ix

'rules of the game' are applied and develop. This question invites us to reflect on the relationship between structural power and the bargaining relations and 'rules of the game' that comprise the EMS and EMU policy process: with, on the one hand, different sources of structural power providing the framework for the policy process and invading its functioning, but, on the other, the constituent bargaining relations and rules of the game having their own dynamics, rooted in such factors as the interaction of corporate self-interests. No one who reads this book can fail to be impressed by the contrast in European monetary integration between the leaps forward in 1978–79 and 1987–91 and the crab-like movements that followed; between the self-confidence of the EMS and EMU policy process between 1988 and 1992 and its subsequent crisis-ridden, beleaguered and defensive character.

The central argument is that the EMS and EMU policy process is best understood as composed of a distinct set of interdependent bargaining relations and rules of the game, embedded in a framework of structures that they have a limited, and fluctuating, capacity to influence. Accordingly, the task is to map out the different sources of structural power in the international political economy and elucidate their nature: world currency relations, financial markets, monetary policy ideas, economic 'fundamentals' and trade interdependence – and to unpack the various bargaining relations that comprise the policy sector and show how they function and how they relate to each other and to the rules of the game.

A work of this type creates big personal debts for its author. I cannot repay all the debts that I owe for the book, not least when many of those who have spoken to me at length would not welcome too close an association with a book that dealt with a policy process of which they were a continuing and intimate part. Within this severe constraint I can at least acknowledge some of these debts. Among the many academics and officials from whose conversation on European integration I have benefited a special place goes to my colleagues Kevin Featherstone, Jeff Harrop, George Michalopoulos and Murray Milgate. Not least, they gave the first draft of the manuscript a close reading and made dozens of valuable suggestions.

A particular debt is also due to the Economic and Social Research Council (ESRC) which awarded a research grant on the *Dynamics of European Monetary Integration*. The ESRC is to be thanked and congratulated for recognizing that politics might be more than a secondary, 'down-stream' dimension of European monetary integration and deserved investigation in its own right. This book is in effect one of two results of that project. The other – a book co-authored with Kevin Featherstone – focuses on the interaction of national actors with the EC, offering a comparative account of national policies on the EMS and EMU. A weakness of the present book is that, though identifying the importance of national–EC bargaining in the 'two-level' policy process, and in particular of the bargaining relationship between the German federal government and the Bundesbank, it has less to say on the details of these relationships. This neglect stems in part from the focus on the level of EC institutions in this book and in part from the fact that the next book is designed as complementary in exploring these relationships in more detail.

To no one is my obligation greater than to my wife, Ann. She provided laughter, distraction and protection whilst I laboured writing the manuscript during a short, intensive sabbatical. In such a context there was never a danger that the EMS and

EMU would make our house a succession of crises, and there was the occasional declaration of a moratorium on writing, by no means always welcome at the time but nonetheless of inestimable value in regaining perspective. My son Thomas remained wonderfully unimpressed by the endeavour, whilst Charles was as ever a source of inspiration and pleasure. The merciful gift that my family bestowed on me was a lack of interest in the EMS and EMU.

To those who facilitated my sabbatical leave special thanks are due: to Kevin Featherstone, who covered so much of my postgraduate teaching, and to Colin Mellors, who took over my share of responsibility for the university's European Briefing Unit and for PICKUP Europe. My secretary, Jean Davison, practised her cheerful, efficient magic to make sure that I had time to write.

It should be emphasized that I have sought to limit the scope of the inquiry by not delving deeply into the important economic debate about the substantive pros and cons of EMU or about whether market failure or government failure explains international monetary cooperation. My interest is not in whether the leading actors had good reasons or incentives for what they did. This limitation reflects in part my own limitations as a political scientist with too general a competence in economics to confidently investigate the intrinsic merits of specialist arguments for and against EMU. It also stems from the focus on the dynamics of the policy process and on the degree of, and reasons for, variability in monetary cooperation and integration. The reasons for action are taken at face value. What is more important to my purpose is to identify why at certain stages certain external pressures, beliefs and actors have proved more important than others, and how and why the policy process has changed. As will become clearer in the text, I am concerned to restore political reasons for support for, or rejection of, EMU to their proper place in explaining its momentum and the constraints on its progress.

Yet anyone who has worked on so important a subject as the EMS and EMU cannot avoid coming to some independent judgements and in the process disagreeing with respected colleagues in one's field. Most fundamentally of all, I believe that the EMS and EMU policy process places the most daunting choice about strategies for European integration that the EC has faced, with potentially formidable consequences. That policy process, and the Treaty on European Union which it created, opted for the high-risk political strategy of the eventual 'big bang' of a single European currency. In effect, it had become the victim of a narrow conceptualization of money as essentially an economic and technical phenomenon. The neglect of the cultural and political dimension of money was in part apparent in the marginalization of policy approaches that treat EMU as an evolutionary learning process for the public – via the creation of an additional parallel currency – about the practical value of moving to a single currency. EMU as embodied in the Treaty on European Union is the triumph of the technical rationalism of officials and economists over the value of practical experience as a vehicle for 'ever closer union', and, as such, risks damaging rather than furthering the cause that it seeks to promote. There was no proper debate about how EMU could build on demonstrating its practical value in the daily lives of European citizens and thereby acquire a broadening political constituency of support. Unfortunately, and here was the real tragedy of EMU, evolutionary approaches to EMU represented a high-risk economic strategy, for reasons spelt out in chapter 1. In other words, the risks – in the one case political and, in the other, economic – seemed inordinately high in whichever strategic direction one looked.

The mechanistic approach to EMU was also apparent in a second sense: in the lack of awareness of the historical relationship between political union and monetary union and of the need to root effective monetary policy in a strong political infrastructure, not least to provide the protective constitutional framework of democratic legitimacy that such policy requires. EMU required the solid basis of a European citizenry accustomed to widespread European-wide political as well as economic transactions. In the absence of a supportive framework of EC political institutions, and an engaged citizenry, EMU constituted a high-risk approach in a constitutional sense too.

The daunting strategic dilemmas of the EMU project – constitutional, political and economic – serve as a reminder that money, the central object of the policy process, has an irreducibly Janus-faced nature, the one face economic and technical, the other cultural and political. Ultimately, the problems of EMU are two-sided. That is why it has proved impossible to construct a plausible unified theory of EMU as a guide to political action; why the elaboration of a technical economic approach to EMU has stimulated political and constitutional argument; and why the final solution of EMU remains so elusive. What needs to be explained is why the EMU policy process ignored the importance of this duality.

I also find myself in what is probably a minority position in emphasizing the role of institutional dynamics, not so much the substantive rules of the game that are designed to guide action but the complex 'gamesmanship' of the EC's unique 'two-level' policy process. This gamesmanship helps to bestow on the policy process its distinctive character: its sense of being locked into a trajectory of development, yet being hedged in by changing domestic political constraints. Furthermore, I believe that the randomness and irrationality of the foreign exchange markets have been on the whole exaggerated, and that, though their structural power is fundamental, it is not the only source of power around. On the continuum between policy and markets that distinguishes the actors involved in EMU the central banks retain a strategic 'gatekeeper' role. With the liberation of the financial markets their power has by no means been eclipsed. Its basis and the manner of its exercise have had to be reconsidered. Also, Council bargaining within the EC and Franco-German bargaining have their own dynamics and contribution to make to the way that EMU evolves.

There are many other places in this book where I have disagreed with colleagues and friends, and no one should read my appreciation of them as their certification of my arguments.

Finally, it should be noted that the time period of writing the book means that I do not refer to the European Union. In writing about EMU beyond November 1993, the month of final ratification of the Treaty on European Union, it will of course be necessary to refer to the EU; though the fact that EMU falls in the EC pillar of the union means that the term EC will continue to apply in respect of EMU.

Kenneth Dyson
University of Bradford
15 December 1993

LIST OF ABBREVIATIONS

AMUE	Association for the Monetary Union of Europe
BDI	Bundesverband der Deutschen Industrie
BIS	Bank for International Settlements
CAP	Common Agricultural Policy
CBI	Confederation of British Industry
CEPR	Centre for Economic Policy Research
CEPS	Centre for European Policy Studies
CERES	Centre d'Etudes de Recherches et d'Education Socialistes
DG2	Directorate General 2 (Economic and Financial Affairs)
DG5	Directorate General 5 (Social Affairs)
DM	Deutschmark (D-Mark)
EC	European Community
ECA	European Cooperation Administration
ECB	European Central Bank
ECJ	European Court of Justice
ECOFIN	Council of Economic and Finance Ministers
ECSC	European Coal and Steel Community
ECU	European Currency Unit
EEC	European Economic Community
EFTA	European Free Trade Area
EMCF	European Monetary Cooperation Fund
EMF	European Monetary Fund
EMI	European Monetary Institute
EMS	European Monetary System
EMU	Economic and Monetary Union
EPU	European Payments Union
ERM	Exchange Rate Mechanism
ERP	European Recovery Programme (Marshall Plan)
ESCB	European System of Central Banks
EU	European Union
EUA	European Unit of Account
FEER	fundamental equilibrium exchange rates
G-5	Group of Five (USA, Japan, Germany, France, UK)
G-7	Group of Seven (USA, Japan, Germany, France, UK, Italy, Canada)
G-10	Group of Ten (USA, Japan, Germany, France, UK, Italy, Canada, Belgium, the Netherlands, Sweden)
GATT	General Agreement on Tariffs and Trade

GDP	Gross Domestic Product
GNP	Gross National Product
IEPA	Intra-European Payments Agreement
IGC	intergovernmental conference
IMF	International Monetary Fund
IT	Information technology
MCA	monetary compensation amount
MTFA	medium-term financial assistance
OEEC	Organization for European Economic Cooperation
SDRs	Special Drawing Rights
SME	Small and medium-sized enterprises
SPD	Social Democratic Party (Germany)
STMS	short-term monetary support
UDF	Union pour la démocratie française
UNICE	Union of the confederations of Industry and Employers of Europe
UNRRA	United Nations Relief and Recovery Agency

Chapter 1

INTRODUCTION

There is something in the nature of historical events which twists the course of history in a direction that no man ever intended.

(Herbert Butterfield, *The Englishman and his History* (1944: 103))

On 25 January 1989 Nigel Lawson, the British Chancellor of the Exchequer and the longest-serving and most experienced Treasury minister since David Lloyd George, delivered a characteristically strong-worded and forthright speech to the Royal Institute of International Affairs in London. Fixing his sights firmly on the active role of Jacques Delors as President of the European Commission, who was then chairing the Delors Committee for the Study of Economic and Monetary Union, he asserted:

It is clear that Economic and Monetary Union implies nothing less than European Government – albeit a federal one – and political union: the United States of Europe. This is simply not on the agenda now, nor will it be for the foreseeable future.

But Economic and Monetary Union (EMU) was most certainly on the agenda; stage one was agreed at the Madrid summit of the next summer, and EMU was to be at the heart of the Treaty on European Union negotiated in 1991. Where he was more accurate was in his view that EMU would be 'deeply divisive'. To quote him again:

Certainly, neither the British Government nor the British Parliament is prepared to accept the further Treaty amendments which the President of the Commission evidently envisages.

The progress of EMU after Lawson's speech illustrates just how complex its dynamics have proved, capable of ready control by neither a British Chancellor and his party nor indeed a president of the Commission who was deeply committed to its cause. Since then, and indeed earlier, EMU has remained at the very heart of European integration: for some, like Lawson, 'a damaging diversion', for others, like Delors and the German Chancellor Helmut Kohl, an indispensable pillar of the emerging European union.

Although a highly technical issue and therefore understood by few, EMU was to go on to provide the highest political drama. At the Madrid European Council in 1989, an isolated British Prime Minister faced the prospect of the resignations of both her Foreign Secretary and her Chancellor in the absence of a clearer and more positive approach to British membership of the Exchange Rate Mechanism (ERM), the key component of the European Monetary System (EMS); conflict about whether and when Britain should join the ERM was at the root of Lawson's resignation in 1989 – he had supported this policy since 1985; whilst the Rome European Council of 1990, and its specific commitments to the details of the two intergovernmental conferences (IGCs) on monetary union and on political union, was to form the direct background

1

to Margaret Thatcher's loss of the Conservative Party leadership. The high political drama of Britain's role in European monetary integration was further highlighted on 'Black Wednesday', 16 September 1992, when huge speculative pressures drove Britain back outside the ERM and undermined the key element of Treasury policy and of the new Prime Minister John Major's attempt to put Britain back at 'the centre of Europe' where it 'belonged'.

Outside Britain, EMU became embroiled in the high drama of the Danish and French referenda of 1992 on the Treaty on European Union. For French opponents of the so-called Maastricht Treaty, who managed to attract nearly 49 per cent of the vote, the single currency represented a German-dominated Europe. Such, however, was not the perception in Germany itself. Chancellor Kohl found himself confronted by widespread public hostility to the loss of the D-Mark and the threat that the extreme right-wing Republican Party would present itself in the 1994 federal and state elections as the 'D-Mark' party and exploit fear and hostility in a populist and electorally successful manner. In the two countries that represented the core bilateral bargaining relationship in the EC – France and Germany – domestic electoral pressures served to undermine the capability of government leaders to prioritize and push through EMU. And to the electoral dramas were added the crises of the ERM itself, in September 1992 and July/August 1993. Delors's battle for fast European monetary integration appeared to have been lost; the scenario for EMU pushed to 1999 and beyond into the twenty-first century.

Technical complexity, high political drama but, above all, an essential component of uncontrollability by any one political actor were the hallmarks of the EMU saga. In fact (as we shall see) only one actor was really in a position to attempt to impose its will with some prospect of success: the German Bundesbank. When we consider bargaining power within European monetary integration, it is very clear indeed that at no stage, not even between October 1990 and September 1992 when Britain was in the ERM, had the British government anything remotely like the power of the Bundesbank or of the French government.

Control and contention in the EMS and EMU policy process

As we shall see throughout this book, the problem of control was a key distinguishing characteristic of the EMS and EMU policy process. Even those actors to which a structural power might be attributed – the foreign exchange market operators and the Bundesbank – had no more than a vicarious sense of short-term control. Within the policy process the institutional events that mattered most were the bi-weekly meetings of the Bundesbank council, not the weekly meetings of the EC Commission or the monthly meetings of the EC's economic and finance ministers in ECOFIN (the Council of Economic and Finance Ministers). The Bundesbank was the institution that was most respected and feared: by other actors in the policy process and by the markets. It had the power of leadership in the policy process that came from its credibility as the authority presiding over the ERM's 'anchor' currency, defined as the currency with the best record on inflation and the only one never to be devalued within the ERM. But that record, and hence its leadership role, was put in question by mounting counter-pressures, particularly the inflationary momentum created by the aftermath of German unification in 1990 and the shift from surplus to deficit in Germany's current account. It was also a market power that was offset by the traditional postwar tendency of the German federal government to defer to the French government within the core political bargaining relations at the heart of European integration. Though prepared to be robust and resolute in the pursuit of its domestic statutory duty to 'safeguard the currency', in this way precipitating the ERM crisis of July 1993, the Bundesbank was coy about being seen as too assertive on the politically sensitive issue of realignment of currencies within the ERM. Foreign exchange market operators, presiding over huge daily turnovers that dwarfed the reserves of central banks, had also an enormous potential power, and could, as in September 1992 and July 1993, exert that power to enormous effect. But (as we shall see in chapter 8) within a range defined by a broad consistency of exchange rates with economic 'fundamentals', they were hesitant and at best divided, and susceptible to 'steering' by the monetary authorities.

Here then is a policy process in which credibility and reputation are at the very heart of power. They are earned by EC monetary authorities and economic policy makers through long, hard work and lost quickly through negligence, mistake or plain bad luck – as the crises of September 1992 and July/August 1993 demonstrated. Accordingly, the climate of the EMS and EMU policy process for European monetary integration tends to be one of beleaguered and anxious actors: often firm in their convictions (as we shall see in chapter 7, about the importance of 'sound money'); even more uncertain about prospects and the outcomes of their decisions; and certainly not sensing that they control the policy process.

The Janus-faced nature of money

A central reason for the problems of control that beset European monetary integration is the degree of contention that surrounds money: never mind the more specific disputes about the respective values of national policy autonomy and European policy coordination (chapter 6), the 'sound money' emphasis on the EMS and EMU as instruments of 'disinflation' (chapter 7), the question of whether the EC (or some part of it) is an 'optimum currency area' (chapter 7), the appropriate 'convergence' criteria and whether economic convergence should precede EMU or will follow it (chapter 8), and the functioning of the foreign exchange markets (chapter 8).

Fundamentally, the roots of the contention surrounding monetary policy lie in the fact that money has an irreducibly Janus-faced nature: an economic and technical face and a cultural and political face. One face, the economic and technical, has dominated the EMS and EMU policy process, with far-reaching implications. Money's value to those who use it in financial and other markets is above all *economic and technical*. It is a unit of account – expressing the relative value of different commodities; a store of value – a means by which today's wealth can be retained for future use; and a medium of exchange – a means of avoiding the constraints of bilateral bartering in buying and selling. In all these respects money serves to reduce transaction costs, the costs of doing business, and thereby enhances efficiency. Economists are, accordingly, at one in believing that 'money matters': that changes in the money stock – of notes, coins and deposits – have a significant effect on the working of the economy. They are also disposed to argue about money in utilitarian terms: to recognize that some ('hard') currencies perform the functions of money better than others ('soft' currencies); and that the geographic areas of states, even the United States, may not necessarily be optimum areas for currency unions. The technical attributes of a currency are clearly very important. The basis of its worth is defined by its performance; and trust, based on performance, is a vital factor in financial markets.

Beyond that basic level of technical consensus, there is major contention among economists about just how changes in money are related to changes in the economy. Monetarists emphasize long-term relationships, arguing that changes in the amount of money affect 'money things', such as prices, rather than 'real things', like output and employment. These 'real things' are determined by 'supply-side' factors operating in the labour and goods markets, in particular productivity, production costs and profits. By contrast, Keynesians stress the way in which, in the short run, changes in the money stock affect output and employment rather than prices. The mechanism is provided by the way in which changes in money alter prices of financial assets, like bonds, and their yields; thereby affecting interest rates, and thus shifting aggregate demand as consumption and investment behaviour adjusts. At the very least, there is a broad consensus around the lowest common denominator that money stock plays a permissive role in the process of inflation. And, therefore, as inflation has become an overriding priority of policy since the early 1970s, control of the money stock has assumed a new importance. But the dispute still hinges on how changes in the money stock are related to changes in macro-economic aggregates and on what is the direction of causation. As we shall see in chapter 7, the Treaty on European Union goes beyond a lowest-common-denominator position in this economic and technical debate. It is, at a substantive technical level, not a broad framework that can easily evolve and adapt but a contentious document whose detailed provisions threaten a dangerous rigidity – and (as the next paragraph but one shows) in one key sense more contentious than the 'hard' ERM on which it builds (and which is explained in chapter 6).

Again at a technical level there are arguments among economists and officials about the goals of monetary policy. The main problem at this level has been the potential policy conflict between 'external' exchange-rate stability and 'internal' price stability. For French policy actors exchange-rate stability has traditionally had an overriding importance (with, for instance, France seeking to lead the Gold Bloc in the 1930s after the departure of Britain and the United States from the gold standard); for German policy actors the ravages of inflation in the 1920s and 1940s have bestowed a primacy on domestic stability. Pursuit of domestic stability may in turn lead to a concern for international monetary coordination. But that concern focuses more on the coordination of economic policies in order to reduce the costs of economic interdependence: namely, that the external effects of other states' pursuit of their domestic economic priorities may be negative for price stability in one's own country. Historically, therefore, German policy actors have given greater emphasis to EC coordination of economic policies than to exchange-rate coordination. The dynamics of the EMS and EMU policy process are locked into the potential incompatibility of internal and external stability and in particular the calculation of the German Bundesbank – as the central bank presiding over the 'anchor' currency – that intervention to support external stability is compatible with its statutory obligation to maintain price stability. Just how bitter the resulting contention can be was illustrated by the ERM crisis of July 1993.

The economic argument about the proper purpose of money is even more fundamental. One argument is that the main purpose of money is to have a stable worth so that it remains generally acceptable and is thus able to perform its technical functions efficiently. This stability can be achieved by maintaining its price against something, whether gold, the US dollar or the D-Mark, and varying its supply. The alternative view is to see money as mainly a lubricant for economic activity. Credit creation requires that the authorities print a generous supply of money and let the markets value the result. As we shall see in the historical chapters (2–5) of this volume, the first of these arguments has dominated European monetary policies, except for short periods, since the late nineteenth century, giving an important degree of underlying stability.

The other face of money is its fundamentally *political and cultural nature*: a facet that tends to be neglected by those who operate in markets (and value it in utilitarian terms) and by monetary economists. Money is political in being a key expression of statehood. States express their sovereignty in issuing and managing their own currency. Hence central banks have a symbolic as well as technical importance, often expressed in their imposing facades – for instance, those of the Bank of England and the Banque de France. Money is also cultural; it expresses nationhood and identity. Currencies like the French franc, the pound sterling and the US dollar possess an emotional and psychological power. They are 'stores of value' in more than an economic sense, with coins often representing elaborate national mythologies. Correspondingly, a single European currency is evocative of a claim to 'statehood' and 'common culture': a claim that was always bound to be disputed, but a dispute for which EC policy makers – blinkered by the technical economics of EMU and the technocratic policy style of the EC Commission – were unprepared.

The importance of attitudes towards money was evocatively captured in an editorial of the French newspaper *Le Monde* on 31 July 1993. In the dramatic context of the ERM crisis the editorial asserted: 'The war between the international speculators and the central banks is a shock between two cultures. . . . One is inspired by liberal Anglo-Saxon ideologies, the other by a more continental, *dirigiste*, ideal.' Developing this view, it argued that, in the Anglo-Saxon view, currencies were simply commodities; the corollary was a tendency to see them in market terms and to embrace floating exchange rates. By contrast, for French policy makers a currency was a 'measure of value within a nation' and was, accordingly, not like other goods. Currencies must, in this view, be assured a certain stability. The contrast is unquestionably overdrawn. Successive British Chancellors of the Exchequer – Howe, Lawson and Major – had argued the virtues of stable exchange rates; since the late 1970s policies of market liberalization had significantly undermined the edifice of French *dirigisme*; whilst *dirigisme* was most certainly not an ideology embraced by the German economics establishment, though the Bundesbank took a cautious approach to market liberalization and treated the financial markets with a degree of scepticism. But what does emerge is the continuing role of long-standing cultural reflexes, even when policy and market conditions have changed.

In adopting a strategy for achieving a single European currency, the Treaty on European Union did more than enter into a contentious technical debate about its merits and the appropriate context of economic policy for its implementation. The treaty's vulnerability came from its own historical roots in an essentially functional view of the value of a single currency. It was based on a provisional victory in an ongoing economic debate: a debate that was in some respects less kind to the treaty after 1991. But the treaty did not possess the strength that comes from a broad-scale mobilization of public opinion and commitment across the EC. In consequence, its implementation – and not just its problematic ratification in 1992–3 – was likely to be deeply compromised by political contention. And that contention promised to be most serious not in the two major EC states with the most historically symbolic currencies, Britain and France, but in Germany – a country with a very functional approach to its currency, yet a currency whose technical success – compared to that of the pound sterling – had made its symbolic importance politically potent.

It was, interestingly, French policy makers – going back to President Valéry Giscard d'Estaing at the birth of the EMS – who were quickest to link European monetary integration to their national tradition. The European Currency Unit (ECU) bore a convenient relationship to France's historic currency of the *ancien régime*, the *écu*, part of the past glory of France, with its symbolism of the shield contained in its decoration with a fleur-de-lys. Whether regarded as an example of political damage-limitation or of cultural imperialism, the attempt to label the single European currency as the '*écu*' was prescient in identifying a key problem of European monetary integration. Unfortunately, that problem was not just French and therefore not conducive to an easy solution: it was reflected in German insistence that the original draft of the Treaty on European Union be corrected by changing references to '*écu*' to ECU.

The problem with the debate about the EMS and EMU and the policy process underlying the Treaty on European Union is that it avoided or evaded the essential ambiguity of money – as a technical commodity and as a political and cultural phenomenon. The elite-level policy debate became trapped in a one-dimensional view, rooted in the belief that it was possible, desirable and sufficient to base the EMS and EMU on technical ideas of 'sound money' and to encapsulate those ideas in a treaty. Adherence to such a view contained both economic and political risks: of a growing detachment from the realities of changing economic 'fundamentals', notably expressed in rising unemployment and lost output, and fast-acting financial markets (as chapter 8 illustrates); of an underestimation of the role of demand management; and of an inability to accommodate political and cultural concerns. The dynamic processes of European monetary integration and union could be contained within the parameters provided by the Treaty on European Union only at great risk to the whole union project.

Here was a vision of union, but one that was overschematic in its insistence on a set of economic ideas about 'sound money' whose limitations and potential costs were not recognized and allowance made for them. The EC policy process was committed to a restrictive pattern of argument, based on too limited and inflexible a set of economic policy instruments to deal with the basic untidiness of economic development – and too little sensitivity to the political costs of being seen to impose one particular type of monetary union without giving adequate opportunity for political attitudes and interests to evolve towards commitment. There was a reluctance to recognize that the appropriate counterpart in EMU to the complex underlying dynamics of financial markets was a legal framework that enabled EMU but contained sufficient flexibility at the level of means, for instance on realignments of currencies; and that a precondition of union was an opportunity for the European publics to learn more about how monetary union can practically benefit them. In political terms EMU remained too much an abstraction, lacking the roots in daily life and affective identification that national currencies continued to possess.

Competing models of monetary union

A central feature of the debate about EMU was the absence of a broad and intensive political debate about alternative types of monetary union. The debate that took place was very much internal to the EC's policy process, involving the technical committees and ECOFIN: more influenced by technical calculations of the economic costs and benefits of rival forms of monetary union than by a political analysis of their costs and benefits. What was striking about the debate was the dismissal of two evolutionary models of monetary union: the 'currency competition' or ' free intercirculation' union, and the 'parallel currency' union. Paradoxically, political argument played an important role in marginalizing discussion about them; they were proposed by the British government, and the British government was not seen as serious about union but rather as seeking to divert the EC from this aim. They were deeply compromised by this political association. The models of a 'currency competition' and a 'parallel currency' union were also (as we shall see) seriously deficient in economic terms. But, leaving aside the all-too-important political question of who proposed them, their political rationale as instruments for achieving EMU was a good deal stronger than recognized in EC debate. It was stronger than that of the model of monetary union embraced in the treaty.

In a competing currency union the currencies of the member states would freely circulate throughout the union. Competition would drive persistently deviant currencies out of circulation. As no government would risk the political cost of its currency disappearing, there would be a political incentive to convergent monetary policies – to common rates of interest and inflation and thus to *de facto* fixed exchange rates. A parallel currency union would also enable states to retain their currencies. The difference would lie in the creation of a parallel currency to circulate alongside the national currencies and of a union monetary authority with responsibility for issuing the parallel currency. Hence each member state's currency would be competing with the parallel currency.

Instead of an evolutionary path that would have allowed publics and customers to learn about the tangible advantages of monetary union, the EC opted in the Treaty on European Union for currency union. The ultimate goal was to be not just an exchange rate union, based on an evolution of the ERM into an 'irrevocable fixity' of intra-union exchange rates: for, by its very nature, the concept of irrevocably fixed exchange rates could never be fully credible – under extreme pressure governments could always opt to alter rates or secede from the union; and the triangle of fixed exchange rates, freedom of movement of capital and national monetary autonomy was (as we shall see in chapter 5) dangerously unstable. A fully credible and therefore maximally efficient monetary union would, accordingly, involve the adoption of a single currency, managed by a single union monetary authority. But, however well buttressed by economic analysis and argument, the currency union model adopted in the Treaty on European Union lacked the political strengths of an evolutionary approach that would enable the practical benefits of union to be learned in a tangible way by an ever-widening public.

The central problem was that the high-risk political strategy of currency union was more than outweighed by the high-risk economic strategy of the competing currency and the parallel currency approaches. This high-risk nature of the evolutionary approach rested on the empirical historical evidence that, even with hyperinflations, there has been precious little replacement of national currencies by other low-inflation currencies; that the transaction costs of switching to another currency remain high; and that, following Gresham's law, consumers will prefer to use the weak currency in transactions – reversing the anticipated outcome of the strategy.[1] In short, in the absence of a European citizenry accustomed to European-wide political and economic transactions and recognizing its established practical benefits, there were only high-risk strategies – and serious dangers of failure for the integration process. Monetary unification before economic and political unification posed historical hazards, as we shall see in chapter 2.

The dynamics of Economic and Monetary Union

It is these elements of contention in the story of the EMS and EMU, coupled with its essential uncontrollability by individual actors, that make it so complex and dynamic a policy process. This process appears to be unpredictable, though by no means random. There is certainly a great measure of contingency at work, of complexity of underlying structure and of evolutionary learning on the part of the many actors involved. Yet patterns of interaction can be discerned in the policy process: patterns that are provided by institutional 'rules of the game', and the principle of a 'zone of monetary stability in Europe', and by the basic structures that enclose and bear down on the policy process, notably world currency relations, financial markets, monetary policy ideas, trade interdependence and economic 'fundamentals'. The possibility that beneath the complexity of EMU resides a deeper simplicity means that EMU offers great potential for developing theory about the EC policy process. Developing a single, all-embracing theory is, however, another matter: the EMS and EMU are too ensnared within contingency, too prone to migrate to the edge of chaos, for this purpose. Here is no simple, repetitive and passive order, offering up the massive stability on which grand theories of linear and orderly change can securely rest.

The dynamics of EMU are at once political and economic. In quite properly stressing the fundamentally political nature of European monetary integration, one should beware of the limitations of narrowly political science theories of European

---

1. For a review of the problems of the parallel currency approach see P. De Grauwe, *The Economics of Monetary Integration* (Oxford: Oxford University Press, 1992), pp. 144–51.

integration. European monetary integration is given much of its distinctive character by the fact that it is embedded deeply in the inherent asymmetries of international monetary politics and the dynamics of change in the international political economy, not least in financial markets and economic fundamentals. As chapter 8 emphasizes, the financial markets, economic fundamentals and trade interdependence are simply too intrusive to be taken as static or given background factors. Turmoil in the ERM in September and November 1992, after five years of stability without currency realignments, followed by the momentous crisis of July 1993, underlined this point all too well. The Treaty on European Union embodied an essentially technocratic political vision of the path to EMU, in the form of an orderly, schematic progression of the member states together towards a single European currency. In this new legal context, the 'hard' ERM was reconceived as the 'glide-path' to EMU. Yet, the most rudimentary historical analysis of past attempts to manage exchange rates reveals that currencies do not 'glide' for long periods without encountering turbulence in foreign exchange markets, sometimes so profound that – to continue the aeronautical metaphor – flight may have to be cancelled. Financial markets have their own patterns of order whose outcomes can appear random and indeterminate to EC policy makers who inhabit a very different pattern of order.

The dynamism of EMU, and the difficulty of abridging it in a single general theory, are reflected in the complexity of values with which it is necessarily associated. Here we return to the Treaty on European Union of 1992. This treaty gave constitutional expression to what had already *de facto* established itself as the *modus operandi* of the EMS. EMU was interpreted as revolving round the core value of order, expressed in the evolution of the ERM into a quasi-fixed exchange-rate regime and into a disciplinary mechanism for domestic stabilization. Priority was accordingly given in the treaty to price stability, 'guaranteed' by an independent European Central Bank. In short, the treaty embodied a specific and, as events were to illuminate, a by no means uncontroversial economic theory, and one that owed its victory to monetary policy leadership by the German Bundesbank.

But practical economic policy making in the real, partisan world of EC liberal democracies involves more complex and difficult 'trade-offs' of values. The argument that price stability is the long-term precondition for economic growth does not readily displace the argument that its short-term costs are too high and have unduly adverse long-term consequences for output and employment. EMU was in practice always going to be a field of contention among values: between price stability and economic growth, expressed as higher output and employment, and between these values and equity in the distribution of economic costs and benefits – *cui bono*. The Treaty on European Union gave some recognition to this issue of 'trade-offs'. Thus it established linkage between the disciplines of 'convergence' to qualify for EMU and the new EC 'Cohesion Fund' and reform of the Structural Funds to redistribute resources to those EC states that were likely to find adjustment especially painful. The issue of 'trade-offs' with economic growth did not, however, properly surface at the highest EC levels till November–December 1992 with the birth of the so-called 'growth initiative'.

In the mean time, EMU had become identified with the hard ERM, and both with a mechanism for rapid disinflation, the consequences of which some states could not realistically tolerate. It had in effect evolved as a rigid framework of deflation rather than as a complex and subtle mechanism for reconciling the conflicting requirements of stability, growth and equity. Such a mechanism presupposed political union, and the Treaty on European Union had made little progress in that direction. Against this background of a narrowly conceived EMU and its rigid policy implications, perceptions of EMU altered dramatically, involving revised and divided views about the fundamental problems that EMU should address. In turn, financial markets began to question the solidity of the whole enterprise: first in the ERM crisis of September 1992 and then in the big crisis of July 1993.[2]

Theme and arguments: the hollow core in the policy process

The central theme of this book is the complex interaction between the structural dynamics of the international political economy and the internal dynamics of the EMS and EMU policy process, with its various interdependent bargaining relationships and its institutional rules of the game. It deals with what the story of the EMS and EMU tells us about the nature of the EC's policy process – its essentially hollow core in the case of EMU – and about the implications of that policy process for European integration. The EMS and EMU policy process is in many respects *sui generis*. It focuses on the complex interactions of a narrow and privileged set of actors: EC heads of state and government; EC finance ministers and their officials; EC central bank governors and officials; EC Commission and Council of Ministers' officials; professional economists; and foreign exchange market operators. How do they interact, and what are the external pressures shaping that interaction?

European integration is understood as not only bound by structural dynamics but also a dynamic process in which actors, governmental and non-governmental, calculate and reconsider the balance of advantage: between, on the one hand, the loss of national decision-making authority and freedom of manoeuvre in domestic policy consequent on integration and, on the other, the public-interest and corporate gains that may follow from merging or transferring such authority to EC institutions. Conversely, when the consequences of integration are perceived to be policy outcomes that bear down negatively on the interests of national actors, they will seek to retrieve some of that authority: as the British and Italian governments did in September 1992, and most of the other ERM members by moving to very wide fluctuation bands in August 1993. In short, the degree of integration in the EMS and EMU policy process rests fundamentally on rational calculation and voluntarism, which in turn is continuously responding to changing circumstances amd policy outcomes, and to the opportunities and threats that they embody. As chapter 9 argues, the will and capability of the actors in the policy process are central to the dynamics of integration. Actors are continually reassessing their own will and capability to integrate, and that of their partners; and, in that field of forces, who is likely to be able to take a leadership role on a given issue at a given time. They are not simply driven by a blind logic. Thus the sudden rise of EMU on the political agenda of the EC in the late 1980s rested on the will of certain states, led by France, to escape from the constraints imposed by the asymmetrical nature of the EMS, along with their recognition that any reform of the EMS would

2. P. Temperton (ed.) *The European Currency Crisis* (London: Probus Europe, 1993).

have to be on terms acceptable to the country with the anchor currency of the ERM, Germany. The initiative also reflected a perception of greater EC capability in monetary policy management engendered by the new stability achieved within the ERM from 1987 onwards. This combination of new-found confidence with German policy leadership was embodied in the 'constitutionalization' of EMU in the Treaty on European Union.

On the other hand, from summer 1992 onwards the progress of European monetary integration revealed the limits of the capability to integrate of EC institutions, like the EC Monetary Committee, and of member state governments. The ERM crises of September 1992 and July 1993 were catalysts for a reappraisal of attitudes. With increasing perceptions of their more limited capability the will of the actors involved came also in question: especially in the case of the British government whose reservations about EMU were more than confirmed when the pound exited from the ERM. In the process the observer was reminded that, in bold efforts to integrate Europe, the problems of treaty-making are secondary to those of implementation. As we shall see in the historical chapters (2–5), study of past efforts at exchange-rate management and monetary union underline the centrality of problems of implementation in the practice of policy and the underlying fragility of international monetary cooperation. By emphasizing the problems of putting the EMS and EMU into effect, we are made to recognize that the process of EMU is an essentially fragile one of continuing negotiation.

Policy actors

The first argument of this book is that the nature of the European integration process in general, and of the EMS and EMU policy process in particular, is shaped by the *will and the capability of the central actors involved*, and that no single theory of integration is able to bring into play in an adequate and yet parsimonious way the key factors that influence that will and capability. This argument is returned to in chapter 9. It follows that a prime requirement in any analysis of the integration process is to identify the main actors in the specific sector under investigation and to map the nature of their relationships with each other.

Yet it is important to present not only the actors but also the scene. The book argues that the nature of the will and the degree of capability of the actors involved in EMU is shaped by four important factors. First, the actors are immersed in a unique *'two-level' game in the policy process*, the subject of chapters 6 and 9. This policy process embodies two distinct and potentially conflicting political pressures on these actors: the incentives to be reliable, honest and respected negotiators at the EC level, and to develop and sustain political support, ideological and electoral, at the domestic level. Sensitivity to this two-level policy process draws attention to an important aspect of the dynamics of EMU. What gives EMU its peculiar dynamic is the pressure on the actors from the demands of repeated bargaining across a widening scope of issues in a continuous fashion through time. The effects on the value system of negotiators and their incentive to contribute to agreement is appreciable. A focus on EC policy making and implementation as a two-level process also alerts us to the role of domestic political and cultural constraints and to the inherent problems of reconciling EC and domestic pressures within the policy process. In effect, EMU takes on its character from the fact that actors are simultaneously engaged in two 'games', with two different audiences, both of which have to be satisfied if the 'super-game' is to be continued. And the super-game is too important to be put at risk: sunk commitments are too high, socializing and learning effects too powerful, knock-on effects too widespread. So, however fundamentally fragile the EC policy process remains in the absence of political union, its institutional structures have major effects on the way in which bargaining is conducted – and distinguish it from the conduct of bargaining in either a national context or the context of other international organizations.

Second, the *prevalence of certain beliefs* among key actors strengthened their will to pursue EMU in the late 1980s and helped propel the process forward. Economic beliefs have been undoubtedly influential and include:

1   the belief that exchange rate volatility, especially when short term and unexpected, increases transaction costs for exporters and thus prevents the EC maximizing the trade benefits from a single European market
2   the belief that, in an increasingly interdependent world economy, EC currencies are more vulnerable to adverse consequences from changes in global currency relations and that control can be restored only through monetary union
3   the belief that devaluation induces higher expectations of inflation among domestic actors and hence offers no long-term advantages in improving competitiveness
4   the belief that the EMS, and more especially an EMU of irrevocably locked exchange rates and then of a single currency managed by an independent European central bank wedded to price stability, would act as a discipline on national monetary policy that would otherwise be inflationary
5   the belief that monetary union would induce a more effective coordination of macro-economic policies.

To these beliefs must be added political beliefs, among which was the commitment of some leading actors – notably Christian Democratic political leaders and French Socialist leaders – to the ideal of European political union. More crucial still, and far more important than any economic belief, was the political belief, embodied most potently in French policy on EMU, that national interests could be protected only if economic power was wrested from Germany. German unification served to further elevate the importance of EMU as a means to ensure the 'Europeanization' of the augmented power of an already economically strong Germany. To this could be added the neo-mercantilist belief, most strongly espoused by French policy makers, that EMU was an essential basis for more effectively influencing global monetary developments. In these respects the pursuit of power has been fundamental to the dynamics of the EMS and EMU policy process.

A third factor that influences the will and the capability of the actors concerned, and the dynamics and essential fragility of the policy process, is *changing structural conditions in the international political economy*. What gives the EMS and EMU policy process its *sui generis* character as a sector of European integration is the fact that it is enmeshed with different forms of structural power. Financial markets have (as we shall see in chapter 8) their own distinctiveness that inexorably impregnates the conduct of policy. The location of power in the policy process is also deeply affected by the inherent asymmetry of currency relations in an exchange rate system like the EMS; policy leadership gravitates to the anchor currency. Just as fundamentally, changing economic fundamentals affect market perceptions of currencies and parities. At the very heart of the EMS and EMU policy process are the problems of matching parities and markets to the perception that fundamentals have changed or are changing: reflected in a decline of competitiveness or in the inappropriateness of policy to a country's position in the economic cycle. These and other structural factors – like trade interdependence and 'sound money' policy ideas – provide the framework within which actors manoeuvre. They shape the agenda and power relationships and, most notably in times of ERM crisis, they intrude deeply into the policy process.

Fourth, the will and capability to sustain the pursuit of EMU is governed by the *experience with the economic and monetary policies associated with the EMS and EMU*. This experience has involved the relationship between policies for monetary integration and changes in output and employment and in inflation. In this sense the EMS and EMU are a continuing learning process, as new information about economic performance is fed into market calculations and central bank strategy and tactics. The imputed relationship between past and present policies and what is actually happening or likely to happen to economic performance is critical to the credibility of those policies and to their prospects. A loss of credibility in this way was responsible for the demise of the hard ERM in August 1993.

Bargaining relations

The second main argument of this book is that, in common with other sectors of European integration, the EMS and EMU policy process can be fully appreciated only as a set of *interlocking bargaining relations* that, in turn, interact with certain key *rules of the game*. The first task is to identify the key bargains and rules of the game in European monetary integration and the power relationships that they express: Council bargaining, for instance in ECOFIN; Franco-German bargaining; EC–central bank bargaining; bargaining between the German federal government and the Bundesbank; and bargaining between the EC and the foreign exchange markets.

We have noted how the will and capability of actors is shaped by the rules of the game. In focusing on bargaining relations, we should not forget that the rules of the game, formal and informal, are important in their own right. They may reflect power relations, but they also channel and constrain the nature and direction of change in the EMS and EMU policy process. From the rules of the game, and the bargains on which they rest, one gains an idea of the character of the EMS and EMU policy process in a substantive sense: its core values (a 'zone of monetary stability in Europe'), basic rules and norms, and not least its highly technical nature (see chapter 6). Also, as we shall have occasion to remind ourselves, the EC's peculiar two-level policy process has enormous implications: sustaining collective action, yet giving the EMS and EMU policy process a brittle and fragile nature – in short bestowing on European union its elusive quality.

In addition to identifying the key bargaining relations in the EMS policy process it is important to identify more precisely how the interests in these bargaining relations interlock with each other. What, to use the language of political scientists, is the 'governance structure' of the EMS and EMU policy process?[3] In the case of the EMS and EMU the governance structure has three essential characteristics:

1   a dimension of coordination in the form of hierarchy at the domestic level, evident in the relations of finance ministries to 'their' central banks (Germany is historically a major exception), and affecting the mutual relations of finance ministers in ECOFIN and central bankers in the Committee of Central Bank Governors – in effect efforts of governments to maximize domestic policy control by exerting hierarchical authority induce a limited and defensive mode of coordination within EMU, affecting Council bargaining and EC–central bank bargaining (see chapter 6)

2   a dimension of coordination by and through financial markets, structured by informal technical trading rules and yet imparting a volatility to the dynamics of EMU as 'news' impacts on trading (see chapter 8) – the way that market operators perceive economic fundamentals matters crucially

3   a dimension of coordination via policy 'networks' as autonomous actors at the EC level seek out appropriate ways in which to structure and manage their mutual dependence. These networks can take on different configurations: of pluralism, clientelism and corporatism. Pluralist policy networks are characterized by internal fragmentation, competition and the complex mutual adjustment of interests; in them no single body monopolizes representation. Clientelist policy networks involve a strong 'patron' and a number of weak 'clients', with clients competing for favours and privileges from the patron in return for services rendered. Corporatist policy networks involve a monopoly of representation for one or more non-competitive bodies, which as a consequence are able to monitor and control the behaviour of their members and achieve privileged and stable access and influence over policy.

Intergovernmental bargaining and trade-offs of national interests within the framework of the EC Council of Ministers and the European Council give an inevitable and, for the EC, characteristic pluralism to Council bargaining. But, behind the birth and development of the EMS and of EMU were the two technical committees, the EC Monetary Committee and the Committee of Central Bank Governors. Both were instruments through which the central bankers were coopted into the very heart of the policy process. This cooptation was also evident in the composition and work of the Delors Committee and in the way in which the two technical committees flanked the work of the Intergovernmental Conference on EMU. Here was unquestionably a corporatist policy network at work, ensuring that the EMS and EMU were based on an exchange process between EC institutions and central bankers. The Committee of Central Bank Governors was recognized as an official intermediary organization with the monetary sector, understood to be able to 'speak' with authority on its behalf and to be indispensable in monitoring and steering the financial markets.

3.   See e.g. V. Schneider, 'The Structure of Policy Networks', *European Journal of Political Research* 21 (1992), pp. 109–29.

In consequence, looked at as a whole, the EMU policy process walks a tightrope: unsettled by the pressures consequent on hierarchical coordination at the national level and on the operation of the financial markets and yet steadied by a corporatist policy network. This sense of clinging to a tightrope is reinforced when we consider the pluralist policy networks of Council bargaining, suspended as it is between domestic economic and political priorities and the desire to maximize the advantages of cooperation, especially of trade interdependence. The resulting picture is of a hollow core at the heart of the EMU policy process: no single actor is capable on a continuing basis of being the policy-brokering centre, promoting compromise or imposing settlements.[4]

Structural power

The third main argument pursued in the book is that the EMS and EMU policy process – its actors, bargaining relations and rules of the game – is embedded in *sources of structural power in the international political economy*. As we shall see, the external dimension of the dynamics of change in the international political economy has been decisively important: in, for instance, giving birth to the European Payments Union (EPU), to the Werner Report of 1970 on EMU, to the negotiation of the EMS in 1978–9 and to the Delors Report and its aftermath. In each of these cases inadequacies in the functioning of the international political economy created incentives to restore internal and external stability by pursuing European monetary integration: respectively the payments crisis facing western Europe, the malfunctioning of the 'Bretton Woods system', the US dollar crisis, and the asymmetrical functioning of the EMS. Equally, the dynamics of change in the international political economy have been important in creating problems of implementation, in revealing the vulnerability of the EMS and EMU.

Structural power is the power to shape the framework within which the bargaining relations that comprise the EMS and EMU policy process take place, in particular the rules of the game and the opportunities for, and constraints on, policy development.[5] It is the power to determine the conditions on which the EMS and EMU policy process operates. In the context of the EMS and EMU structural power has several sources:

1   control over the anchor currency, lending an inherent asymmetry to bargaining relations within the EMS and EMU policy process and expressed in the policy leadership role of the German Bundesbank
2   control over the supply and movement of capital, in this case lending power to the foreign exchange market operators
3   control expressed in the dominant role of a currency or pair of currencies in total foreign exchange transactions, in particular the role and impact of US dollar movements and US dollar/D-Mark transactions
4   control over the key ideas and beliefs informing the policy process, in particular

---

4. J. Heinz, E. Laumann, R. Nelson and R. Salisbury, *The Hollow Core: Private Interests in National Policy Making* (Cambridge, Mass.: Harvard University Press, 1993).
5. S. Strange, *States and Markets* (London: Pinter, 1988), pp. 24–9.

the 'capture' of the EMS policy process by economic ideas of 'sound money' and the prevalence of political beliefs about European union

5   control over the terms of interdependence in the trade of goods and services, which in western Europe increasingly focuses on the EC institutions and the big multinational corporations

6   control over 'economic fundamentals', which means the appropriateness of national and EC policies for economic competitiveness and the position of one or more countries in the economic cycle

7   control over the economic cycle, with the nature of bargaining relations in the EMS and EMU policy process being deeply affected by whether the economic cycle is in its 'upward' or its 'downward' phase

8   control over security, notably embodied in the role of Council bargaining relations and of Franco-German bargaining relations in offering protection against the re-emergence of historic threats, as exemplified by memories of the cumulative misery of two successive world wars in 1914–18 and 1939–45.

One of the most distinctive sources of structural power derives from the basic fact that, short of political and monetary union, EC monetary integration is inherently asymmetric and therefore problematic. It is inherently asymmetric in the sense that power gravitates inexorably to the monetary authority that presides over the currency that acts as the anchor to which all other currencies peg. That authority sets the standards for the achievement of internal and external stability; it has the capacity to manipulate the incentives for other states to cooperate.[6] Its monetary power derives from several sources: the size of its economy; its performance as exemplified by figures on inflation, budget deficit, external balance and productivity growth; and its monetary capability, defined by reference to such factors as its currency reserves and the significance of its currency for international trade and for central bank reserves.[7] On these measures the German Bundesbank emerges as the 'natural' monetary policy leader in the EMS and EMU policy process. Its structural power (or that of a substitute, should the basis of its monetary power decline as a consequence of German unification) is an essential precondition of the stability of the EMS; its willingness to concede that power, or share that power, a precondition for EMU.

But, in focusing on one type of structural power, even that of the foreign exchange markets, one forgets how the interaction of these different sources of structural power generates a sense and reality of lack of control by any one actor – in other words, the hollow core in the EMU policy process. One is tempted to single out certain bargaining relations as taking on a greater relative importance in this context of structural power: in particular that between the EC and the foreign exchange markets and that between the German federal government and the Bundesbank. One notes also how 'sound money' ideas have endowed the central bankers with greater relative power in EC bargaining. Power remains, nevertheless, elusive. The structural power of

6. M. Kaelberer, 'Werner Report, EMS and EMU: Problems and Prospects of European Monetary Cooperation', paper delivered to the Third Biennial International Conference of the European Community Studies Association, May 1993, p. 12.

7. For measures of monetary power see J. Odell, *US International Monetary Policy: Markets, Power and Ideas as Sources of Change* (Princeton, NJ: Princeton University Press, 1982).

the anchor currency is vulnerable to changes in economic fundamentals: a phenomenon that emerged in 1993. Control over the economic cycle is beyond the reach of any single corporate actor. Also, monetary power is not the only source of power in EC policy, particularly in Council bargaining and Franco-German bargaining. In these bargaining relations control over security has been a fundamental consideration. Both sets of relations have been valued as means to preserve security; that valuation was increased by historical experience and memories of mutually disastrous European wars. A critical factor in the Franco-German bargaining relationship has been the willingness of the German federal government to defer to the French government at critical junctures or, if incapable of doing so because of Bundesbank obduracy, to take later action to compensate the French government for loss or humiliation in the monetary sphere (as happened in 1969–70). The Franco-German bargaining relationship has proved an enduringly important element in the EMS and EMU policy process. In this context, and that of Council bargaining, the French government has been able to acquire an agenda-setting role that was not predictable from its monetary power.

What draws together the three arguments outlined above is the theme of the dynamic nature of the EMS and EMU policy process: a process whose policy outcomes and end effects cannot be fully predicted but which is neither random nor chaotic in its development. Broad parameters of change are provided by the nature of the structures that govern policy development, by the interlocking bargaining relations that comprise the policy process and by the 'two-level' policy process and the rules of the game. And yet, in the face of such complexity, the policy process is impregnated by contingency. This sense of complexity and contingency is strengthened by the dimension of voluntarism in the policy process that comes from the fact that, however formidable and intrusive the context of structural power, bargaining relations and the rules of the game, policy actors are ultimately making calculated choices. Their will and capability to pursue integration within the EMS and EMU policy process are in question.

In the dynamic approach advocated here the EMS and EMU policy process involves the interaction of three levels – the intrusive context of structural power, the constituent bargaining relations and rules of the game, and the rational actors who inhabit the process. Two behavioural assumptions underpin the approach: that actors are intendedly but only limitedly rational; and that they remain opportunistic but keen to seek protection from the hazards of opportunism. Both assumptions underline the circumscribed voluntarism of the policy process. Rationality is bounded in the face of the enormous complexity of structural change, the dynamics of bargaining relations and the constraints of the rules of the game. Indeed, in an important sense the institutional arrangements of the EC represent a complex set of mechanisms for helping actors to overcome some of the hazards of bounded rationality. By collective action in Council bargaining, and with the assistance of the EC Commission, they are better able to transcend the limitations imposed by the too narrow territorial terms, and too restricted resource base, of the modern European state. Even so, actors remain capable of defining their corporate self-interests and public interest in an individualist and idiosyncratic manner.

Opportunism cuts both ways. It creates an important degree of unreliability and indeterminacy in the EMS and EMU policy process. Member state governments have the potential to cut and run when short-term interests appear to conflict with European interests. The behaviour of the British government in deciding to exit from the ERM on 16 September 1992 was seen in just this way by some EC partners. On the other hand, as each is potentially the victim of opportunism by others, EMU is valued as a means of protecting against hazards of this type. The provisions of the Treaty on European Union on the move to stage three of EMU can be seen as an attempt, led by the French and Italian governments, to protect against the hazard of opportunism as governments later sought to renege on the commitment to EMU.

The EC's rules of the game serve, therefore, the dual purpose of helping to overcome the bounded rationality of actors and of protection against the hazards of opportunism. As we have seen, they can do so only imperfectly: in part because national actors remain opportunistic (the option of exit defines the fragility of the EMS and EMU policy process); and in part because the sheer complexity of structural power and the dynamics of bargaining relations threaten to overwhelm the capacity of actors, national or EC, to control policy.

Structure

The structure of this book is not built around an artificial and overschematic attempt to separate history and theory. Indeed, such intellectual rigidity would defeat a purpose of the book which is to show how each can beneficially influence the other. Each section is, however, connected by a unity of approach. The early chapters offer continuous narrative 'thickened' by analysis and argument – illustrating with historical examples and the postwar experience of European monetary cooperation and integration just how elusive union is likely to be. This approach involves switching the reader's attention from one episode in monetary cooperation and unification to another. The narrative method brings to the fore the way in which monetary cooperation and unification comprise a sequence of actions in time bounded by contingency. It illuminates the way in which the present-day policies are moulded by the past, and the nature of that moulding; and it uncovers the attempts of actors, often – indeed typically – fumbling and frustrated, to shape and control the future in a world of policy and markets so deeply swayed by the random tides of exigency. A picture emerges of the essentially fragile nature of international and European monetary cooperation and unification in the absence of a supportive infrastructure of political union.

Connecting these chapters is the argument that it is impossible to adequately understand the nature and development of European monetary cooperation and integration in the 1980s and 1990s without the narrative method. For the study of European monetary cooperation and integration must at heart be historical if it is to comprehend the dynamics of change at work and to see where monetary integration has come from and to where it is going. As the later chapters underline, however, the narrative method is not sufficient. European monetary integration must also be analysed and argued about in terms of how it relates to sources of structural power in the international political economy, to institutional rules of the game and to the nature of bargaining relationships. Social science draws our attention to the role of 'impersonal forces' and the possibility of arriving at a more structured understanding of monetary integration than narrative alone facilitates. But first we must come to grips with the dynamics of change.

Part One
HISTORICAL PERSPECTIVES

Chapter 2

LESSONS OF HISTORY (1)

Nineteenth-century currency unions, federal monetary unions, the gold standard and the 'Bretton Woods system'

The ERM is a modern-day gold standard with the D-Mark as the anchor.
(John Major, British Chancellor of the Exchequer, speech to IMF meeting in Washington, DC, September 1990)

A monetary union will prove permanent only if there is a dominant political will to take social measures to deal with the serious economic effects. . . . In the last resort, this calls for a political union too.
(Helmut Schlesinger, president of the German Bundesbank, speech in Rotterdam, November 1991)

A historical perspective is an indispensable starting-point in our attempt to understand the nature of European monetary integration and of the EMS and EMU as policy process. An obvious question concerns the extent to which past attempts at cooperative international monetary management and monetary unification provide insights into the way in which the EMS and EMU can be expected to function. With this question in mind this chapter focuses on the Latin Monetary Union of 1865, the German and United States' experiences of monetary union, the international gold standard, and the so-called 'Bretton Woods system'. In helping to disentangle the myths of the gold standard and of the 'Bretton Woods system' from the reality of how they actually functioned, this historical approach should sharpen our critical faculty when exploring postwar and contemporary policy processes underpinning European monetary integration and unification. It offers insight into the general factors that facilitate and retard cooperative international monetary management and monetary union.

Less controversial, but no less important than attempts to learn by generalization from history, is the importance of history in promoting our understanding of the present in the light of the past. The imprint of history is carried in the collective memory of institutions, like central banks and finance ministries. It is alive in the minds of monetary policy makers as they seek to draw lessons from past experience. In this respect cooperative international monetary management has always represented a learning process, adjusting to the experience of past policies and their legacies and relating them to new information. For good or ill in terms of the consequences, policy preferences and policy processes are immersed in historical reasoning. They can, accordingly, only be understood historically.

But it should not be thought that only some parts of history are relevant to current policy. No part of the historical record, for instance the Latin Monetary Union, is finally dead. For present policy, and the problems that it faces, helps us to rediscover and reinterpret the past; we learn about the past in the light of the present. That process of learning is in its own right a strong reason for re-examining the experience of the gold standard in its various forms and of the Bretton Woods system, and not least the Latin Monetary Union and the experience of federal states like Germany and the United States.

Finally, an historical perspective allows us to broach an issue that forms the core of chapter 6. We need to consider whether EMU is functioning as a 'self-reinforcing mechanism', locked into a path of development that is defined in historical terms. Alternatively, is it the creature of the contingencies of implementation? An historical account, as offered in this chapter and chapters 3–5, offers the prospect of new insights into this issue.

Putting monetary cooperation and unification into effect

This chapter argues that what unites past experiences of international monetary cooperation and unification with the period of the EMS and EMU is that their character and development have been shaped above all by the capacity of monetary policy actors – in particular of the actors responsible for the anchor currency – to deliver on their commitments. In developing this argument we are drawn to the theme of the will and capability of these actors. Monetary policy actors may be far from impotent: but neither do they bestride the money markets like a collosus. Their will has little more impact than their capability to give effect to it; that capability is deeply influenced (as we saw in chapter 1) by sources of structural power in the international political economy – by the anchor currency, financial markets, economic fundamentals, trade interdependence and monetary policy ideas – along with the rules of the game in monetary policy coordination. Perceptions of that capability feed back in the form of judgements, notably of foreign exchange market operators, about the real commitment of policy actors to monetary cooperation and integration. *Par suprem* international monetary cooperation depends on the credibility of public commitments to highly calculative, tough-minded and risk-conscious market operators. It is a continuing test of the will and capability of monetary authorities to operate a given set of rules of the game.

The nature of this test suggests that, once monetary cooperation has been negotiated, the main problem is putting into effect. The policy process of international monetary cooperation is, accordingly, one of the step-by-step implementation of a policy. Policy appears to evolve in an interactive and negotiated process, not least responding to structural change in the anchor currency, financial markets, economic fundamentals and economic ideas.[1] It involves conflicts about the goals of monetary

---

1. These ideas draw on the extensive implementation literature in the field of policy studies. Notable studies are: H. Wallace, 'Implementation across National Boundaries', in D. Lewis and H. Wallace (eds) *Policies into Practice: National and International Case Studies in Implementation* (London: Heinemann, 1984); H. Hyder, 'Implementation: The Evolutionary Model', in Lewis and Wallace (eds) *Policies into Practice: National and International Case Studies in Implementation*; J. Pressman and A. Wildavsky, *Implementation* (Berkeley, Calif.: University of California Press, 1973); S. Barrett and C. Fudge (eds) *Policy and Action: Essays on the Implementation of Public Policy* (London: Methuen, 1981); C.C. Hood, *The Limits of Administration* (London: John Wiley, 1976); A. Dunsire, *Implementation in a Bureaucracy* vol. 1 (Oxford: Martin Robertson, 1978); R. Mayntz, *Implementation*

policy action: in particular, between those – like the German Bundesbank – who prioritize internal stability and economic policy coordination and those – like the French Finance Ministry – who stress external stability by means of firmly pegged exchange rates. And, not least, policy cooperation raises the question of whether it continues to be in the self-interests of the anchor currency to support such cooperation or whether, as in Britain's exit from the gold standard in 1931, its exit from the system promises an enhanced capacity to achieve domestic economic priorities.

Certainly those who are seeking to put policy into effect remain important and, in formal terms, central. But power also resides with those on whom the effectiveness of action depends. In the monetary policy sector foreign exchange market operators have immense resources at their disposal; their perception of the economic fundamentals of participating currencies is critical; economists influence the climate of opinion about policy and hence its acceptability; and political leaders are responsive to diminishing political acceptability and loss of policy control. In consequence the self-interests of key actors may come into conflict with the rules of the game of monetary policy cooperation or at least with the way in which they are applied at a given time. Compliance cannot be assured; power has a tendency, in certain circumstances, to drift away from those in authority when they most need it.

In the context of such dependence on fast-moving financial markets, changing economic fundamentals and the anchor currency, timescale too is important. A system of international monetary cooperation, like the gold standard, may endure for some time. But it will inexorably be beset by the effects of mounting changes in the environment of its operation, coupled with the delays in negotiating change consequent on the multiplicity of participants with differing self-interests. The result is a sense of inertia in the face of growing problems. Policy instruments no longer seem to match the complexity of the monetary problems. Panic action is forced on governments; the monetary sector is remade from the bottom up. This brief scenario seems all too reminiscent not only of the gold standard and the Bretton Woods system but also of the EMS in 1992 and 1993. As this and later chapters demonstrate, putting monetary cooperation into practice has not been facilitated by a neat, clearly organized hierarchical form to the policy process. Hierarchical coordination and control is not a defining characteristic of international monetary policy cooperation; though EMU is designed to strengthen it.

Nineteenth-century European currency unions

The search for historical parallels to the EMS and EMU and for insight into problems of policy implementation takes us back to the nineteenth century – to initiatives for European monetary unions, to the creation of federal monetary unions, and to the gold standard. If the gold standard could be described as the high point of nineteenth-

---

politischer Programme. Empirischer Forschungsbericht (Königstein: Verlag Anton Hain, 1980); K. Hanf and F.W. Scharpf (eds) *Interorganizational Policy Making: Limits to Coordination and Central Control* (London and Beverly Hills, Calif.: Sage, 1978). For insights into the role of agency self-interest see A. Downs, *Inside Bureaucracy* (Boston, Mass.: Little, Brown, 1967).

century international monetary cooperation, extending well beyond Europe, it never really aspired to the ambition of creating a monetary union. That ambition reached its climax in nineteeth-century Europe in two main developments: the Latin Monetary Union and the Scandinavian Monetary Union.

Strikingly, the birth of the Latin Monetary Union in 1865 was an important catalyst for the International Monetary Conference of 1867, at which representatives from twenty countries met to consider the prospect for a global currency. Faced with the new challenge of a French-led monetary union, the eminent editor of *The Economist*, Walter Bagehot, wrote of the danger to Britain of being 'left out in the cold . . . before long all Europe, save England, will have one money'.[2] This comment, like other aspects of this period, has an intriguing parallel with the debate in Britain about EMU from 1988 onwards. In the 1860s arguments raged in the press and in political circles about the issue of British membership of the new monetary union. As in the 1990s, Britain stayed aloof.

The Monetary Conference of 1867 considered two central issues. The first issue was whether a global currency should be based on the gold standard or on a bi-metallic standard incorporating gold and silver. Britain and the United States were on the gold standard; France, and the Latin Monetary Union, were on a bi-metallic one. In order to avoid the problem of the shifting relative values of gold and silver under a bi-metallic system, the conference voted for the gold standard. It also opted for a transition period during which silver would be phased out. In fact, the decision did not bind governments and was not implemented. The Latin Monetary Union remained with its bi-metallic standard. The second issue was the choice of the unit of account, for instance, the sovereign, the franc or the dollar. Here the solution seemed to lie in aligning the gold content of the three main currencies. If each country minted the same weight coins, each currency could circulate in the other countries. Once again, nothing happened. Britain established a royal commission which recommended against a change in the weight of the sovereign; the US Congress never got beyond discussion of the gold content of the American half-eagle. A reminder of this episode is to be found in the British Museum in London: a specially minted coin which had 'ten pence' inscribed on one side and 'one franc' on the other. Again, with parallels post-1988, Britain proposed an alternative route to currency union, in the form of a new currency – the 'International' – to circulate alongside existing ones.[3]

More substantial in effect was the Latin Monetary Union.[4] It was created by a treaty of 23 December 1865, signed in Paris by ministers from Belgium, France and Switzerland. In contrast to the elaborate process that led to the Treaty on European Union of 1992, the establishment of the Latin Monetary Union took just five meetings and one month. The union also incorporated Italy, and in 1868 Greece joined. There were negotiations with Austria and with Spain. Eventually membership grew to 18

---

2. M. Perlman, 'In Search of Monetary Unions', LSE Financial Markets Group, Special Paper no. 39, 1991.
3. Perlman, 'In Search of Monetary Unions'.
4. H. Parker Willis, *A History of the Latin Monetary Union: A Study in International Monetary Action* (New York: Greenwood Press, 1968); R. Bartel, 'International Monetary Unions: The 19th Century Experience', *Journal of European Economic History* 3 (1974), pp. 689–704.

countries, though other countries accepted the gold franc and not the bi-metallic system as the basis of their coinage.

The four countries initially concerned formally agreed on a rate of exchange between gold and silver and to mint identical gold and silver coins and make each other's currency legal tender. Hence their currencies could circulate freely within the union. A date was also fixed for the withdrawal of old coins (for all except some small Swiss cantons 1 January 1869). In accordance with the tenets of strict monetary control, money supply was to be strictly regulated according to a country's population size. Governments were allowed to issue only six francs per head of population. Thus in 1865, France, with a population of almost 40 million, was allowed 239 million francs; Belgium, with only 5.24 million, was limited to 32 million francs; Switzerland, with 2.7 million, was restricted to 17 million francs. The Latin Monetary Union explains why a traveller with the 1878 edition of Baedeker's guide to Paris could read that 'The money of Belgium, Switzerland, Italy and Greece is the same as that of France'.

Through the Latin Monetary Union the other states were, in effect, linking with the French monetary system. Its formation reflected a combination of economic and political developments that centred on French national interests. At an economic level, by the early 1860s France, Belgium, Italy and Switzerland were already *de facto* in a currency union based on French coinage. The French franc, which had been established by Napoleon Bonaparte's Act of 1803, was a metric coin on a bi-metallic base. When Belgium achieved its independence, its franc was modelled on the French franc (1832). The reform of the chaotic Swiss coinage in 1850 was also based on the French franc. Since Piedmont had retained the franc (named the lira) from the Napoleonic occupation, Italy followed suit. French francs constituted a substantial component of the money supplies of these three states. What precipitated the 1865 treaty was the effects of new gold discoveries in North America and Australia on the French bi-metallic franc. As a consequence, France effectively shifted on to a gold standard, but it, and Belgium, found that inferior Italian and Swiss coins began to flow into their countries. This monetary chaos prompted the treaty of 1865. In part then a motive of protection from disruptive external change was at work in French policy. A similar type of motive appeared in French policy for EMU in 1988: in this case the potentially disruptive impact of capital liberalization on the capacity of the French government to manage the domestic economy.

Politically, French imperialist ambitions and worries about Prussian power were very important motives behind Latin Monetary Union. Emperor Napoleon III thought that French influence abroad would increase if the French monetary unit and French monetary policies could become the basis of a wider European arrangement. Here was also a potential rival to the rise of the Sterling Area, which mainly affected areas outside Europe. Again, a similar type of political motive underpinned French initiatives for EMU in 1988: to retrieve French influence and respect by transferring monetary power from Germany (in this case to the EC).

In practice, though the Latin Monetary Union survived, French ambitions for its role were thwarted by shifts of structural power in the international political economy. First, and of decisive consequence for modern Europe, France lost the Franco-Prussian War of 1870–1, its Emperor fleeing from the battlefield at Sedan. The newly united

Germany, augmented by reparations from France, assumed economic as well as military leadership of Europe and, consistent with its national interests, sought to promote the new Mark and undermine the Latin Monetary Union. Second, the Latin Monetary Union's bi-metallic standard was fatally weakened by a fall in the relative value of silver to gold; silver's supply increased after 1867, leaving large quantities of low-value silver coins in circulation. With sterling, based on the gold standard, becoming the dominant currency for international trade and the anchor currency, the Latin Monetary Union's claim to policy leadership languished. Several attempts were made by its members to shore up the structure, but in vain. In 1874 they limited the volume of silver coins; in 1878 silver was eventually given up; in 1885 a new treaty was ratified that cancelled the legal tender acceptance of 5 franc silver coins outside the minting country.

The bi-metallic standard endured as long as it did because of the corporate self-interests of the Banque de France and French financial leaders who had a profitable business in arbitrage between gold and silver that they were loath to forfeit. Once silver was abandoned in 1878, French self-interests were less engaged; hence this date is usually taken to represent the end of the Latin Monetary Union as any kind of potent force. In fact, it survived not only this event but also inflation among some of its members and even tariffs within the union until its formal end in March 1927. But the Latin Monetary Union's formal continuance for this period owed most to the simple practical fact that no country could afford to redeem its coins held by the others. Its lack of any practical importance was attributable not only to structural changes in the international political economy but also to the lack of institutional regulation of the total money supply: this feature enabled governments, like that of France after 1918, to solve their public finance problems by means of the inflationary printing of money.

The second main example of nineteenth-century currency union is provided by the Scandinavian Monetary Union.[5] It was established in the form of a complete gold standard currency union in a treaty of 18 December 1872, with Sweden and Denmark joining in 1873, Norway in 1875. Identical gold coins, the Scandinavian Krona (of 100 *ore*), circulated in all three countries. Also, the three central banks accepted each other's coins and notes as part of a clearing system that they operated; there was in effect a pooling of reserves, with the central banks opening credit lines for each other. A central bank agreement of the early 1880s eliminated gold as an international means of payment within the union. In these respects then the Scandinavian Monetary Union was considerably more advanced technically than the Latin Monetary Union. But it remained based on the political will of its members to cooperate, and that will depended on trust. Political problems of trust were to prove more important than economic in disrupting it. In 1905 Sweden cancelled its membership, following the separation of Norway from Sweden, only to resume the same form of cooperation with Denmark. The Scandinavian Monetary Union lasted until the First World War when different degrees of involvement in the war and national differences in handling the new international monetary problems unleashed by war undermined its functioning. It

5. L. Jonung, 'Swedish Experience under the Classical Gold Standard 1873–1914', in M.D. Bordo and A.J. Schwartz (eds) *A Retrospective on the Classical Gold Standard 1821–1931* (Chicago, University of Chicago Press, 1984).

had at least endured for over 40 years as a symbol of Scandinavian political solidarity. Not least, the Scandinavian Monetary Union represented an alternative to dependency on the power of larger neighbours whose policies were likely to be determined by reference to domestic concerns without any attention to their implications for Scandinavian countries.

The nineteenth-century European currency unions demonstrate clearly the importance of political motives in monetary union. There was either, as with the Latin Monetary Union, one dominant country with political ambitions or, in the case of the Scandinavian Monetary Union, a basis of political solidarity. In both cases importance was attached by policy leaders to unions of a manageable and controllable size and a politically sympathetic nature. Additionally, the catalyst of structural change in the international political economy was critical. A central motive was to retrieve some semblance of control over external events. Interdependency was important, as between the four countries of the Latin Monetary Union or the three of the Scandinavian Monetary Union. Countries had to be sensitive and vulnerable to each other's actions. But interdependency was not in itself sufficient.

What was lacking in these cases was a central institutional structure to assert common interests and to upgrade the role of common interests in negotiations. Negotiations did indeed take place, but there was no supranational dimension to this process. The competitive implications of exclusively domestic preoccupations were inadequately tempered by institutional mechanisms to foster policy coordination. In the case of the Latin Monetary Union there was no mechanism to enable the participating countries to consult and agree on coordinated action. In this respect the EMS and EMU differed in possessing a more solid institutional basis, though not necessarily one fully adequate to their purposes.

Political and monetary union: the cases of Germany and the United States

If some comfort can be drawn from comparing the institutional contexts of the EMS and EMU with nineteenth-century currency unions, a note of caution is introduced by the experience of monetary union in the two main federal systems: Germany and the United States.[6] The relevance of these experiences derives from the fact that the EC is seen by many as a prototype of a federal system. But (as we shall see) American and German experience suggests the prior importance of a framework of political union to support monetary union. If German monetary union suggests that a radical leap to monetary union can succeed, American experience shows how the transition from political union to monetary union can be difficult and protracted. Both federations had in any case the advantage of being relatively homogeneous cultural areas compared to the EC. The lessons for EMU are that monetary unification is likely to prove a slow and tortuous learning process, with the absence of political union and of shared cultural assumptions making that process more difficult.

Establishment of the mark as the currency for Germany was pre-eminently an act of political will. German monetary union gained its first momentum from the statutes of

6. For a good general overview see K. Born, *International Banking in the Nineteenth and Twentieth Centuries* (Leamington Spa: Berg, 1983), pp. 11–15 and 15–19.

the Prussian-led *Zollverein*, the customs union put into effect in 1834, which called for standardization of German coinage. In consequence, internal trade barriers were removed, and exchange rates between the different currencies fixed, in a development that prefigured the EC. But, reflecting the political fragmentation of Germany and the rivalry between the currency system in the north (the *thaler* standard) and that in the south (the *guilden* standard), the ambition for a standardized currency was not realized till after unification in 1871. The oldest German issuing bank, and the immediate predecessor of the Reichsbank, had been the Preussische Bank, which dated back to an original state bank founded by Frederick the Great in 1765. Deprived of silver and coinage reserves, it was unable to take advantage of this privilege, its role as an issuer of notes being suspended in 1806. Even when the newly named Preussische Bank had this role restored in 1846, restrictions were imposed. By then there were already five issuing banks in those German states that were later to form the German Reich: the Prussian banking law had the effect of stimulating the establishment of new issuing banks outside Prussia. Between 1847 and 1857 25 private and public issuing banks were formed in the German states, 18 outside Prussia. Most issuing banks were geographically restricted in operation and engaged in limited activity. But what was significant was that, prior to the war between Prussia and Austria in 1866, Prussian leadership in monetary policy had to a considerable extent already unified German issuing policy. By 1866, of the total 179 million *thalers* in bank notes circulating in the member states of the German Confederation (with the exception of Austria), 125 million were Preussische Bank notes. Albeit in a very different strategic and ideological context, it is plausible to envisage an expanding EMU based on the D-Mark and the Bundesbank.[7]

The stresses and strains of monetary union were apparent before and after German political unification in 1871. In March 1870 the new Prussian-led North German Confederation legislated to forbid the establishment of new issuing banks and the extension of existing privileges to issue notes. Fearing centralized regulation, the southern states of Baden and Württemberg acted promptly to establish their own issuing banks. Though the North German Confederation law was extended to the new Prussian-led Reich, in 1875 Germany still had 34 issuing banks. More importantly, two-thirds of the notes in circulation came from the Preussische Bank.

The key milestone was the 1875 Bank Act which was passed against the opposition of the Reichsrat, the legislative body in which the states were represented at the national level. Its central provision was the creation of the Reichsbank from the Preussische Bank (which Prussia sold to the Reich) and the compromise on the 'mark' as the currency that it would issue. But the new law bowed to the reality that concessions had already been granted to private issuing banks. Hence the Reichsbank could pursue a single central issuing bank only as a long-term strategy and rely on indirect methods, particulary taking advantage of the fact that it was the only issuing

7. On Germany K. Borchardt, 'Währung und Wirtschaft', in Deutsche Bundesbank, *Währung und Wirtschaft in Deutschland 1876–1976* (Frankfurt, 1976); K.-L. Holtferich, 'The Monetary Union Process in Nineteenth-Century Germany: Relevance and Lessons for Europe Today', in M. de Cecco and A. Giovannini (eds) *A European Central Bank?* (Cambridge: Cambridge University Press, 1989), pp. 216–41.

bank allowed to establish branches throughout the Reich and that it was given tax privileges to develop its role. Reichsbank notes were declared legal tender in 1909: after 1910, only four other banks issued notes. In effect, a single currency was in place.

The establishment of a central bank and a unified currency issue was a much more protracted story in the United States, where the Federal Reserve System was not established till 1913. Early American history was a story of competing currencies; evolution rather than a qualitative leap characterized monetary union. At the time of the Declaration of Independence in 1776 the original 13 New England states did not have their own currencies. A wide variety of coins and money systems were in operation, notably Spanish coins. The dollar emerged during the War of Independence not as a coin but as a bank note issued by the Continental Congress of Philadelphia to finance the war. But that body did not have the authority to crack down on states' use of foreign coins. It was not till 1792, after the Constitution had given the federation the power to tax and mint currency, that the United States began to mint its own coins, the gold and silver dollar. Even so, Spanish coins were circulating well into the 1800s.

Institutional problems bedevilled the establishment of a single currency. The plan to found a centralized national issuing bank was the subject of enduring dispute, beginning with the early plan of Alexander Hamilton. Notably, and in contrast to the Treaty on European Union, the US Constitution did not include explicit powers to establish such a bank. Thomas Jefferson, James Madison and others resolutely opposed the establishment of the First Bank of the United States (modelled on the Bank of England) in 1791: with Madison as president, its concession was allowed to expire in 1811. But the exigencies of war with Britain in 1812–14, and the subsequent escalation of state debt, intervened, Hamilton's ideas were revived and in 1816 the Second Bank of the United States was formed. Beset again by constitutional uncertainties as well as financial difficulties, its concession was withdrawn in 1836.

The combination of strong federalist sentiments with the ill-fated experience of the Second Bank of the United States cast a long shadow over monetary union. The number of issuing banks granted concessions by individual states mounted: from 28 in 1800 to 208 in 1815, to 707 in 1845, and to 1,562 in 1860. There were very different kinds of bank notes, which were not recognized as legal tender, and no regulation concerning gold and silver cover for issuing banks. War again, in this case the Civil War, acted as a catalyst for monetary union. The National Banking Act of 1863 gave the union the power to introduce legal regulation of banks and to grant them concessions; it also brought in the legal distinction between state banks and national banks. By 1880 over 2,000 national banks issued notes; by 1905 over 5,600.[8]

It finally took the banking crisis of 1907–8, which forced 243 banks, including 31 national banks, to suspend their payments, for firm action to be taken. The Federal Reserve Act of 1913 gave the United States a central banking system. With it was created the Federal Reserve System, with its twelve Federal Reserve Districts, each of which obtained a Federal Reserve Bank as a note-issuing bank. Central management was provided by a board of governors. The national banks had to belong to the new

8. On the United States M. Friedman and A. Schwartz, *A Monetary History of the United States, 1867–1960* (Princeton, NJ: Princeton University Press, 1963).

Federal Reserve System, though the state banks were not compelled to do so and it was not until the 1960s that the 'Fed' established an effective monopoly in the issue of notes and coins.

A survey of the experiences of Germany and the United States with monetary union provides little consolation for those who press for monetary union without prior political union. The obstacles become all the more apparent when one considers the difficulties of moving from political to monetary union in relatively homogeneous cultural areas like Germany and the United States. These difficulties escalate when one remembers that the context of monetary union is less benign in the EC; there is nothing remotely like the cross-border labour mobility or the scale of the fiscal transfers seen in Germany and the United States, mechanisms of adjustment that enable a monetary union to absorb economic 'shocks' (as we shall see in chapter 7). One is struck by the evolutionary nature of the development of the US dollar and by the fact that a single currency began to take off there only in the 1790s, when a central government was established. In the case of the much more rapid shift to a single currency in Germany – which might appear to offer a more appropriate European model to the EC – the background was a kind of government in Berlin that has no equivalent in the modern EC institutions.

The international gold standard

The gold standard was in important respects the simulacrum of the European Monetary System. It is hardly surprising then that problems in the operation of the EMS have revived interest in the character and functioning of the gold standard. At one level comparisons can be made between the way in which Britain was forced off the gold standard on 21 September 1931 and its enforced exit from the ERM on 16 September 1992. Or, at another level, one can ask whether the conditions that supported the operation of the gold standard were reproduced in the EMS. In practice, one must be careful about what one is comparing: for the classical gold standard differed in certain respects from the interwar gold standard, and the EMS has gone through different stages in its evolution. Also, as we shall have need to repeat, the institutional context of their operations is very different.

The classical gold standard

From the perspective of the ambition to achieve EMU, the operation of the classical gold standard represents the high-point of international monetary integration in historical terms. Its operation displayed some of the characteristics of a common currency system.[9] It appeared to be an immutable link between nominally different currencies, valuing the mark, the French franc, the pound sterling and the US dollar in legally defined weights of gold. The system was not perceived as a regime of adjustable parities, like the EMS between 1979 and 1987 and then after 1992. In practice (as we shall see) these comparisons are limited in value: first, by the differing

9.   J. Foreman-Peck, 'The Gold Standard as a European Monetary Lesson', in J. Driffill and M. Beber (eds) *A Currency for Europe* (London: Lothian Foundation Press, 1991), pp. 3–19.

institutional characteristics of monetary cooperation (the EMS developed within the political and economic framework of the EC, unlike the gold standard or the later Bretton Woods system); and second, by contrasting structural contexts of their operation (for instance, the context of the 1980s was widespread price inflation, that of the 1920s a prolonged fall in the prices of internationally traded commodities). These two differences mean that, compared to the interwar period, two vital extra parameters have entered the calculations of actors in the EMS and EMU policy process: the institutional setting of the EC, and the preoccupation with 'sustainable' growth (that is, recovery engineered without the fatal flaw of the costs of inflation). For these reasons the lessons of history should be read with sceptical caution.

The classical gold standard had two great virtues, as far as its promoters and defenders were concerned. It created a framework of stability, thus generating the confidence required for the expansion of international trade. It did so by keeping the national currencies of different countries at a fixed relative value, and by confirming the interconvertibility between domestic money and gold at a fixed official price. Second, the gold standard had a moral function. Its great virtue was supposed to be that it was automatic, beyond the control of capricious politicians.[10] Money supplies in each country were linked directly to domestic reserves of gold, and balance-of-payments' adjustments were achieved through international shipments of gold. Balance-of-payments' equilibrium was established through the impact of gold flows on domestic conditions. In this way, in-built and automatic sanctions against inflationary policies ensured steady and sustainable growth.

Indeed, the powerful discipline of the gold standard was meant to produce a *de facto* harmonization of monetary policies of different countries, without explicit coordination.[11] Trading imbalances were supposed to be corrected by price adjustments rather than discretionary resort either to protection (hence free trade was an integral part of the system) or to devaluation. In effect, countries gave up independence in monetary policy in favour of the advantages of free trade, free capital mobility and fixed exchange rates. Domestic adjustment also required a commitment to the balancing of budgets in a classical liberal manner. With budget deficits of a modest size, fiscal policies were not a major source of disturbance. The tough rules of the system were seen as the essential defence against the twin dangers of uncontrollable inflation at home and dislocation of the world's trading and financial system. That at least was the theory. Experience of the European inflation of 1920 to 1923 in the absence of the gold standard seemed only to vindicate this view and to underline the paramount importance of restoring the prewar gold standard. The gold standard came to represent, at least in theory, the triumph of rules over discretion.

Two points of comparison arise with respect to the EMS. First, the classical gold standard was a 'British-managed standard', evoking comparison with the EMS as a

10. R. Skidelsky, *Politicians and the Slump: The Labour Government of 1929–1931* (Harmondsworth: Pelican, 1970), p. 384.
11. B. Eichengreen, 'Editor's introduction', in Eichengreen (ed.) *The Gold Standard in Theory and History* (New York and London: Methuen, 1985); A.I. Bloomfield, *Monetary Policy under the International Gold Standard, 1880–1914* (New York: Federal Reserve Bank of New York, 1959); R. Hawtrey, *The Gold Standard in Theory and Practice* (London: 1947); Bordo and Schwarz (eds) *A Retrospective on the Classical Gold Standard.*

'D-Mark zone'.[12] In the nineteenth century Britain seemed a policy model to emulate: a great naval and trading power at the forefront of technology and backed by the institutional efficiency and effectiveness of its banking system. The domestic political commitment to the value of stable money was underwritten by a Bank Charter Act of 1844. This Act not only defined the special powers of the Bank of England, but also laid down limits on the power of any British government to expand the money supply without asking the permission of Parliament. Such permission was requested only once before 1914. Here then was a central bank that enjoyed an unrivalled credibility. The structural power that derived from its management of the anchor currency gave London a clear policy leadership role and underpinned the stability of the gold standard. With the EMS and EMU that role rested in Frankfurt.

Britain had been on a full legal gold standard since 1821 and on a *de facto* gold standard from 1717. With Germany's adoption of the standard after 1871, and the United States in 1879, the stage was set for its global dominance till 1914. London's structural power had several sources. Pragmatically, the fact that Britain was pre-eminent in world trade and finance created a practical case for adopting its monetary standard to facilitate international exchange. Before 1914 British investment overseas was twice as great as that of France, and more than five times greater than that of the United States. London's unrivalled position as the world's most important financial centre pre-1914 meant that the Bank of England had leverage over the international flows of capital and gold that gave it the capacity to exercise leadership in the management of the new international system. Other central banks were essentially reactive, vulnerable and sensitive to the actions of the Bank of England. Parallels with the later role of the Bundesbank in the EMS are again easy to draw.

Second, the operation of the system endowed central bankers with a powerful legitimacy: figures like Montagu Norman, the powerful governor of the Bank of England.[13] The central banks came to have a strong corporate self-interest in the system's perpetuation, for the gold standard endowed central bankers not only with the role of managing the system but also with a powerful legitimizing ideology and monetary mystique. They were able to harness their self-interests to the structural power of an economic idea. Central bankers were after all the custodians of the rules of the game, intervening to reinforce the impact of prospective gold flows on domestic money markets. The instruments at their disposal included discount rates, open market operations, and gold devices (direct interventions in the gold market and changes in the regulations governing convertibility). Even if, as Bloomfield and Nurske claim, there were widespread violations of the rules of the game, during the classical gold standard as well as the interwar period, discretion lay very much in the hands of the central bankers.[14] They were the ones to decide whether or not to act, when to act, which instruments to use and how to use them. One is reminded of the extent to which

12. W.M. Scammell, 'The Working of the Gold Standard', in Eichengreen (ed.) *The Gold Standard in Theory and History*, pp. 103–20.
13. H. Clay, *Lord Norman* (London: Macmillan, 1957). See also Skidelsky, *Politicians and the Slump*, pp. 28–9.
14. Bloomfield, *Monetary Policy under the International Gold Standard, 1880–1914*; R. Nurske, 'The Gold Exchange Standard', in Eichengreen (ed.) *The Gold Standard in Theory and History*, pp. 201–25.

the EMS and EMU evolved ideologically and technically to suit the corporate self-interests of EC central bankers.

But historical studies of the operation of the gold standard have underlined the gap between myth and reality. In the classical period, the system did not operate neatly according to the rules, and cooperative management was sporadic rather than regular. Discretionary behaviour by national monetary authorities was a prominent characteristic, even under normal circumstances. There is little evidence that the Bank of England gave significant weight to the stability of the world economy in formulating its policies. Rather it was narrowly concerned with its reserve position, in fact only occasionally paying attention even to domestic conditions. This lack of respect for rules and of explicit cooperative management of the system was even less apparent after the rebirth of the interwar gold standard.[15] Faced with imposed costs of deflation that were judged too high, countries were disposed either to suspend convertibility of their currency into gold or to impose tariffs on imports.

In addition to this safety valve of discretionary domestic policy action to insulate the economy from the full rigours of the gold standard, three other factors helped to sustain the classical gold standard. They illustrate the structural power of economic fundamentals. The late nineteenth and early twentieth century offered the safety valve of migration to the 'new world', notably the United States, the British dominions and Brazil. By this form of large-scale labour mobility mass unemployment and poverty could be ameliorated, and governments could pursue more deflationary policies than otherwise. For example, 5 per cent of the British population emigrated in the deflationary 1880s. After Austria-Hungary joined the gold standard in the early 1890s, 6.5 per cent of its population emigrated before 1910.[16] A second factor that helped to sustain the system was the way in which the membership of weak or developing states was financed by inward investment from richer states which wanted colonial produce and cheap manufactures. In effect, the gold standard was sustained by a massive transfer of savings to weaker and poorer states.[17]

Finally, the experience of the gold standard in the late nineteenth century underlined the importance of pay and price flexibility to its stability. The spread of the gold standard coincided with the so-called 'great depression' of 1873–96. The notion of this period as a depression is linked with the persistent fall of prices (with the brief exception of 1887–91). More pertinently, the operation of the gold standard can be used to explain this phenomenon. Demand for gold relative to supply increased with the rush of countries to join the gold standard after 1870 and with the absence of new gold discoveries until the end of the 1880s. As the amount of bank notes and deposits was related to gold, the growth of money supply in countries like Britain and the United States slowed down. But the 'great depression' was a myth in two senses: real GDP continued to grow, slowing down as prices began to rise again after 1896, and money wages also continued to grow.[18] The casualties were unemployed people, with unemployment in Britain rising from 5 per cent in 1851–73 to 7.4 per cent in

---

15. Eichengreen, 'Editor's Introduction', in Eichengreen (ed.) *The Gold Standard in Theory and History*, pp. 12–19.
16. M. Panic, *European Monetary Union* (New York: St Martin's Press, 1993).
17. Panic, *European Monetary Union*.
18. S. Saul, *The Myth of the Great Depression, 1873–96* (London: Macmillan, 1989).

1874–95. The 1873–96 period illustrates that deflation need not mean depression, in the sense of the absence of growth, but that, for this to be the case, pay and price flexibility are enormously important. As we shall see in chapters 7 and 8, the effective functioning of the hard ERM and of the Maastricht route to EMU was impeded by changed structural conditions leading to the absence of so much flexibility.

The interwar gold exchange standard

It was the external shock of war in 1914 that broke the classical gold standard rather than its internal functioning (although the rate of growth of Britain's GDP and real wages had fallen since the turn of the century). In the absence of memories of an internal crisis, the story of the early postwar period was the search for what proved to be an 'elusive stability' by restoring the international gold standard.[19] Widespread agreement on the priority to be given to restoring gold to its old position as an international standard of value was manifested in the international conferences held in Brussels (1920) and Genoa (1922). Indeed, as early as 1918, the *First Interim Report* of the Cunliffe Committee had underlined the importance of this commitment to British policy. Gold's political attraction lay not least in the fact that it was synonymous with British monetary policy leadership.

But, as the Genoa Conference recognized, a shortage of gold necessitated the adoption of a gold *exchange* standard.[20] This solution enabled central banks to hold reserves and undertake international settlement not only in gold but also in the form of foreign balances. In practice, prior to 1914 central banks had been used to holding a certain amount of foreign exchange in addition to gold. The major postwar change was one of the proportion of foreign exchange to total reserves. The collapse of the gold exchange standard in 1930–2 was to be characterized by the wholesale liquidation of these foreign exchange reserves.

The real heart of the structural problems of the restored gold standard was to be the absence of a strong anchor. The British government took the decision to return to gold at its prewar parity in April 1925, despite the high-level advice of the economist John Maynard Keynes that such a decision would be too costly in terms of lost output and employment.[21] Keynes argued that rigidities in wage structure would impede the domestic adjustment process to an overvalued pound. Hence the shortage of gold would cause falling output and employment rather than falling wages and prices. The consequent unemployment would lead to expanding budget deficits, undermining confidence in the sterling rate.[22]

---

19. B. Eichengreen, *Elusive Stability: Essays in the History of International Finance, 1919–1939* (Cambridge: Cambridge University Press, 1990).
20. League of Nations, *International Currency Experience* (Geneva, 1944).
21. D. Moggridge, *The Return to Gold, 1925: The Formulation of Economic Policy and its Critics* (Cambridge: Cambridge University Press, 1969); R.S. Sayers, 'The Return to Gold, 1925', in S. Pollard (ed.) *The Gold Standard and Employment Policies between the Wars* (London: Methuen, 1970), pp. 85–98.
22. The classic statements of the system's malfunctioning are 'The Economic Consequences of Mr. Churchill', in J.M. Keynes, *Essays in Persuasion* (London: Macmillan, 1931); the Macmillan Report on Finance and Industry, Cmd 3897 and Minutes of Evidence (London: HMSO, 1931). Keynes played a prominent role in drafting the Macmillan Report.

The political problem of capability to endure these domestic costs of an anchor currency has to be viewed in the structural context of a marked deterioration in Britain's economic fundamentals, particularly as reflected in its trading position. In consequence, it no longer possessed the authority to exercise its former leadership role within the international gold standard system. A large part of its assets had been sold to pay for the war, adversely affecting annual invisible payments; national debt at home had been greatly enlarged; and the rise of new foreign shipping and manufacturing industries, to take advantage of the interruption of British supplies by war, meant that its exports could no longer generate a surplus sufficient to finance international growth on the prewar scale. The British government adopted an overvalued pound against the background of four years of deflation and stagnation. As a consequence, its core industries – coal, iron and steel, shipbuilding, engineering and cotton – were condemned to a desperate situation.

In this new structural context, power could no longer be ascribed to a single anchor country: rather Britain, France and the United States represented different and contending axes of leadership. Everything depended on their will and capability to pull in the same direction. The new powerful creditor nations were France and the United States. France became a major creditor with the *de facto* stabilization of the franc at a fraction of its prewar parity in 1926. Subsequent tensions between the Bank of England and the Banque de France were further fuelled by the French policies of deliberately augmenting its gold reserves and using stamp duties and coupon taxes to discourage foreign investment. In this way France sought to strengthen its political weight abroad and to insulate its domestic economy. These policies added to Britain's difficulties in maintaining the sterling rate. They also gave France an increasingly important influence on developments in the international monetary system. France was a powerful but reluctant member of the gold exchange system, with – at the heart of the system – the Bank of England on bad terms with the Banque de France.

In addition, from 1928, US overseas lending was diverted to a boom on the New York stock exchange, the effects of which began to preoccupy American interest-rate policy. The United States was also disposed to hoard gold and to retain high protection for its domestic economy. Like France, it was inclined to raise interest rates to attract gold, thereby worsening the difficulties of the Bank of England in sustaining an overvalued pound. As a consequence, the dollar became an unnaturally hard currency. In discussions with Norman, Benjamin Strong of the Federal Reserve Bank of New York – effectively the 'foreign ministry' of the Federal Reserve System in New York – insisted that central bank cooperation was possible only if it did not conflict with domestic economic management.

Currency stability among these three countries sharing the anchor role was clearly a structural prerequisite for the effective functioning of the gold exchange standard. But it had no secure basis in coordinated policies and cooperative attitudes about how to tackle structural problems of economic fundamentals. In this respect at least the EMS had a somewhat firmer institutional basis of cooperation to distinguish it from the problems of the interwar gold standard. In the institutional context of the EC it was more practical to imagine a sharing of the anchor role in the ERM, assuming the will of the German Bundesbank to share that role.

The resurrection and demise of the international gold standard during the interwar period is usually dated from Britain's return to gold in 1925 to its departure from the gold standard in 1931. Britain exhausted its gold and foreign exchange reserves in futile attempts to buoy up employment. By the end of 1931 well over twenty countries had followed Britain's example in leaving the gold standard, notably the greater part of the British Empire and Commonwealth and countries under British influence. In this way the Sterling Area (or Bloc) came into being. Its members sought to harmonize their trade policies with Britain's, as well as keeping the bulk of their currency reserves in the Bank of England. The United States broke with gold in 1933, leaving France – bolstered by its huge gold reserves – to lead the rump of Gold Bloc countries (including Belgium, Italy and the Netherlands) still pursuing tight monetary and fiscal policies to maintain external stability.

The interwar gold standard had proved to be a relatively brief and inglorious episode, punctured by convertibility crises and far from conducive to price and income stability. Above all, it had introduced a deflationary bias to policy, narrowing the discretion of national governments to stimulate domestic output and employment.[23] Between 1932 and 1937, by the use of independent and uncoordinated economic and monetary policies, most countries exhibited reasonable cyclical growth. The exception was the Gold Bloc countries.

This period contains some instructive lessons. Given that Britain could no longer provide a secure anchor for the reconstituted gold standard, central bank cooperation became more important to the system's effective functioning and was certainly more extensive than under the classical gold standard.[24] But (as we have seen) central bank cooperation was undermined by structural problems of economic fundamentals and contrasting policy ideas about the relative importance of the goals of external and internal stability. Exchange rates were misaligned, notably those of Britain and France. In this context reserves were insufficient both to foster monetary growth and to defend currency convertibility. Also, from the late 1920s, new trade barriers disrupted the process of domestic adjustment, reducing the pressure on deficit countries to restore balance by greater success in exporting and diverting gold reserves to the most protectionist countries. As Eichengreen has argued, these problems had been to some degree present under the classical gold standard.[25]

But the real changes with the interwar period were structural and rooted in the international political economy. First (as we have seen) the anchor role was more difficult to perform under the transformed economic circumstances. With a shared anchor role for Britain, France and the United States, difficult problems of the coordination of national economic priorities were introduced. Hence there was neither firm policy leadership nor stability. Second, increasingly integrated financial markets were accompanied by a new sensitivity to destabilizing short-term capital flows (flows of 'hot money'), which could in turn be triggered by specific, perhaps even minor

23. M. Kitson and J. Michie, *Coordinated Deflation: The Tale of Two Recessions* (London: Full Employment Forum, August 1993).
24. S.V.O. Clarke, *Central Bank Cooperation, 1924–1931* (New York: Federal Reserve Bank of New York, 1967); B. Eichengreen, 'Central Bank Cooperation under the Interwar Gold Standard', *Explorations in Economic History*, January (1984).
25. Eichengreen, 'Editor's Introduction', in Eichengreen (ed.) *The Gold Standard in Theory and History*, pp. 22–3.

events and rumours. Third, in operating the rules of the game it became apparent that policy actors – with the exception of the Gold Bloc countries – were no longer so single-mindedly preoccupied with external exchange-rate stability and defence of the gold reserve as they had been earlier. Domestic output and employment were not the subject of such precise objectives, but they represented deepening concerns and qualifications to the implementation of gold standard policy. With such qualifications so manifestly at work, for instance within a Labour government so close to the heart of the system, market confidence was reduced and hedging against devaluation encouraged.[26] A new, more overt importance was attached to national discretion in economic management.

Overview of the gold standard

Looked at in historical perspective one is struck by the limited period of time in which the gold standard endured: for the period 1880–1914, and then from 1925 to 1931. In the political bargaining processes of economic and monetary policy it conferred enormous power on central bankers over national governments, not least legitimizing an ideology of central bank independence. With the rise of the international gold standard we see the marriage of central bankers' self-interests with policy priority to external exchange-rate stability as the guarantor of a rule-based monetary policy. Such a policy was designed to give an automaticity to domestic financial rectitude. It was noticeable in the interwar period that central bank cooperation was more regularized than intergovernmental cooperation at political levels. Figures like Norman and Strong did a great deal more to coordinate policy than the political leaders of their countries, though Strong was clearly inhibited by the isolationism of American policy in this period.

But fundamentally, as the interwar period brutally exposed, the stability and effectiveness of the gold standard – and hence of central bank power over policy bargaining – was determined by a combination of structural factors in the international political economy with the political acceptability of the economic outcomes of its functioning. This lesson applies as strongly to the EMS and EMU policy process as to the gold standard. Central bankers were ultimately dependent on the political will and capability of their governments to maintain the system. In the face of ever mounting costs of lost output and employment that will and capability lost market credibility under the gold exchange standard, and the basis of the gold standard in the corporate self-interests of central bankers was exposed. With the political legitimacy of the gold standard in question the central banks were increasingly vulnerable to the financial markets: and with its demise to public criticism of the irresponsible use of privileged access to power.

After the political and economic crisis of 1931 the Bank of England was to remain reluctant to be quite so assertive again *vis-à-vis* government. By contrast, the German Bundesbank institutionalized a very different set of memories of the interwar period: of hyperinflation in the 1920s and the paramount need for a central bank with an heroic style. In this case a new central bank emerged with the will and capability to

26. Eichengreen, 'Editor's Introduction', p. 24.

assert its independence; it could in consequence act as the firm 'anchor' that the EMS required.

In addition to the will and capability of governments to sustain the operation of the rules of the game, the operation of the gold standard depended on central bank cooperation. The will to cooperate was provided by the corporate self-interest of central banks in maintaining the system. But it was, above all, conditioned by structural factors, like the capacity of the anchor currency to provide policy leadership, changing economic fundamentals and new policy ideas and priorities. Faced with domestic political pressures, governments were disposed to attempt to insulate domestic output and employment from the full rigours of the gold standard's operation. It is not surprising if, at the best of times, coordination and control should appear relatively weak. Putting the gold standard into effect was always problematic.

In the interwar period particularly, the limits of cooperation post-1925 were defined by a lack of policy coordination in defining exchange rates in the first place. This lack of cross-national cooperation in relation to the fundamentals of the system played a part in the later absence of consensus on how best to deal with policy problems in its operation. The will to defend rates was reduced when collective commitment had not been engendered by a collective determination of the structure of rates. Crucially, no international agreements backed these misaligned exchange rates. Here, at the level of rules of the game, was a crucial point of difference from the EMS policy process with its rule of cooperative exchange-rate management.

Two parallels between the gold standard and the EMS are interesting. First, there is a parallel between the problems of the operation of the interwar gold standard and the crisis of the ERM in September 1992. Britain had, contrary to the spirit of the EMS, unilaterally determined the rate at which it entered the ERM in September 1990. In consequence, the Bundesbank felt no commitment to a rate that had been imposed on it, yet which had major implications for itself. Second, how the hard ERM operated simulated many of the problems of the gold standard. Both institutionalized disinflation, in a manner that was especially injurious to countries with severe structural problems of economic fundamentals, and both transmitted, through the exchange rate regime, the impact of adverse economic shocks, such as the recession in the United States under the interwar gold standard and the economic effects of German unification under the hard ERM. Looking back over the histories of the two, one may be struck by the 'surprising' fact that the gold standard and the EMS were successful in avoiding crisis for as long as they did.

The Bretton Woods system

With the Bretton Woods system we come to another policy regime that invites comparison with the EMS and EMU: in this case a fixed exchange rate system, with an anchor currency, but – unlike the gold standard regimes – with a new international institutional structure for its management. The Bretton Woods system is an object lesson in the speed with which change in the international political economy can undermine an anchor currency, the US dollar, with a subsequent incapacity to restore international monetary policy leadership and stability. One is reminded just how fragile the anchor role of the D-Mark in the ERM could prove to be, and how much its stability depends on the policy performance of German actors, notably the Bundesbank and the federal government. On the other hand, the institutional character of the International Monetary Fund (IMF) and of the EMS are different enough to suggest that the EMS could evolve in its own way rather than simply replicate the demise of Bretton Woods. The institutional context of rules of the game matters.

Like any system of international monetary cooperation, the Bretton Woods system bore the imprint of the circumstances of its creation and the memories of its authors. The attempt to learn lessons from the experience of the Great Depression of the 1930s was central to the consultations on postwar monetary reconstruction between the United States and Britain. These negotiations began well before the end of the Second World War and culminated in the United Nations conference at Bretton Woods in July 1944.[27] Fresh in the memories of negotiators were the competitive devaluations, rising tariffs, resort to import controls, sharp drop in foreign lending and huge increases of unemployment of the 1930s. These phenomena were linked by them to the collapse not only of economic liberalism but also of liberal political institutions, and were seen as an inseparable part of the backcloth to world war.

By the mid-1930s at least five separate currency areas had evolved (excluding the Soviet Union and developing countries) in place of the single payments area before 1914: the Sterling Area (including northern Europe and the Commonwealth); the Dollar Area of North and South America; the Gold Bloc of western Europe, led by France but by 1936 in dissolution; the Exchange Control Area of central Europe, tied to Germany; and Japan and the Far East. Symbolic of the period had been the conspicuous failure of the World Economic Conference of 1933. Its initial emphasis on the need for stable exchange rates was torpedoed by the US Secretary of State, Cordell Hull, in terms dictated by President Roosevelt:

> The world will not long be lulled by the specious fallacy of achieving a temporary and probably an artificial stability in foreign exchanges on the part of a few large countries only. The sound internal economic system of a nation is a greater factor in its well-being than the price of its currency.[28]

Symbolic of a greater sense of the dangers of competitive behaviour, and closer to the later spirit of Bretton Woods, was the Three-Power Currency Declaration of 1936. Britain, France and the United States pledged to pursue, in concert, stability in their exchange rates by means of a mutual support arrangement. They called for action to develop world trade by relaxing and eventually abolishing quotas and exchange controls, and they invited all countries to cooperate for this purpose. But it was a case of too little, too late as far as fostering international trade and restoring confidence of financial markets was concerned. Declarations were not adequate.

What was needed was a more developed and comprehensive institutional mechanism for achieving and maintaining an open and liberal postwar economic order. The Bretton Woods system was designed to deliver this mechanism in the form of two

27. R.N. Gardner, *Sterling–Dollar Diplomacy* (Oxford: Clarendon Press, 1956); J.K. Horsefield, *The International Monetary Fund 1945–1965* (Washington, DC: IMF, 1969).
28. Quoted in H.V. Hodson, *Slump and Recovery 1929–1937* (Oxford: Oxford University Press, 1938).

new institutions: the IMF and the General Agreement on Tariffs and Trade (GATT). These institutions were to be the guarantors of a new multilateral trading system, based on a system of registered, fixed exchange rates. In contrast to the interwar period, the new system would be underwritten by the structural power and commitment of the United States. The US dollar became the anchor of the new international regime.

The difference between the post-1918 and post-1945 periods becomes clearer when the United Nations conference at Bretton Woods in July 1944 is compared with the Genoa conference of 1922. Failure to reach agreement at Genoa was bound up in the emotive and complex political bargaining about war debts and reparations from Germany. France insisted that the reparations questions had to be settled first; neither Britain nor the United States shared this view about priorities. But in 1944 French views counted for much less, and the views of the United States as the unrivalled international economic power carried the day. Exchange rate stability and free trade were, in the American view, the precondition for expansion of international trade and securing and spreading prosperity. France's 'oppositional' role in international monetary affairs was, in fact, to endure, becoming adopted by the postwar Gaullists and being a notable feature of President Charles de Gaulle's presidency after 1958. That opposition was then to express itself in French support for EMU as a diplomatic instrument to wield against an American-dominated international monetary system.

At the heart of the new monetary regime agreed at Bretton Woods was the gold-dollar standard: in the words of Dam, a 'much diluted form of a gold exchange standard'.[29] Gold remained the ultimate unit of account in the sense that the dollar was pegged to gold (at $35 an ounce) and other currencies were pegged to the dollar. The United States held its reserves in gold; other countries had the choice of holding their reserves in gold or dollars. Gold also provided a part of the endowment of the new IMF. Its founding members were required to contribute gold in the amount of 25 per cent of their quotas or 10 per cent of their net official gold and dollar holdings, whichever was less.

Otherwise, the new gold-dollar standard was very different from the classical gold standard. Gold coins were not to circulate; there were tough restrictions on gold imports and exports; national currencies could no longer be converted at central banks; and citizens of participating countries could not even hold gold for most purposes. Under these new arrangements gold reserves and domestic money supplies were even less closely linked than before. What was left of the gold standard was a system for pegging exchange rates to one another by defining them in terms of fixed weights of gold.

In order to prevent a repetition of a piecemeal and disorderly process of international monetary reconstruction, as exhibited by the behaviour of the British in 1925 and the French in 1926, the Bretton Woods agreement sought to introduce new more stringent rules of the game: collective supervision of exchange-rate policies. Each member of the IMF was required to propose a par value for its currency in terms of gold, to obtain IMF approval for that par value, and to keep the exchange rate for its currency within 1 per cent of the parity corresponding to its par value.

29. K. Dam, *The Rules of the Game* (Chicago: University of Chicago Press, 1982), p. 133.

Subsequently, a government could change its par value only to correct a 'fundamental disequilibrium' and only with the IMF's approval. The main limitation was that the IMF was not allowed to initiate or recommend changes in par values. The system was designed to encourage collective commitment and support. But bargaining relations within the IMF were constrained by the essentially unilateral nature of changes in par values (subject to the consent of the IMF): that is, until the Smithsonian Agreement of 1971.

Two characteristics of the Bretton Woods system are striking: for just how short a time period it actually functioned in anything like the manner intended; and the fact that the extraordinary success in generating the credit for the postwar reconstruction of the west European economies cannot be centrally attributed to it.[30] As a system of rules, it really operated in its full sense only from December 1958 to March 1968, that is from the re-establishment of convertibility of European currencies to the introduction of the two-tier gold price (the first break in the anchoring of exchange rates to the price of gold). Symptomatic of its strength was the fact that the international payments crisis of summer 1947 was not containable within the structure of the Bretton Woods system. Its management involved the new initiatives of the Marshall Aid Programme and the European Payments Union (EPU). In other words, from 1947 to 1958, the Bretton Woods system was not central to the monetary regime of western Europe and the processes of reconstruction there.

Even in the decade of its full operation, the rules of the game of the Bretton Woods system were effectively rewritten and new policy instruments invented. This process of revision reflected repeated efforts to support the fixed rates of the pound sterling and of the dollar in the face of balance-of-payments' difficulties. Innovations included the Gold Pool; extra funds made available to the IMF under the General Arrangements to Borrow of 1962; the swap network by which central banks could automatically borrow foreign exchange from each other; and the American Interest Equalization Tax of 1963, which effectively deterred foreign borrowers from borrowing on US capital markets.[31] In the words of Robert Triffin, they were 'fire extinguishers', designed to prolong the life of a deeply faulted system.[32]

Also, the rules governing the adjustment mechanism did not operate as intended. In practice countries were notably lacking in will to adjust the peg. With the exceptions of the devaluations of sterling in 1949 and 1967, very few adjustments of parity were made by industrial economies: only the devaluations of the French franc in 1957–8 and the 5 per cent revaluations of the Dutch guilder and the German mark in 1961. Factors of national prestige inhibited devaluations, whilst countries feared the threat of revaluation to the competitiveness of their domestic industries. Structural problems of economic fundamentals and misaligned exchange rates began, accordingly, to plague and infect the gold-dollar standard. In the absence of effective collective supervision of, and action on, exchange rates by the IMF, the burdens of adjustment were shifted to the countries with structural problems, epitomized in chronic external deficits. By

30. A.S. Milward, *The Reconstruction of Western Europe, 1945–51* (London: Methuen, 1984), pp. 43–4; S. Strange, *States and Markets* (London: Pinter, 1988), pp. 102–3.
31. S. Strange, *International Monetary Relations*, vol. 2 of A. Shonfield (ed.) *International Economic Relations in the Western World 1959–71* (Oxford: Oxford University Press, 1976).
32. R. Triffin, *The World Money Maze* (New Haven, Conn: Yale University Press, 1966), ch. 7.

seeking approval for changing their exchange rates, governments went through the formal motions but rarely gave the IMF time to reflect and criticize. Hence coordinated management within the system was less effective than intended. In their desire to exercise political discretion to the full governments were prepared to ignore the rules of the game, and the United States, as the anchor currency, was content to play a passive leadership role within the system.

Ultimately, the downfall of the Bretton Woods system was attributable to the structural problem of the anchor currency, the US dollar. The dominance of the dollar reflected the uniquely strong position of the US economy, represented in the early dollar shortage in Europe. In essence, as the anchor, the United States could afford to ignore its own exchange rate. Of greatest importance, the dollar provided the increased liquidity that was required to support the fast-growing international economy. The monetary expansion needed for economic growth required steadily increasing reserves. By running payments surpluses against the United States and accumulating dollar assets, other countries could augment their reserves with the world's most desirable reserve currency. In practice, especially in the 1960s, the balance-of-payments' deficits of the United States were the main source of extra liquidity. This mechanism was the subject of heated debate. As Kenen emphasized, American tolerance of persistent balance-of-payments' deficits was forced on it by demand from abroad for additional reserve assets denominated in dollars.[33] But, in the view of the French government, the United States was abusing its special role to obtain seigniorage by providing reserves to the rest of the world. Hence, after 1965 France made frequent efforts to convert its dollar holdings into gold.

Whatever the merits of the different arguments in this debate, this mechanism seemed to contain the seeds of the destruction of the Bretton Woods system. From 1959 onwards, Robert Triffin insisted that the system was doomed by a central paradox (the so-called Triffin Paradox). On the one hand, the system relied on dollars for liquidity and on the will of other countries to hold gold-convertible dollars in their reserves to sustain stable exchange rates. On the other hand, the volume of dollars in foreign hands would eventually be so much greater than the US gold reserves that the 'overhang' would destroy confidence in the dollar's convertibility.[34] The structural need of the international economy for credit to foster expansion was, in other words, eroding the structural power of the US dollar as the anchor currency. In such a situation, either the dollar would have to be devalued, or the price of gold would have to be raised and a new set of rules agreed.

To this self-destruct mechanism was added another structural factor that placed huge strains on the exchange rate system and that was a harbinger of developments that were to radically transform the context of monetary policy from the 1970s: the rise of the Eurodollar market. The introduction of the new Eurodollar was to serve simultaneously as a major engine of credit creation and as an unregulated and

33. P.B. Kenen, 'The International Position of the Dollar in a Changing World', *International Organization*, 3 (1969).
34. R. Triffin, *Gold and the Dollar Crisis: The Future of Convertibility* (New Haven, Conn: Yale University Press, 1960). In Triffin's view, this paradox could be resolved by replacing the anchor currency with a world currency reserve and central bank. This idea was resisted by the anchor country which reaped the benefits of seigniorage.

disruptive factor in foreign exchange markets. Its emergence reflected the huge inward investment of American corporations in western Europe, with American banks following American corporations in developing business in Europe. There they discovered that they could avoid American rules limiting the interest on short-term deposits. Deposits with American bank branches in London could attract higher interest. In turn, the Bank of England enabled British and foreign banks in London to conduct all forms of financial business in dollars (not in sterling), because there were no serious implications for the balance of payments. Growth of the Eurocurrency market was phenomenal: from $3 billion in 1960, to $75 billion in 1970, rising to over $1,000 billion in 1984 (later growth owed much to the deposits of the oil states in these markets).[35]

Faced with the structural factors of an inbuilt self-destruct mechanism (the Triffin Paradox) and new unregulated financial markets (the Eurodollar market), and with the institutional failure to implement collective management through the IMF, governments attempted to muddle through, against all the odds. As it began to run balance-of-payments' deficits in the 1960s, and as these deficits were aggravated by the consequences of the Vietnam War, the United States became increasingly involved in exchange rate issues. It opposed devaluation of the pound in 1964, fearing that speculative pressures would be deflected on to the dollar. In the Franco-German dispute of 1968 (see chapter 3) Washington took France's side in wanting a revaluation of the mark, in the hope of achieving thereby a partial devaluation of the dollar. The United States could no longer afford to be so passive about exchange rates.

It was also forced to recognize that confidence in the dollar's convertibility was disappearing. In 1968 the US Treasury effectively ceased to allow the Germans and others to draw on US gold reserves. The precipitating event came in August 1971 when Britain requested that the Federal Reserve swap a portion of the Bank of England's dollar holdings for sterling. The United States perceived in this the beginning of a general run on the dollar. On Sunday 15 August the US Administration of President Richard Nixon suspended the convertibility of dollars held in foreign official reserves into gold. Domestically, the emergency economic package was successfully dressed up as a triumph and a fresh start rather than a humiliation.

Externally, the consequences were far more serious and threatening. The gold-dollar standard was now dead; the Bretton Woods regime was to pass away within two years. In the new climate of uncertainty exchange controls proliferated and protectionist pressures increased, contrary to the philosophy of free capital movement and free trade in which the United States believed. Faced with major policy clashes, the Smithsonian Agreement was concluded in December 1971. It was the only example of a global exchange-rate realignment under the Bretton Woods system, albeit the product of acrimonious bargaining. Despite a substantial devaluation of the dollar, or rather because of the subsequent lack of confidence, the new 'paper dollar standard' proved unsustainable. Faced by a worsening balance-of-payments' problem, the British pound was allowed to float downwards in June 1972, effectively marking the end of the Sterling Area. Thereafter the number of countries pegging their currencies to sterling dropped dramatically and, more generally, the disposition to use significant

---

35. S. Strange, *Casino Capitalism* (Oxford: Basil Blackwell, 1986).

proportions of sterling in reserves diminished. In the face of crises induced by a dollar flood, a meeting of 14 countries in Paris in March 1973 abandoned the pegging on the dollar by the major industrial countries. Intended as a temporary measure, the floating-rate experiment was to endure.

The collapse of the Bretton Woods system can be attributed to two problems of structural change: the erosion of the anchor currency's credibility, with weak and irresponsible policy leadership by the United States; and the scale and mobility of capital in new hugely expanding and unregulated international financial markets. The implications for the European Economic Community (EEC) were enormous. With economies so interdependent in trading, they had been able to achieve the benefits of exchange rate stability via the Bretton Woods system, obviating the pressing need for EMU. Now the benefits of internal EEC trade as a motor of growth and employment were threatened by external instability. External pressures pointed, accordingly, in the direction of an EEC monetary initiative. Also, in considering such an initiative EC policy actors were influenced by two lessons of Bretton Woods. First, the Belgians and the French were keen to avoid repeating the asymmetry of the Bretton Woods system by replacing American with German policy leadership. In practice (as chapter 4 shows) they failed to find a satisfactory alternative to an anchor currency arrangement. Second, there was widespread agreement that the rules of the game for an EEC monetary initative would involve more cooperative policy management than in the case of Bretton Woods. Here the EEC was more successful, though national discretion and German policy leadership qualified the nature of 'cooperative' management. But the remaining problem was whether the EMS and EMU could hope to survive the ever expanding scale and volatility of the financial markets any better than Bretton Woods. The ERM crises of January 1987, September 1992 and July 1993 suggested that a different quality of institutional arrangements, short of EMU, was by no means the solution to this problem.

International monetary cooperation after 1973: the G-7

From 1973 onwards we enter the contemporary history of European monetary integration: the stage when it really comes into its own. But, fundamentally, the EMS and EMU cannot be disentangled from their interactions with international institutions like the IMF, the Bank for International Settlements (BIS) and G-7. As a policy process the EMS and EMU is not self-contained; it is part of the 'globalization' of the international economy and of wider issues of international monetary reform. The nature of other international institutions and their implications for the EMS and EMU need to be understood.

Continuity and change in US structural power

The acrimony that accompanied the demise of the Bretton Woods system, symbolized by the Smithsonian Agreement of 1971, persuaded the main EEC countries that their vulnerability to US policies could be reduced only if two conditions were met: that the role of the US dollar must be diminished; and that the United States must be subjected to the same balance-of-payments' discipline as other countries.

But their idea of a more symmetrical international monetary system diverged from that of the United States. For the United States, symmetry meant the newly acquired freedom to alter its exchange rate like other states; the discipline, and costs, of leadership had gone. The greater degree of self-sufficiency of the US economy enabled the pursuit of a policy of benign neglect of the exchange rate in favour of the interests of the domestic economy. A continuity can be traced here to the remarks of Cordell Hull in 1933 (quoted above). Quite simply, United States' policy actors had a different view of foreign exchange market intervention. Their interventions, after 1971 and before the Plaza Communiqué of 1985, tended to be more infrequent, *ad hoc* and restricted in scale than EC governments would have liked. American policy actors were, on the whole, fairly unconcerned about the depreciation of the dollar in the new period of floating exchange rates.

As we shall see, the enormous structural change of the collapse of an international anchor currency was enormously important in shaping the framework within which EEC policy actors developed proposals for European monetary integration. European hopes of more determined American intervention were on occasion raised – as at the Rambouillet summit in November 1975, only to be frustrated in practice. In short, the European and American monetary policy interests appeared to be increasingly divergent in the 1970s – a crucially important background factor in stimulating new EEC initiatives.

In the wake of the Bretton Woods system the United States managed to continue to dominate the international economy, even though deprived of the structural power of being the anchor currency.[36] Structural power had other sources, not least the role of the US dollar in foreign exchange transactions. Having wrested loose from the constraints of the gold-dollar standard, successive administrations could combine retention of considerable structural power with the freedom to act in an irresponsible fashion, pursuing national interests, as they conceived them, with little or no reference to the implications for other countries. For this reason American behaviour in the 1970s and 1980s has been characterized by some international relations experts as that of a 'predatory hegemon', misusing its power in the international political economy in the pursuit of short-term and narrowly defined national interests.[37]

The US dollar's structural power in the international monetary system was underscored by the fact that it was the currency in which three-quarters of all Eurocurrency deals were done and the currency in which oil was priced and most international trade was invoiced. It remained the dominant currency in foreign exchange trading and the most important intervention currency, giving it a disproportionate influence on the world economy. The risks of intervention in foreign exchange markets continued to be borne disproportionately by other countries, like Germany and Japan. EMS countries were, accordingly, enormously sensitive and vulnerable to the volatility of the US dollar. Because persistent depreciation of the dollar imposed costs on all who held reserves of dollars, it encouraged central banks to diversify their currency reserves. Even so, the D-Mark, as the second largest reserve

36. Strange, *States and Markets*, pp. 106–7.
37. D. Calleo, *The Imperious Economy* (Cambridge, Mass.: Harvard University Press, 1982); R. Gilpin, *The Political Economy of International Relations* (Princeton, NJ: Princeton University Press, 1987); Strange, *States and Markets*.

currency, accounted for only 14.8 per cent of national currencies held in foreign reserves in 1986, compared to 66.6 per cent in US dollars.[38] But the chief result of the US dollar's volatility was to polarize EC currencies into weak and strong. So, paradoxically, American behaviour drew the Europeans together in terms of common interest in greater exchange-rate stability and monetary cooperation, whilst the weak dollar pulled them apart.

The Bank for International Settlements (BIS) and G-10

In the absence of any effective new institutional regime at the international level, the institutional legacy of the Bretton Woods system continues to be the 'most important show in town'. The institutions to which it gave birth – notably the IMF and the GATT – and those that it inherited and developed – the Bank for International Settlements – continue to survive. They in turn spawned new coordinating structures, like the Group of Ten (G-10) and the Group of Seven (G-7), that remain central to what is left of international monetary cooperation. These institutions are, accordingly, worth some attention, for they form a central part of the context of the EMS and EMU policy process.

In origin, the BIS was a European bank created in 1930 by the Hague conference in order to manage the payment of German war reparations. It was also the intention of its founders that it should serve as a new instrument of collaboration among central bankers whose currencies satisfied the practical requirements of the gold exchange standard. Central bankers were to collaborate in maintaining monetary stability, in improving the management of credit in their national markets, and in facilitating international capital movements. The BIS was to be in effect a bank for central bankers, organizing cooperation by means of the monthly meetings of governors of the European central banks that were represented on the board of the BIS.

These aims were not to be realized in the 1930s.[39] For the BIS was born in the face of a financial hurricane: in May 1931 Austria's largest bank, the Credit-Anstalt, collapsed in the wake of imprudent lending to buoy up unviable enterprises and avoid unemployment; in June the US President Herbert Hoover announced his plan for a one-year moratorium on all intergovernmental payments. The result was a general liquidity crisis whose resolution was beyond the resources available to the BIS. It went into eclipse, secretive but not powerful.

That the BIS survived throughout the Second World War was testimony to the will of central bankers to maintain a structure through which they could continue their cooperation in a postwar world, as well as to the pragmatic interest of Allied governments and their banks in not giving up interest payments from Germany. Interestingly, with the demise of the League of Nations, the BIS was the last international institution in which regular confidential contacts were maintained between the western democracies and Germany and Italy.

Despite its eclipse in the 1930s and its wartime role in facilitating German

---

38. P. Kenen, *Managing Exchange Rates* (London: Routledge, 1988), p. 62.
39. G. Trepp, *Die Bank für Internationalen Zahlungsausgleich im Zweiten Weltkrieg* (Zürich: Rotpunkt Verlag, 1993); Foreman-Peck, 'The Gold Standard as a European Monetary Lesson', pp. 14–16.

financing of its war effort, in the postwar period the BIS gained an increasingly prominent role, more in line with the hopes of its founders. Its main banking activity was to help the reserve management of central banks, which placed substantial amounts of their foreign exchange reserves with it, normally on short-term deposit. Central bank deposits were worth some $106 billion in March 1993, the BIS's share of world foreign exchange reserves being around 10 per cent. In addition to providing instant access to these deposits, the BIS lent to central banks in an emergency. In both these senses the BIS became important in the functioning of the ERM, for instance during the crisis of August to October 1992.

The key factors in the postwar renaissance of the BIS were the exigencies created by the outbreak of the Cold War and the launch of Marshall Aid. Its banking business grew appreciably, not least with the development of the Eurodollar market. The BIS's balance sheet total expanded from some $1 billion in 1960 to about $38 billion by March 1981.[40] It had also gained profile and experience in the late 1940s and 1950s by acting as agent for the Intra-European Payments Agreements (IEPA) and the European Payments Union (see chapter 3). More importantly from the perspective of international monetary cooperation, the BIS became the main opportunity for the governors of the European central banks to consult monthly on matters of common interest (from the 1960s the United States joined in the informal discussions at the governor level). Beginning in the 1960s, its role developed in two directions: undertaking rescue operations in the form of three-month credits or swaps for currencies beset by intense speculative pressures (for instance, the frequent rescue operations for Britain from 1961 onwards, for the Italian lira in 1964 and for the French franc in 1968) and the longer-term 'Basle Group Arrangements' from 1966, again developed to protect the position of British reserves.

Particularly important as evidence of the disposition of central bankers to work together in the face of the problems of the 1960s was the formation of the G-10 (with Switzerland as the eleventh associate member) out of the membership of the BIS board of directors: in effect, from the European central banks of Belgium, Britain, France, Germany, Italy, the Netherlands, Sweden and Switzerland, plus the United States, Canada and Japan. Though the G-10 included finance ministers as well as governors, its major institutional anchor remained the BIS. From 1963 it was clear that the G-10 was usurping the role of the board of executive directors of the IMF. Its role in seeking to negotiate exchange-rate realignments was demonstrated at the Bonn meeting of November 1968 (see chapter 3). And it was through G-10's work that, in 1969, the first amendment to the IMF's Articles of Agreement was elaborated, entrusting the IMF with the operation of a new Special Drawing Rights (SDR) scheme as an extra reserve asset.

The Group of Seven

With the 1970s the G-10 went into decline. Its decline reflected in part memories of the disastrous Bonn meeting, but more especially American irritation with its operation

---

40. B. Tew, *The Evolution of the International Monetary System* (London: Hutchinson, 4th edition, 1988), p. 121.

in the protracted and acrimonious run up to the Smithsonian Agreement of December 1971. Intra-EEC coordination problems were seen by the US Administration as at the heart of the inefficiency of G-10 as a forum for international monetary bargaining. From September 1973 onwards the more intimate G-5 emerged as the new forum. The G-5 comprised initially only the finance ministers of Britain, France and Germany, along with those of Japan and the United States. Subsequently, from 1985, Italy and Canada were added, making it the G-7.

This development represented something of a setback for the idea of a European 'monetary personality', coming at a time when (as we shall see in chapter 3) the first EEC initiative for EMU was already in great difficulties. President Valéry Giscard d'Estaing's hosting of the Rambouillet conference of the G-5 in November 1973 was resented by those EEC G-10 members who were excluded, including the European Commission. To make matters worse the G-5 was much more secretive than the G-10. The ambitions of the EEC to coordinate economic and monetary policies came into sharp conflict with the activities of an informal structure that involved four of its members going off to settle matters with the Americans and the Japanese. Here was a key test of whether the European Commission was a true spokesperson of the Community as a whole. President Giscard d'Estaing became locked in battle with the Commission over this issue: for him, the G-5 was a meeting of sovereign governments, and, as the Commission was not a sovereign government, it could not participate.[41] The European Council meeting in Rome in 1977 led to an unhappy compromise by which the Commission president would be enabled to attend the London G-5 summit of 1977: but it was to prove an undignified experience for him. Eventually, aided by support from Italy, the five excluded EEC states, and later Germany and the United States, a more satisfactory compromise was agreed for the Bonn summit of 1978. Thereafter, the EEC Commission president and the president of the Council of Ministers (when the presidency was drawn from one of the excluded states) attended as 'observers'; when one of the G-7 EEC states had the presidency, it would in effect wear two hats at the summit.

The G-7's role in global policy coordination to pursue exchange-rate stability had two high points. Of these the first was the Bonn summit of 1978. Here Germany and Japan, as countries with large current account surpluses, were persuaded to embark on fiscal expansion to boost global demand, whilst the United States made promises about its fiscal policies and a commitment to decontrol energy prices.[42] Unhappily, this fiscal expansion coincided with the second oil-price shock. The result was inflation, topping 5 per cent in inflation-conscious Germany in 1979. G-7 coordination had earned a bad name.

The second high point came with the period between the Plaza Communiqué of September 1985 and the Louvre Accord of February 1987 when global monetary cooperation was revived to depress the US dollar in the foreign exchange market.[43] Two things were notable about the Plaza Communiqué: it signalled a change of

41. R. Jenkins, *A Life at the Centre* (London: Pan, 1992), pp. 458–9.
42. R.D. Putnam and N. Bayne, *Hanging Together: The Seven Power Summits* (London: Sage, 1987).
43. Y. Funabashi, *Managing the Dollar: From the Plaza to the Louvre* (Washington, DC: Institute for International Economics, 1988). Also P. Volcker and T. Gyohten, *Changing Fortunes: The World's Money and the Threat to American Leadership* (New York: Times Books, 1992).

American policy away from neglect of its exchange rate, and it illustrated that the IMF's responsibility for the surveillance of exchange rates, under the Second Amendment to the IMF Agreement, was being undermined in favour of the G-7. In fact, as early as mid-1986, the initiative had lost its impetus. The Louvre Accord confined itself to a general commitment to 'stabilize the currency market' within unpublished currency bands. In practice, the original bands were realigned several times: instead of a narrower 5 per cent range at the outset, a wider width of 10 per cent was eventually chosen. Some success could be demonstrated: exchange rates were much more stable between 1987 and 1992 than between 1982 and 1987. But on balance the results brought the G-7 process into disrepute. The consequences included not only an extremely lax monetary policy in Japan, leading to the biggest speculative bubble since 1929 and forcing Japan into economic difficulties, but also the domestic failure of the US Administration to address its structural budget deficit in the interests of international monetary stability. There was a failure to back exchange-rate pronouncements with concrete budgetary, trade and structural policies. On balance, many judged G-7 to have poisoned rather than healed relations between the United States and Japan.

As Funabashi's account underlines, the Plaza Communiqué and the Louvre Accord illustrated the limitations of German involvement in the G-7 process and the *de facto* primacy that had become attached to the EMS.[44] In the first place, the Bundesbank was very reluctant to participate in coordinated intervention to stabilize the US dollar, not least because it was sceptical about its success – an illustration of how the will of policy actors to engage in international monetary cooperation is affected by perceptions of the capability to deliver. Germany's reservations were above all due to concerns about the EMS, specifically the fear that the attempt to manipulate the value of the dollar would create tensions within the ERM. Finally, throughout the G-7 process, both the Bundesbank and the Banque de France consulted and informed the other ERM central banks. The result was an explicit agreement among ERM central banks to limit the repercussions of US dollar interventions stemming from the Louvre Accord on the cohesion of the system. G-7 coordination processes were clearly not independent from consideration of the EMS, which enjoyed primacy for its members.

The key difference between the EMS and the G-7 stemmed from the fact that G-7 lacked 'institutionalization'. To an even greater extent than the EC, it was at the mercy of the policy actors involved. G-7 lacked any real institutional capacity to mould or sanction their behaviour. This weakness was apparent in the absence of rules about how policy should react to deviations of outcomes from objectives. It was also evident in the failure of G-7 to formalize its coordinatory role by developing objective indicators with reference to which the performance of each country could be judged (e.g. exchange rates, budget deficits, interest rates). Here the EMS and EMU policy process was more successful. Efforts at G-7 coordination proved fleeting rather than sustained. In essence the basic structural problem in the international political economy had not altered. As under the Bretton Woods system, effective international monetary coordination continued to depend on American initiative. But successive US administrations proved unwilling or incapable of providing the necessary policy

44. Funabashi, *Managing the Dollar.*

leadership, with the sort of firm commitment to domestic price stability and low budget deficits consistent with an anchor role. With memories of the legacies of the Bonn summit and the Louvre Accord, German and Japanese policy actors also retained an attitude of caution about G-7. For German actors that had come to mean giving priority to domestic stability in order to satisfy domestic policy priorities and to contribute to the stability of the EMS by providing a firm anchor.

Lessons

> For the historian the only absolute is change.
>> (Herbert Butterfield, *The Whig Interpretation of History* (1931: 58))

This chapter's historical account illustrates that there is no evidence of linear progress in the history of international monetary policy cooperation or of cycles that give a neat and consistent shape to the narrative. Turbulence and order coexist as defining characteristics of the history of international monetary cooperation; the concept of equilibrium seems to have little explanatory power. International monetary cooperation migrates between the edges of order and chaos: order reflecting the continuing impact of the initial conditions of such cooperation, notably a valuation of the benefits of external stability that disposes policy actors to respect the established and evolving rules of the game; and chaos as new information and events lead to non-linear change. For lengthy periods there is 'sensitive dependence on initial conditions', the legacy of past events being carried in the memories of the actors and the institutions within which they interact: for instance, an attachment to Bretton Woods bred by memories of the 1930s. Meanwhile, new trends – like the worsening economic fundamentals of the anchor – begin to emerge, at first not recognized by actors but, when recognized, leading to non-linear change. In the process we are reminded of the value of the quotation that prefaces chapter 1: of the discrepancy between the intentions of actors, however great and powerful they might appear, and the results of their actions. Their control over the dynamics of structural change and of bargaining relations is at best imperfect.

These dynamics bring home one of the lessons of history for the EMS and EMU policy process: the discrepancy between intentions (as, for instance, expressed in the Werner Report of 1970, the Brussels Resolution of 1978 and the Treaty on European Union of 1992) and the results of action is to be regarded as the norm, rather than as an exceptional state of affairs. Policy evolves as it is put into practice. It is being regularly renegotiated in the face of unexpected problems consequent on structural changes in the international political economy and on changes in the interests and power of participants in bargaining relationships. The EMS and EMU policy process is, in short, largely shaped by the problems of putting policy commitments into effect and the responses from policy actors that these problems elicit.

In addition to a sensitivity to the dynamics of the EMS and EMU, we can learn more from history: namely, to ask what is general in the unique case. History enables, indeed encourages, generalization. Without generalization there would in fact be no lessons to learn. In what ways then can we generalize from the historical experiences considered in this chapter?

First, the histories of these various episodes of international monetary cooperation and unification can only be very partially understood in terms of a 'self-reinforcing' institutional mechanism. How each has developed and its ultimate fate has been deeply affected by the nature and the consequences of policy decisions taken under its auspices, consequences that are so often unintended and unanticipated. Time and again governments have shown that they were not prepared to sacrifice domestic policy interests relating to output and employment in order to sustain international monetary cooperation and give effect to its rules. Under the gold standard regimes and under the Bretton Woods system they proved that they were willing to bend or ignore the rules of the game for the sake of domestic interests; they were even prepared to put the system itself in jeopardy. Ultimately, as Keynes emphasized, once a fixed exchange-rate system ceases to reflect the competitive power of national economies and is used to force downward adjustment of money costs, it will break down.[45] Beyond a certain point it cannot defy the structural power of economic fundamentals. The ERM crises of September 1992 and July 1993 are illustrations to set alongside the crisis of the gold exchange standard in September 1931. As the interwar gold standard displayed, an international currency regime is in mortal danger if it becomes too rigid an instrument of deflation. A similar situation of mortal danger faced the Exchange Rate Mechanism in 1992–3, as German deflationary measures to deal with the new domestic problems induced by unification spread their effects across the member states. The foreign exchange markets forced recognition of the structural realities of unsound economic fundamentals on the EMS policy process in summer 1993.

Second, an historical analysis reveals that, at the best of times, coordination and control is fragile within any system of international monetary cooperation short of political and monetary union. This observation holds even for the gold standard, in an age predating the structural power of modern capital movements. Central banks were induced by corporate self-interest to cooperate; indeed, as in the interwar period, their cooperation was closer and more intense than that of governmental leaders. But, as national central banks with a limited set of policy instruments at their command, they were forced to give consideration to domestic interests. We have also seen how the limits of coordination and control were set by a lack of cooperation in defining the rates that were being defended, as in the interwar period, or in realignments of these rates, as under Bretton Woods. In this respect the adequacy of the institutional rules of the game in fostering cooperative management was important.

When we compare the gold standard with the EMS and EMU, we are faced with a paradox. At the level of 'safety valves' to ease adjustment to the rigours of the system the EMS and EMU appear notably weaker. Gone is the resort to trade protection and exchange controls, ruled out by EC law. Little alleviation for mass unemployment or progress to even up widely disparate per capita GDP can be expected from cross-national labour migration, which remains small-scale within the EC. And neither official resource transfers via the EC nor private transfers can hope, on their present scales, to overcome the problems of huge differences in incomes and productivity.[46]

45. R. Skidelsky, *John Maynard Keynes, Volume II: The Economist as Saviour, 1920–37* (London: Macmillan, 1992).
46. Panic, *European Monetary Union.*

To these problems in the operation of the EMS and EMU must be added more institutional obstacles to price and pay flexibility than under the classical gold standard, weakening another means of adjustment and meaning that their effective functioning requires major structural reforms, notably to labour markets and the service sector. The context in which deflation is being imposed is in this respect not auspicious. But (as chapter 6 argues) at least at the level of institutional mechanisms of integration the EMS and EMU are far more imposing than the gold standard; they are more capable of adjustment to deal with emerging problems.

As the Bretton Woods system graphically portrays, another factor has allowed inconsistent policies to develop. This period threw up the lesson that fixed exchange rates, freedom of capital movement, free trade and independent national macro-economic policies were inconsistent. Ultimately, at least one of these objectives would have to be sacrificed. Again (as we shall see in chapter 5) that lesson was to be emphasized in the context of the implications of the single European market programme for the European Monetary System.[47]

But central to the question of coordination and control has been the structural power and policy leadership of the anchor. The stability of each episode of monetary cooperation has depended on the credibility of the anchor. In the case of the Latin Monetary Union it was France; of the pre-1914 gold standard, Britain; of the interwar gold exchange standard, the cooperation of Britain, France and the United States; and of the Bretton Woods system, the United States. For the ERM the anchor was to be Germany. There are three lessons to be drawn: about the impact of the rise and decline of economic leadership by an anchor country on monetary cooperation; about the particular problems of joint policy leadership (as in the interwar period) in the face of the scope for disagreement about external and internal policy priorities; and about the vulnerability of the anchor to structural change in economic fundamentals and to the structural power of the financial markets.

The credibility of the anchor will depend on more than the institutional independence, prestige and courage of its central bankers. It will reflect the performance of its domestic economy, notably on inflation, and of the international economic system over which it presides. There is certainly no support from the historical record for the idea that the performance of the domestic economy is simply and solely attributable to the central bank, however independent and wilful it may be. In other words, one should not assume that the central bank that provides the anchor to the system of international monetary cooperation is even capable of resolving its problems of coordination and control at home, never mind internationally. Post-unification Germany, and the tensions in the bargaining relations between the Bundesbank and the federal government (over the budget deficit) and with both sides of industry (over wage costs), was testimony to the way in which deficient domestic policy coordination could undermine the anchor role and unleash turbulence leading to major revision of the ERM.

Third, the historical record displays that, despite the fragility of international monetary cooperation, and despite the dramatic and memorable character of the collapse of fixed exchange-rate systems (1931, 1973 and 1993), the value of stable

47. T. Padoa-Schioppa, *Efficiency, Stability and Equity: A Strategy for the Evolution of the Economic System of the European Community* (Oxford: Oxford University Press, 1987).

exchange rates has continued to be recognized (not least by Keynes himself). Structural change in the form of increasing economic interdependence has kept the value of external stability at the centre of economic policy debate, with multinational business corporations having a special corporate self-interest in promoting this policy goal. As economic interdependence has grown, notably with an increased sensitivity and vulnerability of national economies to international trade, avoidance of volatility in import and export prices and predictability in production and investment decisions have become widely recognized benefits of international monetary cooperation. The era of floating exchange rates in the 1930s is still remembered for the protectionism, barter agreements and restrictive trading blocs that it engendered. With the end of the Second World War internationalism was very much back in business and, backed by multinationals and international institutions like the EC Commission, remained so. In short, policy makers have repeatedly returned to the value of order in external monetary and economic relations. The structural power of trade and economic interdependency within the EC shaped the agenda of bargaining and the development of rules within the EMS and EMU policy process.

Yet, paradoxically, another source of structural power in the international political economy – the growth of international capital flows beyond the control of national governments, symbolized by the post-1960s Eurodollar market – has made exchange-rate stability even more difficult to attain. If there has been something of a loss of faith in international monetary cooperation in the 1970s and 1980s, it had a great deal to do with a sense of diminished capability to manage the structural power of financial markets. Where, as with the Plaza Communiqué of 1985, policy seemed to be successful it was because policy was driving the dollar in the direction that it was already moving. Policy was 'driving the rate' rather than 'leaning against the wind'. Against this background monetary authorities were more hesitant to attempt to put together and operate a more rule-based system of international monetary cooperation in G-7. A much more discretion-based use of their power seemed attractive. By 1993 the EMS and EMU policy process was faced by this dilemma. In the face of the structural power of the financial markets, was it possible to sustain stable exchange rates? Or was the choice between a return to more national discretion in monetary policy (implicit in the very wide 15 per cent fluctuation band adopted in August 1993) and a more rapid, decisive move to EMU?

Although there are some fascinating historical parallels with the ERM, underlying changes in the behaviour of economic fundamentals and in the nature of structural power in the international political economy need to be appreciated. The single biggest discrepancy between the period 1873–96 and the interwar period, on the one hand, and the 1970s–1980s, on the other, has been in the behaviour of prices. Interwar consumer prices reached a peak in 1920. After that the price level – not just the rate of inflation – was on a falling trend. With the 1970s price inflation emerged as the prime enemy. In the three year period 1970–3, before the first oil crisis escalated inflation, the cumulative rates of inflation for EEC countries varied from 25.2 per cent (the Netherlands) and 22.4 per cent (Italy) to 17.7 per cent (Belgium); Britain scored 28 per cent. The effects of inflation on international monetary cooperation were complex. In producing economic divergence rather than convergence it undermined such cooperation. But, on the other hand, as control of inflation came to the centre of the agenda, 'tying one's hands' to a strong anchor currency was identified as a policy instrument of external discipline for this purpose. Hence the EMS and EMU have evolved as instruments of 'disinflation'.

But as instruments of disinflation they have not been able to operate like the classical gold standard. Here we come to a second, related structural change in economic fundamentals. The structural obstacles to pay and price flexibility became much greater in the late twentieth century. Labour market rigidities were engendered by the higher costs of making workers redundant; the cost structures of business were less flexible with the increased burden of social-security costs on EC firms; and an enlarged public sector created new problems of efficiency and inflationary pressures. In this changed structural context the effective functioning of the EMS and EMU raised new and highly politically sensitive issues of structural reform: to labour markets, to social security systems and to the service sector.

Third, structural change in the form of the rise of powerful international financial markets has had enormous effects on the management of international monetary cooperation, not least on the ERM (a topic for chapter 8). By the 1980s capital was moving on a massive scale, taking advantage of a host of new financial instruments, like swaps and options. They became symbols of an innovatory, expansive but riskier banking environment. The growing opaqueness of financial activity meant that it was harder to assess the build-up of systemic risk in foreign exchange markets and more difficult for central banks to act as efficient gatekeepers between policy and those markets.

To this can be added a fourth change: the location of the hegemon within the international monetary system. *De facto*, after the First World War Britain was no longer able to play that role. With the Second World War structural power within the international monetary system passed outside Europe altogether. The BIS and the G-10 helped to retain some semblance of a central role for Europe. But, in reality, American economic power and the fate of the US dollar was the new axis around which the system continued to spin. As we shall see, the functioning of the EMS has remained deeply sensitive and vulnerable to the dollar. In monetary policy the EC's interdependence with the United States continued to be asymmetric despite the collapse of the Bretton Woods system.

Finally, the question arises of whether the new institutional structure of the EC has significantly changed the context of monetary cooperation among the member states. There is an interesting contrast, and link, between the declining fortunes of global monetary cooperation since the late 1960s and the new momentum that has emerged in Europe behind monetary integration and the promise of union. But the issue that is raised by the American and German experiences of forging monetary union is whether the institutional mechanisms of the EC – short of political union – can hope to provide a framework sufficiently robust to support the achievement of monetary union. Political union is not just a matter of large-scale fiscal transfer mechanisms to ease adjustment of uncompetitive areas within a monetary union and of a mechanism to coordinate fiscal with monetary policies. Without such mechanisms the policy tensions could drive the monetary union apart. It also involves a supranational framework of political legitimacy within which a European central bank can root itself.[48] Perhaps

48. D. Wincott, 'The European Central Bank: Constitutional Dimensions and Political Limits', *International Relations*, 11:2 (1992), pp. 111–26.

even more fundamentally, the American and German experiences firmly underline the difficulties of bringing about a monetary union even within a pre-existing framework of political union. They cast very serious doubts on the political wisdom of a narrowly 'monetarist' and mechanistic approach to EMU.

Chapter 3

LESSONS OF HISTORY (2)

The European Payments Union, the 'spirit of the Hague', the Werner Report and the 'snake'

The path to European monetary union will not be a stroll; it will be hard and thorny.

> (Karl Blessing, president of the Bundesbank, 27 January 1963, remarks on NDR radio programme)

L'Europe se fera par la monnaie ou ne se fera pas.

> (Jacques Rueff, French economist)

The postwar pursuit of European monetary integration and union is characterized by a central paradox. In one sense there was fundamental change. New institutions reflected new sources of structural power: notably, the role assigned to the EEC and earlier the European Coal and Steel Community (ECSC) as new means of preserving the security of Europeans (the fragility of which had been so harshly demonstrated by two world wars), and the role of trade interdependence in supporting the European integration process and associating it with the experience of rising prosperity. But, on the other hand, short of political union with institutions enjoying their own political authority and competences to act, the EEC continued to offer a frail centrifugal force. This paradox permeated the postwar history of EMU: an idea that would not go away but whose realization was fraught with immense difficulties.

What is perhaps most striking and instructive is the combination of continuity and change in the vocabulary of EMU: the language of 'cooperation' is now accompanied by that of 'integration' and 'union'. In this transformation of language was secreted a change of ambition among key policy actors and those who influenced them. Cooperation implies working together to some end but doing so on an essentially voluntary basis. No transfer of authority takes place; policy remains firmly fixed at the national level; and wide discretion continues to be enjoyed by national policy makers in observing the rules of the game. But with integration comes the idea of completing an 'imperfect' cooperation by the addition of new institutions so as to better combine the parts into a whole. Here authority is pooled or shared; supranational institutions upgrade the importance attached to common interests in the policy process; and the value placed on reputation as an honest and reliable negotiator exerts a greater influence on the policy process. With the language of 'union' ambition to transform international relations takes its final form. Authority is ceded in an irreversible manner; a new level of government is created with its own legitimacy and autonomy of action; and national policy is framed within independently enforceable supranational rules.

As we shall see in this and the next chapter, the development of the European Community's role in economic and monetary policy reflects the interplay of these three elements: of cooperation, notably in economic policy coordination; of integration, which finds its particular expression in the monetary policy field; and of union, via an irrevocable fixing of exchange rates and/or the creation of a single European currency. What we are witnessing is substantial continuity in the practice of economic policy, but evidence of more significant change in the approach to monetary policy. The EMS and EMU policy process displays simultaneously a sense of being in the sway of the past and yet trying to break free.

The postwar birth of European monetary integration was far from being an isolated sectoral development. It was bound up in a critical juncture of events in the international political economy, most especially in the wider processes of economic cooperation and integration associated with the Organization for European Economic Cooperation (OEEC). The key factor here was the massive structural power of the United States in the immediate postwar international economy. This structural power was brought to bear in the form of American commitment to the reconstruction of western Europe, as exemplified in the Marshall Plan of 1947, and the attempt by US policy makers to tie economic and financial aid to the condition of economic and financial cooperation and, preferably, integration by the west European states. The failure of the United States to realize in full its ambitions for European integration can be readily illustrated.[1] But American aid was crucial in sustaining reconstruction, and its support for west European integration was important psychologically.

American support for European integration coincided with the presence in government of politicians who had direct experience of the failures of the 1930s and the horrors of two world wars on European soil. For these politicians a break with the bonds of the past was indispensable: notably Konrad Adenauer, German Chancellor 1949–63; Robert Schuman, French Prime Minister 1947–8 and Foreign Minister 1948–52; Paul-Henri Spaak, Belgian Prime Minister 1948–51 and Foreign Minister 1948–51, 1954–7 and 1961–6; and Alcide de Gasperi, Italian Prime Minister 1945-53. With the exception of Spaak these figures were Christian Democrats. Here we come to another source of structural change in postwar Europe: at the level of party and ideas. Christian Democracy emerged as a new postwar political movement preaching reconciliation and identifying European union with this principle. Here, additional to external American pressure, was a fresh ideological and party political factor that was to prove of enduring significance. On European union, as well as in other respects, Chancellor Helmut Kohl saw himself as the inheritor of Adenauer's political ideas. Federalist politicians were far from able to use their will indiscriminately, as events were to testify. But they represented a new climate of ideas that was to prove a potent new factor.

Not least there was a pervasive sense that, in international economic and monetary affairs, the mistakes of the 1930s must not be repeated. The economic crisis of 1947 served as a reminder of the inherent limitations of a postwar European reconstruction founded on national action and national markets. Economic cooperation and even integration were, accordingly, more readily accepted as a practical requirement of national prosperity. Propelled by a combination of historical learning and economic crisis, coloured by new political beliefs in union, and sustained by the structural power of American support, European integration became one of the great phenomena of postwar Europe. Economic and monetary policies became bound up with it.

1. A. Milward, *The Reconstruction of Western Europe, 1945–51* (London: Methuen, 1984).

In exploring the history of European monetary integration between 1945 and 1978, this chapter focuses again on the question of what can be learned from the past. Two themes stand out: the problems of putting ambitions for integration and union into effect in the face of the incompatibility of the goals of monetary cooperation; and the importance of the configurations of power on which initiatives and their implementation depend, in particular the problem of effective leadership in monetary policy cooperation. These twin problems were to frustrate early American initiative and undermine the EEC's 1962 Action Programme and the Werner Report of 1970.

The European Payments Union: the United States and currency union

Few episodes reveal more clearly the character of the postwar period and the historic problems of EMU than the debate surrounding the creation of the European Payments Union, its character, its operation and its demise. In this story are exhibited the new hopes of the period and their disappointment. We see both the expression of American structural power and its limitations even at such an early stage in the postwar period. Also, the story underlines how the configuration of power in this policy sector could differ sharply from that in another, namely the coal and steel sector. In this case Britain's role was pivotal, a further reminder that the configuration of power in 1950 was very different from that in 1978–9 (the birth of the EMS) and in 1988–91 (the rebirth of EMU). Monetary history is a record of changing location of leadership roles in the international political economy.

American influence on the design of the Bretton Woods system was a price that the British and French governments had to pay for indispensable postwar dollar credits and generous American funding of the United Nations Relief and Recovery Agency (UNRRA). Total US aid to western Europe totalled $10,098 million between July 1945 and June 1947. But, despite the scale of this aid, it became apparent as early as the payments crisis of 1947 that the resources to purchase dollar imports were being exhausted rapidly. The threat to continuing reconstruction was most vividly symbolized by the British exchange crisis of that August and the ending of sterling–dollar convertibility. Mounting difficulties in international trade and payments posed a serious threat to the continuation of recovery: a payments crisis raised the spectre of a crisis in production. To these new and impending difficulties the Bretton Woods system provided no real answer. Increasingly evident was the threat of a reconstitution of the international political economy of the 1930s with its principle of economic autarky, a danger that the US Administration was determined to avoid.

Most importantly, the payments crisis of 1947 took place against the background of the unveiling of the Cold War and a spreading realization that Soviet power could be extended further westwards by exploiting the economic weakness of western Europe. West European governments proved adept at using this fear of threat to western security – the structural power of the Soviet Union in the military field – as an incentive to American action. Against this background the US State Department began to argue that, in order to consolidate and carry forward reconstruction, and to 'save Europe', a shift from relief measures to a longer-term package of support for western Europe was required. In turn, this support could be used as an incentive to lever the cooperation of west European countries in constructing a more closely integrated

Europe, based on transnational economic collaboration and the competitive stimulus to productivity from a large single market on the American model. In effect, Europe could be reconstituted in the American image. Prewar New Deal ideas were harnessed to the new postwar context of sustaining a beleaguered European recovery, containing Soviet expansion and winning the battle of political ideas and beliefs in Europe.

Such was the perception of leading American policy makers in 1947 and the pre-eminently political calculations that lay behind the launch of the European Recovery Programme (ERP) or the so-called Marshall Plan that year. From 1948 to 1951 the US Congress made over $12 billion available for the ERP. The outflow of dollars represented 2.1 per cent of American GDP in 1948, rising to a peak of 2.4 per cent in 1949. As Hogan demonstrates, this flow of aid was crucially important in sustaining recovery. It facilitated essential imports, eased production bottlenecks, encouraged higher rates of capital formation and helped to suppress inflation.[2]

The payments crisis of 1947 also led US policy makers to give priority to assisting the west European countries in re-establishing convertibility. Convertibility would simultaneously aid the integration of Western Europe and the implementation of the Bretton Woods system. For it was clear in 1947 that the Bretton Woods system was stillborn in Europe. Most trade in Europe in the late 1940s was conducted through some 200 bilateral agreements.[3] Specified bilateral credit lines were typically incorporated in these agreements, beyond which bilateral deficits had to be settled in gold. But European governments tended to be desperate to retain their small gold holdings. Hence deficits forced them to use quotas and high tariffs to restrict imports.

Some means of escape from the constraints of bilateralism was required. The 'dollar gap' exacerbated the problem. All European countries were concerned to earn surpluses in gold, US dollars or any currency convertible into dollars. Only in this way could the demand for imports from the dollar area be satisfied. As the British government discovered when, in 1947, it made the pound sterling convertible for just seven weeks, the price to be paid for a unilateral declaration of convertibility was that other countries would immediately seek to earn a surplus with the country concerned, for the convertible currency had become equivalent to the dollar. After the failed unilateral dash to convertibility by Britain in 1947, the perception gained ground that a return to convertibility required a multilateral framework based on coordinated European action.

The story of European reconstruction involves the unprecedented engagement of senior United States' officials in the promotion of European integration, including the idea of European monetary union. It embraces the European Recovery Programme and the European Payments Union, and in particular the role of the European Cooperation Administration (ECA), the US agency administering the ERP. But the story is one of the difficulties of putting far-reaching ideas of integration into effect. These difficulties had four main sources: first, in a growing American perception that the EPU's

2. For contrasting views on the importance of the Marshall Plan for European integration see Milward, *The Reconstruction of Western Europe, 1945–51;* M.J. Hogan, *The Marshall Plan: America, Britain and the Reconstruction of Western Europe, 1947–1952* (Cambridge: Cambridge University Press, 1987).
3. W. Diebold, *Trade and Payments in Western Europe: A Study in Economic Cooperation, 1947–1951* (New York, 1952).

development could bring two American objectives into conflict – the objective of achieving an integrated Europe, and the objective of achieving a multilateral payments system in the form of the Bretton Woods agreements; second, in the surprising speed with which western Europe was able to restore output and trade and thereby reduce the degree of its structural dependency; third, the variety and complexity of national interests that had to be reconciled; and fourth, the particular power that the British government had within negotiations about the EPU. Ultimately, three of these factors acted as external constraints on American power; the first undermined the internal capability of the United States to exercise its structural power over Europe.

Essentially, the EPU was born out of American failure to turn the Organization for European Economic Cooperation, the body established under American pressure to plan the disbursement of Marshall Aid, into an effective instrument of trade liberalization, market integration and institution building for a united Europe.[4] Successive efforts to achieve multilateral payments agreements within the OEEC framework had come to little: the Agreement on Multilateral Monetary Compensation of November 1947; the first Intra-European Payments Agreement (IEPA) of November 1948; and the second IEPA of July 1949. The initiative stemmed from the ECA's Planning Group, led by Richard Bissell and including Harlan Cleveland. Their ideas were espoused by Paul Hoffman, administrator of the ERP 1948–50, William C. Foster (Hoffman's deputy and successor in 1950) and Averell Harriman, special ambassador to the ERP 1948–50. Central to their thinking were proposals for an inter-European commerce commission, modelled on the American Interstate Commerce Commission, and a European central bank with similar powers to the Federal Reserve Board and operating a single currency. The new initiative was designed to circumvent the obstacles represented by a legacy of traditional European attitudes and loyalties represented in the OEEC. A supranational and technocratic approach was being advocated, in effect the approach to integration that was later to be characterized as 'functionalist'.

By October 1949 the ECA's Planning Group had put together a specific timetable for European monetary union and a European central bank, in conjunction with the economists Robert Triffin and Albert Hirschman. Externally, the French economist Robert Marjolin, a confidant of Jean Monnet, was involved as secretary-general of the OEEC (1948–55). Later (as we shall see) Marjolin was to serve as the EEC commissioner responsible for economic and financial affairs from 1958 to 1967. Triffin was to emerge as Monnet's leading monetary adviser and to play a long-term role in giving visibility to these ideas, as well as in the debate about the EMS in 1978–9. The timetable was based around the assumption that Marshall Aid would come to an end in 1952. Hence, it was radically short: by the end of 1951 a currency union controlled by a European monetary authority, followed in July 1952 by the

---

4. The best general overviews of the EPU are R. Triffin, *Europe and the Money Muddle: From Bilateralism to Near-Convertibility, 1947–1956* (New Haven, Conn.: Yale University Press, 1957); Milward, *The Reconstruction of Western Europe, 1945–51*, ch. 10; J. Kaplan and G. Schleiminger, *The European Payments Union* (Oxford: Clarendon Press, 1989); Hogan, *The Marshall Plan*, pp. 293–335. See also D. Gros and N. Thygesen, *European Monetary Integration: From the European Monetary System to European Monetary Union* (London: Longman, 1992), pp. 4–9.

introduction of a European currency, the *écu* or Europa. The *écu* or Europa would float against the dollar, and all quantitative restrictions on dollar trade would be removed. In a speech of 31 October Hoffman made the first public reference to the demand for 'a single large European market' without quantitative or 'monetary' barriers to trade. But there was no explicit reference to European monetary union.

Already the United States' State Department was beginning to assert its view that to make aid dependent on agreement to a European central bank was likely to jeopardize negotiations. The challenge to sovereignty was too strong and direct to be tolerated, particularly by the British government; preference should be given to use of the more flexible word 'integration' rather than 'unification'. It was also less clear to the State Department that the objectives of promoting European integration and a return to the Bretton Woods system were readily compatible. Faced with potential conflict of objectives, the State Department gave clear priority in negotiations to the Bretton Woods system.

The negotiations on the EPU and their outcome in the treaty signed on 19 September 1950 illustrated a different configuration of power from that in the Schuman Plan for the European Coal and Steel Community, which had just been launched by the French government. In the case of the ECSC power was recognized as laying mainly with France.[5] By contrast, in the EPU negotiations Britain's position was pivotal. American policy was ultimately shaped by a recognition that defence and security considerations dictated that the British government should be a strategic player in these negotiations, however disappointed many US policy makers felt about its failure to take a constructive lead in integrating Europe. In short, the structural realities of European security prevailed. The American negotiating position that Britain must be a part of the new EPU gave great leverage to that country's government. Britain proved in the end to be prepared to accept a definite commitment of the Sterling Area to a pattern of multilateral settlements on a world-wide basis as well as involvement in a European framework. In return, it was able to frustrate the ECA's plan to make the EPU a stepping stone towards European monetary and ultimately political union. The essential commitment entered into with the EPU treaty was to a multilateral payments system in western Europe and embracing the Sterling Area. All that was left of the ECA's ambitions was the creation of a special EPU unit of account, to be defined as having the equivalent gold content to the 1950 US dollar. For Triffin it would provide an element for incorporation in later proposals for monetary union.[6]

Another factor that influenced the balance of power against the ECA in the negotiations was the stronger economic position of western Europe in 1950 than in 1947. By 1950 its foreign trade was already more than 25 per cent above its prewar level and output was rising every year. ECA influence in Europe was, correspondingly, weakened. We saw above how and why its influence had diminished in Washington. The US Treasury saw the prospect of a strong and strengthening EPU endangering the central position of the United States in the international monetary system. The British government was able to effectively exploit the differences between the ECA and the US Treasury to ensure that the EPU's Management Board did not become a strong

5. Milward, *The Reconstruction of Western Europe, 1945–51*, ch. 12.
6. Triffin, *Europe and the Money Muddle*, p. 173.

institution. In other words, the combination of incompatible goals among American policy actors with a reduced capacity for American leadership in Europe killed at birth the first major postwar effort to achieve EMU.

In essence, the EPU provided an official compensating mechanism by which deficits with one country could be offset by surpluses with another. The problem of the lack of transferability of bilateral balances was solved by this means in the absence of currency convertibility via foreign exchange markets. Each month the EPU took over all the bilateral surpluses and deficits of each of its members and worked out its 'cumulative net position' with the union. In this way all bilateral deficits and surpluses among members were simply cancelled out. Only the changes in the 'cumulative net position' of each country with the union as a whole had to be settled. Both members' cumulative net positions and 'credits' made available as one means of settlement were expressed in terms of the new EPU unit of account.

The complex settlement mechanism owed a great deal again to Triffin in his capacity as economic adviser to the ECA. In effect, it represented a compromise between the interests of countries expecting to be in surplus with the union (they wanted settlement in gold or US dollars) and the interests of those anticipating deficits (they preferred credit so as not to lose precious gold and dollars). US dollars and 'credits' were the principal means of settlement. Each country was assigned a quota equal to 15 per cent of the sum of exports and imports in 1949, basing the quota on a 'turnover' figure. The monthly settlement formula related the proportion between dollars (or gold) and credit to the member country's cumulative deficit or surplus expressed as a percentage of its quota. From August 1955 the characteristic dollar–credit ratio changed from 50:50 to 75:25.

The EPU had to face an immediate crisis in 1950–1 when the Federal Republic of Germany developed a large current-account deficit that soon exceeded its quota. The management of this crisis illustrated that the balance-of-payments position of member countries had ceased to be seen as simply national problems and that other countries were prepared to agree to policy measures that were not in their short-term interests in order to save the system. An effective and coordinated response was achieved by the implementation of a package of measures advocated by an expert group of the EPU management board: a combination of tighter monetary policy in Germany with a temporary unilateral suspension of import liberalization and a special EPU credit to Germany. In effect, the EPU management board had begun to develop what was to be later described as 'multilateral surveillance'. At the same time an asymmetry between the settlement terms for creditor and debtor positions revealed the weakness of the EPU. It could deal in 1950–1 with the German deficit crisis. But once that deficit was transformed into a mounting current-account surplus the EPU found that it had no real means to force the German authorities to take compensatory action. This problem was later to plague the IMF and G-7 in relation to Germany.

In effect, two multilateral settlement areas operated until December 1958, kept apart by exchange controls. On the one hand was the dollar area, within which settlement was in US dollars; on the other was the 'soft' settlement area, in which settlement was mainly through the machinery of the EPU or in sterling. In fact, the EPU area accounted for something like 70 per cent of world trade. Its core membership was all 18 OEEC members, but through the sterling and French franc areas it covered much of Africa and Asia as well. Some discrimination in trade and payments against countries in the dollar area did indeed occur. At the same time European exports to the United States increased faster than imports, and the problem of the 'dollar gap' diminished in seriousness. Also, by 1957–8, the cumulative net positions of most member countries became large relative to their quotas, requiring full gold settlement. Hence EPU lost much of its value and importance for debtor countries. They were more impressed by the new scope for international official borrowing and lending, with its promise of greater autonomy of action in national policy. This shift in incentives induced the view that a full return to convertibility was possible. Accordingly, in December 1958 the EPU was wound up, the participating countries made their currencies convertible, and the 'binary payments system' ceded place to a unified and greatly expanded dollar area as the countries of the old 'soft' settlement area undertook a drastic dismantling of exchange controls in favour of a market-oriented international monetary system. The Bretton Woods system had at last come of age, but of the ambitions of 1949–50 practically nothing was left. The forum for policy coordination was the IMF. Yet (as we saw in chapter 2) no sooner had the IMF achieved its full status than it was reduced to 'fire fighting' to protect the system of which it was so central a part.

The European Community: the Treaty of Rome, the Action Programme of 1962 and its aftermath

With the failure of the ambitions of 1949–50, the aspirations to provide a European forum for economic and financial policy coordination, and ultimately for Economic and Monetary Union, passed to the new institutions of the European Economic Community. The European Commission became the natural institutional home for the idea of EMU, continuing to pursue like the ECA an essentially technocratic approach to its realization. Charged with an explicitly supranational role, with a moral force as the conscience of the Community in working towards the treaty commitment to 'ever closer union', and with the executive power linked to its role as the initiator of Community legislation, the Commission has always been attracted to EMU. Between 1958 and 1967 this association was implicit in the role of Marjolin as Commission vice-president and commissioner responsible for economic and financial affairs. As we shall see in more detail later, the Treaty of Rome of 1957 created a twelve-year transition period for completion of the customs union. EMU was not prioritized: but it was never dead. For EMU was always understood to be an issue that would be propelled on to the agenda in the wake of trade liberalization and the achievement of a genuinely common market: in other words, policy linkage would operate. That is why the two main EMU initiatives (symbolized by the Werner Report and the Delors Report) followed respectively on the removal of trade barriers (completed 18 months ahead of plan on 1 July 1968) and on the onset of the completion of the single European market programme. The Commission could if anything be accused of rushing forward with EMU proposals before trade and market liberalization had been given time to demonstrate their practical value.

The continuing story of the EC and EMU is one of the difficulties of giving practical effect to a big and imprecisely defined idea. EMU was and remained an essentially contested concept, contested in meaning (as we saw in chapter 1) and contested in its technical details. Technically, it raises problems of the compatibility of the goals of monetary policy cooperation. A broad distinction can be made between the so-called *economist* and *monetarist* approaches to EMU. German and Dutch policy actors have consistently advocated a priority to the economic dimension of EMU: that is, to convergence of economic performance, notably of inflation rates, budget deficits, government debt and interest rates, as a precondition of monetary union. Additional to 'nominal' convergence of this type, the creation of a single internal market and the development of political institutions with the authority to operate an effective fiscal policy at the EEC level were required. In this perspective, the timescale of monetary union was long; coordination of economic policies was the priority. The capacity for effective coordinated action had to be demonstrated before an irrevocable fixing of exchange rates and a centralization of monetary authority in an EEC central bank. Later this approach was to be labelled 'the coronation theory' of EMU. The 'economist' approach was suited to German interests as a country with a low inflation rate and a surplus on its balance of payments. It served to reduce the risks of imported inflation and hence to help safeguard internal stability.

By contrast, the 'monetarist' approach was consistent with the interests of countries with high inflation rates and balance of payments deficits. French and Belgian officials have tended to emphasize that monetary integration could act as a driving force for wider economic integration. Priority to external stability in the form of fixed exchange rates would force a more effective economic policy cooperation and the strengthening of the EEC's political authority and budgetary competence. It would also involve Germany in financing their balance of payments' difficulties. As we shall see in chapter 9, a neo-functionalist argument was at work here. Integration in one sector, typically a highly technical one like monetary policy, would spillover into related sectors in order to make the original integration viable. In the perspective of the monetarist approach, the timescale of EMU was short. Priority had to be given to an irrevocable fixing of parities, together with the establishment of a European Reserve Fund or some other form of mutual aid in helping to meet balance of payments' problems.

This basic dispute about the proper approach to EMU had profound practical consequences, for it went to the heart of the political issue of who bears the costs of adjustment to EMU. A monetarist strategy opened up the prospect that surplus countries would be indefinitely financing the deficit ones, without being able to force the latter to take firm corrective measures. Hardly surprising then, Germany offered staunch resistance to this view. The economist strategy would, by contrast, place the burden of adjustment on the deficit countries. This broad distinction of approach between economist and monetarist strategies surfaced repeatedly in the policy debates on EMU, providing a thread of continuity running through later debates and a central issue on which compromise had to be found in the Werner Report and later the Delors Report and the Treaty on European Union. Compromise was always likely to favour Germany given its structural power as the dominant EC currency and hence its leadership role in EC monetary cooperation. But it was also uneasy and prone to dissolve under the pressure of events.

The relative lack of progress of EMU as a policy idea in the 1960s was not simply due to the contested character of the goals of monetary cooperation. Above all, the catalyst was needed of a combination of external structural change in the international political economy with internal pressures to place it firmly on the political agenda of the EEC and to encourage Germany to assume a leadership role that was necessary to EMU's progress. Internally, the structural dynamics of trade interdependence was gathering force. But it had yet to reach a scale where its effects and visibility *vis-à-vis* other economic processes at work concentrated political attention on its implications for economic and monetary union. In 1960 the ratio of intra-EEC trade to GDP stood at only about 6 per cent (compared to 12 per cent in 1975 and 15 per cent in 1991). Perhaps even more importantly, the external environment of the early and mid-1960s was relatively tranquil and not as yet radically threatening to German priority to internal stability. The six EEC states continued to notch up substantial balance-of-payments' surpluses through the 1960s. The first major problems of external deficits affected France in 1968 and 1969. Apart from a revaluation of 5 per cent by Germany and the Netherlands in 1961, exchange rates among the EEC currencies remained fixed until 1969. Indeed, symptomatic of the attitudes of EEC governments to EMU was the way in which the Dutch and German governments in 1961 failed to undertake prior consultation with other EEC governments about their revaluation (though they failed also to properly consult the IMF). In effect, the external 'guarantee' of exchange-rate stability and German satisfaction with the status quo in international monetary cooperation kept EMU off, or at least low down, the EEC's agenda.

But, during the 1960s, debates within the EEC, notably in the Council of Economic and Finance Ministers (ECOFIN), demonstrated a concern that the functioning of the EEC's two main policy initiatives of that period, the customs union and the Common Agricultural Policy (CAP), could face disruption from exchange-rate adjustments, like those of 1969. Threat to the *acquis communautaire* was exhibiting its potential to alter the agenda and favour new policy initiatives, a potential not lost on the EEC institutions. Otherwise, against the background of the relative success of the Bretton Woods system, the EEC Commission was starved of political opportunity to pursue the idea of EMU. As that system came under increasing stress from 1966, a stress symbolized by the devaluation of sterling in November 1967, that opportunity began to present itself.[7]

EMU was kept alive in the 1960s by its apostles: notably, Marjolin in the EEC Commission and, connected to Jean Monnet's Action Committee for the United States of Europe, Pierre Uri (economic adviser to the EEC 1958–9) and Robert Triffin. Essentially, the Treaty of Rome of 1957 had been a disappointment for the federalists in respect of EMU. The Spaak Report, on which the treaty had been based, had suggested the desirability of monetary unification; and Uri had been the main author of that report.[8] But the Treaty of Rome contained only very general provisions in this

---

7. M.G. de Vries, *The International Monetary Fund 1966–71: The System under Stress* (Washington, DC: International Monetary Fund, 1977).
8. P. Uri, 'Réflexion sur l'approche fonctionnaliste de Jean Monnet et suggestions pour l'avenir', in G. Majone *et al.*, *Jean Monnet et l'Europe d'aujourd'hui* (Baden-Baden, 1989), p. 76. For the Spaak Report see Comité Intergouvernemental crée par la Conférence de Messine, *Rapport des chefs de délégation aux ministres des affaires etrangères* (Brussels, 21 April 1956).

area, notably:

- Article 2 which set the target of 'establishing a Common Market and progressively approximating the economic policies of the member states . . . ';
- Article 103 which states that short-term economic policies should be considered as a matter of 'common interest' and, therefore, should be subject to 'mutual consultations';
- Article 104 which suggests that 'each member state shall pursue economic policy to ensure the equilibrium of its overall balance of payments and to maintain confidence in the currency while ensuring a high level of employment and the stability of the level of prices'. As a means of achieving this objective, member states should coordinate their economic policies. In the monetary field coordination was to be promoted through a Monetary Committee. This new committee was to have a consultative role, expressing opinions about the monetary and financial situation in each country. Each country was to nominate two members, to meet together with two representatives from the EEC Commission;
- Article 106 stipulates that exchange controls should be eliminated to the extent necessary to make possible the movement of goods, services, capital and people;
- Article 107 underlines that the exchange rate is to be viewed as a problem of common interest;
- Article 108 envisages 'mutual assistance' in case of serious difficulties in the balance of payments by 'the granting of limited credits by other member states, subject to the agreement of the latter'.

Faced by this disappointing outcome, Monnet asked Triffin and Uri to prepare proposals for a European monetary system.[9] Triffin was the link to the earlier ideas of the ECA for monetary union in 1949–50. His proposals gave priority to the establishment of a European reserve fund as a key first step on the way to an EEC central bank and a single currency.[10] These proposals were adopted by the Action Committee for the United States of Europe and promoted in declarations of November 1959 and July 1961.[11] They were identified as a priority for two reasons. First, they were essential if the EEC was to exert an influence in the international monetary system commensurate with its influence in the international trading system via the common commercial policy. Triffin provided the critique of the viability of the gold-dollar standard and of the need for the European countries to protect themselves against its in-built problems. Second, Britain's application of 1961 to join the EEC was seen as presenting a new political opportunity. The issue of 'widening' the EEC had to be accompanied by a new consideration of 'deepening' so that Britain would be joining an 'economic and political union'. But in practice it was to be Monnet's own French government, presided over from 1958 by Charles de Gaulle, that rejected the

9. R. Triffin, 'Note sur ma collaboration avec Jean Monnet', in *Temoignages à la mémoire de Jean Monnet* (Lausanne: Fondation Jean Monnet pour l'Europe et Centre de Recherches Européennes, 1989), p. 531.
10. R. Triffin, *Gold and the Dollar Crisis: The Future of Convertibility* (New Haven, Conn.: Yale University Press, 1960), pp. 131–44.
11. *Action Committee for the United States of Europe: Statements and Declarations 1955–67* (London, 1969), pp. 46 and 60–2.

British application (in January 1963) and that asserted the claims of national sovereignty against the proposals of the EEC Commission. The dynamics of Council bargaining were to offer little opportunity for federal ideas.

Whatever internal political window of opportunity that might have opened in the early 1960s was rapidly closed. This process is illustrated by the fate of the Commission's first major proposal for monetary integration, the *Action Programme for the Second Stage* of 1962.[12] Marjolin, the commissioner responsible for economic and financial affairs, had been close to the ECA's planning in 1949–50 (as secretary-general of the OEEC) and an intimate collaborator of Monnet (they had worked together in the early postwar French national planning commission). Accordingly, it was not surprising that there were striking similarities between the Action Programme and the proposals of the Action Committee for the United States of Europe. The Action Programme was prompted by two events: first, general concern about the disruptive effects of the Dutch and German revaluations of 1961 and the lack of consultation accompanying them (a concern expressed in a report of the EEC Monetary Committee in 1961); and second, the need to provide an effective framework for possible British membership of the EEC.[13] In October 1962 the European Parliament added its call for closer coordination of monetary policies to that of the Monetary Committee. The Commission was responding not only to the pressure of parliamentarians but also to a committee comprising very senior national finance and central bank officials.

The added ingredient was a strongly technocratic and rationalist policy culture within the Commission, articulated in the figure of Marjolin with his background in French national economic planning. This policy culture, strongly influenced by French values, was reflected in both the rationale and the content of the Action Programme. In terms of rationale the Commission was seeking to establish a clear path for stages two and three of the transitional period ending in 1970. In terms of content the Action Programme was a move towards integrated EEC planning based on detailed sectoral studies. By the end of the transitional period, if not earlier, a system of fixed exchange rates and a European reserve currency were to be in place. Meanwhile, in the second stage, a whole variety of measures were to be taken: a system of prior consultation on almost all major aspects of national and external monetary policies; the creation of a Committee of Central Bank Governors, a Budgetary Policy Committee and a Medium-Term Policy Committee; a system of mutual aid; and the extension of the liberalization of capital movements. In essence, the Action Programme of 1962 represented a climate of optimism about integration induced by the success of the first

12. Commission of the EEC, *Action Programme of the Community for the Second Stage* (Brussels, 1962); R. Marjolin, *Le travail d'une vie: mémoires 1911–1986* (Paris: Editions Robert Laffont, 1986). For very good accounts of these discussions see L. Tsoukalis, *The Politics and Economics of European Monetary Integration* (London: George Allen & Unwin, 1977), pp. 56–7; D. Kruse, *Monetary Integration in Western Europe: EMU, EMS and Beyond* (London: Butterworth, 1980).
13. For the EEC Monetary Committee see Commission of the EEC, *Fourth General Report* (Brussels, 1961). On the concern about the consequences of British entry for the future momentum of integration see M. Camps, *European Unification in the Sixties* (London: Oxford University Press, 1967), p. 2.

stage of the twelve-year transition period. It was a programme designed to consolidate and carry forward that success.

The Action Programme had its supporters, notably the private support of the French Finance Minister Valéry Giscard d'Estaing and the Dutch Finance Minister Jelle Zijlstra. These two actors were to play key roles in the launch of the EMS in 1978–9: the one as French President, the other as head of the Dutch central bank. Both wanted to give priority to fixed exchange rates and a common currency. Giscard d'Estaing's policy was motivated by two major political calculations: by a concern for the survival of the CAP, a policy from which France was the major beneficiary; and by the prospect that the creation of a common EEC currency would provide a strong rival to the dollar and sterling. In the first case, the common currency would be an absolute safeguard for the CAP. In the second case, French influence on the reform of the international monetary system would be strengthened. Giscard d'Estaing recognized that the realization of these aims required an effective monetary alliance between France and Germany within the framework of the EEC. Though more cautious, the EEC Monetary Committee also stressed the difficulties posed for EEC policies, like the CAP, by devaluations and revaluations. Hence some progress was made. In May 1964 the Council of Ministers resolved that the principle of prior consultation should be applied in the EEC Monetary Committee to cover all international monetary problems. Also, it agreed to establish the Committee of Governors of Central Banks and the Budgetary Policy Committee. In April the Council had already created the Medium- Term Economic Policy Committee with the task of preparing the medium-term Community economic policy programme.[14]

Events in 1963–4 shifted attitudes towards a generally more favourable view of the benefits of EEC cooperation in monetary policy. Inflationary pressures in France and Italy, coupled with serious Italian balance-of-payments' deficits in these two years, demonstrated the risks that arise from 'unmanaged' economic interdependence. Large inflows of funds into Germany created risks of rising inflation there and external pressures for another D-Mark revaluation. In this context of external threat to domestic stability the German government had a greater incentive to embrace EEC cooperation in economic and monetary policy. Against this background, in early 1965 the Commission adopted fixed exchange rates, seen as the path to a common currency, as a strategic objective.[15] Indeed, it is possible to speak of a political consensus about the importance of fixed exchange rates lasting through the 1960s.

But the larger ambition to move quickly towards EMU was frustrated. Politically, the main problems were caused by domestic political difficulties in France and Germany and the consequent inability to achieve a consensus of policy goals in Franco-German bargaining relations as a catalyst for successful EEC action. The problems with the French government involved more than just its deep internal divisions about the idea of EMU. Council bargaining was immobilized by the crisis of relations between the Commission and the French government, exemplified in the French boycott of the Council of Ministers in 1965–6. Prompted by a clash over a Commission package of proposals dealing with the financing of the CAP (in effect

14. Commission of the EEC, *Eighth General Report* (Brussels, 1965).
15. Commission of the EEC, *Eighth General Report*.

involving an extension of the powers of EEC institutions), the crisis was resolved by the so-called 'Luxembourg Agreement'.[16] This agreement of January 1966 contained a statement in which the French delegation asserted the right of veto in the Council of Ministers 'when very important interests are at stake'. Though the other five members continued to defend majority voting where the treaties stipulated it, two consequences followed. First, the debilitating practice of prolonging bargaining in the Council till unanimity was attained was reinforced; and second, the promotive ambitions of the Commission were frustrated. A drift of power towards supranational Council bargaining style was stopped in its tracks. In its place a renewed emphasis on intergovernmental Council bargaining, with the implicit threat of national veto, created a climate of 'lowest-common-denominator' policy making. The policy activism of the early 1960s gave way to a policy inertia. And the effects were undoubtedly felt in the EMU debate.

This debate was radically altered in January 1966 when the arch Gaullist Michel Debré replaced Giscard d'Estaing as French Economics and Finance Minister. The proposal for a single EEC currency was now presented as a direct threat to French national sovereignty. As far as the French government was concerned, it was now off the agenda. French policy for a radical reform of the international monetary system, and for a displacement of the US dollar's role within it, continued. But the policy instrument for that purpose was no longer the common EEC currency. It was a return to the gold standard and a reassertion of the interwar French policy of hoarding gold. The ideas of the French economist Jacques Rueff had triumphed over those of Giscard d'Estaing. The effect was to further isolate France and undermine the unity of the EEC states on international monetary reform. This lack of EEC unity and French isolation was to be demonstrated in 1968 when only France refused to endorse the plan for the creation of Special Drawing Rights (SDRs) in order to create extra international liquidity. On the other hand, Giscard d'Estaing, still an important political figure as leader of the Independent Republican Party, was being much more publicly explicit in his support for a common EEC currency.[17]

The implementation of the EEC's Action Programme of 1962 was also impeded by the influence of Ludwig Erhard, as Federal Economics Minister in Bonn till 1963 and then as Chancellor from 1963 to 1966. Unlike Chancellor Konrad Adenauer, Erhard, supported by a group of industrialists, favoured a wider European free trade area rather than a customs union of the six. As an avowed 'Atlanticist', he also displayed a marked preference for dealing with monetary issues in the framework of the IMF and for avoiding any further obstacles in the way of British membership of the EEC. His position of opposition to EMU was reinforced by Finance Ministry officials and Bundesbank directors, who argued that a system of mutual aid in the EEC and the creation of a European reserve fund would lessen financial disciplines at the national level and draw Germany into financing at least part of the deficits of other countries. The effects would be inflationary.[18] Hence Germany turned its face away from its necessary leadership role if EMU were to be successfully pursued in favour of focusing its attention on domestic stability.

16. EEC, *Ninth General Report* (Brussels, 1966), sections 13–15.
17. Tsoukalis, *The Politics and Economics of European Monetary Integration*, p. 57.
18. Tsoukalis, *The Politics and Economics of European Monetary Integration*, p. 72.

The Barre Plan and the Hague summit: a changing international political economy and new policy leadership

The frustration of the implementation of the EEC's Action Programme of 1962 was to be displaced by a new mood of optimism and determination in 1970–1. This change of mood reflected a complex set of political and economic changes in 1968–9, leading to the Hague summit of December 1969. One relatively minor but symbolic change took place within the Commission itself in July 1967. Marjolin, the EEC 'planner', was replaced as commissioner responsible for economic and monetary affairs by Raymond Barre, a French economist with stronger neo-liberal ideological credentials. With this change went a difference of approach; pragmatism and realism were now emphasized. The revised approach was embodied in the so-called Barre Plan of 1969.[19] A new mood of caution was reflected in the Commission's emphasis not on irrevocably fixed exchange rates but on parity changes by agreement, and not on a reserve fund but on a mutual assistance system consistent with Article 108. Here, in essence, were the germs of the ideas that were later to inspire the foundation of the European Monetary System. The Commission was showing evidence of having learned from the experience of the Action Programme. Monetary 'cooperation' had replaced monetary 'integration'.

The new proposals of Barre were based on an argument that the EEC had to respond to a new source of structural power: namely that the customs union and the CAP had produced such a degree of economic interdependence among the member states that national economic policy decisions could no longer be effective if taken in isolation. In order to continue to maximize the benefits of economic interdependence, and to improve the performance of national economic policy, three steps were necessary:

1   The procedure for medium-term economic policy programmes required improvement so that greater convergence and compatibility of national economic objectives could be achieved.
2   In order to improve the coordination of short-term economic policies, the system of prior consultations must be extended to all economic policy decisions that might have an influence on other economies. Prior consultation should also take place in the preparation of national budgets.
3   Priority needed to be given to the creation of a Community mechanism for monetary cooperation, which would include both short-term monetary support and medium-term financial aid. In both cases, upper ceilings were required, as well as maximum quotas for each country.

More important in launching EMU were the effects of external structural changes in the international political economy in 1968–9. Particular significance has to be attributed to international monetary crisis: to its economic consequences, to its effects on perceptions of the credibility and durability of the Bretton Woods system and on

19.   Commission of the EEC, *Memorandum to the Council on the Coordination of Economic Policies and Monetary Cooperation within the Community*, Supplement to Bulletin III-1969 (Brussels, 1969), pp. 3–4.

perceptions of the relative economic power of Germany, and to the conclusions that were drawn by leading national and EEC actors about the need for a new EEC initiative. Additionally, domestic political crisis in France fuelled the monetary crisis: first, the May 1968 crisis as workers and students took to the streets in opposition to the government, which wobbled dangerously; and then the resignation of President de Gaulle in April 1969 following the defeat of a referendum on which he had staked his reputation. The May 1968 crisis led to the introduction of exchange controls in France in the face of a speculative attack on the franc. But intra-EEC tensions were further fuelled by a marked deterioration in France's economic fundamentals, signalled by a substantial deterioration of the French balance of payments. Allied to a large and growing German surplus, this deterioration underlined the structural power of Germany within the EEC economy. The result was that financial market operators were driven to speculate on a devaluation of the franc and/or a revaluation of the D-Mark. Volatility in the foreign exchange markets was increased by the British devaluation of November 1967; subsequent deflationary measures there combined with similar measures by the US Administration to spread fears of recession.

Against this background, an emergency meeting of the Group of Ten (G-10) took place in Bonn in November 1968. This chaotic meeting was to have lasting political consequences. In Bonn the governments of Britain, France and the United States put strong pressure on the German government to revalue the D-Mark. The goal of the British government and the US Administration was to ease pressure on their currencies from the financial markets; the French government was concerned also to save face by avoiding a devaluation. But the pressure was in vain.[20] So determined was the resistance to a D-Mark revaluation by the German Economics Minister, Karl Schiller, and the Finance Minister, Franz-Josef Strauss, that the expectation at the end of the meeting was that the French franc would be devalued. Strauss added to French discomfort by publicly expressing the view that the franc would be devalued. Instead, consistent with the priority it attached to external stability, the French government chose the path of deflationary measures and exchange controls.

The main result of the Bonn meeting was to persuade many in the French political and economic establishment that German economic power was to be feared; that German behaviour had been irresponsible and intolerable. Though the French government was not suddenly converted to EMU, indeed the Gaullists reiterated the argument of national sovereignty, Giscard d'Estaing's case for a common EEC currency was strengthened. In Bonn too, figures close to Willy Brandt, the Foreign Minister and chairman of the Social Democratic Party (SPD), were concerned about deteriorating attitudes to Germany. Brandt continued to press the importance of dissociating Germany from old-fashioned, and in the case of Germany, historically tainted ideas of nationalism. Even if the stance on revaluation was not altered, in fact it was repeated in 1969, structural arguments about the centrality of the EEC and Franco-German relations to security made the German government disposed to seek an opportunity to demonstrate its cooperativeness in EEC affairs. The outcome was that

---

20. For a good account of the Bonn meeting see Tsoukalis, *The Politics and Economics of European Monetary Integration*, pp. 70–1. For an insider account see R. Jenkins, *A Life at the Centre* (London: Pan, 1992), pp. 264–70.

the Commission's new initiative on European monetary integration was sown in fertile ground. Paradoxically then, the recriminations linked to the Bonn meeting, and its failure to resolve the international monetary crisis on mutually acceptable terms, served to generate greater internal momentum towards EEC monetary integration.

This internal momentum was further strengthened by President de Gaulle's resignation in April 1969. Following the presidential elections, which were won by Georges Pompidou, Giscard d'Estaing returned as Minister of Economics and Finance. In this context not only was the new Barre Plan ensured a favourable reception, but also EMU was once more a live issue. The Barre Plan of 1969 was seen at the time as well adapted, perhaps all too well adapted, to French interests. German opposition was, nevertheless, muted on this occasion. Surprisingly, at least in the light of later developments, the main opposition came from Italy and the Netherlands. They argued that monetary cooperation in a wider context than the EEC was required, and, once de Gaulle had resigned, that the improved prospects for British entry should not be jeopardized by making entry more difficult for the British government.

In this new political context it proved possible for the Council of Ministers to agree, in July 1969, that the system of prior consultation should be extended to every economic policy measure that could be considered to have an effect on other member states or to endanger the internal or external balance of the country concerned. The EEC Commission, or any member state government, would have the right to ask for such consultation if it believed that a particular policy measure met these criteria. Unfortunately, in practice it was all too often possible to recognize this effect only *after* the policy measure had been decided: a huge limitation on the effectiveness of this policy innovation.

The weakness of the prior consultation mechanism and the impact of international monetary crisis on the whole integration process were amply demonstrated in August 1969. The fixed exchange rates of the 1960s had created an illusion of a *de facto* monetary union. That illusion was shattered by the August crisis. A devaluation of the French franc was followed by a short period of floating of the D-Mark prior to its revaluation in October: again evidence that Germany was prepared to take unilateral action to shield itself from external inflationary pressures. Both countries tried to insulate their agricultural markets from the effects by imposing border taxes.[21] Once more criticism descended on the German government, with the European Commission taking it to the European Court of Justice (ECJ). The chief focus of anger was the threatening implications of the decision to float the D-Mark for the survival of the CAP and even for the customs union. Against the background of these events, and the fears of a return to economic nationalism, a new initiative to promote EEC cooperation in monetary policy seemed to be a *sine qua non* of sustaining, let alone advancing

---

21. Under the CAP the prices of many agricultural products were defined in terms of the European Unit of Account (later the ECU). A devaluation would automatically increase agricultural prices in the country concerned by an equivalent amount. This outcome was politically unacceptable to the French government. Border taxes were an emergency solution to the problem. In order to maintain prices at different levels, a complicated system of monetary compensation amounts (MCAs) was introduced. France typically obtained negative MCAs which helped to keep French food prices below the EC average; Germany had positive MCAs with the opposite result.

European economic integration. The fact that the Hague summit of December 1969 took place against the background of so fundamental a monetary and political crisis was to be decisively important in shaping its innovatory outcome.

As one surveys the record of monetary cooperation and integration in the 1960s, from the Action Programme to the Barre Plan, one is struck by two main impediments to progress: the sharp differences of view among the Six about the goals of monetary policy cooperation, and the unwillingness of Germany to assume a leadership role consistent with its economic and monetary power within the EEC. The German Bundesbank perceived itself to be isolated in its priority to domestic price stability and with more to lose than gain from cooperation. Ideological consensus was lacking; so too was a perception that external currency instability sufficiently threatened German domestic interests that cooperation was required. In short, the kind of structural change that would have altered German perceptions of self-interest was absent.

But in 1969–70 two developments reawakened and complicated the political debate about EEC monetary integration. First, mounting external stresses within the Bretton Woods system placed reform of the international monetary system on the agenda and the issue of a unified EEC policy on the agenda. On international monetary reform France found itself isolated from the other five states which both distrusted French motives and feared the consequences of French policy. Germany, Italy and the Netherlands were not prepared to countenance any monetary policy initiative that might erode a central pillar of Atlantic security by joining in an assault on the position of the US dollar. In this sense French policy on EMU involved the EEC in a conflict about political goals as well as about monetary policy goals of external versus internal stability.

Second, and here again Italy and the Netherlands had particularly strong views, the two French vetos on British entry into the EEC (in 1963 and 1967) diminished the case for pursuing European monetary integration. Sterling was too important a currency to exclude; British entry was central to the EEC's development; and, they argued, no new and more difficult barriers to British entry should be created at this stage. For the Dutch and the Italians British membership offered a counterweight to the domination of the Franco-German axis. Hence, though Britain was no longer a formal part of the European monetary integration process, as it had been in the EPU period, its power in this policy sector was felt indirectly. In this way conflict about the political goal of enlargement and its requirements fed into the EMU debate.

Despite these internal divisions about monetary and political goals, two structural changes in the international political economy prompted a growing recognition of the need for a fundamental reconsideration of the whole framework of monetary cooperation as envisaged in the Barre Plan to include a qualitative leap forward to integration and union. The first structural change was signalled by a growing threat to the Bretton Woods system from international monetary crises. A long period of balance-of-payments' surpluses had kept monetary crisis at bay within the EEC and facilitated the maintenance of fixed exchange rates from 1961 to 1969. But by 1968 the strains were showing, culminating in the August 1969 monetary crisis. Crisis was throwing into question the successes that had been achieved in creating a customs union and the CAP. At the very least, it was putting the need for a concerted EEC response to defend the *acquis communautaire* on to the top of the political agenda.

Also, as the crises of 1968–9 demonstrated, the structural factor of mounting economic interdependence among the Six made for ever greater vulnerability of governments to each other's policy measures. Policy cooperation within the EEC to match this new trade sensitivity seemed a minimum requirement of effective economic and monetary policies. The environment was favourable to a new EEC policy initiative: particularly when to mounting international monetary crisis, and its rapid transmission via increasing economic interdependence, was added a deepening general concern about the capacity of the US dollar to sustain its role as the anchor currency of the Bretton Woods system and to offer the necessary policy leadership for that system's stability and survival. The key question was whether Germany would seek to limit the adverse consequences for domestic price stability from increasing external instability by unilateral action (floating) or by engaging in EEC cooperation.

A vortex of structural changes were at work redefining and reshaping the scope for EEC monetary integration: monetary crises undermining the external stability offered by the Bretton Woods system and the anchor role of the US dollar; mounting economic interdependence and its internal consequences for the EEC; the very different condition of economic fundamentals, notably in France and Germany; and the continuing absence of ideological consensus. The result was that new external presssures for closer monetary cooperation and integration were offset by internal divisions of interest and policy rooted in different economic fundamentals and ideological beliefs.

To this list of pressures must be added the slow but perceptible shift in the position of the German federal goverment on European monetary integration. In the early 1960s scepticism and hostility had been paramount, reflected in the chasm between the views of Erhard and the Commission on economic policy. But, following the Bonn meeting of 1968, and the controversy that followed about German policy, the political goal of using Council bargaining to demonstrate that German policy was firmly anchored in a European framework came to the fore in monetary policy. The will of successive German governments to concede in EEC bargaining in the interests of protecting security had in fact been implicit in the agenda of European integration since the Schuman Plan for the ECSC had been launched in 1950. Now, impelled by the events of 1968–9, it surfaced in the field of monetary policy. This change was, arguably, the most significant of all. Its effectiveness depended, however, on the degree of unity of purpose between the German federal government and the Bundesbank. This bargaining relationship was about to demonstrate its central importance to EMU.

The 'spirit of the Hague': Brandt and Pompidou

In the history of the EC there can be few sharper contrasts than that between the language of the Commission's Fourth General Report of 1970 and that of the Marjolin Report of 1975.[22] The optimism of 1970 was captured in the Commission's reference to the 'spirit of the Hague' and to EMU as the most ambitious European project since

22. Commission of the EC, *Fourth General Report* (Brussels, 1970), p. x of the Introduction. R. Marjolin *et al.*, *Report of the Study Group Economic and Monetary Union 1980*, Marjolin Report (Brussels: Commission of the European Communities, 1975), p. 1.

the Treaty of Rome. Five years later Marjolin, who was by now a former commissioner and who had been asked to review the prospects for achieving EMU by the target date of 1980, concluded pessimistically:

> Europe is no nearer to EMU than in 1969. In fact, if there has been any movement, it has been backward. The Europe of the 1960s represented a relatively harmonious economic and monetary entity which was undone in the course of recent years; national economic and monetary policies have never in 25 years been more discordant, more divergent, than they are today.

Why the burst of energetic action in 1970–1? And why so sudden a collapse of belief in the feasibility of EMU, in fact well before 1975? In seeking the answer to these two questions some basic lessons about the character of the European monetary integration process can be learned.

The new dynamism post-1969 was evident in the Hague summit and its dedication to a relaunch of European integration, in the Werner Report that followed on from the summit, and in the implementation of the unfinished business in the Barre Plan. Externally, we have already identified the catalyst of the 1968–9 international monetary crises, especially that of August 1969, and the mounting loss of faith in the durability of the Bretton Woods system of fixed exchange rates. In the possible and even likely absence of an effective global guarantee of fixed exchange rates, the EEC states had a new incentive to consider a regional guarantee. Internally, domestic political change had infused the Franco-German bargaining relationship with new energy. Following his election in 1969 President Pompidou of France sought to bring closer into the government the Independent Republican Party of Giscard d'Estaing (who returned as Finance Minister) and the Centrists, both of which had a much more positive view of EMU. He was also forced to come to terms with two perceptions of change in the external environment: the evidence of the structural power of German economic strength as exhibited at the Bonn G-10 meeting of 1968; and the paradox of British entry – that it could serve to help balance German power, and yet that it might dilute the commitment to integration.

Together with the effects of the August 1969 crisis, these factors suggested that the new president could gain the political high ground in Europe by a major new initiative. Ideally, such an initiative should test British resolve in relation to the EEC; French doubts on this score related mainly to the role of sterling. Also, by exploiting the gathering weakness of the US dollar, again another preoccupation of French policy, it might be possible to achieve French ambitions for reform of the international monetary system via the creation of an EEC 'monetary personality' on the world stage. These political calculations led to the identification of EMU as the focus for the ambitious new policy initiative. Accordingly, Pompidou took the initiative to call the summit. But it was the conjunction of circumstances that was important, along with a new coincidence of interests between Paris and Bonn.

In fact, at the summit itself Willy Brandt, the new German Chancellor, took the initiative on EMU. He wanted to 'invest the European Community with a new quality'.[23] To the summit Brandt brought the forceful self-confidence of a newly

---

23. W. Brandt, *People and Politics: The Years 1960–75* (London: Collins, 1970), p. 254.

elected Chancellor, committed to change, along with his own peculiar capacity for incorporating wide vistas in his approach to politics. Two political goals were foremost in his mind. As Foreign Minister in the previous 'Grand Coalition' government, he had watched the progress and effects of the Bonn meeting of 1968 with concern. Brandt's sense of the historic constraints on the use of German power following the Holocaust and the Second World War led him to give unqualified support to a strategy of reconciliation. For this reason alone he sought a new initiative within the framework of the EEC that would dispel the impressions left by the 1968–9 monetary crises, improve relations with France and eradicate any threat from monetary disturbances to the European integration process. But, strategically, Brandt needed also a counterpart in the west to his new 'opening to the east', the so-called *Ostpolitik*. This policy change of reconciliation with Germany's eastern neighbours had, in his view, to be accompanied by a flanking measure to the west in order to remove suspicions about Germany's motives.[24] Greater German security to the east must not be bought at the cost of a loss of control over security in the west.

With these political goals in mind, for the first time a German Chancellor committed himself to the establishment of EMU. He did so on terms that were consistent with the long-standing insistence of the Bundesbank on priority to the economic dimension of EMU. In Brandt's view, EMU should be realized in two stages. Stage one would require the EEC to demonstrate its success in formulating common economic policies. On that basis Germany would be prepared to transfer a portion of its foreign reserves to a European Reserve Fund, and a monetary union would be put in place.

The communiqué at the end of the Hague summit was a clear victory for the views of Brandt on EMU and boldly claimed that the EEC had 'arrived at a turning-point in its history'.[25] Again, consistent with a tradition of French policy, President Pompidou had stressed the monetary dimension of EMU. In his view, priority should be given to a pooling of foreign reserves and to the creation of a common monetary policy so that the EEC could be a more effective negotiator in international monetary reform. But, consistent with the Bundesbank's view, the summit communiqué explicitly stated that the development of monetary cooperation should be based on the harmonization of economic policies; the European Reserve Fund was to be the culmination of the process of EMU. The practical need was to draw up a timetable of action. For that reason, the summit asked the Council of Ministers to draw up a plan for the creation of an EMU.

A more cautious assessment was made by Walter Hallstein – the first president of the EEC Commission – who noted the 'significant omissions' of the Hague summit communiqué:

24. H. Simonian, *The Privileged Partnership: Franco-German Relations in the European Community, 1969–1984* (Oxford: Clarendon Press, 1985), p. 82.
25. The most outstanding general survey of the Hague summit and its aftermath is Tsoukalis, *The Politics and Economics of European Monetary Integration*, chs. 6 and 7. On Brandt's role see N. Kloten, 'Germany's Monetary and Financial Policy and the European Community', in W.L. Kohl and G. Basevi (eds) *West Germany: A European and Global Power* (Lexington, Mass.: D.C. Heath, 1980).

We search in vain for measures actually to restore majority voting in the Council of Ministers, or to introduce direct elections to the European Parliament. There is no provision for strengthening the powers of the Commission. . . . Finally, most of the dates fixed for the completion of the talks . . . smack of diplomatic compromise . . . they lie too distant in the future.[26]

Despite such reservations, the new 'spirit of the Hague' was soon given practical demonstration in Council bargaining in January 1970. In accordance with Article 108, the Council of Ministers approved the EEC's system of short-term monetary support, which was to be operated by the Committee of Governors of the Central Banks and to be automatic and unconditional. Thus, of the recommendations of the Barre Plan, only one awaited completion – the provision of medium-term financial assistance (which was agreed in March 1971). The sense of a new dynamism in Council bargaining was still captured in the rhetoric of President Pompidou's press conference speech in January 1971 when he called for a 'European confederation' with a European government. But the speech was stronger on rhetorical effect than content; he no more had an EEC of strong supranational institutions in mind than when introducing the concept of a 'European Union' into the Paris summit of 1972.

The Werner Report: 'monetarists', 'economists' and the principle of parallelism

It was clear from the outset of Council bargaining, even before the Werner Committee began its work, that significant differences of views existed. The German Economics and Finance Minister, Schiller, played up the importance of the institutional reforms required for EMU: an acceptance of majority voting to expedite progress and a transfer of powers to the European Parliament, in short amendment to the Treaty of Rome with all its attendant difficulties. The French government was ominously silent on this issue: for it, an early move to fixed intra-EEC exchange rates was paramount, again consistent with its monetarist approach to EMU. For Germany and the Netherlands, by contrast, the move to such an exchange-rate regime should follow rather than precede economic convergence. In addition, the German government was less than comfortable with the references of the French and Belgian governments, as well as of the Commission, to the creation of an EEC 'monetary personality'. This political goal for EMU seemed to imply a hostility to the role of the US dollar that could be threatening to the Atlantic-based security structure on which Germany and others depended.[27]

In order to fulfil the mandate given to it by the Hague summit, the Council of Ministers established a group under the chairmanship of Pierre Werner, the Prime Minister of Luxembourg, in March 1970. It comprised the chairmen of the EEC Monetary Committee, of the Committee of Governors of the Central Banks, of the Medium-Term Economic Policy Committee, of the Short-Term Economic Policy Committee and of the Budget Policy Committee, along with a representative of the

---

26. W. Hallstein, *Europe in the Making* (London: George Allen & Unwin, 1972), p. 101.
27. See the very good discussion in Tsoukalis, *The Politics and Economics of European Monetary Integration*, pp. 87–90.

Commission. In this way all the member states were represented in the bargaining process that produced the Werner Report. The task of the Werner Group was to make it possible 'to identify the basic issues for a realization by stages of economic and monetary union in the Community'.[28] Its interim report of May revealed just how deep-seated was the disagreement between the advocates of the monetarist approach (France, Belgium, Luxembourg and the Commission) and the advocates of the economist approach (Germany and the Netherlands). The dispute focused on the monetary arrangements that the monetarists in the Werner Group proposed for stage one: a reduction of intra-EEC margins of fluctuation (the introduction of the so-called 'snake') and the creation of an Exchange Stabilization Fund.

In an attempt to resolve this entrenched disagreement, the Werner Group requested the opinion of the Committee of Governors of the Central Banks, a move that gave rise to the Ansiaux Committee (Baron Ansiaux was the governor of the Bank of Belgium). The Ansiaux Committee was diplomatically cautious. It favoured an immediate *de facto* rather than *de jure* narrowing of margins during the first stage and a gradual process of establishing an Exchange Stabilization Fund in line with clear evidence of progress towards economic convergence. This careful diplomatic balancing of the two approaches, combined with deference to the technical expertise of central bankers, was to enhance central bank influence on the final report of the Werner Group in October 1970.

Central to the final Werner Report was the principle of 'parallelism'.[29] In the realization of EMU parallel progress was required in the economic and monetary dimensions within a specific timescale (by 1980) and in stages. Monetary union was to involve

> the total and irreversible convertibility of currencies, the elimination of fluctuation in exchange rates, the irrevocable fixing of parity rates and the complete liberation of movements of capital.

In the view of the Werner Group, a single currency was the preferable final outcome. Also, institutional changes would be required to give effect to an EMU. As they would require modifications to the Treaty of Rome, it would be necessary to convene an intergovernmental conference for this purpose. In the words of the Werner Report, EMU would be 'a leaven for the development of political union, which in the long run it cannot do without'. In this phrase is the first clear mark of German influence.

Consistent with its central principle, the Werner Report envisaged the creation of two new organs of Community decision: the 'centre of decision for economic policy' and the 'Community system for the central banks'. In relation to the 'centre of decision for economic policy', it is notable that much less attention was given to convergence criteria and low inflation than in the Maastricht Treaty. Conversely, a good deal more importance was attached to EEC authority over budgetary policies. In

28. Council-Commission of the European Communities, *Interim Report on the Realization by Stages of Economic and Monetary Union – 'Werner Report'*, Supplement to Bulletin 7-1970 (Brussels, 1970).
29. Council-Commission of the EC, *Report to the Council and the Commission on the Realization by Stages of Economic and Monetary Union in the Community – 'Werner Report'*, Supplement to Bulletin 11-1970 (Brussels, 1970).

1970 'nominal' convergence was less of an issue than it was to become later. The focus was very much on coordination of economic policies. Here German influence was once more apparent. The new 'centre of decision' would need to have a decisive influence over EEC economic policy, including national budgetary policies, and, correspondingly, would need to be directly politically responsible to the European Parliament. In the words of the report:

- the essential features of the whole of the public budgets, and in particular variations in their volume, the size of balances and the methods of financing them or utilizing them, will be decided at the Community level
- regional and structural policies will no longer be exclusively within the jurisdiction of the member countries
- a systematic and continuous consultation between the social partners will be ensured at the Community level.

In the elaboration of the second 'centre of decision' German rather than French influence was again discernible. The 'Community system for the central banks' was to be given an independent role in the conduct of internal and external monetary policies, with the exception of decisions about changes of exchange rates. Though explicitly modelled on the US Federal Reserve System, the affinity with the German model of central bank independence reflected German policy leadership on the key principles of EMU.[30] On the narrowing of intra-EEC margins of fluctuation and the establishment of a 'Monetary Fund' the ideas of the Ansiaux Committee were largely endorsed. In the first stage an experimental, *de facto* narrowing of margins was to be attempted (the 'snake'); if this experiment proved its value, the Monetary Fund could be established to manage the mutual aid mechanism and later to take over the management of reserves. Here was evidence of Franco-German compromise, but one in which the caution of the Bundesbank was the dominant ingredient.

In a diplomatic sense, the principle of parallelism stood as a symbol of the compromise between monetarists and economists on which the Werner Report sought to base its appeal and to garner a consensus for action. But (as we have seen) the substantive content of the report betrayed the degree of German policy leadership: both on the long-term ambitions for political union (with which the French government was uncomfortable) and on the provisions for stage one in respect of the coordination of economic policies and the specific steps towards monetary union.

The publication of the report showed just how brittle and problematic the consensus was and how difficult it would be to steer Council bargaining to a successful outcome. In particular, the French government began to express its reservations about the final objective, finding itself under mounting pressure from the hard-line Gaullists. At the root of the new concern was a sense that the French government had launched an initiative at the Hague summit whose progress it was proving difficult to control in EC bargaining.

In recognition of this new political problem in Council bargaining, the Commission's Memorandum in response to the Werner Report limited itself to

30. K. Klasen, 'Die Verwirklichung der Wirtschafts- und Währungsunion in der EWG aus der Sicht der Deutschen Bundesbank', *Europa Archiv* 13 (1970).

measures required to implement the first stage. These measures – on economic policy coordination and central bank coordination – affected only the functioning of existing institutions. They did not require any new institutions or transfers of competence that would fuel opposition within the French government. At a tactical level this strategy of the Commission was successful in moving forward the decision-making process. But, at the same time, it was a sign that the 'spirit of the Hague' was in retreat. The disappointment of the other five at the French government's new-found hostility to institutional and political reform was intense. It did not, however, shift the French government from its opposition to any consideration of issues of institutional reform. Brandt noted Pompidou's hostility to the institutional reformers who 'cherished vain illusions'.[31] In Pompidou's words:

> If we try to define procedures and competences before making a start, however small, on common intergovernmental action, we shall condemn ourselves to endless ratiocination over principles and, in the end, to doing nothing.[32]

To add to the sense of declining commitment the German government insisted on the introduction of a 'safeguard clause' in the final Council decisions of March 1971 on stage one. Germany's attitude of caution on the monetary aspects of stage one was underlined. The new clause emphasized the reversibility of the new monetary measures after five years if parallel progress in economic policy cooperation and in managing the intra-EEC margins of fluctuation had not been achieved. In other words, stage two was not automatic. This clause revealed the deep-seated reluctance of the Bundesbank to assume a leadership role in EEC monetary policy, a role that – in view of the structural power of the German economy and D-Mark – was an essential precondition for EMU.

The Council decisions of March 1971 did at least complete the implementation of the Barre Plan of 1969 and gave substance to the Werner Report's proposals for stage one. The 'snake' was launched; procedures for economic policy coordination were put in place; and a mechanism for medium-term financial assistance activated (but in this case not automatic, with the EEC able to impose conditions). In chapter 6 the nature and functioning of the procedures for economic policy coordination will be considered. Suffice it to say here that they represent an enduring, but disappointing legacy of the 'spirit of the Hague'. In March 1972, in response to the acute problems besetting the management of the 'snake', an attempt was made by ECOFIN to relaunch EMU. The commitment to fixed exchange rates was underlined; a further attempt was made to improve coordination of economic policies; a readiness to resort to capital controls was stressed; and, to help Italy and appeal to two of the new candidate members, Britain and Ireland, the first step was taken to a Community regional policy.

In addition, the Council asked for a report on the possible functioning of a European Monetary Cooperation Fund (EMCF). Established in April 1973, the EMCF is another enduring institutional legacy of this period. In practice, its functions have remained limited, and its existence shadowy. Essentially the EMCF is operated by the

31. Brandt, *People and Politics*, p. 258.
32. A. Morgan, *From Summit to Council: Evolution in the EEC* (London: Chatham House, 1976), p. 14.

governors of the EC central banks, who constitute its board, and the Bank for International Settlements in Basle acts as its agent. It administers the very-short-term and short-term credit facilities.

When, in November 1973, the Commission proposed a transfer of reserves to the EMCF, as part of the second stage, it was firmly blocked by the French, German and Dutch governments. For the French government, such a proposal was too 'supranational'; for the German government, it was contrary to the principle of parallelism enshrined in the Werner Report. The strongest supporters of the proposal were the Belgian, Italian and British governments; interestingly in the light of later developments, the pro-EEC British government of Edward Heath regarded the proposal as too conservative. Once again, the German position was decisive and unyielding. The basic problem was, in the German view, that the EMCF was ultimately subject to the authority of ECOFIN. It did not possess the independence, or potential for independence, that was promised in the Werner Report and that was so fundamental to German policy interests.

The 'snake' and its legacy: 'animal de la préhistoire' or a system with the future in its bones?

In practice, the most visible manifestation of stage one was the operation of the 'snake' and, in particular, the so-called 'snake in the tunnel'.[33] But the 'snake' was born into a wholly different context from that envisaged in the Werner Report. That new context was provided by the dramatic structural change in the international political economy represented by the unravelling of the Bretton Woods system. As a consequence, the secure anchor that had helped retain a fixed exchange rate system among the EEC states in the 1960s came adrift. With it the problems of narrowing intra-EEC margins of fluctuation grew.

The Werner Report had correctly identified that, even under the circumstances of the 1960s, exchange-rate fluctuations under the Bretton Woods system had meant a greater predictability of the dollar than of intra-EEC rates. Under the Bretton Woods' rules, parities of EEC states were defined in terms of the US dollar, along with the associated margins of fluctuation (originally 0.75 per cent). Implicitly then the bilateral (or cross) rates between any two EEC currencies could move by *twice* the declared fluctuation margin *vis-à-vis* the dollar, as they switched position relative to the dollar. As the Werner Report recognized, this greater predictability of the dollar enhanced its value as a reserve currency and store of value compared to EEC currencies. Hence it had proposed that the bilateral fluctuation margins among EEC currencies be narrowed, at first to 0.6 per cent, and then gradually eliminated.

Following the Council decisions of March 1971, the Committee of Central Bank Governors concluded an agreement to implement this aspect of the Werner Report. Though it was due to go into operation in June, the launch of the 'snake' was in fact postponed till April 1972. The interim period witnessed the worst international

---

33. For useful overviews of the 'snake' see G. Jennemann, 'Der Europäische Wechselkursverbund', in G. Magnifico (ed.) *Eine Währung für Europa* (Baden-Baden: Nomos, 1977); Tsoukalis, *The Politics and Economics of European Monetary Integration*, pp. 112–36; Gros and Thygesen, *European Monetary Integration*, pp. 15–21.

monetary crisis since the Second World War and, as we saw earlier, the clear sign that American support for the Bretton Woods system was collapsing in August. With the US dollar in deep trouble, and speculative attacks persistent, deep division opened up in Council bargaining about how to deal with the crisis. On behalf of the German government, Schiller proposed a joint float of all EEC currencies against the dollar, whilst the French government preferred a resort to capital controls to ward off speculative inflows. As an avowed economic liberal, Schiller rejected capital controls. Fearful of a loss of competitiveness as its currency floated upwards with the D-Mark against the dollar, the French government rejected the German view. Only six weeks after the Council decisions, the deep divisions within the EEC were made apparent as, in May, the German and Dutch currencies were floated and new capital controls were introduced in almost every other EEC country. The French government was once again, as in 1968, confronted with the stark facts of the structural power of the German economy, with Germany willing to resort to unilateral action to secure the goal of domestic price stability.

The Smithsonian Agreement of December 1971, hammered out in difficult negotiations within the G-10, was an important catalyst for bringing the French government back to the Council bargaining table on EMU. On the one hand, it was seen as a success for French objectives in reforming the international monetary system. The dollar price of gold was changed; the outcome suggested that the participating countries were adhering to parities in terms of gold, rather than dollars; and it was the first multilateral renegotiation of exchange rates. Also, following the Smithsonian Agreement, the D-Mark returned to a pegged exchange-rate system. But, on the other hand, the Smithsonian Agreement tripled the margin of fluctuation *vis-à-vis* the dollar to 2.25 per cent. Any two EEC currencies could now move by up to 4.5 per cent against each other. Such an increase in exchange-rate flexibility was threatening to the Community, not least the CAP. The French government – and the Commission – was desperately keen to promote internal action to reverse this development.

German interest in collaborating in Council bargaining was motivated by two concerns: first, an economic concern to restore EEC solidarity in the face of the collapsing Bretton Woods system and increasing doubts about the reliability of the US dollar; and second, represented by Chancellor Brandt, a political concern to restore bargaining relations with France following the effects of the May 1971 decision to float the D-Mark, and, as a counterbalance to the divisive internal effects of his *Ostpolitik* in Germany, to achieve a political success within the Community that would command broader-based domestic support in the run-up to an impending federal election.

These calculations formed the background to the implementation of the Basle Agreement in April 1972 (when the member states agreed to limit intra-EEC margins of fluctuation to 2.25 per cent), to the relaunch of EMU in May (outlined above), to the establishment of the European Monetary Cooperation Fund, and to the Paris summit of October. The Paris summit established EMU as the priority issue for the Community, reiterated the commitment to making a success of stage one, and endorsed an agreed position on international monetary reform. Its principles for monetary reform were fixed but adjustable parities, measures to control short-term capital movements and the reduction of the role of reserve currencies. Though this optimism reflected a renewal of political will, it was obvious even at the time that the capability to realize that seemed increasingly questionable, for the launch of the 'snake' had been fraught with problems from the outset.

The 'snake' was launched in April 1972 as the 'snake in the (dollar) tunnel', four months after the Smithsonian Agreement. In clear gestures of solidarity the new EEC members Britain and Denmark joined the other six members in May (Norway also became associated). In July the strength of the German government's commitment to the fixed rate system was tested by intense speculative pressures. Schiller resigned as Economics and Finance Minister when the government agreed to introduce new capital controls. His successor, Helmut Schmidt (who as Chancellor was to be central to the launch of the European Monetary System) was more of a convert to the monetarist approach to EMU, particularly the value of fixed exchange rates. Capital controls were not desirable, but they appeared now as a necessary price to pay for the advantages of the 'snake'.

Despite this significant change in the balance of German policy, heavy speculative pressures took their toll on the 'snake'. Britain withdrew as early as June (and Denmark from June to October); Italy followed in February 1973. The devaluation of the US dollar in March 1973 did nothing to halt speculative pressure, accompanied as it was by a clear American policy of passivity in relation to the dollar. Against this background, in the final blow to the pegged exchange rate of the Bretton Woods system, the six EEC countries decided in March to engage in a joint float, in other words to give priority to stable exchange rates among themselves. The 'snake in the tunnel' was in effect dead; interventions to maintain fixed margins against the dollar (tunnel) were discontinued. The joint float of March 1973 highlighted the failure of a policy of progressive resort to exchange controls.

Notwithstanding the unity implicit in the joint float, the operation of the 'snake' indicated the emergence of a 'strong' currency group and a 'weak' currency group. Germany, the Netherlands and Norway displayed their credentials as strong currencies by revaluations in, respectively, June, September and November 1973. Countries with 'weak' currencies were forced by the 'snake' to bear the burden of the costs of adjustment. In other words, the tensions of asymmetry in currency relations were revealed in a harsh manner, affecting Council bargaining relations and putting the problem of asymmetry increasingly to the centre of the agenda.

Also, with the first stage of EMU due to end in December 1973, the Council of Ministers found itself unable to agree on the transition to the second stage. The Commission's report on the first stage in April 1973 contained no new ideas, only more meetings of ECOFIN to improve policy coordination, the reintegration of all national currencies in the 'snake', and a possible further narrowing of margins.[34] It was eventually agreed that, from 1 January 1974, 'a' second stage of EMU would come into effect, as opposed to 'the' second stage. What this transition actually involved was left unclear, but what was clear was the view of the French, German and Dutch governments that progress in stage one had been too slow and disappointing to move to the second stage.

34. Commission of the EC, *Attainment of the Economic and Monetary Union*, Supplement to the Bulletin V-1973 (Brussels, 1973).

The main Council decisions of November 1973 were to extend EEC credit facilities (but with no pooling of foreign reserves); to hold monthly ECOFIN meetings; to establish the Economic Policy Committee in place of the committees on Short-Term Economic Policy, Medium-Term Economic Policy and Budgetary Policy; and to make prior consultations obligatory on changes of parity, central rates or intervention points of any EEC currency (in the previous September the Dutch government had revalued the guilder without prior consulation, other than with its Benelux partners). Indicative of the decline of the 'spirit of the Hague' was the Commission proposal that consideration of EMU should be postponed till 1975 when the report on European Union was expected.[35] But progress continued. In October 1974 ECOFIN authorized the issuance of EEC loans on the world market to rescue member states in balance-of-payments' difficulties. A total of $3 billion was envisaged in the first instance. Initially Ireland and Italy, and later Greece, were the main beneficiaries; France took advantage of this loan facility in 1983.

The final blow to the ambition for the 'snake' as an instrument for keeping EMU alive came on 19 January 1974 with the independent floating of the French franc. Only five of the original nine members were left in the system, and they represented a *de facto* D-Mark zone. Taken against German pressure, the French government's decision was a response to the sharply adverse effects of the first oil crisis of 1973. Deteriorating balance-of-payments' and inflationary problems were evidence of a threatening deterioration in France's economic fundamentals and introduced new short-term considerations into French policy. In the words of Giscard d'Estaing, the 'snake' was an 'animal de la préhistoire monetaire européenne'.[36] As Tsoukalis points out, the chief advocate of the monetarist approach had now deserted the system; paradoxically, the German government, traditionally wedded to the economist approach, was left to defend the logic of the 'snake' as the motor for EMU.[37]

But, though deeply wounded, the 'snake' was not dead. France returned in July 1975 at the previous central rate, only to withdraw again in March 1976 as its expansionary fiscal policy exacerbated speculative pressures in the financial markets. What was clear was that the policy of the 'snake' was dominated by Germany. The German government's adherence to the principle of fixed but adjustable exchange rates was manifested in the operation of the 'snake' from 1976 onwards. Inaugurated by a general realigment in October 1976 (the so-called Frankfurt realignment), a total of five realignments occurred before the 'snake' was replaced by the EMS in 1979. But it was an ineffective instrument of collective action against the sharp decline of the US dollar from September 1977, as the German Chancellor Schmidt was soon to recognize. German vulnerability in the face of what Schmidt characterized as 'irresponsible' American policy, coupled with the weakness of the 'snake' as a defensive mechanism to cushion Germany against the behaviour of the US dollar, was to be critical to the EMS initiative of 1978–9.

35. Commission of the EC, *European Economic Integration and Monetary Unification* (Brussels, 1973).
36. Quoted in Tsoukalis, *The Politics and Economics of European Monetary Integration*, p. 130.
37. Tsoukalis, *The Politics and Economics of European Monetary Integration*, p. 130.

The legacy of the 'snake' was not just greater German commitment than at its outset. It was also the beginnings of the emergence of an increasingly vocal grouping of economists who, committed to the value of exchange rate stability by the experience of the period of floating, identified in EMU a more secure basis for a strategy of sustained growth. Here the Commission was itself a catalyst, setting up various study groups of economists. Evidence of the development of their ideas and contribution is contained in the Commission's report on 'European Union' of 26 June 1975 and in the so-called 'All Saints Day Manifesto' issued by nine prominent economists in November 1975. They were prepared as a contribution to the Tindemans Report, which had been requested by the Paris summit of December 1974 as the basis for agreeing an overall concept of European Union.

The Commission's report concluded that the EEC's main objective should continue to be EMU but highlighted the deficiencies of the Werner Group's approach, notably the difficulties of implementing the principle of parallelism.[38] In its view, the EEC had, as a consequence, been condemned to an incremental process of step-by-step evolution when what it needed was a qualitative leap forward. As an alternative the Commission advocated the early introduction of a common, parallel currency, the Europa, to serve initially as a reserve currency for use in official transactions and later to be used as an intervention currency. Behind this attempt of the Commission to regain the initiative on EMU was the influence of Altiero Spinelli, an active European federalist.[39]

In the 'All Saints Day Manifesto' the parallel currency approach to EMU was further developed.[40] The Europa would be more than a reserve currency to help maintain fixed exchange rates. It would be designed to have constant purchasing power by keeping the price level of a representative commodity basket constant in terms of Europas. By allowing it to compete with national currencies in all monetary functions the Europa could be expected to penetrate into general usage in countries with high inflation rates. In this way, the Europa would act as a mechanism of full-scale monetary reform. A weaker version of the proposal was outlined in the two OPTICA reports published by the Commission in 1976 and 1977.[41]

During the 1970s the perceived failings of the 'snake' led to a series of proposals for reform that were later to influence the debate about the EMS. One of the earliest, in September 1974, came from the French Economics and Finance Minister, Jean-Pierre Fourcade.[42] Essentially, this plan was based on a critique of the asymmetry in the functioning of the 'snake'. Instead of a grid of bilateral parities, the new European Unit of Account (EUA) would serve as a pivot and not just for accounting

38. Commission of the EC, *Report on European Union*, Supplement to Bulletin V-1975 (Brussels, 1975).
39. M. Burgess, *Federalism and European Union* (London: Routledge, 1989), p. 83.
40. G. Basevi et al., 'The All Saints' Day Manifesto for European Monetary Union', *The Economist*, 1 November 1975.
41. G. Basevi et al., 'Towards Economic Equilibrium and Monetary Unification in Europe', OPTICA Report '75 (Brussels: Commission of the European Communities, March 1976); G. Basevi et al., 'Inflation and Exchange Rates: Evidence and Policy Guidelines for the European Communities', OPTICA Report '76 (Brussels: Commission of the European Communities, February 1977).
42. *Agence Europe/Documents* no. 817, 17 September 1974.

purposes. The EUA was identical to the fixed-amount basket of EEC currencies and was to be renamed the European Currency Unit (ECU) in 1978. In this way the French government aimed to spread the burden of intervention more fairly, for any country that reached its margin against a Community average would be required to intervene, whether its currency was strong or weak. Despite the plan's failure to generate significant action, it did raise an issue that was to be central to the EMS negotiations, namely the rules for intervention and settlement.

This unsuccessful initiative was followed, in July 1976, by a proposal from the Dutch Finance Minister, Wilhelm Duisenberg, who was later head of the Dutch central bank and a key participant in the Delors Committee.[43] The Duisenberg Plan suggested the creation of a general EEC framework for consultation and surveillance of exchange-rate policies, based on the idea of agreed 'target zones' for exchange rates. Though the proposal foundered on the hostility of Germany to the declaration of any target zone, it did succeed in firmly lodging in officials' minds that policy coordination was likely to remain weak in the absence of some objective indicator to act as a trigger. It was to resurface in the EMS negotiations in the form of the 'divergence indicator'. At least, in March 1977, ECOFIN took action to encourage the Monetary Committee and the Committee of Central Bank Governors to intensify their consultations on exchange-rate issues: from 1977, the Commission began to produce regular analyses of exchange markets.

But overall, whatever the legacy of the 'snake' and whatever the quality of the economic thinking generated by its operation, judgement cannot fail to take account of the sense of disappointed expectations and frustration that surrounded the EMU enterprise when, in 1975, the Marjolin Report delivered its pessimistic verdict. It is not surprising that when, in October 1977, the new Commission president, Roy Jenkins, used a public speech to attempt to relaunch EMU, he was greeted with a mixture of indifference and hostility.[44] His predecessor as president and current commissioner responsible for economic and monetary affairs, François-Xavier Ortoli, was notably cool in the wake of experience with the 'snake'. What at least was clear was that a return to EMU would have to take a much more indirect and less mechanistic form than the Werner Report.

Lessons

Perhaps the main historical lesson to emerge from this study of the history of European monetary cooperation and integration in the early postwar period is that the establishment and development of the EEC created a wholly new context. The importance of this institutional change is brought out when one compares the experience of the EPU with that of the Werner Report. The EPU left no substantial legacy, other than the ideas of Triffin and his associates. Although the 'spirit of the Hague' was reduced to frustrated ambition, a legacy was left. With all its shortcomings the 'snake' had the future in its bones, and it operated to fix the commitment of the

43. N. Thygesen, 'The EMS: Precursors, First Steps and Policy Options', in R. Triffin (ed.) *The Emerging EMS* (Brussels: Bulletin of the National Bank of Belgium, 1979), pp. 87–125.
44. R. Jenkins, 'Europe's Present Challenge and Future Opportunity', first Jean Monnet Lecture (Florence: European University Institute, 27 October 1977).

German government to European monetary integration. Similarly, despite its deficiencies, the mechanism of coordination of economic policy via the Council of Ministers laid a long-term basis for a later shift to 'mutual surveillance'. Also, the development and consolidation of EC policies in other areas helped to increase pressure for monetary policy coordination. In the 1960s and 1970s monetary policy coordination was seen as indispensable to protect the customs union and the CAP, the so-called *acquis communautaire*. From the mid-1980s the single European market was similarly viewed as requiring EMU as a 'flanking measure'. This lesson about the importance of institutional context is reinforced if one turns back to the discussion of the Latin Monetary Union in chapter 2.

The second lesson develops the idea that European monetary integration cannot properly be seen in isolation, not simply from the wider environment of institutional change within the EC but also from the dynamics of structural change in the international political economy: of the strength of the anchor currency, of economic fundamentals, of foreign exchange markets and of trade interdependence. Such external pressures have variously served to prompt and constrain European monetary integration in a powerful manner. They could act to stimulate the integration process, as for instance in 1949–50 and 1969–70; neither EPU nor the 'spirit of the Hague' can be understood apart from their role in forcing agenda change. At the same time, external pressures regularly showed their capacity to disrupt the integration process, for instance in delaying the implementation of the 'snake' and then in derailing its development. It is hard to avoid the conclusion that the monetary integration process has been essentially reactive to the dynamics of structural change in an increasingly fast-changing international monetary system; and that the increased speed of change and scale of the international monetary system has had paradoxical effects for European monetary integration.

A related lesson that emerges clearly from the Werner Report is the tendency for policy on European monetary integration to be based on the presumption that in the international political economy the past will repeat itself. In the case of the Werner Report the assumption was that global coordination of a fixed exchange rate system would continue to operate and to do so effectively. This assumption was soon revealed to be mistaken. Another assumption was that economic development would enable continuing progress towards convergence of economic performance, thus facilitating improved economic policy coordination and monetary integration. Again, the external shocks administered by the collapse of the Bretton Woods system and then the first oil crisis were to show the inadequacy of this assumption. As we shall see, the Treaty on European Union of 1992 was to prove similarly vulnerable to the fragility of its economic assumptions. In particular, the scale of the shock of German unification and its effects on economic fundamentals and convergence was not appreciated. This failure led to the ERM crisis of July 1993.

The problem of the potential speed and scale of structural change in the international political economy leads on to a further lesson, namely the immense difficulties in devising a policy approach to manage the inherent complexity involved in attaining EMU. The characteristic ECA and Commission responses to this complexity were to develop heroic, planned approaches that relied on pre-commitment to timetables and stages. This approach was an essential part of the Action Programme of 1962, of the Werner Report of 1970 and of the Treaty on European Union. But, as the experience of the first two of these initiatives has shown, such a technocratic approach is vulnerable to the very complexity that it is trying to manage: how, for example, can policy goals do other than adjust in the face of changing circumstances? Heroism compounds a sense of failure and stagnation, as the initiatives of 1949–50, 1962 and 1970 demonstrated. The EMS was conceived as a means of avoiding one in-built problem of complexity in EMU: by giving up the approach of trying to coordinate its economic and monetary dimensions ('parallelism') in favour of a qualitative leap to deal with a specific problem, namely the effects of the falling dollar on EC economies. But fundamentally, an approach that stresses timetables and stages for EMU remains vulnerable to the impact of complex structural dynamics and short-term economic considerations on monetary policies. French policy towards the 'snake' was affected in this way in 1973; British policy towards the ERM underwent a conversion in 1992; and in August 1993 the 'hard' ERM collapsed in the face of market pressures. An altered constellation of problems and a transformation of policy preferences can soon override formal commitments. What was not attempted was the evolutionary approach, based on building up practical experience of using and valuing a common currency.

To give a final reinforcement to the theme of the dynamics of structural change, it is worth stressing how the EPU, the Action Programme of 1962, the Hague summit, the Werner Report and the operation of the 'snake' underline just how fragile are the power relations on which European monetary integration is forced to build and just how important and problematic has been the issue of policy leadership. In the EPU negotiations the British government had found itself in a pivotal bargaining position; by 1978/79 it was on the margins rather than a central actor in the power play involved in constructing the EMS. The German government was a sceptical, even hostile participant in the EMU discussions of the 1960s. Under Chancellor Schmidt it emerged as the guardian of the holy grail of monetary integration. But even then Germany's role in the 'snake' was largely dictated by the reluctance of the Bundesbank to assume a leadership role. Valéry Giscard d'Estaing had been a zealot for EMU in the 1960s. Yet in 1973 his zeal was to be transferred from the promotion of a 'European monetary personality' on the world stage to France's role as a sovereign state in the new G-5.

EMU depended on convergent interests among member state governments. That such convergence could be achieved was evident from the Hague and Maastricht summits. The problem was to sustain the commitment entered into as a consequence of short-term policy convergence in the face of the effects of the structural dynamics of economic fundamentals, financial markets and currency relations. These dynamics change political calculations of self-interest and may make it attractive to policy actors, like the Bundesbank, to play an independent game. In the 1970s the French government's shift of position on the implementation of the Werner Report was eloquent testimony to this problem. Equally (as we shall see in chapter 4) the structural dynamics of international currency relations and trade interdependence were capable of reinforcing the will to pursue European monetary integration. That capability was reinforced by the impact of the institutional framework of the EC on the bargaining attitudes of national policy actors.

Chapter 4

AMBITION REGAINED (1)

*Negotiating the EMS – power relations and
policy change*

I consider the new EMS to be primarily a political event.
(Otmar Emminger, 'The Foreign Exchange Rate as an Instrument of Policy',
Lloyds Bank Review 133 (1979: 21))

It would be absurd to think of this practical and extremely useful arrangement [the EMS]
as being a step towards a European monetary union.
(Robert Marjolin, *Le travail d'une vie: mémoires 1911–1986* (1986))

The conventional view is that the creation of the European Monetary System (EMS) in
1978–9 was a radical step forward in the European integration process. Here was the
'qualitative' leap forward in monetary policy integration of which the EC Commission
had spoken in June 1975. In this chapter we are not only concerned with the origins of
the EMS because of the insight that it offers into the power relations on which the
EMS and later EMU policy process was constructed. We are also interested in
establishing whether in fact the creation of the EMS represented a 'qualitative' leap
forward: or whether, to pursue the argument of chapter 3, it was the 'snake' that had
the future in its bones and the EMS that essentially extended and amended it. It is
argued that the birth of the EMS was not in practice a radical discontinuity but part of
a longer-term learning process about the need to unite Europe in the face of
threatening structural changes in the international political economy: notably
represented by 'irresponsible' behaviour of the dominant world currency. The main
historic point of departure of that learning process was not the personal initiatives of
EC Commission president Roy Jenkins in 1977 or of German Chancellor Helmut
Schmidt in 1978 but a more deep-seated structural change: the collapse of the Bretton
Woods system, the dollar crisis and ensuing speculative currency flows. In this
increasingly threatening international political economy German policy actors
concluded that it was more costly for Germany to resort to unilateral monetary policies
and much more attractive to pursue external monetary stability.

The decade of the 1970s was a period of 'ambition lost' as far as the apostles of
European union were concerned. The climate of bargaining within the Council of
Ministers testified to this fact: the rapid collapse of the 'spirit of the Hague'; the
impact of the new currency dislocations and divergences of economic fundamentals,
precipitated by the collapse of the Bretton Woods system and the oil crisis of 1973;
and the setback to the ambitions for union implicit in the veto politics of the
Luxembourg Agreement of 1966, a setback that the Hague summit had conspicuously
failed to overcome. As the 1970s progressed, it was difficult to avoid the judgement
that discordant interests, combined with intergovernmental bargaining and 'veto
politics', had condemned EC Council bargaining to a present and future of inertia and

diminishing credibility. EC institutions and Council bargaining gave the increasing impression of being just another arena for the conflict of national interests; European politics seemed to be settling down to its traditional pattern of contending states whose interests were defined by domestic political and economic constituencies. In this altered context, realism seemed to mean accepting that politicians had changed little; that the state remained the prime source of loyalty and inspiration; that the inspiration for what measure of European cooperation and integration could be achieved was only likely to come from the exigencies and calculations of domestic politics in member states; and that what success European integration enjoyed had its basis in the role of the EC in augmenting and strengthening, not eroding and replacing, the role of the state.[1] A weatherbell of this transformed climate of opinion was Robert Marjolin: an enthusiast for union, he regarded the relaunch of EMU by Roy Jenkins with intense scepticism.

But out of the pessimism of the late 1970s was to come a retrieval of momentum in Council bargaining, and one that had enormously important long-term consequences. Ambition was regained: with the launch of the EMS in March 1979, and with the new drive for EMU following the Hanover Council of 1988. A prior institutional innovation of the 1970s, the European Council, was to play a decisive role in providing this new sense of direction in Council bargaining. Designed to give more coherent political leadership to an expanded EC (the British, Danes and Irish joined in 1973), regular meetings of the heads of government and state were to be centre stage in the two initiatives: the Copenhagen, Bremen and Brussels Council meetings to consider and prepare the EMS; and a whole succession of Council meetings, notably Hanover, Madrid, Strasbourg, two in Rome, and Maastricht to agree EMU. In neither case was ambition regained easily. Great expenditure of time, energy and patience was required, coupled with mutual recrimination. Yet, in each case, the momentum created by the convergent interests and combined wills of a nucleus of powerful governments was such that these heavy costs were borne.

At the heart of this and the next chapter is the question of the nature of the EMS and of EMU as historical phenomena. It is argued that the EMS and EMU represent different types of 'policy learning'. In seeking to understand policies as learning processes, we are drawing attention to the overriding importance of their historical context. Policy is a learning process in the sense that specific policies have their origin in, and derive their character from, specific historical events to which they are a response; and in the second sense that policy makers are continually needing to relate new ideas and information to the accumulated experience of policy and decide what kinds of adjustments to policy are required. Propelling this learning process are the dynamics of structural change in the international political economy; these dynamics are expressed in the historical events and new ideas and information that affect policy development. But the idea of policy as a learning process points to a 'self-reinforcing' dimension in policy change.

From this perspective the dynamics of policy change in European monetary integration and union have their basis in evolving perceptions of policy failure. Policy learning is driven by these perceptions. A process of policy learning is indicated when the goals or instruments of policy are adjusted in the light of past experience and new

1. A. Milward, *The Rescue of the European Nation State* (London: Routledge, 1992).

information.[2] In other words, we are studying the way in which ideas about economic and monetary policy are changing: ideas about policy goals, about policy instruments and about the precise use of policy instruments. In doing so, we are able to make judgements about 'levels' of policy learning and change.[3] At the lowest level, there are incremental changes in the way that policy instruments are used – say specific interventions or interest rate changes; then we can identify the 'higher-order' incrementalism of developing new policy instruments, like new mechanisms of intervention or the adoption of wider or narrower margins of fluctuation; and, finally, can be found the level of radical or 'heroic' policy change, in which a new rationale for policy is defined based on changed policy goals as well as instruments. Characteristically, 'heroic' change involved the opening of the policy process to new actors and ideas.

By exploring how and why ideas about European monetary policy have changed at these three levels (goals, instruments and their use), we are offered a more refined insight into the nature of policy change in European monetary integration. In the process it is possible to explore the configurations of power behind the two key initiatives of 1978–9 and 1988–91. What do they tell us about the will and capability of different policy actors in the integration process? The actual rules of the EMS and of EMU and the problems of putting them into effect are a matter for chapter 6. Here we are simply interested in explaining why the initiatives took the form that they did and what that tells us about the nature of the integration process and of the EMS as a policy process.

A new strategy and tactics for EC Commission leadership: Roy Jenkins and the 'qualitative leap'

> The lesson he [Jean Monnet] taught me was always to advance along the line of least resistance provided that it led in the right general direction.
>
> (Roy Jenkins, *A Life at the Centre* (1991: 463))

The launch of the EMS in 1979 is usefully viewed as an historical episode in a protracted learning process about the importance of stable exchange rates to the EC member states, and, far more difficult, about the political will to accept, and be capable of living within, the subsequent constraints of external stability on domestic economic and monetary policies. As we saw in chapter 3, the operation of the 'snake' had already underlined to countries, not least France, which had withdrawn twice, the very great difficulties involved in accepting these constraints. The result was a European Community that was divided into two groups: a German-oriented 'snake' (its economy accounted for over two-thirds of the collective GDP of the group of countries involved); and the 'non-snake' countries (including notably Britain, France and Italy) whose currencies were floating individually. In effect, a 'two-tier' Community had evolved: on the one hand, a core of states with strong economic fundamentals, notably

---

2. The classic statement of the 'policy learning' approach remains, H. Heclo, *Modern Social Politics in Britain and Sweden* (New Haven, Conn.: Yale University Press, 1974).
3. P. Hall, *Policy Paradigms, Social Learning and the State: The Case of Economic Policy-Making in Britain* (Harvard, Mass.: Centre for European Studies, unpublished paper, 1989).

moderate inflation and stable currencies; and, on the other, states that combined high inflation, substantial balance-of-payments' deficits and currency depreciations. Political disquiet about this situation was reflected in the rather rapid dismissal of the Tindemans Report on European Union at The Hague European Council in December 1976; it had recommended an acceptance of the reality of a two-tier Community and the need to build on the 'snake' as a means of bringing about convergence of economic and monetary policies and of creating a 'zone of monetary stability' in an unstable world.[4]

Part of the momentum behind the learning process involved in the creation of the EMS was provided by this disquiet about the political implications of a two-tier EC in monetary policy. For the French government in particular it underlined once again the structural power of Germany in the economic construction of European integration. The Belgian, French and Italian governments attached political priority to developing a form of European monetary integration based on a symmetry that the 'snake' did not possess. Economically too, the 'snake' represented an inadequately integrated EC, with some currencies floating and others participating in the joint float *vis-à-vis* third currencies. It symbolized also a divergence of economic fundamentals in the 1970s, rather than the economic convergence on which the Werner Report had been based. In short then, the 'snake' was widely viewed in EC circles as an example of policy failure rather than as a success. The argument that it required improvement or some new initiative was likely to find wide acceptance within the framework of Council bargaining.

The inside political story of the launch of the EMS begins with Roy Jenkins. Against this economic and political background of Council bargaining, his strategic perception was that monetary integration represented the 'line of least resistance' for a Commission initiative to restore leadership to the EC. In January 1977 he took up office as the new president of the European Commission. The first real political heavyweight to be appointed to the position, at least since Walter Hallstein, his appointment enjoyed the strong political backing of President Giscard d'Estaing of France and Chancellor Schmidt of Germany. Interestingly, and of relevance to what followed, all three had a political background in economic and monetary policies: Roy Jenkins as the British Chancellor of the Exchequer 1967–70, Helmut Schmidt as Economics and Finance Minister 1972–4 and Giscard d'Estaing as Finance Minister for long periods in the 1960s and early 1970s. Embattled and frustrated during his first few months by the constraints of his office, by his unfamiliarity with the ways of operating of Council and Commission bargaining, and by the sense of inertia that permeated the Council bargaining at that time, Jenkins sought out a theme that could provide a new initiative to galvanize the Community and to leave a lasting political mark on its development.

By July 1977 the 'big idea' of his presidency was beginning to emerge, as Jenkins worked out a political strategy that would meet the harsh realities that he faced. That strategy was worked out over the summer and autumn and informed by a number of considerations. First and foremost, Jenkins recognized that economic problems were central to the EC member states, notably the problem of diverging economic

---

4. L. Tindemans, *European Union* (Brussels: Ministry of Foreign Affairs, External Trade and Cooperation in Development, 1976).

fundamentals. An initiative was needed that would help to promote convergence. In turn, internal economic divergence and a relative deterioration of the fundamentals of the EC economies in the world economy was linked, in his view, to the new era of floating exchange rates and currency instability: to the negative effects of external instability on intra-EC trade and growth. In the 1960s the EC economies had performed at least as well as those of the United States and Japan. With the 1970s relative performance had fallen well behind. A key difference between the EC economy and those of Japan and the United States was that exchange-rate fluctuations were *internal* to the former and external to the latter.

The prospects for a successful Commission initiative and productive Council bargaining were further brightened by an emerging consensus about economic policy goals in key EC capitals. Underlying this consensus was the new fear of inflation, the conversion of policy actors in countries like France to the importance of the goal of internal stability and admiration for the success of Germany in meeting this goal. As early as the 1976 federal elections Chancellor Schmidt had attempted to direct national pride to the achievements of *Modell Deutschland*. This emerging 'model' character of Germany was best displayed in the 'Stabilization Plan' of the new Barre government in September 1976. Here was a French government committing itself unequivocally to the goal of internal stability in economic policy, to an *assainissement* (cure) of the economy in order to establish currency stability. An economic policy consensus underpinning Franco-German bargaining provided an essential basis for a new EC initiative. It had not been apparent in the 1960s when (as we saw in chapter 3) the market- and domestic stability-oriented thinking of Erhard confronted the priority to external stability and the *planification* and *dirigisme* of the Gaullist governments. It was to disappear again between 1981 and 1983, as a new French Socialist government sought to implement its programme for an independent revival of output and employment.

Jenkins's political approach was also based on his view that he could exploit the new capacity for flexibility and leadership that had been instituted within Council bargaining. Since 1974 the European Council had established itself as the most authoritative decision-making centre in the Community. Three times annually, the heads of state and government met to impart a sense of political direction to the work of the EC institutions. However fluctuating the performances of these summit meetings, the European Council was seen by Jenkins as the necessary base for any new initiative. This approach was reinforced by the fact that, as an 'outsider' with hardly any previous experience of the EC institutions, notably the Commission itself, Jenkins felt more comfortable in direct face-to-face bargaining with fellow politicians rather than with EC bureaucrats. He was strengthened in his view by advice from Jean Monnet that major advances in European integration were not likely to come from working within the established institutional channels. Jenkins was, in consequence, prepared to accept setbacks to his initial ideas in the Commission and in the ECOFIN Council, knowing that the European Council was ultimately the most important arena of Council bargaining – and that, within that arena, gaining the support of Schmidt and Giscard d'Estaing, the indispensable underpinning of Franco-German bargaining, was critical. In the political story of the EMS the European Council meetings of 1978 at Copenhagen, Bremen and Brussels are accordingly decisive. Chastened by his first unhappy summit encounters, notably the London European Council, Jenkins came round to the view that the best that he could hope for was fluctuating influence in Council bargaining by focusing his energies on this arena and bilateral meetings in preparation for the summits.

A third factor that gave Jenkins confidence in his approach to Council bargaining was the presence of EC-conscious elites in at least three national capitals. In Belgium Leo Tindemans as Prime Minister – aided and abetted by his Foreign Minister Henri Simonet – gave the unqualified support of the Belgian presidency of the European Council to the new Jenkins initiative, not least as a means of reopening debate on the neglected Tindemans Report. They provided an early point of contact to Jacques van Ypersele, who had drafted the section of the Tindemans Report dealing with EMU. The outstanding Belgian monetary policy expert, van Ypersele, served as monetary policy adviser to the Belgian Finance Minister and chairman of the EC Monetary Committee during the crucial negotiations. He acted as a catalyst in discussions within the EC Monetary Committee in early 1978 and then as a major power broker in the technical negotiations on the EMS in the autumn. Van Ypersele was close to the Jenkins's orbit and helped to bring the powerful figure of Robert Triffin – who had retired back to Belgium from the United States – into that orbit.

In France the combination of President Giscard d'Estaing with Raymond Barre as his Prime Minister from the autumn of 1976 created the most 'European-minded' French government since the inception of the Fifth Republic in 1958.[5] As we saw in chapter 3, Barre had served as EC Commissioner for economic and monetary affairs and authored the EC's influential Barre Plan. The involvement of Bernard Clappier, governor of the Banque de France, in European integration went back to his role in the drafting of the Schuman Plan of 1950, which had launched the European Coal and Steel Community. Along with Dr Horst Schulmann, he was to play a key role in preparing the confidential paper for the Bremen summit.

With a European-minded government came the capacity of the French state to integrate its action in economic and monetary policy. This capacity was embodied in the Inspectorate of Finance, the prestigious *grands corps* that occupied the commanding heights of economic and monetary policy.[6] In 1974–6, for instance, the following policy actors had shared membership of the Finance Inspectorate: François Ortoli, president of the European Commission; Giscard d'Estaing, French President (and his secretary-general in the Elysée); Jean-Pierre Fourcade, French Finance Minister; Jacques de Larosière, director of the Trésor in the French Finance Ministry; as well as the deputy governor of the Banque de France and the Prime Minister's adviser on economic and financial affairs. This common corps membership extended to the French financial institutions: to the directors-general of the Crédit Lyonnais, of the Banque Nationale de Paris and of the Union des Assurances de Paris, as well as the secretary-general of the Société Générale.[7]

5. P. Ludlow, *The Making of the European Monetary System* (London: Butterworth, 1982), pp. 19 and 33. This book constitutes the most thorough and most authoritative account of this episode.
6. X. Beauchamps, *Un état dans l'état: le ministère de l'économie et des finances* (Paris: Bordes, 1976); M.-C. Kessler, *Les grands corps de l'état* (Paris: Presses de la Fondation Nationale des Sciences Politiques, 1986).
7. *Anciens élèves de l'École Nationale d'Administration 1975* (Paris: ENA, 1976).

In Germany Schmidt had proved since 1972 a much firmer supporter of EMU than his predecessor as Economics and Finance Minister. As he stated in 1974, the 'snake' was not least important as a means of keeping EMU alive.[8] His economic policy adviser as Chancellor, Horst Schulmann, had served in Brussels, as had the state secretary in the Finance Ministry, Manfred Lahnstein. Lahnstein was to play a key role in the negotiations between the Bremen and Brussels councils. Though these figures could be expected to play their national roles with gusto, notably in the case of France, there was a new basis of goodwill in Council bargaining to the cause of European monetary integration on which Jenkins could count, or at least take a risk. Belgium, France and Germany were to provide the axis around which the EMS developed.

A final element in Jenkins's approach was his recognition that a leadership role by the German government, by Schmidt in particular, was decisive for the success of the kind of initiative that he had in mind. Precisely because the initiative would be in the realm of economic affairs, the support of the government that presided over the most powerful and successful of the EC economies – *Modell Deutschland* – was critical. The highest-level political commitment in Bonn was all the more important in the case of monetary policies, where the prerogatives and the deep-seated caution and even hostility of the Bundesbank could be readily anticipated. Its president from 1975 to 1980, Otmar Emminger, was on record as regarding the 'snake', indeed fixed exchange rate regimes in general, as a serious threat to internal monetary stability; it created an obligation to intervene in foreign exchange markets that, in Germany's case, could fuel inflationary pressures.[9] Schmidt was, by contrast, a known advocate of European monetary integration. His reaction was, therefore, from the outset critical to the success of Jenkins's initiative. On the will and capacity for action of Schmidt depended the solution to the EC's problem of leadership in economic and monetary policy that had so bedevilled the 1960s and 1970s.

Further reinforcing the central leadership role of Germany was the perception that, with all its European credentials, the French government was held back by two factors: relatively weak economic fundamentals and the dual domestic political challenge to the President – within the presidential majority from the Gaullists, who were more insistent on the resolute defence of 'French interests' and 'national independence', and from the resurgence of the Left (including the prospect of Communist Party ministers in government after the March 1978 Assembly elections). The consequence for Council bargaining was that the French government's European enthusiasm was restrained and that external apprehension, not least that of Schmidt, about developments in France mounted.

But, crucially, the EMS initiative benefited from two pieces of good fortune. In the first place, large American balance-of-payments' deficits in 1977 weakened the US dollar; the trade deficit moved from $9.5 billion in 1976 to $31 billion in 1977. Between October 1977 and February 1978 the dollar declined from DM 2.30 to 2.02, a devaluation of 12 per cent. By September 1978 it had dropped to DM 1.76, another 12

8. L. Tsoukalis, *The Politics and Economics of European Monetary Integration* (London: George Allen & Unwin, 1977), p. 130.
9. O. Emminger, 'Deutsche Geld- und Währungspolitik im Spannungsfeld zwischen innerem und ausserem Gleichgewicht', in Deutsche Bundesbank (ed.) *Währung und Wirtschaft in Deutschland 1876–1975* (Frankfurt-am-Main, 1976), pp. 485–554.

per cent devaluation. Ensuing heavy currency flows into the D-Mark imposed high costs on Germany for pursuing a unilateral monetary policy. The effects of the sharp appreciation of the D-Mark were apparent within the EC, with the French franc and the Italian lira tending to move down with the US dollar and not up with the D-Mark. German competitiveness was undermined and the Bundesbank exposed to the danger of fuelling domestic inflation if it intervened in a sustained way to prevent D-Mark appreciation. Yet more seriously, the crisis of the US dollar seemed on a scale that could presage a serious dislocation of the international economic system, with the prospect of deeper injury to German interests. Insult was added to injury when the US Administration pressed Germany to act as a 'locomotor' for the world economy by domestic reflationary measures that would help correct the US balance of payments. Schmidt became increasingly embittered at what he viewed as the irresponsibility of the Carter Administration.

Here was the external catalyst for Schmidt's commitment, privately expressed to Jenkins in February 1978, to 'propose, in response to the dollar problem, a major step towards monetary union; to mobilize and put all our currency reserves into a common pool . . . and to form a European monetary bloc'.[10] In fact, the EMS was to form one strand in a wider initiative both to protect the German economy and to bring back some leadership and coordination to the international economy. As Ludlow has noted, the Bremen European Council meeting was followed immediately by the Bonn G-7 summit. In return for the safety net of the EMS, which would satisfy German interests by sharing the burden of intervention and slowing the appreciation of the D-Mark, Schmidt was prepared to make concessions on reflation as part of a coordinated package of action at the international level.[11] Whatever his anger with the US Administration, he recognized that cooperation via G-7 offered the best chance of securing measures that would promote the strong US dollar that Germany wanted to see. In turn, a durable EMS depended on a strong US dollar. The outcome was, not least, that Schmidt emerged as the leading international statesman on economic issues.

But though Schmidt's initiative was immediately inspired by external economic pressures and a new national monetary self-interest in the goal of external stability, two political goals inspired his interest in European monetary integration: his perception of the need for united EC action to fill the vacuum of international economic statesmanship left by American 'irresponsibility'; and his desire to use European integration to make Germany a more 'calculable' (*berechenbar*) actor and thereby rehabilitate it. The EMS fitted into a wider political concept of Germany's role in Europe after the horrors of the Second World War and the Holocaust. In this respect his thinking fitted that of many leading German figures of his generation, of politicians who had directly experienced war and the deprivations and suffering that it brought. In Schmidt's eyes, Germany had to be, above all, a reliable and constructive partner in integrating Europe. The EMS would serve as an additional anchor for West Germany's ties to the EC and as an instrument for deepening those ties. It was a theme that Schmidt was to develop most eloquently in his speech to the Bundesbank council in November 1978.

10. R. Jenkins, *European Diary, 1977–1981* (London: Collins, 1989), p. 224.
11. Ludlow, *The Making of the European Monetary System*, pp. 128–32.

Good fortune also came in the form of two Council presidencies that were supportive of an EC monetary initiative. Jenkins was assisted by the strong support that he received from the Belgian presidency of the European Council in the second half of 1977 and from the German presidency in the second half of 1978. The Tindemans Report had already identified the 'snake' as a basis for promoting convergence; van Ypersele also contributed ideas to the Jenkins's initiative. But, more importantly, the German presidency was able to hold Council bargaining to the ambitious timetable for agreeing proposals that had been set at the Bremen summit on its own initiative.

Despite these many advantages the progress of the new initiative on European monetary integration was far from smooth. Publicly, its inception can be dated from Jenkins's speech of October 1977 at the European University Institute in Florence.[12] Both Robert Triffin, the Belgian-born economist and the *doyen* of economists promoting European monetary integration (see chapter 3), and van Ypersele contributed their advice. However, the prime mover behind the speech was Michael Emerson, an economist and Commission official (brought in by Jenkins), who was to continue to be a key influence on the economic research underpinning the single European market and EMU initiatives of the 1980s. Through him the ideas contained in the MacDougall Report on the role of public finance in European integration were brought to bear on the draft.[13] Stable exchange rates and a common currency were put back at the centre of the agenda, but the Jenkins's initiative emphasized that they were to be accompanied by a more active, redistributive role for an expanded EC budget, the budget of a 'slim-line federation' consuming some 5–7 per cent of GDP (cf. the 20–5 per cent in Germany and the United States). Though in one sense the role of fiscal transfers was modest in relation to existing federal systems, it was very ambitious when compared to current Community expenditure, which was below 1 per cent of GDP. This aspect of the Florence speech helped, if anything, to reduce its impact. In the words of *The Economist*, it was 'A Bridge Too Far'.

Problems quickly followed within the Commission and with ECOFIN. Within the Commission opposition came from two main sources: from François-Xavier Ortoli, who exerted his influence to the full as former Commission president and commissioner responsible for economic and monetary affairs; and from the German commissioner Willi Haferkamp, who had held the economic and monetary portfolio in Ortoli's Commission. Ortoli and Haferkamp were wedded to the old gradualist, step-by-step approach; both were also fortified by a sense of a much greater familiarity with the mores of the EC institutions than Jenkins had or could possess. In Jenkins's own honest account: 'I was an enthusiast for the *grandes lignes* of Europe but an amateur within the complexities of its signalling system'.[14]

It was eventually Ortoli's paper, committed to the traditional approach of parallel and comprehensive progress towards economic convergence and monetary union, that

12. R. Jenkins, 'Europe's Present Challenge and Future Opportunity', first Jean Monnet Lecture (Florence: European University Institute, 27 October 1977).
13. D. MacDougall *et al.*, *Report of the Study Group on the Role of Public Finance in European Integration* (MacDougall Report), volumes 1 and 2 (Brussels: Commission of the European Communities, 1977).
14. Jenkins, *European Diary, 1977–1981*, p. 2.

went forward as the official statement of the Commission's position. In so far as there was anything significantly new in the Ortoli proposals, it involved a revival of the idea of a target zone for managing exchange rates, on the lines of the Duisenberg Plan of 1976 (see chapter 3). In contrast, Jenkins had sought a 'qualitative leap' towards monetary union, one that Ortoli judged to be 'politically absurd'.[15] By a bold approach Jenkins aimed to break through the inertia on EMU and to use a common monetary policy to establish improved conditions for a more rapid economic convergence of the member states. This sense of a setback for Jenkins was further reinforced when the November meeting of ECOFIN signalled a pronounced disinclination to accept even the ideas of Ortoli, with the German Finance Minister, Hans Apel, displaying a notable hostility. Neither economic nor political conditions were judged to be propitious. There was, in short, a clear sense of a lack of political will in Council bargaining to give new momentum to EMU.

From Brussels to the 'spirit of Bremen': the activation of Council bargaining

The rest of the story of launch of the EMS is one of how, after so unpromising a start, the European Council began, albeit with difficulty, to build and consolidate a collective will for action in the field of monetary policy. There were three landmarks – the European Council meetings at Copenhagen, Bremen and Brussels, with the EMS forming the central issue at the latter two. But again the first European Council meeting at which the new monetary initiative was discussed – the Brussels Council of December 1977 – was far from encouraging. Giscard d'Estaing was cool, and Schmidt reserved.[16] The chances of success for Jenkins's initiative looked poor.

Schmidt's conversion to enthusiasm, announced privately to Jenkins in February 1978, was the great turning-point. Two factors were decisive in translating that enthusiasm into practical effect: one directly, the other indirectly. Of direct importance were attributes of Schmidt's approach to politics: his attribution of primacy to economics and his belief in the importance of 'concentration' for the realization of any great scheme. Both attributes stood, in his mind, in antithesis to the political approach of his predecessor, Willy Brandt. Once Schmidt's powerful mind had latched on to the acute external threat posed by the fast-falling US dollar, then his political approach led him towards dedicating his enormous energies to an initiative in monetary policy.

At this point a factor of 'background' importance enters the picture. Schmidt was already on record as a dedicated champion of the 'snake' and the longer-term ambitions that underpinned it. He had just written the introduction to the German edition of Monnet's *Memoirs*, in which he addressed the Action Committee for the United States of Europe's declarations of support for EMU.[17] Along with Jenkins's initiative, there was much in his experience to dispose him to propose 'a major step towards monetary union'.

15. R. Jenkins, *A Life at the Centre* (London: Pan, 1992), pp. 463–4 and 468–9.
16. Jenkins, *A Life at the Centre*, p. 469.
17. J. Pinder, *European Community: The Building of a Union* (Oxford: Oxford University Press, 1991), p. 125. H. Schmidt, preface to J. Monnet, *Erinnerungen eines Europäers* (Munich, 1978).

The sense of a turning-point in Council bargaining was further completed when, in March 1978, the Left was defeated in the French National Assembly elections: meaning no prospect of Communist ministers in the French government to worry Schmidt. Giscard d'Estaing's Republican Party and its allies in the centre-right Union pour la démocratie française (UDF) did unexpectedly well, strengthening his own position *vis-à-vis* the Gaullists within the presidential majority. In short, the French President's long-standing predilections for European monetary integration had apparently been given a freer rein than ever before.

The change of political atmosphere in Council bargaining was registered at the Copenhagen European Council in April. Here, late in the proceedings, in a private after-dinner conversation, Schmidt announced his plan to dissolve the 'snake' and to develop a new arrangement in which the European Unit of Account would be used far more extensively, a European Monetary Fund would be created and a partial pooling of official reserves would take place.[18] The new system would entail intervention obligations for all EC states. Already the plan had been cleared at a bilateral meeting between Schmidt and Giscard d'Estaing at Rambouillet, though notably Schmidt had not cleared the plan with his own cabinet or – perhaps even more significantly – with the Bundesbank. The French President spoke of the plan as a 'new Bretton Woods for Europe'. What emerged at Copenhagen was the sense of an initiative operating at the highest and most discrete level of confidential personal diplomacy, very much akin in its approach to that of the Schuman Plan. The power and effectiveness of the Franco-German bargaining relationship was demonstrated to its greatest effect.

This preference for secrecy was reflected in the press conference that followed the summit. No impression was given of substantial progress. In fact, in private, Schmidt, Giscard d'Estaing and the British Prime Minister, James Callaghan, had agreed at Copenhagen to entrust the development of these ideas to a confidential group of three nominated advisers: Schmidt nominated Dr Schulmann, Giscard d'Estaing nominated Bernard Clappier and Callaghan nominated Kenneth Couzens, a senior Treasury official. Again, this procedure kept the scepticism and even hostility of Emminger at the Bundesbank away from the development of policy. It also bred resentment in some national capitals, notably The Hague.

In the months leading up to the next European Council in Bremen, the key preparatory work was done in the EC Monetary Committee and by the Clappier-Schulmann-Couzens working party. Van Ypersele used his position as chairman of the Monetary Committee to raise the key issues involved in EC monetary reform; via its report to the ECOFIN Council, the ministers of finance were drawn more fully into the discussions. At the heart of these issues was the idea of transforming the 'snake' into a completely new Community system by introducing an obligation to intervene based on either the European Unit of Account or a trade-weighted basket of currencies, as opposed to the existing 'parity-grid' system (see later for a more detailed discussion). By the time of the Bremen summit there was broad agreement within ECOFIN about the need to create a stable exchange rate system.[19]

18. Jenkins, *European Diary, 1977–1981*, p. 246; Ludlow, *The Making of the European Monetary System*, pp. 88–94.
19. Ludlow, *The Making of the European Monetary System*, pp. 97–103.

The progress of the secret talks revealed the particular problems that the British government had with Schmidt's initiative. These problems had surfaced at the Copenhagen summit when Callaghan had expressed his preference for a pound/dollar initiative within the framework of the IMF and shown reluctance about the establishment of the secret high-level group of three. Couzens rapidly became a marginal and eventually a humiliated figure, his reservations, not least about the technical problems involved, confirming a lack of political commitment at the highest levels of the British government. There was strong support in the Foreign Office and from Harold Lever, the economic and financial policy adviser to the Prime Minister. Mild support was even forthcoming from the Bank of England, which saw in a new EC monetary system a useful discipline on the behaviour of the government. But negotiations were maintained firmly in the hands of the Treasury whose senior ministers were strongly opposed.

Just before the Bremen summit, Callaghan was to indicate in a newspaper interview that he regarded the plan as an act of German self-interest, 'thinly disguised by a veil of Community spirit'.[20] He was in fact giving public articulation to a Treasury view. In his autobiography, the British Chancellor of the Exchequer of the time, Denis Healey, argues that his opposition had been confirmed once he noted that the new monetary system would require the weaker countries to intervene in the currency markets to prevent the stronger currencies from rising: in effect, German self-interest writ large.[21] This conclusion derived from comments made by Lahnstein and confirmed a key German incentive for embracing external stability: namely, that a joint EC float against the US dollar would share the burdens of the depreciating dollar among the member states. Perhaps more importantly, the Treasury calculated that a fixed exchange rate with the D-Mark would deprive the British government of much needed flexibility to tackle domestic priorities for expanding output and employment. Later, just before the Brussels European Council, the Treasury was to fully state its objections, adding that sterling was unusual in being sensitive to a different degree to movements in the oil price in view of Britain's large energy resources; and that Britain enjoyed stronger trading and financial relationships with non-European countries.[22] So it was the Schulmann-Clappier paper that formed the basis for discussions at the Bremen European Council meeting in July, and a resentful and suspicious British government that took part.

The French government was, by contrast, very receptive to the Schmidt initiative. Its incentives for monetary cooperation reflected a traditional French priority to external stability (symbolized by France's attempt to lead the Gold Bloc in the 1930s) and President Giscard d'Estaing's view that fixed exchange rates were essential to stabilize and lubricate trading relations and investment, a view shared with the EC Commission.[23] Also, French economic policy goals had (as we saw above) shifted closer to those of Germany. External discipline was seen as a useful discipline to enforce an internal stability that had proved elusive with a flexible exchange-rate system.

20. Ludlow, *The Making of the European Monetary System*, pp. 111–14.
21. D. Healey, *The Time of My Life* (Harmondsworth: Penguin, 1990), pp. 438–9.
22. United Kingdom Government, *The European Monetary System* (London: HMSO, 1978).
23. M. Loriaux, *France after Hegemony: International Change and Financial Reform* (Ithaca, NY: Cornell University Press, 1991), p. 253.

The influence of the Schulmann-Clappier paper, and therefore of the Franco-German bargaining relationship, was reflected in the fact that it was published virtually intact as an Annex to the Bremen communiqué. Its chief characteristic was its explicit endorsement of the idea of a completely new Community arrangement that would not simply amount to the 'snake' by another name. At Bremen the European Council agreed to accept this plan as the basis for developing a reform and attached an introduction to the paper in which a timetable of 31 October was settled for technical refinements so that definite decisions could be taken at the European Council in Brussels in December. In order to encourage compromise in Council bargaining, reference was added to the need for concurrent studies of the action needed to strengthen the position of the economies of less prosperous states in any new monetary system. The aim was to create incentives for their participation. The German presidency was most keen on a timetable that would allow the reform to come to fruition during its term of office: whilst the Irish and Italian governments argued strongly that both domestic political support and the need to promote economic convergence indicated that they required new measures of financial support as a basis for participation.

The Schulmann-Clappier paper's most controversial statement was that 'The European Currency Unit (ECU) will be at the centre of the system'. Room was left for differences of interpretation; indeed, Clappier and Schulmann appeared not to share a common view of the ECU's future role. For Schulmann the ECU was, first and foremost, a means of denominating the central rates and a means of settlement between central banks. For Clappier, consistent with the Fourcade Plan of 1974–5 (see chapter 3), it was the basis on which the new intervention system was to be established.[24] Here was to be a central issue for consideration in the EC Monetary Committee and ECOFIN. Impressively, the paper's stress on the creation of a European Monetary Fund (EMF), no later than two years after the start of the scheme, received a warm endorsement from Giscard d'Estaing and Schmidt. But it contained the germs of another dispute. Not surprisingly, both these disputes were to focus around the technical reservations of the German Bundesbank.

Another notable fact about the Bremen summit was the gap between Schmidt's reference at the press conference to 'a system of monetary union within the European Community' and the content of the formal communiqué which spoke of 'the creation of a closer monetary cooperation (European Monetary System) leading to a zone of monetary stability in Europe'. The policy implications of 'cooperation' and 'union' were very different (as we noted in chapter 3).

From the 'spirit of Bremen' to the 'gloom of Brussels': the power of the Bundesbank

Despite reservations about the secretive and assertive character of Franco-German bargaining and initiative, symbolized by the Schulmann-Clappier paper, and the sense of key and difficult issues pending, a clear sense of political direction and structure had been given to Council bargaining by the Bremen European Council. Now, with

24. Ludlow, *The Making of the European Monetary System*, p. 107.

echoes of 1970, the 'spirit of Bremen' infected and gave way to the normal Council bargaining processes of the EC. To centre stage came the technical committees – the Committee of Central Bank Governors and the Monetary Committee – and ECOFIN. In short, the technical issues were digested by finance ministry officials, central bank officials and finance ministers – and, above all, the Bundesbank came to centre stage to provide policy leadership on the technical issues. Here was the moment of greatest danger to the impulse for radical reform.

Once the technical committees got to work, the Bundesbank's position was brought to bear to great effect: with the determination of an independent institution that was proud of its success and had the authority that flows naturally from that success. Its views revolved around a concern to minimize the risks to internal stability inherent in a proposal of this kind. They can be summarized as follows:

1   Only countries, like France, that had clearly demonstrated their commitment to stability should be regarded as suitable candidates for any revised exchange-rate regime.
2   Flexibility about parity changes should be built into the system so as to minimize exposure to intervention by the central bank.
3   Credit facilities should be limited, not least so that the discipline on monetary authorities was maintained.
4   Limits should be placed on the Bundesbank's obligation to intervene and the possibility of partner countries using D-Marks to intervene.
5   The intervention system should be based on the 'parity grid' rather than the 'basket'.
6   The creation of an EMF would not affect the Bundesbank's autonomy to determine its own monetary policies.[25]

This position proved powerful because it was coherent and technically well-argued and was enormously influential in the final EMS bargain. The influence of the Bundesbank came from the basic structural fact that German leadership was indispensable to the effective functioning of any new EC monetary system: *de facto* that leadership role would have to be played by the Bundesbank. That fact meant that in Council bargaining, power gravitated to the Bundesbank.

In the technical bargaining two actors were important power brokers: Lahnstein, as state secretary in the German Finance Ministry, in brokering a deal acceptable to both Schmidt and Emminger in Germany and between Germany and its partners, and the Belgian government, which via van Ypersele, as chairman of the Monetary Committee, helped to broker an agreement between the French and the German positions (in fact between the 'non-snake' and the 'snake' countries) on the implications of the ECU being at the centre of the new system.

Between the two European Council meetings, Schmidt and Giscard d'Estaing used their regular bilateral summit in September 1978, symbolically in Aachen, to review progress and to seek to arrive at provisional agreement. Though this Franco-German bargaining session was to attract the ire of the British government as an attempt to stitch up on agreement on German terms (the EMS as a 'DM-zone'), it served

25. Ludlow, *The Making of the European Monetary System*, pp. 181–2.

essentially to ratify known positions in the technical committees. In particular, the Aachen summit agreed that, though the ECU would be used as the formal means of denominating the central rates, interventions would be based on a parity grid. The ECU might, however, 'serve a useful purpose as an indicator of divergence', and, it was agreed, the system should avoid putting the pressure for adjustment on just one currency. In effect, French negotiators had already agreed that a 'basket-centred' currency system would be too technically complex (with frequent and potentially dangerous changes in the relative weightings of currencies) and was in practice far from achieving the objective of limiting the difficulties of the weaker 'non-snake' countries. The Bundesbank had, in other words, scored an early victory for its enduring view that the greatest onus should be on weaker currency countries to take action to support their currencies.

But, even with the Franco-German compromising apparent at the Aachen summit, a combination of factors served to make for difficult negotiations in September and October: the determination of the French government that the EMS should be more than an amendment to the 'snake'; the resolution of the Bundesbank on such issues as membership of the new system, the creation of the EMF and the size and distribution of credits; the argument of the Irish and Italian governments for very large flanking measures of financial support as the basis for an acceptable compromise; and the general desire of the British government, led on this issue by Denis Healey, to discredit every aspect of the proposed new system and yet not to be left out of continuing negotiations about the future of the system, should it come into being.

Such, however, was the general will in Council bargaining to reach agreement within the strict timetable that the British government found itself isolated. It was in the end to be the only EC government that did not commit its currency to the new Exchange Rate Mechanism (ERM), as it became called, though formally it remained a part of the EMS. Assisted by the French President, who was keen to balance German strength in the proposed system, the British government was able to gain agreement on the idea of an EMS that all could join and that would contain an ERM in which it was not necessary to participate. Britain could, therefore, belong to the EMS, including for instance the ECU basket and the transfer of reserves. But (as we shall see) the ERM was to constitute the heart of the new system.

The other crucial problem was the Bundesbank. Before the Brussels European Council, on 30 November, Chancellor Schmidt took the extraordinary step of delivering an impassioned and robust speech to the Bundesbank council.[26] Its main theme was challenging to the Bundesbank: that the basic rationale for the EMS was historical and political, not technical, and that accordingly the Bundesbank's independence would be abused if it sought to take up a veto position. The influential aspect of the speech was not so much its content – with references to the Holocaust and to the peculiar requirements of reponsibility borne by Germany's political leadership – or any implicit threat to act to curb Bundesbank independence. Most potent of all was the clear demonstration that the traditional bargaining relationship

---

26. O. Emminger, 'Deutsche Geld- und Währungspolitik im Spannungsfeld zwischen innerem und ausserem Gleichgewicht', pp. 13–14 and 364. Also D. Marsh, *The Bundesbank: The Bank that Rules Europe* (London: Heinemann, 1992), pp. 194–5.

between the German government and the Bundesbank was destined to take on a new form as European integration extended to the monetary field. Sitting astride different bargaining relations – in the European Council, in Franco-German relations and with respect to the Bundesbank – the German Chancellor had acquired a new potency: the potency of a linking-pin among different, now interconnected bargaining relations. The Bundesbank had its foretaste of what life would be like operating in a new field of political bargaining pressures in the nascent EMS policy process.

In fact, though the Brussels European Council of December 1978 accepted the recommendations on the internal mechanics of the EMS put to it, it did not provide a happy launch consistent with the 'spirit of Bremen'. It was an instance of sour and depressing Council bargaining, characterized by last-minute objections of the French government – on the issues of financial transfers to Ireland and Italy and of the future of the monetary compensation amounts (MCAs).[27] President Giscard d'Estaing took a very restrictive view on subsidized loans and in effect blocked extra Regional Fund aid; in addition, he made a dismantling of the MCAs a precondition for the launch of the EMS. Ireland and Italy left with disappointed expectations, but within a few days agreed to enter the EMS in any case; then, without any clearly stated reason, in March 1979 the French government removed its objection on the MCA issue, enabling the EMS to come into operation on 13 March. The Brussels summit had demonstrated once again the impact of domestic political conditions on Council bargaining: in this case, the impact of increased strains between the President and the Gaullists within the presidential majority and the effort of the President not to be outflanked by the Gaullists in his demonstration of loyalty to the interests of French farmers. In retrospect, of course, no actual damage was done to the main substance of the EMS agreement as spelt out in the Brussels Resolution of 5 December.

The EMS bargain

In order to understand the nature of the agreements that established the EMS it is necessary to explore the Council bargaining process in the final run-up to the Brussels European Council. Here a key role was played by van Ypersele, chairman of the Monetary Committee, in engineering a compromise that gave the 'snake' and 'non-snake' countries something of what they wanted.[28] A central element in this compromise was played by the new 'indicator of divergence'. This device was designed to emphasize the new importance of the ECU as a central element of the system and to underline the point that the EMS was not simply a new version of the 'snake'. It involved the calculation of ECU margins for each currency (maximum divergence spread around the central rate); the fixing of a 'divergence threshold' in ECU (75 per cent of the maximum spread was chosen for this purpose, so that in normal circumstances a currency would attain this threshold before it reached its bilateral limit); and the establishment both of a 'presumption to act' on the part of the

27. Jenkins, *A Life at the Centre*, pp. 483–90.
28. On the technical aspects of the negotiations and final agreements see the excellent coverage in Ludlow, *The Making of the European Monetary System*, pp. 158–69 and 230–43; J. van Ypersele and J.-C. Koeune, *The EMS, Origins, Operation and Outlook* (Brussels: Commission of the European Communities, European Perspective Series, 1985).

monetary authority of a currency which breaches its 'divergence threshold' and of an obligation for central banks to consult if the divergence remains after more than five days.

Consistent with the spirit of the Duisenberg Plan, an attempt was being made to devise an objective indicator as a trigger for European monetary policy coordination. But it was not made clear what the division of tasks was to be between the new 'divergence indicator' and the parity grid. In other words, a great deal of discretion was left to the monetary authorities and – led by the German Bundesbank – they could be expected to exercise that discretion with caution, in other words by not according a central role to the 'divergence indicator'. The idea that this new objective indicator would serve as a source of symmetry in the functioning of the EMS was to be disappointed because the Bundesbank had no self-interest in a symmetrical EMS that would impose heavy costs of intervention on itself and thereby jeopardize its priority to domestic stability.

Also crucial to the argument that the EMS was not simply a revised 'snake' were the credit mechanisms and the proposed new EMF. Yet in neither case were radical breakthroughs achieved. The Bundesbank took up a very tough position in September and October, not least arguing that maintenance of the strict timetable for negotiation depended on observing legal constraints. A transfer of German reserves to the new EMF would require special German legislation, and, it was argued, creation of new credit mechanisms beyond those set up under the EMCF of 1973 would constitute treaty amendment and require the special and protracted amendment procedure of Article 236 of the Treaty of Rome. Hence it was decided that the EMF was a matter for the future and that attention should focus on alterations to the existing credit mechanisms. The Bundesbank's appeal to the limitations of EC legal powers proved an effective device, then and later, for gaining its way and preserving its self-interests within the new EMS.

Very-short-term financing referred to the credit facilities that central banks made available to each other via the EMCF so that they could intervene in Community currencies. The amount of such credits was already unlimited, so discussion focused on their duration before settlement was required; duration was raised from 30 to 45 days after the end of the month of intervention. This facility was to remain, as in the 'snake', the core of the intervention system of the EMS. In practice, however, countries were gaining only a very limited extra time in which to adjust their policies in order to stop an outflow of funds.

On the matter of short-term monetary support (STMS) and medium-term financial assistance (MTFA) the German government conceded to the views of the 'non-snake' countries about the total amount of credit that should be involved: 25 billion ECUs, with a credit ceiling of 11 billion ECUs for the MTFA and of 14 billion for the STMS. Utilization of the STMS was to continue to be available for three months, but could now be renewed twice for a period of three months.

Though the STMS and the MTFA had been increased by a factor of three, it should be noted that they were only the same size as the combined IMF quotas of the participants. These extra credits and the new duration of the very-short-term facility were to prove a far from adequate means of overcoming the asymmetry in the functioning of the new EMS. In any case, in the early years of the EMS the monetary authorities were to display a marked preference for responding to major imbalances by realignment of currencies rather than by using the enlarged credit facilities.

Less impressive still was the attempt to establish the role of the ECU as a reserve asset and means of official settlement. Here major restrictions were inserted, again notably at the behest of the Bundesbank. In the Brussels Resolution participating states in the ERM agreed to provide to the EMCF, through revolving three-month swap arrangements, 20 per cent of their gold – revalued at six-month intervals to reflect market value – and dollar reserves in exchange for an equivalent sum denominated in ECU. Other EC states could also, on a voluntary basis, join the scheme (as Britain did in July 1979). This arrangement was undoubtedly advantageous. Since the early 1970s gold reserves had been in effect banned as an official means of settlement. The new swap arrangements, which redenominated them into ECU, made them partially usable. In other words, the usable international reserves of the countries participating in the EMS had potentially been increased.

But in two senses the EMS fell short of radical change. First, the new arrangement did not amount to reserve pooling and an enhanced role for the EMCF beyond the 'bookkeeping' function outlined in chapter 3. The depositing central banks continued to own and manage, on behalf of the EMCF, 'their' gold and dollars and to receive interest on them. Additionally, the Committee of Central Bank Governors was responsible for a noticeably restrictive agreement of March 1979, restrictive that is in its interpretation of the Brussels Resolution. According to this agreement, the new ECUs would not be fully usable. Creditor banks would be obliged to accept up to 50 per cent settlement in ECU, the balance being 'settled by transferring other reserve components in accordance with the composition of the debtor's central bank reserves' (Article 16.1 of the 13 March 1979 agreement).[29] Behind this important qualification to the functioning of the new EMS stood the power of the Bundesbank, which was concerned that most of the ECUs created through the swaps would end up in its hands. It was not until 1987 that this acceptance limit on settlement in ECUs was finally removed.

The Brussels Resolution did not take a clear position on the use of realignments of currencies and the criteria that would guide their use. In the real world such a statement of criteria would have been a hostage to fortune; it would have helped to build up anticipation of change in the financial markets. Certainly, no reference was made to any ambition to eliminate realignments. There was only the Bremen conclusions which stated that the new arrangement must be 'at least as strict as the snake'. The one clear rule enunciated in the Brussels Resolution was that realignments were to be subject to mutual consent: in effect, a system of collective management.

But perhaps the most crucial bargain of all was at the German domestic level. The German federal government felt obliged to provide a reassurance to the Bundesbank that the commitment to a 'zone of monetary stability' and the adoption of the new 'divergence indicator' did not imply 'unlimited' intervention. 'Imported inflation' had long been the risk that most worried Otmar Emminger as president of the Bundesbank. With the ERM the dilemma between internal and external stability was posed in a new, potentially more acute form. Emminger was well aware of the ERM's central

29.   Van Ypersele and Koeune, *The EMS, Origins, Operation and Outlook*, annex.

weakness and major threat to the Bundesbank's priority: that the central bank of a country receiving a currency inflow had no certainty that the central bank of the country whose currency's value was the lowest in the ERM regime would tighten monetary conditions enough to stop its capital outflow. Accordingly, there was no guarantee that the combined money supply of the two countries would not rise and eventually threaten price stability in the 'inflow' country: in other words, in Germany.

Recognizing the force of this concern, in a speech to the Bundestag in December 1978 the German Economics Minister, Otto Graf Lambsdorff, made it clear that the Bundesbank would not be obliged to intervene if, in the judgement of its president and his colleagues, it would constitute a threat to their statutory requirement under the Bundesbank Act of 1957 to maintain domestic monetary stability.[30] In effect, he was giving public support to the substance of a letter from Emminger, written to the German government and arguing that the Bundesbank must be able to opt out of any obligation of unlimited intervention in support of weaker currencies.[31] This domestic bargain between the federal government and the Bundesbank was not only central to the politics of creating the EMS, but also crucial to its later functioning. Other central banks knew its substance. Unlimited intervention was never part of the EMS's policy repertoire, and the Bundesbank was to be the judge of whether and when intervention had reached unmanageable proportions, as for instance it did in notifying the German government by the weekend of the devaluation of the Italian lira in September 1992 that it had spent some DM90 billion in intervention and that it could go no further. As policy leader in the EMS, Germany was in a position to enforce its interpretation of the 'rules of the game' strictly and (as we shall see in chapter 6) to dictate the terms on which realignments took place.

Lessons

One of the central lessons to be drawn from the experience of launching the EMS was about the nature of the EC policy process in relation to this issue. In effect the policy process comprised a set of interconnected bargaining relations: between the member state governments within the framework of the EC institutions; between France and Germany, notably in the Schulmann-Clappier meetings; between the EC and the central banks; and, crucially, between the German federal government and the Bundesbank.

We have also noted a basic ambiguity: between the importance of key actors in activating the bargaining processes and providing a linking-pin between different bargaining relations; and the ultimate submergence of their contribution in these complex bargaining relations. Roy Jenkins and Helmut Schmidt were able to exert a propulsive influence because their policy ideas and political and economic circumstances colluded to make that possible. The Commission president recognized that, for him to make a mark on the integration process, a 'big idea' was indispensable. Though he was undoubtedly wise to have chosen monetary integration for that purpose, a risk was involved, and, by the time of the Brussels summit of December

---

30. Deutscher Bundestag, *Stenographischer Bericht*, 122 Sitzung, 6 December 1978, pp. 9485ff.
31. On this letter see *Central Banking*, autumn 1992.

1977, it seemed that he might have miscalculated. For, in addition to a big idea that fits the line of least resistance, a personal initiative requires one all-important extra ingredient, good fortune. And good fortune came in the form of the external challenge of the collapsing dollar and its implications for Germany's domestic economic interests. That circumstance brought Schmidt into the picture. The personal support and commitment of the German Chancellor was critical. For nothing could be done without the German government's backing: that backing created a window of opportunity that the French government could not afford to miss. German equivocation on EMU had always been the central stumbling block to progress. Now there was a Chancellor who, in the interests of German competitiveness that was endangered by external exchange-rate instability, was prepared to take on the Bundesbank's opposition. At that point Jenkins's role receded into the background. His role, expertise and skills were not relevant to the central problem of policy leadership in EC monetary policy cooperation and integration: that the EMS would have to rest fundamentally on a bargain between the German federal government and the Bundesbank. Schmidt's individual contribution at this domestic level was every bit as important as his role in the European Council. The magic combination then was a big idea, a line of least resistance and good fortune. Good fortune held out during the negotiations. But the line of least resistance proved to be alive with friction, represented above all by the Bundesbank's efforts to protect its interests and the efforts of countries with weaker currencies to gain EC support for their burdens of adjustment under the new system.

An appreciation of the underlying matrix of power relationships behind the launch of the EMS is deepened by a recognition of just how effective a damage-limitation exercise was fought by the German Bundesbank in the final run-up to the Brussels European Council. Behind the complex patterns of bargaining relations and political manoeuvrings stood the structural power of the Bundesbank, rooted in the fundamental reality of German monetary power, the fact that the D-Mark was the natural anchor currency for an EC monetary arrangement and the exclusive responsibility of the Bundesbank for safeguarding its value. The inevitable result was a bias to asymmetry in the EMS policy process. Clearly, the Bundesbank did not and could not win an outright victory; that would have involved opposing compromise and blocking its own government's initiative. And it was very much on the defensive, its power that of veto rather than of agenda setting. Yet (as we have seen) the final package bore its imprint in the area of the all-important technical details. The impact of the Bundesbank on the agenda-setting phase was avoided only by keeping the preparation of the Bremen summit away from the normal technical committees of the EC. The Schulmann-Clappier paper was a deliberate attempt to sustain political momentum during the launch. But, even so, the idea of change at the level of basic policy goals did not surface in a clear, unequivocal fashion. In its absence the position of the Bundesbank was strengthened in the later technical negotiations.

To what extent then did Jenkins achieve his 'qualitative leap'? The answer must be that, at the level of goals, he was unsuccessful. The Brussels Resolution adopted the language of Bremen: a 'scheme for the creation of closer monetary cooperation leading to a zone of monetary stability in Europe'. Here was no talk of 'union', in the manner of the Werner Report, even of 'integration'. Nor was there any reference to the idea of an enlarged EC budget to transfer resources in the interests of economic convergence, an idea taken up in Jenkins's speech in Florence. Again, there was no support for economic convergence in the form of new ideas for closer economic policy cooperation, building on the Werner Report.

The EMS was essentially a limited, defensive mechanism to improve monetary stability: a 'shock absorber' mechanism to deal with external problems, specifically the US dollar and tailored above all to German interests as the price of German policy commitment and leadership. It did not involve a fundamental change of policy paradigm in the conduct of monetary affairs. Change occurred essentially at the level of policy instruments and the proposed use of these instruments. Even here, reflecting the absence of anything much more than symbolic change in basic policy goals, there was no reserve pooling in a European Monetary Fund (which was not to come into existence till 1981 and did not in fact appear), and no new credit facilities were created. The Bundesbank had successfully blocked the EMF and gained confirmation that intervention credits had to be settled in a short time and that the new scheme had no commitment to fixed exchange rates and unlimited intervention.

Above all, the EMS was not based on the creation of a new supranational standard for the achievement of external and internal stability. In so far as one could speak of change at the level of goals, it involved the statement that 'A European Currency Unit (ECU) will be at the centre of the EMS'. But its use as a means of settlement was to be limited by the later agreement of March 1979; its use as the basis of the 'divergence indicator', potentially the major change at the level of policy instruments, was undermined by a lack of clarity about the role of this new indicator in relation to that of the parity grid, whilst *de facto* the D-Mark operated as the standard for the achievement of both forms of stability. Without operational and effective policy instruments, the goal represented by the central role of the ECU in the new system was more symbolic than practical. Ambition had been regained, but in a modest form. In retrospect, one can see just how much the 'snake' had had the future in its bones, and just how much the critical momentum for European monetary integration had its catalyst in the demise of the Bretton Woods system and the structural consequences for trading and policy relations among the EC states.

Chapter 5

AMBITION REGAINED (2)

Negotiating and implementing the Treaty on European Union – power relations and policy change

We should be under no illusions – the present controversy over the new European monetary order is about power, influence and the pursuit of national interests.
(Wilhelm Nölling, president of the *Landeszentralbank* of Hamburg, speech to US–German economic policy group, 7 March 1991)

Keeping the franc's parity with the D-Mark is a precondition of this (preservation of the European Monetary System). Without a common monetary system, there is no Europe.
(President François Mitterrand, on nominating Edouard Balladur as Prime Minister, 29 March 1993)

If the EMS had few claims to represent a 'qualitative leap' in the content of EC policy, its enduring significance lay in establishing a new policy process. The pattern of bargaining relations that had been called into play during the launch of the EMS congealed to form the infrastructure supporting the EMS policy process, and (as we shall see in chapter 6) the new institutional rules of the game had lasting consequences for the attitudes and behaviour of the participating policy actors. The subsequent story of the EMS – and of the relaunch of EMU on the back of the EMS – is of the complex interaction of these bargaining relations: between member state governments in the framework of the EC institutions (Council bargaining): between the French and German governments (as over the Franco-German Economic Council); between EC institutions and the central banks (for instance, over the Nyborg agreement and in the Delors Committee); between the German federal government and the Bundesbank; and between the EC monetary authorities and the foreign exchange markets (as over the adoption of a very wide 15 per cent fluctuation band for most ERM currencies in August 1993).

The key question is why the EMS policy process did not simply continue to proceed on the basis of pragmatically refining its policy instruments (as at Nyborg) but, in the late 1980s, shifted gear to embrace a radical change of policy content: indeed, to constitutionalize a commitment to a specific and controversial path to EMU. This chapter is concerned, first, with examining the complex of pressures and influences at work in propelling EMU on to the agenda of the EMS policy process; and second, with showing how new events, ideas and information were used by actors in the policy process to seek to engineer a change in the location of power in the EMS – with enormous implications for the future of European integration.

In effect, unlike in 1978–9, we are looking at a policy learning process characterized by radical, heroic change: characteristics that help us to understand some of the later problems of putting EMU into effect – problems that we analyse in the next chapters. For the very reason that, unlike the birth of the EMS, EMU constituted a 'paradigm' change in policy, the policy process involved does not connect as closely and directly to the experience and lessons of the 1970s: of the 'spirit of the Hague' or of earlier fixed exchange-rate regimes: in short, to what we have considered in the previous chapters.

But the past was by no means absent. As we saw in chapter 4, the priorities in the EMS policy process carried the imprint of the experience of the 1970s: those priorities, represented in the hard ERM, were expected to form the glide path to EMU. In the bargaining about EMU policy, for instance in the work of the Delors Committee, reference was made to the Werner Report. The idea of a timetable for stages towards EMU and, on this occasion, of building 'automaticity' into the final transition to stage three of union, can be understood as elements of direct learning from the experience of the 1970s. Also symptomatic of a learning process from the 1970s was (as we shall see) the omission of reference to creating 'a centre of decision for economic policy' at the EC level.

Fundamentally, however, the relaunch of EMU was an historical child of the mid- and late 1980s:

- of the experience of operating the EMS and the lessons that were drawn about its limitations, especially in the form that it developed from 1983
- of the political lesson, drawn most strongly in France, that the EMS involved an asymmetry of power that imposed undue costs on some countries and that could be corrected only by shifting authority to the EC level
- of domestic experiences with economic policy, notably the inflationary consequences of devaluation, and a subsequent convergence of economic policy ideas around a shared priority to price stability and stable exchange rates (i.e. the idea that external and internal stability were mutually supportive)
- of the impact of new 'sound money' policy ideas on the evolution of the EMS and its transformation into EMU, notably the virtues of 'tying one's hands' in domestic policy
- of the confidence and ambitions that were fed by the Single European Act and the implementation of the single European market programme (what follows its '1992' target?)
- of the extension of the single market's idea of economizing on transaction costs to monetary policy and its appeal to the business sector
- of the fuelling of confidence and ambition by a phase of economic growth from 1988 to 1991 that paralleled the period from the Delors Committee to the European Council meeting in Maastricht, and later,
- of the impact of German unification in 1989–90 on perceptions about the relationship between national interest and European integration.

It was a complex story whose plot reveals the impact of a range of beliefs and reasons to act on key policy makers, allied to the exigencies of policy development, and intertwined (as we shall see in later chapters) with deeper external and internal structural factors that gave an added momentum to the EMU policy process.

Before analysing the behaviour and motivations of pivotal actors in promoting EMU, it is important to underline one key factor that influenced the EMS and EMU policy process. The economic context of the bargaining relations about EMU was that the EC member states found themselves synchronized on the 'up-side' of the economic cycle. Between 1987 and 1990 the average annual rate of growth of the EC's real GDP was 3.3 per cent. It was possible to attribute some of this expansion to the climate of confidence and optimism engendered by the launch of the EC's single market programme. In such a context the sense of economic risk and of incipient policy conflict was reduced. Also, and of crucial significance for the course of the treaty negotiations, the bargaining relations between the EC monetary authorities and the foreign exchange markets shifted to the margins of the policy process. Paradoxically, neglect of this key bargaining relationship was later to prove the Achilles' heel of the Treaty on European Union.

Mounting stresses, strains and conflicts in the EMS and EMU policy process came from two sources: the sharp desynchronization of the British economy in 1990, followed by negative GDP growth in 1991 (−2.5 per cent) and 1992 (−0.6 per cent) and, more gradually, from mid-1990 the slip of other EC states into the 'down-side' of the cycle, gathering force and effect in 1992. With recession and policy conflict the bargaining relations between the EC monetary authorities and the foreign exchange markets came to centre ground. More ominously still, by 1993 the policy process was faced by the mounting perception that the EC was facing not simply the temporary difficulties of the 'down-side' of the economic cycle but a deeper structural problem: of declining performance in relation to the United States and Japan, and of the flight of investment to much lower-cost economies, not least in east central Europe. With so transformed an economic context the policy process was confronted with the possibility that, in negotiating the Treaty on European Union, it had been addressing the wrong questions.

The inheritance and role of the Delors Commission: a transformation in Council bargaining relations

When the negotiation of EMU is compared with the negotiation of the EMS differences emerge not only in the scope and ambition of policy but also in the policy process, in the inheritance of policy and in the general background of policy. In a very significant sense, Jacques Delors was more blessed by good fortune than Roy Jenkins had been. On becoming Commission president in January 1985, Delors inherited an EMS that had become, by general consent, a successful venture in multilateral action to stabilize exchange rates. There had been an initial turbulent phase of seven realignments between 1979 and 1983; only four more followed (one in 1985, two in 1986 and one in 1987) before a long phase without realignments (1987–92) began. The emphasis was increasingly on domestic monetary policies that would underpin exchange-rate stability; that meant a greater effort to achieve economic convergence (e.g. in inflation rates) and a greater willingness to coordinate monetary policies. In other words, the EMS had evolved into an instrument of external discipline; that discipline was provided by convergence of national policy priorities around German objectives and performance. By 1985 even the British Chancellor of the Exchequer, Nigel Lawson, had become convinced of the superior merits of the discipline of membership of the ERM to any other technique for achieving monetary stability (though the Prime Minister, Margaret Thatcher, had not). There was a measure of consensus on economic policy goals that had eluded Jenkins, despite the benefit of the Giscard–Schmidt partnership.

There was also a degree of inherited dynamism in EC Council bargaining that Jenkins would not have recognized. The European Council meeting at Fontainebleau in June 1984 had already imparted a momentum to the idea of a package deal that would incorporate the liberalization of the internal market and reform of decision-making processes within the Community.[1] The French presidency of the Council from January to June 1984 had proved to be a decisive turning-point. It had displayed a transformation in the approach of the French government to European integration, with President François Mitterrand deeply engaged in the notion of a *relance européenne* for the 1980s. Reflecting a European idealism that he had espoused since the 1940s, he aligned French interests – in the monetary field now aligned with German priority to internal stability – with the idea of European federalism.[2] That Mitterrand did so then, rather than when he came to office in 1981, had everything to do with economic and political circumstances in France: economically, the collapse of the new Socialist government's attempt to implement an independent economic policy programme dedicated to increasing output and employment; and politically, the decline of the Communist Party which enabled Mitterrand to align himself with the moderate wing of the Socialist Party (including Michel Rocard).

In the ERM crisis of March 1983 the French government had chosen continued membership of the ERM and the costs of a programme of austerity to restore confidence in the franc and avoid further devaluations rather than attempt to maintain existing policies behind import barriers, capital controls and repudiation of the EMS.[3] Successive devaluations of the franc in September 1981, June 1982 and March 1983 involved a cumulative change of nearly 30 per cent in the franc–mark rate over an eighteen-month period. This episode constituted a critical learning experience for the French political establishment, in particular that German policy makers would respect the French government only if it had a strong currency. The policy of the *franc fort* had begun, to be pursued with an impressive bipartisan continuity. As Minister of Economics and Finance in the Socialist government (1981–4), Delors had not only been a vocal advocate of continued ERM membership but also learned at first hand the powerful constraints and costs imposed on national economic policy making by the asymmetry of the EMS.[4]

Delors's appointment as president of the Commission was a case of the right person at the right time. He was a political heavyweight, well known in Community circles (as chairman of the European Parliament's Committee on Economic and Monetary Affairs 1979–81), familiar with ECOFIN as a consequence of his ministerial portfolio

1. M. Gazzo (ed.) *Towards European Union* (Brussels: Agence Europe, 1985), vol. 1, pp. 96–7.
2. F.O. Giesbert, *Le Président* (Paris: Editions du Senil, 1990). In fact, in the 1970s Mitterrand had aligned himself with the left-wing CERES (Centre d'Etudes de Recherches et d'Education Socialistes) group and, partly in consequence, opposed the Tindemans Report.
3. P. Favier and M. Martin-Roland, *La décennie Mitterrand* (Paris: Seuil, 1990); G. Robin, *La diplomatie de Mitterrand ou le triomphe des apparences, 1981–1985* (Paris: Editions de la Bievre, 1985); P. Bauchard, *La guerre des deux roses: du rêve à la realité, 1981–1985* (Paris: Bernard Grasset, 1986).
4. A. Moravcsik, 'Negotiating the Single European Act', in R. Keohane and S. Hoffmann (eds) *The New European Community* (Boulder, Colo.: Westview Press, 1991), p. 51.

in the French government and – despite a complex relationship with Mitterrand – able to count on the new-found enthusiasm of the French government for its 'European vocation'. Jenkins had not had the same familiarity with the ways of the EC; nor could he count on as much support from the British government.

Like Jenkins, Delors cast round for the 'big idea' to inspire his presidency.[5] But unlike Jenkins, he was from the very outset attracted to monetary policy, both by career background and by the prospects for building on the emerging success of an established policy, the EMS. Delors's future leadership on this issue was deeply influenced by the fact that his career had begun at the Banque de France (1945–62), by his chairmanship of the European Parliament's Committee on Economic and Monetary Affairs in the very early years of the EMS, and by his period as Economics and Finance Minister. Though he scouted the prospects for a major initiative in this area, it was clear from his initial consultations with heads of governments that prior developments were already making the internal market the natural choice for the big idea and that liberalization of capital movements was a precondition for getting EMU on the agenda. Delors presented his big idea to the new Commission in December 1984 and, in his maiden speech to the European Parliament on 14 January 1985, announced the goal of 'completing the internal market' by 1992. From the outset he was aware that he was putting in place the conditions for an EMU initiative.

Symptomatic of the momentum that had built up was the speed with which the next European Council meeting in Brussels endorsed the goal of a single market by 1992 and called upon the Commission to draw up a detailed programme with a specific programme. The subsequent White Paper produced by Lord Cockfield, the new commissioner responsible for the internal market, was unanimously accepted by the European Council in Milan in June 1985. This ambitious programme of reform involved some 300 legislative proposals to remove the various 'non-tariff' barriers to trade that still stood in the way of a truly 'common market': physical barriers (border controls); technical barriers (like trading standards and company law); and fiscal barriers (indirect taxation).[6] It was the recognition that realization of this programme required a review of decision-making processes that in the end led the Italian presidency to force through the Milan summit an intergovernmental conference to consider appropriate treaty revision in the face of solid British opposition and the reservations of Greece and Denmark about 'complete liberalization'. Mrs Thatcher placed her faith in the Germans to block any reference to the EMS and EMU in the treaty revision. The IGC was to agree the proposals on which the Single European Act of 1986 was based; in turn, that Act was to shift the centre of gravity in the EMS and EMU policy process – from a reliance on intergovernmental bargaining in Council to a more supranational style of bargaining in which the common interests and momentum established in agreeing the Act facilitated a new cohesion in promoting a major advance in EC monetary integration.

5. J. Delors *et al.*, *La France par l'Europe* (Paris: Bernard Grasset, 1988), pp. 47 and 50–1.
6. Commission of the European Communities, *Completing the Internal Market: White Paper from the Commission to the European Council* (Luxembourg: Office of Publications of the European Communities, June 1985).

The Single European Act, the complete liberalization of capital movements and the relaunch of EMU

It is important to note that throughout this process – the launch of the big idea of the completion of the internal market and the proceedings of the IGC leading to the Single European Act – the idea of monetary reform remained close to, even central to, Delors's thinking. Before the Milan summit he was trying to place monetary reform, along with other issues, on the agenda.[7] It resurfaced in the Commission White Paper which envisaged a European Financial Area in which, in addition to the creation of a single market in financial services, there would be freedom of movement of capital. It noted, with prescience, that free capital movement would be likely to introduce a new disruptive factor into the functioning of the EMS.

Even more strikingly, the Commission proposals to the IGC sought to revive progress towards the European Monetary Fund by suggesting that its establishment should require only the unanimous approval of the group of states that would choose to participate.[8] This proposal, amounting to a two-track Community, was halted by an informal meeting of ECOFIN which insisted on prior consultation before any further monetary proposals were put before the IGC. Opposition was led by the British and German governments, albeit in different manners. For the British, opposition was principled; the proposal smacked of the surrender of sovereignty. For the Germans, the proposal was premature; progress was first needed in establishment of freedom of capital movement and in economic convergence.

By contrast, the French and Italian governments felt that the Delors's proposal was too weak. What emerged at the IGC was a demonstration of why their bargaining position was weak on EMU. They were reluctant to make the rapid move to capital liberalization that Germany was clearly setting as a precondition for opening negotiations on EMU. As we shall see, by 1988 the French and Italian governments were to succeed in redressing this element of weakness in their position: the British government was to be left isolated in its opposition of principle.

From the perspective of relaunching EMU, Delors and the French and Italian governments could judge the Single European Act to be a success. It brought the EMS within the scope of the treaties, rather than – as until then – a mechanism set up alongside and not formally a part of the Community. The Commission now had formal responsibilities in the operation of the EMS. Also, in the preamble to the revised treaty, EMU was for the first time made a formal treaty objective (with a gloss added about 'cooperation in economic and monetary policy' to suit a dismayed and disappointed Mrs Thatcher). Pursuing the Commission's role as the guardian of the treaty, Delors was to make full use of this new legal resource in the bargaining that was to follow. Finally, the creation of a European Financial Area, with freedom of capital movement, could be expected to raise a whole series of issues about the development of the EMS and give Delors additional bargaining advantages. Delors's important contribution was to use these new bargaining resources to maximum effect.

At the same time, governmental opposition had forced Delors to drop his monetary reform proposals by the autumn of 1985. As he admitted to the European Parliament

7. Moravcsik, 'Negotiating the Single European Act', p. 60.
8. M. Gazzo (ed.) *Towards European Union*, vol. 1, pp. 8 and 25–6; vol. 2, p. 86.

in July 1985, the differences between the member state governments were 'too great for progress to be possible'.[9] Delors recognized that the main substantive bargaining in the IGC would have to involve the internal market, majority voting to expedite its implementation, and increases in the structural funds to help compensate the weaker and peripheral economies.

More problematically, the Single European Act placed the EMS under the unanimity rule of Article 236a: 'in so far as further development in the field of economic and monetary policy necessitates institutional changes the provisions of Article 236 shall be applicable'. The move from the EMS to EMU would of course require institutional change (the establishment of a European central bank), would therefore be subject to the amendment procedures of the Treaty of Rome, and could accordingly be vetoed by the British government (even though it was not a member of the ERM). An inner group of states committed to EMU could not move ahead without the approval of others, notably the British government. The prospects of a two-tier EC that had been implicit in the Commission's proposals had been significantly reduced. So, though Delors was given new bargaining resources, the Single European Act erected new barriers to be negotiated.

With the Single European Act negotiated, and an ambitious new work programme in place, Delors moved to secure momentum for a relaunch of EMU with two initiatives. One – the Padoa-Schioppa Report – was designed to provide a coherent rationale for a new initiative in the monetary field in the wake of the economic consequences of creating the internal market. The other – priority to complete liberalization of capital movements – sought to unblock a key source of opposition to the relaunch of EMU and encourage a more constructive leadership role by Germany on this issue. In April 1986 the Commission asked a group of experts under the chairmanship of Tommaso Padoa-Schioppa, who from 1979 to 1983 had been director-general of DG2 (economic and financial affairs) of the Commission; Michael Emerson, who had earlier played a part in the launch of the Jenkins's initiative and who remained a senior Commission official, joined the group. In essence, the Report of 1987 argued that the combination of freedom of capital movement under the '1992' initiative with the commitment to stable exchange rates under the ERM left no room for independent monetary policies.[10] Existing and planned policies meant a qualitative change in the operating environment of monetary policies. They required a review of institutional arrangements for the coordination of monetary policies if stability and an effectively functioning single market were to be ensured.

The Padoa-Schioppa Report did not advocate a 'precipitous' move to monetary union; it was judged to be too high-risk a proposition without a change of economic and political attitudes. But what was important was its insistence on a fundamental contradiction between the retention of independent monetary policies, on the one hand, and retention of stable exchange rates in the new framework of capital mobility, on the other. After all, a key weapon of monetary authorities in the face of speculative attacks in the markets – exchange controls – was being removed. It was a message that

9. Official Journal, *DEP*, no. 2-8328, 9 July 1985, p. 42.
10. T. Padoa-Schioppa *et al.*, *Efficiency, Stability and Equity: A Strategy for the Evolution of the Economic System of the European Community*, with a preface by Jacques Delors (Oxford: Oxford University Press, 1987).

enjoyed a significant influence in Council bargaining and gave a new cogency and sense of purpose to economic arguments for a relaunch of EMU. With ever larger capital flows from one member state to another, there was a new risk to exchange rate stability. Why not eliminate that risk once and for all?

The work of the group led by Padoa-Schioppa was paralleled and followed by two other developments. First, there was a notable growth of work on the EMS's problems and prospects and on EMU by academic economists, notably those with a specialization in monetary economics and international economics. This work had various strands, including a stress on the costs of inflation and the deleterious effects of devaluation on long-term competitiveness, with a subsequent emphasis on price stability as a policy objective and on the role of the EMS as an automatic disciplinary mechanism for linking national policy performances to the 'strongest' currency, that is lowest performing in terms of inflation. Along with this academic rationale for the primacy to be accorded to the hard ERM as an instrument for price stability went the argument of economists like Francesco Giavazzi that, in the absence of capital controls, it would be impossible to maintain a stable exchange rate system like the ERM.

In the debate about EMU the London-based Centre for Economic Policy Research (CEPR) served as an important catalyst in bringing together young economists and organizing influential conferences and publications that integrated the contributions of economists and central bank officials.[11] The CEPR was a new platform, established in 1983, through which primarily European economists like Francesco Giavazzi (University of Bologna), Alberto Giovannini (Columbia University, New York), Paul De Grauwe (University of Leuven), Luigi Spaventa (University of Rome) and Charles Wyplosz (INSEAD, France) were able to disseminate ideas about EMS reform. They also played an important role in developing the ideas that underpinned the research for the EC Commission's *One Market, One Money* study of October 1990 (see chapter 7). An additional and related influence was work centred on the Centre for European Policy Studies (CEPS) in Brussels. Daniel Gros, who was in DG2 (Directorate General 2) working with the Delors Committee, and Niels Thygesen (University of Copenhagen), who was a member of the Delors Committee, became the key figures linked to the CEPS. From 1986 they organized a working group of central bankers and economists to study the problems of, and prospects for reform of, the EMS.[12]

A second development was the emergence of a new source of political support outside the confines of the EC's institutions. In late 1986 the two 'founding fathers' of the EMS, former Chancellor Helmut Schmidt and former President Valéry Giscard d'Estaing, launched the Committee for the Monetary Union of Europe. Composed of political figures, central bankers, private bankers and economists, it was dedicated to propagating the cause of EMU. In pursuit of that purpose the Committee for the Monetary Union of Europe published, in April 1988, its proposals for EMU, including the institutional design of a European Central Bank.[13]

11. Notably F. Giavazzi *et al.* (eds) *The European Monetary System* (Cambridge: Cambridge University Press, 1988).
12. D. Gros and N. Thygesen, *The EMS: Achievements, Current Issues and Directions for the Future* (Brussels: Centre for European Policy Studies, 1988), CEPS Paper 35.
13. Committee for the Monetary Union of Europe, *A Programme for Action* (Paris: Crédit National, 1988).

Linked to this initiative was the establishment of the Association for the Monetary Union of Europe (AMUE); its president was the president of Philips, its vice-president the chairman of Fiat, and banks like Société Générale and Paribas were well represented in its membership, alongside employer organizations, such as the Italian Confindustria, and chambers of commerce, as in France. By April 1990 over 200 companies were active members. The AMUE used conferences, research on business attitudes to a single currency (first published in October 1988) and publications to press home the message that industry and commerce stood to benefit considerably from the savings of transaction costs and the trading stability that would ensue from a single currency. Its influence was also brought to bear via overlapping membership on national employer organizations, like the Confederation of British Industry. Along with the Committee for the Monetary Union of Europe, AMUE articulated the significance of two structural changes in the international political economy for EMU: increasing trade interdependence with the single market and the vulnerability of EC currencies in world currency relationships.

But far more important than the advocacy of new policy ideas in Community circles was the problem of negotiating the relaunch of EMU in the context of powerful governmental constraints on Council bargaining: notably, the principled opposition of the British government and the reluctance of the German government in the face of the known views of the Bundesbank. For this purpose Delors moved to bring forward the complete liberalization of capital movements in accordance with Article 13 of the Single European Act. In doing so, he could count on the strong support of the British and German governments, both of which had liberalized capital movements. Delors was also reassured that support would come from the French government which, by early 1988, was looking for ways to relaunch EMU. Under the presidency of Giscard d'Estaing major reform of the French financial system had begun. Now, the new centre-right government of Jacques Chirac between 1986 and 1988 was giving added priority to domestic policy reforms to create a dynamic financial sector in France as an essential component of a modern economy. In the context of fast-growing and global financial markets there was a new recognition in the French government that advantages could be gained by competitive 'deregulation' and that exchange controls were becoming more difficult and costly to operate. Consequently, the gap between French, German and British positions on monetary policy was narrowing considerably – a crucial precondition for successful Council bargaining on EMU.

The passage of the Directive on the complete liberalization of capital movements, adopted in June 1988, was remarkably quick: only seven months from the publication of the proposal to its adoption.[14] As we shall see, it became a key component of Council bargaining at the crucial Hanover summit of June 1988. The Directive was to enter into force on 1 July 1990 (with derogations for some member states till the end of 1992). Significantly, 1 July 1990 was to be adopted at the Madrid summit of June 1989 as the date from which stage one of EMU was to commence. In the words of the Commission: 'The decision to liberalize capital movements provides the key underpinning for the creation of a single market in financial services'. Clearly the

---

14. *Official Journal* L178, 8-7-1988.

financial sector could not be seen as integrated if exchange controls served to prevent the transfer of money from one member state to another.

The Commission was also very aware that the integration of capital markets could act as a catalyst for the relaunch of EMU. Exchange controls had been a key policy instrument of the French and Italian monetary authorities in stabilizing their exchange rates. They were now denied it and were, accordingly, persuaded that urgent and probably radical action was needed to strengthen the EMS. With the new incentive of agreement on an issue close to its interests, the German government was better disposed to think constructively about EMU. It was also under pressure to respond constructively to a major policy concession by other governments. There was, in short, an intimate linkage in Council bargaining between the Directive on the complete liberalization of capital movements and the relaunch of EMU.

Crucial to the relaunch of EMU was a transformation of Council bargaining relations, away from a 'lowest-common-denominator' style, with governments defending their autonomy to pursue domestic interests, to a more supranational style. Here the European Commission played a key role in orchestrating the EMS policy process towards an upgrading of common interests in Council bargaining relations. This capacity to nudge the EMS policy process in the direction of radical change derived from the new leverage given to the Commission by the process of fulfilling the terms of the Single European Act, especially the momentum to implement the single market programme. Though itself the product of a pre-eminently inter-governmental style of bargaining, the Single Act was paradoxically to generate a new dynamism of supranationalism that the Commission was able to exploit. The new wild card was the abolition of exchange controls. The key to Commission influence in Council bargaining in the EMS policy process came from its early recognition that the abolition of exchange controls represented a watershed event. So powerfully would the bargaining relations between the EC monetary authorities and the foreign exchange markets be transformed that the EC central banks and the EC institutions would need to give urgent attention to radical reform of the EMS: and that urgent attention could be assured only if initiative came from the highest level of Council bargaining.

The Basle-Nyborg Agreement: central bank bargaining and policy reform

The event that precipitated a new debate about monetary reform in the bargaining relations between the EC institutions and the central banks came earlier – in January 1987 when, despite relatively sound economic fundamentals in France, the rapid fall of the US dollar and upward pressure on the D-Mark precipitated an ERM realignment, involving a revaluation of the D-Mark and the Dutch guilder and a devaluation of the French franc. The event was a crisis in two senses: a crisis of the *franc fort* policy, and a crisis for the new centre-right French government of Jacques Chirac, whose Gaullist national pride was affronted. His government attributed the crisis to the inadequacy and unfairness of the intervention mechanisms of the EMS in dealing with speculative pressures and encouraged new French initiatives for reform of the EMS so that there would be more equitable burden-sharing. The crisis was seen as justifying urgent initiatives to correct the problem of asymmetry in the EMS. These initiatives took three forms: the Basle-Nyborg Agreement of September 1987, a limited non-institutional reform of the EMS's policy instruments that was worked out within the Committee of Central Bank Governors; the proposal of November 1987 for the Franco-German Economic Council; and the Balladur paper, submitted to ECOFIN in January 1988 and involving a more radical critique of the asymmetry in the functioning of the EMS.

In practice, though French pressure was of overriding importance, it was not the only factor at work in the negotiations for the Basle-Nyborg Agreement. As early as May 1986 the Commission had proposed a timetable for the complete removal of capital controls as part of the single European market programme. Central bank officials and finance ministry officials did not need the Padoa-Schioppa report to recognize that the new scale of capital movements would require a review of the adequacy of the EMS's instruments of policy coordination. Their main concern was to produce a reform that would ward off a new high-level Franco-German initiative and political intervention in the EMS as a result of new Council bargaining: in other words, to satisfy the French.

The Basle-Nyborg Agreement was a classic compromise, pragmatic in the manner of central bankers.[15] It was based on bargaining between the two main coalitions that comprised EC–central bank relations: the weak-currency countries (France, Belgium and Italy) and the strong-currency countries (Germany, the Netherlands and Denmark). The French wanted an automatic financing mechanism for intramarginal interventions and, via more equitable burden-sharing in intervention, progress towards greater symmetry in the EMS. By contrast, the Bundesbank was preoccupied by developments in the German money supply. It also argued that increased resort to central bank intervention was likely to prove counterproductive once the markets had identified unsound economic fundamentals behind a currency. The prime requirement for stability of the EMS was that each member country should establish the reputation for price stability of Germany: that required domestic reform and action, not reform of the EMS intervention mechanism. Both coalitions could agree on the need to arrive at an agreement that would demonstrate a positive attitude to European cooperation and, not least, that would enable the central banks to retain control over events and prevent a worse outcome: the intervention of Council-level bargaining. But a formidable constraint on the bargaining process was provided by the intense scepticism and suspicion of the Bundesbank which feared for its autonomy of action and its capacity to discharge its prime responsibility for the German money supply.

The Basle-Nyborg Agreement was susceptible to different interpretations. On the one hand, the Banque de France sought to claim that it had succeeded in developing the policy instruments of the EMS in a manner that had originally been staunchly opposed by the Bundesbank: the credit facilities of the EMCF were extended in time (the deadline for settlements was raised from 45 to 75 days) and enlarged; and a new recognition was accorded to the use of very-short-term financing for intramarginal interventions on certain conditions. Such measures had formed a key part of the Fourcade Plan of September 1974 (see chapter 3). Jacques de Larosière, governor of

15. On Basle-Nyborg see D. Gros and N. Thygesen, *European Monetary Integration* (Harlow: Longman, 1992), pp. 94–5 and 99. For the Bundesbank interpretation of the agreement see K.O. Pöhl, *Pressegespräch mit Bundesbank Präsident Pöhl* (Frankfurt: Deutsche Bundesbank Presse und Information, 14 September 1987).

the Banque de France, spoke of the intervention mechanism as now 'presumably automatic'. Another safeguard that the Bundesbank had built into the EMS Agreement of March 1979 (see chapter 4) was dropped: the acceptance limit for settlements in official ECUs was raised from 50 per cent to 100 per cent. Initially accepted for two years, this provision was extended.

But, on the other hand and more persuasively, the president of the Bundesbank could point to the general recommendation in the Basle-Nyborg Agreement that less reliance should be placed on interventions to stabilize currencies (always a concern of the Bundesbank) and a more active use made of changes in interest-rate differentials and the strengthening of monetary policy coordination. In other words, according to Karl-Otto Pöhl, the costs of preserving existing parities would actually be reduced. The key words were 'a more active, flexible and concerted use of the instruments available, namely, exchange-rate movements within the fluctuation band, interest rates and interventions' so that member states achieve 'sufficient convergence towards internal stability' to 'foster exchange-rate cohesion'. The fact that the new procedures stood up well under the immediate crisis generated by Wall Street's 'Black Monday' on 19 October 1987 served to confirm the view of the Committee of Central Bank Governors that this limited and pragmatic response was adequate. What followed – the relaunch of the EMU – had little to do with central bankers.

In broad terms the view of the central bank governors was that there was no need to consider a radical revision of policy goals; an amendment to policy instruments and their use would be satisfactory. This view circumscribed the scope of the Basle-Nyborg Agreement. But (as we shall see) the Hanover summit was a quite different matter. There the commitment to radically new policy goals (understood to be based on the Single European Act) was taken as an assumption (though contested by the British government). That this assumption should have taken root so rapidly is one of the most extraordinary aspects of European integration in the 1980s. It involved a displacement of authority over monetary policy as political leaders, via ECOFIN and the European Council, asserted their dominance over the area of policy goals. The centre of gravity shifted from EC–central bank bargaining to Council bargaining, and Council bargaining offered new scope for the broader interests of heads of state and government and foreign ministers to affect policy.

Franco-German bargaining and the Franco-German Economic Council

Even more alarming for the Bundesbank was the activation by the French government of direct Franco-German bargaining relations to achieve 'coordination' and 'harmonization' of Franco-German economic policies. These words were used in the draft treaty negotiated by the two governments in November 1987 to commemorate the 25th anniversary of the 1963 Franco-German treaty on cooperation. This treaty was conceived by the German Chancellor and the Foreign Minister as an important political gesture of the dedication of both countries to European cooperation. The tough interest politics came from two sides: the French government, with Jacques Chirac as Prime Minister and Edouard Balladur as Finance Minister, had a strong Gaullist sense of French national interest; whilst the German Bundesbank fused together its sense of German public interest with corporate self-interest in its determined efforts to water down the final treaty. What was clear to the Bundesbank was that the French government wanted access to policy making in the Bundesbank itself, undermining the independence that was so critical to its power within the bargaining relations between itself and the German federal government.

The politics of the Franco-German Economic Council was locked in the interaction between two bargaining relations: that between the French and German governments, and that between the German federal government and the Bundesbank. Like French bargaining in summer 1987 over the Basle-Nyborg Agreement, this proposal had its roots in the shock to the pride of the new Gaullist government of Chirac from the currency crisis of January 1987. By focusing its initiative at this level the French government hoped to bypass the Bundesbank and create for it a *fait accompli*. It also used the tactic of suddenly insisting at a late stage that a document that was initially intended to be ceremonial should be elevated to the status of a treaty binding in international law. The Bundesbank was excluded from the bilateral bargaining at intergovernmental level and shocked by this mode of proceeding. Although it had been informed of the original contents of the draft treaty in November 1987, it did not receive a copy of the document till the day before its scheduled signature in Paris on 22 January 1988.

The proposal with which the Bundesbank was faced was for a Franco-German Economic Council that would meet four times a year, alternately in France and Germany, to discuss economic policy. Its members would include the French and German Finance and Economics ministers, the president of the Bundesbank and the governor of the Banque de France. Two aspects were of special concern to the Bundesbank: that the two central banks were put on an equal footing when the Banque de France was legally subordinate to the French government; and that both were bound by the treaty to objectives of economic coordination determined by the Franco-German Economic Council. The first of these two provisions would result in a serious asymmetry of power in the new Council, with only one actor being independent of government and hence ineffectual in its capacity to defend stability. The second provision failed to specify that economic policy coordination would be subordinated to the objective of price stability, and hence was completely unacceptable. It ignored the policy authority that German law ascribed to the Bundesbank council.

With such a treaty in effect, the Bundesbank would have been unable to take interest rate decisions without first consulting the French. Faced by this prospect, the Bundesbank moved on to the domestic political offensive against the German federal government in late January 1988. Its first step was to broadcast the legal opinion of its staff that the treaty would break the Bundesbank Law of 1957 under which it was independently responsible for 'safeguarding the currency'. On 4 February, as the Bundesbank council convened for an unusually long session of five hours, Chancellor Kohl conceded before the Bundestag that the treaty must in no way undermine the independence of the Bundesbank and its statutory responsibility. The next day, in the wake of the Bundesbank council meeting, the Bundesbank wrote to the Finance Ministry demanding a binding assurance that the treaty would not impinge on its independence. Faced with an avalanche of professional legal and economic opinion supporting the stand of the Bundesbank the federal government decided that the treaty must be amended. In the form put to the Bundestag in November, the treaty declared that the independence of the Bundesbank was in no way being limited.

The outcome of the Franco-German initiative, and the subsequent history of the Franco-German Economic Council, underlined the sensitivity and vulnerability of the German federal government to the domestic power of the Bundesbank. Though the Bundesbank was deprived of any role in agenda-setting, it was able to empty the treaty of any real meaning in relation to economic 'coordination' and 'harmonization'. Once again, following their victory in the March 1993 Assembly elections, the French Gaullist-led government of Edouard Balladur sought to revive the Franco-German Economic Council. But, when in June 1993 the new Finance Minister Edmond Alphandéry announced that he was calling a meeting of the Council to discuss a coordinated lowering of interest rates, he was rebuffed by his German counterpart Theo Waigel, who abruptly cancelled because of pressing domestic commitments. The underlying factor remained Bundesbank irritation at attempts by the French government to exert public pressure on it. Attempts to activate Franco-German bargaining relations repeatedly fell against the hurdle of the bargaining relations between the German federal government and the Bundesbank and the resources of legal authority, technical expertise and public approval on which the Bundesbank could draw in handling those relations.

Council bargaining before and at the Hanover summit

More important than the bargaining relations between the EC and the central banks in the relaunch of EMU was the linkage between direct bilateral Franco-German bargaining relations and the arena of Council bargaining. In this arena the alliance of French and Italian initiative with the active support of the German Foreign Minister was critical in carrying the day.

The process was initiated with the sharply critical paper that was presented to ECOFIN by the French Finance Minister Balladur in January 1988.[16] The assumption that underpinned the blend of political argument and economic analysis in this paper was that the Basle-Nyborg Agreement was a far from adequate response to the deep-seated problems of the EMS. These problems were defined in terms of French experience since 1983. France had made substantial improvement in reducing its rate of inflation; yet it had not been rewarded within the EMS for doing so. Instead, the continuingly greater strength of the D-Mark in the ERM had forced France into a prospect of protracted low growth. In short, the functioning of the EMS as a new instrument of economic policy discipline had been an unpleasant learning experience for France.

Given this experience, Balladur concluded that 'The rapid pursuit of the monetary construction of Europe is the only possible solution'. He delivered a strong attack on the asymmetry that was built into the EMS and reflected in the uneven way in which the burden of the costs of adjustment was borne. In effect, Balladur meant that Germany escaped the costs; France, as in January 1987, had to bear them disproportionately.

16. E. Balladur, 'Europe's Monetary Construction', Memorandum to ECOFIN Council (Paris: Ministry of Finance and Economics, 8 January 1988).

Ultimately it is the central bank whose currency is at the lower end of the permitted range which has to bear the cost. However, it is not necessarily the currency at the lower end of the range which is the source of the tension. The discipline imposed by the exchange-rate mechanism . . . produces an abnormal situation when its effect is to exempt any countries whose policies are too restrictive from the necessary adjustment.

Again, the ideas of the Fourcade Plan of 1974 were much in evidence; the costs of intervention must be assigned more fairly. Looking ahead, Balladur raised questions about a single currency and a European central bank but did not indicate a clear commitment to fundamental institutional reform.

This theme was rapidly taken up by Guiliano Amato, the Italian Minister of the Treasury, in a memorandum to ECOFIN on 23 February.[17] In this case there was no clear focus on a single currency or European central bank. The critique was wide-ranging and focused on the theme of the risk that the Italian government was taking in agreeing to eliminate exchange controls in the context of an EMS that suffered from a 'structural fault' that the German government had persistently failed to tackle, namely its large external surplus. Essentially, German economic and monetary policies appeared as driven by domestic self-interest, reflected in a disposition to avoid revaluation of the D-Mark. There was no interest in any EC public good underpinning its policies. As a consequence, the EMS lacked an engine of growth. Amato emphasized the importance of a 'common and homogeneous attitude to inflation' but that the shared objectives of economic policy should include growth as well as price stability. In the context of the EMS crises of 1992 and 1993 these two criticisms – of asymmetry and of the lack of an engine of growth – were to be revived. And by the time that the crisis of Italy's exit from the ERM struck in 1992, Amato had become Italian Prime Minister.

The final and crucial key to the relaunch of EMU was provided by the self-interests of the German presidency of the EC in the first half of 1988. A decisive element was the desire of the German Foreign Minister, Hans-Dietrich Genscher, to use the presidency for the purpose of giving urgency to his ambition for European union. Genscher sought to use the French and Italian critiques of the EMS to take forward the theme of the rapid pursuit of the monetary construction of Europe. In essence, he saw a window of opportunity for the German presidency to carry forward the agenda of European integration, created by the new mood of optimism about the implementation of the single European market programme and the important EC budget deal agreed at the special European Council meeting in February.

Genscher's credentials as a European federalist had been well demonstrated in his leading role in the Genscher-Colombo initiative of 1981 and the Stuttgart Declaration of June 1983. The Genscher-Colombo initiative had been a Council declaration calling for greater movement towards European unity; the 'Solemn Declaration on European Union' issued at the Stuttgart summit during the previous German presidency had included, among other demands, a call for the reinforcement of the EMS. Again, Genscher wished to take advantage of the presidency, with the important difference that, on this occasion, the French government's position had changed. The French

17. G. Amato, 'Un Motore per lo SME', *Il Sole 24 Ore*, Rome, 25 February 1988. Reprint of Memorandum to ECOFIN Council, 23 February.

Prime Minister, Pierre Mauroy, had launched a public attack on the Stuttgart Declaration.[18] Now, on a broader political front, the French government seemed altogether better disposed towards European unity.

What was striking about Genscher's initiative of February 1988 was the title of the paper: 'A European Currency Area and a European Central Bank'.[19] It went considerably further than the Balladur and Amato papers in this respect, including the suggestion that the ECU could serve as initially a parallel currency and later, after a transition period of several years, as the single currency. The rationale for the proposal was twofold: that a single currency and a European central bank were 'economically necessary' for the completion of the internal market; and that, echoing here a traditional French view, Europe's dependence on the dollar would be reduced. Also, reflecting Italian concerns, Genscher proposed two mutually supportive pillars for EMU, reflecting the situation in Germany where policy was driven by two acts: the Bundesbank Act of 1957, with its guarantee of Bundesbank autonomy in realizing price stability; and the Law for Promoting Stability and Growth of 1967, in this case establishing four objectives of federal macro-economic policy – price stability, high employment, external equilibrium and growth. Such a framework should be transferred to the EC level, but not forgetting that the European central bank should be dedicated to price stability and enjoy independence for this purpose. In order to expedite progress, Genscher – supported by President Mitterrand – suggested that the Hanover summit in June should establish a group of between five and seven independent experts with 'professional and political authority' to work out more detailed proposals.

Genscher's influence should not be underestimated. As the dominant figure in the junior coalition party, the Free Democratic Party, on which the government of Helmut Kohl depended, and as a long-serving Foreign Minister and deputy Chancellor, Genscher's political role was pivotal in Bonn. On issues of European integration he could count on the support in principle of Chancellor Kohl, whose political career had also been dedicated to the cause of European federalism. This ideological factor at the centre of the Bonn government could by no means determine what followed in the sphere of EMU; structural changes in the international political economy and the monetary power of the Bundesbank were crucially important. But it created a background to policy, a disposition to respond to opportunities in a particular way. It also showed that, in contrast to the EMS initiative of 1978, the key agenda-setting role was played this time by the Foreign Minister rather than the Chancellor, and (as we shall now see) the Finance Minister. This process reflected both the strength of the principle of departmentalism within the German federal government (with a consequent potential for ministerial leadership) and the nature of the leadership style of Chancellor Kohl, a style that was much more relaxed and less 'hands-on' than that of his predecessor and less confident in the field of economic and monetary affairs.

At the more practical level of sectoral Council bargaining the paper submitted by

18. Robin, *La diplomatie de Mitterrand ou le triomphe des apparences*, p. 219.
19. H.-D. Genscher, 'A European Currency Area and a European Central Bank', Memorandum to the General Affairs Council (Bonn: Ministry of Foreign Affairs, 26 February 1988).

German Finance Minister, Gerhard Stoltenberg, to ECOFIN on 15 March 1988 was even more significant.[20] It was more defensive on the issue of asymmetry in the EMS and more cautious about the dangers in a period of transition to EMU. But what was novel was that Stoltenberg took up the issue of exchange controls which had been raised in the Amato paper and indicated that a deal could be done. Adoption of the Directive on the complete liberalization of capital movements was viewed as strategically important and, despite Italian concerns, as needing to be undertaken in an irrevocable manner, without safeguard clauses. On that basis the German government would be prepared to consider proposals for institutional reform leading to EMU. Here was precisely the linkage that Delors had been working to achieve. On 13 June the German presidency achieved agreement on the new Directive, putting Chancellor Kohl in a relaxed and confident mood for the summit on 27–8 June.

Once it became clear that the German presidency wished to give pride of place to EMU at the Hanover summit and that Genscher's proposal embodied a procedure that would bypass the EC's technical committees, the central bank governors became aware that overdue caution and scepticism could lead to their exclusion from the early negotiations, as had happened during the phase of the Schulmann-Clappier working party in 1978. The procedure finally adopted at the European Council meeting embodied a compromise. Delors was keen to avoid the inertia that would follow from entrusting progress exclusively to the technical committees; but Kohl and the German Finance Minister – with the recent experience of the Franco-German Economic Council initiative fresh in their minds – were concerned to keep the Bundesbank reasonably happy, and the Bundesbank had expressed publicly its worries about the Genscher initiative. Genscher's idea of a group of independent experts was, accordingly, qualified by agreeing that a committee would be established under the chairmanship of Delors and consisting of the twelve central bank governors acting 'in a personal capacity', one additional member of the Commission, and three independent persons.

On the substantive remit of the Delors Committee's work there was also compromise. Delors could take heart from the fact that the conclusions of the Hanover Council meeting incorporated the statement: 'The European Council recalls that, in adopting the Single Act, the member states confirmed the objective of progressive realization of economic and monetary union'. In consequence, the Delors Committee was not asked to report on the question of the desirability of EMU. Its task was to examine the means of achieving this union in time for the meeting of the European Council in Madrid in June 1989 and for prior consideration by ECOFIN. On the other hand, against the wishes of President Mitterrand and of the Genscher paper, Margaret Thatcher and the Danish Prime Minister, Poul Schluter, succeeded in ensuring that a specific reference to a European central bank was not included in the instructions to the committee (though the committee was not expressly barred from considering this issue). It was understood that consideration of a draft statute for a European central bank would be reserved for the Committee of Central Bank Governors. In consequence, parallel with the Delors Committee, an informal group drawn from

---

20. G. Stoltenberg, 'The Further Development of Monetary Cooperation in Europe', Memorandum to ECOFIN Council (Bonn: Ministry of Finance, 15 March 1988).

central bank officials and legal experts (and under the chairmanship of Professor Jean-Victor Louis) met to develop a blueprint for such a draft statute.[21]

Two factors distinguished this phase in the relaunch of EMU from the birth of the EMS. The first was the pivotal role of the French government, driven by its perceived national interest in wresting power from the Bundesbank, in the wake of the humiliating experience of the asymmetrical functioning of the EMS. This factor was allied (as we saw earlier) with the greater capacity of the European Commission, post the Single European Act, to infuse Council bargaining with a more supranational style and draw the German government into cooperation on EMU via the incentive of complete capital liberalization. The scope and intensity of French initiatives was impressive, symptomatic of the resolution with which its government pursued its goals of reducing the costs of economic interdependence to it and augmenting its influence on monetary policy. The results of this difference in the lead national actor, and of the more influential role for the Commission, were also important. Initiated by Chancellor Schmidt, the EMS had eventually emerged as a limited defensive mechanism to absorb exchange-rate shocks: in short, as consistent with German national interests. But the basis of EMU was in French and Italian national interest in scaling down the power of the Bundesbank and in the Commission's capacity to use the leverage of the abolition of exchange controls and joint commitment to complete the single market to focus Council bargaining on a supranational level. The watershed event behind the EMS had been the fast-falling US dollar. Behind the relaunch of EMU were two such watershed events: the January 1987 EMS crisis (the basis of French initiative), and the abolition of exchange controls (the basis of Commission initiative). Later, in November 1989, a third watershed event would intervene to intensify French concern to contain German power: the breaching of the Berlin Wall.

The Delors Report: The impact of Karl-Otto Pöhl

The Delors Report was ready for submission to ECOFIN in April 1989, symbolically on the tenth anniversary of the EMS, and following eight meetings since September.[22] If Franco-Italian initiative and Commission orchestration in the context of Council bargaining had played an important part in putting EMU back on the agenda in 1987–8, the Delors Committee served as arena in which, informally, EC–central bank bargaining came to the fore. It proved to be an important policy learning process, not least for the Commission.

German influence – in the form of the Bundesbank president, Pöhl – was central to the Delors Report. The degree of Bundesbank influence was apparent not only in its overwhelming success in getting its specific concerns recognized in the report but also in the way in which it functioned as the model for designing the European System of Central Banks (ESCB) that was proposed by the report. Its policy was clearly set out

---

21. See Gros and Thygesen, *European Monetary Integration*, p. 317. Also for details, J.-V. Louis, *Vers un système européen de banques centrales* (Brussels: Editions de l'Université de Bruxelles, 1989).
22. Committee for the Study of Economic and Monetary Union, *Report on Economic and Monetary Union in the European Community* (the Delors Report) (Luxembourg: Office for Official Publications of the European Communities, August 1989).

in a paper that was annexed to the main report.[23] In particular, Pöhl insisted that the Community should have the power to limit the budget deficits of member states in an EMU, otherwise large Italian-type deficits could create inflationary pressures for the Community as a whole. Also, he objected to any precise statements about the period of transition and to any timetable for the beginning of stage two. The Bundesbank was not in principle opposed to EMU, but it was insistent about the conditions for moving forward with monetary integration. This stance was reflected in its irritation at the appointment of Padoa-Schioppa as secretary to the Delors Committee; the Bundesbank had doubts about the depth of his commitment to the primacy of price stability and viewed the Padoa-Schioppa Report as a plea for enhanced authority for ECOFIN at the expense of the central banks.

By contrast, much less attention was given to the concern that was expressed in two other papers annexed to the report: one by the governor of the Irish central bank and the other by Delors.[24] This concern focused on the need for augmented fiscal transfers to less well developed regions in line with the principle of cohesion; here the doubling of the EC Structural Funds as a flanking measure to enable weaker economies to adapt to the single European market was seen as a precedent.

But, however great the influence of the Bundesbank on the proposed policy instruments to give effect to the goal of EMU, the very nature of the goal required radical change in the nature and use of these instruments. The members of the Committee were inexorably involved in a process of paradigm change in monetary policy. In other words, the influence of the Bundesbank president and of the other central bank governors was constrained by a radically changed political context.

There were two interesting similarities between the Delors Report and the Werner Report of 1970: the definition of EMU and the principle of parallelism. First, their definitions of EMU were indistinguishable. In the words of the Delors Report, a monetary union 'constitutes a currency area in which policies are managed jointly with a view to attaining common macro-economic objectives'. According to paragraph 22, it involved:

- the complete liberalization of capital transactions and full integration of banking and other financial markets
- total and irreversible convertibility of currencies
- the elimination of margins of fluctuation and the irrevocable locking of exchange-rate parities.

Although the Delors Report noted that the locking of parities did not necessarily imply the introduction of a single currency, it differed from the Werner Report in recommending its introduction as soon as possible after parities were locked. Once the condition of irrevocably locked exchange-rate parities was achieved, the currencies of the member states would in any case be no more than the 'non-decimal denominations of a common currency'.

23. K.O. Pöhl, 'The Further Development of the European Monetary System', in collection of papers annexed to the Delors Report, pp. 131–55.
24. J. Delors, 'Regional Implications of Economic and Monetary Integration', in collection of papers annexed to the Delors Report, pp. 81–9. Also M. Doyle, 'Regional Policy and European Economic Integration', in collection of papers annexed to the Delors Report, pp. 61–79.

In addition, the Delors Report returned to the principle of parallelism: developments to secure economic convergence would have to accompany steps towards monetary union. Although economic and monetary union were seen as distinct in theory, it argued that they should be pursued together in practice. Economic union was defined in terms of four basic elements:

1   the single market, within which persons, goods, services and capital can move freely
2   competition policy and other measures aimed at strengthening market mechanisms
3   common policies aimed at structural change and regional development
4   macro-economic policy coordination, including binding rules for budgetary policies.

The point was also made that a high degree of agreement between member states on the economic goals that they wish to pursue was indispensable. This agreement involved 'the combination of a large degree of freedom for market behaviour and private economic initiative, with public intervention in the provision of certain goods and services'. Here again, in the insistence on economic convergence, the German influence was apparent.

Beyond these general similarities there are some interesting contrasts of detail about policy instruments between the Delors Report and the Werner Report. The Delors Report emphasized the achievement of convergence by means of medium-term guidelines for budgetary policies, coupled with the authority (of ECOFIN in cooperation with the European Parliament) to apply binding rules in the form of upper limits to national budget deficits. By contrast, the Werner Report had focused on a centralization of budgetary authority at the EC level in a new 'centre of decision for economic policy' so that the Community could promote adjustment within the EMU by using much larger-scale fiscal transfer mechanisms to even out the differential effects of external shocks. Again reflecting the Bundesbank view, and the monetarist climate of economic ideas (see chapter 7), more reliance was now placed on price flexibility and factor mobility than on the active use of discretionary budget policy to achieve adjustment.

Given the composition of the Delors Committee, it is not surprising that its report gave priority to minimizing the dangers of fiscally irresponsible behaviour by politicians. Whilst the idea of binding rules on national budget deficits was to prove highly controversial (for it was judged to be a direct assault on national sovereignty), the need for constraints remained very much alive and was to influence strongly the Treaty on European Union of 1992. But, given the reduced ambitions for EC budgetary authority, the Delors Report was able to stay clear of any implications that political union was a necessary prerequisite of EMU. ECOFIN could provide an adequate mechanism for dealing with both the transition to EMU and the operation of EMU.

The Delors Report was also much more explicit than the Werner Report about the new institutions that would be required. At the heart of EMU would be a federal institution, the ESCB, in which official reserves would be pooled. In essence, national central banks would be ranged around a new common institution with its own balance sheet and with responsibility for setting monetary policies that the national banks would implement. Its structure would comprise a policy-making Council, comprising the national central bank governors and the members of the ESCB Board, the latter being appointed by the European Council and responsible for overseeing the execution of the Council's policy. On the Bundesbank model, the ESCB would be committed to the objective of price stability and expected to support the general economic policy established at the EC level. It would also be independent from instructions of national governments. At the same time, to introduce an element of accountability, the Council would have to report to the European Council and to the European Parliament. It was a tribute to the prestige of the Bundesbank among central bankers that the proposals on institutional design occasioned no important disagreement.

Although the European Council had instructed the Delors Committee to 'propose concrete stages', this aspect proved most contentious. Pöhl was particularly vocal in his opposition to the idea of a transition period in which monetary authority was shared between the national level and the emerging ECSB. The resulting confusion of responsibilities was liable to jeopardize effective policy making and upset financial markets. In the end reference was made to two transition stages: stage one was to begin on 1 July 1990 with the introduction of the provisions of the Directive on liberalization of capital movements; but no agreement was reached on the date of commencement of stage two, other than that it would start when the necessary treaty amendments came into force. No time period was put on the duration of stage two, though the emphasis on a gradual transfer of authority during stage two suggested that it would be long and open-ended.

The inability to be precise about the timetable – a point of difference from the Werner Report – was accompanied by a vagueness about the details of both stages, especially stage two. Stage one was to be essentially a continuation of the EMS, with entry into the ERM by Britain, Portugal and Greece and with a somewhat enhanced research and advisory role for the Committee of Central Bank Governors; stage two would see the establishment of the ECSB to oversee the transition to a common monetary policy and would involve realignments 'only in exceptional circumstances' and a narrowing of margins of fluctuation as 'economic convergence permitted'. Stage two was defined as 'a training process leading to collective decision-making, while the ultimate responsibility for policy decisions would remain at this stage with national authorities'. It was generally recognized that this aspect of the report was inadequate and that it would play an important part in the considerable amount of preparatory work that would be required before an intergovernmental conference began to revise the Treaty of Rome.

On the issue of the role of the ECU the Delors Report represented a compromise. On the one hand, the Bundesbank was utterly opposed to the promotion of the ECU as a parallel currency. In Pöhl's view, a parallel currency involved a serious risk of inflation, consequent on an additional source of money creation. Although the report deferred to this view of the Bundesbank, it did propose that

- the ECU has the potential to be developed into a common currency
- the official ECU might be used as an instrument in the conduct of a common monetary policy.

Overall, the balance sheet of the Delors Report was a mix of positive and negative for Delors. On the negative side, he had had to concede a significant amount to the pragmatism and gradualism of the Bundesbank president and other central bank governors. Hence, on publication of the report, it was possible for the governor of the Bank of England, Robin Leigh-Pemberton, to welcome both its unanimous view that there must be much greater convergence of economic performance before any firm move towards EMU and the absence of a timetable for the completion of the three stages. Pöhl made very clear the Bundebank's corporate interests in arguing that it could live very well with the status quo. Privately, he and other Bundesbank officials persistently complained that the French government was trying to 'get a grip on the D-Mark'.

On the positive side, the composition of the Delors Committee added an authority to its recommendations that could not have been achieved by a traditional committee of EC 'wise men' of the type that had originally been proposed by Genscher. Perhaps even more importantly, the central bank governors had been locked, albeit in a personal capacity, into a set of proposals that offered a route forward to EMU, including a deadline for the start of stage one.

In retrospect, the Delors Committee could be seen as riding the crest of a wave. A learning process about the need to move beyond the EMS had begun before the Committee started its work. Among central bankers, the governors of the central banks of France, Italy and Spain – Jacques de Larosière, Carlo Ciampi and Mariano Rubio – were most outspoken in their advocacy of dropping the illusion of independent monetary policies at the national level. Though their pro-European views were controversial, there was unanimity around the proposition that capital liberalization meant the removal of territorial control of national monetary systems. The integration of EC markets, particularly the effects of freedom of capital movement, put at risk German control of its monetary policy as well as everyone else. Consensus about the relative success of the EMS in achieving its goals was accompanied by growing doubts about whether this success could continue in the absence of a fundamental reappraisal not only of policy instruments but also of policy goals. In practice, then, the Delors Committee had displayed a will to cooperate in the pursuit of EMU that could certainly not have been expected three years earlier. Everything now depended on retaining the political momentum of the Hanover summit.

It was clear well before the Delors Report was published on 17 April 1989 that political momentum was subject to two main countervailing forces: fear of, and respect for, the Bundesbank, and the intransigence of the British government on the issues of sovereignty, accountability and the character of a united Europe. The two forces differed in nature. Opposition from the Bundesbank was of the variety 'yes, but . . . ': ultimately it could be overruled by the federal government, which contained a potent level of support for a federal Europe. The British government's hostility was, by contrast, one of principle and did not seem amenable to compromise. It did not enjoy the fear and respect engendered by the Bundesbank; too many years of bitter summit battles about the British contribution to the EC budget and of perceptions of negative, unconstructive British attitudes to successive initiatives, not least to the EMS, had ensured that a leadership role had not been achieved. But the British government did have the ultimate deterrent of vetoing a treaty amendment to enable the establishment of the institutions for an EMU.

At the Hanover summit British strategy had been essentially defensive: to minimize threat. The position of the British government was elaborated in two major speeches during the deliberations of the Delors Committee: Margaret Thatcher's speech at the College of Bruges on 20 September 1988, and the speech delivered by the Chancellor of the Exchequer, Nigel Lawson, at Chatham House, London, on 25 January 1989. In her Bruges speech the British Prime Minister justified her opposition to a European central bank; this was not 'the key issue'. Her language to describe European union was one of 'cooperation' rather than 'integration': 'willing and active cooperation between independent sovereign states is the best way to build a successful European Community.' The Prime Minister referred to 'arcane institutional debates' resulting from the fact that 'some in the European Community seem to want . . . a European super-state exercising a new dominance from Brussels', which would 'suppress nationhood' and lead to an 'identikit European personality'. For Lawson, EMU 'implies nothing less than a European government – albeit a federal one – and political union: the United States of Europe. This is simply not on the agenda now, nor will it be in the foreseeable future.' EMU was presented as a diversionary tactic, designed to deflect attention from the rigorous pursuit and completion of the single market. But the fact of the matter was that the British government was isolated and on the defensive. Its faith that the presence of the governor of the Bank of England and the president of the Bundesbank on the Delors Committee would sabotage progress towards EMU proved ill-founded; the governor's contribution had been 'ineffective'.

Council bargaining from the Madrid summit, via Ashford Castle, to the Rome summit

The Madrid summit

Against this background the meeting of the European Council in Madrid in June 1989 took on a decisive importance. EMU returned to the level of Council bargaining. The management of the Madrid summit was facilitated by the tactical decision of the Spanish Prime Minister, Felipe Gonzalez, to drop one controversial issue – an agreement on a charter of fundamental social rights – so that EMU could dominate the agenda. The triumph of the summit was to avoid a split over EMU and to take one big decision: a commitment to call an intergovernmental conference (IGC) to revise the treaty to accommodate EMU, as proposed by the Delors Report.

Three factors made for a somewhat more conciliatory approach by the British Prime Minister. First, as over the EC budget deal at the Brussels summit of February 1988, the sense of British isolation had increased, not least with the adverse reactions in other EC capitals to the substance and personal style of the Bruges speech. Second, there was, additionally, a sense of a victory for the British government in keeping the social charter off the agenda. A successful negotiation could be readily proclaimed, without the danger that other countries would move ahead without Britain. For here was the limitation on Britain's power of veto: that other countries could proceed without Britain. The Foreign Office stressed that success in negotiations would be to slow down advance towards EMU and to gain some influence over its precise path. Third, the Madrid summit was the occasion of a concerted attack by the Foreign

Secretary, Geoffrey Howe, and the Chancellor of the Exchequer, on the unwillingness of the Prime Minister to be specific about the conditions under which Britain would join the ERM. They were emboldened to act in part by the setback that the Conservative Party had just suffered in the European Parliament elections; in part by alarm about the lack of internal governmental discussion in preparation for the Madrid summit; and in part by the calculation that such a concession would help to detach stage one of EMU from stages two and three. In effect, Mrs Thatcher was boxed in at Madrid by her two most senior ministers and isolated; both threatened resignation if clarity about British intention to join the ERM by the end of 1992 were not achieved. Neither was to be forgiven.

The Prime Minister's more conciliatory stance was apparent during formal summit discussions when she accepted that the Delors Report's approach by stages to EMU was correct and its analysis invaluable and that stage one could make an early start. In relation to the ERM a shift of attitude was discernible in the move away from the vague formula for ERM entry of 'when the time is ripe' to five conditions: one applying to Britain – lower inflation – and four applying to the EC – abolition of all exchange controls, progress towards the single market, liberalization of financial services, and agreement on competition policy. But the underlying reality remained that on EMU Mrs Thatcher's aims were not accommodating. She sought to prevent the Delors Report becoming the only basis for further negotiation, and to block an IGC on monetary union and stages two and three of the Delors Report. Here, unlike on the ERM, there were no profound differences of view about tactics within the British government.

Fundamentally, the key to Council bargaining at the Madrid summit was provided by the strength of support from the French, German, Italian, Spanish and Belgian governments for two key proposals of Delors: that embracing stage one of the Delors Report should mean agreeing to stages two and three; and that there should be an intergovernmental conference. There were some nuanced forms of support: thus the governments of Greece, Ireland and Portugal sought more EC financial support to offset their problems of adjustment as a condition of agreement; and those of Denmark, Luxembourg and the Netherlands questioned the pace of the plan. But Mrs Thatcher stood alone in her principled opposition to both proposals, clashing sharply with President Mitterrand whose government was about to take over the presidency. In the final four-point compromise she managed to gain two concessions, to the irritation of Mitterrand, and sought to claim that there was no automaticity about the move to or timing of stage two. The key points of agreement were

- a restatement of commitment to reach EMU in stages
- acceptance that the Delors Report 'defines a process designed to lead by stages to EMU' (Mrs Thatcher was successful in avoiding a definite commitment to stages two and three of the Delors Report)
- stage one should begin on 1 July 1990
- an intergovernmental conference to lay down the subsequent steps 'would meet once the first stage had begun and would be preceded by full and adequate preparation' (Mrs Thatcher frustrated President Mitterrand's desire for a commitment that the conference should finish by 1992).

Despite these concessions, the bargain achieved at the Madrid summit was decisive for the progress of EMU. Building on the new momentum, the European Commission decided in September to launch the *One Market, One Money* study, under the direction of Michael Emerson and with Daniel Gros as one of the economic advisers. The aim was to strengthen its bargaining position in the forthcoming preparations for the IGC. Meanwhile, ministers and officials in the framework of ECOFIN and the General Affairs Council were mandated to get on with the job of preparing an inter-governmental conference to convene sometime after July 1990, and in the process to begin the hard job of defining what the later stages would look like and how they were to be achieved. The French presidency sought to secure the political momentum by convening a high-level group of officials from national finance and foreign ministries to prepare the questions for the forthcoming IGC. In essence, the so-called Guigou Report of October (named after its chairwoman, Elisabeth Guigou) served to draw in those who would later be involved in the detailed IGC negotiations, an effort at 'socialization' into the issues, as well as to meet the requirements of the Madrid Conclusions.[25] The exercise underlined the resistance of British officials to the idea of a single European bank to operate a single currency. It also drew forth a huge amount of policy-making activity in the Treasury and the Bank of England to develop counter-proposals to the Delors Report, embodied in the Treasury paper of November and the Bank of England paper of December.

The competing currency plan

In essence, the alternative approach of a competing currency plan, mapped out in London under John Odling-Smee at the Treasury, combined a stress on evolution, competition and cooperation. Intellectually, its roots were in the ideas of Friedrich Hayek, with which the British Chancellor had great sympathy. The Treasury advocated an evolutionary approach as opposed to the formal step-by-step of the Delors Report.[26] According to this approach, only stage one of the Delors plan would be implemented and the complexities and difficulties of treaty amendment avoided. The single market in financial services and freedom of movement of capital would enable an effective competition among currencies and drive down the transaction costs of switching currencies. As individuals and corporate actors would prefer to hold the currencies of lower-inflation countries, national policy makers who valued maximizing the use of their currency would have an incentive to avoid inflationary policies. Hence national monetary policies would be drawn into competition; the country with the highest credibility in fighting inflation would derive benefit in the form of the lowest interest rates. The Treasury argument was that, by eliminating currency competition, an ESCB would encourage an overall monetary policy stance close to the average EC performance; its own proposal would lead to a policy stance closer to the best.

25. High-Level Group of Representatives of Governments of the EC Member States, *Report on Economic and Monetary Union* (the Guigou Report), Paris, 31 October 1989.
26. HM Treasury, *An Evolutionary Approach to Economic and Monetary Union* (London: HMSO, November 1989). The essentially tactical motivation is made explicit in M. Thatcher, *The Downing Street Years* (London: Harper Collins, 1993), p. 716.

Though this pragmatic approach to EMU was designed to appeal to the Bundesbank and thereby forge a powerful alternative to the strategy mapped out at Madrid, it was rejected by Pöhl. The Bundesbank was particularly worried that increased currency substitution would undermine the effectiveness of national monetary policies. At the meeting of the Committee of Central Bank Governors in December 1989, Pöhl also proposed a mechanism by which market forces might reward monetary policy virtue. But it was different. His idea was that central banks would make their monetary growth targets explicit, specific and comparable. Market judgement would then penalize the wicked and reward the virtuous. The central problem of the British proposal was, however, political: at the level of inter-governmental bargaining, rather than bargaining with the Bundesbank. It was not at all clear whether, and how, currency competition could lead to monetary union in the sense of a common currency: the basic fact of political life in Council bargaining was that political will had already settled on the concept of monetary union as the adoption of a single currency. Precisely because the British proposal appeared as a diversionary tactic, which was how the Prime Minister conceived it, it did not receive the attention that was expected.

The Strasbourg summit

The failure of British policy to redirect the process of policy change or to undermine its momentum was clear at the Strasbourg meeting of the European Council in December 1989. For, since June, a profound change had begun to take place in the context of Council bargaining about EMU. The rush of events in eastern Europe, notably in Germany with the breaching of the Berlin Wall in November, had led to a renewed political perception of the crucial importance of EC solidarity in the face of a watershed in postwar history. Central to this perception was a heightened recognition of the need to anchor a larger and more powerful Germany even more firmly in the west and of the importance of a strengthened EC for this purpose and for the wider purpose of dealing more effectively with the consequences of the collapse of the Soviet empire in the east. In the face of this new rationale for accelerating the momentum of integration, endorsed not least by the US President, George Bush, the capacity for resistance of the British government was reduced.

It was eroded by another factor. Since the Madrid summit Howe had been replaced as Foreign Secretary, and in October, amidst bitter exchanges about the undermining of his policy by the Prime Minister and her anti-ERM adviser Alan Walters, Lawson had resigned. In losing two troublesome ministers Mrs Thatcher had become yet further boxed in; she could not afford to lose another. The result was that EC policy, in particular the negotiating positions for the Strasbourg summit, was now determined in the collective context of cabinet.

But the central problem at the Strasbourg summit was not caused by the British government. It stemmed from deep suspicion and alarm in the French government that the immersion of the German government in events in the German Democratic Republic and beyond in the east was reducing its interest in, and enthusiasm for, EC integration. Increasingly critical German reactions to EMU, including signs of the Bundesbank's enthusiasm for the British government's evolutionary approach, had preceded the summit and irritated the French government. At the summit Chancellor Kohl was at pains to demonstrate that there had been no let up in his enthusiasm: to demonstrate his unswerving reliability as a negotiator in Franco-German and EC Council bargaining.

The result was that the British Prime Minister lost the argument on the date for the IGC. It was to be convened by the end of 1990 to negotiate amendments to the Treaty of Rome for EMU. She could only console herself with her publicly expressed view that the IGC could take 'years and years' to complete. In this Mrs Thatcher was rebutted by the Italian Foreign Minister, Gianni De Michelis, whose government was to hold the presidency in the second half of 1990: his timetable was to complete the IGC by the end of 1991 so that a European central bank could be established in January 1993, as both Mitterrand and Delors hoped.

Following pressure from Kohl, it was also agreed that accountability should be ensured by considering new powers for the European Parliament in relation to EMU (a strange position given the much-praised independence of the Bundesbank from political pressures). This emphasis on new powers for the European Parliament reflected a reawakening of interest in the idea of institutional reform to meet the challenge of new events in the east, an idea that was to resurface in the forthcoming Irish presidency.

ECOFIN: Ashford Castle and the decisions of March 1990

The next key event was the EC Commission's paper to the informal ECOFIN meeting at Ashford Castle in March 1990.[27] It represented the first attempt of the Commission to give an opinion on how EMU might be attained. The Commission's paper departed from the Delors Report in three respects: it explicitly proposed a two-year stage two (1994–6); it moved away from the idea of binding EC rules on the upper limits to national budget deficits in favour of national legislation to curb excessive deficits and the principle of setting guidelines on curbing deficits at the EC level; and it was noticeably more positive in its commitment to the role of the ECU as the single currency and its development during the transitional stage of six years (1990–6). Behind these modifications was a mix of political calculation (for instance, to steer a course between Pöhl and his critics on budget deficits) and of the influence of the academic economists close to the Commission. In particular, binding rules on national budget deficits were now seen as involving a politically impractical centralization of economic policy and as economically impractical given the enormous difficulties involved in fiscal fine-tuning. The economic advice that underpinned the Commission paper reflected a lack of faith in fiscal policy instruments.

Another factor at work was the desire of the Commission, led by Delors on this issue, to regain some of the political initiative lost within the Delors Committee by a strong direct impact on Council bargaining. This impulse was apparent in the softening of the principle of strict parallelism in economic convergence and monetary union. On the other hand, in the face of opposition led by one of the senior Commissioners, Sir

---

27. Commission of the European Communities, 'Economic and Monetary Union', paper for the informal ECOFIN Council at Ashford Castle, Brussels, March 1990.

Leon Brittan, Delors was not successful in using the Commission paper to launch a bid for a major increase of aid for the poorer regions of the EC. Behind the paper was a considerable wrangle within the Commission about what constituted a rational political strategy to achieve the unanimously agreed goal of a 'Euro-fed' bank with guaranteed political independence. Brittan was keen not to widen the gulf with the British government. And there was always the calculation – based on experience – that, though the Commission might propose, the Bundesbank would ultimately dispose.

Despite these limitations, the Commission paper was important in helping the Commission to regain the initiative in 1990. Annexed to it was the detailed analysis of the benefits and costs of EMU prepared as part of the *One Market, One Money* study. Its basic message was that the costs would be most heavy in the early stages whilst the process of economic convergence and credibility of the emerging system remained incomplete; the main benefits, notably elimination of exchange transaction costs, would come later, once the single currency was introduced. This distribution of costs and benefits in time suggested the economic and political merits of a short period of transition to EMU. The Commission had begun a process, to be completed with the publication of *One Market, One Money* in October 1990, of actively persuading key decision makers and policy 'influentials' about the merits of EMU.[28]

The Ashford Castle meeting was important in another sense. For the EC Monetary Committee, made up of officials from national finance ministries and central banks, tabled a detailed paper that made clear the urgency with which a majority viewed the need for progress on EMU. Most strikingly, it set out the principles that would have to be enshrined in the new treaty and gave unequivocal support not only to a European central bank and single currency but also to a rapid transition to the single currency in the early part of stage three. The paper from the EC Monetary Committee made clear just how advanced preparations were for the IGC. Also, the determination displayed at Ashford Castle to agree a treaty for full EMU showed the new British Chancellor of the Exchequer, John Major, just how isolated his government was and how limited its room for manoeuvre. Delors and colleagues in ECOFIN noted a less aggressive and intransigent response than that of his predecessor, Lawson, to the Delors Report. In short, Ashford Castle introduced not only a new note of optimism into Council bargaining on EMU, but also a difference of view about the tactics to deal with EMU between the British Prime Minister and Major. Major was keen to play a full part in negotiating the new treaty with the aim of securing agreement on a procedure of 'opting-in' so that governments could maintain their discretion about whether and when to join in full EMU; his Prime Minister was determined to resist the principle of EMU.

A further sign of a new momentum towards EMU was provided in March 1990 by the decisions of ECOFIN to strengthen coordination procedures. These decisions affected the functioning of both ECOFIN itself and the Committee of Central Bank Governors and sought to prepare them for the onset of stage one of EMU in July by following closely the proposals of the Delors Report (paragraphs 51–2). In the case of ECOFIN, the procedure of multilateral surveillance was introduced as a new element

28. Commission of the European Communities, 'One Market, One Money', *European Economy* 44, October 1990.

of stage one: it involved an appraisal of the extent to which individual member states were achieving convergence or divergence. In the case of the Committee of Central Bank Governors, an attempt was made both to augment its analytical capacity and to develop its role as an EC-level institution. The Committee was expected to adopt a more coordinated approach, by for instance agreeing coordinated intermediate monetary targets (as proposed by Pöhl) and a more effective monitoring of the effectiveness of national monetary policies. It was also to achieve a more visible, public profile, by providing new reports to the European Parliament and the European Council and by giving collective opinions on policies of individual countries. In fact already, at a crucial meeting in December 1989, the Committee of Central Bank Governors had agreed a number of steps designed to transform itself into the forerunner of the European central bank system, to ensure that it played an independent and assertive role in the EMU policy process and to coordinate monetary targets in the name of price stability. Pöhl aimed to use a refashioned and strengthened Committee of Central Bank Governors to better promote the policy interests and concerns of the Bundesbank in the move towards EMU.

German unification, political union and the Dublin summit

The significance of these moves was in fact completely overshadowed by the rapid development of the debate about political union in the period preceding the European Council meeting in Dublin in April. Chancellor Kohl's initial period of introversion, as he was caught up in the early rush of events following the internal collapse of the GDR regime, gave way to a new optimism in March after the victory of his centre-right allies in the first (and only) national democratic elections there and the prospect of unification and the first all-German elections. He took the initiative in pressing his EC colleagues 'to construct a European roof over a united Germany' in order both to overcome mistrust of a united Germany and to emphasize his own country's commitment to a 'European Germany' and not a 'German Europe'. At a series of rapidly convened meetings of EC foreign ministers the momentum for political union built up, with a paper from the Belgian foreign minister and joint proposals from the French and German foreign ministers. When, following their bilateral summit in Paris in April, Kohl and Mitterrand proposed an accelerated move to political union, including an IGC on political union to run concurrently with the IGC on EMU, it was clear that this topic would dominate the Dublin summit – and that, again, the British Prime Minister would be isolated. In Paris Kohl spoke unequivocally of a 'United States of Europe'.

Reaction within the Commission to the rapid emergence of political union was mixed. Indeed, it did not develop a collective voice. It was clear that the momentum behind political union in Franco-German bargaining and in Council bargaining had become unstoppable; the Danish Foreign Minister, Uffe Ellemann-Jensen, had joined in by using a speech at Chatham House in London to attack the British government's hesitant attitude to political union and failure to see the 'writing on the wall' (though, just before the Dublin summit, the powerful Danish parliamentary commission responsible for scrutiny of EC business decisively rejected the Franco-German proposals).

But two concerns preoccupied the Commission. First, as good officials, many in the

Commission feared that the Franco-German proposals had not taken account of the formidable technical obstacles to their timetable. They noted that there was much more confusion over the meaning of political union than over the concept of EMU, and two years' work would have gone into the 'full and adequate preparation' of the IGC on EMU before it began work. Nine months' preparation for political union would not be adequate. Additionally, there was a fear, articulated by Sir Leon Brittan, that this initiative could slow down progress towards EMU; that linkage of this kind would prove damaging to the EMU project. Given his enormous personal commitment to EMU, Delors shared this concern.

Concern was also apparent among economic policy advisers to the Commission. From their perspective, and that of Delors, the main contribution that the initiative for political union could make to EMU would be a substantial augmentation of the budgetary power of the EC, particularly its redistributive capability, on the lines of the MacDougall Report.[29] But a substantially improved fiscal transfer mechanism – disproportionately funded by a German government that was now in the process of taking on huge new financial commitments in the east – was not what Kohl had in mind when he spoke of political union.

Once again, Mrs Thatcher used the Dublin summit of April to argue the case for restricting political union to moves towards 'closer cooperation between sovereign member states' and to argue that powers of national parliaments, electoral systems and heads of state must be kept off the agenda. The two key decisions on union were first, that EC foreign ministers should meet to define concrete terms for political union and report back to the next Dublin summit in June, and second, that the IGC on EMU – and a parallel one on political union – should end in time for their results to be ratified by member states before the end of 1992. In May the EC foreign ministers gave the go-ahead to institutional reforms but emphasized that the IGC would not be establishing the final stage of full federal union. This conclusion chimed in with the more cautious approach of the Commission which preferred what Delors described as 'a second stage of the Single European Act'.

The 'hard ECU'

Just before the June meeting of the European Council the British Chancellor of the Exchequer, John Major, sought to regain the initiative on EMU by presenting to his colleagues in ECOFIN his proposal for the 'hard ECU'.[30] The idea derived from the City of London (from Paul Richards at Samuel Montagu) and was presented to the Treasury as the 'City view' by Sir Michael Butler, a former British Permanent Representative to the EC. In fact, the claim that the 'hard ECU' plan embodied the 'City view' stemmed from the fact that it had been endorsed by the European Committee of the British Invisible Exports Council, the City's 1992 Committee. Its leitmotif of a market-driven approach, building on the Treasury paper of 2 November 1989, was ideologically acceptable to the Conservative government, and it seemed an

---

29. See e.g. Gros and Thygesen, *European Monetary Integration*, pp. 460-66.
30. Bank of England, *The Hard ECU in Stage 2: Operational Requirements* (London: Bank of England, mimeo, December 1990).

advance on the earlier evolutionary approach in that it filled a vacuum of ideas about how to make an effective contribution to the forthcoming IGC by proposing institutional changes.

The 'hard ECU' would be distinct from the existing ECU, from which it would differ, first, in being issued by an official institution, the European Monetary Fund, against national currencies, and second, in not being allowed to depreciate against any national currency in a realignment. In effect, the ECU would cease to be a basket currency and would become one traded on foreign exchange markets in its own right. The EMF would manage the ECU in open market operations in such a way that it would always be at least as strong as the strongest national currency. Its advantage as an extra, parallel currency would lie in its more stable purchasing power. The proposal was an advance in incorporating an institutional dimension: the creation of the EMF to manage the 'hard ECU' from the start of stage two and to provide some sort of common monetary policy. But the question of a single currency would not arise unless and until the 'hard ECU' had displayed its success in the market.

Though the Spanish government showed interest, and the former French Finance Minister Balladur articulated a similar proposal, the general response in ECOFIN and the technical committees to the 'hard ECU' proposal was one of considerable scepticism. First and foremost, it was seen as a politically motivated distraction from the central issues in the EMU negotiations: like the fundamental problem that, without a European central bank managing a single currency, freedom of capital movement would be a force for currency instability. Second, it was by no means clear why the 'hard ECU' was more likely to take off as a widely traded EC currency than the present D-Mark or how, in the context of generally fairly low inflation levels within the EC, people could be persuaded to use the 'hard ECU' rather than national currencies. Third, it was viewed as technically flawed, not least by the Bundesbank: it would boost the supply of money in the EC and thus stimulate inflation. In response, the British government argued that any creation of 'hard ECU' could only be in exchange for national currencies; hence there would be no increase in the money supply. This drew forth the retort from the Bundesbank that national governments could allow their own money supplies to rise in compensation. But, above all, the political presentation of the 'hard ECU' plan was handicapped by the British Prime Minister's continuing reservations of principle about stage three. Without the commitment to stage three, the 'hard ECU' plan lacked basic credibility. In consequence, the proposal was sidelined.

New problems: from the second Dublin summit to the Rome summits

During the Irish presidency EMU continued its momentum. Progress was maintained at the June summit in Dublin, with the agreement that on 13 December in Rome the IGC on EMU would commence; that the IGC on political union would negotiate in parallel; and that their work should be completed so that ratification could take place by 1 January 1993. The Italian presidency in the second half of 1990 had, therefore, a favourable inheritance. A sense of momentum was sustained by the decision of the British government in October to join the ERM, a decision that seemed consistent with accepting the logic of stage one of EMU and that offered the prospect of improving

British influence on negotiations. But ERM entry had been in effect forced on a British Prime Minister who was left with too few allies to continue to resist.

In practice, however, the Italian presidency was to face substantial problems on the EMU front. They arose from the predictable conjunction of two forces of resistance: from the Bundesbank, which had become increasingly concerned about the risks involved in EMU, and from the British Prime Minister, who staunchly resisted any linkage between ERM entry and EMU. For this reason the Rome summit of October 1990 was critical. It was critical because it was preceded by deepening suspicion, notably on the part of the French government, that the German government was becoming cautious. This suspicion had solid foundation: the Bundesbank was recoiling from its bitter defeat at the hands of the federal government on the question of the terms of the currency union between the two German states in the summer. German monetary union had starkly underlined the limits of the power of the Bundesbank and shown how the effective discharge of its responsibilities could be undermined by decisions of the federal government; in this case a decision that was motivated by party political strategy and tactics, not the needs of the German economy. A repeat performance of economic 'irresponsibility' was, in the view of the Bundesbank, all too possible with EMU, particularly as, at the level of the European Council, bargaining was in the hands of economically illiterate heads of state and government and foreign ministers. With EMU the danger was that a visionary Europeanism would ignore basic economic realities.

Accordingly, the state of domestic bargaining relations between the federal government and the Bundesbank had reached a new low. On 19 September 1990 the Bundesbank took the unusual step of issuing a lengthy official statement on EMU and one that, in the light of later events like its role in the ERM crisis of July–August 1993, can be seen as pregnant with consequences for European monetary integration.[31] In its view, the new problems posed by German monetary union must be brought under control before EMU could be contemplated. Scepticism was voiced about the feasibility of carrying out both undertakings at once. Also, there were certain 'unconditional, not negotiable, requirements' in the area of economic convergence that must be met as a precondition. The German Finance Minister confirmed his support for the caution of the Bundesbank.

To further underline Bundesbank concerns, in October Pöhl made clear that Britain's unilateral entry into the ERM in that month had further complicated life for the Bundesbank. Sterling's continuing role as a reserve currency, combined with the view that the British government had 'overvalued' sterling in the ERM and that its price stability record was very poor, persuaded the Bundesbank that the price of supporting the pound in the ERM could be dangerously costly to it. To the inflationary costs of German unification was now added the potential intervention costs consequent on sterling's entry into the ERM. Again, in the light of the Bundesbank's role in the sterling crisis of September 1992, this declaration of the Bundesbank's view was pregnant with consequences. In September and October 1990 a new, more assertive posture by the Bundesbank had become a potent factor in Council bargaining.

The division of opinions in Council bargaining came to a head at a meeting of

---

31. Published in *Monthly Report of the Deutsche Bundesbank*, October 1990, pp. 40–4.

ECOFIN in Rome in September. At issue was the date at which stage two was to start. There were those, like the finance ministers of Belgium, France and Italy, who understood that the April summit had implied that stage two would commence on 1 January 1993, to coincide with the completion of the single market. But the Dutch and the German ministers advised against the fixing of any dates, arguing that economic convergence should determine the rate of progress (in effect the argument of the Bundesbank). The fallback position of Theo Waigel, the German Finance Minister, and Pöhl was that stage two could begin in 1994 provided that certain conditions were met – on inflation, interest rates and budget deficits. The European central bank would be set up only at the end of stage two. When set alongside the interest displayed by the Spanish Finance Minister in Major's 'hard ECU' plan, it seemed that there was a real risk of derailment of the EMU negotiations. In consequence, the French government and the Italian presidency were alarmed. It seemed that on EMU the French and German governments had drifted apart. For Delors it was important that a date be set for stage two; the Communication of the Commission on EMU of 21 August had suggested January 1993 to coincide with the completion of the single market. But the precise date, 1993 or 1994, was less important than that stage two should be brief. On that issue no progress was being made.

Against this background, the October meeting of the European Council in Rome acquired a critical significance. The two key power brokers were Chancellor Kohl and the Italian Prime Minister, Giulio Andreotti. Both were pushing for an historic decision on EMU. In particular, Kohl wished to use what he presented as the window of opportunity before the first all-German elections in December and before the full economic impact of German unification was felt domestically. He was already aware that the unexpectedly bad economic situation in eastern Germany could, in the near future, prejudice Germans against the idea of taking on additional commitments and risks in the EC. Hence there was a need for haste. Andreotti and Kohl were also keen to clear the main EMU business out of the way so that the European Council meeting in December could focus on the difficult and contentious issues involved in providing a mandate for the impending IGC on political union. For Kohl, European political union was, if anything, more important than EMU. The result was an unpleasant surprise for Waigel and Pöhl – and for Mrs Thatcher, who felt ambushed by the presidency's insistence on a timetable for EMU (and remembered her similar experience at the Milan summit of 1985 when another Italian Prime Minister, Bettino Craxi, had suddenly obliged her to vote on whether an IGC should be established). Kohl proposed that stage two should begin on 1 January 1994.

Two key decisions were taken in Rome, both against the wishes of Mrs Thatcher. Stage two was to begin in January 1994, on some fairly relaxed conditions:

1   that the single market had been achieved
2   that all restrictions on capital movements had been removed
3   that the revised treaty had been ratified
4   that all member states had taken the measures necessary to enable them to take part in the ERM (a softening of the condition in the Delors Report)
5   that a process had begun that would make the governors of the national central banks independent by the start of stage three

6   that governments would not be able to finance budget deficits by printing money

7   that the EC would not bail out any member.

With an eye on Pöhl and Waigel, who had to be carried along in the bargain, Kohl was successful in adding a further condition for the transition to stage two:

> The European Council recalls that in order to enter stage two other satisfactory and durable progress towards real and monetary convergence, in particular price stability and the consolidation of public finances, should have been made.

These conditions were to profoundly influence the final Treaty on European Union, with the text of some of the points being embodied in it.

Also, the Rome summit concluded that the European central bank would be established at the start of stage two rather than, as Waigel and Pöhl wanted, at the end. Its role in stage two would be to strengthen coordination of monetary policies, 'to oversee the development of the ECU', and to practise using the instruments and procedures that it would need when it operates monetary policy in stage three. Additionally, no more than three years after stage two starts, the European Council was to consider a progress report before deciding the date of stage three, 'which will occur within a reasonable time'. These decisions represented a mandate to the forthcoming IGC. They also involved the isolation of the British Prime Minister in her defence of a national currency. For it was clear that, whatever the domestic hesitations and the reservations and hostility of the Bundesbank, the German government had, in principle, accepted that the ECU could replace the D-Mark, sometime before the end of the 1990s.

There had been no clear intention to isolate and exclude Mrs Thatcher, let alone ambush her, at the Rome summit; rather that isolation was the outcome of the combination of her own political will to remain within the existing framework of 'cooperation' with the momentum given to EMU by the French, German and Italian political leaders. Indeed, the prime ministers of Denmark and Luxembourg, and Jacques Delors, were concerned about this outcome. The outcome was indeed a critical event in precipitating a change of governmental leadership in Britain. An angry and embittered Mrs Thatcher returned to proclaim to her Parliament that Britain had 'surrendered enough', to accuse the European Commission of trying to 'extinguish' democracy and to dismiss the prospects for the 'hard ECU' plan that was central to the government's own negotiating position. The result was the dramatic resignation of the deputy Prime Minister, Sir Geoffrey Howe, and his devastating speech in the House of Commons on 13 November. By the end of the month John Major, who as Chancellor had persuaded his colleagues at Ashford Castle that he had a more constructive and open approach, was Prime Minister. And his new government gave top priority to giving practical expression to the new Prime Minister's desire to see Britain playing a more innovative and less defensive role at the 'centre' of Europe.

What was undoubtedly true was that the sense of Mrs Thatcher's weakening political authority at home, particularly after Lawson's resignation as Chancellor in October 1989 (precipitated by the attack of the Prime Minister's economic adviser on the ERM as 'half-baked'), contributed to a diminished effectiveness of her negotiating position in the European Council. There was a certain symmetry between Mrs Thatcher's isolation in the EC and her isolation within the British cabinet on EC policy. The British government entered the IGCs with a greater authority that came from the attempt to combine a constructive approach with cabinet and Conservative Party unity. Ultimately, the Achilles' heel of Major's strategy was to prove to be party unity. But during the IGCs the full force of this problem did not display itself: party disunity's destructive potential for Major's strategy emerged in the ratification process of the Treaty on European Union.

The bargaining process in the intergovernmental conference on EMU and the Treaty on European Union

With the European Council meeting in Rome on 14–15 December 1990 the two IGCs were launched. Although Delors used the summit to complain about recalcitrant states, notably Germany, the atmosphere was positive and promising. EMU was on track and speeding ahead, and in a much better state of health than the debate about political union. Already almost three years of debate and analysis had preceded the IGC on EMU. It was far better prepared than the IGC on political union, where the French and German governments had very contrasting approaches: Germany favouring a strengthening of the European Parliament, France seeking to fortify the role of the European Council and to reduce the role of the Commission. On political union the Commission had not developed a central role in shaping the agenda: and, during the IGC on political union, it was to be very much on the defensive, particularly as the Luxembourg presidency established a closer working relationship with the Council of Ministers' Secretariat than with the Commission in producing the draft treaty for a 'European Union' with three pillars. Two of these pillars – foreign and security policy and interior and judicial policy – were to be intergovernmental in character, excluding a central role for the Commission and the Court of Justice in policy development. Delors felt excluded and betrayed, not least by the French government which was a central architect of these ideas.[32]

Commission influence

The distinguishing feature of the IGC on EMU was the degree of coherence given to its negotiations by the long phase of preparation that had proceeded it. Essentially, bargaining was structured by the tabling of two main sets of papers: the Communication of the Commission of 21 August 1990 and, incorporating the conclusions of the Rome summit in October, its 'draft treaty amending the Treaty establishing the European Community with a view to achieving economic and monetary union' of December; and the draft statute for the European System of Central Banks, presented by the Committee of Central Bank Governors.[33] Both drafts

32. F. Laursen and S. Vanhoonacker (eds) *The Intergovernmental Conference on Political Union* (Dordrecht: Kluwer, 1992).
33. Commission of the European Communities, *Intergovernmental Conferences: Contributions by the Commission* (Luxembourg: Office for Official Publications of the European Communities, 1991), pp. 5–62. Committee of Governors of the Central Banks of the Member States of the European Economic Community, *Draft Statute of the European System of Central Banks and of the European Central Bank* (Basle, 27 November 1990).

were to be extremely influential. The draft from the Committee of Central Bank Governors was to be incorporated without amendment as a Protocol annexed to the Treaty on European Union.[34] The third paper, the 'hard ECU' plan of the British government, was to be without influence, despite support from the Spanish government. The main impediment to a favourable reception was the plan's failure to deal with stage three. A factor that helped maintain momentum in the work of this IGC was not only the role of the Commission's preparatory work in structuring bargaining but also the overlapping membership of the IGC and the EC Monetary Committee in helping to draw together different bargaining relations. As a consequence, the members of the IGC had already been heavily involved in the preparatory work in the EC Monetary Committee, and the Monetary Committee had already built up a strong corporate support for EMU, evident at the Ashford Castle meeting of ECOFIN in March 1990. The combination of close liaison and overlapping membership between the IGC and this key technical committee of the EC with so much preparatory work did a great deal to smooth negotiations in the IGC.

Despite this favourable context for negotiations, certainly compared to that of the IGC on political union, tensions and difficulties abounded. The striking point is simply that these problems did not succeed in derailing progress. The negotiations in the IGC on EMU were given added momentum by the conclusions of the Rome summit in October. And it was a tactical advantage for the Commission to be the first with a draft on the table and, unlike in the IGC on political union, to have that draft taken as the basis for negotiations by the Luxembourg presidency. Within the IGC itself the Commission was able to have some influence. Thus the Commission fought off the French government's proposal that member state governments should be given a right of initiative in EMU, via ECOFIN (a proposal that was consistent with the French position in the EPU negotiations). In the context of the general reverse that Delors was experiencing on EPU during the Luxembourg presidency, preservation of the Commission's right of initiative on EMU was an important victory. It was an issue on which Delors intervened personally against the French government, with the support of the small states. German support was also forthcoming particularly when, in January 1991, the French Finance Ministry began to speak of a stronger ECOFIN as a *gouvernement économique*.[35] In fact, what the French government had in mind was a role for ECOFIN as a forum for a dialogue about the different objectives of economic policy. But the German government reacted in a hostile fashion to French talk of ECOFIN as 'the centre of economic government', seeing in this proposal a means both of undermining the authority of the ESCB and of developing an interventionist approach.

In other respects too the Commission was influential within the IGC negotiations. With the support of the Dutch presidency in the second half of 1991, the Commission gained a greater role for the European Parliament in EMU. According to Article 109b

34. Council of the European Communities/Commission of the European Communities, *Treaty on European Union* (Luxembourg: Office for Official Publications of the European Communities, 1992).
35. P. Bérégovoy, 'Pas d'indépendance monétaire de la banque centrale dans l'ignorance des exigences politiques', *Auszüge aus Pressartikeln,* Deutsche Bundesbank, 22 November 1990.

of the Treaty, the ECB was to present an annual report to the Parliament and may be requested to appear before its competent committees. The Commission also influenced proposals on capital liberalization with third countries. Again with strong Commission support, the proposal of the British and German governments that, as a sanction for excessive budget deficits, EC Structural Fund aid should be withheld, was defeated. Delors's personal influence was further apparent in the Protocol on Economic and Social Cohesion, including its provision for the new Cohesion Fund to support environmental projects and trans-European networks. Fundamental to this Protocol was the idea of matching support for weaker EC countries that were fulfilling programmes of economic convergence as part of EMU. Within the negotiations Delors put his political weight behind what he regarded as a key linkage between EMU and economic and social cohesion. But otherwise the Commission retained a low-profile, background role in the IGC itself. Its key concern was its own competencies in EMU.

The other arena of Commission influence was on the negotiation of texts in the EC Monetary Committee, notably the protocol on the excessive deficit procedure and the protocol on the convergence criteria. Here it was less successful. Whilst it recognized that some yardstick was probably necessary for the identification of excessive deficits, it sought, in vain, to avoid precise figures for the convergence criteria and their proliferation in number. The Commission emphasized that the determination that a deficit was excessive was a matter of judgement about the sustainability of its fiscal position. This judgement could not be made in isolation from an assessment of the overall economic situation and development. What the Commission did recommend was the so-called 'golden rule' of public finance: that public borrowing should not exceed investment expenditure.

The influence of the two technical committees: the convergence criteria, the ESCB and the stages of EMU

The IGC was essentially the focus at which a huge amount of bargaining was brought together and specific points of difficulty finally reconciled. It is, however, essential to remember that the contribution of the two technical committees was decisively important, and that, through these two committees, the influence of the German Finance Ministry and the Bundesbank was decisively brought to bear on the final shape and content of treaty provisions – on convergence criteria, the independence of the central bank and the minimal responsibility of the European Monetary Institute in stage two.

Negotiations on the *convergence criteria and the excessive deficit procedure* were delegated to the EC Monetary Committee. Here there was strong conflict of positions, with the convergence criteria eventually being adopted by majority vote. The lead was taken on this issue by German and Dutch officials, with backing from Spain. For the Spanish government the preference for tough convergence criteria derived from a desire to place itself in a strait-jacket that would facilitate and legitimize difficult fiscal decisions at home. Tough convergence criteria were (as we have seen) a traditional theme of Dutch and German governments in the debate about EMU. The alternative view was advocated by the Italian government, with support from DG2: that the new treaty was a constitution and that it was not sensible to make the treaty rigid and inflexible by inserting precise, detailed figures about, for instance, budget deficits and public debt, into the treaty. It suspected, quite rightly, that the adoption of tough criteria, for instance on long-term interest rates, was proposed in order to reduce the prospects for Italian eligibility in the absence of radical domestic action. Quite simply, given the domestic priority to low inflation, German officials had little economic incentive to see countries with weak currencies in an EMU; every incentive to ensure that the final EMU bargain reflected German economic priorities and institutions writ large; and the capability, resting on the structural power of its economy and currency and its role as the anchor of the ERM, to get its way in negotiations.

Within the EC Monetary Committee and the IGC the British government played a key role in helping to achieve an agreement on provisions for excessive deficits that were at once tough and flexible: tough in detail, yet flexible in interpretation. According to Article 104c and the Protocol on the Excessive Deficit Procedure, member states shall avoid excessive deficits. 'Excessive' is defined as over 3 per cent for the ratio of the planned or actual government deficit to GDP, and over 60 per cent for the ratio of government debt to GDP. The aim to be tough was demonstrated in the form of sanctions. Failure to comply with requests of the Council to reduce a deficit can be followed by a request to the European Investment Bank to reconsider its lending policy to the state in question and by a requirement that the state must make a non-interest-bearing deposit 'of an appropriate size' with the Community.

But Article 104c also made it clear that allowance could be made for a situation in which the deficit is 'declining substantially and continuously' or is 'exceptional and temporary' (a reference to the problems consequent on German unification), as long as the excess comes 'close to the reference value'. In effect, the treaty was seeking to give strong incentives to budgetary prudence whilst recognizing that dynamics of the budgetary situation and judgement must finally determine the capability of states to qualify for stage three.

Beyond criteria on deficits and debts, quantitative precision was given to two other nominal criteria in the Protocol on the Convergence Criteria, referring to Article 109j:

- an average rate of inflation, over a period of one year before the examination, at no more than 1.5 percentage points above that of the three best performing member states in terms of price stability
- an average long-term interest rate, over a period of one year before the examination, that does not exceed by more than 2 percentage points that of the three best performing member states in terms of price stability.

To these nominal criteria was added a further test of convergence: that a member state had respected the 'normal' fluctuation margins of the ERM for at least two years, without severe tensions. In particular, it should not have devalued within the ERM on its own initiative within the same period. Behind these figures was the work of the EC Monetary Committee and the clear imprint of the goals and interests of the German Finance Ministry and the Bundesbank. Despite their toughness, it was clear that the insistence of the Delors Report on mandatory upper limits on budget deficits had been replaced by a decision to operate stage two and the transition to stage three on the basis of peer-group pressure in ECOFIN rather than strict compulsion.

Even more significant was the impact of the Committee of Central Bank Governors in the area that had been reserved for them since the Hanover summit of 1988: *the architecture of the European Central Bank*. In this area negotiations were delegated to the EC central bank governors who were given autonomy and succeeded in having every detail of their proposals accepted. To this extent the Treaty on European Union incorporates an EMU for central bankers. Once again the German Bundesbank was able to exert a formidable influence through this body. In effect, the Protocol on the Statute of the European System of Central Banks and of the European Central Bank is the Bundesbank writ large. In some respects the ESCB appears stronger than the Bundesbank; in others weaker. Its strength is apparent in an even more clear-cut determination of the primacy of price stability as its objective. According to Article 2 of the Protocol dealing with its objectives:

> In accordance with Article 105(1) of this Treaty, the primary objective of the ESCB shall be to maintain price stability. Without prejudice to the objective of price stability, it shall support the general economic policies in the Community . . .

Here is an even less equivocal commitment than that of the Bundesbank whose main responsibility, as defined in the Bundesbank Act of 1957, is 'the safeguarding of the value of the currency'. In addition, the legal status of the ESCB's objectives, and its independence, is even more secure than that of the Bundesbank. The Bundesbank's mandate rests on simple legislation; that of the ESCB is written into treaty form, making revision – or the threat of it – less credible.

Where the ESCB is potentially weaker is in its operational efficiency, its capacity for rapid decision-making and implementation. The Protocol makes the Governing Council the repository of all major monetary policy authority and ensures that the six-person executive board is in a minority on this council. The other members of the Governing Council are to be the governors of the national central banks. In turn, the executive board has to rely on the national central banks for the implementation of policy. Hence the governors of the national central banks are left in a pivotal position, not least able to pursue their own corporate interests in preserving as much operational autonomy as possible for themselves, and hence the granting of independence to these governors before stage three was such an important issue if political interference in the ESCB was to be avoided.

In addition to price stability, independence was the second clear policy goal around which the Committee of Central Bank Governors could unite. This goal was underlined by the stipulation in Article 7 of the Protocol that the ECB officials shall not seek or receive instructions from another EC body, a national government or any other body, and by the appointment of executive board members (by the European Council) for a term of eight years, not renewable, and of governors of national central banks for a minimum of five years. Two other provisions are designed to safeguard the ECB's independence in the pursuit of price stability. Article 21.1 forbids the ECB to engage in the direct monetary financing of public deficits, in the form of credit facilities or purchase of debt instruments from local or national governmental bodies or EC institutions. Article 109 makes it clear that, in the absence of a formal agreement on an exchange-rate system for the ECU with non-EC currencies (i.e. a Bretton Woods type of agreement), ECOFIN must not adopt positions on exchange-rate policy that prejudice the primary objective of price stability. In the case of a formal agreement, it must have consulted with the ECB 'in an endeavour to reach a consensus consistent with the objective of price stability'.

The ESCB was the single most powerful institutional development to emerge from the Treaty on European Union. Here was a body entrusted with the tasks of defining and managing the monetary policy of the Community; with holding and managing the foreign exchange reserves of the member states; and with conducting foreign-exchange operations. Initially, national central banks were to transfer foreign reserve assets (other than their own national currencies, ECUs, IMF reserve positions and SDRs) up to an amount equivalent to 50,000 million ECU; thereafter, the Governing Council would determine the proportion to be called up by the ECB (Article 30 of the Protocol). The ECB was also endowed with the authority to conduct open market and credit operations (Article 18) and to require credit institutions to hold minimum reserves with the ECB and national banks in pursuance of its monetary policy objectives (Article 19). Though these policy instruments are impressive, they do not amount to a clear-cut subordination of the national central banks in a hierarchical relationship to the ECB. For what is missing from the Treaty on European Union is provision for the ECB to impose reserve requirements on national central banks. In the absence of such a requirement, the ECB is not in the same relationship to national central banks that national central banks enjoy in relation to commercial banks.[36]

The result of the impact of central bank governors through the Committee of Central Bank Governors and through their membership of the EC Monetary Committee was a Treaty on European Union that gave precedence to a monetary orthodoxy. In doing so they were both reflecting their interpretation of Germany's outstanding economic performance, an interpretation that focused on the role of the Bundesbank in ridding that country of the costs of inflation, and ensuring that the transition to EMU would at least safeguard, and in important respects enhance, their corporate power. Some central bankers, like those of the German Bundesbank, may have deeply mistrusted EMU. But, given the political drive behind the EMU negotiations, their strategy was to safeguard what they could and to make use of the process to promote the cause of price stability and central bank independence in order to reduce external inflationary pressures on their domestic policy priorities. In these policy goals the Bundesbank was undoubtedly successful. And it was successful because these goals were incorporated at the decisive points in the negotiating process: in the composition of the Delors Committee, in the delegation of the design of the ESCB to the central bankers, and in the delegation of work on excessive deficits and convergence criteria to the EC Monetary Committee.

The imprints of the technical committees, and of influence of the central bankers, were also to be found in the outcomes of the negotiations on the other key issues with which the IGC was left: *the nature of stage two, and the conditions for the transition to stage three*. These imprints reflected their victory in gaining acceptance for the principle of the 'indivisibility' of monetary policy in the treaty negotiations. Stage two represented an elaborate compromise on the questions of the entry conditions and its length and substantive content. German and Dutch officials wanted to toughen the

---

36. For a good discussion of this issue see Gros and Thygesen, *European Monetary Integration*, pp. 377–84.

entry conditions for stage two, on the argument that convergence should at least accompany further integration, and to emphasize the decentralized and voluntary character of monetary policy during the transition. At this point the foreign exchange markets were brought into the bargaining process. The financial markets must not be confused about who was responsible for what; the effects could be destabilizing. And it would undermine the long-term authority of the ESCB if an institution with that name but with feeble powers were to be created in stage two. Above all, Dutch and German officials argued that ultimate responsibility for monetary policy must remain in national hands. The bargain was worked out in the Committee of Central Bank Governors which, in October 1991, submitted to the IGC a Draft Statute of the European Monetary Institute. This Draft Statute was accepted in the Treaty on European Union as the Protocol on the Statute of the European Monetary Institute. EMI was to be the key institutional innovation of stage two and to have three main objectives: to strengthen coordination of monetary policies, including reporting on progress in convergence, taking over the tasks of the EMCF amd monitoring the functioning of the EMS; to prepare for the establishment of the ESCB in stage three; and to oversee the development of the ECU. Essentially, it was to absorb the Committee of Central Bank Governors and the EMCF, but with little in the way of enhanced policy responsibility.

But two changes were of significance. According to Article 8 of the Protocol, members of EMI (the central bank governors) may not, in that capacity, 'seek or take any instructions from Community institutions or bodies or governments of members states'. This requirement of independence applied even to those central bank governors who, at the national level, still did not possess guaranteed independence. Also, on one issue the Committee of Central Bank Governors was overruled. The Committee had wanted to elect one of their members as the president of the EMI Council. Article 9 of the Protocol provides that the European Council shall appoint to this position, in effect the one full-time member of the EMI Council. Some increase of visibility could be expected as a result of these changes, and there was a new potential for independence of action in EC monetary policy. But, at the end of the day, EMI's powers appeared to be limited and basically consultative: in essentials a victory for the Bundesbank.

The basic price of the emphasis on the 'indivisibility' of monetary policy and the Bundesbank's victory in securing this principle was a weakening of the substance of stage two. Stage two's content did not meet the hopes of the EC Commission or match up to the recommendations of the Delors Report. Some gains were made. Thus the ECU was 'hardened'; during the transition the currency composition of the ECU basket was to remain unchanged. But on other issues stage two appeared a 'soft' transition. There was, for instance, no provision for a narrowing of the fluctuation margins within the ERM as a means of reinforcing coordination in stage two. In line with the recommendations of the Delors Report, French and Spanish officials pressed in the negotiations for some pooling of reserves in stage two in the interest of an effective intervention policy *vis-à-vis* third currencies. Here again, little progress was made; the EMI was simply enabled to operate as agent for, and at the request of, national central banks in their foreign exchange management. Reserve pooling was, in other words, voluntary. In effect, management of the transition was being left primarily to the national level.

In return for such important concessions, French and Italian officials made two significant gains: first, the treaty opted for a relatively short and firm timetable for stage two, relative that is to the Delors Report (stage three would begin either three or five years after the commencement of stage two on 1 January 1994), and second, the entry conditions for stage two were relaxed. Compared to the conclusions of the Rome summit of October 1990, two conditions were removed: the process of making central banks independent could start during stage two and the 'no-bail-out' rule would apply only from the start of stage two. But, building on the German concern about convergence expressed in the Rome summit's conclusions, it was decided that, before the start of stage two, each state shall adopt 'multiannual programmes intended to ensure the lasting convergence necessary for the achievement of economic and monetary union, in particular with regard to price stability and sound public finances'. ECOFIN and the EC Monetary Committee had gained a new task: the right to comment on convergence programmes and, through peer-group pressure, to seek to influence national budgetary policies to respect the requirements of convergence.

On the crucial issues of the length of stage two and the conditions for the transition to stage three the IGC had little specific guidance for its negotiations, either from the Rome summit or from the Delors Report. The treaty provisions on these issues constituted an elaborate compromise, involving first and foremost France and Germany and, less centrally, Britain and Denmark. In the lesser compromise the British and Danish governments succeeded in negotiating separate protocols enabling them to opt out of stage three of EMU. Initially, the British and Danish requests had been met by a text of the Dutch presidency that sought to insert a general clause permitting all states only to opt into EMU when the European Council deemed the conditions to have been met. The other ten governments in ECOFIN rejected this general clause as too weak an affirmation of their commitment to EMU, so that the British and Danish governments had to accept separate protocols. The British government had at least met its prime objective in the IGC negotiations: to demonstrate that the treaty did not involve a commitment to EMU. Such a commitment would have deeply divided the Conservative Party and done so just before an election where success was seen to depend above all on party unity.

The key compromise was between the French and German governments. For the German negotiators insistence on tough convergence criteria as a precondition for EMU went along with a reticence about a precise timetable, for it could not be foreseen just when the criteria would be met. For the French, backed by the Italians, a firm timetable has the virtue of forcing convergence, both by harnessing political will to corrective action and by its effects on markets that come to anticipate the timetable. The final compromise came late in the negotiations. Its essential feature was the combination of tough convergence criteria with a firm timetable for entering stage three. According to Article 109j of the treaty, stage three would be achieved by one of two means:

- by a decision of the European Council, acting by qualified majority, and to be taken not later than 31 December 1996, that a majority of member states fulfil the convergence conditions, thus enabling it to set a date for the beginning of stage three; or

- before 1 July 1998, the European Council, again acting by qualified majority, shall determine which member states meet the conditions and can go on to stage three, which shall start on 1 January 1999.

This outcome was seen as a triumph for French diplomacy. But it was made possible by the decision of Chancellor Kohl to defy domestic criticism and give the go-ahead to a deal that would demonstrate that, with the Treaty on European Union, European union was now irreversible. The French government had, as a consequence, acquired what they sought: an apparently automatic transition to stage three, no later than 1 January 1999.

The progress of the IGC negotiations: where power lay

Despite the elaborate preparations for the IGC, the progress of the negotiations was far from smooth. The public launch of the Commission's draft treaty in December 1990 was accompanied by an internal row in the Commission. Delors was accused of not securing full and proper consent for the document prior to publication. But far more significant was a renewed assertiveness of the Bundesbank and clear evidence that Germany's bargaining positions in the IGC were being strongly influenced by it. By late January it was plain that the main issue was not the British 'hard ECU' plan, to which there was an adverse reaction because of its failure to address the mechanism for stage three. The central debate was about the nature of stage two, with Delors wanting to establish the ESCB at the start of stage two and the Dutch and German officials adamant that the principle of the 'indivisibility' of monetary policy (for which also read the maintenance of the authority of the Bundesbank) required that its introduction be deferred to stage three. It was also apparent at this early point in the negotiations that Delors had lost to the Dutch and Germans over the argument about whether sanctions should be deployed against countries that were guilty of excessive deficits.

An important impact was made by a German draft of March.[37] Although the German Foreign Ministry had succeeded in weakening the draft's original conditions for moving to stage two, the draft bore the imprint of the Finance Ministry's authorship and Bundesbank approval. Delors attacked the draft as an abandonment of the commitments entered into at the Rome summit, but largely in vain. It was the occasion for a rare row between Delors and Kohl. The British government had also to accept that German support for the 'hard ECU' plan was firmly ruled out. The draft underlined that the German government's political will was firmly behind EMU but that serious technical concerns had to be addressed. In particular, it was proposed that in stage two the Committee of Central Bank Governors should become the Council of Central Bank Governors, a change that the Commission and the French government viewed as essentially cosmetic.

The Bundesbank was in any case making its own views known: that fiscal deficits must be brought under control and central banks made independent as preconditions of EMU, and that, given likely variations in the will and capability to realize these

37. *The Economist*, 9 March 1991, pp. 43–5.

preconditions, it was likely that a 'two-speed Europe' would result.[38] Appearing before the economic committee of the European Parliament on 19 March 1991 Pöhl referred somewhat incautiously to the aftermath of German monetary union as a 'disaster'. The remark was directed at the risks of EMU but sparked a breakdown of relations with the German Chancellor, who concluded that Pöhl was trying to undermine him. At a personal level relations between the Chancellor and the Bundesbank president had reached a very low point.

But, despite concern about this rift, Bundesbank officials continued to press their points. The recently appointed vice-president of the Bundesbank, Hans Tietmeyer, who had earlier, as a top economics official in Bonn, been a close confidant of Kohl, made public his dislike for Delors's approach of setting target dates as a means of testing Germany's commitment.[39] He also stressed that, as a number of states (he cited Britain, Italy and Greece) did not yet fit into a *Stabilitätsblock* (stability bloc), a 'two-speed Europe' would be a price to pay for EMU. Convergence had to precede monetary union. And, according to Tietmeyer, 'a stable currency is more important than a united currency'. There was, of course, nothing new in these injunctions from the Bundesbank. But what was clear was that the conjunction of a 'mismanaged' German monetary unification in 1990 (in the view of the Bundesbank) with a dash to EMU had created a defensive and increasingly assertive Bundesbank. The Bundesbank was conscious of escalating burdens: the financing of German unification, the Gulf war and the reconstruction of eastern Europe and the Soviet Union. Now, with the IGC, its own authority was on the line in a way that it had never experienced before.

In a general sense it might seem difficult to pin down influence in the IGC negotiations. Influence can be expected to vary across issues. Thus the British failed to get a general 'opt-out' clause for stage three; but, on the other hand, the British representative, Nigel Wickes, was important in negotiating the 'tough but flexible' criteria on excessive deficits. Pierre Bérégovoy, the French Finance Minister, was able to carry the day on the final timetable for stage three. Yet, overall, the key intellectual contribution and impact on the final EMU bargain came from the Germans, in combination with the Dutch, in particular from Horst Kohler, state secretary in the German Finance Ministry. Kohler was abrasive and tough and carried the persuasion that derives from a clear conception of what the German government wanted and the Bundesbank would wear and from a recognition of his colleagues in the IGC that ultimately his government had the one veto position that really mattered. This leadership role for Germany was replicated in the Committee of Central Bank Governors (in the shape of Pöhl and his influence on the draft statute of the ESCB) and in the EC Monetary Committee (of which Kohler was a member). The German government did not carry all before it on every issue. But it did represent the pivot around which a balance had to be found.

As early as the informal meeting of ECOFIN in May it was becoming apparent that a solution might be found for one of the bargaining problems: that of keeping Britain on board whilst enabling its government to avoid a commitment to EMU. Delors was by then suggesting a declaration or protocol to the treaty that would grant Britain an

---

38. *Financial Times*, 27 February 1991.
39. *Auszüge aus Pressartikeln*, Deutsche Bundesbank, 17 April 1991.

'opt-out' yet not prevent other countries from moving ahead. But more important still was the effort of the Luxembourg presidency to present a draft treaty that would unblock the Franco-German dispute on stage two and the timing of the creation of an ESCB and enable the German government to strike a mutually acceptable bargain with the Bundesbank. This proposal centred on the idea of two subperiods to stage two: the first (1994–5) would see something akin to the German proposal for a Council of Central Bank Governors; and the second (1996 to stage three) would begin with the establishment of the ESCB. Having made a concession to Germany, including the idea of sanctions against countries with excessive budget deficits, the draft proposed that a decision to move to stage three and to set a date for its start could be taken by the end of 1996. Both the French and German ministers showed signs of softening their positions: Theo Waigel, the German Finance Minister, could take pleasure from the broad agreement that the ESCB would be modelled on the Bundesbank and from the deferral of the date for the establishment of the ESCB; and Pierre Bérégovoy, the French Finance Minister, was convinced that the German government was preparing itself to accept a timetable. The other new idea was that each country should prepare convergence programmes to submit to ECOFIN, before stage two, to affirm their will to achieve economic convergence.[40]

By September–October the outlines of a bargain on the convergence criteria and on stage two were becoming clear. The Bundesbank's strength on these issues was manifested in August when there were signs that the German Finance Ministry was relaxing its views on the convergence criteria in favour of the view – popularized by Graham Bishop of Salomon Brothers – that market pressures could be relied on to discipline budget deficits.[41] It struck back powerfully. An informal ECOFIN meeting of September showed that ministers were in a mood to make concessions, and in October the 'tough but flexible' compromise on the convergence criteria was achieved. The particular criteria selected were not the product of rigorous economic calculation. They were set at their particular levels for two reasons: because the figures were close to the average performance of the best-performing EC countries in 1990, and because the Bundesbank was keen to agree figures that would constitute a prospectively too high hurdle for the EC states collectively to jump.

The new draft treaty of the Dutch presidency in November underlined the negotiating success of the Bundesbank in gaining acceptance for both tough convergence criteria and sanctions against countries with excessive budget deficits. Only two key issues were left to a late stage. The nature of the 'opt-out' clause for stage three was clarified at the informal ECOFIN meeting at Scheveningen in early December. Norman Lamont, the British Chancellor of the Exchequer, was unsuccessful in achieving a general 'opt-out' clause and had to make do with a special exemption. He also sought to introduce a revised version of the 'hard ECU' plan that met with a frosty reception: not least because of his professed scepticism about the whole EMU project.

More important was the remaining issue of the date and conditions for the transition to the all-important stage three. Here, at the very final stage of the European Council meeting in Maastricht, the French government won a significant tactical

40. *The Economist*, 18 May 1991, Finance Section.
41. G. Bishop *et al.*, *Market Discipline CAN Work in the EC Monetary Union* (London: Salomon Brothers, November 1989).

negotiating victory, a victory that in turn owed much to Chancellor Kohl. With the 'opt-out' achieved, the capacity of the British government to exert influence on these questions was diminished. In other words, the price of the 'opt-out' was an acceptance that the other governments could determine the final timetable for EMU.

The Maastricht summit

The mood of the German delegation at the Maastricht summit in December was affected by a surge of anxiety in the German press about the implications of EMU for domestic currency stability, represented most starkly by shrill headlines in the most popular daily newspaper, *Bild Zeitung*, and on the front cover of the weekly news magazine *Der Spiegel* ('*Angst um die D-Mark*', 'fear for the D-Mark'). But Kohl rejected the caution of many of his colleagues. He was personally committed to ensuring that EMU, as a key component of European union, was made irreversible. Hence when, on the eve of the summit, in bilateral negotiations President Mitterrand and Andreotti approved an ingenious formula to stop less enthusiastic countries from blocking the final transition to EMU, they found that they were pushing against an open door. Pierre Bérégovoy proposed to his colleagues in ECOFIN a formula that combined a firm timetable for stage three with qualified majority voting in the European Council to determine whether sufficient states had met the convergence criteria. A 'critical mass' of countries was required for a decision by the end of 1996: though in this case the date for the beginning of stage three is not actually specified (it could be deferred into the next century). Otherwise, 'the third stage shall start on 1 January 1999' (Article 109j of the Treaty) for just those countries that met the criteria, by a decision of the Council before 1 July 1998. Both ECOFIN and the European Council meeting at Maastricht underlined that the irreversibility of EMU was the central preoccupation of ten of the twelve member states. Ultimately, this principle formed the central axis of the negotiation and of Franco-German compromise. By combining irreversibility with acceptance of two-speed EMU the formula made it easier for Kohl and Waigel to argue that a key concern of the Bundesbank had been met: namely, that not all states were likely to be ready for EMU at the same time, or even ever.

EMU was but part, though arguably the central part, of the Treaty on European Union that emerged from the Maastricht summit. The IGC was successful in keeping the negotiations on EMU separate from those in the IGC on European political union. At Maastricht, however, the problems that had bedevilled the negotiations on political union threatened to spill over to affect the fate of the whole projected treaty. Two threats were most apparent: from the German government's late insistence on linkage between success in concluding the EMU negotiations and greater progress on political union, notably enhanced powers for the European Parliament, and from the difficulty of agreeing so complex and wide-ranging a package deal in such a summit meeting, not least with major disagreement over issues like the social chapter – with the British government taking an intransigent stand of opposition in principle – and the nature and scale of measures to compensate those states – like Spain – that would have the greatest problems of adjusting to the convergence criteria for EMU.

At the end of the day the commitment of the Dutch and German governments to achieving a treaty agreement carried the day. Kohl brokered a difficult agreement over the social chapter, in practice the biggest and most difficult negotiating issue at the summit. The Dutch presidency's contribution was in resorting to the use of a tough and unusual negotiating method for European Council meetings: rapid majority voting on individual sections of the draft treaty. Ruud Lubbers, the Dutch Prime Minister, justified the use of this method by reference to the need to meet a predetermined political deadline for the treaty, to the pressure to equip the EC to move on to other more pressing substantive issues, especially in eastern Europe and the Soviet Union, and to the psychological factor of huge 'sunk costs' by all the participants in the negotiations. All the political leaders were made aware of the risks of failure at a time when external pressures for change were mounting. This procedure proved expeditious in the case of EMU, for the principle of EMU had been accepted before the IGC ever got underway and the recommendations of the central bankers formed a cornerstone of the treaty. It did not, however, prevent Norman Lamont from walking out of ECOFIN when the Dutch Finance Minister demanded a line-by-line debate on the British protocol.

But, in the final analysis, there was a palpable sense that the German government had sacrificed most in conceding the principle of the irreversibility of EMU in treaty form. Just as Helmut Schmidt had been so powerful an actor at the Bremen and Brussels summits of 1978, so Helmut Kohl's perception of the implications of changing political conditions proved the most potent factor at the Maastricht summit. In Kohl's mind there were two basic considerations at work. First and foremost was his sense of being a man of his political generation, of a generation that was not directly implicated in National Socialism and war but was nevertheless marked by it. The consequence was a political vision that sought to escape from the sense of shame and loss by building new safeguards against a repetition of the European tragedies of the early twentieth century. Among these safeguards, an irreversible process of European union was central. In addition, 1990 had brought a new factor. German unification had created a new reality, the perception of an even stronger and assertive Germany pursuing its own interests within the EC and in eastern Europe. Kohl recognized the risks in this new situation. Fear of German power could cause the EC to degenerate into a game of alliances against Germany, a game that would undermine the EC and harm Germany. In this altered context Kohl was at pains to emphasize that German national interest was better secured by an EC in which the members were strong together than by seeking, vainly, to be strong alone.

For Kohl then the Maastricht negotiations were a strategic issue to be determined from the perspective of 'high' politics, even if there was a domestic price to pay. It was a rare issue for Kohl: one on which he was prepared to display bold political leadership. And he needed to be brave, for the Bundesbank's interpretation of German unification was very different; it constituted a huge burden that militated against the added risks of EMU. Ultimately, what happened at Maastricht cannot be understood without reference to the political ideals of Chancellor Kohl and the effects of German unification on his political strategy for Europe.[42] What united the two episodes of the

42. For the continuity in Kohl's thinking on the importance of a federal Europe, see Die politische Redaktion des Saarländischen Rundfunks (ed.) 'Auf dem Weg zum Bundesstaat Europa', *Europäische Perspektiven* (München: Wilhelm Goldmann Verlag, 1979), pp. 67–78; H. Kohl, 'United Germany in a Uniting Europe', St Anthony's College, Oxford, and the Konrad Adenauer Foundation, 1992.

birth of the EMS and the relaunch of EMU was their demonstration of the capacity of the European Council to exert an independent political will in the name of integration and union.

Problems of treaty ratification and policy implementation: the reassertion of the power of the foreign exchange markets and of the Bundesbank

On 7 February 1992 the foreign and finance ministers of the member states convened in Maastricht to sign the Treaty on European Union. That meeting, and the period that immediately followed it, represented a high point in optimism about EMU. This optimism was reflected in Council bargaining in ECOFIN where the IGC and the treaty appeared to act as catalysts for a change of attitudes and behaviour. Its bargaining was characterized by a strengthening mutual solidarity: in part a function of the sense of ownership and euphoria that came from having made so ambitious a treaty and in part the result of a newly acquired sense of responsibility to make 'their' treaty work. The work on mutual surveillance and on convergence programmes was conducted with a new sense of purpose: governments like those in Italy and Spain were emboldened to achieve budget consolidation with a new vigour.

There were undoubtedly some economic problems on the horizon. Bond yield differentials started to widen after a period of narrowing, followed by the collapse of the ECU bond market, which had been seen as the commercial precursor of monetary union. This evidence of scepticism within financial markets about the Maastricht project was linked to mounting concern about the escalating costs of German unification and the effects both on the policies of the Bundesbank and on its relations with the federal government.

In particular, foreign exchange market operators were able to read the continuing negative signals about EMU from the Bundesbank. Its scepticism was evident in a statement, published in February 1992 and authored by Tietmeyer, in which the priority of convergence over any timetable was asserted and the inadequacy of the provisions for a supportive political union noted. More vociferous criticisms came from Bundesbank council members. Already, in December 1992, two had expressed severe reservations.[43] Reimut Jochimsen, president of the *Landeszentralbank* in North-Rhine Westphalia, had spoken of the Maastricht agreement as 'suicidal' because it was too deficient in building political union and too rigid in its timetable. Dieter Hiss, president of the Berlin *Landeszentralbank* and a former economic policy adviser to Chancellor Schmidt, questioned whether the culture of economic stability of Germany, based as it was on Germany's uniquely painful experiences of the ravages of inflation, could be exported to the EC. Then, in his book *Abschied von der D-Mark*, Wilhelm Nölling, president of the Hamburg *Landeszentralbank*, attacked the economic incompetence of the Kohl government and argued that the existing EMS was a better basis for integrating the east European economies into the west than the new hurdles being created by EMU.[44] Schlesinger too used a book to question whether the budget

43. For a summary of Bundesbank council member reactions see D. Marsh, *The Bundesbank: The Bank that Rules Europe* (London: Heinemann, 1992), pp. 248–51.
44. See in English W. Nölling, *Monetary Policy in Europe after Maastricht* (London: Macmillan, 1993).

deficits of many countries made possible their serious candidacy for EMU; whilst his predecessor Pöhl was quoted as being bitter about the way in which Kohl had made too many concessions on EMU without an adequate supportive edifice of political union so that economic, financial and social policies could be properly coordinated.[45] The Bundesbank felt obliged to adopt a more public note of scepticism that was not lost on the foreign exchange markets. In so doing it had the welcome support of sixty members of the German economics establishment, including Karl Schiller, who signed a petition against a too hasty and ill-considered EMU.

But in May 1992 no one could have then predicted the awful scale of the problems that were to beset the EMU project before its final ratification.[46] By the end of 1992 the EC was in the grip of economic and political malaise; the Commission was in retreat and the Treaty on European Union was beset by a double crisis – of ratification and of policy implementation. Treaty ratification had not been achieved by the target date. Britain and Italy had been ejected from the ERM in the September crisis and a series of humiliating and large-scale currency realignments, the first since 1987, had been forced on the system by market pressures. Spain devalued twice, Portugal once and France very narrowly escaped devaluation. By the end of November the D-Mark had been revalued by 13 per cent against the lira, 15 per cent against sterling, and 12 per cent against the peseta. This scale of change was well outside the previous experience of the ERM. Fast-changing political and economic conditions, leading to the most momentous crisis yet experienced by the ERM (in July 1993) had conspired to end the period of the so-called 'new' or 'hard' EMS, to produce a partial disintegration of the ERM, to cast a cloud of gloom over prospects for European union, and to diminish the authority of the European Commission and its president. Council bargaining was reduced to a defensive and reactive character.

Changing political conditions: new problems of legitimacy

The change in political conditions was marked by the crisis generated by the rejection of the Treaty on European Union in the first Danish referendum in June 1992. This rejection had all the hallmarks of a watershed event. Though the rejection was by a slender majority in a small state, it acted as a catalyst for the mobilization of opposition in other member states, notably in Britain but also in France and Germany. Political and economic consequences followed. Economically, the new risk to the EMU project cast doubt on the ERM itself and the hard-won investment of many of its members in establishing the credibility of their parities. In turn, the reduced credibility of the ERM threatened to keep interest rates high, at a severe cost in output and employment.

Politically, the difficulties of ratification suggested that the limits of public tolerance for elite initiatives had been sorely tested. There was substantial public aversion to a process of constitutional change that had been determined not by

45. H. Schlesinger, *Staatsverschuldung ohne Ende* (Darmstadt: Wissenschaftliche Buchgesellschaft, 1992). For Pöhl's views see D. Balkhausen, *Gutes Geld und Schlechte Politik* (Düsseldorf: Econ Verlag, 1992).
46. On the ERM crises of 1992 and 1993 see P. Temperton (ed.) *The European Currency Crisis* (London: Probus Europe, 1993).

wide-ranging and intense public debate but in inconspicuous IGCs, according to the private conventions of diplomatic negotiation. Doubts surfaced about the democratic credibility of an elite-driven process of union that had failed to engage large sections of the political class as well as the citizens of Europe. Ominous too was the EC-wide fall in support for 'efforts being made to unify western Europe', registered in the regular Eurobarometer spring and autumn surveys. In spring 1991 80 per cent supported such efforts, with 11 per cent against; in spring 1992 the proportions were still 76 to 16 per cent; by the autumn the majority was 73 to 19 per cent. The spring 1993 survey confirmed the fall in support, with 41 per cent supporting Maastricht, 24 per cent opposed and 35 per cent not knowing; 38 per cent would be indifferent if the Maastricht Treaty were scrapped; 47 per cent were unhappy about democracy in the EC. Particularly disturbing was the spring 1993 finding that, though overall 52 per cent of Europeans favoured a single currency, 60 per cent of Germans were opposed to this project, with only 29 per cent of them in favour. This finding, along with French opinion polls showing that in September 1993 53 per cent of French people rejected the Maastricht Treaty, pointed to a deep political problem at the very heart of the EMU project.

In response to the Danish referendum the member states decided to press on with ratification – 'business as usual' – and to seek ways of addressing Denmark's problems without a renegotiation of the treaty. President Mitterrand sought to regain the initiative, domestically as well as within the EC, by calling a referendum on the treaty for September. But in fact the French referendum was to prove a cause of prolonged crisis and uncertainty rather than a vehicle to restore the EC's flagging fortunes. By August the prospect of a French rejection had become apparent. The consequence was an increasing belief that the Treaty on European Union could be doomed – with further adverse economic consequences for the credibility of parities in the ERM. In practice, the French referendum result produced a narrow majority for the treaty but not before the protracted uncertainty had led operators in the foreign exchange markets to seek refuge in the D-Mark. The main casualties of the new speculative pressures were the British pound and the Italian lira on so-called 'Black Wednesday', 16 September 1992, the first two currencies to leave the ERM.

Ejection from the ERM was in turn a profound political crisis for the government of John Major, accompanied by open recrimination from within the British government against the Bundesbank's failure to support the pound effectively. Its consequences for EC business were all the more serious because the British government held the presidency during the second half of 1992. Subsequently, in November the British government only very narrowly avoided defeat in the House of Commons on the issue of proceeding with the treaty; the price was a decision by the Prime Minister to delay final ratification until after the second Danish referendum – a decision that further aggravated relations with EC partners.

The energy of the EC was sapped by continuing uncertainty and internal crisis management not only in relation to ratification of the Treaty on European Union and to the ERM but also by prolonged and acrimonious debate about the financial package (the so-called Delors II) to accompany the treaty in the interests of the poorer countries. At least there were two positive political signs by the end of 1992. The Edinburgh summit of December achieved agreement on the the new financial package, ten of the twelve states had by then ratified, and an interpretation of the treaty had been agreed to meet Danish concerns without a renegotiation.

Changing economic conditions

The changing economic conditions in 1992 were at least as alarming for the fate of the EMU project. EMU became increasingly embroiled in the tensions and conflicts associated with the 'down-side' of the economic cycle and with a new climate of uncertainty and instability in the foreign exchange markets. Two notes of official alarm were sounded in summer 1992. In June the annual report of the Bank for International Settlements argued that EMU was likely to be doomed on technical grounds. There was likely to be a steady erosion of political consensus for EMU as the real costs of 'too rigid' exchange rates and contractionary fiscal policies for output and employment became manifest, and as the effects of capital liberalization were brought to bear on the ERM. Meanwhile, a leaked and gloomy report from the IMF spelt out in more detail the costs of EMU in lost employment and output. On average, growth in the period 1993–6 would be diminished by 0.4 per cent per annum at best, and at worst, if markets lacked confidence in EMU, by 0.8 per cent per annum. Belgium and Italy were likely to be especially hard hit by the effort to apply the convergence criteria, notably to curb 'excessive' deficits.

These authoritative voices of doom influenced foreign exchange market sentiments and were soon reinforced by mounting evidence of the onset of general EC recession. After seven years of sustained growth in the EC economy at 2.5 per cent or more, EC-wide GDP grew by only 1.2 per cent in 1991 and 1.1 per cent in 1992. Thereafter, the Commission's growth projection was steadily revised downwards: from 0.75 per cent to 'slightly negative growth' for 1993. As an indicator of impending recession, EC unemployment rose from 8.4 per cent of the labour force in 1990 to 10.1 per cent in 1992, and an estimated 11 per cent for 1993. As Delors and his colleagues recognized, without sustained growth the prospects for EMU were bleak. For with recession the capacity of the member states to fulfil the convergence criteria was weakened. Recession brought falling tax revenue and burgeoning public expenditure, and hence the prospect of rising and excessive deficits. In 1990 six countries had met the budget deficit criterion: Britain, Denmark, France, Germany, Ireland and Luxembourg. By 1993 only Denmark, Ireland and Luxembourg, the three smallest states, were projected to meet this criterion, and of them only Luxembourg to meet all four convergence criteria. Market operators were quick to recognize that the treaty did not guarantee speedy convergence and therefore make it safer than before to hold traditionally weaker currencies. Hence the Italian and Spanish governments did not succeed in sustaining a new credibility from the Treaty on European Union. The all-important economic good fortune that had sustained the progress of EMU from 1988 to 1991 vanished; a catalogue of economic misfortunes filled the agenda.

Three economic developments were central to the problems of the ERM in 1992, in addition to the onset of recession and the effects of political events. Two were unleashed by domestic factors, in the United States and Germany. The first development was *the external factor of the US dollar's decline*: traditionally an indicator of impending tension and conflict in the ERM. By July 1992 the gap between US and German short-term interest rates was the highest for 30 years, reflecting the efforts of the US Federal Reserve to revive the persistently sluggish US economy by interest rates just a little above 3 per cent. As a result, the position of the D-Mark in the ERM strengthened, putting extra pressure on other ERM currencies. Also, collectively locked into the ERM embrace, the ERM countries found that their competitiveness with the USA was being undermined. The strength of the D-Mark threatened other ERM members with overvalued currencies in relation to the dollar and loss of export competitiveness and jobs. In fact, the onset of the ERM crisis can be dated from 21 August when the market operators scored their first victory: 18 central banks tried to prop up the US dollar by intervention and failed.

The second economic development involved *new problems in the anchor currency of the ERM* in the wake of German unification. The credibility of the D-Mark's role as the anchor currency of the ERM was being undermined, first, by a twin deficit problem, of budget deficit and current account deficit; second, by domestic German inflation above that of other member states like France; and third, by devaluations within the ERM which exposed the German economy as uncompetitive. Perceptions of the mismanagement of German unification worked like yeast in the foreign exchange markets, and the fermentation brought to the surface by summer 1993 new images of an ERM anchored around a currency that was itself underpinned by a problem of poor economic fundamentals. German domestic policy action to tackle that problem proved incompatible with the domestic policy needs of its ERM partners. The immediate damage was done by the Bundesbank as it raised its interest rates to a postwar high in the effort to combat the inflationary effects of German wage agreements and the accelerating budget deficit. It did so with two rationales: a domestic rationale that stressed the irresponsibility of the federal government and both sides of industry and its statutory responsibility to 'safeguard the currency'; and a rationale for the EC that argued that the stability of the ERM depended ultimately upon its effective performance in maintaining its place as the anchor of the system. The consequence was that, as long as the D-Mark remained more attractive to foreign exchange operators, fellow members of the ERM were required to follow the Bundesbank in raising rates. And they had to endure the additional costs of paying an extra interest-rate risk premium to attract currency holders whose rational disposition was to hold the only ERM currency that had never been devalued. In February 1993 the risk premium carried by short-term French rates was some 5 per cent. Irritation with the Bundesbank boiled to the surface at the informal ECOFIN meeting in Bath in September 1992, when Lamont used his chairmanship to put great and persistent pressure on an angry president of the Bundesbank to reduce interest rates. Indeed, by June 1993, market perceptions of the weakening fundamentals of the German economy had enabled a core of ERM countries, notably Belgium, France, Ireland and the Netherlands, to reduce their three-months' interest rates below German levels. The Bundesbank was beginning to need to look more anxiously over its shoulder at the foreign investors holding D-Marks, in turn an inhibition on its capacity to reduce interest rates.

In the third economic development, foreign exchange market operators were confronted with economic and political information which suggested *deteriorating economic fundamentals* in some cases and, in most cases, that *the domestic costs of sustaining existing ERM parities, the 'hard' ERM and meeting the new EMU convergence criteria would prove prohibitively high.* The result was a collapse of market confidence that extended from a group of currencies to embrace the ERM as a whole. The first victims were the British and Italian currencies. Defence of sterling's parity was manifestly incompatible with economic recovery, particularly as high interest rates already made it impossible to tackle the fundamental problem of a huge mountain of personal indebtedness built up during the credit boom of the late 1980s. Behind the problems of the lira was an intractably high public sector debt. In the absence of a will and capability to undertake a planned realignment to address the problems of the lira and sterling, an absence that was demonstrated at the ECOFIN meeting in Bath, market operators began to sell pounds and lira on a scale that the ERM could not accommodate. Attention was to shift to other currencies – the peseta, escudo and punt – and, most importantly of all, the French franc. In each case the solution to domestic economic problems seemed incompatible with the Bundesbank's high interest rate policy. The ERM became locked into a situation of interest rate crises.

To add to the woes of the ERM, the continuing depreciation of the pound after it was floated in September 1992 created an impression of the return of competitive devaluation, putting added pressure on such currencies as the French franc and the Irish punt (the latter was forced to devalue within the ERM in January 1993, the fourth realignment since September, in the wake of a further British interest rate cut). These currencies had to bear the dual burden of high German interest rates and devaluations by major trading partners. The British and then the Irish governments sought to put the issue of asymmetry back on to the agenda, but against the staunch opposition of the Bundesbank. Meanwhile, the threat of huge speculative pressures persisted, with Spain as a major target. The Spanish government, faced with a large current account deficit and unemployment over 20 per cent, had to endure three devaluations of the peseta between September 1992 and May 1993. It seemed, to say the least, that EMU in the form of the Treaty on European Union, was not an imminent prospect. But the more immediate critical issue – which came to a head in July 1993 – was whether the French authorities could prevent a devaluation of the franc, an event that would drastically undermine the credibility of the treaty's EMU strategy.

At the heart of the problems of the EMS was the conjunction of the declining US dollar, the fiscal and monetary pressures induced by German unification and a rigid political determination to maintain fixed exchange rates – all within the context of mounting recession and economic divergence. German unification was a profound idiosyncratic shock that could be effectively countered only by a real appreciation of the D-Mark: a development that was ruled out by the politics of the 'new' EMS. Appropriately, the Bundesbank was pressing for a general realignment well before the 1992 crisis, a proposal that was successfully resisted by the French government. Economic policy advice was also unequivocal: that a fixed rate regime without capital controls and with unsound fundamentals was inherently fragile and vulnerable. In 1992 a more fragile EMS (minus the policy instrument of capital controls) met an external shock without making appropriate exchange rate adjustments: the result was delayed and bungled realignments. The outcome was a vicious circle of competitive deflation and political conflict over interest rates and mismanaged realignments. With real short-term interest rates of around 7 per cent, prospects for recovery from recession were nil. Exchange-rate policies began to lose credibility in key countries, led by Britain, as it became clear that their price in output and employment was too damaging in political and economic terms.

Central to the problems of German unification for the EMS was the failure of German policy makers to achieve an appropriate fiscal, monetary and labour-market balance in the context of new inflationary tendencies: French policy makers had to bear a significant responsibility for the determination to eschew a degree of exchange-rate flexibility. Because of these errors of policy judgement the ERM had begun to operate in a way that was not only self-destructive but also threatening to the prospects of EMU. It was, above all, clear that only a very large reduction in German interest rates could deflect speculative pressures and stimulate recovery. The first small sign that the Bundesbank was prepared to respond to this requirement came with a cut in its leading interest rates in February 1993. But, given continuing domestic inflationary pressures and lax fiscal policy, the prospects were only for cautious, step-by-step rate reductions. In July/August 1993 the ERM's existing policy mechanism of 'narrow' bands was to succumb to a full-scale interest rate crisis as the gap between the rate cuts needed for economic recovery and the domestic approach of the Bundesbank became manifestly unbridgeable.

Reappraising the route to EMU

In the wake of the September 1992 crisis, the two key technical committees – the EC Monetary Committee and the Committee of Central Bank Governors – set to work to undertake special reviews of the policy instruments and functioning of the EMS, as well as to examine the nature of stage two (which was due in January 1994). There were predictable divergences of view. Some French policy makers wanted to narrow margins of fluctuation in the ERM (in return for strengthened monetary cooperation); the Bundesbank argued that any change should be in the direction of wider margins (a change that was to be accomplished in August 1993). The Bundesbank had once again to fight off pressures for 'greater symmetry' of burden-sharing between weak and strong currency countries. Despite the careful diplomatic balancing attempted in the reports of the two committees on the 1992 crisis, submitted to the informal ECOFIN meeting in Kolding in May 1993, victory for the views of the Bundesbank was very clear.[47] The EMS was judged to be fundamentally sound rather than in need of significant reform. The basic failures had been to manage it as a *de facto* monetary union and its lack of sufficiently tight surveillance of exchange rates to enable the member states to be given an early warning of the need for realignments. Other member states should be given the right of initiative in raising questions about particular countries' central rates and should be assisted by the availability of new objective indicators, particularly of external competitiveness. Perhaps most symptomatic of Bundesbank influence was the argument that the onus is on the member state in difficulties to take appropriate action, with interest rate adjustment its most

47. Committee of Governors of the Central Banks of the Member States, 'The Implications and Lessons to be Drawn from the Recent Exchange Rate Crisis' (Basle: 21 April 1993); and the Monetary Committee of the European Community, 'Lessons to be Drawn from the Disturbances on the Foreign Exchange Markets' (Brussels: 13 April 1993).

promising instrument. Intervention by central banks was seen, by contrast, as of limited utility, with new emphasis being placed on the voluntary character of support from other central banks.

Two main elements of agreement emerged. The Bundesbank was successful in its demand that more frequent parity changes should be reintroduced and that the EMI must function as a mechanism for improved early identification of currency misalignments so that, unlike in September 1992, necessary changes can be made before they are forced by market operators. In addition, the obligations of the Basle-Nyborg agreement on central banks to support individual currencies were if anything diluted: 'other member states will determine to what extent and how they can support these efforts through appropriate voluntary actions', in the words of the EC Monetary Committee.

The Commission's role was essentially limited to that of trying to keep up political pressure on the technical committees to achieve an agreement that would significantly strengthen monetary cooperation and, in the process, do something to augment stage two of EMU. Beyond that there were two central concerns: to sustain as much solidarity as possible in ECOFIN (itself a taxing business); and to promote an EC-wide growth initiative. In February 1993 ECOFIN showed signs of relaxing its approach to EMU; it was agreed that a review of whether countries had met the convergence criteria could be delayed until the end of 1996, giving them the maximum amount of time to adjust. Already, at the Edinburgh summit the Commission had succeeded in gaining endorsement for a growth initiative, though one that was generally recognized to be very small in relation to the scale of the problem of recession. The basic limitation that the Commission faced was that, whatever repairs were agreed to the policy instruments of the ERM or resources acquired for new infrastructure projects, their impact would be far less than the interest rates of the Bundesbank. And the Commission had no authority over the Bundesbank; whilst the Bundesbank perceived itself as more a victim of events than a colossus dictating economic terms to states and markets.

Though many contrasting proposals were made, the central thrust of development after September 1992 was towards a new tactical flexibility about the route to EMU. At issue was the nature and degree of tactical flexibility needed. In the technical committees the message was very much one of modest repairs to the EMS and a relook at stage two of EMU with the objective of avoiding future currency misalignments. The 'spirit of Basle-Nyborg' prevailed (though the crises of 1992 and 1993 showed that it was not made flesh). Politically, its underpinning was provided by two key factors: by the commitment of the French Socialist government and its centre-right successor in March 1993 to strengthen monetary cooperation as the centre-piece of economic strategy; and by the Bundesbank's desire to return to a more flexible ERM. In the view of most economists and foreign exchange market operators such modest tactical flexibility was completely inadequate in the absence of sharp and durable reductions in Bundesbank interest rates. Otherwise, an interest rate crisis would follow as the ERM forced countries to sustain high interest rates that were inappropriate to the needs of their domestic economies. That crisis struck at the heart of the ERM in July 1993.

Two more radical scenarios for development were on offer. The first involved recognizing that the central problem was that differences in economic fundamentals were likely to endure and that speculative pressures were a fact of life. A solution could be found by moving to wider bands of fluctuation, thereby building much greater flexibility into the operation of the EMS. With realignments being more frequent and not permitted to exceed the width of the bands, one-way bets would be more hazardous for speculators.[48] This solution was the one adopted in August 1993.

The second scenario argued that the fundamental problem was not currency misalignments but a stage two that was too long and would act only as an invitation to repeated speculative attacks, sapping the will to achieve EMU. Its solution required a new fast-track to a mini-EMU, whether inside or outside the Treaty on European Union and based on the strongest currencies in the ERM: Germany, France and the Benelux countries, and possibly Austria and Switzerland.[49] Public support for such an initiative came from Pöhl, the former president of the Bundesbank, and from Schmidt, the former German Chancellor.

But, as they recognized, the fast-track proposal ran up against two big problems: the stern opposition of the Bundesbank, expressed forthrightly by Helmut Schlesinger, its president, in January 1993; and Delors's commitment, as a loyal servant of the EC, to making the treaty-based approach work. It raised profound questions about the political development of the EC. France was presented with the potentially unwelcome political prospect of a very unequal partnership with Germany, deprived of the counterweight of other Latin countries and Britain; with a new core group that would be more eastern- than southern-oriented. From a wider EC perspective, the fast-track proposal left unclear what exchange-rate policies would be pursued by those left out and how they could hope to persuade the markets of their capacity to join later.

Paradoxically, the fast-track proposal put Schlesinger in the position of defending the Treaty on European Union against something worse, though of course he continued to differ from Delors in having a much longer-term and negative view of the prospects for EMU. A side-effect of the mini-EMU idea was a new pressure on the ever-more beleaguered Bundesbank to commit itself even more strongly to making sure that the ERM in its existing form was a success. But, in the absence of a cataclysmic event like the collapse of the ERM, or of failure to ratify the Treaty on European Union, the prospects for such a new qualitative leap forward ever reaching the EC agenda remained remote. Even with such an event, it remained highly doubtful that the German federal government would feel that it had the domestic political strength to take on the Bundesbank on so fundamental an issue at such a difficult time in its economic and electoral fortunes. With a spate of local, state and then the federal election in 1994, and a challenge from the Republican Party promising to save the D-Mark, the federal government was forced into a posture of caution on EC initiatives. Indicative was the way in which, at the 1–2 August emergency ECOFIN meeting, the new state secretary in the German Finance Ministry, Gert Haller, dismissed the fast-track as 'a joke'.

48. J. Williamson, 'How to Reform the EMS', *International Economic Insights*, November–December 1992.
49. Considered in J. Pisani-Ferry, 'After the Monetary Turmoil', *International Economic Insights*, November–December 1992; and in G. Bishop, *Capital Liberalization* (London: Salomon Brothers, December 1992).

The most likely prospect remained that the agenda of the EMS and EMU policy process would continue to be dominated by the problems of putting into practice the EMU timetable agreed at Maastricht. The legacy of German unification and its mismanagement in the form of high German interest rates, sluggish economic growth and adverse public attitudes in Germany, coupled with the corporate self-interests of the Bundesbank in retaining its authority, suggested that continuing implementation problems and renewed failure were likely to bedevil the EMS and EMU policy process. Most likely was a 'long, hard and frustrating slog' to EMU. This process would be characterized by a degree of solidarity in the EC technical committees, governed by their corporate self-interest in keeping EMU within their own orbit and politicians at bay.

But just how difficult that task would be was revealed in July and August 1993 when an overwhelming crisis, centred on the French franc, formally wrecked the 'hard' ERM. The humiliation of the French government was avoided by the device of adopting a very broad 15 per cent band for all members except Germany and the Netherlands. The main immediate political effect was a recognition in both the German and the French governments that 1999 was now the most likely date for any move to EMU and that a substantial review of the EMU schedule was required. But, more than anything else, this crisis revealed the extent of German power over EMU in a public fashion.

Two other events in October 1993 underlined the centrality of Germany in EMU: the decision of the special EC summit to locate the EMI in Frankfurt (a recognition that progress had to be on German terms), and the judgement of the German Federal Constitutional Court on the Maastricht Treaty. Though enabling Germany to ratify the treaty, which could then come into force on 1 November, this judgement raised difficulties. First, the court underlined that the realization of the convergence conditions prevailed over any timetable (a view regularly reiterated by Hans Tietmeyer of the Bundesbank), and second, it ruled that, once stage three had been entered, Germany could leave the EMU if the stability conditions proved not to be satisfied. To add to the sense of major hurdles to be cleared, the court welcomed the German government's acceptance of the provision that, before agreeing to stage three, it would seek the agreement of the federal legislature. As far as Germany was concerned, 'opt-in' to stage three was the reality, not automaticity. More radically still, with the court's ruling 'opt-out' was viewed as a feasible proposition in stage three. The EMU policy process had to contend with the German Federal Constitutional Court's reservations as well as with the Bundesbank, and to face up to its subordination to the underlying political reality of one and most probably two German federal elections (in 1994 and 1998), in a new, changing and less certain republic, before stage three.

Lessons

EMU was bound up in a profound shift in EC–national policy linkages from 1984 onwards. This shift was reflected in the way that Council bargaining functioned:

1 in the way in which a coalition of Christian Democratic and Socialist governments in France, Germany, Italy and Spain forced the pace of integration

2   in the momentum imparted to Council bargaining by intensified Franco-German bargaining relations, with Mitterrand driven by a widespread French fear of German domination of Europe and Kohl by a mixture of ideological commitment to a federal Europe and diplomatic priority to reassuring Germany's neighbours

3   in the effect of German unification in strengthening the will to bind the new Germany more tightly into the EC and giving added vigour to Franco-German bargaining

4   in the psychological advantage given to proponents of EMU by the new legitimacy afforded by the Single European Act and by the political leverage offered by the commitment to total capital liberalization

5   by the presence of a Commission president with the will and capability to be a major actor in Council bargaining and able to use a dynamic and expansive interpretation of new (and old) legal and political commitments.

EMU as policy learning: diplomacy, central banking and treaty amendment

The Treaty on European Union's provisions on EMU reflected the nature of the EMS policy process, the power relationships on which it was based and the specific trajectory of policy learning that the EC had traced in economic and monetary policy. One of the most striking attributes of the relaunch of EMU was its character as a policy learning process. As we have seen, there is a connection that holds together the 'snake', the EMS and the EMU project of the Maastricht Treaty; the one is a vehicle to the other, constituting an enduring learning experience that has imparted a gradual accretion of institutional strength to the process of European monetary integration.

But, in order to understand the specific character and dynamics of EMU, it is important to focus on the specific circumstances out of which it flourished from the mid-1980s: the ideological consensus and convergence around the priority to price stability; the incentive of other EMS members to borrow monetary stability from Germany that had begun to affect the operation of the EMS since 1983; the consensus that the EMS had been a relative success around which integration could build; an emerging recognition of the incompatibility of free capital movement, fixed exchange rates and national economic policies; a new irritation with the unequal distribution of the costs of adjustment in an asymmetrical EMS; and the eager impulsion imparted by the single European market programme and its provisions for complete capital liberalization. Behind these factors was the imprint of the past: like memories of accelerating inflation and of its debilitating effects in the 1970s or the 'Euro-sclerosis' debate of the early 1980s. Above all else, however, EMU was reborn out of a specific conjunction of events which stimulated a rapid learning process among national and EC policy makers about operating the EMS and launching the single market programme in 1988 and onwards.

It was the conjunction of watershed events (the 1987 ERM crisis, the liberalization of capital movements and German unification) with policy learning that made monetary policy 'high' Council bargaining politics, taking it outside the normal range of its functioning in the hands of technical experts in finance ministries and central banks. As we saw in chapter 4, the launch of the EMS was a case of policy learning that, in its fundamentals, was retained in the hands of these technical experts. Policy learning was at the level of designing new policy instruments and reconsidering the usage of existing policy instruments. Essentially, the EMS was a mixture of strategic change with gradualism. It did not involve radical change in the goals and language of policy. The relaunch of EMU after the mid-1980s was different because, on this occasion, government leaders via the European Council were prepared to assert the primacy of a radical change of policy goals and to insist on that primacy, at Hanover, Madrid, Dublin and Rome. Though it coopted central bankers, the mandate of the Delors Committee represented a displacement of authority over policy.

In another sense the negotiations on EMU and on the EMS were intriguingly similar: in both cases the process of policy learning was remarkably self-contained. There were external actors pressing for a commitment to EMU, including the Committee for the Monetary Union of Europe and academic economists. But neither they nor the business associations like UNICE (Union of the confederations of Industry and Employers of Europe) were central to the process of policy innovation and negotiation. At best they were helpful in mobilizing support or legitimizing innovation. More fundamentally, the EMS and EMU policy process bore the imprint of the confluence of two professional cultural worlds: those of central banking, represented in the Delors Committee and in the technical committees of ECOFIN, and of diplomacy, as embedded in the conventions of IGC negotiations as a method of treaty amendment. Their strongly internationalized professional cultures were receptive to EMU but not necessarily representative of, or closely attuned to, popular attitudes and emotions

Here we come to the central political problem of the Treaty on European Union: the elite-driven commitment to radical policy change in so central an area of public policy, with such wide-ranging effects and symbolic importance, was not accompanied by significant party political or media engagement and the generation of widespead public interest and enthusiasm. That this did not occur had everything to do with the nature of the policy-making structures at the EC level and the weak basis of democratic legitimacy for EC policy. Party political involvement is primarily within the arena of the European Parliament, but its activities neither relate closely to the activities of parties in domestic politics at the national level nor excite media attention because of a perceived lack of political power. The low level of voter turn-out and lack of enthusiasm for direct elections to the European Parliament is in any case hardly surprising, for they do not amount to popular participation in choosing a European government or determining the direction of EC public policy.

Only with the ratification process was EMU brought fully into the realm of electoral competition and high media profile; but the flow of ideas was decidedly one-way, downwards. And the reaction, as registered in Britain, Denmark and France, was of widespread public disenchantment and grudging endorsement. An EC-oriented elite had produced a radical shift in the location of authority over policy without seeking to engage public interest and enthusiasm. Subsequently, the whole EMU enterprise fell victim to the limitations of the EC's political structures as a mechanism for democratic engagement. EMU had little prospect of taking effective root in the absence of a basis of legitimacy in strong democratic EC institutions that would be capable of inspiring and sustaining a genuine European consciousness.

At the heart of the bargaining that produced the Treaty on European Union was a compromise: concession by the Bundesbank and its allies on the radical policy goals espoused in Council bargaining, in return for a Bundesbank-led definition of policy goals and design of EMU institutions and policy instruments. Whether that central compromise, and hence the treaty itself, would prove adequate as the route to EMU in the face of changing circumstances was the open question. Was the Treaty on European Union based on too narrow and rigid an economic theory to withstand a harsher climate of falling output and rising unemployment? It was certainly a monument to a remarkably closed policy process.

Bargaining and power

The second key attribute of EMU as a policy process is what it reveals about bargaining relations at the EC level. Three central characteristics of the policy process were apparent: first, how actors found themselves enveloped within a complex interconnected set of bargaining relations; second, how power gravitated towards those actors who at key points in the policy process were able to act as linking pins between different bargaining relations; and third, how the relative significance of bargaining relations shifted with different stages in the policy process. The bargaining relations were in principle the same that characterized the launch of the EMS. But the experience of operating the EMS and the new momentum imparted by the single market programme, especially capital liberalization, had altered their quality. There was a new will and sense of capability to act boldly, even heroically, that united the Commission and the overwhelming majority of members of the European Council.

Power shifted as the policy process evolved. In the agenda-setting stage the framework of Council bargaining within the EC institutions and the Franco-German bargaining relationship were pre-eminent. The ascendancy of these bargaining relationships meant a priority to political goals: whether retrieving lost monetary power (a French preoccupation) or binding states in an ever closer union (an idea that enjoyed much support in Bonn). Though initiative in both these bargaining relations was very much French-centred, it was still apparent that policy leadership depended on the German government and the Bundesbank. In the more technical stage of policy preparation EC–central bank bargaining and German government–Bundesbank bargaining came to the fore; and with policy implementation EC–central bank, EC–financial markets and German government–Bundesbank bargaining occupied centre stage.

In other words, power had a habit of drifting back towards the Bundesbank, but to a Bundesbank that was by no means a free actor. It experienced the constraints of trying to assert its corporate interests and view of the public interest in a framework of multiple, overlapping bargaining relations. The capacity of an actor to make a difference came when that actor could operate as a linking pin, holding together different bargaining relations. This applied to Delors in the stage of agenda-setting; to Delors and Pöhl in the stage of policy preparation (in the Delors Committee); and to Kohl in the final framework of intergovernmental bargaining (at Rome and then Maastricht). Thereafter, the phase of policy implementation revealed the central linking-pin role of the president of the Bundesbank. That role was caught up (as we shall see) in the evolving corporatist policy network of the Committee of Central Bank

Governors as it prepared to become the European Monetary Institute (EMI). It was also embroiled in the mounting tensions with the foreign exchange markets, which looked to the Bundesbank for policy leadership. When that leadership was judged to be lacking, as in July 1993, the victim was the ERM and not the Bundesbank.

The basic reality was that EMU was caught in powerful crosswinds. From one direction, there was the impetus provided by structural changes in the international political economy: by trade interdependency and capital liberalization, by the efforts of EC states with weaker currencies to reduce the costs of an asymmetrical EMS, and by the vulnerability of EC currencies in world currency relationships. Here were themes that were likely to endure and sustain EMU at the centre of the EC's agenda. And in the changing terms of trade interdependency, as represented in the single market project, the EC institutions had acquired a new potency as sources of structural power, as Delors demonstrated in 1987/88. But, on the other hand, divergent economic fundamentals, the weakening of the ERM's anchor currency and the scale and volatility of foreign exchange markets put a series of question marks over EMU. Beset by such complex structural changes, the EMS seemed as likely to prove fragile as previous attempts to manage stable exchange rates. The Bundesbank may have continued to possess structural power, but it was just one among several sources of structural power and hence far from in commanding control. And it was difficult to envisage that it would voluntarily relinquish that power to an EC central bank. Hence so much rested on the political will and capability of the German government to make the ultimate leap to EMU.

Two long-term distinguishing characteristics of bargaining power on EMU are identifiable. One is the contrast with the debate about the launch of the European Payments Union in 1949–50 when British power to shape the agenda and outcomes was very evident. The launch of the EMS showed just how far that power had waned in relation to the Franco-German axis. With the relaunch of EMU after the mid-1980s British bargaining power was even less apparent. This contrast has its roots in enormous structural changes in the international political economy. The other contrast is with the negotiations for the Single European Act. In the latter case the British government had constructive ideas to bring to bear, above all the single European market. Here its enthusiasm was engendered by the possibility of a symmetry between a radical 'Thatcherite' domestic programme of neo-liberalism, dedicated to competition, and an EC deregulating its internal market. EMU was altogether different. The sense of a compromise among the 'big three' of the Community that underlay the Single European Act was absent in the case of EMU. For EMU confronted the British Conservative governments with an asymmetry: between the ambition for union and the parallel themes to neo-liberalism in 'Thatcherite' ideology – national identity and sovereignty. More practically, British influence was reduced by its absence from the ERM between April 1979 and October 1990, and then again after September 1992. And Britain's entry into the ERM coincided with the onset of the damage to its functioning from German unification: an experience that reduced rather than stimulated enthusiasm for EMU. When seen from the perspective of the EMS and EMU, the history of European integration looks very different from how it appears from the perspective of the Single European Act.

Implementation problems

The final characteristic of the EMU policy process to emerge is the nature of its problems of implementation. It became rapidly clear that these problems were not simply little local difficulties. They were above all structural problems that went to the heart of the union project. The Maastricht Treaty was part of these problems rather than a framework within which to solve them. These problems – of political legitimacy and of international economic competitiveness – raised fundamental questions about the EC policy process and the nature of the economic ideas that it had 'constitutionalized'. We shall need to return to these questions in the conclusion.

Part Two
THEORETICAL PERSPECTIVES

Chapter 6

PUTTING THE EMS AND EMU INTO PRACTICE (1)

The 'rules of the game', the 'two-level' policy process and the structural power of the 'anchor' currency

It is in public institutions that men express their will to control events, and therefore it seems to me that historians will go wrong if they try to resolve political and constitutional history into other elements. . . . The history of institutions must in some sense be central.

> (Sir George Clark, Regius Professor of Modern History, Inaugural Lecture, University of Cambridge, 1944)

Beginning with this chapter there is a shift of approach to the study of European monetary integration. Earlier chapters have offered a narrative 'thickened' with analysis. The focus alters in this and succeeding chapters to a social scientific, expository approach: of analysis and explanation 'thickened' with narrative. With the shift of approach goes a change in the object of attention: from the strategies and tactics of key actors to the 'impersonal forces' and sources of structural power at work on the EMS and EMU policy process. Such forces may not be as immediately and clearly visible as the actors that strut the stage of policy. Yet they are no less important for that reason. Indeed the narrative account of earlier chapters has repeatedly drawn attention to their presence. It is now time to more precisely identify these 'impersonal forces' and sources of structural power, to analyse their nature and functioning, and to assess their significance. In the next two chapters the structural power of economic forces occupies centre stage: economic ideology, financial markets, economic fundamentals and trade interdependence. Here, the institutional arrangements of the EMS and EMU – the 'rules of the game' that they embody and their structures – are the focus of attention, and, secreted behind their operation, the structural power of the 'anchor' currency.

In chapters 3–5 a central question was who chooses the nature of the game and the rules by which it is played? We now turn to the significance of the 'rules of the game' in the EMS and EMU policy process. Institutions are important in a twofold sense: as a link to history, for they provide continuity between past, present and future, and as a link to policy, for policy choices and the nature of the European integration process are shaped by the past and the institutions that incorporate and represent that past. They are an essential component of the policy learning process, which (as we noted in earlier chapters) has been so indispensable a component of European integration and the EC policy process.

In addition, in looking at the role of institutions in structuring the EMS and EMU as policy process, we are reminded that monetary policy is pre-eminently a sector that combines a very high technical complexity with political and economic sensitivity: capable of being at one and the same time 'low' politics and 'high' politics, a field of professional judgement for central bank and finance ministry experts, and yet one whose outcomes can have enormous implications for electoral prospects and for output, employment and price stability. In remembering that the EMS and EMU are pre-eminently institutions we are sensitized to the way in which their technical character – their rules governing policy instruments and how they may be used – are embedded in political and cultural contexts. We are also reminded just how important their technical character is.

This chapter provides a case study of the role of institutional arrangements and the structural power of the anchor currency in structuring two key interdependent bargaining relations in the EMS and EMU policy process: Council bargaining, and bargaining between the EC and the central bankers. Accordingly, ECOFIN and the Committee of Central Bank Governors are the focus of our attention.

The EMS and EMU as systems of institutional regulation: why policy coordination, and why the primacy of monetary policy coordination?

In referring to the EMS and EMU as systems of institutional regulation, attention is being drawn first and foremost to the EC's rules of the game for economic and monetary policies: rules, for instance, about economic policy coordination (like mutual surveillance), about exchange-rate management (establishing and changing central currency rates, the nature and use of margins of fluctuation, and the kinds of policy instruments to be deployed), about convergence criteria in the transition to EMU and about fiscal deficits and the operations of the ESCB with EMU. Chapters 4 and 5 have illustrated the nature of the political bargains on which these rules have rested. In this chapter we ask just how important they are in practice, and how and why they have changed.

The rationale of institutions suggests their importance.[1] Rules are designed to provide incentives for certain kinds of behaviour: in the case of the EMS for behaviour that promotes 'monetary stability in Europe' (the Brussels Resolution of December 1978) and in the case of the ESCB behaviour consistent with the mandate 'to maintain price stability' (Article 105 of the Treaty on European Union of 1992). They also have the purpose of deterring behaviour: like the inability to engage in unilateral devaluation or revaluation within the ERM, or the constraints that EMU places on excessive fiscal deficits, thereby narrowing the room of national budgetary manoeuvre. Institutionalization of monetary policy coordination gives to the bargaining process a framework of rules that limit 'free riding' and tie down expectations. It makes coordination more effective because it is locked into a system that organizes reciprocal exchange of sacrifices for opportunities. In its absence, 'free riding' can more readily

---

1. During the 1980s institutions underwent a renaissance as a method of analysis in the social sciences. See, for instance, the influence of J. March and J. Olsen, 'The New Institutionalism: Organizational Factors in Political Life', *American Political Science Review* 78 (1984), pp. 734–49; R. Scott, 'The adolescence of institutional theory', *Administrative Science Quarterly* 32 (1987), pp. 493–511; P. Hall, *Governing the Economy: The Politics of State Intervention in Britain and France* (Oxford: Polity, 1986); D. North, *Institutions, Institutional Change and Economic Performance* (Cambridge: Cambridge University Press, 1990); S. Steinmo, K. Thelen and F. Longstreth (eds) *Structuring Politics: Historical Institutionalism in Comparative Analysis* (Cambridge: Cambridge University Press, 1992).

destroy policy cooperation. What made the EMS distinctively different from the Bretton Woods system was the fact that it was locked into the institutional framework of the EC and of the single European market. Its weakness remained that exit from the ERM, as by Britain and Italy in September 1992, was always an option.

At heart, the purpose of the EMS and of EMU is to modify the behaviour of national policy makers in the form of explicit constraints on the conduct of their fiscal and monetary policies. Their rules enforce mutuality, for, in principle, they apply to all participants. Thus each country in the ERM is obliged to defend the agreed margins of fluctuation. Mutuality does not, of course, imply symmetry. This point is crucial. In practice (as we have seen) the underlying inherent asymmetry of international monetary cooperation, based as it is on the stabilizing role of an anchor currency, means that the burden of adjustment is thrown on to the weak currency countries that are losing reserves rather than the strong currency countries with an injection of liquidity. Much of the history of the bargaining relations within the ERM, and earlier the 'snake', is a story of the tensions between mutuality and asymmetry.

Institutions are also important in defining the parameters of change in bargaining. As participants become socialized into the formal and informal rules of the system, they tend to develop a trained incapacity to think outside its frame of reference. Consequently, change takes on the typical form of incremental adjustment to the established rules. Once the rules are established, with all the heavy 'sunk costs' in putting them into place, they develop a momentum of their own. They shape the direction of bargaining, policy learning and institutional change. In effect, the institutional attributes of the EMS and EMU impart a self-reinforcing character to the European integration process.[2] Through the mechanism of entrenched institutional rules the legacy of specific events and power relations at a given time locks European integration into a particular path of development (as we saw in chapter 5).

As institutions the EMS and EMU represent interconnected webs of formal and informal rules. The technical complexity of the formal rules is perhaps the easiest aspect of their institutional character to comprehend. Here we are dealing with a hierarchy of rules: from the treaty provisions of the Treaty of Rome (notably Articles 2, 103, 104, 106 and 109), the Single European Act and the Treaty on European Union, through European Council conclusions and resolutions (like the Brussels Resolution of 1978, the Madrid Conclusions of 1989 and the Rome Conclusions of October 1990), to decisions of ECOFIN (notably those of 1964, 1974, 1990 and 1993) and agreements (like the Basle Agreement of 13 March 1979 and the Basle-Nyborg Agreement of 8 September 1987 concluded by the Committee of Central Bank Governors). These rules embody the bargaining strength of different actors in the context of the structural power of the anchor currency, and changes of these rules reflect the interests of those with significant bargaining power.

Informal rules are no less important in structuring bargaining relations. They are

2. On institutions as 'self-reinforcing mechanisms' and institutional change as characterized by 'path dependence' see D. North, *Institutions, Institutional Change and Economic Performance*, ch. 11. His ideas derive from W. Arthur, 'Self-Reinforcing Mechanisms in Economics', in P. Anderson, K. Arrow and D. Pines (eds) *The Economy as an Evolving Complex System* (Reading, Mass.: Addison-Wesley, 1988).

simply more elusive. They are represented by conventions and codes of behaviour that have evolved in the working of the EMS and EMU and that are rooted in the wider cultural fabric of the EC. The operation of the bargaining relations on which the EMS and EMU are based is deeply affected by inherited beliefs, values and attitudes about how policy actors should behave. Such informal rules are likely to be a factor of continuity, encapsulating the understandings of each other that actors have accumulated over time as they interact repeatedly on EC business in forums like the European Council, ECOFIN, the EC Monetary Committee and the Committee of Central Bank Governors. They evolve for different reasons.[3] Some informal rules are an extension and elaboration of formal rules to handle specific problems. Thus, after 1979 the members of the ERM delegated responsibility for a common policy towards the US dollar to the German Bundesbank. Others represent shared ideological preferences that generate internally enforced codes of conduct, for instance the use of the ERM as a rule to enforce domestic monetary discipline in order to attain price stability.

Unquestionably the best and most potent example of an informal rule as an extension or elaboration of formal rules is the 'anchor currency' rule. In the past, fixed exchange rate systems have tended to operate on the basis that one currency acts as the ultimately secure foundation of the system. All other currencies peg to the anchor; all, save the anchor, are free to change their exchange rates (the so-called N–1 problem). The EMS was no exception. As we saw in chapter 4, Giscard d'Estaing and Schmidt had originally planned that the ECU would function as the 'central point' of the EMS: an intention proclaimed at the Brussels summit. In practice, revealing the underlying asymmetry of the ERM, the Bundesbank subverted this rule. In the words of Karl-Otto Pöhl in 1991: 'The Bundesbank turned the original concept [of the EMS] on its head by making the strongest currency the yardstick for the system'.[4] The attributes of an anchor currency are well known. It is a dominant medium of exchange within the system; its country base possesses domestic money markets that are sufficiently liquid to cope with international capital flows; its manufacturers are recognized to have a leadership role in the market-place (so that the current account balance is important); and, above all, its policies, especially on inflation, must command credibility in the financial markets (not least by making the currency 'devaluation-proof'). Linked to the anchor currency rule is a set of expectations: that an anchor currency is never expected to be devalued against any other in the system; in turn derived from another expectation, that the inflation rate in the anchor country will be at least as low, taking a period of several years, as any other in the system. Otherwise, an excess of inflation will threaten or cause a devaluation, making the currency no longer a credible anchor. So, crucially, the operation of the EMS has been linked to certain important expectations about the behaviour of the Bundesbank and its capacity to control the development of the German economy.

The anchor currency rule has significant consequences for interest rate policy.

3. North, *Institutions, Institutional Change and Economic Performance*, ch. 5.
4. Speech in St Paul's Church, Frankfurt, on 27 August 1991. Interestingly, Pöhl had originally written: 'That the ECU stands as the central point of the system has more than symbolic importance. Long term, this can lead to wide-ranging consequences . . . ' in 'Neuer Anlauf für Europa', *Weltwoche*, 6 June 1978.

Interest rates in the anchor country generally set the minimum rates for the whole system. Since the anchor currency country is never expected to opt for devaluation, it does not require a risk premium in its interest rates to encourage market operators to hold its currency. The risk premium has to be paid by other countries whose currencies (and monetary policies) lack the credibility of the anchor. Furthermore, the anchor currency country is free to set its interest rates solely according to the needs of its domestic economy. Under the 'new' EMS (as we shall see) the Bundesbank and other ERM central banks interpreted the anchor rule to mean that Germany should set interest rates to control its own domestic inflation, while all other states set their rates to maintain fixed parities with the anchor. Strictly interpreted in this way, the anchor currency rule could be used to justify the Bundesbank in setting interest rates in a selfish fashion, without regard for the economic conditions in other member states.

There are also informal rules that embody social norms, defining for instance the importance of reputation with one's colleagues in EC bodies, honesty and integrity in one's dealings, and mutual solidarity and support in the form of assisting the success of each other's presidencies of the Council or of avoiding a loss of influence over policy from one's specialist council to the European Council. The significance of such social norms has been enormous within the bargaining relations of EC policy sectors and is probably very underestimated. They have had a general effect on the functioning of the European Council and the Council of Ministers. In the case of central bankers the norms of honesty and integrity take on a particularly magical quality. They help to explain the degree of solidarity that has become so typical of the Committee of Central Bank Governors and the EC Monetary Committee.

More generally, such rules of the game have evolved to facilitate a convergence of national interests with a more supranational policy style in bargaining relations. At the heart of this process has been the role of national self-interest and of a learning process about how national self-interest is best promoted within the institutional context of the EC. On the one hand, there are the national interests of each successive presidency in being seen to run an impartial presidency that can distinguish between national interest and Community interest; and in being effective in securing agreements, creating in turn a pressure for decision-making deadlines. The result is a set of informal rules that emphasize the importance of an impartial presidency and a productive presidency. On the other hand, member states are part of a learning process as the presidency rotates. As a consequence, respect for these informal rules is regularly reinforced and diffused.

Institutions like the EMS and EMU are based on the will and capability of a given set of actors, in this case principally finance ministries and central banks, to cooperate and to coordinate their policies. The will to coordinate economic and monetary policies at the EC level (or, for that matter, in G-7) is built around three considerations. First, there is the incentive to reduce transaction costs, the costs of making and enforcing effective policies – the counterpart of friction in economic and monetary policies. An aim of policy coordination is to improve the quality of the information on which policies are based and to ensure that specific economic and monetary policies can be enforced more effectively. In a situation of interdependence among policy makers, with each affected by the behaviour of others, the problem of incomplete and uncertain information can be effectively addressed only by some measure of institutional regulation. For this reason, theorists of the 'new institutional economics' argue that the search for institutional regulation is a response to the 'bounded' rationality of actors: to the fact that economic and monetary policy makers are intendedly rational but only limitedly so.[5] Institutions are a means of transcending the constraints that limited cognitive competence places on policy. A further rationale for institutional regulation is the desire to erect safeguards against the hazards created by the incentives to opportunistic, 'beggar-my-neighbour' policies in the absence of institutional regulation: represented, for instance, by 'competitive devaluations'. Institutions are a means of achieving credible commitments and minimizing evasion of collective responsibilities. They give expression to the value placed on certainty in bargaining relationships.

In the language of the new institutional economics, the EMS and EMU represent mechanisms to organize transactions so as to economize on 'bounded' rationality, whilst simultaneously safeguarding against the hazards of opportunism. In this perspective there is clearly a strong emphasis on the role of utilitarian calculation in generating and sustaining institutional regulation of bargaining. Such an emphasis accords with the narrative accounts of the EMS and EMU in previous chapters. But the new institutional economics is also at pains to point out that institutional regulation introduces new incentives into bargaining relations: incentives to dignified conduct, to place value on trust, honesty and reliability, and to care for one's reputation and that of others. Institutions introduce a new ethical component into policy calculations. In short, the EMS and EMU are not simply to be understood in terms of calculative self-interest. They bring new values and mores to bear on economic and monetary policy bargaining, additional to the content of their formal rules. The informal rules are (as we noted) at least as important.

A second factor behind the will for policy coordination is ideological conviction, the normative views that actors hold about how the world ought to be organized.[6] The promotion and acceptance of institutional regulation by the EC owes something to the notion that the relations among the states and people of Europe should be organized in a different, more cooperative manner so that a peace and prosperity that has eluded Europe in the past can be better realized in the present and future. Ideological conviction about the importance of European union has been linked to each of the main initiatives for economic and monetary cooperation and integration; at work is a spirit of altruism in bargaining relations. Altruism can be seen as another facet of utility maximization, but one in which actors gain utility from the well-being of others expressed in terms of justice and fairness. The result is that self-imposed standards of conduct come to play a role in bargaining relations in the EMS and EMU policy process. Later in the chapter we shall consider the influences of ideology on the EMS and EMU policy process.

Third, the will for policy coordination is rooted in what theorists of the new institutional economics term 'asset specificity'.[7] Asset specificity refers to the

5. Notably O. Williamson, *The Economic Institutions of Capitalism: Firms, Markets, Relational Contracting* (New York: The Free Press, 1985).
6. This point is emphasized in North, *Institutions, Institutional Change and Economic Performance*, pp. 20–2.
7. O. Williamson, *The Economic Institutions of Capitalism*, p. 53.

idiosyncratic attributes of a specific transaction, specifically whether these attributes involve a sense of identity between the actors involved in a given transaction and, correspondingly, a high value placed on continuity and the maintenance of close face-to-face contacts in their mutual relationships. In the case of monetary policy the will to create institutional regulation and deepen bargaining can be traced back to certain attributes of the sector:

1   the sense of a distinct, even unique professionalism among central bankers (a central banking culture that transcends national boundaries)[8]
2   a basic similarity of policy objective (in particular, an aversion to inflation) and a broad consensus about the factors that shape the behaviour of the economy
3   the absence of the complexity of political and constitutional obstacles to policy coordination to be found in economic policy, underlining the relatively simple structure of the sector and the essentially automatic nature of the implementation of monetary policy decisions
4   the view that the exchange rate is not simply another price like any other but, uniquely, the link between *all* prices quoted in the national currency and those quoted in other countries' currencies
5   the argument that, because exchange rates are very flexible whereas the prices of goods are sticky, changes in nominal exchange rates affect real rates and thus may impose heavy costs on the level and character of activity in the economy[9]
6   the thesis that pegging or fixing exchange rates offers an unusually effective rule for disciplining domestic monetary policy and purchasing credibility for that policy.[10]

Together, or individually, these points can be – and are – used to justify monetary policy coordination, and underline the reason why, within EMU, monetary policy coordination and, within monetary policy coordination, exchange-rate management (the ERM) have achieved primacy over economic policy coordination. Monetary policy coordination can be described as the preserve of a genuine 'policy community' whose actors share a common identity and interest. It is more than simply a 'network' of actors who recognize that, in relation to certain policy issues and problems, they are mutually dependent and must accordingly interact.[11] As we shall see next, however, the primacy of monetary policy coordination has to do with more than asset specificity. For factors of capability as much as of will have determined the dynamic way in which policy coordination has changed, in particular variations between economic policy coordination and monetary policy coordination within EMU and in policy coordination over time.

8.   W. Scammell, 'The Working of the Gold Standard', in B. Eichengreen (ed.) *The Gold Standard in Theory and History* (London: Methuen, 1985), pp. 103–20.
9.   P. Kenen, *Managing Exchange Rates* (London: Routledge, 1988), pp. 7–8 and 83–5.
10. F. Giavazzi and M. Pagano, 'The Advantages of Tying One's Hands: EMS Discipline and Central Bank Credibility', Discussion Paper no. 235 (London: Centre for Economic Policy Research, 1986).
11. On the distinction between 'policy community' and 'policy network' see M. Wright, 'Policy Community, Policy Network and Comparative Industrial Policies', *Political Studies* 36 (1988), pp. 593–612.

In analysing the EMS and EMU as systems of institutional regulation, it is important to bear in mind a distinction between two kinds of rules for policy coordination.[12] On the one hand, there are rules for 'policy optimizing' in a context where increasing economic interdependence means that the effectiveness of one country's economic and monetary policies is undermined by the impact of other countries' policies.[13] The economic and monetary policies pursued by one country create spillover effects on other countries. An example would be the impact of a large unilateral shift in fiscal policy or exchange-rate policy by another country. In such a context national economic and monetary policies are likely to be suboptimal. The best prospect for optimizing national policies lies in coordination. Then each actor is given greater foreknowledge of what other actors plan to do, thereby better informing national policy decisions, and an opportunity is opened for more mutual influence in policy making. Institutional regulation helps to internalize the effects of economic interdependence.

On the other hand, there are rules for the pursuit of shared goals: for instance, of exchange-rate stability as a public good (the ERM) or of price stability as a public good (the Treaty on European Union).[14] Typically, behind these commitments to shared goals is the experience of actors with past economic and political shocks: in the case of the EMS, the shock of the collapse of the dollar in 1977–8; in the case of EMU, the memories of the huge costs of inflation and the role of misbehaviour by governments in increasing these costs. Whereas rules for 'policy optimizing' behaviour are essentially procedural, spelling out new means of coordination, rules for achieving a public good involve substantive agreement about what should be done in common. They are, at least in theory, less vulnerable to the hazards of opportunism as actors seek to impose the maximum costs of cooperation on others and maximize the benefits for themselves.

As we shall see, rules for policy optimizing are the defining characteristic of economic policy coordination in the EC. The introduction of the first medium-term economic policy programme in 1967 did not in fact lead on to a commitment to shared goals. By contrast, the notion of a shared commitment to specific public goods as the basis for coordinated action found a more ready reception in EC monetary policy coordination. We have already noted the reasons for this asymmetry in the development of economic and monetary policy coordination. What we can note for now is that the different character of the system of institutional regulation in the two areas was likely to have important implications for the effectiveness of policy coordination.

Though we have established that in principle the rules of the game are very

12. For this distinction see Kenen, *Managing Exchange Rates*, pp. 75–7.
13. On the 'policy-optimizing' approach to coordination see B. Eichengreen, 'International Policy Coordination in Historical Perspective', in W. Buiter and R. Marston (eds) *International Economic Policy Coordination* (Cambridge: Cambridge University Press, 1985).
14. On the 'regime-preserving' or 'public-goods' approach to coordination see R. Cooper, 'Economic Interdependence and Coordination of Economic Policies', in R. Jones and P. Kenen (eds) *Handbook of International Economics* (Amsterdam: North Holland, 1985), vol. 2; Kenen, *Managing Exchange Rates*, ch. 6.

important indeed, we are left with two interrelated questions. First, just how much do the rules of the EMS and EMU matter in practice; have they been effectively enforced? Second, how do the actors involved in the EMS and EMU actually treat these rules: do they abide by them or avoid and evade them with impunity? The questions are interrelated, for, in answering the second question, we are providing a substantial part of the answer to the first. The argument of this chapter is that the capacity of the Bundesbank to provide effective leadership by the anchor currency country is critical to the effective enforcement of the rules of the game of the EMS and EMU; that, correspondingly, the rules of the game must reflect its interests as a policy actor; and that that capacity for rule enforcement and the way that the actors involved treat the rules are a function of two factors – whether their ideological dispositions and self-interests accord with the EMS and EMU as institutions, and whether changing political and economic conditions, notably in the financial markets, reinforce or undermine those ideological dispositions and the capacity to make the rules effective. Rule enforcement is most effective when political and economic conditions and ideological convictions and self-interests are supportive of the policy goals that the EMS and EMU embody and hence of the use of the associated policy instruments – like interest rate policy and intervention – in a coherent and consequent manner.

Do the rules of the game matter? Financial markets and the 'two-level' policy process

The central argument of this chapter is that the rules of the game matter but that they occupy a complex and changing relationship to three phenomena that deeply influence the effectiveness of their functioning. These phenomena are first, the extent to which the economies of member states face similar or different trends and problems (in other words, the issues of economic fundamentals and convergence); second, the financial market forces that impinge on the functioning of the EMS and progress towards EMU; and third, the nature of the 'two-level' policy process in which these systems of institutional regulation are embedded. Ultimately, the character of the EMS and EMU as systems of institutional regulation and bargaining is not separable from these three phenomena. The EMS and EMU live in a constant and changing state of cooperation, tension and conflict with them. Only by recognizing these relationships and building them into analysis can one properly appreciate the fundamentally dynamic nature of change in European monetary integration.

And yet, in emphasizing economic convergence, financial markets and the two-level policy process, one should not lose sight of the pressures on actors that derive from their immersion in these systems of institutional regulation – pressures that induce policy coordination and that involve standards by which the behaviour of individual actors can be appraised by their peers. Through the EMS and EMU ideological motivations to cooperate are given expression, whether a normative view of the importance of European union or of the need for cooperation in order to more effectively secure price stability. In the case of the EMS cooperation is valued as a means of reducing the costs of exchange-rate volatility and as a mechanism to enforce monetary policy discipline; EMU is viewed by its advocates as a more effective institution for reducing these costs and enforcing discipline. In the process, reputation, trust and concern for the behaviour and experiences of others come to loom larger in the utility function of the actors involved. Correspondingly, ECOFIN and the two main technical committees – the EC Monetary Committee and the Committee of Central Bank Governors – can be seen as embodying a degree of altruism in which individual actors (finance ministry officials and central bankers) gain some measure of utility from the well-being of their peers. As institutions the EMS and EMU are monuments to the importance that a body of EC actors profess to attach to specific values.

Of course, how the EMS and EMU develop is shaped by the relative bargaining power of different actors in the two-level policy process, notably their monetary power and domestic policy reputation – factors that point to the primacy of the Bundesbank and its values and interests. Bargaining outcomes are in turn deeply influenced by the health of the economic fundamentals of different EC economies, by the degree of convergence of economies, by the assessments of financial markets as well as by the functioning of the two-level policy process in which the EMS and EMU are embedded. Ideology, as it is affected by the policy outcomes attributed to the EMS and EMU, can act as a key source of institutional change once, for instance, the costs of lost output and employment at the national level come to be seen as outweighing the benefits of the EMS or EMU. In that case institutional change ceases to be incremental; it can mean either challenging the existing terms of cooperation (for instance, arguing that the EMS is too asymmetrical in its functioning) or even challenging policy cooperation *per se*.

The implications of the way in which the EMS and EMU are embedded in the operation of impersonal forces like financial markets and processes of economic convergence or divergence are essentially a theme for chapter 8. Here we simply need to note that, fundamentally, the effectiveness of the rules of the game depends on the bargaining relations between the EC monetary authorities and the foreign exchange markets. The behaviour of operators in financial markets derives its character from the experience of being part of an intensely fast-changing competitive market, in which choice is more likely to be governed by incentives and pressures to maximize wealth, or at least to achieve a satisfactory outcome that can be justified to the owners of capital: whether one is operating on a corporate account or for clients. It can be taken as axiomatic that relative price changes, for instance in the US dollar/D-Mark rate or in interest rates, will affect preference for holding one currency rather than another; they alter the incentives of market traders and, in the monetary policy sector, are arguably the most potent source of institutional change (for instance, in 1987 and 1992–3). As was argued above, changes in relative prices can help trigger ideological changes with major implications for the functioning and development of the EMS and EMU.

Attention to financial markets reminds us that utilitarian calculations of rational self-interest impact directly on the EMS and EMU. Institutional change and market pressures may operate in a broadly single and coherent direction, as they did so notably from 1987 to 1992. Yet they can also come into sharp conflict, bringing the very different rationales of institutional regulation and the market into a sharper focus. At that point, the way in which the EMS and EMU develop is determined by the relative benefits and costs that they present to their central actors. Do the costs of intervention to support parities come to outweigh the benefits of the system in its existing form? Are the costs in foregone output and employment too high a price to pay for expressing a positive valuation of European union? In short, when the price of institutional regulation in the form of the EMS or EMU is low, European integration will loom larger in the choices of governments and central bankers. When and as that price rises, as in 1992–3, European integration is likely to account for less of the behaviour of the main actors involved.

The functioning of the rules of the game underpinning the EMS and EMU is also deeply affected by the complex relationships of cooperation, tension and conflict that are engendered by the two-level nature of economic and monetary policy processes within the EC. In effect, two levels of policy coordination have to be reconciled, each with a different character and associated with different expectations and obligations. As policy actors are embedded in both levels, that of the EC and that of national policy making, they have an incentive to seek to reconcile these two sets of expectations and obligations. They may, however, find it difficult to do so, and the tensions and conflict involved can be intense, as for the British government over entry into, and exit from, the ERM and over the deeply divisive debate about ratification of the Treaty on European Union in 1992–3.

The nature of compliance with the requirements of economic and monetary coordination at the EC level is governed by two characteristics of the EC level of policy making and implementation. First, formal third-party enforcement has been absent in the case of the EMS, whether in the form of the EC Commission or the European Court of Justice. Its absence has reflected a lack of trust, for it is clear that enforcement would be undertaken by agents whose own utility functions come to influence outcomes and whose own costs rise with an accretion of functions. But lack of third-party enforcement will in turn be likely to diminish trust and confidence in the application of agreements. In such a context actors find it easier to justify evasion and avoidance of rules. The efficacy of the EMS as a system of institutional regulation could, as a consequence, be expected to suffer. This point underlines the inherent fragility of the EMS short of full EMU.

But, in the absence of third-party enforcement, cooperation and compliance have been facilitated by a second factor: that the European Council, ECOFIN and its technical committees represent repeated or 'iterated' games in which the possibility of cooperation among the participants in making their choices is much more evident than in 'one-off' games.[15] In one-off games, or games with a finite duration of time, the strategy of participants is affected by the continuing incentive to defect; the calculation is that one can enjoy the public good created by the cooperative activities of others without incurring the costs of participation.[16] Where a game of cooperation is continued indefinitely among the same players, as in the institutional framework of the EC, it will tend to pay the participants to live up to the terms of agreements, because the gains accruing over repeated games exceed the benefits that could be derived from a single defection. In such a context, if the gain from cooperation and compliance in a specific case is very small, it may actually prove preferable to cooperate and comply even though the gain from defection could actually be higher.

15. R. Axelrod, *The Evolution of Cooperation* (New York: Basic Books, 1984).
16. M. Olson, *The Logic of Collective Action* (Cambridge: Cambridge University Press, 1965).

Also, in repeated games reputation, integrity and trust become valuable assets in bargaining. They evolve as part of an unwritten constitution that guides the behaviour of the actors towards each other and sets broad limits to that behaviour. Again, in a context of iterated games involving a great diversity of national, political and economic interests, consensus takes on a greater practical value than the simple majority as a rule of the game.[17] To lose credibility as a committed participant by offending against these rules of the game is to forfeit bargaining strength. Hence, in the EMS, self-enforcement via ECOFIN and the two main technical committees has played a more significant part than third-party enforcement. It has depended on the capacity of participants to become well informed about each other's behaviour through these institutional structures, for instance via mutual surveillance, and thus able to monitor and police enforcement. With the provisions of the Treaty on European Union the capacity for monitoring and policing enforcement is reinforced, notably in relation to excessive budget deficits. Yet discretion continues to lie very much with the national governments to self-enforce agreements. In such circumstances, the strategy of the EC Commission is to seek to build up trust and a sense of collective 'ownership' of agreements within ECOFIN and the twin committees.

The dynamic imparted to cooperation and compliance by the endlessly repeated nature of gamesmanlike behaviour at the EC level has undoubtedly been important. Its importance has rested not least in the way that it has undermined the claims of either intergovernmentalism or supranationalism to offer adequate explanations of European integration. According to the one theory, European integration rests on inter-governmental bargains, based on the lowest common denominator of interests and strictly delimited sharing or pooling of sovereignty. Its dynamic is essentially provided by domestic political interests and calculations.[18] According to the other theory, integration derives its dynamics from 'a cumulative pattern of accommodation in which the participants refrain from unconditionally vetoing proposals and instead seek to attain agreement by means of compromises upgrading common interests'.[19] Leadership derives from institutions, like the Commission, that stand 'above' national govern- ments. Another variant of this theory – cooperative federalism – argues that European integration has been characterized by the 'pooling' and mixing of national sovereignty with Community powers so that both levels lose any clear separation between them.[20] Neither type of explanation offers a satisfactory account of the

17. North, *Institutions, Institutional Change and Economic Performance*, pp. 47–53.
18. For an up-to-date presentation of this approach see A. Moravcsik, 'Negotiating the Single European Act', in R. Keohane and S. Hoffmann (eds) *The New European Community: Decision Making and Institutional Change* (Boulder, Colo.: Westview Press, 1991), pp. 41–84. As applied to the EMS and EMU see M. Kaelberer, 'Werner Report, EMS and EMU: Problems and Prospects of European Monetary Cooperation', paper delivered to the Third Biennial International Conference of the European Community Studies Association, Washington, DC, 27–29 May 1993.
19. E. Haas, 'Technocracy, Pluralism and the New Europe', in S. Graubard (ed.) *A New Europe?* (Boston, Mass.: Houghton Mifflin, 1964), pp. 64–6.
20. See, for example, S. Bulmer and W. Wessels, *The European Council: Decision-Making in European Politics* (London: Macmillan, 1987), p. 10. On the role of the Council presidency, see E. Kirchner, *Decision-making in the European Community* (Manchester: Manchester University Press, 1992); G. de Bassompierre, *Changing the Guard in Brussels: An Insider's View of the EC Presidency* (New York: Praeger, 1988).

integration process that we have studied in the last few chapters; neither captures the subtle process of change at work as well as the insights from game theory. These insights underline just how much the framework of national governmental action has been altered by the rigours of intensive and repeated gamesmanship at the EC level. As a consequence, benefits and costs of cooperation have had to be reassessed on a utilitarian basis.

And yet the domestic sources of policy remain far more important than the theory of supranationalism or of cooperative federalism allows. That other level – the national – is potent, whether in reinforcing integration or thwarting its progress. For the domestic context provides the primary reference point for the national politicians and officials that make up ECOFIN and its technical committees, and of course for the heads of state and government meeting in the European Council. At the heart of this primacy to the national level is the fact that the electoral and parliamentary legitimacy of government continues to rest there. Governments are forced to consider the balance of parliamentary support for their European policies, especially when they find themselves dependent upon coalition support. Thus we have seen how President Giscard d'Estaing was frustrated by the need to share power with a Gaullist party that did not share his own enthusiasm for EMU. Above all, national elections hold the key to power – the answer to the question of who sits in the European Council and in ECOFIN. National electoral costs and benefits are never far from the mind of the politician, whose job it is to win votes: and, with twelve national governments, there is regularly an impending election to alter the centre of gravity of political behaviour in Council bargaining. Consideration of the French National Assembly elections of 1978 affected the timing of the EMS initiative: whilst a different outcome might have led to its abandonment before the idea was formally launched. Similarly, Chancellor Kohl's attitude to EMU at the Rome summit in October 1990 was influenced by the impending first all-German federal elections and concern about the implications of the mounting costs of German unification.

The problem for theories of European integration is that there is not a single, simple relationship between the two levels of action that comprise the integration process. How that relationship operates in one policy sector or over one issue may not be replicated in another; over time, the relationship can take on very different characteristics in the same sector or over the same issue. Rather than a universal characteristic to the two-level policy process, one finds a variety of states and, moreover, states that are often unstable, temporary and contingent – a point to which we return in chapter 9. As we have noted, the complex dynamics that underpin the EMS and EMU mean that the two-level policy process can shift rapidly from a condition of mutual support to a condition of tension or of bitter conflict and mutual recrimination. One has only to compare the solidarity within ECOFIN of early 1992 with the acrimony and ill-will that took over by September, culminating in the exit of the British pound and the Italian lira from the ERM, or with the poisonous atmosphere in which ECOFIN met in August 1993 to reform the ERM so that it could continue to survive the onslaughts of the foreign exchange markets. The theory of cooperative federalism is wrong in arguing that the EC has involved the loss of any clear separation of the two levels. The argument runs ahead of the evidence which can offer partial but not full support. On some policy issues at some times it seems notable just how much the scope for discretion of both levels has been restricted; the two levels appear to be interlocked.[21] Where domestic and market dynamics enable the characteristics of cooperative federalism to take hold, the impact can be profound. Such was the experience of the relaunch of EMU between 1988 and 1992. In putting together the EMU project, ECOFIN and the two main technical committees achieved an unprecedented degree of mutual solidarity and self-confidence.

But, despite the institutional arrangements of the EMS, one can still justifiably speak of the importance of *state* economic and monetary policies. National governments continue to retain a broad scope for their own discretionary action to mark them as centres of substantial economic and monetary policy making. This is not to argue that the conditions for realizing national governmental priorities were always or equally favourable. It is to note two things: that the potential constraints represented by participation in the institutional regulations of the EMS and EMU do not necessarily always translate into practical limitations; and that national governments are keenly aware of their scope for discretionary action and prepared to make full use of it within the operation of the EMS or EMU. By changes to the rules of the game in August 1993 they succeeded in broadening that discretion.

If the impact of EC-level institutional regulation was one side of the coin of integration, the other was the continuing resilience of national actors' attachment to, and concern for, the domestic level. An example was provided when sterling's 'divergence indicator' went through its lower limit in late August 1992. This flashing red signal was ignored by the British government in the weeks before 16 September. It is also useful to note the way in which sharp rises in very-short-term interest rates helped the Banque de France to win the 'battle of the franc' during the September 1992 crisis. This policy instrument was effective because, in French institutional conditions unlike in British, the authorities were able to insulate the domestic economy by invoking a domestic rule of the game to stop the commercial banks from passing on rate increases to commercial and personal borrowers. The means for doing so were provided by the five- to ten-day repurchase rate, the rate at which commercial banks borrow short-term money from the Banque de France as a last resort, similar to the Bundesbank's Lombard rate. By increasing the repurchase rate the Banque de France could push up money market rates without triggering an increase in the commercial banks' base rates. In the process, the costs were borne by the commercial banks.

An expression of the continuing vitality of the member states in the EMS and EMU policy process is that the rules of the game at the domestic level remain important and vary in significant ways from country to country. Thus the Bundesbank can make life a bit harder for the speculator than can the Bank of England. It insists that banks selling foreign currency to it must have collateral in the form of securities on deposit with Germany's state (*Land*) central banks. These securities are the 'Lombard' which German banks can also use as collateral for obtaining emergency liquidity from the Bundesbank. When a bank sells a foreign currency to the Bundesbank, the transaction is counted against the Lombard to cover the settlement risk. This rule helps to slow down the process of speculation.

21. On 'cooperative federalism' as 'interlocking politics', in which similarities are explored between German federalism and the EC, see F. Scharpf, 'The Joint-Decision Trap: Lessons from German Federalism and European Integration', *Public Administration* 66 (1988), pp. 239–78. Also Kirchner, *Decision-making in the European Community*.

The rationale for limitations on international policy coordination has been formalized and most forcefully expressed by various economists, though more in the context of evaluating the G-7 and the value of policy coordination to the United States.[22] The essential elements of this rationale are as follows:

1   that policy coordination is based on unjustified assertions about the degree of interdependence among industrial economies, especially in the case of the United States, giving the false impression that sustained growth requires international policy coordination

2   that, in a world of sovereign states, governments have the right and the responsibility to pursue monetary and fiscal policies that they believe to be in their best interests (and should not seek to use policy coordination to abrogate their responsibility)

3   that it is a mistake to rely on other governments to assume their share of the burden of adjustment in a framework of institutionalized policy coordination because it is unrealistic to expect them to take domestic policy action inconsistent with their perception of what is needed to maintain their own sustainable growth

4   that international policy coordination can diminish the credibility of central banks vis-à-vis market operators by providing new incentives for them to renege on counter-inflationary strategy

5   that competition between governments is preferable to 'cartel-like collusion' for it optimizes policies by rewarding those governments that attract internationally mobile factors of production by 'supply-side' measures and forcing others to adjust in order to halt the drain of economic activity[23]

6   that flexible exchange rates are an important policy instrument for adjustment and that coordination based on fixed rates imposes policies on individual countries that are not sustainable in the long term

7   that, in a fixed exchange-rate regime, capital mobility will equalize nominal interest rates so that, in a high inflation country, real interest rates will be lower, prompting an unwanted expansion, and hence tending to raise inflation differentials and divergence of real exchange rates. In other words, coordination in fixed rate regimes like the ERM is not, according to Walters, the best means to tackle inflation; it is doomed to fail.[24]

As we have seen from the above analysis of policy coordination in the EC, particularly of the behavioural consequences of repeated bargaining in a formal institutional

22.   M. Feldstein, 'The End of Policy Coordination', *The Wall Street Journal*, 9 November 1987; S. Fischer, 'Macroeconomic Policy', in M. Feldstein (ed.) *International Economic Policy Cooperation* (Chicago: Chicago University Press, 1988); R. Dornbusch, 'Doubts about the McKinnon Standard', *Journal of Economic Perspectives* 1 (1988); P. Krugman, 'Louvre's Lesson – Let the Dollar Fall', *The International Economy*, January/February 1988.

23.   R. Vaudel, 'Coordination or Competition among Macroeconomic Policies?', in F. Machlup *et al.* (eds) *Reflections on a Troubled World Economy: Essays in Honour of Herbert Giersch* (London, 1983), pp. 3–28; R. Vaudel, 'International Collusion or Competition for Macroeconomic Policy Coordination? A Restatement', *Recherches Economiques de Louvain* 51 (1985), pp. 223–40.

24.   A. Walters, *Britain's Economic Renaissance* (Oxford: Oxford University Press, 1986).

context, the 'realism' of much of this rationale is myopic. Its strength is that it does appreciate the continuing focus of loyalty and commitment to the state, and that it brings out the element of voluntarism that guides the approach of governments and central bankers and the disincentives to cooperation that they face. Also, some aspects of the rationale against policy coordination are persuasive: for instance, the rationale for policy competition and the so-called 'Walters effect'. But the rationale for policy competition only underlines the case for 'subsidiarity' in economic and monetary policies; the point that coordination destroys monetary discipline only reinforces the importance of central bank independence to support the credibility of counter-inflationary strategy; and the argument that a 'Walters effect' is at work may only confirm how unstable monetary policy coordination in the EMS is short of EMU and strengthen the case for a faster move to EMU. The real problem with the rationale against policy coordination is that it is better tuned to the limitations of the G-7 process; it fails to come to grips with the specific institutional nuances of the EC, and not least to the underlying structural dynamics of the single European market and close trade interdependence.

The rules of the game in economic policy coordination: the context of bargaining in ECOFIN

For reasons that have been outlined in a previous section, policy coordination has been less strongly developed in the field of economic policy than in monetary policy. Judged against the principle of parallelism propounded in the Werner Report, and against those 'economists' who argue that economic convergence must precede monetary union, this imbalance in progress towards EMU is a cause of disappointment and concern. If the Treaty on European Union has brought nearer the achievement of the Werner Report's 'Community system for the central banks', there is but a muffled echo of the report's proposal for the 'centre of decision for economic policy' with its responsibility to the European Parliament.[25] Indeed, it can be argued that economic policy coordination has been achieved less via the institutional mechanisms of economic policy coordination than by the *ad hoc* process of adjustment of national economic policies to meet the requirements imposed by realignments within the ERM. Thus, following devaluations within the ERM in 1982 and 1983 respectively, the Belgian and Italian governments began the process of dismantling wage indexation (termed the *Scala Mobile* in Italy). But, though policy convergence has been promoted through the indirect route of monetary integration, economic policy coordination remains an underdeveloped area.

Historical background

Historically, perhaps the most important characteristic of economic policy coordination within the EC has been the preoccupation with developing and refining rules of

25. Council-Commission of the EC, *Report to the Council and the Commission on the Realisation by Stages of Economic and Monetary Union in the Community – 'Werner Report'*, Supplement to Bulletin 11-1970 (Brussels, 1970).

procedure. Prior to the Treaty on European Union, the EC had not succeeded in establishing one or more policy goals to guide economic policy coordination, let alone agreeing the appropriate economic policy instruments that governments should use and the way in which they should be used. Again, indirectly, other EC initiatives have been important in bringing some measure of coordination. For instance, the single European market programme contained a commitment to harmonize indirect taxation (value-added tax and excise duties) and, in establishing freedom of capital movement, it denied to future governments resort to the policy instrument of exchange controls.

But the problem has not simply been that the search for agreed policy goals has proved elusive. The search has never been allowed to become too intensive. Beyond the indirect impacts of the EMS and the single market programme, it can be argued that the Treaty on European Union constituted only a limited breakthrough to a new level of economic policy coordination. Again, change took an indirect route. The treaty's provisions represented an attempt to agree a minimum level of economic policy coordination consistent with the requirements of a monetary union. In other words, the new provisions for economic policy coordination were essentially a by-product of the activities of the actors involved in promoting monetary union.

As we saw in chapter 3, Articles 103 and 104 of the Treaty of Rome created a constitutional basis for economic policy coordination. According to Article 103, short-term economic policy was a matter of common interest and, therefore, should be subject to mutual consultation. To achieve the economic objectives spelt out in Article 104, member states are asked to coordinate their economic policies. In practice, it has taken either economic crisis (as in 1963–4, 1968–9 and 1973–4) or the commitment to transform the EMS into EMU (as in 1970–1 and 1989–90) to force governments to attend to developing institutional regulation of economic policy coordination.

In the wake of the crisis precipitated by Italy's serious balance-of-payments' crisis of 1963, and not least the irritation at the Bank of Italy's preference for seeking support from the IMF rather than the EEC, ECOFIN decided to put new procedures for coordination in place. They included a Medium-Term Economic Policy Committee, with the task of preparing the first medium-term EEC economic policy programme (the first appeared in February 1967); a Budgetary Policy Committee comprising senior officials from national finance ministries and Commission officials; the Committee of Central Bank Governors; and a recommendation on anti-inflation measures that included, for the first time, a quantitative upper limit (of 5 per cent) on annual public expenditure growth. In 1966 ECOFIN adopted, as recommendations, guidelines for short-term economic policy. In practice, the medium-term economic policy programmes were to remain little more than a compilation of national forecasts provided by the national governments, imperfect in their overall consistency; and the guidelines were lacking in any precision about measures to be adopted, in effect more like declarations of intent.

Again, the crises of 1968–9 facilitated the implementation of much of the Barre Plan. In 1969 ECOFIN agreed that the system of prior consultation should be extended to every economic policy measure that could be considered as having an effect on the economies of other member states or endangering the internal or external balance of the country concerned. In such cases the right to ask for consultations rested with either a member state government or the EEC Commission. Once more, the limitation of such commitments was speedily underlined. In August the French franc was devalued, and in October the German mark revalued, without any prior consultation.

The commitment to give some content to stage one of the Werner Report was the central factor behind the ECOFIN decisions of 22 March 1971: one strengthening collaboration among the central banks (considered in the next section) and the other on coordination of short-term economic policies. In effect, they completed the implementation of the rest of the Barre Plan (see chapter 4). Thereafter, ECOFIN met three times a year, adopted common guidelines for economic policy and – in March 1972 – instituted the Steering Committee to pull together the work of the technical committees. Behind these decisions was a confidence in the important role that fiscal fine-tuning could play in economic stabilization, a confidence that was widely shared within the OECD. In practice, however, the economic policy guidelines were extremely vague. The EEC anti-inflation programmes of 1972 and 1973 were strong on intent but weak on any specifics about what was to be done and on detailed commitments from governments.[26]

Behind the ECOFIN decision of February 1974 on 'the attainment of a higher degree of convergence of economic policies' was a complex of pressures: the search to give some sort of content to stage two of EMU and a recognition of the inadequacy of the rules adopted in 1971; the disruptive effects of the inflationary and balance-of-payments' difficulties unleashed by the oil crisis; and irritation with the behaviour of a member state government, in this case the Netherlands, which had revalued the guilder in September 1973 without proper prior consultations with its EC partners. Prior consultations were henceforth made obligatory on changes of parity, central rates or intervention points of any EC currency; ECOFIN was to meet monthly; and an Economic Policy Committee was to replace the three committees dealing with budgetary policy, short-term economic policy and medium-term economic policy.

Two points are striking about the functioning of the institutional structure. It is noticeable that the Economic Policy Committee, and its predecessors, did not develop the sense of shared purpose and identity that was established in the EC Monetary Committee or the Committee of Central Bank Governors.[27] The policy issues and problems were much more variable. Correspondingly, membership changed with the issue or problem at hand, and no enduring personal rapport or sense of continuity and shared experience evolved. Its profile was low both in the launch of the EMS and in the relaunch of EMU, certainly lower than that of the two other committees. As we noted in chapter 5, the convergence criteria were worked out within the EC Monetary Committee, whose prestige was furthered by the overlap between its membership and that of the IGC on EMU.

Also, ECOFIN had tended to meet only once a year in the 1960s. In 1970 one meeting of ECOFIN contrasted with fifteen meetings of the Agriculture Council and twelve of the General and Foreign Affairs Council. In that year there had been more meetings of the Labour and Social Affairs Council and the Transport Council (three each). It is hardly surprising then that solidarity and a rich texture of informal rules

26. L. Tsoukalis, *The Politics and Economics of European Monetary Integration* (London: George Allen & Unwin, 1977), pp. 137–42.
27. P. Ludlow, *The Making of the European Monetary System* (London: Butterworth, 1982), pp. 15–16.

had failed to evolve. By 1975, however, the number of ECOFIN meetings had risen to eight. Thereafter, it was to remain the third most important Council, measured by the number of annual meetings, after agriculture and foreign affairs.

The judgement of the Marjolin Report of 1975 on the continuing failure of the machinery for economic policy coordination stands as definitive:

> Each national policy is seeking to solve problems and to overcome difficulties which arise in each individual country, without reference to Europe as an entity. The diagnosis is at national level; efforts are made at national level. The coordination of national policies is a pious wish which is hardly ever achieved in practice.[28]

ECOFIN and EMU

The launch of the EMS in 1978–9 and the relaunch of EMU from 1988 onwards did in fact represent new departures in economic policy coordination, albeit in different ways. Both reinforced the managerial responsibilities of ECOFIN; and both intensified cooperation and the role of peer-group pressure. With the EMS, collaboration in exchange-rate management had the indirect affect of drawing ECOFIN and the EC Monetary Committee into deliberation on the economic policy measures to accompany currency realignments. With the launch of EMU, for the first time changes in rules of procedure were firmly severed from a context of crisis and mutual recriminations, of the kind seen in 1963–4, 1968–9 and 1973–4.

Also, and arguably more important, the Treaty on European Union was preceded by an evolution of the informal rules underpinning the operation of ECOFIN. EMU's relaunch was in part a story of an increasing concentration of a sense of mutual responsibility and accommodation within ECOFIN. As the negotiations proceeded, a greater sense of collective identity emerged. This new sense of responsibility and solidarity was reinforced by the mandate given to ECOFIN by the Madrid summit of 1989; in July 1990 stage one of EMU was to commence. The informal ECOFIN at Ashford Castle in March 1990 served as a barometer of this process of change. In effect, the ECOFIN decisions of March 1990 on strengthening the coordination procedures anticipated some of the content of the Treaty on European Union. Central to these decisions was the introduction of multilateral surveillance as a new procedure in the work of ECOFIN in stage one.

After the Madrid summit the factor of anticipation of treaty change was a new ingredient in the development of the work of ECOFIN. It found its expression in the two main areas of provision of new rules for economic policy coordination in the Treaty on European Union: multilateral surveillance (Article 103) and the 'excessive deficit' procedure (Article 104c and the Protocol on the excessive deficit procedure). Under the multilateral surveillance procedure member states were required to forward information about important economic policy measures to the EC Commission: the Commission was in turn to submit reports to ECOFIN on the performance of each member state so that 'sustained convergence' and consistency with the 'broad guidelines of the economic policies of the member states and the Community' could

---

28. R. Marjolin *et al.*, *Report of the Study Group Economic and Monetary Union 1980* (Brussels: Commission of the European Communities, 1975).

be monitored; and ECOFIN could, by qualified majority, make recommendations to a member state and even make these public. In the treaty provision was made (Article 103.5) to tighten up the rules for multilateral surveillance; states not respecting the broad guidelines of economic policy to be established as legally binding for stage two will be subject to public recommendations from ECOFIN. Also (as we noted in chapter 5) member states are required by the Treaty on European Union to avoid excessive deficits. A protocol spelt out the substantive criteria on budget deficits and government debt that would form the basis for monitoring by ECOFIN. And, if public recommendations prove ineffective, ECOFIN may decide – by a two-thirds majority (excluding the votes of the member state concerned) – to impose a range of sanctions.

In 1991, when the IGC was still deliberating, the Luxembourg summit decided to adopt a procedure for considering country-specific 'convergence' programmes that would spell out measures intended to promote price stability and sound public finances. Along with multilateral surveillance, the procedure of convergence programmes was seen as an important new mechanism for making economic policy coordination more effective. Again two factors were at work: a recognition that stage one was already underway and had a clear termination date, and anticipation of treaty change. Also, convergence programmes had an important political rationale: they went some way to satisfy the concerns of Dutch and German negotiators at a delicate stage in the treaty-making process; and they offered to some governments, like those of Italy and Spain, an opportunity to use EC-approved targets as an external political discipline to justify unpopular economic policy measures at home. Article 109e.2 required that, before stage two began on 1 January 1994, each member state shall have had a multi-annual convergence programme assessed by ECOFIN. With multilateral surveillance and convergence programmes ECOFIN had, during stage one, strengthened its collective commitment to making economic policy coordination more effective as a component of EMU. The result was an increasingly strong rapport between ministers in ECOFIN and officials in the EC Monetary Committee. By 1992 each monthly ECOFIN session included two sessions devoted to reviewing specific convergence programmes.

One dynamic at work in ECOFIN is similar to that to be found in other specialist Councils: namely, that it is jealous of its prerogatives. Since the inception of the European Council meetings in 1974, it has had reason to be concerned at regular intervals about those prerogatives. For in pushing for the establishment of the European Council, President Valéry Giscard d'Estaing and Chancellor Helmut Schmidt were particularly concerned to have a mechanism for improved international economic policy coordination. Economic policy issues have had a habit of reappearing on the agenda of the European Council, most strikingly with the launch of the EMS and then the relaunch of EMU. ECOFIN has found that, as a specialist Council, it has not been able to enjoy the autonomy and sense of sovereignty over its own affairs possessed most notably by the Agriculture Council. It has reason to fear the European Council whose conclusions are binding for ECOFIN even if they do not reflect ECOFIN's views. The activism by the European Council, at Hanover, Madrid and later, helped to create an unusual pressure to agree within ECOFIN to protect its own corporate interests; if those interests were not identified and clarified at an early stage, ECOFIN could find itself with a worse outcome than if mutual agreement were prioritized.

Essentially, the members of ECOFIN could agree on the need to safeguard their autonomy in the EMU negotiations and to enhance their management responsibilities. Those aims were substantially achieved in the IGC. They also motivated opposition within ECOFIN to the proposals in the Delors's White Paper on Competitiveness, Growth and Employment of 1993 on part-financing the construction of European energy, telecommunications and transport networks by means of 'Union bonds', to be issued by the EC itself rather than through the European Investment Bank. In outflanking the EIB, itself an agent of ECOFIN, the Commission appeared to be acquiring power at the expense of ECOFIN.

ECOFIN and the two-level policy process: the limits of economic policy coordination

In assessing the development of economic policy coordination one needs to bear in mind the ambivalence that is imparted to the behaviour of actors in ECOFIN by the two-level policy process. Ministers are subject to two potentially conflicting pressures: to be a hero as part of a successful negotiating effort (e.g. on EMU) or managerial exercise (in operating the EMS or managing the transition from the EMS to EMU) and to be a hero by standing up on behalf of domestic problems to Brussels.

On the one hand, a new sense of shared interests and responsibilities and of corporate identity had evolved within ECOFIN as part of the EMU process. Multilateral surveillance meant that the level of exchange of information was higher; convergence programmes involved stronger peer-group pressure – an instance was provided by the challenges to the British programme, presented in summer 1993, for underestimating the degree to which its budget deficit was structural and thus exaggerating the capacity of cyclical economic recovery to reduce it down from 8 per cent to the Maastricht target. A cause and symptom was to be found, among other things, in the self-interest of members in ECOFIN and its technical committees in not losing influence to another forum, the European Council, whose decisions might well be less agreeable than its own. This development was further encouraged, post-1989, by ECOFIN's new managerial role in determining credits for eastern Europe and the Soviet Union and its successor.

The sense of shared interests and responsibilities was further promoted by a set of informal rules that had been spawned around the role of the presidency. Rotation of the presidency twice a year generated a sense of common ownership and identification with this institution and with facilitating its success in achieving decisions: for, in a long-term sense, each government has a self-interest in maintaining the goodwill of others so that its presidency will gain support and therefore be seen to be a success. The result is an inbuilt pressure to agree texts and to display a capacity for action.

On the other hand, ECOFIN is composed of ministers who owe their presence there to the domestic parliamentary, party and electoral arenas. This sense of responsibility to a domestic constituency is reinforced by press and broadcasting coverage, for press and broadcasting are organized and operate on a domestic basis. Consequently, there are pronounced limits to cooperation.

Three factors define the limits of economic policy coordination by affecting the way in which the two-level policy process operates: economic divergence, economic ideology, and domestic managerial, political and constitutional obstacles to budgetary leadership. These factors conspire to shape just how wide a margin of manoeuvre finance ministers and central bankers seek to retain or retrieve.

As we shall see in chapter 8, *differences in the nature and scale of domestic economic problems* have persistently undermined the capability, and ultimately the will, of governments to unify around and sustain a single set of economic and monetary policies. In the 1970s, and beyond, contrasting rates of inflation was a major factor in fuelling domestic suspicions about the implications of EMU: was the price of EMU that low-inflation countries would have to take on the inflationary policies and practices of others (a continuing German concern); or was the price that overly harsh and ultimately unsustainable costs of high unemployment and lost output would be imposed on high-inflation countries? Two examples will suffice to illustrate the impact of economic divergence on policy coordination. In the period 1990–2 the unusually high levels of personal indebtedness in the British economy added an extra dimension of difficulty to the British economy in adjusting to the ERM and formed a crucial domestic background to 'Black Wednesday' in September 1992. Even more importantly, German unification created a huge special domestic problem in the very anchor of the ERM: an economy with a huge structural imbalance, escalating budget deficit and public debt, inflationary pressures and consequently very high interest rates.

But ultimately, economic divergence and contrasting problems are not *per se* incompatible with economic policy coordination. They affect how it operates. Economic divergence, and the problems that it throws up, can be dealt with by policy cooperation, notably by reviewing and revising exchange rates (something that governments were in practice unwilling to act on before 'Black Wednesday'). It is precisely the combination of economic divergence with close economic interdependence, and thus mutual sensitivity and vulnerability, that makes policy coordination so important.

Also important is the will of governments to cooperate: and that will is anchored in *economic policy ideologies* and the views that these ideologies contain about how economies behave. Earlier chapters have revealed just how contrasting economic ideologies were in the 1960s and early 1970s. They underpinned the tensions between the French and German governments about EMU and between the EEC Commission and the German government. Symbolic was the clash between Robert Marjolin as EEC Commissioner for economic and monetary affairs and Ludwig Erhard as German Economics Minister and then Chancellor. Marjolin was steeped in the planning ideology of the French National Planning Commission, in which he had worked with Jean Monnet in the early postwar period; Erhard was the great political spokesman of the 'social market economy'. Although the ideological divide between French and German governments softened in the 1970s and 1980s, German distrust of DG2 of the Commission (economic and monetary affairs) was to remain a continuing theme: Chancellor Schmidt was suspicious of Ortoli; Karl-Otto Pöhl distrusted Padoa-Schioppa. Only for a brief period under Wilhelm Haferkamp did DG2 come under a German figure: but then not an imposing or effective one. Traditionally, DG2 had incorporated a French/Belgian/Italian axis that coloured its economic ideology. German officials were notably underrepresented in DG2; German economists played little role in its advisory structure. With the 1980s a softening of this divide occurred: Henning Christophersen as commissioner responsible for economic affairs from 1989 was a former Danish Liberal Party leader and Minister of Finance, and, throughout the 1980s, Michael Emerson brought a great deal of authority to the economic policy research of DG2.

But, far more important was a convergence of economic policy ideology that greatly facilitated economic policy coordination: not least, because it was a process of convergence around German policy ideas (price stability) and institutions (central bank independence) – in other words, German leadership. DG2 was an active participant in this convergence. Convergence of economic ideology was, however, no simple and continuous process. By 1992–3 new doubts had begun to arise about how EC economies were actually behaving: could requisite adjustments be made within the ERM by changing domestic prices and wages, or were changes of nominal exchange rates more effective; were interest-rate changes for the purpose of economic stabilization too costly to output and employment, or was economic stability essential to sustained recovery? In attempting to answer those questions officials and economists were posing a potential challenge to the orthodox economic ideology, notably in the direction of 'renationalizing' economic policy.

Finally, at the heart of the two-level policy process is the complex array of *domestic political obstacles to economic policy coordination*. Domestic political institutions become the vehicle through which the impact of divergent economic trends and problems and contrasting economic ideologies are brought to bear on the actors involved in the two-level policy process. In the history of European economic policy cooperation a few particular domestic institutions have left an imprint: the Bundesbank at all times; the French Gaullist party, notably during the 1960s and 1970s; and the British Labour Party (during the EMS negotiations of 1978) and the British Conservative Party (during the EMU negotiations and ratification of the Treaty on European Union). When faced with critical decisions on economic policy coordination, government leaders in Britain and France have had to consider party militants opposed to EMU; they have also had to take account of imminent elections and their implications for retaining room for domestic political manoeuvre. In 1993 the Spanish government was forced to reconsider its attitude to economic policy coordination as a national election approached, unemployment mounted and its majority was in danger. In Germany the prime domestic political obstacle was not, prior to the early 1990s, party political or the prospect of electoral defeat for a government but the independence, authority and prestige of the Bundesbank. Previous chapters have charted the profound implications of that German domestic relationship for economic policy coordination.

Treaty rules and the path to EMU

The Treaty on European Union did not provide a self-sufficient body of rules to promote compliance with the requirements of economic policy coordination, in particular the convergence of the budgetary performance of member states. The need to develop accompanying rules for this purpose was apparent from the functioning of the convergence programmes. Budgetary discipline is prescribed by the treaty. But the treaty leaves open the question of whether national budgetary systems have the institutional capacity and supportive cultural context to meet this requirement.[29] EMU has important implications for the rules of the game, for budgetary structures and procedures, at the national level. The credibility of compliance requires a substantial review of these as well as the formal agreement of convergence programmes. Without rules that support strong budgetary leadership at the national level the behavioural changes required for EMU will not be achieved. In other words, the nature of domestic budgetary bargaining relations, and the rules within which they are conducted, are likely to profoundly affect the prospects for EMU.

Against this background, strengthened rules for economic policy coordination have not produced a simple, smooth path to EMU. By 1993 it was clear that the path was tortuous. Review of convergence programmes was in practice a haphazard process. Sometimes there was a wide-ranging, and for the government concerned often uncomfortable, discussion in the EC Monetary Committee and in ECOFIN. There were governments that were keen to use ECOFIN to help to put through more rigorous economic policy programmes than they felt were possible if they relied simply on their own domestic political authority and budgetary procedures. In 1991, for instance, the Italian government sought to use ECOFIN's critical review of its convergence programme to gain its authority for tough budget measures in 1992. Overall, however, convergence programmes proved different in contents, often over-optimistic (as with the Greek programme of 1993 which forecast a reduction of the budget deficit from 9.4 per cent of GDP in 1992 to 1.6 per cent in 1996), and had varying timetables. The presentation of many involved little more than a monologue. In recognition of the difficulties that governments were having in meeting the convergence criteria, ECOFIN decided in February 1993 to extend the convergence programmes to 1996 and to set common standards for measuring the economic performance targets. In July it established a more formal framework for monitoring convergence, testing it in reviewing the (mutually coordinated) French and German programmes in November.

The messy reality of economic policy cooperation post-1992 was influenced to no small extent by that fact that all governments recognized, implicitly rather than explicitly, a characteristic of the convergence criteria in the Treaty on European Union that was emphasized in chapter 5: that an element of discretion was allowed in their interpretation. The rules of the game for proceeding to the third and final stage involved ultimately a political judgement by the Council of Ministers about which countries had done enough to proceed, and whether enough countries had done so. In this important sense the outcome is not automatic. And a favourable political judgement on these issues depended on the degree of mutual confidence and solidarity that could be sustained in ECOFIN. This calculation held together the pro-EMU governments with the Commission in a beleaguered but nonetheless, by 1993, still solid coalition of mutual support.

---

29. K. Gretschmann (ed.) *Economic and Monetary Union: Implications for National Policy Makers* (Maastricht: EIPA, 1993).

The broad economic policy guidelines and the Delors's White Paper

Within the framework of the route to EMU traced in the Maastricht Treaty the perceived importance of macro-economic policy coordination was increased by the impact of the ERM crises of 1992–3 and by the new budgetary pressures induced by the 'down-side' of the economic cycle. With the formal collapse of the 'narrow-band' ERM in August 1993 central bank and finance ministry opinion shifted emphasis to the importance of long-term convergence; whilst the severity of the output-employment crisis, and evidence of its structural and not just cyclical nature, created a new challenge of how to achieve a coherent EC strategy that could combine convergence, Maastricht-style, with new measures to associate EMU with job creation and economic expansion.

One dimension of improved economic policy coordination was supposed to be provided by the new broad economic policy guidelines for the member states, drawn up in conformity with Article 103.2 of the treaty. The aim was that these guidelines, approved by the European Council, would form the framework for a more effective mutual surveillance during stage two of EMU and for assessing individual convergence programmes. But on the guidelines the Commission was forced on to the defensive by ECOFIN, their final form being a diluted form of the original. Early Commission efforts to set specific targets for recovery met fierce opposition in ECOFIN – like a reduction of two to three percentage points in average EC short-term interest rates, an average increase in real wages of one percentage point below the rise in productivity, and the creation of 15 million jobs by 2000, thereby halving EC unemployment. Belgian, French, Italian and Spanish finance ministers were in principle willing to embrace such targets. However, strong objections surfaced from the British, Dutch and German ministers. In their view the EC had no legal instruments to meet such targets, the levers of macro-economic policy still remaining with individual states. The only specific target to which ECOFIN warmed was an average inflation rate of no more than 2–3 per cent by 1996. At least that target was for the first time spelt out in a legally binding document. Otherwise the guidelines limited themselves to a general call for lower interest rates, wage restraint, and lower budget deficits and government debt. A deterioration of public finances was to be avoided in 1994; from 1995 the EC was to aim at making its debt position sustainable.

The Commission's retreat on the macro-economic policy guidelines was complemented by a struggle for power and influence between ECOFIN and the Commission over the Delors's White Paper on Competitiveness, Growth and Employment, commissioned by the European Council. Concerned by the economic downturn and accelerating unemployment, the European Council had called on Delors to map out an EC-wide strategy for tackling recession. In the context of this exercise, two key questions affected the Commission's relations with ECOFIN: the problem of coherence between the convergence criteria of the treaty and any new expansionary budget strategy to create jobs that might emerge, and ECOFIN's concern to protect its own prerogatives over financing of the resulting action plan. The EC Commission faced two interrelated difficulties in fulfilling its mandate in time for the Brussels summit of December 1993. Its own political weakness after the fiasco of the ratification difficulties of the Maastricht treaty meant that it could do little more than offer a menu of non-binding measures from which member state governments could pick to suit their own perceptions of national need. The result was a White Paper that was noticeably more hands-off in approach than the Delors Report of 1989.

To compound its difficulties, the Commission found itself internally divided on the appropriate substance of the White Paper. On the one hand, the Social Affairs Directorate DG5 embodied an essentially social democratic vision of the importance of labour market regulation and consensus and identified work-sharing as a source of jobs; on the other, DG2 was wedded to the idea of much greater labour market flexibility and 'pricing people into work' as solutions to unemployment, along with rigorous priority to price stability and control of public finances. Delors had his own priorities, rooted in his view that the EC must enthusiastically embrace and master technological change, investing in a new infrastructure of European energy, transport and telecommunications networks and promoting research and development and training. From this melange of views, and given the very different ideological perceptions of the member state governments, it proved difficult to forge a single clear and intellectually coherent message for the White Paper, other than that a collective approach was indispensable.

Before and during the Brussels summit of December 1993 the struggle for power and influence between ECOFIN and the Commission came to a head. Despite the travails of putting it together, and late public attacks from within the British government, the White Paper was endorsed at the summit: in effect, signalling a shift towards labour market deregulation. But the divisive issue involved how the gap in the 20 billion ECU per annum funding of the trans-European networks between 1994 and 1999 was to be bridged. Delors proposed that the EC should raise 8 billion ECU per annum for this purpose by issuing new 'Union bonds', additional to the existing budgetary allocation and the EIB's lending. A powerful nucleus of ECOFIN ministers, led by Britain, Germany and the Netherlands, saw in this proposal an attempt to create a new fiscal role for the Commission, bypassing the EIB (ECOFIN's agent) and breaking free from ECOFIN control. Despite Delors's claim that there was nothing new in principle or scale in such EC borrowing, referring to comparable facilities in 1975 and 1979, it was decided at the summit to remit the detailed elaboration of an action plan to ECOFIN, including the question of how to mobilize the extra 8 billion ECU per annum. It was clear that the new Maastricht Treaty rules had done little, if anything, to remedy the long-standing tension between the Commission and ECOFIN over macro-economic policy coordination. If anything, tension had grown.

The rules of the game in monetary policy coordination: the evolution of the EMS and the Committee of Central Bank Governors

In earlier chapters we have noted how, historically, international economic policy coordination has lagged well behind monetary policy coordination, being in effect more a by-product of the latter than a dynamic factor in its own right: in this chapter we have identified the main reasons for this lack of 'parallelism' between these two types of coordination. In the case of EMU, the rules of the game sought to protect the ESCB from the political and market pressures emanating from large budget deficits and governmental debts. Otherwise, multilateral surveillance constituted too soft a rule to enable the EC to fashion a coherent and suitable fiscal stance for Europe as a whole.[30] The rules of the game in economic policy coordination were, in other words, narrow and incomplete.

The historical perspective in the early part of this volume also reminds us that the rules of the game in international monetary policy coordination have never enjoyed an unchallenged and unequivocal authority over the behaviour of governments and central bankers. As chapter 1 pointed out, there was widespread violation of the rules of the game during the operation of the classical gold standard, pre-1914, as well as under the gold exchange standard of the interwar period.[31] In reality, the cooperation of central banks was sporadic and discretionary action a distinguishing characteristic, with insulation of the domestic economy from external disturbance as a typical priority. Examples of discretion included decisions about the scale and timing of changes to interest rates and about whether and how to use open-market operations.

Again (as we saw in chapter 3) the birth of the EEC and the stipulations of Articles 106–8 of the Treaty of Rome had little real impact on the behaviour of member states with respect to their exchange rates. Though, according to Article 107, the exchange rate is to be viewed as a problem of common interest, the revaluations of the German D-Mark and the Dutch guilder in 1961 were based on no proper consultation at the EEC level. Agreement on a system of prior consultations in 1969 was immediately flouted as France devalued the franc and Germany revalued the D-Mark. In 1971 the decision to float the German D-Mark was taken in defiance of EEC partners; the Dutch decision to revalue the guilder in 1973 involved consultations only with its Benelux partners.

The decision of ECOFIN on 22 March 1971 to strengthen monetary policy coordination in pursuance of the proposals of the Werner Report was also without much practical consequence. The Committee of Central Bank Governors was asked to establish general guidelines on trends in bank liquidity, the terms for supply of credit and the level of interest rates.[32] As a consequence, the committee established expert groups to monitor exchange-rate developments and trends in national money supplies. It also collaborated with the EC Monetary Committee to set up a working group on harmonization of monetary policy instruments: but little more than survey work appeared. In practice, analytical work on monetary policy and money supply projections was left to the national level. The work of the Committee of Central Bank

---

30. Note the speech in May 1992 at the City University, London, by Erik Hoffmeyer, chairman of the Committee of Central Bank Governors and governor of the Danish central bank, who criticized the skewed relationship between the rules for monetary policy and those for fiscal policy in the Treaty on European Union; the former are supranational, the latter intergovernmental in nature. See also P. Kenen, *EMU after Maastricht* (Washington, DC: The Group of Thirty, 1992).

31. See respectively A. Bloomfield, *Monetary Policy under the International Gold Standard, 1880–1914* (New York: Federal Reserve Bank, 1959); R. Nurske, 'The Gold Exchange Standard', in the League of Nations, *International Currency Experience* (Geneva: League of Nations, 1944), pp. 27–46.

32. N. Thygesen, 'International Coordination of Monetary Policies – With Special Reference to the European Community', in J. Wadsworth and F. Leonard de Juvigny (eds) *New Approaches to Monetary Policy* (Alphen aan den Rijn: Sijthoff & Noordhoff, 1979), pp. 205–24.

Governors remained essentially reactive to views of, and information volunteered by, national central banks; national central banks were defensive about information and coordination; hence the central secretariat lacked anything but the most rudimentary resources.

Until the 1980s, though there might have been a central bank culture, it did not take the form of an ideological consensus about the goal of monetary policy. Some central bankers subscribed to a neo-Keynesian view that monetary policy had as a goal the stabilization of the business cycle; others, led by the Bundesbank, saw the goal as solely price stability. A certain sense of solidarity was to be found, not least in maintaining an arm's-length relationship with the European Commission (which had no exclusive right of initiative in its work as in other EC policy areas and which was geographically distant from Basle). But that solidarity was qualified by a lack of the kind of ideological consensus that was to emerge in the 1980s.

Also, the presence of a central banking culture does not mean that central banks are monolithic institutions. They incorporate a wide range of people, with governors from different backgrounds – some like Carlo Ciampi, Eddie George and Schlesinger career central bankers, others from various backgrounds (like Pöhl from economic journalism, Pöhl and Hans Tietmeyer from senior posts in the Bonn finance ministry, Jacques de Larosière and Jean-Claude Trichet from the French Trésor, Guido Carli from the IMF or Wim Duisenberg from government office). Career central bankers included those whose role had been primarily in domestic issues and others, like Tietmeyer and de Larosière, whose experience involved international issues.

The 'snake' and then the EMS undoubtedly contributed to a learning process about the importance of establishing and respecting clearer rules of the game for monetary policy coordination: although, in the case of the 'snake', acute inflationary pressures and balance-of-payments' crises were not conducive to the development of institutional regulation; indeed its scope diminished with defections from the system, notably by Britain and France. Internally there remained two central problems in the application of the rules of the game of the EMS. First, they tended to lack precision, leaving much room for interpretation. And the process of interpretation was very much led by the most powerful actor, the Bundesbank. Thus, for instance, the divergence indicator did not prove to be important in practice.

Second, the nature and impact of institutional regulation and bargaining within the EMS was shaped by the reluctant role of the Bundesbank. As Norbert Kloten, a member of the Bundesbank council, stated: 'the Bundesbank never wanted a dominant role in Europe's monetary policy making. . . . She was forced to accept that role.'[33] The presence of so reluctant an actor at the heart of the EMS was not a recipe for institutional dynamism. It helps to explain why the European Monetary Cooperation Fund was not transformed into the proposed European Monetary Fund, as was intended should happen in 1981; why large short-term and medium-term credit facilities were hardly used at all; why interventions at the margin and very-short-term financing through mutual central bank credit played a decreasing role (with the exception of the time around the January 1987 realignment and the crises of 1992 and

---

33. N. Kloten, 'Die Europäische Währungsintegration: Chancen und Risiken', *Auszüge aus Presseartikeln* 81, Deutsche Bundesbank, 1988, pp. 1–7.

1993); why the most profound of all ERM crises in July 1993 was met by the policy instrument of substantially broadening the margins of fluctuation (thereby reducing pressures for intervention by the Bundesbank); why the intention that official intervention should be wholly in European currencies (rather than in US dollars) was ignored; and why the official ECU did not play its prescribed role. The dynamism was essentially a political one, embedded, as we have seen, in the 'high politics' of Franco-German relations and in the European Council. Despite all its ostensible power, the Bundesbank was to find itself locked into political as well as market dynamics over which it experienced little sense of control.

At its birth in 1979 the EMS comprised a loose system of rules to serve a very general purpose – 'a zone of monetary stability in Europe'. Its chronology can be divided up into periods based on the transformation of the rules of the game, along with a changing emphasis in the specification of the policy goals that were to serve this general purpose. Until August 1993 this transformation was in essence a story of a process of narrowing of the scope for discretion in using policy instruments. Rules, formal but above all informal, evolved, demonstrating the will and capability of the member states to tackle the causes of uncontrolled inflation and to gain a measure of protection from the outcomes of potentially huge and increasing speculative movements in foreign-exchange markets. They demonstrated their belief that the goals of internal and external stability were mutually reconcilable. In this process of rule elaboration the Bundesbank was the policy leader, though in the initial launch it had been a reluctant participant. For the use of the D-Mark as a preferred intervention currency, and the consequent large build-up of D-Mark reserves, was not sought or imposed on the EMS by the Bundesbank.

The formal rules of the EMS are laid down in various sources: the Brussels Resolution of 5 December 1978; the Basle Agreement of 13 March 1979; and the Basle-Nyborg Agreement of 12 September 1987. Although they have undoubtedly been important in setting the parameters of the system, it will be clear from the account above that informal rules have been far more important in the evolution of the system. The formal rules were described in chapters 4–5: on the ECU and its functions; on the exchange-rate and intervention mechanisms; and on the credit mechanisms. Here it is helpful just to note the intentions of the founders as spelt out by one of the key figures in the EMS negotiations, Jacques van Ypersele, and to provide more details on the key formal rules.

Ypersele gave emphasis to the fact that the EMS was not to be dominated by a particular country, in the manner of the Bretton Woods system. It was to be a 'democratic' rather than an 'autocratic' arrangement: thus, for instance, according to the Brussels Resolution, 'adjustments of central rates will be subject to mutual agreement by a common procedure which will comprise all countries participating in the exchange-rate mechanism and the Commission'.[34] In pursuit of this purpose, two principles had been incorporated into the institutional design: 'flexibility' and 'symmetry'. 'Flexibility' meant provision for realignments so that different trends of inflation in member states could be accommodated. The formal rules did not, however,

34. J. van Ypersele, 'Operating Principles and Procedures of the EMS', in P. Trezise (ed.) *The EMS: Its Promise and Prospects* (Washington, DC: Brookings, 1979).

specify the criteria that were to guide realignments. 'Symmetry' was fostered by having a common point of reference in the ECU, a weighted basket of all participating currencies, rather than in a grid of bilateral parities. The innovation was that central rates and intervention limits were defined in terms of the ECU and that when a currency crossed the 'divergence threshold' (based on the ECU basket formula) there was a presumption that the authorities concerned would act to correct this situation. The credit facilities were to ensure that low-inflation countries would contribute to a 'symmetric' adjustment process.

In practice, these principles were not respected; the rules based on them were ignored or, by informal means, revised. From 1983 onwards realignments lost their attraction in favour of other informal rules. Symmetry was never an obvious characteristic of the EMS. Instead, debate shifted to the question of whether, *de facto*, the EMS was a zone of German economic 'dominance' or one of complex asymmetry with German 'leadership' of the system.[35] The Bundesbank's special position was apparent from the fact that most of the intervention activity within the EMS was undertaken by other central banks.

The basic formal 'rules of the game'

At the heart of the EMS were the rules of the game for the management of the exchange-rate mechanism (ERM): rules on how central rates were to be established and changed; on the nature of the margins of fluctuation; and on the policy instruments, notably intervention, for the purpose of keeping rates within the margins. As we have seen, the central rates are defined in terms of a common basket of currencies, the European Currency Unit (ECU). These values for each currency are then used to define a central rate for each pair of currencies, thereby locating the centre of the band for the bilateral exchange rate between them. There are, however, no formal rules for realigning central rates in the ERM in the form of 'objective indicators' to structure the negotiating process (like the 'equilibrium' exchange rate or changes in reserves).

In addition, the rules of the game of the ERM defined it as a system within which, as under the Bretton Woods system, exchange rates were confined within 'narrow' and 'hard' bands. The conventional spread from one side of the central rate to the other was 4.5 per cent: a width of margin of 2.25 per cent. Historically, this choice of width had its origins in the attempt of the participants in the 'snake' to make their currencies at least as predictable as the US dollar following the widening of margins against the US dollar from 1 per cent to 2.25 per cent by the Smithsonian Agreement of 1971. This choice of margin was to endure till 1993. The Italian lira was allowed a margin of 6 per cent, a 'broad' band approach adopted by Spain and Britain on their entries

35. See, for instance, the contrasting positions in F. Giavazzi and A. Giovannini, 'Models of the EMS: Is Europe a Greater Deutschmark Area?', in R. Bryant and R. Portes (eds) *Global Macroeconomics* (New York: St Martin's Press, 1987), pp. 237–65; P. De Grauwe, 'Is the European Monetary System a DM-Zone?', Discussion Paper no. 297 (London: Centre for Economic Policy Research, 1989). D. Gros and N. Thygesen, *European Monetary Integration: From the European Monetary System to European Monetary Union* (London: Longman, 1992).

into the ERM, respectively in 1989 and 1990. This 6 per cent margin was a recognition that some governments required greater tactical flexibility to accommodate domestic and external problems of adjustment. It could, not least, frustrate foreign exchange speculators who – though expecting a currency to realign – could not be sure in the case of a broad band whether the band might prove wide enough to accommodate the realignment: in other words, the actual market rate might not move at all. Equally, the broad band was understood as a temporary measure, a learning process in adjusting to the disciplines of the system; Italy moved to the 'narrow' band in 1990. Unilaterally, the Benelux countries pursued a strategy of an even narrower margin, with France also attracted by this idea. The Danish government even proposed to the IGC in early 1991 that the margin be narrowed to 1.5 per cent for all participants in stage two. This proposal met resistance from governments which preferred to retain discretion to move unilaterally in this direction. But, in contravention of the expectation of a progressive narrowing of margins, the ERM crisis of July/August 1993 was to precipitate a decision of ECOFIN to greatly widen the margin of fluctuation to 15 per cent, for all countries other than Germany and the Netherlands.

These bands – broad or narrow – remained 'hard' in the sense that intervention by central banks was mandatory in order to prevent exchange rates from falling outside the bands. Hard bands are basically a statement of commitment, designed to gain greater credibility in foreign-exchange markets. In the case of the width of the margins some countries succeeded by unilateral action in establishing a new informal rule. In June 1990 (till August 1993) the Belgian franc followed the Dutch guilder by moving to an even narrower spread of 1 per cent, with the intention of so building market confidence that they could virtually eliminate their interest-rate differential with Germany.

The main rules of the game on policy instruments related to intervention. From the outset the formal rules of the game of the ERM distinguished between two types of joint foreign-exchange intervention by the central banks: marginal intervention, which takes place when a currency is at the extreme limit of its permitted fluctuation band; and intramarginal intervention, which occurs before such a situation is reached. In the case of *marginal intervention*, the two central banks whose currencies are up against their absolute limits are obliged to intervene to prevent the exchange rate falling outside its permitted range. The rules specify that the intervention is unlimited in quantity. But it is limited in duration (the Basle-Nyborg Agreement raised the period from 45 to 75 days after the end of the calendar month in which the intervention takes place). Thus, if the Bundesbank is obliged to purchase French francs, the Banque de France is required to reimburse it in D-Marks or ECUs within that specific period of days. In other words, the Bundesbank is required to acquire francs only for this duration. After that, it must be repaid out of French foreign exchange reserves, with the French central bank accepting all of the foreign exchange risk incurred by the intervention of both central banks. Following the July 1993 crisis, the Banque de France was left with negative net foreign currency reserves.

By contrast, though *intramarginal intervention* was practised extensively from the beginning, in fact more extensively than marginal intervention, it was not adequately regulated till the Basle-Nyborg Agreement. Central banks had recognized from the outset that joint intervention before currencies reached the absolute limits of their bands was the only sensible way to reverse the momentum of a speculative attack. And, the divergence threshold was designed as a signal for intramarginal intervention. But even the Basle-Nyborg Agreement placed very limited requirements on the Bundesbank (or any central bank with a strong currency) to assist weakening currencies. Its 'presumption' to act did not amount to an automatic requirement to do so. Moreover, if willing to engage in such joint intervention, the amount that it is expected to purchase is limited to a maximum of 200 per cent of any country's 'debtor quota' in the EC's short-term monetary support mechanism. This maximum might well amount to only a day or two of really heavy selling of a currency, as in the case of the British pound in September 1992.

The rules of the game on intervention are particularly important and more specific than those on realignments. They have two characteristics. First, so circumscribed are the rules in terms of both time and quantity that it is clear that intervention can be of use as a palliative only in dealing with short-term problems. In the case of marginal interventions, they enable a breathing space of about three months before all support needs to be financed out of the embattled central bank's own reserves. At that point market operators recognize that the intervention mechanism is becoming exhausted, and events take their own course. Yet, as happened in September 1992 and early 1993, Franco-German cooperation could evolve its own dynamism within the framework of the rules: in this case a joint declaration of the Bundesbank, the Banque de France and the French and German finance ministries that they had every intention of ensuring that the franc was not devalued.

Second, the formal rules of the EMS left open the issue of the appropriate mix between intervention, domestic policy adjustments (including interest rates) and capital controls. Later policy changes were to reduce the degree of discretion, notably by elimination of capital controls and by the provisions of the Basle-Nyborg Agreement relating, for instance, to a more active use of interest-rate differentials. But coordination of the use of discretionary policy mixes by national authorities was always likely to be problematic: the scope for bungling was considerable.

Ultimately, however, the Achilles' heel of intervention was that the Bundesbank could not in fact commit itself to unlimited intervention. To do so would be to sacrifice its monetary policy mandate and independence. As a matter of institutional self-interest and public interest it continued to express its unwillingness to undertake massive unsterilized intervention, even for a short period. For this reason, the very-short-term credit facility was never unlimited; the Bundesbank sterilized its interventions (as it was permitted to do); and intervention was not allowed to affect German interest rates. This continuous theme of the Bundesbank was reasserted following the ERM crisis of 1992 and deeply influenced its attitude to the management of the crisis of July 1993.

1979–83: the informal rule on realignment

In its initial period of operation, 1979–83, the EMS evolved a set of informal rules that were remarkably well adjusted to the acute problems that beset it at birth. Indeed, so problematic were economic conditions at its birth that it is hard to envisage that its founders would have possessed the compound of will and capability to take the requisite decisions and actions after 1979. This observation only underlines the point about the importance of good fortune in the launch of new projects for European integration. American interest rates rose sharply as part of a tightening of domestic monetary policy; the second oil price shock involved great inflationary pressures (peaking at an average of about 10 per cent in 1981–2) and a threatening combination of balance of payment, budget deficit and unemployment problems; following the elections of a Socialist President and huge Socialist majority in the National Assembly, the French government embarked on an independent fiscal strategy of reflation. By the end of 1979 two realignments had already occurred. External economic shocks and diminishing internal political consensus meant a phase of acute turbulence and the demise of the Brussels Resolution's idea of a new phase of institutional reform in the form of the European Monetary Fund in 1981. In this context the rules of the game that evolved were defensive and minimalist.

Two key informal rules were to take shape in this first stage and to endure. First, it was accepted as an operating procedure that coordination of exchange-rate policy *vis-à-vis* the US dollar would be delegated to the Bundesbank. In practice, as a consequence, the Bundesbank intervenes much more in the US dollar markets than in the markets for EMS currencies. Second, realignment was influenced by a unilateral and informal rule of the Bundesbank: that it was better to let the D-Mark appreciate than to permit the domestic money supply to rise. This rule of the Bundesbank was to provide a factor of continuity in its policy towards the EMS. With prudent management of central rates it would be possible to insulate the German economy from the inflationary potential of the system. Planned realignments were preferable to large-scale interventions.

But a third informal rule was to prove decisive in defining the character of the early period of the EMS between 1979 and 1983: the rule that 'stable but adjustable' rates were to be maintained by facilitating realignments that compensated for losses of competitiveness by a country but that did not confer a competitive advantage on any country. Here was a case of an informal rule extending and elaborating the formal rules. Realignments had, in other words, a preventive role: to remove serious misalignments among currencies.

In making realignments at least, it seemed that the EMS was behaving according to the formal rules: more visibly than ever before, in the EC or the IMF, realignments were a joint responsibility, involving a real collaborative discussion of the participants. In all, seven realignments took place between 1979 and 1983, involving 27 changes of ECU central rates, with an average size of 5.3 per cent. They offset nearly 90 per cent of inflation differentials.[36] Though individual changes tended to be relatively small scale, their cumulative impact could be significant, as in the most important bilateral link, that between the D-Mark and the French franc, which changed by 30 per cent between September 1981 and March 1983.

36. Commission of the European Communities, *European Economy: One Market, One Money* (Luxembourg: Office for Official Publications of the European Communities, October 1992), p. 42. See also N. Thygesen, 'Exchange-Rate Policies and Monetary Targets in the EMS Countries', in R. Masera and R. Triffin (eds) *Europe's Money: Problems of European Monetary Coordination and Integration* (Oxford: Clarendon Press, 1984). H. Ungerer, O. Evans and P. Nyborg, 'The European Monetary System: The Experience 1979–82', Occasional Paper (Washington, DC: International Monetary Fund, 1983).

As far as the application of the rules was concerned, it was clear that countries were not always successful in negotiating the scale of parity adjustment for which they had been looking, including the French government in March 1983; and that, as a price of agreement in ECOFIN, commitments to domestic policy adjustment were made, again involving the French government as well as Italy and small states like Belgium and Denmark. This linkage to domestic policy adjustment was insisted on by the Bundesbank and helped to keep alive the idea that the EMS could contribute positively to long-term economic convergence.

Another enduring feature of EC monetary policy coordination was the degree of informal coordination between French and German policy makers on realignment issues involving a change of their bilateral rate and on accompanying economic policy adjustments. In effect, coordination between French and German policy makers, outside the formal EMS machinery, became an inner informal rule that applied as soon as their bilateral rates became an issue. In such cases, as in September 1981 and June 1982, ECOFIN could expect to be presented with a *fait accompli*.

1983–7: a new informal rule of 'tying one's hands'

In the chronology of the EMS March 1983 was a watershed event. Not only was it the date of a comprehensive realignment embracing all participating currencies, but also it represented (as we saw in chapter 5) a dramatic turning-point in the development of French economic and EC policies. Faced with a domestic political crisis about the policy costs of the EMS and the prospect of its breakdown, the French government decided to make the EC the central reference point for its economic policy making and to redefine its view of the EMS. Thereafter, the 'new EMS' began to evolve. The new EMS did not, at least at this stage, involve a development of its formal rules. At its heart was the evolution of a new informal rule: that the EMS was an instrument of domestic policy discipline. Basically, the French government led a process of redefinition of the EMS that, for domestic policy reasons, was widely shared among the members of the ERM.

The ostensible rationale was economic: that the most effective way to promote competitiveness, and hence sustained economic growth and employment, was by controlling inflation; that devaluation was a source of inflationary pressures and should, therefore, be avoided as a policy instrument; that a policy of resolute fixing of the exchange rate to the strongest currency (the D-Mark) was a superior policy instrument for convincing employers and trade unions and the financial markets of the commitment to bring down inflation; and that, by 'tying one's hands' and achieving credibility for anti-inflation policy in this way, it would be possible to lower the unemployment costs of disinflation. In practice, the ratiocination for this 'strong currency' policy and strategy of competitiveness through competitive 'disinflation' was provided later by economists.[37]

---

37. Notably, F. Giavazzi and M. Pagano, 'The Advantage of Tying One's Hands: EMS Discipline and Central Bank Credibility', *European Economic Review* 32 (1988), pp. 1055–82. The view of inflation on which the argument is based goes back, however, to work by Barro and Gordon published in 1983 (see chapter 7).

More immediately, the motivations of the French government were as much political as economic. First and foremost, the French political establishment achieved an impressive degree of unity around the aim of achieving the respect of German policy makers. This aim was indispensable to securing French influence in the most important element of French policy: the Franco-German bargaining relationship. A relationship of equality had not been apparent in the functioning of the EMS since 1979 (and was not to be gained by exit from the system). By outperforming Germany in price stability it would be possible to acquire the respect of the financial markets and financial market power and to translate that respect into influence on Germany. The ambition of the Banque de France, articulated by its governor Jacques de Larosière, was to share the anchor role in the ERM with Germany. In other words, France would be respected by German policy actors and others only if it had a strong currency: hence the staunch commitment to the *franc fort*. The much-criticized asymmetry of the EMS – the product of the anchor role of the D-Mark – was now presented as its attraction. It was a credible peg for a stability-oriented monetary policy.

Between March 1983 and January 1987 the EMS settled down to become a much more stable system, despite the instability of the US dollar, and to display some success in promoting nominal convergence. The two main indicators of success were inflation and realignments. Inflation declined from an average of around 7 per cent in 1982 to only just over 1 per cent in 1986; the standard deviation fell from 4 to 2 per cent. And only four realignments took place, involving 12 parity changes of a lower average size (3.8 per cent) than in 1979–83. They compensated for only 52 per cent of the loss of competitiveness due to higher inflation in the devaluing countries. Between March 1983 and April 1986 there was only one realignment, involving the Italian lira. The background was provided by domestic policies that contributed to disinflation by reducing budget deficits, though much more in some countries like Denmark and France than others like Ireland and Italy. In fact, this period differed from its predecessor in a diminished role for relating realignments to the consideration of domestic policy adjustment in ERM bargaining; more reliance was placed on the commitment of national governments to push through domestic measures, symbolized by the Italian government's move to modify the wage indexation mechanism (the *Scala Mobile*) in 1985. In effect, governments had 'internalized' the requirements of realignment. The EMS was being used to bear down on inflation, as a cost-controlling discipline for weaker economies.

1987–93: the 'hard' ERM – the franc fort, Basle-Nyborg and stage one of EMU

The events of January 1987 and their sequel represented the second great watershed event in the development of the EMS. Once again, the Franco-German bargaining relationship was pivotal. Against the background of a rapidly falling US dollar, the French franc came under unsustainable pressure. Reactions within the French government were angry indeed: for France's economic fundamentals were basically sound. In such circumstances, not least over three years of budgetary *rigeur*, the French government concluded that there must be a deep fault in the EMS if the onus of adjustment fell so heavily and disproportionately on it. Within the Bundesbank there was alarm at the way in which, to an unprecedented degree, it had been drawn into a huge support operation for the franc. The intervention support for the French franc was much greater than anything previously undertaken by the EMS. It was, accordingly, the occasion for an outburst of mutual political recrimination between the French and German finance ministries.

Two issues were raised: first, what changes were required to the rules of the EMS to deal with such extraordinary speculative pressures; and second, given the impending commitment to freedom of capital movement under the single European market programme and the consequences for the future scale of speculative movements, could the EMS hope to survive in its present form? In chapter 5 we reviewed the genesis, content and implications of the changes to the formal rules of the game in the Basle-Nyborg Agreement. They helped to give definition to the idea of a new period of more active and concerted policy coordination, particularly in more flexible use of intramarginal interventions and more active use of interest-rate differentials. The implication was that resort to marginal interventions would decline and that more use of the other two instruments would replace the traditional reliance on capital controls.

But far more important was the emerging commitment to a new informal rule about central rates: that, against the new background of capital liberalization, the mere possibility of realignments would be likely to generate unsustainable speculative attacks. The new EC policy of freedom of capital movement had two implications: it removed a traditional and much-used policy instrument for protecting central rates, capital controls; and, by encouraging a very rapid process of financial integration, it promised to stoke up speculative pressures. The only credible defence was to transform the ERM into a 'fixed-rate' system; the only way to achieve that credibility was by demonstrating that politicians were prepared to take whatever action was required to sustain the central rates, and by strengthening the policy instruments available to the EMS for that purpose. This informal 'fixed-rate' rule took root slowly but firmly, again led by the French policy of the *franc fort*. It found its expression in the Delors Report of 1989, which spoke of 'an understanding that [exchange rate realignments] would be made only in exceptional circumstances'. The only formal change made was the move of the Italian lira from the wide 6 per cent to the narrow 2.25 per cent band.

Domestic factors were critical to the reformulation of the EMS, under the leadership of the French Trésor and the corporate self-interests of the Inspectorate of Finance. By 1988 French policy had advanced to a new stage under the combined impact of the humiliating reverse of January 1987 and the prospect of capital liberalization. Behind the Balladur paper of January 1988 was a new rationale for developing the EMS into EMU. Once again, the new policy represented a powerful compound of political and economic motives. Basically, the French government sought to regain influence and power by shifting the locus of authority in European monetary policy from the Bundesbank to a new European institution. Only in this way would monetary policy no longer be oriented to domestic economic conditions in Germany but to wider European conditions, and German dominance replaced by symmetry. The same objective – price stability – would have a different, and more acceptable, outcome because the policy would differ in domain. Better an EMU with a European central bank than an EMS led by German interests. The *franc fort* policy had come to have a new dimension – and it was to be regarded with equal fervour by the Gaullist Finance Minister Edouard Balladur (1986–8) as by his Socialist predecessor and successor Pierre Bérégovoy and by Balladur again when he returned as Prime Minister in 1993.

Strength and continuity were given to the French commitment to EMU by another factor: the corporate self-interests and functioning of the Inspectorate of Finance. This *grands corps* gained its status and prerogatives not only from the fact that the Finance Ministry was part of its territorial domain but also because of its success as represented by the presence of its members in prestigious positions in French politics (including Giscard d'Estaing and Michel Rocard), across the French administration and in international institutions, from the IMF to the EC Commission. EMU offered the Inspectorate of Finance a new opportunity to offset the loss of monetary independence experienced in the EMS by seeking out new career openings and influence thorough an extended network at the EC level. Added strength and cohesion were given to French EMU policy by the role of the Inspectorate of Finance as dissemination mechanism for policy ideas across institutional boundaries.

Although the period 1987–92 is typically characterized as 'the EMS without realignments', it was always clear on closer inspection that the new informal rule had severe weaknesses. The 'fixed-rate' rule was never endorsed by the Bundesbank. In effect, the Bundesbank was an unwilling accomplice. Disagreement and misunderstanding did not break out suddenly in September 1992. The Bundesbank's concern surfaced on two occasions. In the autumn of 1989 Pöhl suggested publicly that realignments might be appropriate, evoking a sharp political reaction. Thereafter, the Bundesbank was more private and discrete in its lobbying but nonetheless consistent. In spring 1990, in a series of confidential discussions with Dutch, French and Italian officials, the Bundesbank tried, unsuccessfully, to bring about a broad ERM realignment. Informal soundings were again made in 1991. A key factor in holding back the Bundesbank was a desire to avoid a confrontation with the French Finance Ministry, which was implacably opposed to a devaluation of the franc. This factor underlined the leading political role of the French government in the EMS. Then, in October 1990 Pöhl made it clear that he believed that the British government had entered the ERM at the 'wrong' rate; in September 1992, as market storms gathered around the lira and the pound, his successor, Helmut Schlesinger, used a newspaper interview to express his doubts about the wisdom of trying to defend indefensible central rates. These statements from the Bundesbank evoked heated public recriminations. Above all, they were a manifestation of a fact of fundamental significance: that the informal rule on which the 'new EMS' was supposed to rest was deficient in force because the most powerful actor within the institutional structure of the EMS lacked confidence in it.

The 'EMS without realignments' was essentially the product of the political calculations of EC governments. It was not endorsed by academic economists, including those who subscribed to the rule of 'tying one's hands' in the ERM. For academic economists the essential feature of the new EMS was its fragility and instability in the face of potentially huge speculative pressures; the required feature of a transition period to EMU was that it should be short – and the transition period provided for in the Treaty on European Union was long.[38] In this respect the treaty added to the problem with its so-called 'no-realignment' rule. Article 109j laid down as a precondition for EMU that member states should keep their parities unchanged for two years before the irrevocable locking of rates in stage three. This new formal rule envisaged a stage of exchange-rate stability. But the no-realignment rule would only frustrate timely adjustment of parities, the value of which was emphasized in the two reports on the September 1992 crisis by the EC Monetary Committee and the Committee of Central Bank Governors. Article 109j threatened excessive rigidity and repeats of the 1992 crisis.

With this third period, the original principle of flexibility had been eroded in two key senses: capital and exchange controls were being rapidly removed, and realignment was being ruled out – albeit not ultimately convincingly – as a policy instrument. Given this new limitation on national discretion in monetary policy, the incentives for monetary policy coordination were increased. For reasons that we explored in chapter 5, the institutional characteristics of the period after 1987 were reinforced by its merging into stage one of EMU on 1st July 1990. From that point the EC technical committees and ECOFIN were committed to setting their work in the context of EMU, with a new emphasis on *ex ante* coordination and prior consultation.

1993: towards a more flexible two-tier ERM

August 1993 represented another watershed event in the development of the ERM and in shaping the prospects for EMU in the 1990s. Formally, it involved the decision by a special emergency meeting of ECOFIN, requested by the German monetary authorities, to widen the margin of fluctuation to 15 per cent for all currencies, other than the Dutch guilder and the D-Mark which maintained their old 2.25 per cent margin. This decision meant the formal collapse of the 'hard' ERM. Though the decision was initially presented as a temporary change with the objective of returning to a narrowing of bands by 1994, by December the EC's Economic Affairs Commissioner Henning Christophersen was admitting that a return to narrow bands was no longer to be seen as a condition for entering stage three of EMU. The background to the decision was the most momentous crisis in the history of the ERM, with the French franc pinned to its floor in the ERM and massive central bank interventions incapable of lifting it off that floor or deterring foreign exchange market operators from their belief that the domestic interest rates required to maintain the franc's parity were fundamentally incompatible with tackling the deepening problem of falling output and employment in the French economy. The crisis was in essentials one of interest rates, based on the perception of foreign exchange market operators that the domestic policy needs and interests of the two key ERM countries, France and Germany, were diverging rather than converging.

But the roots of the July 1993 crisis went deeper to an even more significant watershed event, German unification in 1990 and its economic mismanagement.

---

38. D. Begg *et al., Monitoring European Integration 1: The Impact of Eastern Europe* (London: Centre for Economic Policy Research, 1990); R. Portes, 'EMS and EMU after the Fall', *The World Economy*, January 1993.

Thereafter, problems of domestic stability had come to haunt the anchor currency of the ERM, forcing the Bundesbank to hike interest rates to record levels. As Bundesbank interest rates represented the interest-rate floor for the system, and with other states bringing inflation under better control than Germany, the rest of the ERM was forced to accept high real interest rates. The requirements of the ERM became even more onerous and impractical as the EMS entered the down-side of the economic cycle. Domestic requirements were for sharply falling real interest rates; ERM requirements were impelling high real interest rates. The British pound and the Italian lira were the first victims in the September 1992 crisis, exiting from the ERM; the Spanish peseta and Portuguese escudo were forced into repeated devaluations; the Irish punt followed with a devaluation in January 1993; and the French franc was under repeated siege before its eventual moment of truth in July 1993.

Already, in the wake of the September 1992 crisis, the EC Monetary Committee and the Committee of Central Bank Governors had undertaken special reviews of the EMS. Their conclusions were that the EMS was not in need of significant reform. But their two reports, submitted to ECOFIN in May 1993, were symptomatic of a recognition that the ERM had to be more flexible. Notably, in the light of what was to happen in July and August, the Bundesbank argued in the negotiations for temporary wider margins (in the order of 12 to 20 per cent). Unable to secure agreement on that basic change, otherwise the Bundesbank got what it wanted in the two reports. They referred to the need for more frequent planned realignments; for a surveillance mechanism to be set up to provide an early warning of the need for realignments; for fuller discussion in ECOFIN and the technical committees, based on the availability of objective indicators to measure the strength of particular currencies and the right of any country to raise questions about another country's central rate; and for intervention to be seen as a voluntary matter, of limited utility and second in importance to domestic policy adjustment by the monetary authorities of countries whose currencies were in difficulties. A very minimum flexibility was built into an ERM that was understood to be otherwise unchanged in fundamentals: to be based on narrow and hard bands.

The ERM crisis of July 1993 transformed that understanding. With a margin as wide as 15 per cent the hard ERM had been suspended in favour of 'managed floating'. This outcome to the crisis represented a victory for the Bundesbank and demonstration of its capacity for policy leadership. The French government had preferred as a solution the German proposal for the exit of the D-Mark from the ERM, a signal that the D-Mark was the problem, not the French franc or the ERM. This proposal proved unacceptable to other ERM members who identified their link with the D-Mark as their essential national interest in the ERM. Led by the Netherlands, they threatened to stick with the D-Mark. The outcome would have been that the Franch franc would have been left to depreciate alone. In gaining acceptance for a 15 per cent margin for most members, the Bundesbank had satisfied its key interests: in enabling it to take the necessary domestic monetary action to safeguard internal stability without having to be so concerned about its effects on other ERM members; and in reducing pressures for Bundesbank intervention as other currencies were given much wider freedom of manoeuvre. The Bundesbank gained greater discretion in domestic monetary management and less exposure to the ill-effects of intervention on the German money supply. The gain for other ERM members was greater flexibility to alter interest rates with reference to domestic economic needs without the external constraints of the hard ERM.

Two key questions remained. First, was so broad a band of fluctuation consistent with the purpose of the EMS – a 'zone of monetary stability' – and with continued progress to EMU? In the views of Giscard d'Estaing and Schmidt, the two founders of the EMS, the answer was a decided no. The ERM crisis was a crisis of European integration, reflecting a lack of dynamism and purpose in Franco-German bargaining relations; it was a defeat at the hands of the foreign exchange market operators.

Unquestionably, the change to one of the basic policy instruments of the ERM in August 1993 threatened to undermine its purpose and set back progress to EMU. But just how serious this threat was depended on the answer to the second question: whether and in what ways the *informal* rules governing the use of the bands of fluctuation would alter. The ERM members, other than Germany and the Netherlands, were faced with a dilemma: whether to prioritize the use of the new discretion to rapidly lower interest rates and encourage domestic recovery; or whether to maintain *de facto* narrow bands of fluctuation and closely shadow the D-Mark as a demonstration of policy resolve to the foreign exchange markets and to claim a secure place in the group of EC countries that would eventually form an EMU. How the EMS and EMU developed would depend crucially on the informal rules relating to the use of the new band of fluctuation; on how the foreign exchange markets reacted; and on political will and political decisions about the future route to EMU. A two-tier ERM seemed the most likely route to EMU. The Bundesbank sought to exert leadership on this policy issue, 'recommending' that other ERM countries should use caution in cutting interest rates. Such policy leadership was clearly self-interested; it was designed to shield the Bundesbank from pressures to cut its own interest rates sharply and thereby undermine its goal of domestic stability. But Bundesbank self-interest appeared to coincide with the perceived self-interests of most other ERM countries in demonstrating their *de facto* capability of remaining in a narrow band with the D-Mark. The prospect of competitive devaluation proved less attractive than that of competing to be in the *de facto* top tier of the ERM. That strategy required a credible commitment to price stability and to a Community-wide coordination of monetary policies based on the priorities of the Bundesbank. In short, the new flexible broad-band ERM was likely to contain an inner circle or upper tier of countries pursuing narrower, non-binding bands with the D-Mark. By December 1993 the Belgian and French currencies had crept back inside the old narrow band, a demonstration of the policy resolve. By then it was also clear that Christophersen and Hans Tietmeyer of the Bundesbank shared the view that there should be no rush to set a date for a return to narrow bands.

It also seemed possible that, consequent on the crises of 1992 and 1993, the stage two of EMU, scheduled for 1 January 1994, might take on a different form and significance.[39] The European Monetary Institute could be expected to seek a new role as an early warning system for ERM realignments in the context of any return to

---

39. See e.g. N. Thygesen, 'Towards Monetary Union in Europe – Reforms of the EMS in the Perspective of Monetary Union', *Journal of Common Market Studies*, December 1993.

narrow bands; to try to encourage member states to entrust to it the task of managing their foreign exchange reserves; even more radically, to become empowered to manage the domestic money market operations of participating central banks through bilateral contracts; and, perhaps most importantly of all, to search out a new role as a vehicle for developing ideas about a fast-track to EMU for a few within the Maastricht framework. Even with the continuation of a flexible broad-band ERM, EMU as envisaged in the Treaty on European Union was far from dead. Article 3 of the protocol on convergence criteria states simply that 'the criterion on participation in the exchange rate mechanism . . . shall mean that a member state has respected the "normal" fluctuation margins . . . without severe tensions for at least two years before the examination.' That criterion was, if anything, now easier to fulfil.

The Committee of Central Bank Governors: stage one of EMU

Despite the ERM crises of 1992 and 1993 the EMS remained formally an aspect of EMU, dedicated to implementing stage one as envisaged at the Madrid summit and putting in place stage two as outlined in the Treaty on European Union. In essence, stage one as outlined in the Delors Report was not radical; it represented a continuity with the EMS post-1987. It was, after all, unlike the transitions of 1983 and 1987 in lacking – till 1992 – a crisis to precipitate radical institutional change. In the words of the Delors Report, stage one 'would aim at a greater convergence of economic performance through the strengthening of economic and monetary policy and coordination within the existing institutional framework'.[40] As far as monetary policy coordination was concerned, the most important features of stage one were the attempts to strengthen the role of the Committee of Central Bank Governors and to achieve a full participation of all EC currencies in the ERM. It was, however, very questionable – as events were to prove – whether improvements to monetary policy coordination were anything like adequate to deal with the potentially destabilizing effects of the entry of the Spanish peseta in June 1989 and of the British pound in October 1990. Both countries introduced new and large problems of domestic policy adjustment to the rigours of the ERM, particularly Britain with its large burden of private debt relative to other EC countries and its balance of trade problem.

With the ECOFIN decisions of March 1990 new procedures for monetary coordination by the Committee of Central Bank Governors were put in place for stage one, replacing those of 1971 and 1974. These procedures envisaged a more active coordinating role for this Committee, based on a strengthening of its analytical capacity and its subcommittee structure, and a more visible public profile, enhanced by new annual reports and the possibility of making collective opinions public. Stage one involved also a measure of accountability to the European Council and the Economic and Monetary Committee of the European Parliament. In effect, it was the first stage in a transfer in the focus of the work of the Committee of Central Bank Governors from the informal and voluntary coordination of national central banks to the EC level.

40. Committee for the Study of Economic and Monetary Union, *Report on Economic and Monetary Union in the European Community* (the Delors Report) (Luxembourg: Office for Official Publications of the European Communities, August 1989), para. 50.

Symbolic of the search for a new, more visible profile was the publication of its first annual report on EC monetary and financial conditions in April 1992.[41] At the heart of the report was an emphasis on the difficulties of coordinating monetary, fiscal and wage policy in the interests of exchange-rate stability. Criticism was not levelled at monetary policies, though tensions in trying to coordinate short-term interest rates were recognized. The Committee of Central Bank Governors was concerned by excessive fiscal deficits and failure to contain wage pressures, particularly in member states 'which play a pivotal role in shaping the economic and financial conditions in the Community'. Fiscal policies and wage behaviour were putting too much stress and strain on monetary policies and threatened the stability of the ERM. Without substantial improvements in these two areas of concern inflation would remain too high (5.1 per cent in 1991, a disappointingly small decline of 0.7 per cent from the previous year). In other words, a veiled warning was being delivered to Germany. A more explicit warning was that current fiscal and wage problems threatened to create high levels of interest rates that ran counter to the need of many EC countries to engineer economic recovery. As an illustration of this view, and of a more assertive stance, in April the committee specifically criticized Spain for a lack of control in public expenditure and for failure to moderate wage behaviour.

In June 1992, in a speech in London, the chairman of the Committee of Central Bank Governors, Erik Hoffmeyer, took this theme of a lack of coordination further by criticizing the 'structural flaws' in the Treaty on European Union. Monetary policy coordination was to become supranational, but economic policy coordination would remain intergovernmental; the weak links between centralized monetary policy and decentralized fiscal policies reflected in turn the lack of clarity in the treaty about the political framework for European union; consequently, EMU would prove vulnerable to tensions and dissatisfaction at the national level. This speech reflected the new reality for the Committee of Central Bank Governors after the Maastricht summit and the paradox of success. The treaty's provisions had been a substantial victory for it. Now, however, the Committee of Central Bank Governors found itself exposed in a novel way and worried about its capacity to discharge its new role in the absence of a secure and strong EC political framework with which it could work and share responsibility for the European economy. Hoffmeyer remained firmly pro-EMU and thus differed from the negative view of the annual report of the Bank for International Settlements in June 1992. But both Hoffmeyer's speech and the BIS annual report had one factor in common: they reflected the concerns expressed by the Bundesbank.

As in the case of ECOFIN, the Treaty on European Union induced anticipatory behaviour within the Committee of Central Bank Governors. Already (as we noted in chapter 5) the relaunch of EMU by the European Council in 1988 had stimulated a more active bargaining position and more solidarity by this committee. Solidarity was encouraged by two factors: first, a new and more assertive ideological consensus around price stability as the goal of monetary policy and around the notion of central bank independence as the prerequisite for success in sustaining price stability; and second, the desire that the policy ideas and corporate concerns of central bankers

---

41. Committee of Governors of the Central Banks of the Member States of the European Community, *Annual Report (July 1990–December 1991)*, April 1992.

should not be neglected in favour of initiative and control of the policy process on EMU by the European Council and ECOFIN. Here we see replicated a factor that encouraged greater solidarity within ECOFIN during the same period: the desire not to lose managerial responsibility to another body. We are also reminded that ideological consensus was based on the German Bundesbank model: in other words on German leadership. Within the Committee of Central Bank Governors the overwhelming prestige of the Bundesbank was reflected in its work on the two draft statutes of the EMI and the ESCB. In practice (as we saw in chapter 5) the Committee of Central Bank Governors was remarkably successful in influencing key aspects of the Treaty on European Union, with work on the statutes for the EMI and the ESCB delegated to it.

The debate about a European monetary policy

The treaty provided that, with stage two, the Committee of Central Bank Governors would be transformed into the EMI, with responsibility not only for monitoring the EMS but also for strengthening the coordination of monetary policies and for preparing for a common monetary policy under the ESCB. Hence it was learning to come to terms with an augmentation of its authority in January 1994. This prospect had by 1992 concentrated its mind on consideration of how the common European monetary policy would operate. The focus of this bargaining was one of its three permanent subcommittees: that for monetary policy, which in turn established working groups to consider different problems, including the emotive issues surrounding the design of future European bank notes. Work was intensified, with new contributions from its own secretariat, including the new Economic Unit, and the Commission; whilst the chief economists of the key central banks began informal meetings. But progress in negotiations was slow.

A difficult issue in stage one was the effort to set coordinated and consistent quantitative objectives for money and credit aggregates as a basis for mutual surveillance of national monetary policies. In practice, a negotiated outcome proved very difficult to achieve, to the consternation of the Bundesbank. The difficulty stemmed, not least, from different views about the value and reliability of the information contained in monetary aggregates, compared for instance to the value of a fixed exchange-rate policy as a discipline on inflation or – as the Bank of England advocated after 1992 – of inflation targeting. A higher profile in the analysis of monetary trends proved difficult to establish, a failure that did little to reassure the Bundesbank about EMU.

Other issues relating to the future European monetary policy proved equally contentious among the central banks, exposing big differences of bargaining position between the British, French and German central banks. One such issue was minimum reserve requirements. The Bundesbank argued strongly that, as in Germany, minimum reserves on bank deposits should be introduced throughout the EC to provide harmonized and more effective monetary control. By this means the future ECB could force commercial banks to deposit non-interest bearing deposits with it as a means of effecting monetary discipline. Such a possibility was contained in Article 19 of the statute of the ESCB and was seen by the Bundesbank as an indispensable additional anchor for monetary stability. The Bank of England in particular was concerned by the implications of a more hierarchical relationship between the ECB and the national central banks.

In fact, the issue of minimum reserve requirements was an aspect of a wider debate, which focused on two main models for operating a European monetary policy. The model of a decentralized system was proposed by the Banque de France and supported by the Bank of England and justified by reference to the principle of 'subsidiarity' in Article 3b of the Treaty on European Union. According to this model, the operation of monetary policy would be kept as far as possible at the level of the existing national central banks as part of the new ESCB. In this way, decisions could be taken at the lowest possible level, consistent with the treaty. The Bank of England backed this position for three reasons: corporate self-interest in preserving as much autonomy as possible within any future ESCB; consistency with the domestic political priorities of the Conservative government, which gave great emphasis to the novelty and importance of the principle of 'subsidiarity' within the new treaty; and the attraction of an arrangement, akin to the US Federal Reserve System, in which the Bank of England – like the Federal Reserve Bank of New York – could provide the operating arm for a European central bank with its headquarters in Germany. Decentralization would also be a protection for specifically British institutions, like the discount houses which channel liquidity from the Bank of England to the British banking system.

By contrast, the Bundesbank championed an alternative model based on German arrangements. Monetary operations such as repurchase agreements could be organized through national central banks in much the same way that the state central banks in Germany assemble and process bids for central bank funding. The Bundesbank backed a federal rather than highly centralized ESCB as consistent with the principle of 'subsidiarity' but rejected the idea of a 'loose currency board'. Its central principle was the indivisibility of monetary policy, a principle that the Committee of Central Bank Governors had insisted on in the EMU negotiations (as we saw in chapter 5). Above all, the Bundesbank feared that the model promoted by the British and French central banks would lead to national central banks setting slightly different interest rates from those established by the ECB. The result would be competitive distortions in the operation of monetary policy and an undermining of price stability. Having conceded on the creation of the ECB, the Bundesbank was in no mood to see regulation any less strict than that in Germany.

Constraints on, and prospects for, central bank coordination: between government discretion and independence

As we saw in the case of economic policy coordination, monetary policy coordination is embedded in the complex politics of the EC's unique two-level policy process. It is also exposed to the traditional preference of EC governments (with Germany as the classic postwar exception) for hierarchical control over 'their' central banks. The result is that central bank coordination has been vulnerable and fragile to national institutional arrangements and to changing domestic economic priorities: above all, to the willingness of national governments to let their central banks cooperate. Attitudes to EMU among actors within the Committee of Central Bank Governors and the EC

Monetary Committee reflected, at least in part, different national institutional contexts: some were encouraged by the fact that a 'structural congruence' was possible between domestic and EC monetary policy arrangements; others were suspicious, even hostile, recognizing the scale of the gulf between domestic monetary arrangements and prospective EC arrangements; whilst yet others took hope from the fact that their domestic arrangements were clearly moving in the direction of proposed EC arrangements. This division was most apparent over the key issue of central bank independence, provided for in the case of the ESCB and before stage three for the national central banks. Germany had no problem on this issue; two successive British Prime Ministers, Margaret Thatcher and John Major, entertained deep reservations about granting full independence to the Bank of England (though notably their Chancellors, Lawson and Lamont, did not), and implicitly even more to an independent ECSB; whilst the Belgian, French and Spanish governments were by 1993 moving ahead with plans to give independence to their central banks well ahead of the Maastricht timetable.

Without independence for national central banks there were great constraints on voluntary coordination in the Committee of Central Bank Governors: they were forced to look continuously over their shoulders at their national governments. Hence, as far as the Committee of Central Bank Governors was concerned, it was crucial to the success of the EMI that, as soon as possible after 1 January 1994, such independence should be granted. In its absence the development of an effective common institutional regulation of monetary policy, of formal and informal rules, was inhibited. Governments, like the British, that were unwilling to concede independence to their central banks were equally opposed to delegating authority to them for the purpose of central banking coordination. On the other hand, independent central banks like the Bundesbank were suspicious of the credibility of bargains arrived at with central banks which, in the last resort, did not possess the capability to deliver. To complicate the problems of coordination of monetary policy further, even the Bundesbank had problems about delegating authority to its president acting in the Committee of Central Bank Governors: for its own authority was concentrated in the Bundesbank council, not the president. Together, these factors served to undermine the strength of central bankers as bargaining partners in European integration.

For these reasons it was clear that effective coordination and maximum impact on EC bargaining required a transformation of the Committee of Central Bank Governors into a new type of institution, initially the EMI and the ESCB. But, just how effective a coordinating and bargaining role the EMI could play would depend on the number of central banks to which independence had been granted. With legislation to grant independence completed or underway in Belgium, France and Spain in 1993, there was a prospect of a significant, and growing, group of independent central banks: bearing in mind also that already the Danish, Irish, Italian and Portuguese central banks had a substantial amount of independence. The combined weight of the independent and semi-independent central banks, plus the lesson of the ERM crisis of 1992 that a tighter surveillance of exchange rates was needed, suggested that the EMI could develop a more active and influential bargaining role than had originally been envisaged. Of particular interest was likely to be its use of its right under Article 109f, acting by a two-thirds majority, to 'formulate . . . submit . . . and make recommendations' to the monetary authorities on monetary and exchange rate policies. Where these formal recommendations were backed by all the independent central banks, their credibility would be likely to be far greater with the foreign-exchange markets than that of any hostile government.

Overall, the progress in forging new rules, formal and informal, for monetary policy coordination has been impressive with the EMS and the proposals in the Treaty on European Union. During the 1980s a series of factors conspired to facilitate institutional development and the bargaining strength of the EC central bankers: the perceived success of the EMS in stabilizing exchange rates and fostering nominal convergence; the desire to sustain that success by strengthening the EMS when it was faced by crisis, as in 1983 and 1987, and then by the threat of destabilization as a consequence of capital liberalization; and ideological consensus about the primacy to be accorded to price stability and central bank independence. Together, these factors promoted radical institutional change in the form of EMU and a role as model for the Bundesbank. They also ensured that violations of the rules of the game were nothing like so marked as in the 1960s and 1970s.

But the crisis of September 1992 revealed that the institutional development of the EMS and of EMU had not removed some fundamental centrifugal tendencies of the EC's two-level policy process. As the exit of the British government from the ERM that September displayed, governments have the all-important discretion not to pursue the domestic policies that are required to sustain the central rates. In this respect nothing seemed to have changed since the 'snake' of the 1970s, when the British government withdrew in June 1972, Italy in February 1973, and France in January 1974 and then again in March 1976. But in fact the notable feature of the EMS was the degree of loyalty that members displayed to the system: the exits of the British pound and the Italian lira in September 1992 were in fact the first in over 13 years and were followed by a closing of ranks. In this respect at least there was evidence that, as an institution, European monetary coordination had significantly developed.

In two other senses, government discretion was obviously potent in the operation of the EMS. First, the rules of the EMS stated that realignments of central rates will be subject to mutual agreement, and that procedure was respected. However, the formal procedure was not specific about decisions on central rates for new members of the ERM. In October 1990 the British government chose to enter the ERM and did so at a central rate that it selected. That act of unilateralism had significant consequences: for the Bundesbank was not convinced that it could be committed to provide full support for a rate that it had not played a part in determining and that, moreover, it regarded as wrong. Of course, seen from another angle, this episode of disagreement about Britain's central rate underlines the strongly cooperative norms that had emerged within the functioning of the ERM and the belief that these norms had not been understood and respected in October 1990.

Second, governments were strongly motivated by the desire to save face. Reputation was a two-sided affair in a two-level policy process. A concern for one's reputation among one's colleagues in the ERM was matched by a concern about one's image within one's political party, with coalition partners and with the electorate. This phenomenon could be observed in the way that debate about realignments within the EMS focused on the composition of the upward and downward adjustments involved.

In the early 1980s and in January 1987 the French government put pressure on the German government to revalue as part of a package so that the scale of devaluation of the franc could be 'hidden'. The implication was that Germany had a problem, as well as France. Face-saving was also a key factor in the unwillingness of governments to contemplate realignment in summer 1992 and in the French government's preference for a wide 15 per cent margin rather than a package deal that included a devaluation of the franc in August 1993. Defence of parities had become infected by national symbolism: it involved the pride and reputation of governments who had committed themselves to the informal rule of fixed rates more in order to achieve respect than out of European idealism. National power was measured in terms of the degree of strength of one's currency within the ERM (the *franc fort* model); the desire to augment it was apparent in the professed will of the French government to share in the anchor role in the ERM with Germany (a will professed just before the July 1993 crisis) and in Prime Minister John Major's view of summer 1992 that the British pound had the potential to replace the D-Mark as the anchor in the 1990s.

The penalties for hubris were paid quickly: for ignoring rational economic arguments that the shock effects of German unification required a real appreciation of the D-Mark and that the workings of the sclerotic EC labour markets would place potentially excessive pressure on adjustment via alterations in relative nominal wages.[42] Governments had the all-important discretion to prevent a review and revision of central rates, as in spring 1990 and August and September 1992, and were repaid for their economic folly. In September 1992 the Bundesbank offered an economically sensible bargain for coordination of a general realignment with an interest rate cut. The bargain was rejected. One is reminded that the central informal rule on which the third stage of the EMS was based (fixed rates) had its roots more in political calculations of national interest and in the factor of pride than in economic theory or in some logic of European integration. And EC governments proved vulnerable most of all in their pride – and as delicate as Humpty Dumpty, once that was meddled with by the foreign-exchange markets.

Whilst economists were disunited about the weighting to be given to different causes of instability in the ERM, they could agree that a fixed-rate rule was doomed. It would either come into hopeless conflict with underlying fundamentals (whether defined in terms of economic variables like the current account, inflation or unemployment or of the state of the financial system – like its capacity to absorb the budget deficit or the overhang of private debt); or, perhaps even independently of fundamentals, as in the case of France, it would fall victim to self-fulfilling expectations of operators in the financial markets.[43] A fixed-rate regime offered a 'one-way bet' to operators in the financial markets once expectations of a sizeable realignment had built up. The question is whether rates will change in a rational and controlled manner or whether change will be forced on the authorities; not whether

---

42. Portes, 'EMS and EMU after the Fall'.
43. For the dispute on the relative importance of 'self-fulfilling expectations' and 'fundamentals' see respectively R. Portes, 'EMS and EMU after the Fall: A comment' and J. Williamson, 'The Fall of the Hard EMS', *The World Economy*, No.3 (1993), pp. 377–9.

fixed rates can be made permanent outside a monetary union.[44] And underlying that question is the deeper issue of whether governments can be relied on to make a rational and controlled response to changing economic fundamentals and shifting perceptions in foreign exchange markets. In 1992 EC governments were treating the EMS as if it were *de facto* a monetary union, an illusion that could not be sustained. In so doing they were unwittingly conspiring to offer the markets a one-way bet. For foreign-exchange market operators, and economists, knew that there was no such thing as a regime of permanently fixed exchange rates, other than within a fully established monetary union.

The corporate solidarity of central banks

What ultimately was interesting in EC–central bank bargaining relations was the degree of corporate solidarity that EC central bankers were able to retain in the face of these centrifugal pressures. Solidarity was an important resource for them in their bargaining position with other EC bodies. It was to be expected that the functioning of the Committee of Central Bank Governors would be affected by the 1992 crisis and its aftermath, by the structural dynamics of economic divergence and of the down-side of the economic cycle as this showed its effects after 1991. In its operation the pressures and tensions of soft and hard currency blocs resurfaced. The countries of the soft currency bloc were cast in the role of *demandeurs* for change; those of the hard currency bloc as vetoers. But what was perhaps surprising was the degree of corporate solidarity that remained, reflected in the tortuous attempt to share out blame for the 1992 crisis in its report of April 1993. That solidarity may not have shown a clear-cut commitment to linking reform of the EMS to EMU: for instance, the emphasis on more frequent realignments in its April 1993 report gave no attention to the provision in Article 109j that a currency must stay within the 'normal' fluctuation margin for at least two years as a precondition of eligibility for stage three.

Four factors induced cohesion among central bankers. The first was enduring ideological consensus around the primacy of a single policy goal, price stability. Second, central bank culture was forged in the peculiar disciplined world of confronting financial markets. Central banks were the actors most exposed to financial market pressures: in the front line in trying to sell government debt or defend exchange rates. That discipline had become harsher with market liberalization. The financial markets were much more effective censors of economic and monetary policies than before, as the experiences of 1992–3 underlined. Central banks recognized that the basic requirement was either to convince the markets by taking credible action or to do what they intimated. Stronger market discipline drew them together rather than apart and underlined their bargaining strength.

A third factor was the corporate self-interest of the Committee of Central Bank Governors in preventing the slippage of initiative to the European Council, where heads of government and state and foreign ministers could not be trusted to be well

---

44. J. Williamson and M. Miller, *Targets and Indicators: A Blueprint for the International Coordination of Economic Policies* (Washington, DC: Institute for International Economics, 1987).

informed on economic and financial issues. ECOFIN shared that corporate interest and was able to embed it in the treaty in the provision that ECOFIN will decide on stage three (thus keeping the foreign ministers at bay). Finally, it should not be forgotten that the EC central bank governors came together more frequently than finance ministers: in fact for two-and-a-half days per month in Basle, for the monthly meeting of the board of the Bank for International Settlements, for the G-10 governors' meeting and for a half-day of the Committee of Central Bank Governors. In this context the scope for peer-group pressure to build up is increased.

The prospects for the EMI in stage two

The launch of the EMI to replace the Committee of Central Bank Governors embodied a paradox. Here, on the one hand, was a body with modest powers to prepare for stage three, to strengthen the coordination of monetary policies, and with more formalized rights to be consulted before national policy decisions were taken. Also, in contrast to its predecessor, the EMI possessed an independently appointed and full-time president. Independence was further underlined in Article 8 of the Protocol: its council members (central bank governors) were not to seek or take instructions from EC institutions or national governments in the performance of their tasks. With the establishment of central bank independence in Belgium, France and Spain by 1994, the potential for a more authoritative and self-confident body was reinforced. It might even benefit from the treaty provision that national central banks could delegate some of their operations to the EMI.

On the other hand, there were few other grounds to judge the EMI as a qualitative leap forward in European monetary integration. First, the recent traumatic ERM crises and lack of progress towards meeting the convergence criteria indicated that stage two would be lengthier than some EC politicians and officials had anticipated; and that the centre of gravity would shift not only away from preparation of stage three to other functions but also to the role of ECOFIN in promoting economic convergence and the recovery on which EMU depended. Equally constricting on any qualitative leap forward in integration was the doctrine of 'indivisibility' on which the Bundesbank had insisted. In consequence national monetary sovereignty was to be left intact till stage three.

Given the likely length and difficulties of stage two, the central problem was likely to involve the EMI's role in monitoring the functioning of the EMS. The scale of the turbulence and size of speculative pressures revealed in 1992 and 1993 suggested that some greater pooling of authority was required in this sphere than had been anticipated in the treaty negotiations or in the central bankers' report on the 1992 ERM crisis. Such a potential existed in the provision of Article 6.4 of the Protocol that national central banks could entrust the EMI with the task of managing their foreign exchange reserves. Indeed, as a member of the Delors Committee, Alexandre Lamfalussy, the president of the EMI, had advocated a more radical step: that in stage two the new EC monetary authority should be empowered to enter into bilateral contracts to manage the domestic money market operations of central banks. These kinds of changes would involve a centralization of central bank operations rather than a transfer of authority from the national level. But first they would have to overcome the deep-seated reluctance of national central banks to dilute their role.

With no capacity to impose substantial authority of its own, the EMI was thrown back on practising the arts of persuasion and leverage. Much would depend on its ability to make constructive use of new opportunities: of the evidence of structural weakness in the EMS and of consequent threats to the EC's wider functioning; of the spread of national central bank independence and their subsequent greater reliance on each other; and of the possibility that the Bundesbank's incentive to share its monetary sovereignty might increase if the D-Mark came under increasing pressure because of unsound fundamentals and proved unable to sustain its role as anchor. The optimistic scenario involved a strengthened EMI based on an inner club of low-inflation countries whose central banks were independent and which, one by one, returned to the discipline of a hard ERM. The pessimistic scenario was a failure to make progress on economic convergence and expansion, a diminishing political will to support union (if the German and French elections of 1994 and 1995 respectively returned less-federally-minded political leaders) and measures to renationalize policies.

Conclusions

It seldom wins and then by the skin of its teeth. It crawls, it goes into hiding but keeps on, putting down its quickly drying track on the historical landscape.

(Günter Grass, *From the Diary of a Snail* (1972: 6))

This chapter has demonstrated that the EMS and EMU policy process, and the bargaining relations that comprise it, is locked in a double paradox: between the inherent fragility of exchange-rate systems, exposed as they are to the dynamics of structural change in the international political economy, and the institutional durability given by the framework of the EC; and to the complex tensions typical of the distinctive two-level policy process that characterizes the institutional functioning of the EC and that gives it, short of European political union, an inherent fragility. Hence there is a constant dialectic between change and stability, summarized in the elusive stability that defines the EMS and EMU policy process in the absence of the institutional robustness of a European political union.

So, whilst this chapter has highlighted the importance of the rules of the game in economic and monetary policy coordination in the EC, it has also drawn attention to the complex dynamics of change that affect their development and operation because they are embedded in the unique two-level policy process of the EC. The way in which the formal and informal rules have evolved is inseparable from this two-level policy process, as we have seen in the cases of ECOFIN and the Committee of Central Bank Governors. This observation raises questions about the nature of institutional change within the EC.

As we witnessed in chapters 2–3, exogenous factors in the form of war – as in 1914 with the suspension of convertibility – and economic crisis – as in 1931 – have been obvious sources of discontinuous institutional change in international monetary policy coordination. Radical changes in formal rules followed and would do so in the face of similar exogenous developments in the future. But the single most important point about institutional change to emerge from this chapter is that, within the EC, institutional change has been overwhelmingly incremental. The EC has provided a new type of institutional context that has made possible repeated new bargains and compromises among its constituent actors: repeated bargains have meant that reputation, honesty and integrity have taken on a new importance in the dynamics of economic and monetary policy coordination. Compared, for instance, to the Bretton Woods system or the gold standard, the EC has offered a more hospitable environment for accommodating evolutionary institutional change. The consequence has been that the actors directly involved have been able to derive increasing returns from the EMS. In effect, the EMS has provided a path of development that has been able to accommodate economic and financial problems – and might even have enough resilience to endure economic decline.

When we consider the launch and development of the EMS or the relaunch of EMU, we observe that these processes consisted of a gradual alteration of formal and informal rules. As we saw in chapter 4, the launch of the EMS was not fundamentally radical in altering the formal rules of monetary policy coordination. But from thereon informal rules gradually evolved within ECOFIN and the technical committees that altered its character and prepared the way for changes of formal rules, limited in the case of the Basle-Nyborg Agreement and radical with the Treaty on European Union. This gradual evolution of informal and formal rules was interwoven with the effects of two other factors: the unanticipated consequences of choices made within the operation of the EMS (thus the commitment post-1983 to using the ERM as a disciplinary device for domestic policy raised new questions about German 'dominance' of European monetary policies, articulated by Balladur and Amato in 1988); and the external changes in the context of the operation of the EMS (notably the threat posed by rapid falls of the US dollar in 1977–8 and 1986–7 and the introduction of freedom of movement of capital in the late 1980s). These two factors provided new opportunities for agenda-setting and influence by the European Commission and increased its bargaining power (as we saw in chapter 5). They also acted as catalysts for national governments and central bankers to redefine their self-interests and to conclude that existing institutional arrangements for policy coordination were inadequate. Ultimately, however, fundamental institutional changes in the EMS were an aggregation of many specific and small alterations over time in the perceptions of self-interest and opportunity on the part of the various actors involved.

Looked at from an institutional perspective, there is an understandable temptation to conclude that specific changes in the formal and informal rules of policy coordination may change the history of the EMS and EMU but that they will not change its direction. The institutional evolution of the EMS shows that history matters, but that historical change has an inbuilt tendency to follow the admittedly not always well-defined contours provided by institutional regulation and the structural power of the anchor currency that underpins that regulation: in short, that institutional change, and history, is 'path dependent'. Institutions impart a self-reinforcing character to change. Reflecting the structural power of the anchor currency, they also provide a context of predictability in which the complex bargaining relations that comprise the EMS and EMU policy process evolve.

This stress on underlying continuity is attributable to another facet of the EMS and

EMU policy process: the presence of a corporatist policy network. It is most developed in the bargaining relationship between the EC and the central banks, with three factors combining to support it: the corporate self-interest of the central banks in keeping the European Council and, if possible, even ECOFIN out of the sphere of business where it judges itself to be professionally competent; the common professional culture, abetted by ideological consensus; and the behavioural effects of repetitive bargaining.

But this account of the role of the EC as a mediating institution, facilitating continuous bargaining and compromise, has also drawn attention to the degree of tension and conflict that has marked the history of the EMS: most strikingly in March 1983, January 1987, September 1992 and July 1993, as well as in the 1960s and 1970s. Again, exogenous and endogenous factors have precipitated tension and conflict: the effects of the rapid fall of the US dollar in 1986–7 and 1992 have generated repeated tensions as the D-Mark strengthened within the EMS; the inflationary pressures introduced into the anchor country, Germany, by unification and the consequent effects on levels of interest rates within the ERM as the Bundesbank pushed up its rates to choke these pressures; and the incompatibility between the external discipline imposed by ERM membership on such occasions and domestic needs and pressures to restore output and employment. These factors express themselves through the two-level policy process and shape the degree of mutual solidarity that is possible. Very practically, they reveal the limitations on the capacity of actors in ECOFIN and the technical committees to achieve compromise solutions: witness the bruising bargaining in ECOFIN in August 1993 leading to the decision to widen the bands of fluctuation. Their freedom to bargain and still maintain the loyalty of domestic political support is restricted, as the government of John Major discovered in the autumn of 1992.

Ideological convictions are another source of tension and conflict that infect economic and monetary coordination within the EC: convictions about European union or about national independence; and convictions about the proper goals of economic and monetary policies. The first ideological cleavage, between European union and national independence, is manifested in the different positions adopted by Christian Democratic parties, which are pro-union, and the British Conservative and French Gaullist parties, where national independence represents a cultural inheritance that constrains economic and monetary policy coordination. It was noticeable that, before the crucial Maastricht summit in December 1991, the Christian Democratic heads of government met to coordinate their position and affirm their overriding ideological commitment to European union; meanwhile, the British Conservative government negotiated an opt-out on stage three of EMU. Ideological commitment was important and divisive. It endowed actors with a will to pay, if necessary, a high price for what they believed. For some actors that high price included a willingness to move ahead faster to EMU as an inner core, in the name of union; for others, it involved the willingness to pay the price of exclusion, in the name of national independence.

The second potential cleavage – on convictions about economic and monetary policy – raises the decisive question of whether the EMS had evolved, and the Treaty on European Union been negotiated, on the basis of an economic theory that would prove controversial and potentially damaging. EMU, in the form that is outlined in the treaty, and the earlier informal rule that the EMS was a disciplinary mechanism, were embedded in an ideological commitment to price stability. The expression of this commitment was the informal rule on no realignments and the formal rules on convergence criteria and excessive deficits. But such an ideological commitment could be difficult to sustain; its price might even prove too high for those who are ideologically committed to European union. Making sacrifices for price stability is one thing in the face of the ravages of rampant inflation: but the value of the trade-off changes as inflation drops and actors are left to bear the costs of unemployment and lost output. To the extent that the new formal rules of EMU are built on an incentive system that involves an ideological commitment to price stability, there is a risk that the rules will be subverted.

A further tension within the EMU negotiated in the Treaty on European Union is between the institutional regulation of economic policy coordination and the institutional regulation of monetary policy coordination. The risks of a failure to adequately address the problem of fiscal coordination had been outlined by Alexandre Lamfalussy, general manager of the Bank for International Settlements (and later president of the EMI), in the annex to the Delors Report:

> The combination of a small Community budget with large, independently determined national budgets leads to the conclusion that, in the absence of fiscal coordination, the global fiscal policy of the EMU would be the accidental outcome of decisions taken by member states. There would simply be no Community-wide macroeconomic fiscal policy.[45]

In the treaty economic policy coordination was strengthened but remained intergovernmental in character; monetary policy coordination was to become supranational, involving a different order of institutional change. By 1993 it was not clear just how precisely this tension would manifest itself. Such an asymmetry of institutional development within EMU opened up the prospect of a restructuring of the overall rules in both directions. In short, if EMU eventually emerged, it was likely to have a different equilibrium from that envisaged in the Treaty on European Union.

In the final analysis, it is clear that factors endogenous and exogenous to the EMS have caused tension and on occasion outright conflict, as well as fostering cooperation, in economic policy and monetary policy coordination. They have influenced the way in which the rules of the game, formal and informal, have evolved and been applied in practice. Analysis of the rules underpinning the EMS has revealed the importance of national political interest and calculation in shaping their evolution (like the role of the *franc fort* behind the informal rules on the ERM as a disciplinary mechanism and on no realignment); crises have drawn out the potential for tension and conflict within the EMS, even the collapse of its key policy instrument of narrow bands in August 1993; and the exits of the British and Italian governments clarified the limits of the integration process and the underlying vulnerability and fragility of the ERM. The crisis of September 1992 was a story of failure of communication and of mutual recrimination on a grand scale. The institutions of the EMS, notably ECOFIN and the

---

45. A. Lamfalussy, 'Macro-coordination of Fiscal Policies in an Economic and Monetary Union in Europe', in Committee for the Study of Economic and Monetary Union, *Report on Economic and Monetary Union in the European Community*, p. 101.

EC Monetary Committee, failed to function effectively either in averting the impending crisis by a planned realignment or in managing the crisis. It was decisive bilateral Franco-German action, beyond the established rules on intervention, that eventually saved the ERM. In 1992 both promised 'massive' intervention, and the Bundesbank resorted, for the first time, to intramarginal intervention on behalf of the franc. Bilateral Franco-German collaboration on the EMS was hardly new. But the form that it took in 1992 showed just how important the institutional arrangements of the EMS were for these two countries.

Paradoxically, the episode of the September 1992 crisis highlighted the importance of institutional regulation; cooperative norms had become strongly established in the functioning of the EMS. Whilst in the future powerful exogenous and endogenous forces – mediated by the two-level policy process and by financial markets – could destroy the ERM in its hard form and postpone EMU in its Maastricht version, it is impossible to escape the conclusion that economic and monetary policy coordination within the EMS policy process has been locked into a particular path of development from which it had not, even after the July 1993 crisis, been derailed. Other possibilities in its development can be stressed, like a *de facto* EMU based on the D-Mark; certainly, no law of historical inevitability is at work. The disruptive power of financial market forces was, for instance, all too apparent in 1992–3, not least in the face of institutional rules that lacked credibility. But one could still speak of the history of the EC's economic and monetary policy coordination in terms of a coherent sequence of causes and effects: argue that the rules of the game and their evolution have provided a key to this coherence; and point to the leadership role of the Bundesbank in an inherently asymmetrical system of monetary policy coordination as the main structural source of that coherence. Of course, if the structural power of the Bundesbank were eroded, and no adequate substitute as anchor found, that coherence would vanish.

As we survey the importance of institutional rules of the game, we are reminded of one of the central lessons of chapter 2 – that, though rules may give a certain overall pattern and coherence to policy development, they do not mean that putting the EMS and EMU into practice has involved a neat, clearly organized and hierarchical pattern. The story of the EMS and EMU is of an interactive and negotiated policy process, framed by the rules of the game but not simply contained within them. Capability of the policy actors involved to deliver on their commitments, themselves embodied in rules, is decisive. It is tested by reference to the adequacy of the economic ideology underpinning the rules; to the extent to which the operation of the rules is compatible with economic fundamentals; by how adequately and effectively financial market operators perceive that the rules are being applied to ensure strong fundamentals; and by the consistency of policy with trade interdependence. The 'impersonal forces' of European monetary integration take more forms than just the institutional rules of the game, as we shall see in chapters 7–8. A more encompassing structural power is at work.

Chapter 7

PUTTING THE EMS AND EMU INTO PRACTICE (2)

The power of 'sound money' policy ideas

If all economists were laid end to end, they would not reach a conclusion.

(George Bernard Shaw)

Chapter 6 showed that, important though they are, the rules of the EMS game and the two-level decision structure of the EC do not provide a single, simple institutional explanation of the nature and patterns of change in the EMS and EMU policy process. Our attention was brought back repeatedly to different bases of structural power: to the role of economic ideas, of economic fundamentals, of trade interdependency, of financial markets and of powerful world currencies like the US dollar. In speaking of the 'impersonal forces' of the global economy we are not speaking of a single simple phenomenon. The structural power of financial markets, and the role of competitive forces in rewarding rational actors, is clearly important. But the way in which they operate is shaped by other sources of structural power: the power of trade interdependency and of economic fundamentals, like differential inflation rates or debt levels or contrasting balance of trade positions; and the climate of economic ideas. They help to define the relationships between governments and markets and influence the expectations of each about the behaviour of the other. In short, the context of the bargaining relations that comprise the EMS and EMU policy process is provided by the structural power of financial markets, world currency relationships, economic fundamentals, trade interdependency and economic ideas.

The objective of this chapter is to examine critically one of these economic dimensions of the EMS and EMU and the way in which it affects the policy process. What has been the role of economic ideas in structuring bargaining relations within the EMS and EMU policy process? In the process a set of assumptions are being tested: that the climate of ideas amongst policy professionals is important in relation to economic management; that economic ideas possess a degree of autonomy in their development; and that policy actors are 'cocooned' within sets of economic policy ideas that shape and constrain their choices and create 'focal points' for agreement.[1] The argument is nuanced. On the one hand, the EMS and EMU policy process has been captured by a mainstream economics whose intellectual history involves a return to 'sound money' policy ideas; and, with the Treaty of European Union, the EC has in effect 'constitutionalized' a set of economic ideas that, preoccupied with price stability,

1. On the influence of the climate of ideas on economic policy management see H. Nau, *The Myth of America's Decline: Leading the World Economy into the 1990s* (New York: Oxford University Press, 1990). On the role of transnational 'epistemic communities' in fostering cooperation see P. Haas (ed.) 'Knowledge, Power and International Policy Coordination', special issue of *International Organization* 46 (1992).

risk neglecting sensible and effective demand management at the Community level. In this respect the treaty is more than a general procedural framework for achieving EMU; it is programmatic in an economic sense, imbalanced in the repertoire of policy instruments that it bestows on the EC and vulnerable to changing circumstances, like a fall in total EC spending as EC monetary policy is tightened. But, on the other hand, the adoption and gradualist approach to EMU of the treaty owed more to a difficult process of compromise among domestic political objectives than to any strictly economic rationale for an extended transition period in stage two. Political conditions were central to the influence of a particular transnational 'epistemic community'.

Though 'sound money' policy ideas might be ascendant, it was not possible to speak of a single unified economic theory underpinning the EMS and the Treaty on European Union or of a consensus among economists and officials about how 'sound money' is best put into effect. Within the burgeoning economic literature on European monetary integration and union there were deep divisions across a wide range of issues – from the appropriate relationship between economic convergence and monetary union to the desirable role and extent of fiscal policy coordination in EMU. On perhaps only one issue was there something approaching an economic consensus: that the stage two of EMU as proposed in the treaty was far too long and would prove destabilizing.[2] More characteristic were often fundamental disagreements about the appropriate policy instruments for EMU. An example was the difference between mainstream monetarists, who argued for money supply targeting, and central bankers, who, though committed to 'sound money', preferred to retain discretion in the use of their policy instruments like interest rate changes. It was central bankers rather than any 'epistemic community' of monetarists who captured the EMS and EMU policy process.

But what united central bankers and monetarists was 'sound money': the preoccupation with price stability and with the monetary aspects of the economy. The important feature of much of this theoretical disagreement during the negotiations within the EMS and EMU policy process between 1988 and 1991 was that it was conducted within this framework of ideas. Both the EMS, as it evolved from 1983, and the Treaty on European Union rested on this foundation of sound money ideas. The reference point of the EMS and EMU policy process remained the intellectual impact of sound money ideas. Indeed the new EMS and EMU involved a transfer to the EC level of an ideological ascendancy of sound money ideas that had previously been established at the national level in the core EC member states. So it is worthwhile beginning with a brief historical outline of these ideas and the conditions that gave rise to their ascendancy within the mainstream ideas underpinning the EMS and EMU policy process in the 1980s.

2. See the argument on the superiority of a strategy of 'shock therapy' over gradualism in P. De Grauwe, *The Economics of Monetary Integration* (Oxford: Oxford University Press, 1992); the otherwise heated debate between R. Portes, 'EMS and EMU after the Fall: A Comment', J. Williamson, 'The Fall of the Hard EMS', *The World Economy*, no. 3 (1993), pp. 377–9; and G. Bishop, *EMU in 1995?* (London: Salomon Brothers, 1992); Bishop, *Is There a Rapid Route to an EMU of the Few?* (London: Salomon Brothers, 1993).

Monetarism and 'sound money'

The main vehicle through which sound money ideas re-established themselves was monetarism. Monetarism is an economic ideology in the sense that it links certain propositions about economic actors and the behaviour of the economy to normative views about the long-term benefits of a competitive economy and of highly restricted government intervention in the economy. Its roots go back to the quantity theory of money which formed the basis of classical monetary economics from the eighteenth century. But in its modern form monetarism flowered in the United States, where its central ideas had an affinity with the pronounced spirit of radical liberal individualism in the political tradition. In short, cultural receptivity played an important part in its appeal there. The term was first used by Karl Brunner in the 1960s, while monetarism became most closely associated with the writings of Milton Friedman.[3]

The relationship to political tradition was important in either facilitating or restricting monetarism's later dissemination, particularly to western Europe. In this respect an important distinction must be drawn between the doctrine of monetarism and the sound money policy ideas and techniques that were taken up by governments across western Europe during the 1970s and 1980s. Monetarist doctrine exported most successfully to Britain, being adopted by the Thatcherites who came to dominate economic policy making after the election of the Conservative government in 1979. Policy transfer was helped in this case by the Thatcherite ideology of the 'enterprise culture' as well as by a deeper national political tradition of 'arm's-length government' and the limited state.[4]

Elsewhere in continental Europe, the combination of an entrenched state tradition, emphasizing a primacy of public-service values, with the strength of Christian Democratic and Social Democratic political ideologies created greater cultural resistance to monetarism. But, though the ideological appeal was more limited, the policy instruments of sound money were adopted widely. They were, for instance, taken up by the German Bundesbank before the British Treasury; they came to be adopted by the French Socialist government by 1983. It was not possible to adopt these policy instruments without radically reconsidering the goals of policy; so, implicitly, a new economic policy orthodoxy took root in the EC states by or during the 1980s.

Though cross-national policy transfer played a role, the real catalyst for the adoption of sound money ideas was national economic crisis: in Britain in the mid-1970s, before the election of a Conservative government in 1979; and in France in 1983. In fact, in both cases crisis and the adoption of sound money policy instruments occurred under socialist governments: in the form of monetary targets in Britain and external exchange rate discipline in France. This transformation of policy ideas was to be explained by the way in which economic crisis brought to a head a process that had been underway since the 1960s: namely that changing economic circumstances and problems had been revealing the inadequacy of the prevailing

3. K. Brunner, 'The Role of Money and Monetary Policy', *Federal Reserve Bank of St Louis Review* 50 (1968), pp. 8–24; T. Mayer (ed.) *The Structure of Monetarism* (New York: W.W. Norton, 1978).
4. K. Dyson, *The State Tradition in Western Europe* (Oxford: Basil Blackwell, 1980).

orthodoxy – Keynesianism. The background to Keynesianism had been provided by the problem of recession, of unemployment and falling prices, that characterized the interwar years. Its great achievement was to create a political consensus about the appropriate policy instruments to deal with that problem: namely, an active use of fiscal policy in the form of adjustments of tax and public expenditure.

But the weakness of Keynesianism derived from its inability to generate a similar consensus, or sense of conviction, about what could be done about the new problem of accelerating inflation, whose cause was generally attributed to the 'wage–price spiral': the upward pressure of wage settlements on prices, and the upward pull of prices on wages.[5] The paramount need to focus on this economic problem was further under-lined by the two oil crises of the 1970s. In their wake 'stagflation' – the combination of low growth and high unemployment with high inflation – came to dominate economic debate. In effect monetarism was able to fill a policy vacuum and to provide the intellectual catalyst for the kind of sound money ideas that were later to dominate the EMS and EMU policy process. It did so by returning to the idea that by managing the money supply it was possible to control prices. Friedman argued that, after a time lag, prices reflect movements in the money supply. Also, fiscal policy instruments were much less effective and reliable policy instruments in stabilizing the economy than Keynesianism predicted; not least, budget deficits have little net effect on aggregate demand because government borrowing 'crowds out' private borrowing and associated spending. The key requirement was a long-term discipline on the rate of growth of the money supply.

The central theoretical underpinning of monetarism was provided by the argument that a market-clearing mechanism exists in the economy to ensure that there is a unique unemployment rate consistent with stable inflation. This rate is predetermined by the supply side of the economy, by the efficiency of markets and firms. If unemployment is cut below this 'natural' rate by a fiscal and/or monetary boost, then inflation will not only rise but also accelerate until unemployment reverts to its starting-point. The 'acceleration' principle implied that there was no permanent trade-off between inflation and unemployment: that government was not able to influence either output or unemployment over the medium term by such means. Instead, the attempts of governments to spend their way to full employment led to increasingly rapid inflation, without discernible benefits as unemployment soared from one business cycle to the next. Governments might just as well focus on price stability as the single and ultimate objective of economic management; use monetary policy instruments for this purpose; treat budgets as exercises in prudent housekeeping rather than as instruments for balancing the economy; and deal with unemployment and output problems by 'supply-side' measures to induce greater competitiveness (like measures to reduce rigidities in the labour market or in the service sector). As Friedman argued, the economy gravitates towards a 'natural rate of unemployment' which in the long run is largely independent of the rate of inflation and cannot be changed by monetary policy.[6] The existence of this natural rate of unemployment

5. J.K. Galbraith, *A History of Economics: The Past as the Present* (London: Hamish Hamilton, 1987).
6. M. Friedman, 'The Role of Monetary Policy', *American Economic Review* 58 (1968), pp. 1–17.

means that price stability does not lead to higher unemployment in the long run. So, a key practical consequence of monetarism was that it ruled out of order any debate about the trade-off between unemployment and inflation: extra inflation cannot be justified by any long-term gain in employment.

Another practical consequence of monetarism was its opposition to discretion in the conduct of policy. The subsequent debate was about the appropriate techniques for controlling inflation, with emphasis on the importance of a clear rule that would force a 'nominal strait-jacket' on the economy. Ideally, monetary policy should simply be a technical matter of controlling inflation; policy should be taken out of the political process. This result could be achieved by a rule of central bank independence, linked to a further rule that central banks should aim at medium-term domestic monetary targets: or by the discipline of being anchored to a strong anchor currency by means of a fixed exchange rate system: or by an inflation target and the subordination of a mix of monetary and exchange rate policies to that target.

The relative value of these policy instruments was hotly disputed within the sound money approach. Friedman was a long-standing apostle of floating exchange rates, not least so that countries could pursue independent macro-economic policies.[7] In this respect neither he nor his disciples could be expected to view the EMS with any enthusiasm. The policy instrument of exchange rate changes was too important a means of domestic economic adjustment to be sacrificed, other than in a strictly defined 'optimum currency area' (a concept that we shall consider below). So, though monetarism provided a broad ideological framework supporting sound money, it did not lead to automatic support for the policy instuments contained in the EMS and EMU.[8] The common ground among monetarists was to be found in a single-minded devotion to a clear rule as the basis of policy. For some that rule was a money supply target; for others, it was an exchange rate target.

The other practical consequence of the ascendancy of sound money ideas was to be observed in the distribution of power in the making of economic policy. In order to understand the political significance of economic policy ideas one must ask *cui bono* – who benefits? Sound money appealed to the corporate self-interests and *amour propre* of central bankers (it revalued their policy instruments, provided them with a means to protect themselves from outside interference and gave a sense of mission and mystique to their purpose); of financial institutions with money to lend (and likely to benefit from the use of high interest rates to squeeze inflation); and of the growing number of people, notably retired people, with savings that they wished to protect against the ravages of inflation. In the debate about the development of the EMS and about EMU, sound money served to legitimize and empower the role of central bankers, with results that we have seen in previous chapters. More generally, sound money asserted the political interests of savers who, in increasingly affluent societies, were of mounting importance to governments (being numerically and electorally far more 'important' than unemployed people).

7. M. Friedman, 'The Case for Flexible Exchange Rates', in Friedman, *Essays in Positive Economics* (Chicago: University of Chicago Press, 1953).
8. Note the stern opposition to the ERM of Mrs Thatcher's economic policy adviser, in A. Walters, *Britain's Economic Renaissance* (Oxford: Oxford University Press, 1986); Walters, *Sterling in Danger* (London: Institute of Economic Affairs, 1990).

Borrowing credibility and gaining reputation

The main intellectual foundations for the new EMS and for EMU were provided by a new view of inflation as a problem of credibility and reputation and by evidence about the relationship between central bank independence and price stability. With the 'credibility' approach to inflation the refinements of game theory were applied to sound money policy; inflation was viewed as the product of an interaction between what the government wants to achieve and what the public expects the government to do. In their seminal work Barro and Gordon speak of a 'time inconsistency': that, though a policy of no inflation is best in the long run, there are short-run incentives for the government to deviate from this policy by creating surprise inflation – whether to court popularity by a speedy increase of economic activity or to lower the value of public debt. Hence the government's professed commitment to price stability commands little credibility with the public; the public anticipates surprise inflation.[9] The key question is how can government achieve greater credibility: the answer is that it must make its policy time-consistent by a long process of building up reputation; and that it will be able to do this only if it limits its own freedom to act in monetary policy. In this way public expectations of inflation will be radically reduced.

This answer was specifically tailored to the EMS by Giavazzi and Pagano, again applying the insights of game theory. They provided a politically useful rationale for the asymmetrical nature of the EMS by arguing that this asymmetry had value as a disciplinary device.[10] Credibility for a counter-inflationary strategy could be achieved by countries with traditionally high rates of inflation by pegging their exchange rates to the strongest currency, the D-Mark. They would then be forced to follow the Bundesbank's policy standard and would be able in the process to borrow its reputation as a central bank committed to price stability. In return for the loss of policy autonomy they would gain credibility for their commitment to fight inflation. Also, by tying their hands to the D-Mark anchor the monetary authorities of high-inflation countries could lower the unemployment costs of disinflation compared to the alternative of pursuing an independent programme for economic stabilization. Again the mechanism involves changed expectations: the government's greater credibility will lead to a fall in inflationary expectations and thus have a critical bearing on the cost at which it can carry through its policy.

This theory commanded wide respect within EC central banks, notably in the Benelux countries, France, Italy and Spain. Politically, it provided an economic rationale for living with the inherently asymmetrical EMS and the policy leadership of the German Bundesbank. The EMS achieved a new legitimacy as the basis for

9. Notably, R. Barro and D. Gordon, 'A Critical Theory of Monetary Policy in a National Rate Model', *Journal of Political Economy* 91 (1983), pp. 589–610; R. Barro and D. Gordon, 'Rules, Discretion and Reputation in a Model of Monetary Policy', *Journal of Monetary Economics* 12 (1983), pp. 101–22.
10. F. Giavazzi and M. Pagano, 'The Advantage of Tying One's Hands: EMS Discipline and Central Bank Credibility', *European Economic Review* 32 (1988), pp. 1055–82; F. Giavazzi and A. Giovannini, *Limiting Exchange Rate Flexibility: The European Monetary System* (Cambridge, Mass.: MIT Press, 1989); J. Melitz, 'Monetary Discipline, Germany and the European Monetary System: A Synthesis', in F. Giavazzi *et al.* (eds) *The European Monetary System* (Cambridge: Cambridge University Press, 1988), pp. 51–79.

counter-inflationary strategy. By tying the hands of politicians and central bankers and thus providing an automatic discipline in the manner of the gold standard, the EMS seemed to provide the answer to a central problem of sound money policy: the will and capability of policy makers to resist incentives to create inflation.

One aspect of this problem that was especially relevant to the EC states had been identified by Frenkel and Johnson in 1976.[11] Their 'monetary theory of the balance of payments' was an extension of monetarism to 'open' economies where money supply and demand are interrelated among countries through international payments. In such a context, even under flexible exchange rates, the issue arises of whether individual countries can pursue independent monetary policies. The growing internationalization of capital markets raised the question of whether it would be possible to achieve domestic money supply targets. After 1979 the efforts of the British government to pursue an independent monetary policy based on such targets provoked disillusionment; by 1982 official policy was beginning to recognize the importance of the exchange rate and the long and acrimonious process of conversion from the merits of money supply to exchange rate targeting was underway.[12]

Central bank independence

The conclusion that a government that keeps discretionary power over monetary policy cannot make a credible commitment to price stability was reinforced in the work of Alesina and of Neumann.[13] This work draws on the theory of the political business cycle. This theory assumes that politicians are seeking to maximize their own preferences, above all for short-term electoral gains, rather than the 'public good'. Hence they have a natural tendency to economic stimulation and to generate cycles in the economy that are synchronized with the timing of elections. Politicians are also assumed to have ideological preferences that dispose them to prefer inflation as a presumedly effective means of tackling unemployment. This combination of political self-interest and ideology means that, as long as politicians are given the opportunity for political manipulation of the money supply, they cannot be trusted to avoid the temptations of monetary expansion and inflation.

Alesina's work sought to use empirical research to demonstrate a clear relationship betweem price stability and central bank independence, pointing out that the two most independent central banks – those of Germany and Switzerland – had the lowest rates of inflation. The argument that major institutional reform in the form of central bank

11. J. Frenkel and H. Johnson (eds) *The Monetary Approach to the Balance of Payments* (Toronto: University of Toronto Press, 1976).
12. See the seminal paper by M. Artis and D. Currie, 'Monetary and Exchange Rate Targets', *Oxford Economic Papers* 33 (1981), pp. 176–200. A partisan though interesting insight into the acrimonious dispute between the two monetarist rules – represented by the Prime Minister's economic adviser, Alan Walters, and the Chancellor of the Exchequer, Nigel Lawson – is to be found in N. Lawson, *The View from No. 11: Memoirs of a Tory Radical* (London: Bantam Press, 1992).
13. A. Alesina, 'Politics and Business Cycles in Industrial Democracies', *Economic Policy* 8 (1989), pp. 55–98; M. Neumann, 'Central Bank Independence as a Prerequisite of Price Stability', in Commission of the European Communities, *European Economy: The Economics of EMU*, Special Edition 1 (Luxembourg: Office for Official Publications of the European Communities, 1991), pp. 79–91.

independence was a necessary condition for price stability became central to the debate about EMU after 1988. Here was another example of how influential academic economics can be when they serve to legitimate political realities – the new EMS and German policy leadership in the case of the credibility approach to inflation and the power of the Bundesbank as a role model in the EMU debate in the case of the central bank independence approach. Again, both approaches strongly appealed to the corporate self-interests of central bankers and legitimized a German-centred EMS and EMU.

Despite this grip on the policy process, these theoretical arguments raised some serious questions. It was not obvious that credibility and reputation could be achieved speedily or indeed at all by simply borrowing it through the hard ERM or making one's central bank independent. It had to be earned and demonstrated over time by resolute national action. In the case of central bank independence the issue was not only one of institutional design but also one of the presence of a coalition of interests capable of giving the bank political protection and of a supportive economic culture that prioritizes stability.

Devaluation

To arguments about the virtues of tying one's hands to the D-Mark and of central bank independence was added a re-evaluation of devaluation as a policy instrument. European Commission analysis distinguished between the short-term and long-term effects of devaluation.[14] In the short term it protects a country from output and job losses through its direct effect on real exchange rates. But the long-term costs are that real wage adjustment is delayed and inflationary expectations may be shifted upwards. Consequently, competitivness is eroded. With repeated devaluations a vicious circle of inflation, macro-economic instability and problems of competitiveness is likely to endure. Hence in committing themselves to a hard ERM or to EMU, EC states were benefiting by renouncing the costs of the misuse of devaluations. It must be emphasized that not all sound money economists accepted this analysis and evaluation of devaluation, any more than the arguments for tying one's hands to an anchor currency. In addition to a core of mainly British monetarists who were hostile to the inflexibility of the ERM and EMU, other sound money economists were prepared to recognize that the judicious use of devaluation to deal with external shocks, like German unification, was too important a benefit to be abandoned.[15] But the important point was that the mainstream economic thinking behind the EMS and EMU had ceased to view devaluations as a costless and flexible policy instrument.

The story of the EMS and of EMU was then one of a capture of their intellectual rationale by sound money ideas. This capture was reflected in the way that debate about EMU came to focus more narrowly on the 'fiscal conditions for a monetary union' than on the idea that the EC should develop an active, coordinated fiscal stance and concern itself with the growth of demand. It was apparent in the informal rules of

14. Commission of the European Communities, *European Economy: One Market, One Money*, 44 (Luxembourg: Office for Official Publications of the European Communities, October 1990), pp. 138–40 and Annex D, especially p. 291.
15. De Grauwe, *The Economics of Monetary Integration*, ch. 2.

the EMS from 1983 onwards (see chapter 6); and in the importance assigned in the Treaty on European Union to price stability as the mandate for the ESCB, to central bank independence, to the 'no bail out' rule and to the convergence criteria, notably on excessive deficits. Characteristic of this ascendancy of sound money ideas was the emphasis on rules that were expressed in nominal, not real terms. In neither sound money ideas nor the treaty was there any ambition to control output and employment directly: only to ensure respect for key financial rules on, for instance, budget deficits, public debt and inflation. Sound money's dominance was not total: for political compromise in Council bargaining involved a recognition that 'economic and social cohesion' was a prime aim of EC policy, with the creation of a new policy instrument for this purpose – the Cohesion Fund. But economic and social cohesion was not added to the convergence criteria, thereby legitimizing a more active fiscal role for the EC. It provided a weak flanking measure to the main event – an EMU based on sound money.

Critical perspectives on EMU: the traditional theory of 'optimum currency areas'

The structuring of the policy debate about the EMS and EMU in the 1980s and early 1990s around sound money ideas gave an impressive sense of coherence and stability to the policy process. It suggested a powerful structural logic at work: that the policy process could be understood in teleological terms. The EMS and EMU appeared to be logical developments serving the purpose of putting in place an increasingly robust mechanism for establishing a more credible and therefore more effective policy against inflation in the EC. But the consensus was never as solid nor as durable as it then seemed; the motives at work were more complex and political. There was continuing dissent from monetarists who favoured flexible exchange rates, like Walters, and from neo-Keynesians who feared that a strait-jacket of disinflation was being placed on the EC. Though they had little success in influencing the Treaty on European Union, economic developments after 1991 gave a new momentum to these critiques. It appeared that the treaty was being implemented at painful cost and that it embodied a consensus of the 1980s that was being increasingly challenged by events, notably a problem of inflation in the anchor currency that demanded domestic policy action in Germany (high interest rates) that was poisonous for other ERM members that no longer had a serious inflation problem. The result was that many economists who had earlier supported the hard ERM as a way of bringing down otherwise unmanageable inflation in these other ERM members were forced to reconsider their views.

One challenge came on the question of whether the policy of tying one's hands was effective and sensible. Empirical evidence did not strongly support the value of the EMS as a disciplinary mechanism.[16] During the 1980s the Scandinavian countries and Switzerland made a lower sacrifice than the EMS countries (minus Germany) in terms of unemployment; Britain, outside the ERM, did better than France but worse than

16. P. De Grauwe, *The Cost of Disinflation and the European Monetary System* (London: Centre for Economic Policy Research, Discussion Paper no. 326, 1989); D. Gros and N. Thygesen, *European Monetary Integration* (London: Longman, 1992), pp. 127–33.

Italy; whereas Spain, also outside the ERM, did worse than either France or Italy. Even more disturbing was the evidence that, in the case of France, more unemployment was needed to cut inflation than had been needed before the hard ERM had taken hold. The gap between French and average EC inflation rates had narrowed: but the gap between French and average EC unemployment rates had widened. Blanchard and Muet calculated that to lower unemployment by a mere 3 per cent would require a 30 per cent improvement in French competitiveness, suggesting a radical fault at the heart of French economic policy strategy.[17]

The theory underpinning the notion of the EMS as a disciplinary mechanism had some notable weaknesses. First, the hard ERM would always be an imperfect exchange-rate commitment: for implicit in an exchange rate is the possibility of its change, and change had been regularly used till 1987 (and was to return in 1992–3); the ERM also operated with margins of fluctuation whose effects the theory ignored. After 1987 the ideas of a 'hard currency bloc', centred on the D-Mark and the Dutch guilder, and a 'soft currency bloc', represented by the French franc, never fully disappeared. Second, the theory rested on a view that changes in domestic wages and prices offered an alternative mechanism of economic adjustment to changes of nominal exchange rates. But, in the view of neo-Keynesian economists, the 'stickiness' of wages and prices suggested that reliance on this mechanism was likely to be slow and severely painful, leading to a build up of pressures for either exchange-rate adjustment or protection for domestic markets. It was likely to lose credibility as an influence on behaviour when the costs of pursuing it (exhibited in lost output, higher unemployment and electoral threat to incumbent governments) came into conflict with other policy goals. This loss of force in the commitment to use the EMS as a disciplinary mechanism was apparent even before the British government's withdrawal from the ERM in September 1992. The implications of that commitment, in the form of sustained high interest rates, were increasingly seen by operators in foreign exchange markets as incompatible with the government's need to tackle a protracted domestic recession and to restore domestic political confidence.

This weakness in the functioning of the EMS as a disciplinary mechanism, as underlined so vividly in 1992, cast a more fundamental doubt on the power and adequacy of the theoretical model upon which the EMS/EMU edifice had come to rest. Events in 1992 and 1993 were not kind to this model. The longer the British recession continued and the more persistent high unemployment proved in France, the more difficult it was to argue that the costs of using the EMS as an instrument of disinflation were only temporary: as the rest of the EMS countries slipped into recession from 1992, this concern spread to France and other countries. It seemed increasingly possible that the recession not only involved a temporary deviation in output below its trend but also was permanently moving its trend lower. In other words, commitment to the sound money paradigm underpinning the EMS and the Treaty on European Union was being bought at the cost of a permanent loss of output and employment. This process could be explained by economists in terms of 'hysterisis' effects, such as long-term unemployment permanently demotivating large

---

17. O. Blanchard and P.-A. Muet, 'Competitiveness through Disinflation: An Assessment of the French Macro-Economic Strategy', *Economic Policy* 6 (1993), p. 12.

numbers in the labour market; decline in investment reducing the stock of plant and machinery; and a diminished size of the manufacturing sector making the future growth of demand unsupportable without a balance-of-payments' crisis. The sound money paradigm implicit in EMU as defined in the Treaty on European Union came into question as recession and high unemployment promised to be protracted; questions arose about whether the benefits of further 'competitive disinflation' were any longer worth the extra cost in output and employment.

Some of the most trenchant criticisms of the EMU project as specified in the treaty came from the theory of 'optimum currency areas'. This theory has a much longer pedigree than credibility theory, predating not only the EMS but also the first launch of EMU at the Hague summit. It remains the traditional starting-point for discussing issues concerning monetary union. But its value was questioned in the EC Commission's *One Market, One Money* study, which attached greater importance to the new credibility theory.[18] It had little impact within the EMS and EMU policy process of the late 1980s. Politically, this situation was not surprising, for whereas credibility theory stressed the benefits of EMU, the optimum currency area theory had concentrated on the costs of monetary union.

The theory of optimum currency areas had been developed to deal with one main question: by what criteria do we define the appropriate geographic area for a single currency? The seminal work was done by Mundell (1961), McKinnon (1963), Kenen (1969), Krugman (1991) and, in the context of the EMU debate, by Ingram (1973), Eichengreen (1991) and Masson and Taylor (1993).[19] Their work rested on the assumption that when a country joins a monetary union it loses an important instrument of adjustment – the exchange rate. So the question arises of how the costs of adjustment can be dealt with in its absence. The debate focused on the definition of the criteria that were necessary for a smooth and effective functioning of a monetary union and on the issue of how to weigh and evaluate these criteria in coming to a judgement. Though the debate was ultimately inconclusive, in the sense that it did not yield any final agreement, the debate about monetary union was undoubtedly enriched by this body of theory. Unfortunately, as far as EMU was concerned, the theory of optimum currency areas was, on the whole, less friendly to the view that the EC was an appropriate area for a monetary union than the credibility theory. On the other hand, it did not suggest that the gold standard area had qualified as an optimum

18. Commission of the European Communities, *European Economy: One Market, One Money*, pp. 45–7.
19. R. Mundell, 'A Theory of Optimum Currency Areas', *American Economic Review* 51 (1961), pp. 657–65; R. McKinnon, 'Optimum Currency Areas', *American Economic Review* 53 (1963), pp. 717–25; P. Kenen, 'The Theory of Optimum Currency Areas: An Eclectic View', in R. Mundell and A. Swoboda (eds) *Monetary Problems of the International Economy* (Chicago: University of Chicago Press, 1969); P. Krugman, *Geography and Trade* (Cambridge, Mass.: MIT Press, 1991); J. Ingram, 'The Case for European Monetary Integration', *Princeton Essays in International Finance* 98 (1973), Princeton University, NJ; B. Eichengreen, 'Is Europe an Optimum Currency Area?', *National Bureau of Economic Research Working Paper no. 3579*, January 1991; P. Masson and M. Taylor, 'Fiscal Policy within Common Currency Areas', *Journal of Common Market Studies* 31 (March 1993), pp. 29–44; P. Masson and M. Taylor, 'Common Currency Areas and Currency Unions: A Survey of the Issues', in Masson and Taylor (eds) *Policy Issues in the Operation of Currency Unions* (New York: Cambridge University Press, 1993).

currency area, or more strikingly still the United States.

Factor mobility

Over time, some six criteria were established as relevant to the assessment of the potential for a monetary union, each emphasized by different theorists: factor mobility (by Mundell); openness (by McKinnon); trade integration (by Kenen and Krugman); international financial integration (by Ingram); wage and price flexibility (by sound money economists); and fiscal policy (by Eichengreen and by Masson and Taylor). According to Mundell, the appropriate criterion for a monetary union was the degree of factor mobility – mobility of capital and labour – within an area. A high degree of factor mobility provides the mechanism for reducing the costs of adjustment that is lost once exchange rate changes are sacrificed in a monetary union. As early as 1957 James Meade had argued that low labour mobility in Europe meant that exchange rates should remain flexible within that area.[20] One of the key points stressed within the theory of optimum currency areas remains that labour mobility is much lower among the states of the EC than within the United States, reflecting cultural barriers and language differences. Sizeable out-migration of unemployed workers, rather than regional changes in real exchange rates or in-migration of companies attracted by low wages, explains how US states like Michigan adjust to regional 'shocks'.[21] Hence economists tend to argue that lack of labour mobility remains a powerful obstacle to an EC monetary union.[22]

There is no dispute about the proposition that large-scale labour mobility across member state boundaries is not feasible as a main instrument of adjustment. But the negative implications for EC monetary union have been countered by the argument that labour mobility is much more likely to be required as a consequence of regional 'shocks' than as a consequence of 'country-specific shocks', the former being more significant than the latter; and that movements of labour between regions (but within countries) are over ten times more important than migration between member states. At the same time regional labour mobility does not seem to operate with the same strength in all member states.[23] Also, it has been stressed that most EC trade takes place within specific industries (like automobiles, chemicals and investment goods) so that 'shocks' affecting individual industries tend to be shared across countries; and that the single European market programme is further reducing the degree to which industries in different member states are subject to differentiated 'shocks'.[24] In neither case then – regional 'shocks' or 'industry-specific shocks' – is exchange-rate adjustment a relevant and very useful instrument. And, so the Commission argued, 'asymmetric

---

20. J. Meade, 'The Balance-of-Payments Problems of a European Free Trade Area', *Economic Journal* 67 (1957), pp. 379–96.

21. Eichengreen, 'Is Europe an Optimum Currency Area?'.

22. E.g. M. Feldstein, 'The Case against EMU', *The Economist*, 13 June 1992, pp. 23–6; and the German 'gang of sixty' economists who published a manifesto against EMU in H. Giersch *et al.*, 'Manifesto gegen EWU', *Frankfurter Allgemeine Zeitung*, 11 June 1992.

23. P. De Grauwe, 'Is Europe an Optimum Currency Area? Evidence from Regional Data', manuscript, Catholic University of Leuven, 1991.

24. Commission of the European Communities, *European Economy: One Market, One Money*, pp. 142–5.

shocks' were likely to diminish with the progressive realization of a single market.

At the heart of this debate remained the question of whether country-specific shocks would continue to be important within the EC. In the face of repeated country-specific shocks EMU is *a priori* welfare-reducing, because national monetary policies can no longer be used to absorb them. German unification in 1989–90 was a reminder that such shocks could occur and that their effects could be profound. But there was also a case for arguing that the United States and the EC's 'core' were not very different from each other with respect to 'supply shocks', and that the future EMU was more likely to be characterized by common shocks.[25] EMU performs at its best in the face of common shocks; countries are denied the opportunity to pursue beggar-my-neighbour policies by using exchange-rate changes to export the adverse consequences of the shock from themselves to others. The United States and the EC had in common the fact that each had a core region, in the case of the EC comprising Germany, the Benelux countries, France and Denmark. Here intra-industry trade is prevalent; common shocks produce similar experiences and require similar policies. Each also had a 'periphery' whose trade with the core was more inter-industry and where the experience induced by common shocks was different. Here country-specific shocks were more likely; such shocks would also tend to be much larger in size. The key differences were that the economic weight of the EC's periphery was relatively larger than that of the United States' periphery, and that the United States' periphery was more economically integrated into its continental economy than that of the EC. Though this evidence might be used to support the argument that the EC's core was no less a good candidate for a monetary union than the United States, other differences – like those of fiscal structure – need to be considered.

Trade integration and economic openness

McKinnon's seminal paper focused on the degree of openness of economies by arguing that, in the case of small countries whose trade constituted a large proportion of GNP, frequent changes of exchange rate would produce price instability – simply because imported goods, whose prices change directly with the exchange rate, make up such a large part of the overall price index. Such countries will prefer stable exchange rate regimes and to rely on other adjustment mechanisms than exchange rates. In effect, intra-EC trade interdependency constitutes an economic fundamental determining why some countries, like Ireland and the Benelux states, are more likely to be attracted by the benefits of EMU than others, like Britain.

Building on this theme of the structural power of trade interdependency, it can be suggested that the costs of monetary union decrease and the benefits increase with the intensity of trade within a given geographic area.[26] But the average intra-EC exports of the four major EC economies as a percentage of their GDP was less than the domestic significance of Canada's exports to the United States: in 1990 the figures were 16.1

25. T. Bayoumi and B. Eichengreen, 'Shocking Aspects of European Monetary Unification', *National Bureau of Economic Research*, Working Paper no. 3949, January 1992.
26. P. Krugman, 'Policy Problems of a Monetary Union', in P. De Grauwe and L. Papademos (eds) *The European Monetary System in the 1990s* (London: Longman, 1990), pp. 52–4.

per cent for Germany, 12.5 for France, 9.5 for Britain and 9.4 for Italy. So the argument that increased openness made monetary union more attractive did not yield an unequivocal case for an EC-wide monetary union.

The link between the degree of industrial diversification and monetary union has also been explored. Thus Kenen argued that countries characterized by a low degree of product diversification would be more vulnerable to country-specific shocks; hence they should retain exchange-rate flexibility. By contrast, a high degree of product diversification meant that industry-specific shocks would not translate so easily into country-specific shocks and that less pressure would be placed on labour mobility as a means of adjustment. Again, it was possible to argue that EC countries tended to have highly diversified industrial structures; and that, consequently, monetary union was a more feasible proposition.[27]

But it is important to treat with caution the assumption that increased trade integration and greater economies of scale consequent on a single European market will make for smoother adjustment to shocks in an EMU. Krugman has argued that the experience of the United States shows that an internal market induces a greater regional concentration within industrial sectors than is as yet to be found within the EC. The concentration of the US automobile industry in Michigan is a case in point. With a similar development within the EC a sector-specific shock is more rather than less likely to lead to a country-specific shock. In the absence of US-style adjustment mechanisms (fiscal transfers and labour mobility), the resort to devaluation may seem an indispensable instrument to adjust to these shocks.

Financial integration

Ingram was important in trying to shift attention away from a preoccupation with labour mobility as a defining criterion for a monetary union by emphasizing the potential importance of another aspect of factor mobility – the mobility of financial capital. With greater mobility of capital goes an increased degree of financial integration; in turn, financial integration means that an alternative adjustment mechanism is available. A shift in the balance of payments is then accompanied by a flow of transactions in a wide range of financial instruments, helping to offset this shift. In this way the external balance ceases to be a policy problem of governments; it is automatically adjusted through movements of capital responding to market inducements. From this perspective, the provisions of the single European market programme on freedom of movement of capital were realizing a key criterion for a monetary union. On the other hand, it was all too possible that freedom of capital movement would destabilize a regime of stable exchange rates: one result might be an accelerated dash for monetary union; another a heightened scepticism about the credibility of a monetary union.

---

27. Commission of the European Communities, *European Economy: One Market, One Money*, p. 46.

Wage and price flexibility

Wage and price flexibility was a criterion added by sound money economists who argued that the traditional theory of optimum currency areas had neglected the scope for market adjustments. Labour mobility or large fiscal transfer mechanisms are less important in so far as wage and price flexibility at the regional level acts as a means of responding to a problem of adjustment. Though domestic wages and prices change more slowly than nominal exchange rates, a strategy of relying on wage and price adjustment avoids the inflationary implications of resorting to devaluation.[28] It is also superior to reliance on fiscal policy in that it removes rather than alleviates the distortion of relative prices that lies at the heart of the problem of adjustment. After EMU the expected real rate of return in one country relative to others will be vital in shaping regional employment prospects; disruptive effects on employment opportunities will be minimized only if there is convergence in supply-side conditions and not just nominal convergence of the kind proposed in the Treaty on European Union.[29] In the absence of greater labour market flexibility to cushion EMU adjustment is likely to take the form of large shifts in capacity utilization and employment.[30] This view that a monetary union can achieve adjustment by relying mainly on wage, price and labour market flexibility is challenged particularly by neo-Keynesians who argue that it is sometimes too agonizingly slow and painful a process to be practical; that price and wage 'stickiness' is a fact of life.[31]

Fiscal transfers

Neo-Keynesian theorists were, by contrast, keen to emphasize that, in the absence of large-scale labour mobility or of wage and price flexibility as found in the United States, fiscal transfers could serve as an important instrument to cushion countries or regions from shocks once exchange-rate adjustment had been abandoned within a monetary union. In other words, the capacity and potential of the fiscal policy mechanism could be a key criterion for determining whether a given geographic area was suitable for a monetary union. This view could be traced back to the MacDougall Report of 1977, a major study of fiscal federalism initiated by the EC Commission and that drew attention to the huge scale of difference in size between the federal budgets of the United States, Canada and Germany and the EC's tiny budget. In the wake of the Treaty on European Union, MacDougall was to restate the paramount importance of a much enlarged EC budget as a means of correcting regional imbalances.[32] Implicit was the argument that, for EMU to be successful, the convergence criteria needed to

28. D. Gros and N. Thygesen, *European Monetary Integration* (London: Longman, 1992), pp 237–8; De Grauwe, 'Is Europe an Optimum Currency Area?'.
29. This point is made by two EC Commission economists in B. Connolly and J. Kroger, 'Economic Convergence in the Integrating Community Economy', *Recherches Economiques de Louvain* 59 (1993), no. 1–2.
30. Note here S. Englander and T. Egebo, 'Adjustment under Fixed Exchange Rates: Application to the European Monetary Union', *OECD Economic Studies* 20 (Paris: OECD Publications, 1993).
31. P. Kenen, *Managing Exchange Rates* (London: Routledge, 1988), pp. 19–20 and 33–4.
32. D. MacDougall, 'Economic and Monetary Union and the European Community Budget', *National Institute Economic Review* 140 (1992), pp. 64–8.

be supplemented by a much greater stress on 'economic and social cohesion', going beyond the provisions of the treaty for, for instance, a new Cohesion Fund for environmental and infrastructural projects. More important were such ideas as an EC-wide system of social security transfers to directly assist poorer households.[33] In this way some minimum insurance against differentiated shocks could be provided.

The need for a system of fiscal taxes and transfers between member states was mainly legitimized by reference to the United States, in work by American scholars. Thus, Sala-i-Martin and Sachs sought to show that the US federal tax and transfer system served as an important 'shock absorber' by automatically increasing federal tax payments from, and lowering transfer payments to, those regions that were prospering relative to the national average, and conversely increasing transfers to, and reducing revenues from, those regions that were below the national average.[34] They estimated that for every decline in US state income of $1 the federal budget transfers back 40 cents. This system was estimated to cushion over one-third of the effects of region-specific shocks on disposable income. It functioned in effect as an automatic stabilizer. Eichengreen argued that less flexible labour markets in the EC than in the United States meant that an even larger federal fiscal tax and transfer mechanism was needed. His estimate was that EC taxes compensated for no more than 1 per cent of an income loss from an unfavourable shock hitting a member state.[35] These figures on the United States' economy have been challenged: thus it has been pointed out that in fact income transfers there play only a small role in dealing with transitory shocks; most of these transfers relate to persisting differences in prosperity.[36]

But, whatever the arguments about the realities of the United States' experience, it is clear that the EC's fiscal structure is not remotely like that of the United States. Monetary union does not start against the background of an EC-wide income tax and social security system to shift resources from better-off to worse-off individuals; whilst the redistribution between member states is limited in scale overall, though for the poorer regions the flows could be substantial, approaching 5 per cent of their GDP – a scale similar to that of Marshall Aid. Thus in 1991 the total size of the EC budget was just slightly above 1 per cent of the EC's GDP; the Structural Funds, which – particularly in the form of the European Regional Development Fund and the European Social Fund – are the main instrument of redistribution, accounted for only about ¼ per cent of the EC's GDP. Ultimately, such sums are too small to enable the

---

33. For examples of such proposals see I. Begg and D. Mayes, 'Social and Economic Cohesion among the Regions of Europe in the 1990s', *National Institute Economic Review* 138 (1991), pp. 63–74; C. Bean *et al.*, 'Policies for 1992: The Transition and After', in *The Macroeconomics of 1992* (Brussels: Centre for European Policy Studies, CEPS Paper no. 42, 1990); C. Wyplosz, 'Monetary Union and Fiscal Discipline', in Commission of the European Communities, *European Economy: The Economics of EMU*, pp. 165–84.

34. X. Sala-i-Martin and J. Sachs, 'Fiscal Federalism and Optimum Currency Areas: Evidence for Europe from the United States', in M. Canzoneri, V. Grilli and P. Masson (eds) *Establishing a Central Bank: Issues in Europe and Lessons for the United States* (Cambridge: Cambridge University Press, 1992), pp. 195–219.

35. B. Eichengreen, 'One Money for Europe? Lessons from the US Currency Union', *Economic Policy* 10 (April 1990), pp. 117–87.

36. J. von Hagen, 'Fiscal Arrangements in a Monetary Union: Evidence from the US', mimeo, Indiana University, March 1991.

EC to exert a stabilizing role by redistributing resources. In the view of some neo-Keynesians, and of an unpublished 1992 study of DG5 of the EC Commission (the Social Affairs Directorate), the public finance role of the EC would need to be developed in a radically new form or national governments would have to be given a higher degree of fiscal flexibility than the treaty envisaged. Otherwise, with the introduction of EMU, the combination of inadequate interregional fiscal flows with wage and price inertia would condemn less competitive EC regions to low growth and substantially higher unemployment.[37]

For others, however, the differences between the EC and the United States put in question the merit of basing arguments about fiscal conditions for a monetary union on a comparison with the United States. The EC is, fundamentally, not a federal state and remains a long way from becoming a state on the US or German model. The absence of the required combination of political will and capability to establish a federal union suggests that the model of fiscal federalism remains simply unrealistic as a basis for designing EMU. So, though interregional fiscal flows need to be developed, active national fiscal policies are likely to remain the main mechanism of adjustment to shocks within EMU. In this perspective, the main danger lies in the contractionary fiscal bias that the Treaty on European Union's convergence criteria introduce into national budgeting, especially for countries with high levels of debt. With such constraints the price of inappropriate fiscal policies may be too high for the benefits of monetary union.[38]

The challenge to the economic model underpinning the treaty

The scale of the theoretical challenge to the consensus underpinning the Treaty on European Union was in retrospect hardly surprising. For ultimately, though credibility theory and the theory of the political business cycle had captured the EMS and EMU policy process, the main axis of debate about monetary unions in international monetary economics remained the theory of optimum currency areas. The EMS and EMU policy process was unable to avoid confrontation with the theoretical and practical implications of the fact that the EC did not constitute an optimum currency area. The credibility theory on which the new EMS and the treaty were based proved to be none too robust in the face of evidence that suggested that the discipline of the hard ERM was not the only instrument for delivering price stability or the sole or even prime reason for the convergence of inflation rates. Convergence of inflation rates could as well be explained by a homogeneous group of countries reacting similarly to an external inflation shock as by an independent effect of the ERM.[39] With confidence in the ERM as a particularly effective disciplinary device weakened, the theory of optimum currency areas did not offer much of a secure guide to policy. With time it had been stretched to incorporate more and more criteria, as we saw above. The

---

37. Sala-i-Martin and Sachs, 'Fiscal Federalism and Optimum Currency Areas'. On the DG5 study see 'EMU May Cost Jobs, Says Study', *Financial Times*, 16 August 1993, p. 14.

38. C. Bean, *Economic and Monetary Union in Europe* (London: Centre for Economic Policy Research, Discussion Paper no. 722, October 1992).

39. M. Artis and D. Nachane, *Wages and Prices in Europe: A Test of the German Leadership Thesis* (London: Centre for Economic Policy Research, Discussion Paper no. 296, March 1989).

corollary is that it provides an ever more complex body of contested theories. At best it yielded the conclusion that, if there were an optimum currency area in Europe, it was not coterminous with the EC. Thus it might add non-EC Austria and Switzerland to Germany, the Benelux countries, France and Denmark.

But, above all, it was the emerging view that the reduction of inflation in the 1980s had been bought at the cost of a permanent loss of output and employment – even for the strongest, most convergent economies – that most challenged the economic philosophy on which the treaty rested. As we have seen, sound money ideas had reasserted the interests of savers against government policies that tolerated or induced inflation. These interests were not likely to vanish from the agenda, not least as sound money had gained a solid footing in public and private institutions, and savers were an interest (much larger than the unemployed) that governments could not afford to ignore. Even so, new problems were forcing other priorities on the attention of governments and the EC, with rising unemployment and fears of threats to public order, not least from a resurgent extreme right, raising concerns about the hazards of the inflexibility built into the hard ERM and the treaty's approach to EMU. As the real world of the EC changed, so economic ideas were reassessed. 'Competitive disinflation' seemed no longer an adequate economic strategy: more flexible and active demand management, a more active labour market policy in the form of new employment and vocational education and training measures and greater labour market flexibility emerged as more relevant to the purpose of associating the EC with job creation and not mass unemployment, with prosperity and not recession. Hence (as we saw in chapter 6) there were problems in getting the Delors White Paper of 1993 to sit easily beside the Maastricht convergence criteria.

Even the thesis that central bank independence explained low inflation was challenged.[40] There was evidence to suggest that the nature of the institutions of the labour market was at least as important as central bank independence in affecting the rate of inflation. To put it another way, central bank independence only operates efficiently either when it is combined with a system of strongly coordinated wage bargaining in which negotiators take account of macro-economic factors (like the inflationary effects of wage increases) or when a highly decentralized wage bargaining system forces the attention of individual union members on effects on the competitiveness of the firm. This combination of coordinated wage bargaining with central bank independence – rather than central bank independence in its own right – can be seen as the efficient secret of the German economy. The key point is that a system of either coordinated or decentralized wage bargaining appears to lower the costs of a given rate of inflation measured by unemployment and lost output. In neglecting labour market institutions and emphasizing central bank independence the Treaty on European Union was condemning the EC to an EMU that would be excessively costly. It was in any case by no means clear that an independent central bank would function so smoothly outside the specific cultural conditions of Germany.

40. P. Hall, 'Bank's Independence Not the Complete Answer', *The Independent*, 23 January 1993. On the importance of labour market institutions see M. Bruno and J. Sachs, *Economics of Worldwide Stagflation* (Oxford: Basil Blackwell, 1985); L. Calmfors and J. Driffill, 'Bargaining Structure, Corporatism and Macroeconomic Performance', *Economic Policy* 6 (1988), pp. 13–61.

In Germany an economic culture that was scarred by the memories of two devastating inflations was supportive of such an institution; elsewhere an economic culture of stability had weaker historical foundations.

By 1993 the Treaty on European Union's economic rationale was beleaguered. On the one hand, sound money economists were by no means as unanimous in their support, with the critics in the ascendant. Some rejected any logical linkage between the credibility theory and the EMS and EMU or between central bank independence and the EMS and EMU. For them the benefits of low inflation could be attained by domestic institutional reform rather than importing the Bundesbank's reputation via the ERM and by relying on national money supply targeting or inflation targeting rather than sacrificing policy autonomy. On the other hand, neo-Keynesians pointed to the permanent costs of the disinflationary strategy on which the treaty rested. A larger gap had opened up between, on the one hand, the institutional rules of the game and the institutional momentum that we considered in chapter 6 and, on the other, the structural context of economic ideas where mounting controversy raged.

The treaty seemed to have been born at a turning-point in economic development. Instead of each successive business cycle taking inflation to new heights, as in the 1960s and 1970s, inflation appeared to be declining from one cycle to the next. A protracted and widening gap between actual output and productive potential and severe increases in unemployment suggested that the central economic problem was now an inadequate level of private and public spending – the problem that had earlier exercised the mind of John Maynard Keynes. In addition, the very success in reducing inflation meant that, compared to the 1970s, it was harder to secure the kind of negative, or at least very low, real interest rates that recovery required: particularly against the background of the use of high interest rates by the Bundesbank to deal with the stresses of German unification. A changed context of low inflation, high real interest rates and accelerating unemployment intimated that the central problem was now demand deficiency. In trying to frame a solution attention was likely to shift to the role of budget deficits as 'shock absorbers' and to convergence of supply-side conditions (institutional convergence), with implications for the credibility and relevance of the treaty's convergence criteria and timetable for EMU. Fiscal policy coordination might then cease to be an epiphenomenon of monetary union. With the tide turning, the treaty seemed to be stranded on the wrong beach.

Economic policy ideas and practice

Looked at historically, it remains interesting to ask who among economists influenced the economic ideas on which EMU rested and the form that this influence took. In identifying the pedigree of key ideas, like the credibility theory and the theory of the political business cycle, we have already gained some insight into the question of 'who'. The American roots of monetarism, and of much of the debate about the new EMS and EMU, cannot be denied. But the ideas of sound money as they developed within this context had also a very recognizable European pedigree. They illustrated the continuing significance of different national traditions of economic policy ideas – and, at the national level, a greater or lesser degree of structural congruence between national economic debate and the debate within EC institutions about EMU.

Cross-national policy networks and diffusion of ideas: the 'epistemic community'

An important new aspect of the EMU debate of the 1980s was the big pan-European research network represented by the Centre for Economic Policy Research (CEPR). Established in 1983 under the direction of Richard Portes, the CEPR was to prove influential not simply in bringing new American thinking to bear on European economic debates but, even more importantly, in organizing the exchange and development of economic policy ideas within Europe, particularly with reference to the EMS and EMU: not only among economists but also with central bankers and finance ministry officials. Among the 140 or more economists linked through the CEPR were such key figures in the EMU debate as Francesco Giavazzi (University of Bologna), Paul De Grauwe (University of Leuven), Jacques Melitz (Paris) and Charles Wyplosz (INSEAD, France). Moreover, economists linked to the CEPR had an important input into the background studies for the EC Commission's *One Market, One Money* study.[41] The ideas that were developed and disseminated in this network, notably the idea of tying one's hands, had – for reasons of corporate self-interest – an appeal to many central bank officials.

One Market, One Money was itself symbolic of a major change since the first EMU launch in 1970, namely, the organization of economic policy advice. Its central focus and coherence came from two factors: first, the priority that it accorded to price stability, and second, the importance that it attached to the reputation and credibility of monetary institutions, to be gained by central bank independence. Though such ideas had an American origin (the work of Barro and Gordon, for instance), *One Market, One Money* reflected the receptiveness of continental European economics to ideas that stressed institutions and their importance for the credibility and reputation of monetary policies. At heart continental European economics embodied a traditionally close relationship between law and economics, and law sustained a sensitivity to institutional questions that was not so central a hallmark of Anglo-American economics. The economists behind EMU were then strongly institution-focused in approach in a continental European manner.

The influence of the *One Market, One Money* study was complex and subtle. At the level of research and dissemination the link to the Centre for European Policy Studies in Brussels was important. There Daniel Gros had been a DG2 official serving the Delors Committee and an economic adviser to DG2 when the study was undertaken; Niels Thygesen had been a member of the Delors Committee. At the level of political influence DG2 used its link to UNICE, the organization that brings together national employers' associations, like the German Bundesverband der Deutschen Industrie (BDI) and the Confederation of British Industry (CBI). Through UNICE's EMS/EMU group the national associations were brought at an early stage into DG2's work for *One Market, One Money*. At this level the work on the micro-economic benefits from savings on transaction costs with a single currency was more influential. The corporate sector stood to benefit from elimination of the costs of hedging against exchange-rate

---

41. Commission of the European Communities, *European Economy: The Economics of EMU.*

uncertainty, of commission fees and of in-house costs of maintaining foreign exchange departments. In the estimate of the EC Commission the total direct transaction cost savings (corporate and non-corporate) amounted to between one-quarter and one-half of 1 per cent of the EC's GDP: roughly equivalent to the Commission's earlier estimate of the size of the direct savings from the abolition of frontier controls as part of the single market programme.[42] Subsequently, national employers' associations gave great weight to the transaction cost argument in lobbying at the domestic level for EMU, for instance, the CBI in Britain. Their influence on national finance ministries was, however, not very significant. Thus the British Treasury did not share the CBI's enthusiasm about the significance of transaction cost savings with a single currency. Also, national employers' associations were, over time, subject to other influences: like the concern of members about the price to be paid for EMU (in the form of high interest rates), as for instance in France, or the shift of the BDI from great enthusiasm to a more reserved and cautious approach. Despite these reservations the Commission had succeeded in launching a process of learning from above.

The significance of network-building and cross-national diffusion of economic policy ideas can be exaggerated: the image of a transnational 'epistemic community' difficult to sustain. For, on closer inspection, the national basis of economic policy ideas remained solidly entrenched: reflecting in part the self-containment induced by linguistic barriers; and, not least, the extent to which these ideas were linked to the working environment and needs of domestic politics. In the case of two countries in particular there was a notable asymmetry between the ideas of the EMU economists in the orbit of the EC Commission and national economic debate: Britain and Germany. Under Nigel Lawson and John Major the British Treasury was happy to buy the idea of tying its hands via the ERM, but did not see that this idea necessarily entailed the leap to EMU; and to buy the argument that transaction cost savings meant that the single EC market programme was a top priority, but not to view the transaction cost savings of a single currency as significant enough to outweigh the costs of loss of national policy autonomy. For the Treasury, unlike for the EC Commission, the key debate revolved around the question of whether the EC was an optimum currency area, and the answer would be provided by the capacity of member states to meet strict convergence criteria. For the Commission (as we have seen) the key debate focused on the importance of institutional arrangements for establishing the credibility and reputation of monetary policy.

The dialogue of the deaf was, if anything, more pronounced in the case of Germany. There economists remained, on the whole, rooted in the 'national economy' tradition, oriented to maintaining what they saw as basically domestic explanations for Germany's postwar economic success. Essentially inward-looking, German economists were slow to participate in the EMU debate. When they did so, it came in the publicly visible form of a manifesto against EMU, signed by 60 of their number and published in the *Frankfurter Allgemeine Zeitung*.[43] More active was the Bundesbank itself where, as in the case of the British Treasury, the economic policy ideas were derived at least in part from the literature on optimum currency areas (economic convergence

---

42. Commission of the European Communities, *European Economy: One Market, One Money*, Annex A, pp. 251–68.
43. H. Giersch *et al.*, 'Manifesto gegen EWU', *Frankfurter Allgemeine Zeitung*, 11 June 1992.

as the essential prerequisite for a monetary union) but also from a home-grown experience of the importance of institutional credibility in fighting inflation.

Symmetry between the economic policy ideas of the EMU economists in and around the EC Commission and national policy debate was more pronounced in the cases of France, Italy and Belgium. Here an increasing number of economists were seeking to persuade their national politicians of the importance of the goal of domestic price stability. The ERM and EMU seemed to offer an ideal opportunity to hitch this objective to the strength of elite political support for European union: by using the argument that the ERM and EMU could be used to import priority to price stability, first by a commitment to match the discipline of the Bundesbank and then by Europeanizing this discipline by an appropriately designed European central bank. In fact the main focus of this domestic debate was internalized to the finance ministry/central bank nexus rather than a public phenomenon. Thus the main linkage at the level of ideas was between the Trésor in the French Finance Ministry and the Banque de France and the Italian Treasury and the Bank of Italy, on the one hand, and the EC Commission, on the other. In the Italian case, for example, the Treasury had Francesco Giavazzi as economic adviser, and, within the Bank of Italy, Tommaso Padoa-Schioppa as deputy director-general.

The European-centred nature of the EMU debate is clear from the extent to which economic policy ideas from the early 1980s come to focus on emulation of Germany: on borrowing Germany's monetary reputation. The attraction lay in tying one's hands to the sound money policy of the German Bundesbank; in turn, the sound money policy of the Bundesbank owed little to American monetarist economists. For German economic policy makers, especially in the Bundesbank, had a long history of resistance to the postwar dominance of Keynesian economic ideas. Keynesian ideas had been introduced as late as 1966 when the Grand Coalition brought to power a Social Democrat Federal Economics Minister, Professor Karl Schiller, and then had had little time to establish their credibility before the oil crisis of 1973. So, predating the US monetarist revolution, Germany could lay claim to a traditional postwar, and at the time rather idiosyncratic, view that macro-economic stability and growth depended on a carefully regulated monetary policy – administered by an independent central bank. Its sound money policy was by no means fashionable, at least not till the 1970s. The sound money policy of the EMS and EMU, as refined by European economists, is to be seen more as as a process of policy borrowing from the German Bundesbank than as importing American monetarist doctrine.

Economics as partisan analysis

In identifying the networks through which economic ideas about the EMS and EMU were disseminated it is also important to remember that academic economists were only a part of a complex process. Their ideas were important as standard sources of reference, but ultimately the ideas were brought to bear on policy makers by economic journalists and by institution-based economists, that is those employed in finance ministries, central banks and financial institutions, as well as in think-tanks. Thus, as we have seen, Michael Emerson was a pivotal figure within the European Commission; Tommaso Padoa-Schioppa within the Commission and then the Italian central bank; whilst economic journalists – like Sam Brittan at the *Financial Times* – and economists with financial institutions – such as Jean-Michel Charpin at the Banque Nationale de Paris – could be important barometers of official attitudes as well as important disseminators of ideas.

The importance of institution-based economists and economic journalists was all the more important because of the lack of clear-cut policy advice from international monetary economics. As an academic field it had had great difficulty keeping up with the enormous changes affecting its object of interest.[44] Above all, the importance of institution-based economists derived from their role in providing partisan analysis: endowing their institutions with influence by connecting specific policy ideas with the fundamental dispositions or values of those in positions of power.[45] Practised as partisan analysis, economics is subordinated to the play of power; it is a technique of persuasion in the bargaining relations that comprise the EMS and EMU policy process.

But economic policy ideas are by no means powerless in their own right. The structural power of economic policy ideas derives, first, from the fact that policy makers become dependent on them for their reputation and capacity to be persuasive. As their reputations could be won or lost by the success or failure of the economic policies that they chose, they could hardly afford not to listen, least of all when their opponents were arming themselves with partisan policy analysis. In the 1980s sound money policy ideas came to dominate partisan economic analysis; from it the key policy positions on the EMS and EMU were derived. The direction of influence was not (as we shall see) simply linear: from academic economists to policy makers. The values and dispositions of European policy makers were to be an active presence in the development of policy proposals.

Second, the structural power of economic policy ideas is revealed in the way that they come to imprison policy actors. Policy actors may hold tenaciously to an economic policy idea because it reflects their corporate self-interests or because of enormous psychological 'sunk costs' in promoting an idea. These factors were to be influential in encouraging EMS and EMU policy actors to be reticent in using their new-found scope for flexibility in monetary policies after the July 1993 ERM crisis.

Institution-based economists were much closer to the calculations and constraints of political power. With that came a greater eclecticism and pragmatism than the academic economist usually practised. Nowhere was this pragmatism and eclecticism more apparent than in the very practical sound money policy ideas of the Bundesbank. In the words of Helmut Schlesinger: 'Pragmatic monetarism as accepted in the Federal Republic must not be confused with rigid adherence to scholarly doctrine'.[46] Long experience with annual money supply targets since 1974 had taught the Bundesbank to respect their value but recognize their limitations. Their value lay not in the ease with which they could be effected but rather in their symbolism as a statement of determination and in their use to legitimize tough action, like an increase in interest

44. Krugman, 'Policy Problems of a Monetary Union', pp. 48–51.
45. C. Lindblom, *The Policy-Making Process* (Englewood Cliffs, NJ: Prentice-Hall, 1968), pp. 32–4.
46. H. Schlesinger, 'Zehn Jahre Geldpolitik mit einem Geldmengenziel', *Offentliche Finanzen und monetäre Okonomie* (1985).

rates. The Bundesbank stuck to a few simple economic policy beliefs: that the money supply is linked to inflation; that a high public-sector deficit causes high interest rates; that the balance of payments matters; that intervention to maintain fixed exchange rates produces hazards for domestic stability; and that deregulation of financial markets should be viewed with suspicion.[47] These beliefs deeply influenced its role in the two main interdependent bargaining relations in which it was involved: in the bargaining relations between the EC and the central banks, and in the bargaining relations between it and the German federal government.

But the real pragmatism came in acknowledging that the money supply targets of the Bundesbank could not effectively substitute for the need for responsible behaviour by other domestic actors: by government in controlling budget deficits and public debt, and by the 'social partners' in aligning collective bargaining to macro-economic realities. Ultimately, too, it recognized that its capacity to use its independence effectively – to 'face down the government' – depended on the persistence of a culture of economic stability: that is, on the strength of public support for a counter-inflationary monetary stance. It had, in other words, a sense of its own limitations, and hence of the limitations of the sound money policy approach underpinning the Treaty on European Union. Again in the words of Schlesinger: 'Monetary policy cannot reverse a grave misdirection of fiscal and wages policies. Anti-inflation policy cannot be reduced to the problem of providing a proper set of technical instruments.'[48]

This essential pragmatism and eclecticism of the Bundesbank was vital to the consistency of its approach and its sense of the cultural and historical relativity of economic policy ideas. But it was not the originator of the economic theories on which the new EMS and EMU were based. These theories were the prerogative of institutional economists who were commentators rather than, as with the Bundesbank, participants in real decisions of European significance. Other central bank economists may have been much closer to the cutting edge of theoretical advance in European monetary integration. But their theoretical activity seemed more like compensation for not being in actual control of their monetary policies. The Bundesbank's impact on the approach to EMU embodied in the Maastricht Treaty was to protect its corporate and political interests in restricting the size of any EMU and thus retaining German dominance of European monetary policies.

Economic analysis and political objectives

The argument that the EMS and EMU policy process reflects the structural power of sound money is subject to an even more fundamental qualification than that provided by the pragmatism and eclecticism of institution-based economists. The record of the policy processes of the EMS and EMU supports the view that economic policy ideas were not so much important in independently driving policy in a certain direction as in legitimizing what politicians and their officials had chosen to do in pursuit of their own essentially political or corporate motives.

47. On these beliefs see D. Marsh, *The Bundesbank: The Bank That Rules Europe* (London: Heinemann, 1992).
48. J. Dempsey, 'German Bank Chief Airs Treaty Worries', *Financial Times*, 17/18 April 1993.

These political and corporate motives were sometimes rational. In the case of French policy from 1983 onwards the political objectives were paramount: to enhance control over policy and to gain greater respect from, and thus bargaining leverage with, other EC governments; to dissociate French Socialism and the reputation of the President from negative historical images of monetary chaos and defeat derived from the Popular Front of the 1930s and revived by the experiences of devaluation in 1981–3; and to provide the Inspectorate of Finance with an alibi (ERM discipline) to impose its values on the government after the 'mistakes' of 1981–3.[49] Similarly, behind the British government's adoption of the currency competition plan in 1989 was the political calculation that it could serve as a diversionary tactic in the EMU negotiations.[50] But, most importantly of all, the convergence criteria of the Maastricht Treaty embodied the political interest of German actors in restricting the size of the eventual EMU and continuing to dominate European monetary policy. Seen against the background of these interacting calculations of political interests the treaty is properly to be seen as not first and foremost an exercise in economic reasoning but rather as a political exercise in postponing conflict between two key interests – between German interest, on the one hand, and, on the other, the interest of EC countries with 'softer' currencies in enhancing their reputation and policy influence by being in stage three.[51]

The political motives were also often deeply emotional, whether based on a deep conviction about European union or about national sovereignty: Helmut Kohl and Margaret Thatcher stand as the striking contrast. It was above all the non-rational political factors that produced either a powerful community of interests, as between Kohl and Mitterand, or a dialogue of the deaf, as between both and Mrs Thatcher. In the final analysis, economic policy ideas were only likely to succeed to the extent that they were consistent with such deeply held political passions. And, of course, their appeal was also dependent on their consistency with rational political calculation. *One Market, One Money* was a classic illustration of the role of economic ideas as legitimator of policy. Like the earlier Cecchini Report on the single European market, it was an example of economic research *after* the decision of political principle had already been taken.[52] Economic policy advice was being organized to legitimize policy. Similarly, in the cases of France and Italy, the role of economists was not so much to preach the logic of economic policy ideas to political leaders and officials (though they did play that role) as to make acceptable at the level of economic ideas and national debate the paramount political facts about the EMU policy process: that the D-Mark was the anchor currency, endowing Germany with policy leadership; that Germany would never give up an independent central bank in the name of EMU; and that, accordingly, the EMS and EMU would have to be designed on German terms.

49. On these motives see P. Favier and M. Martin-Roland, *La Décennie Mitterrand* (Paris: Le Seuil, 1990); J. Attali, *Verbatim* (Paris: Fayard, 1992); P. Simonnot, '1983: l'autre politique déjà', *Le Monde*, 29 June 1993, pp. 25, 30, 31.
50. M. Thatcher, *The Downing Street Years* (London: Harper Collins, 1993), p. 716.
51. P. De Grauwe, *The Political Economy of Monetary Union in Europe* (London: Centre for Economic Policy Research, Discussion Paper no. 842, September 1993).
52. Commission of the European Communities, *European Economy: The Economics of 1992* (Luxembourg: Office of Official Publications of the European Communities, March 1988).

Conclusion

The Treaty on European Union has a Janus-like quality. On the one hand, its gradualist nature is rooted in the pre-eminence of political objectives in its design, particularly German interest in retaining both reputation and dominant influence in any transition to stage three. On the other hand, the treaty stands as the EC's great monument to the 'sound money revolution' in economic thought. The policy ideas that it legitimizes have helped transform the whole context of economic and monetary policies, shifting the location of power in the EC – towards the bargaining relations between the EC and central banks and the primacy of the German Bundesbank – and redirecting the efforts of policy actors to new goals (price stability and fiscal discipline). The revolution in European integration consequent on EMU appeared to be more profound than that of the single European market: not only at the level of institutional reform but also at the level of policy effects. Previous major policy innovations have been associated with the idea of early, if not immediate benefit: whether the customs union, the EMS or the single market. With EMU the costs in lost output and employment preceded the benefits, a trade-off in time that is always difficult for democratic politics and new to a big project of European integration. It was, therefore, a new departure for EC integration: in ideological terms and in terms of political strategy.

Not least, sound money policy ideas endowed Germany (or rather the Bundesbank) with authority as a source of knowledge about how to manage a modern EC economy effectively. The new, or rather renewed prestige of the German model confirmed its leadership role in the new EMS and EMU. Hence power in the EC policy process was displaced not only to the central banks, but also to the Bundesbank in particular and to the bargaining relations between the Bundesbank and the German federal government. There was, in short, a collusion of ideas and power in the policy process.

The victory of sound money ideas was not primarily attributable to the EC Commission and Jacques Delors. Because the EMU initiative occurred during the years of Delors's presidency and of a renewed prestige and confidence of the Commission, it is tempting to trace what happened to their influence. The crucial fact is that the victory of sound money in the Treaty on European Union was the product of forces of which the EC Commission and Delors were largely a reflection. These forces were formidable singly, and overpowering in their convergence: the increasing power of savers as a political interest (with the prospect that over-60s would represent a majority of voters by 2015); the experience of the role of acute inflationary pressures in generating economic crises at the national level; and the combination of the traditional intimacy of the bargaining relations between central bankers and governments with the new mutual interest in collusion occasioned by the fight to contain and defeat inflation.

The most striking indicator of change in the political and economic context of economic ideas was the new saliency of the interests of savers. Correspondingly, greater value has been placed on price stability and liberalization of markets; and pension and investment funds have acquired a new significance as actors in financial markets (see chapter 8). Economic crisis was a second factor: not so much a single shared event as a succession of national crises, each of which drew attention to the need for a new budget discipline in the interests of containing inflation and promoting competitiveness. In Britain the crisis dated from the mid-1970s; in France from 1982–3; whilst in Germany it was more deeply historically embedded in the 1920s and 1940s. The lessons were generalized to the EC level in the form of a sound money EMU, behind which stood a coalition of modernizers at the national and EC levels: not least, modernizers in Italy and Spain who, in the absence of a deep-seated crisis before 1992, sought to use the EMS and EMU policy process to force similar effects at the national level.

Third, central bankers had uniquely close ties to the EMS and EMU policy process. As we shall see in chapter 8, their gatekeeper role to the financial markets endowed them with a technical expertise on which governments depended – and liberalization of capital movements has made this role more rather than less significant; whilst chapter 6 has already shown their unusually close connections to the EC policy process through dual representation in both the Committee of Central Bank Governors and the EC Monetary Committee. The victory of sound money ideas was closely linked to the privileged position of the central banks in the EMS and EMU policy process; ideology and corporate self-interest enjoyed a symbiotic relationship.

Whilst it is appropriate to speak of the victory of sound money ideas in the negotiations on the Treaty of European Union, some important qualifications about their structural power are in order. First, economic theorizing about the EC as a monetary union has been far from monolithic and is far from having a simple, one-way relationship to politics. Within the literature on optimum currency areas, between Keynesians and monetarists, and among more mainstream sound money economists, there have been divergent perceptions of problems and solutions. Economics has continued to comprise different networks of information and advice, enjoying a complex interactive relationship with those in power. On the one hand, influence has gravitated to those economists and networks that are able to speak directly to the political needs of policy makers – and the political need to contain and defeat inflation has been paramount in the 1980s and into the 1990s for long-term structural reasons. In broad terms, sound money ideas have conferred prestige on institutional economists linked to finance ministries, central banks and financial institutions, if only as mediators between academic ideas and political convictions and calculations. They have most directly addressed the need to clothe corporate self-interest in a public mission.

On the other hand, the fundamental fact is that economic ideas are difficult to control; their power is subtle, elusive and contingent on economic and political circumstances. Here we come to the paradox of the power of economic ideas. That power rests in their capacity to convey knowledge that politicians need and to give authority to the actions of politicians. It derives also from the psychological effects of 'sunk costs' in pursuing a particular policy; it has to be seen to succeed. Yet economists have no real control over the factors that determine a politician's perceptions of need. Hence the use of economic ideas to legitimize a policy – like the approach to EMU in the Maastricht Treaty – does not imply that economic factors have been the prime inspiration for that policy. Political actors and central bankers possess their own power over economic policy ideas, the power of patronage. This factor has been decisive in the EMU bargaining relations where long-term political themes in French and German policy resurfaced: French national interest in containment of German power and the power of the *grands corps*, and German national interest in continuing to dominate European monetary policy. It was not so much economic beliefs about the errors of devaluation or the benefits of tying one's hands that put EMU back on the EC's agenda as the political belief, represented most forcefully in France, that Germany's economic and monetary power must be controlled and balanced by shifting decision-making authority to the EC level. What is, however, important is that, once launched, EMU – like the EMS already – was captured by sound money ideas.

Second, the particular quality of the impact of sound money ideas was influenced by the policy style of the EC Commission which in turn, through the exclusive right of initiative of the Commission in EC policy, infected the bargaining relations at Council level and wider policy debate. That policy style also fitted in well with some national policy styles, notably in France. Sound money's own legacy to the EMS and EMU policy process was to endow its debates with a degree of technical abstraction that hindered rather than assisted the process of mobilizing popular support. The presentation of the benefits and costs was overwhelmingly couched in macro-economic theory. Missing was the emphasis on the benefits to the convenience of the citizens of the member states and to small and medium-sized businesses, for which the transaction costs of changing currencies and the inefficiencies of the intra-EC payments system were a serious problem. Though small and medium-sized businesses were much more important to EC employment than the large multinational companies, it was the latter that dominated the economic debate in the Association for the Monetary Union of Europe and via national employer organizations and UNICE. Paralleling the failure to involve and mobilize SMEs (small and medium-sized enterprises) was the neglect of the micro-economic dimensions of EMU, for instance in the EC Commission's *One Market, One Money*. The result was a collusive, elitist debate that left the EMS and EMU policy process in a vacuum of political legitimacy. Technical economic arguments must somehow translate into mobilizing political ideas that can be communicated as relevant to the practical interests and concerns of citizens. That translation was not achieved in the case of the EMU policy process.

This problem was exacerbated by the dominance of the EMS and EMU policy process by an intellectual model of technocratic rationalism. Its roots were partly in macro-economics, and partly in the bureaucratic culture of the EC Commission as policy initiator. Pragmatism and caution did not figure strongly in its value system. As we have seen, there were overwhelming economic and political obstacles in the way of an evolutionary approach to EMU as a learning process in using a common currency, giving citizens and small businesses the opportunity and time to experience the practical benefits of EMU. Politically, such an evolutionary course was not helped by its espousal by the British government; it was suspected, rightly, that it was designed as a distraction. In any case, it was of limited intellectual appeal to many of those involved in the policy process.

Caution might also have been prompted by the observation that strong, prestigious currencies tend, as in the United States, to reflect a cohesive domestic market. The EC market was not very cohesive. Its financial markets might be increasingly integrated, with major consequences for monetary policy. By contrast, however, cross-national labour mobility was not well established as a safety valve for problems of adjustment.

It was far from clear that EC markets would work in some cases at all (e.g. the labour market) or quickly enough (e.g. in the downward adjustment of wages and costs) to enable anything other than a mini-EMU to work (and then with difficulty). Fiscal transfers were still only on a small scale. The processes of structural reform, of completing the single market and of developing fiscal transfer mechanisms appeared not to have gone far enough, and consolidated their benefits, as preconditions for an EC-wide transition to EMU. Instead, the imprint of technocratic rationalism married to macro-economic theorizing dominated the EMS and EMU policy process.

Despite continuing doubt and dispute about what is fundamentally important in economic management, the forces that we have described above seem to point to a continuity in the ascendancy of sound money ideas: after the EC Commission lost its confidence and prestige in 1992, and even after Delors. These forces suggest a structural change in the location of power over policy linked to the ascendancy of these ideas. The importance of the Treaty of European Union lies in the way that it institutionalizes certain rules in the EMS and EMU policy process, giving to sound money an EC constitutional authority that it lacks in national law. A powerful in-built bias is thereby given to the economic foundations of European integration.

But, in the real world of contending interests and political pressures, trade-offs among values will be difficult to avoid: economics will continue to register these difficulties in its theoretical disputes. Stability is the guiding principle of the sound money policy ideas underpinning the treaty, and the stages of EMU are meant to provide an institutional safeguard for this value. Given the factors that we have outlined, it will clearly remain of enormous significance in guiding the policy process. Yet it cannot stand in splendid isolation. There are other values around which political action and economic policy ideas are properly mobilized: wealth-creation, in the sense of measures to promote output and employment, through active demand management, an improved infrastructure (of training and of research and development) and greater efficiency (of labour markets and of public and other services); and equity, expressed in terms of a greater emphasis on the treaty's dedication to 'economic and social cohesion', in the form of fiscal transfers. These two values were expressed respectively in the Delors White Paper agreed at the Brussels summit of 1993 and in the Delors II budget package agreed at the Edinburgh summit of 1992. But in practical terms they remained modest when set aside the impact of the stability-oriented policy approach.

If the EC is to reflect the real complexity of economic policy values, and to be responsive to democratic politics, its policy process for EMU must provide a broad framework for policy development. Such a policy process would be a complex and subtle mechanism for reconciling the conflicting requirements of stability (to satisfy savers), wealth-creation (to satisfy those in manufacturing and commerce) and equity (to satisfy those, like unemployed and under-employed people, who are disadvantaged by change). The Treaty on European Union was not that mechanism. Mounting political objection to the painful costs of a myopic stability-oriented policy, combined with inertia of the EMS and EMU policy process in responding, created the threat of a crisis that would simultaneously demystify not only the ideology legitimizing central bank power but also the ideology of European integration itself. EC integration will be known by its consequences, and the political and corporate company that it has kept.

Chapter 8

PUTTING THE EMS AND EMU INTO PRACTICE (3)
The structural power of financial markets, economic 'fundamentals' and trade interdependence

> A central bank which never fights, which at times of economic tension never raises its voice, which in the age of the mass welfare state wants to be friends with everyone: that central bank will be viewed with mistrust.
>
> (Karl Blessing, president of the Bundesbank, 10 November 1967)

Much of the distinctive character of the EMS and EMU policy process as a sector of European integration is provided by two related facts: that it involves a complex bargaining relationship between EC monetary authorities and the foreign exchange market operators, and that its context involves the structural power of the financial markets, of the economic fundamentals of its members and of their trade interdependency. The character of the foreign exchange markets – notably their globalization and volatility – means that the policy process differs from that to be found in other sectors of European integration. This difference is embodied not least in the content of the bargaining relationship, with its preoccupations with credibility, reputation and trust. By its rules of the game, and changes in these rules, the EMS and EMU policy process seeks to influence the behaviour of market operators. Thus, narrow bands encourage one-way bets; very wide bands shift the centre of gravity to the 'market makers'. Experience of how the rules of the game on intervention are operated may tempt market operators to test the resolve of the authorities to defend ERM currencies or discourage them. Foreign exchange market operators focus their attention on the economic fundamentals of the EC economies; how these fundamentals develop and how they are perceived by operators is critical to the functioning of the EMS and EMU policy process. With the rules of the EMS game, and with the new convergence criteria of the Treaty on European Union, EMS and EMU policy makers sought to transform the content of the bargaining relations with the market. Hence it is tempting to attribute a *sui generis* character to the EMS and EMU as policy process, with respect not simply to its strategic importance within the overall project for European union but, above all, to its *modus operandi*.

There is nothing perhaps so unusual in the fact that the policy actors in the EMS and EMU are bound up in the impersonal forces represented by the institutional dynamics of the EC's two-level policy process: or even in the fact that their interaction is structured by a particular climate of sound money economic ideas, when the dominance of those ideas derives from deeper underlying forces in the polities and economies of advanced industrial societies. But, alongside the structural power of the anchor currency, the foreign exchange markets, and the values and interests that they reflect, represent an altogether different context for the operation of the policy process. These markets are acutely sensitive to relative price changes, notably in interest rates, and to the implications of political and economic news for judgements about economic fundamentals and future price changes. Their volatility is legendary, the question being whether that volatility is excessive or not.

Also, the foreign exchange markets function as, in effect, a continuing referendum on the political will and capability of monetary authorities to pursue a particular policy, whether to staunchly defend a particular set of parities in the ERM or to pursue economic convergence rigorously for the sake of EMU: and they are a referendum in which the enfranchised are wealth holders (or those who act on their behalf) with an interest in assessing and managing financial risks with the objective of improving returns. In other words, their functioning reflects the confidence of market operators in different currencies and those who manage them: the reward of that confidence is a greater freedom of manoeuvre for the monetary authorities concerned. The penalty for its absence is a sense of monetary authorities being at the mercy of markets.

To volatility and investor confidence as vital factors in the operation of foreign exchange markets must be added the 'fungibility' of money, that is, its ability to be transferred from place to place, and from purpose to purpose. As we shall see, two forces have been decisive in this respect. Liberalization and the new information and communications technologies have massively enhanced the flexibility and speed of operation of the foreign exchange markets. Here are markets which, to a greater degree than any other, are global, and where the problems of regulation are more acute than anywhere else. Politicians and finance ministry and central bank officials in the EMS and EMU policy process face operators in foreign exchange markets whose outlooks are international and global in scope: for whom the EMS and EMU is but part of a much larger field of forces, not least the US dollar/D-Mark rate and the US dollar/Japanese yen rate. The combination of liberalization, notably the removal of exchange controls, with continuing market innovation has had enormous implications for the EMS and EMU policy process and for the conduct of national economic and monetary policies.

Policy and markets: the role of central banks

European monetary integration can be defined as a sector in which actors are arranged on a continuum: some closer to the heart of policy, to the actual making and implementation of decisions on the design and use of monetary policy instruments; others involved with the financial markets, in particular foreign exchange transactions, and yet whose decisions on purchase and sale of currencies have direct bearing on the policy process. At one end are the heads of state and government in the European Council, alongside the foreign ministers, embodying the highly political sensitivity of monetary policies; at the other end are the market operators, the corporate treasurers and the pension and investment fund managers. The market operators are highly professional, well informed and competent to judge their own self-interests. Doing most of their business in wholesale markets, the average size of their deals can be huge: for instance, in April 1992 the average size of D-Mark/pound sterling option deals was some $32 million. Their importance can be related to their role in enabling investors to economize on transaction costs, particularly the information costs of searching out investment opportunities and verifying their productivity and then monitoring their performance.[1] This role has enabled them to accumulate considerable power. In between the two ends of the continuum, as gatekeepers between the markets and policy, stand the central banks, but as gatekeepers who are positioned, as public-law institutions, closer to policy than to the market operators and who, traditionally and with the exception of the Bundesbank, have been in an essentially hierarchical bargaining relationship with their governments.

Two underlying factors have decisively influenced relationships within this sector. As we saw in chapter 7, sound money had, by the mid-1980s, endowed European monetary integration with a degree of community at the level of economic ideas, reflected later in the Treaty on European Union. Also, a complex combination of policy, technological and internal market changes had served to liberate market operators from the constraints of national public authorities. In effect, market operators are in a privileged position with respect to European monetary integration, not least because governments are dependent on them to help finance deficits. This privileged position was above all strengthened by policies to liberalize capital movements. So, paradoxically, as policy has thrust ahead to EMU, seizing the political initiative in a bold fashion, the market operators have gained greater power. In the bargaining relation between EC monetary authorities and the financial markets the market operators had a privileged position. The big questions were just how privileged that position was; and what was the relative significance of this bargaining relation compared to the other bargaining relations that constituted the EMS and EMU policy process.

The different actors involved in European monetary integration have assessed its problems and prospects from their own perspective on the continuum between policy and the market. Investment fund managers exhibit, quite properly, a great faith in market rationality and the virtues of market discipline. Those who operate in the financial markets – the commercial banks, corporate treasurers, pension and investment fund managers, and hedge fund managers – are concerned to make money within the framework of the rules of the game, or by finding ways round them, and to avert risks that might follow from the behaviour of the monetary authorities. Heads of government, finance ministries and central banks are, by contrast, making and operating the rules, and, in the process, seeking to control financial markets, or at least some of the effects of their operation.

But, in practice, the reality is far from so simple. First, many of the actors in the European monetary integration process find that they are looking two ways. Perhaps the best examples are provided by the central banks and the commercial banks; they are acting closest to the interface of policy and markets. Here again there are interesting cross-national differences. France, for instance, provides an example of a relatively well-structured policy process. Its commercial banks, public and private, are particularly sensitive to the policy of the Banque de France: being tied to the Banque de France, and the Banque de France in turn locked into the Trésor of the Finance Ministry, by a web of interpersonal relations: interpersonal relations that are held

---

1. H. Leland and D. Pyle, 'Information Asymmetries, Financial Structure and Financial Intermediation', *Journal of Finance* 32 (1977), pp. 371–87; N. Strong and M. Walker, *Information and Capital Markets* (Oxford: Basil Blackwell, 1987).

together and smoothed by common membership of, and personal identification with, the Inspectorate of Finance as a common career reference.[2] Most symbolic of this elite network was the fact that two successive governors of the Banque de France, Jacques de Larosière and Jean-Claude Trichet, were former directors of the Trésor. In short, in France sensitivity to policy seems to reach further along the continuum of actors involved in European monetary integration than in most other countries. Even so, as the ERM crisis of July 1993 underlined, neither the Banque de France nor the commercial banks could in the last analysis escape the contingencies of the financial markets.

Second, the relationship between the monetary authorities and the market operators is very far from being an exclusive one. Market uncertainty is not the only uncertainty facing the monetary authorities, and the policies of the monetary authorities are not the only source of instability and risk facing financial market operators. Thus economic fundamentals may change, for instance in the form of differential inflation rates; shocks – like German unification – may intervene to test the credibility of the commitment of monetary authorities; and the monetary decisions of the managers of the anchor currency may, as in July 1993, take both other monetary authorities and market operators by surprise. Market operators have an eye on each other, as well as on the monetary authorities. Governments are sensitive to public opinion, as mediated through the media, to internal party mood and to electoral support. Fundamentally, the matrix of calculation is simpler for market operators, who are basically out to make profits and protect their positions. Governments must bear in mind party support, electoral majorities and their reputation with their EC partners as well as their reputation with the markets. In this important respect the chain of reasoning applied by Barro and Gordon and Giavazzi and Pagano (discussed in chapter 7) lacked key elements of realism. The 'game' between the monetary authorities and the financial markets was not the only one being played by either party.

Third, there is an asymmetry in the speculative pressures that affect different currencies within the ERM. One of the problems of integrating the pound sterling into the ERM was the fact that there are many more holders of this currency than of, for instance, the French franc. The one remained a world-class currency; the other was not. Hence the potential for speculative runs on sterling that would prove difficult to manage was greater. The traditional strength of ERM currencies, other than the pound sterling and of course the much more significant D-Mark, was that the only large holders of these currencies were nationals of the country concerned. Thus anyone wanting to speculate against one of those currencies had to borrow it in order to sell them. In consequence, the volume of speculation was likely to be rapidly turned round as nationals continued to need their currency for domestic transactions and to repay their debts. In practice, with elimination of exchange controls, this strength began to be eroded. But asymmetry was still apparent in foreign exchange turnover with the US dollar. In April 1992 turnover with the US dollar as a percentage of total daily turnover in the foreign exchange markets varied from 25.4 per cent in the case of the

2. On the Inspectorate of Finance see e.g. E. Suleiman, *Elites in French Society* (Princeton, NJ: Princeton University Press, 1978); J. Saint-Geours, *Pouvoir et finance* (Paris: Fayard, 1979).

D-Mark to 9.5 per cent and 2.3 per cent in the cases of the pound sterling and the French franc respectively.[3]

The complexity of strategic interaction between actors on the policy-market continuum is well captured in the case of the central banks. With respect to European monetary integration their policy aims have been clear: to defend their autonomy and stabilize financial markets, and to promote their influence by capturing specific areas of policy (through central bank independence). The method employed by the central banks was to ensure that they remained privileged interlocutors of finance ministers and heads of government in the context of a very small and exclusive policy community. This privileged access and exclusivity depended on a subtle political balancing act: keeping in line politically, for instance in the Delors Committee and during the IGC negotiations, and keeping out of political debates and contest, and relying on governments to undertake effective political persuasion of publics that an EMU based on central bank independence was in the public interest. The consequence was that the central banks were able to emerge as privileged actors within an exclusive policy community, their privilege based on their technical expertise in the management of monetary policy.

But they were also to be caught up in a tension between their policy aims, notably defence of their autonomy, and their methods, maintaining a close, privileged and non-confrontational relationship with government. This tension was more readily resolved on their own terms under the gold standard, when governments adopted the preferences of central banks. With EMU, however, the political initiative was much more overt. The gold standard exhibited the power of the central banks; EMU defined its limits. Yet in both cases power implied political restraint, a dependence on politicians to protect their autonomy. In 1992–3 the central banks were left uncomfortably exposed as the public relations efforts of governments to sell the Treaty on European Union ran into difficulties.

The other tension that beset the role of the central banks was between policy and markets. Central banks are much closer to the financial markets than finance ministries and certainly heads of government and foreign ministers. They can be viewed as 'informed insiders' in foreign exchange markets, using their superior knowledge about how they and the government will use ERM policy instruments to limit the costs and maximize the effectiveness of intervention. How that role is best performed is a matter of some dispute: EC central banks have been far from monolithic in their internal views of the value of the hard EMS and of EMU. In one view, the informational advantage of central banks *vis-à-vis* the market operators is enhanced when they are able to hide their hand, resorting to secrecy about policy and remaining ambiguous about exchange rate targets.[4] Correspondingly, this advantage of information

---

3. Bank for International Settlements, *Central Bank Survey of Foreign Exchange Market Activity in April 1992* (Basle: BIS, March 1993), p. 10.
4. On the effectiveness of central bank intervention see U. Bhattacharya and P. Weller, *The Advantage to Hiding One's Hand: Speculation and Central Bank Intervention in the Foreign Exchange Market* (London: Centre for Economic Policy Research, Discussion Paper no. 737, 1992); K. Dominguez, 'The Informational Role of Official Foreign Exchange Intervention Policy: The Signalling Hypothesis,' in Dominguez (ed.) *Exchange Rate Efficiency and the Behaviour of International Asset Markets* (New York: Garland Publishing, 1992); J. Stein, 'Cheap Talk and the Fed: A Theory of Imprecise Policy

asymmetry is reduced once, as with the ERM, central banks are committed to the defence of stable and explicit parity rates. Influential support for this view comes from George Soros, the most famous hedge fund manager, who pointed out that his capacity for placing successful speculative bets is enhanced by the attempts of monetary authorities to defend stable parities, as in the ERM. Within EC central banks too there have always been those closest to the markets who have been most acutely aware of the loss of room for manoeuvre in relation to the markets as the ERM hardened.

But, in another view, the transparent rules of the hard ERM have an advantage over, say, those of the Louvre Accord of 1987 and certainly over floating rate regimes. The central banks can more effectively deal with the markets under such a regime because clear expectations reduce the potential for disagreement among policy makers, help boost the confidence of market operators in their commitment and help to pre-empt the problems of control that arise as market operators evolve their own, quite possibly false interpretation of the 'real' rules, against which the monetary authorities are then tested.[5]

Beneath this dispute about method are different models of how foreign exchange markets are best managed: by a 'managed float' of currencies, in which the advantages of ambiguity about policy can be pursued; or by stable exchange rates that clarify expectations and generate trust. Even more fundamentally, the dispute reveals contrasting views about how the markets operate and the conditions under which they operate properly. In facing the foreign exchange markets central banks, for all their experience and professionalism, are hampered by limited knowledge of the processes at work.

Despite this limitation EC central banks have certain tactical advantages in dealing with market operators. They can operate discreetly during 'thin' markets, for instance Tokyo overnight, to move a particular rate more sharply than would be possible in London or New York, thereby setting the tone for a day's trading. Faced with a crisis situation they can seek to use very high day-to-day lending rates to inflict losses on speculators. More fundamentally, a central bank knows about sensitive economic data before it is made public. With this advantage it can anticipate the reactions of market operators and operate a 'bear squeeze', a way of causing substantial losses to those who have bet against a particular currency. There seems to be an element of paradox in the fact that, whilst central bank intervention is trivial in relation to daily foreign exchange market turnover, it can exert significant effects.[6] Such effects are possible when intervention is broadly consistent with economic fundamentals; then it is likely

---

Announcements', *American Economic Review* 79 (1989), pp. 32–42; M. Obstfeld, 'The Effectiveness of Foreign Exchange Intervention: Recent Experience, 1985–88', in W. Branson *et al.* (eds) *International Policy Coordination and Exchange Rate Fluctuation* (Chicago: University of Chicago Press, 1990); The Jurgenson Report, *Report of the Working Group on Exchange Market Intervention* (Washington, DC: US Treasury, 1983); D. Adams and D. Henderson, *Definition and Measurement of Exchange Market Intervention* (Washington, DC: Board of Governors of the Federal Reserve System, Staff Study no. 126, 1983).

5. P. Kenen, *Managing Exchange Rates* (London: Routledge, 1988).
6. For an analogous piece of reasoning see J. Dow and I. Saville, *A Critique of Monetary Policy* (Oxford: Oxford University Press, 1988).

to fall on receptive ground. The 'steer' given by the authorities becomes decisive when market operators crave a signal, and they are receptive to central bank signals when their expectations are not unanimous or held with certainty.

As we shall see, two factors blunt the effects of central bank intervention, in addition to the modesty of its scale: first, when intervention is inconsistent with economic fundamentals, and thus lacks credibility, and second, when the operation of technical trading rules drives the market operators away from a respect for economic fundamentals. In such circumstances, mistakes at the level of policy are characteristically a central cause of loss of control and crisis.

At the same time, central banks are informed insiders in the policy community. They seek to ensure that policy on the EMS and EMU takes account of anticipated reactions of operators in foreign exchange markets, and they are more sensitive than governments to the implications of a mismatch between economic fundamentals and exchange rate policy for the behaviour of the markets. Thus, in 1992, the Bank of England was quicker than the Treasury to see that the sterling parity was not sustainable. The central banks have certain tactical advantages within the policy community. By for instance emphasizing the risk that their governments may not be able to finance their deficits without policy change, central banks can use their informational advantage about financial markets to increase their influence on policy. Once again we are reminded that central banks benefit from 'information asymmetries': *vis-à-vis* markets and *vis-à-vis* governments.

But the constraints on their power should not be underestimated. Central banks are very imperfectly informed about foreign exchange markets. Their policy instruments, particularly resources for intervention, are limited in relation to the scale of the markets. And they do not fully control the process of 'signalling' policy intentions and capability to the market; here the announcements of finance ministers and heads of government and 'rumour' operate to provide the markets with 'news'. Information asymmetry does not readily translate into control.

Innovation and change in the foreign exchange markets

Prior to this chapter we have been essentially concerned with the policy actors in European monetary integration. This bias is quite appropriate because European monetary integration has (as we have seen) been driven first and foremost not by market operators but by political actors. Nevertheless, the foreign exchange markets have been a crucial context within which initiatives in European monetary integration have taken place and the EMS and EMU policy process evolved. Perceptions of politicians and officials about the nature, operation and development of these markets have been central to their calculations – for instance, in the relaunch of EMU in 1988. Of perhaps even more importance, some of the most important problems of putting the EMS and EMU into practice revolve around the foreign exchange markets.

Despite this structural power of the financial markets EMS and EMU policy development and implementation has not been able to benefit from a single agreed theoretical account of how foreign exchange markets operate or from extensive and sound empirical work on the market operators themselves, their behaviour and above all motivations. Are these markets efficient or not; do they change in a linear and predictable or non-linear and dynamic fashion; does order or chaos reign there? In the absence of a simple, definitive answer to these questions, economic theory cannot adequately brief policy makers about how their activities influence market operators. A central problem in putting the EMS and EMU into practice is that policy makers, and academic economists, have differed in their assumptions about operators in the foreign exchange markets – whether they are rational, responding rapidly to new information, or prone to overconfidence about their forecasts or to overdue reliance on historic images of currencies; whether they are risk-averse or risk-seeking. Politicians have on occasion even feared political motives at work in the markets: with, for instance, the former EC Commissioner and French Prime Minister Raymond Barre forecasting an 'Anglo-Saxon attack' on the EMS and EMU by ambush of the French franc.[7]

The foreign exchange market is distinctive among financial markets in being created and structured by government intervention. At heart the market is shaped by the fact that governments have decided to create their own currencies and national institutional structures to act as monopoly suppliers of each currency. Hence the national central banks are able, by employing specific policy instruments, to determine the value of their currencies. Despite the enormous shift to globalization and deregulation that has occurred in the foreign exchange markets, it remains important not to lose sight of their domestic political and institutional context – which (as chapter 1 emphasized) endows national currencies and their value with a great deal of emotional and psychological significance. Foreign exchange markets, global and deregulated as they are, remain embedded in very different market organizations, cultures and rules: in London and Paris, let alone London and Tokyo.

Another distinctive feature of the foreign exchange markets is the way that they are intertwined with other financial markets, like the stock market, the bond market and the retail market: all markets that have become more international, liquidity-driven and thus capable of adjusting more quickly to economic indicators. In effect, all international financial transactions pass through it, involving enormous volumes of daily trading. Also, there is an interdependence with goods markets, in the form of financing international trade. In addition to dynamic effects from these ancillary markets, internal dynamics are generated by the behaviour of the current and the capital accounts of the balance of payments, and shocks affecting them; and by central bank foreign exchange interventions and whether they serve to stabilize the market or not. These complex interdependencies underline the difficulty of any adequate intellectual modelling of the functioning of foreign exchange markets and help us to understand the appeal of nouns like 'complexity', 'chaos', 'volatility' and 'randomness' to characterize them.

Borrowing from Chaos Theory it seems plausible to argue that foreign exchange markets are essentially non-linear and indeterminate in their dynamics, their operation punctured by events – like a newspaper interview by a central bank governor – which

---

7. See *Financial Times*, 11 February 1993, p. 2. Barre's concern was shared in public comments made by the French Finance Minister Michel Sapin and the German Chancellor Helmut Kohl.

can produce unpredictable and extraordinary results.[8] Foreign exchange markets appear as a world of 'shattering cascades and unserviceable intricacies'. This view of the character of foreign exchange markets gains some support from the 'news' approach. In this view the arrival of new information has decisive effects on the markets: whether election results (like the Danish referendum of June 1992), official announcements, rumours or economic data (on, for instance, inflation or the money supply).[9]

Alternatively, borrowing from Complexity Theory, there is a deep simplicity of evolving rules that give an element of order to the complex foreign exchange markets.[10] An example might be provided by the argument that speculatory pressures are generated by technical trading rules as they have evolved among market operators. In this case operators are seen as engaging in speculation because they deem a currency worth buying, based on the expectation that they can pass it on at a higher price in the future – even if this behaviour defies economic fundamentals.[11] The longer-term result may be 'speculative runs', which reflect rational and self-fulfilling expectations of market operators regardless of the fundamentals. Such a phenomenon appeared to affect the Spanish peseta after the Maastricht summit and before the Danish referendum.

But, whether chaotic or simply complex, foreign exchange markets do not seem to represent tidy, repetitive and passive systems, readily amenable to official control. Full respect for this reality was not built into the provisions of the Treaty on European Union with respect to the timetable for EMU and the provision for realignment. In September 1992 the markets brought it to the attention of politicians in a way that economists – despite their best efforts (as we saw in chapter 7) – had failed to do.

Another distinctive feature of the financial exchange markets is the role that 'Europe' played, at least in name, in their postwar development. The Eurocurrency markets – like the Eurodollar market, the Euromark market, the Euroyen market and the Eurosterling market – began a new process of offshore banking, which saw vast amounts of US dollars and other hard currencies deposited and lent outside the domestic financial markets of these currencies, with London as the major centre of this activity – although formally these markets had no geographical base or national home. The prime catalysts for their rapid growth were provided by the efforts of US banks to escape domestic regulatory restrictions on their activities and their attempt to meet the

8. For attempts to apply Chaos Theory to financial markets see E. Peters, *Chaos and Order in the Capital Markets* (London: John Wiley, 1991); A. Medio, *Chaotic Dynamics: Theory and Applications to Economics* (London: Oxford University Press, 1992).
9. R. Macdonald, *Floating Exchange Rates: Theories and Evidence* (London: Unwin-Hyman, 1988).
10. On Complexity Theory see R. Lewin, *Complexity: Life at the Edge of Chaos* (London: Dent, 1993); M. Waldrop, *Complexity: The Emerging Science at the Edge of Order and Chaos* (London: Viking, 1993).
11. J. Frankel, 'The Dazzling Dollar', *Brookings Papers on Economic Activity* 1 (1985), pp. 199–217; M. Obstfeld, 'Rational and Self-Fulfilling Balance-of-Payments Crises', *American Economic Review* 76 (1986); M. Obstfeld, 'Competitiveness, Realignment and Speculation: The Role of Financial Markets', in F. Giavazzi *et al.* (eds) *The European Monetary System* (Cambridge: Cambridge University Press, 1988); G. Evans, 'A Test for Speculative Bubbles and the Sterling–Dollar Exchange Rate: 1981–84', *American Economic Review* 76 (1986), pp. 621–36.

growing needs of American multinational corporations as they expanded in Europe. In the process international banking activity grew apace, and the Eurocurrency markets emerged as the world's largest source of international loans, offering cheaper funds from banks not restricted by reserve requirements, and a flexibility unhampered by exchange controls or interest-rate ceilings. They developed into a major engine of credit creation for the world economy and (as we saw in chapter 2) put increased pressure on the Bretton Woods system. The Eurocurrency markets grew from $3 billion in 1960 to $75 billion in 1970. In the early 1970s two events served to give these markets an added scale so that, by 1984, they were worth $1,000 billion. With the advent of floating exchange rates and the liberalization of capital controls international capital flows boomed; this process was expedited as the oil-producing countries deposited the proceeds from a quadrupling of oil prices in 1973 in the Euromarkets.

The consequences of this growth were spectacular. International banking activity grew relative to the domestic banking markets; financial firms began to think of themselves as global operators. The centre of gravity of foreign exchange markets shifted from the observable flows of trade in goods and services (the current account) to the capital account. Currencies became investments to be bought and sold by those who might have no underlying trade with the country or countries concerned. A survey by the Bank of England noted that, in 1985, around 90 per cent of the value of transactions in the London foreign exchange market were not related to trade. In the process the role of official financing of payments' imbalances, by for instance the IMF, declined in favour of private capital flows that are sensitive to interest rates. The power of the global market operators and their portfolio preferences was thus established, with monetary authorities more concerned about the threat of capital in- or outflows than the current account.[12]

The Eurocurrency markets were in practice only a part of a much wider set of changes that gave a distinctive radicalism to the changes affecting the foreign exchange markets from the 1960s: the first major changes since the end of the nineteenth century. These changes were interactive and included:

1. developments in information and communications technologies (IT) which have altered the processes of work, as vast volumes of trade can be undertaken instantaneously using computer screens rather than the trading floor, and enabled new and more sophisticated financial products to be offered, notably in the currency forward, futures and options markets
2. demands for new types of financial services as the size of wealth portfolios relative to income has risen in most developed economies and as world trade has grown and multinational business corporations have become more active, reflected in the Eurocurrency markets and the currency swap market
3. changing political attitudes to regulation in the form of deregulation of exchange controls, interest rates and market access, with the United States' authorities leading the way, followed by London's 'Big Bang' of 1986, and thereby gaining an advantage in market innovation

12. Bank for International Settlements, *Recent Innovations in International Banking* (Basle: BIS, 1986).

4   inventiveness by the foreign exchange market operators as they seek competitive
     advantage in the face of new or established market entrants by developing new
     market niches, notably in derivatives, and respond to increased risk and
     uncertainty in the markets.[13]

Unabated innovation in the foreign exchange markets has radically reduced transaction
costs, notably through information technology (IT) and screen-based trading systems,
thereby encouraging market trading; it has made access to instant information a critical
determinant of market competitiveness; it has shifted attention from goods markets to
asset markets as elements in international transactions; it has opened up and linked
financial markets to the benefit of both borrowers and lenders by means of, for
instance, currency swaps; it has blurred the traditional distinction betweem banks and
other types of financial intermediary and made non-bank intermediaries much more
important; and, at the macro-economic level, it has eroded the capability of national
monetary authorities to control the money stock by its effects on the demand for
money. Currency transactions have exploded in scale and complexity, with 24-hour
trading in global markets for which geography has become increasingly irrelevant. The
radical increase in capital mobility meant that economic interdependence grew at a
faster pace in the financial markets than in goods markets during the 1980s.[14] In the
process the pattern of international capital flows has become strikingly different from
that of the late nineteenth century: then the bulk went into real assets, like railways;
now financial assets have become more important sources of profitability.[15]

     Indeed the scale and complexity of the foreign exchange markets have become
distinguishing hallmarks in their own right, particularly when allied to their volatility.
We have noted (chapter 6) that foreign exchange and other financial markets are
distinctive in their flexibility: compared to the 'stickiness' of prices and wages in goods
markets. The volatility of financial markets and the rigidity of goods markets make for
difficult and potentially mutually destabilizing problems of adjustment. This volatility
combines with the hugely increased scale of the foreign exchange markets in an age of
liberalized capital movements to give a seemingly awesome power to these markets.

The structural power of the financial markets and of the US dollar, the D-Mark and the ECU as world currencies

The awesome potential power of the financial markets is obvious when one compares
the size of central bank reserves with daily turnover in the foreign exchange markets.
In April 1992, for instance, an average daily turnover of $300 billion in the London
foreign exchange market was matched by $44 billion of Bank of England reserves.

13. See for instance K. Ohmae, *The Borderless World* (New York: Harper Business, 1990); R.
     O'Brien (ed.) *Finance and the International Economy 5* (Oxford: Oxford University Press,
     1991); R. O'Brien, *Global Financial Integration: The End of Geography* (London: Pinter,
     1992); D. Thornton and C. Stone, 'Financial Innovation', in K. Dowd and M. Lewis (eds)
     Current Issues in Financial and Monetary Economics (London: Macmillan, 1992).
14. S. Cooper, *Cross-Border Savings Flows and Capital Mobility in the G7 Economies*
     (London: Bank of England Discussion Papers no. 54, March 1991).
15. P. Turner, *Capital Flows in the 1980s: A Survey of Major Trends* (Basle: BIS Economic
     Papers no. 30, April 1991).

According to the IMF, the total non-gold reserves of all the industrial countries amounted to $555.6 billion in April 1992, against the background of a daily net turnover of $910 billion in the nine biggest foreign exchange markets in that year. The fast-increasing scale of the markets is apparent when one compares central bank reserves to the volume of financial assets held by foreign investors. Total cross-border equity holdings in the United States, Europe and Japan increased from $800 billion in 1986 to $1,300 billion in 1991, whilst total cross-border ownership of tradable securities grew to $2,500 billion.[16] In a quantitative sense then, the official instruments to defend currencies seemed progressively enfeebled. Power was slipping away from the public authorities to the markets as market operators escaped regulatory control with liberalization and as intervention appeared less and less capable of leaning against the winds of the markets.

The diminishing effectiveness of central bank reserves has also to be seen against the background of the rising intra-EC trade flows that have been stimulated by the customs union and, more recently, by the single market programme. These trade flows are dealt with later in this chapter. Here it is important to note that changes in the lead/lag structure of the mass of payments for this trade can create very large capital flows. 'Reserve coverage' can be measured by the ratio of one day's trade payments for an EC country relative to its central bank reserves; it expresses its ability to moderate swings in the lead/lag payment structure. The potential size of these swings has mounted with financial market innovations, with companies able to hedge their exposure via the capital markets and a variety of 'derivative' products. But reserve coverage has fallen sharply for most EC countries, notably the original six members. Thus a one-day adverse swing in France's current trade payments would absorb almost 6 per cent of its reserves in 1992, compared to 3 per cent in 1972; an adverse five-day swing for Belgium would deplete its reserves by one-third.[17] The implications for power in the bargaining relations between the EC monetary authorities and the financial markets are enormous.

The Bank for International Settlements has provided a succession of authoritative pictures of the scale and nature of foreign exchange market activity: in March 1986, April 1989 and April 1992.[18] Only four countries took part in the survey of average daily turnover in March 1986: for these countries turnover increased by 116 per cent between 1986 and 1989. In April 1989 estimated global daily turnover for the 21 countries surveyed was $620 billion. By April 1992 it had grown to $880 billion, an increase of 42 per cent since April 1989 and an increase that was not matched by a similar order of expansion of world trade. Though there had been a slowdown in growth of daily turnover, the figures were staggering in their magnitude.

16. The figures in this paragraph are taken from the IMF study undertaken after the autumn 1992 ERM crisis. See International Monetary Fund, *International Capital Markets: Exchange Rate Management and International Capital Flows* (Washington, DC: IMF, 1993).
17. G. Bishop, *Capital Liberalization: The End of the ERM and the Beginning of EMU* (London: Salomon Brothers, 1992), pp. 33–4.
18. For the figures in the next paragraphs see Bank for International Settlements, *Central Bank Survey of Foreign Exchange Market Activity in April 1992*. A useful general survey is 'Foreign Exchange', *Financial Times*, 26 May 1993, Section III.

They also revealed important changes in the nature of market activity. The traditional centre of gravity was the 'spot' market, that is a transaction between two currencies for settlement on the same day or the next day. Its share of total daily turnover dropped from 58 per cent in 1989 to 48 per cent in 1992, and its global turnover increased by only 15 per cent. The major growth was concentrated in the so-called 'derivative' markets which have grown as exchange controls have been relaxed. In particular, the percentage of total turnover accounted for by the 'swap' market rose from 22 per cent to 40 per cent, making it the second largest market category. The swap market is used to hedge financial risk arising from funding and portfolio decisions by the actual exchange of two currencies, now and then in reverse at a future date, at rates agreed at the time of contract. It is a market in which dealers are very active and where business is heavily concentrated on the US dollar (which was involved in 95 per cent of turnover). Transactions also grew more rapidly in the 'outright forward' market (like 'spot' transactions except that they are for settlement more than two days hence), in the 'futures' market (contracts for fixed amounts of foreign currency for delivery on a given date at rates agreed in the contract that are traded on exchanges), and in the 'options' market (in which contracts give the purchaser the right to buy or sell a specified amount of foreign currency at an agreed rate at some date in the future). It was notable that the D-Mark future priced in US dollars was the most heavily traded contract in the futures market and that US dollar/D-Mark contracts accounted for 34 per cent of turnover in the options market. They were further indicators of the structural power of the US dollar and the D-Mark as world currencies, a factor that is underlined below.

The US dollar, the D-Mark and the ECU

This structural power of the US dollar was demonstrated by the significant impact of US dollar movements on domestic output and price levels in the EC states. The size and direction of this impact varied from country to country, relating to structural differences in dependence on dollar-priced imports, in the importance of dollar-induced changes in domestic trade and in wage rigidity. In other words, the effects were significant but asymmetrical. In the case of Britain and Germany, for instance, US dollar appreciation – as in the period 1980–4 – boosted output and had only a limited effect on their inflation; in France and Italy it had a negative effect on output and an inflationary effect on prices.[19] The result of this power of US dollar movements, and its asymmetrical effects, was to create problems of policy coordination and tensions within the EMS and EMU policy process. The problems of coordination were apparent in differences of incentive to pursue global exchange rate management between the French and German governments; the tensions within the policy process reflected the pressures on the D-Mark/franc and D-Mark/lira rates as the inflationary effects of the US dollar proved stronger for France and Italy than Germany. It also meant that the domestic motives inspiring German leadership of the

19. G. Michalopoulos, *Macroeconomic Consequences of the US Dollar Exchange Rate Movements for the EC Economy: An Empirical Analysis* (University of Reading: PhD thesis, 1991).

ERM's dollar policy were not necessarily benign for other EC states which were experiencing contrasting effects from US dollar movements. The structural power of US dollar movements was a source of constant and shifting difficulties as sharp depreciation followed fast appreciation.

The US dollar remained predominant in foreign exchange market turnover in April 1992, most of all (as we have seen) in the swap market. A measure of its significance was the fact that local currency/US dollar transactions amounted to 72 per cent of foreign exchange transactions in Germany and 71 per cent in Britain. It was involved in 83 per cent of all transactions, down from 90 per cent in 1989. A decline also took place in the share of the Japanese yen: from 27 per cent to 24 per cent. The most striking fact, after the predominance of the US dollar, was the rise in the share of total turnover involving the D-Mark. In April 1989, with 27 per cent, it was just very slightly behind the yen as the third most important currency. By April 1992 it accounted for 38 per cent of daily turnover, an increase of 11 per cent in share of gross turnover, making it easily the second most important world currency. The D-Mark was the only currency, apart from the US dollar, traded in large quantities against a wide range of other currencies. Together the US dollar and the D-Mark were involved in 95 per cent of all trading against the pound sterling and the French franc. By currency pairs, US dollar/D-Mark transactions accounted for 25.5 per cent of total daily average turnover in the foreign exchange markets, the US dollar/pound sterling for 9.5 per cent.

The importance of the D-Mark in the European currency markets was particularly pronounced. Trading of the local currency against the D-Mark exceeded local currency transactions against the US dollar in Austria, Ireland, Luxembourg and Portugal, all having small markets. For several other more medium-size European markets local currency/D-Mark transactions represented nearly half of local currency/US dollar business: Italy, the Netherlands, Spain and Sweden. In the case of France local currency/D-Mark transactions were over 90 per cent of local currency/US dollar business; the figure for Britain was, by contrast, 32 per cent. The relative significance of the D-Mark becomes clear when one compares the share of other key ERM currencies in total foreign exchange turnover. Whereas the D-Mark accounted for 38 per cent, the pound sterling and the French franc represented 14 and 4 per cent respectively (the ECU 3 per cent). One significant European currency was in fact outside the ERM: the Swiss franc with 9 per cent of total turnover.

In contrast to the US dollar and the D-Mark, the ECU failed to develop into a major world currency. As we saw in chapter 4, the ECU is defined as a basket of currencies of the countries that comprise the EMS. In addition to its official use as an accounting unit and as a bookkeeping device of central banks for exchanges of reserves, from 1981 the private ECU market began to develop in an initially spectacular fashion in the international bond market. But the initially high hopes were disappointed. By 1993 the ECU could not claim to be an important currency in the international bond markets. Originally its basket definition was expected to attract small investors who wished to hedge against risk. But, as long as the ECU contained currencies that offered risk of inflation, it was unlikely to play that role. At the end of 1989 only 4.4 per cent of the outstanding stock of bonds issued in the international markets were denominated in ECU. The ECU's role as a vehicle for current transactions was even less impressive, reflecting the fact that the handicaps to its development remained formidable. The private ECU was not legal tender, and its supply not legally organized. By 1992 neither Britain nor Germany had given full legal status to the ECU as a foreign currency: whilst nearly all EC governments obliged firms to publish their annual accounts in their national currencies, and taxes were stated and billed in national currencies. Above all, the fact that it was not any country's national currency meant that use of the ECU involved transaction costs that firms preferred to avoid. Unsurprisingly then, the ECU's share of net total foreign exchange market turnover in April 1992 was only 3.8 per cent, up from 1 per cent in 1989.

The City of London

Paradoxically, whilst the D-Mark significantly exceeded the importance of the pound sterling in the European currency markets, the geographical concentration of the global foreign exchange market in Europe was in London. London's share of global trading rose from 25 per cent in 1989 to nearly 30 per cent in April 1992. The shares of Germany and France were, by contrast, 5 per cent and 3 per cent respectively, below Switzerland's 6 per cent. Globally, the market had become more concentrated, with 55 per cent of total turnover attributable to three centres – Britain ($300 billion), the United States ($192 billion) and Japan ($126 billion). Compared to London's $300 billion Germany could muster only $57 billion and France $36 billion. With 60 per cent growth of business, London's relative importance had grown.

But, reflecting the fact that the pound sterling was less widely traded than the US dollar, D-Mark or yen, domestic currency transactions represented less than one-quarter of total trading in London. Foreign currency trading was so substantial that a larger share of trading in both US dollars (26 per cent) and D-Marks (27 per cent) took place in London than in the United States (18 per cent) or Germany (10 per cent) respectively. London was also the second most important site, after the domestic markets, for the trading of French francs and Swiss francs. It is not therefore surprising that foreign banks and dealers accounted for some 80 per cent of total turnover in the London market, with North American institutions alone representing 40 per cent. Altogether ten financial institutions held a combined share of 44 per cent of the London market, reflecting the extent to which market activity was concentrated not only in London but also among a few top players there.[20]

Newly important players: the hedge funds

Another important feature of the changes affecting the foreign exchange markets was that transactions involving non-bank institutions had expanded more quickly than those involving the commercial banks. Between 1989 and 1992, the proportion of interbank business in the London foreign exchange market declined by 9 per cent. In the early 1980s foreign exchange dealing was dominated by commercial banks and corporate treasurers, trading currencies mainly for their own books and taking

20. Bank of England, *Bank of England Quarterly Bulletin*, November 1992, for figures on the London foreign exchange market in April 1992.

short-term positions. By the late 1980s, foreign exchange business was attracting the insurance, investment and, most importantly, pension fund managers who, backed by massive funds and portfolios, changed the nature of currency dealing in ways that posed problems for the monetary authorities. Foreign exchange began to be treated as an asset class in itself, separate from any debt or equity security. Some fund managers invested directly in the currency market, believing that exchange rate movements made currencies as profitable as other financial instruments; more importantly, others bought currencies to hedge themselves against the risk that their underlying financial assets would lose their value with currency movements by using the 'forward' foreign exchange markets. They played the market more aggressively, taking longer-term positions and helping to shift power away from the spot market to the forward markets. Thus, by 1992, EC institutional investors had on average about 20 per cent of their portfolio invested overseas, compared to 6 per cent in 1980 and well ahead of the 5–7 per cent of the US and Japanese institutions.[21]

A key factor in precipitating this change in the market has been the combination of the liberalization of capital movements with the rise in the stock of financial assets, particularly to finance pensions for an ageing population. The rise in the stock of assets is illustrated by British financial institutions: in 1980 the pension funds, investment companies, investment trusts and unit trusts had assets that amounted to 52 per cent of GNP; by 1990 they accounted (at £600 billion) for 108 per cent of GNP: pension funds represented 50 per cent of that figure.[22] Competing on the basis of the investment returns earned by active portfolio management, pension funds – like Phillips and Drew, Schroder Investment, Prudential Portfolio and Gartmore – were increasingly interested in international diversification of their portfolios: these portfolios were huge and growing. The IMF quoted an estimate that the share of foreign currency denominated assets in the portfolios of the world's 300 largest pension funds would increase from about 7 per cent in 1992 to some 12 per cent by 1995.[23] On that basis global pension fund assets would rise to around $7,200 billion in 1996, with $880 billion in cross-border investments.

To these financial institutions must also be added the role of the hedge funds in the foreign exchange markets. The distinctive feature of their power as market operators is the methods that they use: namely, the use of their capital to indulge in highly leveraged positions – or margin trading – typically in a very-short-term and aggressive way and directed at smaller markets. Hedge funds were particularly attracted to the currency markets by their liquidity. Very large returns could be generated by placing huge leveraged bets in these markets. Among hedge fund managers George Soros attained the status of a legend, achieving spectacular rates of growth for his five investment funds, led by Quantum which in 1990 grew by 68 per cent. Between its inception in 1969 and 1993 Quantum had eight years of more than 50 per cent growth. Over one-third of its profits came from taking positions in currencies. Soros's most spectacular coup was against sterling in 1992: betting $10 billion on the foreign exchange markets he made a profit of almost $2 billion, with the Bank of England as

21. International Monetary Fund, *International Capital Markets.*
22. Bishop, *Capital Liberalization*, p. 5.
23. International Monetary Fund, *International Capital Markets.*

chief victim. In June 1993 his publicly aired views that the value of the D-Mark would fall and about the 'futility' of the Bundesbank's effort to maintain high interest rates anticipated the market. The guru status of Soros gave him the capacity to move markets.[24] Where the hedge funds led, the bigger institutions were tempted to follow. But, more ominously, competition from other big players coaxed Soros into taking bigger risks. Within the markets themselves there was fear and mistrust of Soros.

Problems for policy makers

For four reasons these changes within the market and their structural power posed problems for policy makers. First, central banks have always sought to confine the scope for speculative trading by commercial banks via prudential rules that control their ability to take risks in the market. As we saw in chapter 6, such rules are if anything tighter in France and Germany than Britain. With the shift of financial power to investment fund and pension managers and liberalized capital movements the force of such rules was blunted. Also, fund managers take longer-term decisions that are more difficult for the central banks to reverse. The short-term view of the bank currency dealers made them more sensitive to action by the central bank to raise overnight interest rates or to intervene in the market to trigger moves in the exchange rate. Fund managers were more interested in managing risk than making short-term gains. They came into the market to sell currencies on a long-term basis. Additionally, the growth of derivative markets like options, as fund managers seek to safeguard their long-term positions, has created another factor that can reinforce prevailing currency flows. Banks that had sold options to fund managers who were safeguarding against the prospect of a currency devaluation are disposed, once that currency begins to edge beneath its floor within the ERM, to start selling into the market to avoid recording a net loss once it had to acquire the currency at the option price.

Above all, the presence of such huge funds, diversifying their portfolios in order to maximize returns and minimize risks from devaluation, creates for monetary authorities the prospect that a sustained loss of confidence will precipitate a major capital outflow, reflected in a fall in the equity market and a decline in bond prices. In such a context, the commitment and credibility of the authorities become their most potent weapon in the markets – not their foreign exchange reserves whose growth has lagged massively behind that of the foreign exchange markets. The EC's total foreign exchange reserves, at $322 billion in June 1992, appeared diminutive in relation to the rising stock of financial assets within the EC (worth some £600 billion in Britain alone) and its potential for mobility within the single European market.[25] It is instructive to compare the EC's total foreign exchange reserves (and those of the G-7 countries in 1992 – $350 billion) with the ten leading financial institutions in London, each of which on a busy day could have an active flow in the order of $1.5 billion to $3 billion.[26]

24. G. Soros, *The Alchemy of Finance* (New York: Simon & Schuster, 1987).
25. Bishop, *Capital Liberalization*, p. 3.
26. J. Blitz, 'How Central Banks Ran into the Hedge', *Financial Times*, 3 October 1992, p. 2.

Foreign exchange markets and economic fundamentals

Against this background the question of whether the foreign exchange markets operate properly or not has become of enormous practical importance. Specifically, are they rational and efficient mechanisms of adjustment?[27] There is general agreement that the foreign exchange markets are volatile: but are they characterized by 'excessive' volatility? The answer revolves around the issue of whether the behaviour of market operators is based first and foremost on recognition of, and respect for, economic fundamentals, or whether it reflects autonomous changes in market sentiment, occasioned perhaps by the impact of non-economic 'news' or by the operation of technical trading rules within the market, but represented above all by the phenomenon of self-fulfilling expectations. If the answer is that economic fundamentals are sometimes, perhaps often, not respected, then the judgement must be not only that they produce a misallocation of resources but also that the route from the EMS to EMU is so littered with traps that only rapid and decisive action to move to stage three is likely to have a chance of success. The theoretical and empirical research on this topic has been primarily conducted in the context of floating exchange rates rather than of the ERM: but, given that the ERM is an island of stable rates in a tossing sea of floating rates, its relevance is clear.

Volatility and its sources

The arguments that foreign exchange markets are excessively volatile, involve idiosyncratic behaviour and produce irrational effects on exchange rates have been hotly debated in the literature on international monetary economics. That they are not susceptible of final resolution is not perhaps surprising. Thus it can be argued that foreign exchange markets are excessively volatile.[28] They produce malign effects in other markets, particularly goods markets and the labour market, as short-term speculative pressures driven by rapid adjustment to new information push exchange rates out of line with economic fundamentals (the phenomenon of 'overshooting'), and as excessively volatile exchange rates collide with sticky prices and wages elsewhere in the economy. The problem can, of course, be seen very differently: that the volatility of the foreign exchange markets results from inefficiencies in other markets; and that the foreign exchange markets act as an important early-warning signal of the need for adjustment. It is, in other words, the foreign exchange markets that are efficient. The problem lies with other markets which are less efficient because too slow to adjust.[29] Where one stands on this argument depends on where one sits – in

27. For an overview see R. Levich, 'Is the Foreign Exchange Market Efficient?', *Oxford Review of Economic Policy* 5 (1989), pp. 40–60.
28. A classic statement remains R. Dornbusch, 'Expectations and Exchange Rate Dynamics', *Journal of Political Economy* 84 (1976), pp. 1,161–76. Also W. Buiter and M. Miller, 'Monetary Policy and International Competitiveness: The Problems of Adjustment', *Oxford Economic Papers* (Supplement), 33 (1981), pp. 143–75. For a critique see M. Beenstock, 'Exchange Rate Dynamics', in D. Llewellyn and C. Milner (eds) *Current Issues in International Monetary Economics* (London: Macmillan, 1990).
29. See K. Chrystal, 'Operation of Foreign Exchange Markets', in Dowd and Lewis (eds) *Current Issues in Financial and Monetary Economics*, p. 71.

manufacturing industry or in an investment or pension fund, for instance – or on the markets with which one has the most sympathy.

Speculative pressures and rules of exchange-rate management

In so far as unstable behaviour is seen as a problem within the foreign exchange markets, there is a further argument about its prime source or sources. This argument is more susceptible to empirical resolution. On one side, the monetary authorities' own policies and behaviour can be seen as a critical factor in either stabilizing or destabilizing the foreign exchange markets. In order to stabilize the markets they have a number of instruments at their disposal. For instance, clear rules and hard bands, as in the case of the hard ERM, help to anchor expectations; market operators know what to expect of the authorities, that for instance they will definitely intervene at a particular point. On the other hand, stable, managed exchange rates can also invite market operators to make one-way bets of the sort that provoke speculative crises, once it becomes clear to these operators that a change in economic fundamentals (say as a result of differential inflation rates) or the effects of a shock (like German unification) had made present exchange rates disequilibrium rates. By acting to sell and buy currencies, before the authorities realigned, potentially huge overnight profits could be earned.

In order to stabilize expectations and avoid such speculative runs, the authorities have two other tools to deploy: to anticipate the markets by pre-emptive realignment, a move that in the EMS places great political demands on solidarity and efficient management (demands that were not met in autumn 1992 and autumn 1993, or indeed earlier), and by making realignments on a scale that are accommodated within the band of fluctuation so that speculators may find that with realignment the market rate does not move at all (it might even be driven in the opposite direction as those who had sold a currency before devaluation begin to repurchase it). A parity change should never be larger than the width of the band: a golden rule of exchange-rate management.[30] In these ways, along with the tactical flexibility outlined earlier in this chapter, the authorities can alter expectations as they earn respect in the markets. The important feature of the EMS crisis of 1992 was that it revealed that the authorities forfeited much respect, as a result of intransigence and poor communications.

Dogged intransigence and unpredictability of medium-term policies are the two main ways in which the authorities can contribute to destabilization of the foreign exchange markets. Two great catalysts for changes in market behaviour remain first, the perception of market operators that the authorities are failing to adjust policies adequately to changes in economic fundamentals or shocks so that policy comes to lose credibility, and second, the perception that the authorities are not really serious in their commitment to a policy, like the present exchange rate (if, for instance, they fail to take adequate measures to tackle the budget deficit or to raise interest rates to protect it). Resolve of basic policy must be continuously demonstrated in word and action; whilst flexibility to changes in underlying economic conditions must be apparent. The market operators are influenced not only by the transparency of the rules

---

30.   J. Williamson, 'Exchange Rate Management', *Economic Journal*, January 1993.

of the game but also by what the authorities actually do, or fail to do, to apply the rules. In this respect the foreign exchange markets are a continuing referendum on the will and capability of the authorities.

But, on closer inspection, the problem of volatility in the foreign exchange markets looks potentially more intractable. For it remains possible that speculative 'runs' against certain currencies in the ERM may not be supported by economic fundamentals and the perception of disequilibrium exchange rates. In other words, speculative attacks could take place on 'healthy' currencies. Pointing to the internal dynamics of expectations rather than to fundamentals, it can be argued that multiple rational expectations equilibria are possible in foreign exchange markets. Essentially, self-fulfilling expectations are at work and can generate crises by the simple act of predicting and then producing the collapse of a pegged exchange rate.[31] In other words, market operators can produce a speculative crisis with little or no help from the authorities. We have pointed out above the role of factors internal to the dynamics of the foreign exchange markets: the impact of technical trading rules, and the role of news. These factors too can serve to fuel the role of self-fulfilling expectations. In the context of the US dollar's rate with the pound sterling and the D-Mark during the 1970s and 1980s it is possible to identify speculative 'bubbles'.[32] Thus the appreciation of sterling in 1980–2 and of the US dollar in 1982–5 did not seem to be a rational response to a change in economic fundamentals.

The question remains of just how significant speculative crises have been in the history of the EMS and to what extent the evidence supports the underlying importance of economic fundamentals or the role of self-fulfilling expectations. In the history of the EMS two crises are typically cited as driven mainly by speculative pressures – January 1987 and September and November 1992. It is important first to note that speculative runs were not very important in the earlier phases of the EMS when realignments were frequent and small, and that between 1987 and 1992 no speculative crisis occurred.

However, the capacity of market operators to mount one-way bets against the EMS had undoubtedly grown with three factors: the liberalization of capital movements; the huge increase in the scale of internationally mobile financial assets, like pension funds; and the new commitment to a hard ERM. These changes have to be set against the relatively tiny foreign exchange reserves of the central banks. The 1987 crisis did undoubtedly reveal the power of speculative runs in a new form. A concern about economic fundamentals was present in the market: the risk of higher wage inflation in France against the background of public sector strikes there. But in fact higher inflation did not materialize. In this case it can be argued that the outcome owed much to the pressures exerted by the markets, and that the markets misjudged the economic fundamentals and were driven by external instability linked to the weakness of the US dollar, generating a self-fulfilling crisis in the ERM. In short, the ERM crisis of 1987 underlined the structural power of the US dollar as a world currency.

31. Obstfeld, 'Rational and Self-Fulfilling Balance-of- Payments Crises'.
32. For evidence of these speculative 'bubbles' see Evans, 'A Test for Speculative Bubbles and the Sterling–Dollar Exchange Rate: 1981–84'; and, on the US dollar and the DM, see R. Meese, 'Testing for Bubbles in Exchange Markets: A Case of Sparkling Rates?', *Journal of Political Economy* 94 (1986), pp. 345–73.

In many respects the case is more clear-cut in 1992. Once again, the rapid fall of the US dollar was a key precipitating factor, generating a great deal of speculative behaviour. But, on this occasion, the market operators judged correctly that realignment was overdue in the context of changes in economic fundamentals to which the authorities had been blind and which gave diminishing credibility to their policies: like the scale of the problem of the budget deficit and public debt in Italy, and the mismatch between high interest rates and deep and protracted recession in Britain. With the authorities displaying at the informal ECOFIN meeting in Bath in early September that they were unwilling to make an orderly and rational realignment, market operators identified an opportunity to make substantial gains by switching out of and into different ERM currencies. Rapidly confirmed rumours about deep personal divisions at the Bath meeting, particularly between the British Chancellor and the president of the Bundesbank, added to the impression that ERM policy was insufficiently coordinated. In this case misjudgement by the authorities played a much more significant role than any autonomous process of self-fulfilling expectations in the market. The dynamics of news and technical trading rules were at work, as ever, so that short-term expectations fed on themselves: more important in this case were the miscalculations and inefficiences within the ERM policy process.

Just as the exits of the British pound and the Italian lira from the ERM were pre-eminently to be explained in terms of economic fundamentals, the longer-drawn-out crisis of the French franc in 1992–3 lends itself to the same explanation. In the case of the French franc internal market dynamics were at work: news about the Maastricht referendum, coupled with the operation of technical trading rules as traders sought to repeat the huge overnight gains already earned, fuelled speculation. But, for a period, the fact that the authorities were defending relatively strong economic fundamentals, notably on inflation and the balance of payments, gave resolution and credibility to their actions in defence of the franc, and made possible strong concerted action with the Bundesbank. Ultimately it was the Achilles' heel of a real economy mired in recession and cocooned in imported high interest rates that broke market confidence.

In a context in which at least some key economic fundamentals are sound (like inflation, the budget deficit and the balance of trade), even if others are not (like unemployment), the expectations of market operators are – at least for a period – more amenable to influence by the authorities. Herein lies the basic difference between the experiences of the British pound and the French franc in 1992. With so many unsound fundamentals in the British case market operators rapidly achieved a unanimity and certainty about its fate. Unsound fundamentals generated self-fulfilling expectations. But with the French franc the market operators were slower to achieve such unanimity and strength of expectation of a realignment, for the franc had achieved an inflation performance and current account performance that excelled the anchor currency, the D-Mark. As events proved, however, such unanimity and strength of expectation could prove fragile in the face of the effects of deepening recession: as recession made the budget deficit an unsound fundamental; as devaluations by major trading partners like Britain, Italy and Spain ate into France's competitiveness, another fundamental to which market operators attached importance; and as recession led to a worsening conflict between external and internal objectives, between the high nominal interest rates required to maintain the franc's central rate in the ERM and the low real interest rates needed to boost domestic output and employment.

It seems then that the randomness of change in the foreign exchange markets can be exaggerated. Randomness may be an element in their functioning, not least when they react to totally unexpected news, like the rejection of the Treaty on European Union in the first Danish referendum or adverse opinion polls before the French referendum on Maastricht. They bounce about in response to new information.[33] But the foreign exchange markets operate at the 'edge of chaos' rather than behave chaotically. Here, to use the language of Complexity Theory, is no simple, repetitive, passive order. Yet there is some order and predictability, represented by the presence of certain informal and adaptive rules, like technical trading rules and the rule that rates must reflect economic fundamentals.

The rule that exchange rates must reflect underlying fundamentals suggests itself as another golden rule that the authorities need to respect in managing the foreign exchange markets. This rule suggests that two mistakes are to be avoided: the defence of parities that are perceived by markets to be misaligned; and the surrender to speculative pressures when parities correspond well to fundamentals. Unfortunately, it offers no magic solution to the problems of the EMS and EMU. In the operation of the foreign exchange markets there is a constant interaction between economic fundamentals and the way that market operators perceive them. But what matters most is how market operators perceive the fundamentals and come to expect realignments.[34] The notion of sound fundamentals is in fact far from being a precise one in the minds of market operators. Their expectations of realignment rise with the degree of deviations of currencies from their central rates and with the proximity of a past devaluation. In short, there is always the potential for speculative runs to have their own dynamics that overwhelm the authorities. The question is whether the system is sufficiently robust to withstand turbulence.

The idea of 'fundamental equilibrium exchange rates' (FEER) is a technical, prescriptive construct of academic economists to overcome this problem.[35] Defined as the exchange rate that would balance trade flows with long-term capital flows and allow the economy to reach full employment, it is too difficult an idea to operationalize in the conduct of policy. Even put in another way, that the market operators will challenge a disequilibrium exchange rate, it is difficult to assess how big a disequilibrium has to become before it is judged in the market to be indefensible. The key judgement for the authorities is to identify that point before the market operators and to do something about it. But neither the authorities nor the market operators have much of a precise idea of the range of disequilibrium. The authorities can at least take some comfort from the fact that, within that range, market operators are likely to crave signals from the authorities, giving the authorities at least an opportunity to give a 'steer' to the market.

33. R. Meese and K. Rogoff, 'Empirical Exchange Rate Models of the Seventies: Do They Fit Out of Sample?', *Journal of International Economics* 14 (1983), pp. 3–24.
34. Soros, *The Alchemy of Finance*; Z. Chen and A. Giovannini, *The Determinants of Realignment Expectations under the EMS – Some Empirical Regularities* (London: Centre for Economic Policy Research, Discussion Paper no. 790, June 1993).
35. See Williamson, 'Exchange Rate Management'. Also J. Williamson, *The Exchange Rate System* (Washington, DC: Institute for International Economics, 1985).

The structural power of economic fundamentals and problems of convergence

With respect to economic fundamentals the Treaty on European Union represented an important landmark in the bargaining relations between the EC monetary authorities and the foreign exchange markets. In committing itself to the goal of EMU by the end of the 1990s, the EC – propelled by the central bankers – gave specific and detailed priority to a set of formal economic fundamentals that the authorities erected as preconditions for the move to stage three. In effect, the convergence criteria constituted a new signal to market operators, standards by which they could judge not only the prospects for EMU but also the health of particular currencies. Was an individual currency making progress towards meeting the convergence criteria; what were its prospects for doing so? What, accordingly, were the prospects for the EMU project; and what did these prospects imply for the viability of the ERM rates and even for the EMS as a system? The exercise in 'self-binding' commitment by the EC monetary authorities, in tying themselves to the mast of a specific accounting definition of convergence, was an invitation to the markets to make judgements about EMU and, with their own interests in mind, for market operators to act accordingly.

Here was a paradox: the convergence criteria were designed to stabilize market expectations; yet they invited a continuing market referendum on the credibility of the commitments that they contained as operators formed their perception of economic fundamentals based on new economic data, political comment and rumour – as well as absorbed the authoritative comments of the Committee of Central Bank Governors in their new annual reports on progress towards convergence. Implicit was the possibility of a gap of perception between the policy actors and the market operators: with the policy actors preoccupied with the 'nominal' convergence criteria, whilst the market operators sought out other economic fundamentals, like the 'desynchronization' of economic cycles in different countries and the mismatch between monetary policies and unemployment, that determined their assessment of financial risk. And inherent in that gap was the prospect of crisis, which materialized as early as autumn 1992.

Market operators were sensitive not least to the domestic and indeed EC-wide controversy that the convergence criteria engendered. Underlying the Treaty on European Union was a particular judgement of what constituted the necessary convergence for EMU to be possible. The criteria were (as we saw in chapter 7) a legal monument to sound money ideas: a partial statement, drafted under the influence of central bankers, that indicated a view that certain economic fundamentals were more important than others – in particular, that nominal convergence should be given priority over real convergence or institutional convergence. The Treaty on European Union rested on the premise that convergence of the development of costs and prices, and their underlying determinants, must be the priority. In line with the spirit of nominal convergence it focused on targets for convergence of inflation rates, budget deficit and public debt ratios, and long-term interest rates. Two chains of reasoning were decisive: that prolonged fiscal deficits and a rising debt-to-GDP ratio would put an upward pressure on real interest rates and provide an incentive for the authorities to resort to monetary financing or inflation as methods to reduce the real debt stock; and that low and stable inflation was a requirement if an acceleration of unemployment was to be avoided. The other two types of convergence were neglected in the treaty: institutional and real.[36] In practice, the structural power of these neglected economic fundamentals, for instance of labour market institutions and unemployment conditions, was to make a deep imprint on the EMS and EMU policy process.

Institutional convergence

Institutional convergence involves the attempt to narrow the historic differences between economic systems and the institutional – and cultural – attributes that underpin their functioning. From this perspective each EC economy can be seen as the result of a specific historical path of development, embodied in the nature of, for instance, its financial system, its patterns of government–industry relations, the nature of its corporate governance, its industrial relations system, the organization of its service sector, its welfare state arrangements, and its sectoral specialization and foreign trade patterns.[37] Economic fundamentals are embedded in historically conditioned factors; they reflect national variations and the imprint of cultural variables and historic crises.

In so far as economic performance reflects domestic institutional arrangements, then the maintenance of differing domestic arrangements can be expected to yield regularly diverging performances. For instance, price inflation is affected by the extent to which the labour market is flexible and the degree of competition and efficiency in the service sector. With entrenched labour market rigidities, aspects of which date back to the 1940 system of national wage negotiations, and lack of competition in the service sector, where the old professional syndicates continued to play a role, Spain was forced to sacrifice twice as much unemployment for a one percentage fall in inflation as other EMS countries.[38]

The question of the significance of this issue was neglected in the treaty and the preparatory work, for instance in the *One Market, One Money* study of the EC Commission. The major way in which institutional convergence entered the EMS and EMU policy process was in the form of the Bundesbank-inspired model of central bank independence. Otherwise, institutional convergence entered through the back door: in part through the implication, spelt out explicitly in the annual reports of the Committee of Central Bank Governors, that achievement of nominal convergence

36. On the three basic types of convergence see R. Anderton *et al.* 'Macroeconomic Convergence in Europe: Achievements and Prospects', in R. Barrell (ed.) *Economic Convergence and Monetary Union in Europe* (London: Sage/NIESR, 1992), pp. 1–30.
37. Useful classic references here are M. Polanyi, *The Great Transformation: The Political and Economic Origins of Our Time* (Boston, Mass.: Beacon Press, 1944); A. Shonfield, *Modern Capitalism* (London: Oxford University Press, 1965); K. Dyson, 'The Cultural, Ideological and Structural Context', in K. Dyson and S. Wilks (eds) *Industrial Crisis* (Oxford: Martin Robertson, 1983), pp. 26–66; and D. North, *Institutions, Institutional Change and Economic Performance* (Cambridge: Cambridge University Press, 1990). Also, in relation to EMU, see H. Plaschke, 'Economic and Monetary Union: The Pitfalls of Convergence', Aalborg University, April 1993, unpublished manuscript.
38. B. Larre and R. Torres, 'Real and Nominal Convergence in the EMS: the Case of Spain, Portugal and Greece', in Barrell (ed.) *Economic Convergence and Monetary Union in Europe*, pp. 174–90.

would require supply-side measures to promote flexibility in the labour market and liberalization and competition in the non-traded sector, particularly services; and in part in the form of the Protocol and the Agreement on Social Policy (excluding Britain) which envisaged convergence in the regulation of the working environment, working conditions, industrial relations and social protection.

Institutional convergence in the form of exporting the Bundesbank model to the EC level raises the serious problem that institutions are not likely to operate in the same way in a different institutional and cultural context. The ESCB will not have a large-scale fiscal transfer system or an EC-wide system of collective bargaining to support its role; nor can it assume that the cultural context will be one that so favours price stability as that in Germany with its historical experiences of hyperinflation. The context of its operation is, accordingly, likely to be one of much greater controversy, a controversy that will be fuelled not only by the lack of the firm cultural support enjoyed by the Bundesbank but also by the fact that, denied ameliorative action through federal fiscal transfers and a parallel structure of institutional support in collective bargaining, it will be forced to depend on its own limited policy instruments – at potentially great economic, social and political cost. We shall need to return to this question when considering the relationship between institutional and cultural convergence.

One striking expression of the problems of institutional convergence is to be found in private-sector indebtedness in EC countries. Here there is a striking structural difference between Britain and its EC partners. The structure of the British housing market encouraged private ownership by generous tax incentives. It also involved loans for home ownership at variable rather than – as in France and Germany – at fixed rates of interest. Disaster followed as the effects of two events were superimposed: domestic financial liberalization in the 1980s caused an explosion of levels of personal indebtedness: then, the external discipline after entry into the ERM in 1990 imposed sustained high interest rates on British borrowers. As a consequence, in 1990 personal borrowing amounted to 37 per cent of gross income in Germany, 45 per cent in France and 78 per cent in Britain. Personal interest payments as a proportion of income reached 10.5 per cent in Britain, compared to only 3 per cent in Germany and 3.5 per cent in France.[39]

With variable rate mortgages allied to mortgage tax relief in Britain there was a sharp political sensitivity towards the active use of short-term interest rates as a means of stabilizing exchange rates, and a greater political reluctance to cede control of interest rates to an independent central bank. The effects on the capability of the British authorities to abide by the discipline of the rules of the ERM was considerable and was a major contribution to the crisis of September 1992.[40] Structural reform

39. Committee of Governors of the Central Banks of the Member States of the European Community, *Annual Report 1992* (Basle: Committee of Central Bank Governors, April 1993).

40. The British government's record within the ERM was criticized by the chairman of the Committee of Central Bank Governors, Wim Duisenberg, in April 1993. During its brief period in the ERM, it had reduced interest rates on nine occasions, 'a couple of times too many'. See P. Marsh, 'UK Record within ERM Criticized', *Financial Times*, 21 April 1993, p. 1.

seemed, therefore, a requirement of a sustainable British re-entry into the ERM. There was little evidence of a political will to take radical action to restructure the housing market, by phasing out mortgage tax relief and encouraging the rented sector. But market-led developments were more encouraging, with a growing vogue for fixed-rate mortgages by 1993. Two factors were at work: the effect of the interest-rate shock on borrowers, and the rapid growth of the sterling swap market, which enabled building societies to reduce their exposure to interest rate fluctuations.

The issue of domestic will and capability to engage in institutional reform to promote convergence was present also in relation to industrial relations and the labour market. Here again there are significant differences in national institutional structures: between for instance relatively centralized collective bargaining and legally codified 'social partnership' in Germany and an emphasis on more unstructured collective bargaining and the principle of voluntarism in industrial relations and labour market practices in Britain.[41] Labour market changes in the 1980s pointed to a process of convergence: symbolized by changes in unemployment benefit regimes and in the powers of trade unions and the phasing out of wage indexation.[42] Belgium and Denmark led this process within the ERM, Britain outside the ERM – with, overall, the British government as the pacesetter in seeking labour market flexibility, American-style, in order to create new jobs. Increased competition, external to as well as internal to the EC, was a potent factor in inducing such convergence: along with, and primary to, the downward pressure on costs exerted by the discipline of the ERM.

In practice the domestic will and capability to pursue systematic and sustained institutional reform among ERM member countries was limited. The open question was whether, in the 1990s, a combination of diminishing competitiveness and foreign exchange market operators averse to risk would prove an increasingly potent factor in directing domestic political attention to the need to tackle more resolutely labour market rigidities that are inimical to price stability and output and employment growth. Or whether the 'corporatist' model of collaboration of 'social partners' outlined in the Social Chapter appended to the Treaty on European Union, would prove potent in producing a legislative convergence around a different ideology. Whilst these external factors can certainly help to change individual aspects of labour market institutional structures, it is less evident that the basic national institutional frameworks will cease to provide the underlying direction of development of labour market behaviour. The fundamentals of labour markets would not easily give way to EC legislative programmes or to trade and macro-economic pressures.

We are reminded by the institutional perspective on convergence of the extent to which 'civics' – represented by the efficiency and adaptability of institutions – helps to

41. On the limits of convergence in labour markets see J. Goldthorpe (ed.) *Order and Conflict in Contemporary Capitalism* (Oxford: Clarendon Press, 1984). On the enduring impact of cultural variables and historical crises on industrial relations see A. Ferner and R. Hyman (eds) *Industrial Relations in Europe* (Oxford: Basil Blackwell, 1992); C. Crouch, *Industrial Relations and European State Relations* (Oxford: Oxford University Press, 1993).

42. R. Anderton *et al.*, 'Nominal Convergence in European Wage Behaviour: Achievements and Explanations', in Barrell (ed.) *Economic Convergence and Monetary Union in Europe*, pp. 31–57.

explain economic performance.[43] As Rousseau put it, it is in the end the law that is written in the hearts of the people that counts. From this perspective large-scale fiscal transfers, or the import of specific policy instruments for instance in the labour market, are likely to have less effect on economic convergence than the historical legacy of cultural traditions. In some EC countries, like Germany, and some regions, like the north of Italy, long traditions of public-spiritedness and civic engagement facilitate the efficiency of institutions and of markets. In other countries, like Greece, and other regions, like the Mezzogiorno of Italy, a culture to support economic stability and market and institutional efficiency is not part of the historical legacy. The implications of such a long-term historical view of the structural determinants of economic performance for the EMS and EMU policy process are immense. This policy process appears to be caught up in long-term national and regional historical trajectories. In the face of attempts to radically alter the formal rules of the game, informal constraints on their operation can be expected to prove tenacious.

From the perspective of culturally conditioned economic fundamentals only a limited part of the EC seems historically capable of achieving the nominal and real convergence that EMU requires: a more limited part than many of the signatories to the Treaty on European Union recognized. And it is not without interest that the conjunction of the Treaty on European Union with the lira's humiliating exit from the ERM in 1992 played an important role in acting as a catalyst for a new mood of radical institutional overhaul in Italy, an overhaul that involved the governor of the Bank of Italy, Carlo Ciampi, taking over as Prime Minister in April 1993. The task for Italy to achieve economic convergence by means of radical institutional change was enormously complex and difficult. As a country with a 'civic-minded' North and an 'uncivic' South, the outcome was likely to be finely balanced between success and failure.

Potent as culture is in shaping economic fundamentals and performance, problems of cultural convergence were very much off the agenda of the EMS and EMU policy process. Institutional reform mattered more and, notwithstanding inherited cultural patterns, could alter the behaviour of policy makers. In importing the idea of central bank independence, other EC countries would not of course be able to replicate the stability-oriented culture of Germany. But, by altering who takes monetary decisions such institutional reform would deliver historically lower inflation rates, even if not lower than in Germany. Hence, as a convergence criterion, central bank independence appeared crucial: subject to the important provisos that other supportive institutional reforms would have to follow and that national cultures could not simply be rewritten by institutional imports.

Real convergence

Equally missing in the Treaty on European Union was a direct and urgent concern about basing EMU on a real convergence of living standards, production costs and working conditions: of, for instance, real unit labour costs, of rates of productivity

---

43. This point is developed in relation to Italy in R. Putnam, *Making Democracy Work: Civic Traditions in Modern Italy* (Princeton, NJ: Princeton University Press, 1993).

growth, of unemployment and of GDP per capita. The formal convergence criteria did not embody indicators of 'economic and social cohesion'. Real convergence was seen as a long-term process and not as a necessary condition for a successful transition to stage three. Indeed, it pointed to a treaty that, in terms of economic ideology, would have been very different: based on priority to investment in the modernization of capital stock to assist convergence of rates of productivity growth; on reform in the direction of an EC-wide system of collective bargaining with the purpose of putting in place a wages policy that contributes to an amelioration of unemployment as well as countering inflation; and on radical increases in fiscal transfers to even up GDP per capita. Rather (as we saw in chapter 7), the treaty's stress on nominal convergence has a deflationary bias, not least as a consequence of the deficit and debt criteria. The treaty was unable to anticipate the deflationary implications of German unification, and its domestic mismanagement, for the EC economy as a whole. Without that crucial economic insight the edifice of policy measures that were put in place for EMU was left looking woefully deficient. The costs to output and employment of nominal convergence were but marginally addressed in the treaty's Protocol on Economic and Social Cohesion; or in the 'growth initiative' launched at the Edinburgh summit of December 1992.

Unemployment is perhaps the most visible and symbolic illustration of the EC's capacity to achieve real convergence and to do so at a low, 'tolerable' rate. To an even greater extent than GDP per capita it is highly politically sensitive, directly linked to social concerns about poverty, deprivation and crime. Disturbingly, the EMS has been associated with rising unemployment, though it is by no means clear that this rise is to be mainly attributed to it. Perhaps more seriously, the EMS appears to have done little, if anything to ameliorate unemployment. In the case of the original ERM members average annual unemployment as a percentage of the labour force had been 4.8 per cent in the five-year period 1974–9. Thereafter it rose steadily: to 8.7 per cent in 1980–5; and 9.1 per cent in 1986–90. In 1990–2 it fell back slightly to 8.2 per cent, only to begin its climb upwards with the onset of recession in 1993.[44] France, which had experienced unemployment rates of under 6 per cent in 1978 and 1979, was not to see its annual unemployment rate fall below 9 per cent between 1984 and 1992. It needed more unemployment to cut inflation than had been necessary earlier: a quite contrary outcome to that predicted from the theory of tying one's hands that we considered in chapter 7.[45] Dispersion of unemployment around the EC average actually grew during the period between 1987 and 1992. For the original ERM narrow band countries the dispersion was 2.2 per cent in 1987–8 and 2.6 per cent in 1990–2; for the EC as a whole 2.7 per cent in 1987–8 and 3.2 per cent in 1990–2.[46] Real

44. These figures are computed from Commission of the European Communities, *Unemployment in the Community Regions in 1991* (Luxembourg: Office of Official Publications of the European Community, Eurostat Rapid Report, 1991) and from Committee of Governors of the Central Banks of the Member States of the European Economic Community, *Annual Report 1992*, p. 34.
45. O. Blanchard and P.-A. Muet, 'Competitiveness through Disinflation: An Assessment of the French Macro-Economic Strategy', *Economic Policy* 16 (1993), p. 12.
46. Committee of Governors of the Central Banks of the Member States of the European Economic Community, *Annual Report 1992*, p. 34.

convergence was notable both by its absence and by its gravitation around a disturbingly rising average. In 1986–90 the EC average was 9.9 per cent, compared to 7.1 per cent for the total OECD, 5.8 per cent for the United States and 2.5 per cent for Japan.

The figures on *GDP per capita* as an indicator of 'real' convergence are more useful than those on unemployment, given that there are significant cultural and institutional differences among countries and regions of the EC. Thus Greece and Portugal do not register high rates of unemployment (both were consistently below the EC average in 1987–92), even though they lag well behind the rest of the EC in prosperity. The scale and persistence of disparities in GDP per capita remain a source of great concern; yet they appear to have had no substantial impact on the EMU treaty provisions. Some encouragement might be gained by noting that, between 1980 and 1990, the member states saw their GDP per capita move towards the EC average, with the exception of Luxembourg, whose lead at the top widened, and Greece, whose situation at the bottom deteriorated.[47] But, at the regional level, only 40 per cent of the EC regions achieved a GDP per capita closer to the EC average over the decade.

More seriously, the disparities in GDP per capita remained very much larger than in the United States. In 1989 GDP per capita in the most prosperous US state (Connecticut) was just double that in the poorest (Mississippi); the most prosperous EC region had a GDP per capita three and a half times that of the least prosperous. In 1990 the dispersal ranged from 35 per cent of the EC average in Ipeiros (Greece) – down from 39 per cent in 1989 and 42 per cent in 1980 – to 183 per cent in Hamburg (Germany) – up from 173 per cent in 1989. In France the Ile-de-France around Paris had improved its relative position from 158 per cent in 1980 to 162 per cent in 1989 and 166 per cent in 1990. In 1990 the disparity between member states still remained formidable: ranging from Luxembourg (124 per cent), West Germany (117 per cent) and France (112 per cent) through Britain and the Netherlands (both 101 per cent) to Ireland (68 per cent) and Greece (47 per cent).

These figures on GDP per capita are significant in underlining that the experience of the EMS has been mixed. Under the ERM devaluation as an instrument to improve competitiveness has given way to a process of relying on downward pressure on domestic costs and prices from the commitment to a stable exchange rate structure and price stability. Unfortunately (as we have seen) these external pressures for adjustment come up against the structural power and constraints of differing national institutional arrangements and cultural patterns. The consequences for economic fundamentals and performance are, accordingly, more variable than economic theories that are blind to space and time are prepared to concede.

The GDP per capita figures are also important in identifying a group of member states that, in the absence of a large-scale fiscal transfer system and major cross-national labour mobility, is more likely to be able to withstand the adjustment problems consequent on the nominal convergence conditions for EMU: Luxembourg,

47. Commission of the European Communities, *Per Capita GDP in the Community Regions in 1990* (Luxembourg: Office for Official Publications of the European Community, Eurostat Rapid Report, 1993). Also I. Begg and D. Mayes, 'Cohesion as a Precondition for Monetary Union in Europe', in Barrell (ed.) *Economic Convergence and Monetary Union in Europe*, pp. 220–40.

Germany, France, Denmark, Belgium, Italy, the Netherlands and Britain. All are close to, or well above, the EC average. For Spain, Ireland, Portugal and Greece EMU would seem to require a radically different approach to fiscal transfers; whilst even for states like Italy, Germany (with the eastern *Länder*) and Britain new pressures on national fiscal transfer systems are likely to be felt. At least in a federal state like Germany the adjustment process to a German monetary union will be facilitated by labour mobility in a common cultural area and huge fiscal transfers from west to east. In that context it is more possible to envisage a prospect of steady 'real' convergence than in the EC as a whole.

Finally, it is worth noting *real unit labour costs*. For the EC as a whole real unit labour costs fell continuously from 1981 to 1989, then rising again till 1991. But in the case of Britain, France, Germany and Italy convergence did not prove a smooth process. The gap in their real unit labour costs closed between 1983 and 1987. Thereafter it opened up as a consequence of two main developments: first, French real unit labour costs fell rapidly, falling below those of Germany by 1986, and second, Britain (from 1988 to 1991) and Italy (from 1989 to 1991) experienced a sharp rise in real unit labour costs, most sharply in the British case. Since 1988–9 their divergence from French real unit labour costs was pronounced, underlining their loss of competitiveness and diminishing confidence in their ERM parities.

Real convergence seems to have an important relationship to institutional convergence, a relationship that was not identified and explored in the EMU negotiations. As we have noted, the different historical trajectories of countries like Britain, France and Germany – let alone them and Greece and Portugal – suggest deep-seated barriers to institutional convergence, and thus presumably to real convergence.

Nominal convergence

If real convergence seems a very-long-term affair, taking place at contrasting speeds in differing national and regional institutional contexts, nominal convergence has made more progress within the EMS. Indeed, the basic credibility of the strategy built into the Treaty on European Union rests on the capacity of the commitment to nominal convergence to force institutional convergence and real convergence at a faster pace. There is some limited support for this thesis in the history of convergence within the EMS during the 1980s.

Notable progress was made in convergence of *price inflation* towards German rates, particularly by Belgium, Denmark, France, Ireland and the Netherlands.[48] This process was further facilitated in the early 1990s as inflation increased in Germany as a consequence of unification. In fact between 1990 and 1992 deviation from the EC average price inflation fell from 3.4 to 2 per cent, with – in 1991 and 1992 – price inflation higher in western Germany (4.2 and 3.7 per cent) than in Belgium, Denmark, France, Ireland and Luxembourg.[49] For these countries the rate of increase of unit labour costs relative to Germany was reduced, involving an increase of their

48. Anderton *et al.*, 'Macroeconomic Convergence in Europe', pp. 5–7.
49. Committee of Governors of the Central Banks of the Member States of the European Economic Community, *Annual Report 1992*, pp. 11–12 and 34.

competitiveness. Inflation news remained an important factor in the foreign exchange markets. Once differential inflation performance suggested a decline in competitiveness, as in the cases of Britain, Italy and Spain, the currency was defined as 'weak'. It was no accident that the pound, lira and peseta were the chief victims of the 1992 ERM crisis.

Interest rate convergence was another indicator of the prospects for stability within the ERM and for progress towards EMU. The Treaty on European Union gave a great deal of attention to long-term interest rates: not only because central bankers stressed their importance in the investment process, but also because they represented expectations about future short-term interest rates. Thus, they are an early indication of whether market operators expect short-term rates to converge. As convergence of short-term rates is a necessary precondition for EMU, what happens to long-term rates reflects the expectations in the market about the likelihood of EMU. Over the 1980s the process of convergence of long-term interest rates was less marked than of short-term rates, with long-term rates in Germany and the Netherlands remaining notably lower. From 1990 to summer 1992 convergence speeded up, reflecting a new confidence about the prospects for EMU, a process that was to be broken with the crisis of the summer and early autumn. Again, Britain, Italy and Spain shared less fully in this process of convergence.[50]

With the exception of Italy, the process of convergence of short-term interest rates was one of the most striking characteristics of the original ERM members in the 1980s. The Netherlands led the way, followed by Belgium and France. Short-term rates embodied a rate premium to cover the risk of devaluation in not holding the anchor currency, the D-Mark. By establishing a credible monetary and fiscal policy mix to underpin their exchange-rate commitment ERM members sought to follow the Dutch lead in reducing the rate premium. Following the 1992 ERM crisis, only the Dutch authorities were able to avoid a significant widening of short-term interest differentials, with (in ascending order) France, Denmark and Ireland among the original narrow band countries suffering. By early 1993, fortified in the markets by the resolution that they had displayed in the 'battle for the franc', the French authorities were able to restore convergence of short-term rates with Germany and, in June, for the first time to reduce them below the German rate.

Though the market operators clearly appreciated the importance of interest-rate differentials, they were disposed to discount the relevance of convergence of long-term interest rates to the EMU project. In a fixed exchange rate regime with capital mobility interest rates will inexorably be prone to converge. But *fiscal convergence* was another matter. Fiscal convergence, buttressed by convergence plans, was sufficiently important to merit specification in its own Protocol as well as in the substance of the Treaty on European Union. With the major exception of Italy there was some convergence of fiscal deficits as a percentage of GDP over the course of the 1980s, particularly after 1983. By 1990 four states met the two fiscal convergence criteria later to be agreed at Maastricht – Britain, France, Germany and Luxembourg – with Denmark and Spain in close proximity. Their deficits represented less than 3 per

---

50. Committee of Governors of the Central Banks, *Annual Report 1992*, pp. 18–22.

cent of GDP, their general government debt less than 60 per cent. By 1993 only Luxembourg was expected to meet the targets.[51] Albeit trailing significantly behind Britain (whose deficit more than doubled in 1992 to over 6 per cent of GDP), France and Germany had significantly increased their borrowing requirements, with only the Netherlands and Portugal making some progress in reducing deficits. Government debt did not reflect a similarly sharp deterioration for these countries. Even so, Belgium, Italy, Ireland and the Netherlands had huge tasks before them if they were to meet or even approximate the debt criterion. Fiscal convergence ran into reverse under the double blow of mounting recession (which reduced tax income and raised social spending) and high interest rates (which increased the burdening of servicing the government debt). With a fiscal deficit of well over 10 per cent of GDP and a debt level at some 100 per cent of GDP, Italy seemed condemned to fail. And even Germany's chances of qualifying under the fiscal convergence criteria seemed to be worsening.

The Treaty on European Union embodied the faith of central bankers in the importance and efficacy of nominal convergence: that the will to achieve consistent price stability and to reduce budget deficits and government debt would force institutional convergence (led by central bank independence) and real convergence. There is some evidence to support this faith. As the ERM was accepted as a disciplinary mechanism in the 1980s, governments, as in Belgium, Denmark and Italy, began to tackle structural reforms of the labour market with a new vigour, and by the early 1990s many were looking with more determination at structural reform of the welfare state. The Italian government's dismantling of the *Scala Mobile* (wage indexation) became particularly symbolic of this process.

But the evidence remained limited. Powerful cultural and institutional factors, deeply ingrained in national habits, could not be dismissed as epiphenomena; nor could their impact on real convergence be easily discounted. Rather, institutional and real economic fundamentals were the underlying factors at work: industrial relations systems and productivity growth rates were important in shaping inflation rates; and a whole complex of factors in the system of government–industry relations, the industrial relations system, the finance system and corporate governance influenced productivity growth rates. Overall, the treaty endowed the EC with very limited instruments with which to tackle the problems of convergence. For the ESCB those limitations could prove very serious indeed.

Against this background, operators in the foreign exchange markets – sensitive and averse to risk as they are – were quick to conclude that EMU was most likely to proceed on the basis of a narrow group of relatively homogeneous countries: hard currency countries with Germany as the fulcrum. Whereas the nominal convergence criteria had become the central focus for ECOFIN and the European Council, the market operators operated with a broader view of economic fundamentals. For them the key fundamentals were competitiveness (as measured by comparative trends in unit labour costs – a figure that combines a nominal factor, wage inflation, with a real

---

51. International Monetary Fund, *World Economic Outlook* (Washington, DC: IMF, April 1993). Also D. Marsh, 'Maastricht Budget Targets Prove Elusive', *Financial Times*, 27 January 1993, p. 2.

factor, productivity) and the capacity to reconcile internal and external equilibrium (for which a range of indicators were relevant – such as the current account balance, unemployment, interest rates and political news). In short, the real economy was very much part of market calculations, along with the functioning of political institutions.

The structural power of trade interdependence: the single financial market and the foreign exchange markets

We have seen how the bargaining relations between the EC authorities and the financial markets were deeply affected by the structural power of economic fundamentals that, in part for historical and cultural reasons, were not amenable to uniform or rapid convergence, and also how these relations were further complicated by capital liberalization and developments within the markets themselves. But it should be noted that the EC's own policies had created a structural context of increasing trade integration that provided a coherent and rational basis for the EMS and EMU. Whatever doubts might be entertained about the convergence criteria, many market operators in the City of London (like Graham Bishop at Salomon Brothers) and on Wall Street (like George Soros) were more persuaded by this logic for EMU than many British politicians.

In the long term the most impressive structural factors promoting EMU were trade and financial market integration within the EC and the economic openness and vulnerability that they revealed. Between the early 1960s and the late 1980s a quite extraordinary increase took place in intra-EC trade. In 1985–90 intra-EC trade among the twelve member states accounted for 59.8 per cent of their total trade, compared to 45 per cent in 1960–7. This growth was by no means continuous, with a ten-year period of stagnation till 1982. Nevertheless, it demonstrated the increasing degree of interdependence among the EC economies and underlined the value of a framework of stability for that trade. For some EC countries that interdependence was pronounced, with intra-EC trade as a proportion of total trade rising (in 1985–90) to 72 per cent for Belgium, Luxembourg and Ireland, to 68 per cent for the Netherlands and to 62 per cent for France. Again, taking intra-EC trade as a percentage of total trade, disparities between the twelve member states have narrowed over the years. Britain is a useful illustration. In 1960–7 intra-EC trade represented only 27 per cent of its total trade, compared to 45 per cent for Germany: by 1985–90 the percentages were 50 per cent and 53 per cent respectively.[52] Intra-EC trade as a percentage of total trade was in effect a long-term economic fundamental of major importance. Here was a source of structural power that kept EMU on the agenda.

Interestingly, seen from another perspective, intra-EC trade suggested the need to refine the picture of economic openness and of the configuration of costs and benefits of EMU for different EC states. The importance of intra-EC trade (imports and exports) can also be measured in terms of GDP. Here again the evidence of expanded importance is clear. In 1992 intra-EC trade (measured as exports) accounted for nearly 13.3 per cent of their combined GDP, compared to 6 per cent in 1958 and 11.5 per

---

52. See *Eurostat Statistical Yearbook: External Trade 1990* for figures in this and the next paragraph.

cent in 1979, against an economic background in which GDP had nearly tripled in real terms. But there were significant differences in relative openness as measured by intra-EC imports and exports as a percentage of GDP (table 8.1). For some states their degree of openness and external vulnerability indicated that EMU would assume a positive attraction: Belgium (82.5 per cent), Ireland (71.4 per cent) and the Netherlands (59.3 per cent). Other states occupied a more intermediate position: Germany (26.5 per cent), France (21.8 per cent), Britain (21 per cent) and Italy lowest of all at 17 per cent. The weight of intra-EC exports to total GDP also showed variation in 1992: 13.9 per cent for Germany, 11.3 for France, 10.2 for Britain, 8.4 for Italy and 8 for Spain. In fact, other than for Ireland, Belgium and the Netherlands, the structural determination of EMU by intra-EC trade is not obvious. With intra-EC exports at only 13.3 per cent of combined GDP in 1992, openness is less significant than Canada's trade with the United States, where monetary union is not an issue.

Table 8.1: Intra-EC imports and exports as a percentage of combined EC GDP in 1992

Belgium	82.5
Ireland	71.4
Netherlands	59.3
Germany	26.5
Denmark	26.3
France	21.8
Britain	21.0
Spain	18.3
Italy	17.0
EC 12	26.6

Source: EC Commission, *European Economy* (1992)

An aspect of convergence that bore down more directly on the financial markets was the creation of the single financial market in the EC, as a key aspect of the single European market programme. The EC Commission's White Paper on *Completing the Internal Market* of 1985 identified two key requirements for the creation of an integrated European Financial Area: the liberalization of capital movements, which in turn would underpin the creation of a single market in financial services, particularly banking and insurance.[53] A range of restrictions hindered intra-EC trade in banking and insurance: not least, exchange controls (outside Britain, Germany and the Netherlands), restrictions on the financial instruments (like options and swaps) that could be traded, differences in supervision and restrictions on establishment.[54] A whole battery of EC legislative measures were in place by the end of 1992: the directive on the complete liberalization of capital movements (1988); the second non-life insurance

53. Commission of the European Communities, *Completing the Internal Market* (Brussels: COM(85)310, 1985).
54. For details on the hindrances to a single financial market see R. White, 'The Finance Industry and the Community's Regulatory Environment', in M. Castello-Branco and J. Pelkmans (eds) *The Internal Market for Financial Services* (Maastricht: EIPA, 1987).

directive (1988); the solvency ratio directive (1988); the second banking directive (1989); the 'own funds' directive (1989); the second life assurance directive (1990); the third non-life insurance directive (1992); the third life assurance directive (1992); the investment services directive (1992); and the capital adequacy directive (1992). The pension fund directive, scheduled for 1993, was hindered by the problems of reaching a common position. Central to the many complex provisions of this legislation was the establishment of the principle of freedom to provide services (banking, life and non-life insurance, and investment services) based on the granting of a single licence by a member state – the 'single passport' concept. Supervision would then be by the home country. All measures were to be implemented by mid-1994.

The outcomes were anticipated to be: increased competition and greater choice for the consumer among lower-priced services; a spate of mergers, acquisitions and joint ventures; and a new capacity of the EC's long-term savings to flow towards higher rates of return and away from perceived risk. As we have seen, the background was provided by the build-up of long-term financial assets within the EC, particularly as pension funds have grown at a huge rate in the 1980s and seek the benefits of international diversification of their portfolios.[55] The EC's capital liberalization promised to create a new economic fundamental to which the foreign exchange markets will become increasingly sensitive in the 1990s: both bringing home directly to the market operators the speed and depth of interdependence and making the task of steering the markets in the run-up to EMU more difficult. Most crucially, all financial market operators were directly affected: pension funds, life assurance, mutual funds, and banking and securities firms.

Accelerating sectoral interdependence is also a force prompting institutional convergence among national financial markets and in the structures of corporate ownership and control. On the defensive is the German 'insider' model of corporate governance, with its reliance on internal, committee-style supervision of management decisions, involving bankers, workers and other companies; its paucity of companies whose equity is publicly quoted and traded on the stock exchange (and thus vulnerable to takeover); and its concentration of ownership, particularly in the hands of other companies.[56] Liberalization of financial markets is prompting companies to seek the new opportunities for raising equity capital by becoming listed companies whose shares are traded and in which ownership is less concentrated. In the process convergence around the Anglo-American 'outsider' model, in which takeover is the major discipline on managers, seems the most likely prospect. Interestingly, in the 1980s and early 1990s legislative initiatives in most EC states (Britain is an exception) and from the EC Commission had tended to emulate the German insider model. But market pressures, themselves the product of other legislative initiatives, are pointing towards the spread of the outsider model.

---

55. Bishop, *Capital Liberalization*, pp. 4–6 for details.
56. On the contrast between the German 'insider' and Anglo-American 'outsider' models of corporate governance see C. Mayer and J. Franks, *Corporate Control: A Synthesis of the International Evidence* (London: London Business School, November 1992). On the impact of the German model on legislative action at the EC and national levels see K. Dyson, 'The Cultural Context of the Single Market', *Political Quarterly* 64 (1992), pp. 84–98.

Conclusions

At the heart of the problems of the EMU policy process, and of putting EMU into practice, is the restricted conception of institutional convergence that is enshrined in the Treaty of European Union – with its focus on exchange rate stability and central bank independence; a central bankers' conception of nominal convergence; and its premise that the commitment to nominal convergence can force the other forms of convergence, institutional and real. There is a partial truth here; policy and market changes can build up a self-sustaining momentum for institutional reform.

But the question remains of just how effective will reliance on a restricted, accounting conception of nominal convergence prove. As we shall see in chapter 9, the history of European integration underlines the risks of relying on spillover effects from one area of integration to related areas. More appropriate than spillover is the metaphor of 'pollination': whether the seeds of integration germinate successfully in proximate sectors, like labour markets and budget policy, depends on the fertility of the soil there; in integration, fertility requires a critical mass of actors with the will and capability to act. It is by no means self-evident that the necessary will and capability is at hand.

With spillover far from automatic, the risk remains that the ESCB will find itself politically exposed, without adequate instruments to operate a low-cost policy of economic stability. EMU, as designed in the treaty, could in fact prove to be a very high-cost policy in lost output and unemployment. The crucial point is that pursuit of EMU on these terms could put additional strains on the political legitimacy of EC institutions. Ultimately, EMU cannot be achieved in this manner: for credibility with the market operators is not possible in the face of such strains. The casualty promises to be not just EMU and the EMS but the credibility of the EC as a whole.

Despite these serious reservations about the narrow and problematic approach to convergence in the Treaty on European Union, two underlying structural forces give long-term support to the EMS and EMU policy process: the economic convergence brought about through intensifying intra-EC trade, and the convergence taking place in the financial sector in the framework of the single European market programme. Together, these forces create a powerful underlying disposition to a managed exchange-rate regime, like the ERM, and to securing such a regime as firmly as is possible, via EMU. They also underline (as we have seen) the problems of putting EMU into effect: with the huge increase in scale of the stock of mobile financial assets; and with the problem of 'leads' and 'lags' in financing intra-EC trade. Here, in effect, are two economic fundamentals that point the EMS and EMU policy process towards a strategic dilemma in the 1990s: either persisting and probably deepening problems of managing the EMS and the treaty-based transition to EMU or a fast-track to EMU.

This chapter has emphasized how the bargaining relations between the EC monetary authorities and the foreign exchange markets have been influenced by the complex and changing relationship between policy and markets. Deep-seated political, economic, technological and demographic changes have transformed this relationship. But, ultimately, the foreign exchange markets remain political. They are created by governments which express their 'statehood' in the issuance and management of national currencies. That political act brings these markets into being. Correspondingly, governments have the right to remake the markets, for instance by deciding to issue and manage a single European currency. This fundamental political decision is the prerogative of governments. As we made clear above, there has been a discernible shift of power on the continuum of policy and markets, under the impact of a complex cluster of technological, ideological and market-driven changes – throwing international and global market operators into centre stage. But it is important to keep a sense of proportion in evaluating the significance of this change in the distribution of power.

In characterizing the bargaining relations between the EC monetary authorities and the foreign exchange market operators three points need to be borne in mind. First, though central bankers have undoutedly ceded power to the markets, they retain a potential power that is not to be underestimated. They continue to act as gatekeepers between the markets and policy, a position that gives them a strategic importance that they are quick to appreciate and exploit. Not least, central bankers possess a technical expertise about financial markets, notably the bond market, that governments would be foolish to ignore. Just how successful they are in translating that expertise into influence depends, of course, on the credibility and reputation that a central bank has acquired through its own action. In the case of the German Bundesbank that credibility and reputation has proved more impressive than in the case of the Bank of England.

Second, the foreign exchange markets are no more radically unpredictable than they are simple, repetitive systems. They migrate between order and chaos: attracted by the magnetic pole of the rules of the game and the attempt to take advantage of them, but capable of being driven by their own momentum towards chaos. This process is remarkably rule-governed: the rule that exchange rates should reflect fundamentals; the rule that the monetary authorities must demonstrate their commitment by timely and resolute action; the rule that parity changes should never be larger than the width of the band; and the technical trading rules of the market operators, including the rule that how the market operators perceive the fundamentals is basic to decision taking in the market. It is when, as post-German unification, the EC monetary authorities ignore these rules that the bargaining relation with the foreign exchange markets imposes shock-effects on the EMS and EMU policy process.

Third, the 'market' is very far from being a collective entity. In political rhetoric it is readily anthropomorphized, for instance into an Anglo-American conspiracy against EMU. Power is pictured as residing with a pack of predatory shirt-sleeved speculators. In practice (as we have seen) the foreign exchange markets are highly professional, complex and fast-evolving but not fundamentally chaotic or random. Here is a huge engine of credit creation, on which governments and industries have become dependent to facilitate expansion and trade. It is not surprising that, as a consequence, the foreign exchange markets have a privileged position when it comes to arbitrating on policy.

But the foreign exchange markets are no single, impersonal force. They comprise a complex collection of thousands of individual traders, working for competing firms and fearful of the consequences of being overexposed to financial risks. In their behaviour certain rules matter: technical trading rules, for instance, and the rule that economic fundamentals matter. Within limits they are uncertain about what economic fundamentals really tell them and divided about their expectations of the future, not least about the prospects for the EMS and EMU. In that range market operators are sensitive to steering from the monetary authorities. In order to continue to steer successfully, the monetary authorities have to have credibility (which might be enhanced by central bank independence but still has to be earned in action). They have to ensure that their policies are consistent with the broad fundamentals of competitiveness and the economic cycle. By doing so they will maximize their capacity to act effectively. Neither the informal rules of the game under the ERM after 1987 nor the rules for EMU embodied in the Treaty on European Union served to maximize that capacity: not least as the 'shock' of German unification spread its effects across the EC and as the British government, mired in recession, confronted that shock with an economic cycle 'desynchronized' from that of its EC partners and an overvalued currency in the ERM.

Part Three
CONCLUSIONS

Chapter 9

THE HOLLOW CORE

*The EMS and EMU policy process, theories of integration and
the dynamics of union*

Man is both free and in bonds. *Free*, for he must always move on; old forms are all the
time decaying; man must, and he can, use his will and choose. *In bonds*, for he cannot use
his will indiscriminately, nor choose according to the dictates of his constructive cunning
or his fancy. We are incessantly freeing ourselves from our past, but at the same time it
maintains a sway over us.

(Pieter Geyl, *Debates with Historians* (1955: 277–8))

In chapters 6–8 we focused on the big 'impersonal forces' at work in European
monetary integration: on how the anchor currency, economic ideas, economic
fundamentals, foreign exchange markets, world currency relationships, trade
interdependence and the institutional rules of the game have given some semblance of
structure to the EMS and EMU as policy process. In chapter 5 we saw how the shift
from the up-side to the down-side of the economic cycle affected the functioning of
the policy process. These structural factors have also helped to endow the policy
process with its *sui generis* character: defined by the climate of sound money ideas;
the scale, volatility and intrusiveness of the foreign exchange markets; and the inherent
asymmetry in monetary politics.

Not only has it become clear that there is no single source of structural power that
provides us with an 'efficient' secret of the functioning of the EMS and EMU policy
process, but also the examination of each source has brought us back to the
importance of policy actors in their own right. The rules of the game, not least the
two-level policy process, may structure choices; they do not make them. Economic
ideas are as much instruments available to actors and rationalizations of their actions
as contexts of decision. Economic fundamentals are matters for definition and
judgement by actors; within crucial margins they remain uncertain about them. Trade
interdependence and the degree of economic openness to the rest of the EC is but one
dimension of judgement about the appropriateness of a monetary union; actors may be
more swayed by the implications of a particular economic policy idea. And foreign
exchange markets are far from being a monolithic force, but themselves comprise
corporate actors facing risk and uncertainty.

The significance of policy actors becomes clear when one looks at how the
two-level policy process operates. In this institutional context actors face the problem
of reconciling different audiences and interests at the two levels.[1] In 'game-theoretic'

1. On the concept of a 'two-level' policy process, see R. Putnam, 'Diplomacy and Domestic
   Politics: The Logic of Two-Level Games', *International Organization* 42:3 (1988), pp. 427–69.
   On 'interlocking politics', see F. Scharpf, 'The Joint-Decision Trap: Lessons from German
   Federalism and European Integration', *Public Administration* 66:3 (1988), pp. 239–78. For a
   general survey and critique of the intergovernmental relations literature, see K. Goetz,
   Intergovernmental Relations and State Government Discretion (Baden-Baden: Nomos, 1992).

terms the EC's institutional structure creates, at one level, a 'supergame' of repeated Council bargaining, removing the incentive to cheat on one's EC partners by the threat of being punished in later or even simultaneous bargaining; at another level, domestic 'trigger mechanisms' in the form of the withdrawal of political support if the costs of integration are judged to outweigh the benefits. Optimizing a trade-off between the gains from being a reliable and trusted negotiator in 'repeated games' of Council bargaining and the costs of forfeiting domestic support involves in effect judgements about the severity of the punishments implied by different trigger mechanisms. It opens up a range of possibilities in the way in which the 'policy game' is played; there is no single determinable outcome.

In this chapter, building on the previous three, we shall argue the importance of not ignoring the dimension of voluntarism in the European integration process in general, and consider the implications of this argument for our view of the EMS and EMU policy process. The scene remains important. But the nature of much of that scene has been shaped by the few leading actors in this policy process, and the script of that policy process is something that they have had a hand in writing (as we have seen in chapters 3–5). They remain in a crucially important sense tied like bondsmen to the unrolling action which is unlikely to simply illustrate their own will. At one level inhabitants of a policy process like EMU have a sense of being shackled, bricked up by history, institutions and structural forces. Yet their will and capability – their calculations and choices, however limited their capacity for rational action – remain essential features of the dynamics of the policy process.

This thesis about the need to rescue the dimension of voluntarism is developed by re-examining the explanatory power of theories of European integration, old and new, in relation to the EMS and EMU as policy process. A distinction is made between these traditional 'structural' theories and a 'dynamic' approach. In the one case, monetary integration is seen as the development of specific structural factors that constrain actors to behave in a certain way: for instance, elite collusion generated by spillover from one policy sector to another or 'transaction cost economizing'. In the other, the emphasis is on the ultimately voluntary character of the integration process: actors are seen as essentially rational beings, sometimes cooperating, sometimes in conflict, above all with complex interests and motives. The basic argument is that an approach that emphasizes interacting bargaining relations at the sectoral level – themselves in key respects *sui generis* – has the merit of capturing both the structural factors and the element of voluntarism in the EC policy process. It leaves open the question of their relative importance in different sectors at different times over different issues.

Structural explanations of the process of European monetary integration

This chapter begins with the argument that EC integration theory and policy studies have been too dominated by a 'structural bias', leading to an 'overdetermined' view of the integration process. An approach that focuses on the sectoral dynamics of European integration, by identifying the interlocking bargaining relations that comprise each sector, serves to help rehabilitate voluntarism. Such an approach reconciles the need to incorporate the necessarily complex processes of integration with the need to find a way of incorporating impersonal forces into a more dynamic account of the policy process. There are costs: parsimony is sacrificed. But the benefit is a greater agility in capturing processes of calculation and change; a capacity to continually reassess the significance of specific causal factors; and, as this case study of the EMS and EMU has argued, an improved ability to identify the role of the EC's unique two-level policy process in shaping the dynamics of the integration process. Ultimately, the basic presupposition of this approach is that the actors matter a great deal and have interests and motives that cannot be fully revealed by a single structural theory.

The key questions as far as the policy process is concerned are *why* the leading actors in the EMS and EMU engage in these forms of political bargaining, and *how*. Before we return to these questions later in the chapter, it is important to review the explanatory power of structural theories of integration, old and new.

1   the global structuralist explanation
2   the 'statecraft' explanation
3   the intergovernmental bargaining explanation
4   the neo-functionalist explanation
5   the neo-federalist explanation
6   the transaction costs explanation
7   the 'path dependency' explanation

The global structuralist explanation

Seen from an international political economy perspective, the EMS and EMU are embedded in the *complex interdependencies and processes of change within the world economy*. The policy process is, in other words, not self-contained, even though small and privileged; its external dimension is critical to is functioning. EC states can be viewed as continuingly susceptible and vulnerable to the actions of a dominant power, in this case the United States.[2]

Applying the perspective proposed by Susan Strange, how the EMS and EMU function might be said to reflect the entrenched structural power of the United States in the *global financial structure*, a power that was symbolized by the Bretton Woods system and that has outlasted it.[3] Ultimately, US domestic policy has been the key determinant of the availability of credit internationally and of the terms on which currencies are exchanged for each other. The main factor in the development of European monetary integration might be seen as not so much the decline of US power in the global financial structure as the misuse of that power. Thus the origins of the EMS coincided with a new sense among European leaders, led by German Chancellor Helmut Schmidt, that the United States was exploiting rather than managing the global financial structure, by borrowing from rather than lending to the system: in other words by pursuing its own short-term interests at the expense of the long-term

2.   R.O. Keohane and J.S. Nye, *Power and Interdependence* (Boston, Mass., and Toronto: Little Brown, 1977).
3.   S. Strange, *States and Markets* (London: Pinter, 1988).

interests of all in the health of the global financial structure. In the process American behaviour was jeopardizing new efforts at international monetary coordination and forcing a European response.

The strength of this theoretical approach lies in the link between transformation of the EC policy process for monetary integration in 1978–9, 1987–8 and 1992–3 and rapid falls in the US dollar. Both the development of the EMS policy process and the resurgence of the EMU issue can be seen as inextricably linked to changes within the global financial structure – in particular to 'external' shocks. These shocks proved to be the key to new phases of development in European monetary integration. It is also helpful in pointing to problems of the EMS and EMU. Both can be seen as born of a reaction against the irresponsible use of American power. At the same time, their functioning is trapped within the constraints posed by American power in the global financial structure and by the asymmetrical effects of US dollar movements on EC states: note, for instance, the external shocks to, and subsequent turmoil in, the EMS in 1986–7 and 1992 from a collapsing dollar. In short, American power in the global financial structure creates both the context of, and the problems for, the EMS and EMU policy process. From 1978 onwards European monetary integration has been involved in the valiant effort to restore a measure of responsible international monetary leadership. Failure to achieve this objective has served to propel the process further towards full monetary union.

Whilst explanations that consider the distribution and use of power within the international political economy provide useful contextual information, they fail to address the internal characteristics of the policy process *per se*. It is these internal characteristics that enable us to understand why the Bundesbank and the Banque de France give priority to EMS coordination over G-7 coordination.[4] Even if EC governments and central banks are sensitive and vulnerable to American action, and the perceived 'irresponsibility' of American policy grows, it cannot be taken for granted that EC actors have either the will or the capability to pursue and deepen European monetary integration. Once analysis begins to focus on the problems of will and capability attention shifts towards the domestic and EC levels, for instance to the effects of institutional factors and domestic economic performance and political calculation.

The 'statecraft' explanation

Looked at from a very different theoretical perspective, the development of European integration can be interpreted as the expression of the increased *power* of postwar European states.[5] In essence, this approach embodies a traditional 'realist' mercantilism, giving primacy to political purposes of the state, particularly wealth maximization as the basis for securing and extending political power. The fundamental proposition of this approach is that states need to be strong and cohesive enough to activate European integration and to deliver effective policy outcomes.

4. Y. Funabashi, *Managing the Dollar: From the Plaza to the Louvre* (Washington, DC: Institute for International Economics, 1988).
5. A. Milward, *The Rescue of the European Nation State* (London: Routledge, 1992).

In this perspective, the symbiosis between European integration and national political power is the key determinant of the pace and scope of development of European integration. Integration is not so much a supranational development as an exercise in 'extra-nationality', creating new EC institutions as arms of nation states so that the latter can do things that they could otherwise not achieve.[6] European integration is characterized in terms of 'statecraft', an essentially teleological approach that attributes explanatory power to the purpose of reasserting a capacity for governing competence, attributed to those who act on behalf of states. It takes on the character of an imperative created by the efforts of nation-states to make themselves once more accepted and effective political units.

This approach tends to a view of European integration as limited, piecemeal and 'controlled'. It raises the empirical question of whether actors are in practice motivated by such a purpose or by other, more complex considerations of interest, perhaps specific to individual actors. Also, it fails to address the issue of the 'bounded' rationality of those who act on behalf of states: do they in fact have the capacity to control outcomes and steer the integration process imputed to them? A more adequate behavioural assumption for integration theory would be, following Herbert Simon, that actors are intendedly but only limitedly rational.[7]

This assumption of bounded rationality gives credibility to the importance of EC institutions as definers of interests and constraints for actors.[8] By participation in the institutions of the EC their capacity for rational action is augmented. But a changed institutional context, as for instance after the Single European Act, has implications for behaviour. The central idea informing institutional arrangements at the EC level is that the self-regarding and egotistical behaviour of states cannot guarantee outcomes in the public interest of Europe as a whole. Perhaps even more importantly, the assumption of bounded rationality points to the possibility that integration has at least as much to do with unintended and unanticipated consequences. Precisely because the analysis of Milward focuses on the early period when states were putting together the first treaties on European integration, it fails to fully capture the consequences for integration of the institutional development of the EC itself (into the new reality of a two-level policy process). It also exaggerates the capacity for national control of integration outcomes (in the face of the bounded rationality of actors). Each successive move forward in European integration transforms the context within which actors operate. Thus the development of the EMS and EMU has been paralleled, particularly since the Madrid Council of 1989, which legitimized stage one of EMU, by a new (albeit qualified) sense of solidarity in ECOFIN; the factors of corporate self-interest and institutional momentum that supported this solidarity are documented in chapter 6.

The origins of the EMS, with its limited and defensive nature and based on voluntary and informal cooperation, seem to be readily explained in terms of structural arguments about state power. Carefully orchestrated by the German Chancellor and the

---

6. A. Milward, *The Reconstruction of Western Europe 1945–51* (London: Methuen, 1984).

7. H. Simon, 'Rationality in Psychology and Economics', in R. Hogarth and M. Reder (eds) *The Behavioral Foundations of Economic Theory*, supplement of *Journal of Business* 59 (1986), pp. 209–24.

8. D. North, *Institutions, Institutional Change and Economic Performance* (Cambridge: Cambridge University Press, 1990).

French President, a prime motive was the desire to disengage from what was perceived to be the potentially disastrous consequences of 'irresponsible' American economic management, reflected in the declining US dollar. By Europeanizing clearly defined aspects of monetary policy, it was hoped to better insulate the EC states from the currency turbulence characteristic of the late 1970s. The creation of a zone of monetary stability in Europe can clearly be seen as consistent with reassertion of the state, in the sense of allowing national policy objectives in expanding trade to be more effectively realized.[9]

But the limitations of this approach are apparent in the policy process underpinning the adoption of EMU, 1988–91. The French view of EMU, apparent as early as the Balladur paper presented to ECOFIN in 1988, was to use it to wrest political control of monetary policy away from the Bundesbank. In practice, whilst French support for EMU was motivated in this way, control over the integration process proved a more difficult matter. The terms of integration were largely determined by Germany as the anchor currency, not least via the prestige and weight of the Bundesbank in the Committee of Central Bank Governors. Members of the Committee of Central Bank Governors were dominant in the Delors Committee, and the Committee of Central Bank Governors also produced the draft statute for the European central bank – a bank that, on the Bundesbank model, was to be independent and whose paramount objective was to be price stability. Trade-offs here were more complex, not least involving a fair measure of autonomy for the Committee of Central Bank Governors, which in effect in stage two of EMU as envisaged by the Maastricht Treaty is transformed into the European Monetary Institute that prepares for stage three. It is far from clear that the German government was acting consistently with the thesis of increased state power in agreeing to EMU, given that it was signing up to lose its most prestigious institution and a currency whose postwar success seemed to have made it a central symbol of a new German national identity. The Maastricht European Council of December 1991 was important in underlining the extent to which the German Chancellor was prepared to assert his leadership on behalf of his commitment to the ideal of European union. Overall, it is difficult to see how the adoption of EMU, which involved acceptance of centralized control of monetary policy – at the core of sovereignty – by an independent supranational institution, could be simply described in terms of states restricting and controlling a limited process of integration.

The intergovernmental bargaining explanation

Complementary to the above thesis, the emergence of European integration can be seen as an *intergovernmental process*.[10] From this perspective, European integration is

9. Well captured by one of the participants in the EMS negotiations: see D. Healey, *The Time of My Life* (Harmondsworth: Penguin, 1990), pp. 438–40, especially on the motives of the German Finance Minister.
10. A. Moravcsik, 'Negotiating the Single European Act', in R. Keohane and S. Hoffmann (eds) *The New European Community: Decisionmaking and Institutional Change* (Boulder, Colo.: Westview Press, 1991, pp. 41–84. A similar approach to the EMS and EMU is to be found in M. Kaelberer, 'Werner Report, EMS and EMU: Problems and Prospects of European Monetary Cooperation', paper delivered at the Third Biennial International Conference of the European Community Studies Association, Washington, DC, May 1993.

again minimalist and based on a lowest-common-denominator bargaining that rests on the principle of unanimity in policy making and the protection of sovereignty. National governments act as gatekeepers between the EC Commission and domestic politics. More cooperation than integration, EC policy involves a relatively closed process of accommodation, dictated by the relative power of national governments and their experience of operating purely national strategies. Failure of national strategies is of key importance in shifting attention to the opportunities afforded by policy coordination at the EC level. In other words, European integration reflects an autonomous process of *convergence of domestic policy interests and preferences* among member governments. It is propelled by, and embedded within, a *policy learning process* that pushes and constrains national governmental actors to identify a mutual interest in collusion.[11]

The birth and early history of the EMS lends much support to this theory. Roy Jenkins's initiative as Commission President (October 1977) and Chancellor Schmidt's espousal of the idea (from February 1978) were rooted in a recognition of the much lesser ability of the smaller EC states to manage floating exchange rates to their advantage than in the case of the United States. International monetary arrangements and developments following the collapse of the Bretton Woods system seemed to have conspired to frustrate the effectiveness of national policies. Similarly, the disillusioning experiences of March 1983 and January 1987, for the French and Italian governments in particular, can be seen as turning-points in the development of the EMS, affecting the perception of objectives and of required policy instruments. Following the March 1983 realignment the emphasis was increasingly on nominal convergence and coordination of monetary policies to underpin exchange-rate stability; following the January 1987 realignment, when the declining US dollar was the precipitating factor, the response via the Basle-Nyborg Agreement was to reform intervention policy and credit arrangements. The events of 1983 involved a classic process of political exchange: a French domestic stabilization programme in return for guarantees of defence of the franc by other EC central banks.[12] The events of 1987 saw German commitment to institutional reform of the intervention and credit mechanisms in exchange for greater commitment to economic convergence on which, in their view, progress within the EMS had been disappointing.[13] In short, the inspiration and momentum of the EMS seemed rooted in the convergence of national interests based on essentially national learning experiences about the value of external stability.

In the case of EMU it was not so clear that strict limits on future transfers of sovereignty guided choice in the IGC and at the Maastricht summit. Lowest-common-denominator bargaining undoubtedly characterized the British and Danish 'opt-outs' on stage three. Similarly, the German Constitutional Court's ruling of

11. On learning as a determinant of policy the classic statement remains H. Heclo, *Modern Social Politics in Britain and Sweden* (New Haven, Conn.: Yale University Press, 1974). See also M. Weir and T. Skocpol, 'State Structures and the Possibilities for "Keynesian" Responses to the Great Depression in Sweden, Britain and the United States', in P. Evans *et al.* (eds) *Bringing the State Back In* (Cambridge: Cambridge University Press, 1985), pp. 107–68.
12. F.-O. Giesbert, *Le Président* (Paris: Editions du Seuil, 1990).
13. K.-O. Pöhl, Pressegespräch mit Bundesbank Präsident Pöhl, Deutsche Bundesbank, Presse und Information, Frankfurt, 14 September 1987.

October 1993 supported key tenets of the intergovernmentalist argument in claiming a right for the German government to opt-out *within* stage three, should the stability conditions of the Maastricht Treaty fail to be satisfied.

But, in the overall thrust of EMU policy development, the EC Commission and the Committee of Central Bank Governors played an important role, not least the Delors Committee, in establishing the key parameters of the debate. Here, in terms of policy formation, was a significant difference from the genesis of the Single European Act. The creation of the Delors Committee weakened the ability of national governments to act as gatekeepers and control the content of early EMU policy proposals. There was in practice very little difference between the proposals of the EC Commission, presented to the IGC on monetary union as the basis for its business, and the final Maastricht Treaty details (the British opt-out was one key difference). Also, the French and Italian governments' insistence on the 'automaticity' of a fixed timetable in progressing towards EMU was difficult to square with the intergovernmentalist thesis.

Policy learning was not simply grounded in the actual national experience of monetary policy failure. It involved a new EC-inspired learning process about prospective monetary policy failures consequent on the implementation of the single market programme, in particular freedom of capital movement. The Padoa-Schioppa report for the European Commission pointed to the 'inconsistent triangle': of the policy objectives of freedom of capital movement, stable exchange rates and independent monetary policy, only two of which could be achieved simultaneously.[14] In short, if implementation of the single market was to be reconciled with stable exchange rates, EMU was indispensable. The important point is that most EC governments chose to prioritize the single market programme and stable exchange rates over national monetary policy autonomy and that that choice was embedded in an EC-wide rather than autonomous national learning process.

The EMU policy process is also in part a story of how policy actors made use of new economic ideas, most of which are contained in the 'One Market, One Money' report, and of how these ideas were disseminated through cross-national networks.[15] Such ideas included the importance of credibility to effective monetary policy and of institutional conditions (specifically central bank independence) for credibility. The EMU debate in effect empowered at least some central bank governors to seek independence via a new route. Similarly, the idea of economizing on transaction costs via a single currency appealed to the interests of employer and industrial organizations and formed a key part of their supportive role in the EMU debate. Ideas of this type became part and parcel of a transformation of the bargaining relations underpinning European monetary integration, as actors reassessed the gains and losses of EMU.

The neo-functionalist explanation

'Neo-functionalism', again rooted in political science, has bequeathed to European integration theory the concept of *spillover*.[16] According to this concept, the

14. T. Padoa-Schioppa, *Efficiency, Stability and Equity: A Strategy for the Evolution of the Economic System of the European Community* (Oxford: Oxford University Press, 1987).
15. Commission of the EC, 'One Market, One Money', *European Economy* 44, October 1990.
16. E. Haas, *The Uniting of Europe* (London: Oxford University Press, 1958), pp. 103–10 and 271 ff.

consequences (intended or not) of integration in one policy sector spill over, via internal linkage, to related sectors and create there, among national elites (in the case of the EMS and EMU national economic and financial elites), a shift of attitudes, interests and expectations to the EC level. Integration is seen as driven by the interdependent nature of economic problems so that solutions to one lead inexorably to recognition of the need for joint action to deal with others. It follows an impersonal process of spillover: in this case from the single market to EMU (the idea of EMU as a *necessary* flanking measure for the single market). We noted above the linkage between capital liberalization and moves to EMU, and the emphasis of the Padoa-Schioppa report on the way in which the single market had created the new situation of the inconsistent triangle which the EC had to address. The argument that the survival and development of other joint EC policies, notably in agriculture, was conditional on exchange-rate stability within the EC was advanced as early as the 1960s. Within this process the general public's role is to provide a 'permissive consensus'.

This theoretical approach also rests on the assumption of actor rationality and suggests a degree of automaticity to the integration process, denying significant room of manoeuvre to actors and their scope for choice. The metaphor of 'pollination' is in this respect more apt; it draws attention to the more apt question of just how fertile for integration related policy sectors are. Spillover neglects problematic issues of will and capability. Also, in stressing the link between problem solving and the shift of activity and expectations to the supranational level, neo-functionalism underestimates the power of states and the loyalties that they engender. Its value lies primarily in drawing attention to changing opportunities for leverage. Thus, in 1988, the German Finance Minister Gerhard Stoltenberg accepted a linkage between approval of capital liberalization (Italy was notably reluctant) and German acceptance of EMU as a central EC agenda item for the Hanover summit. But ultimately, such linkage depends on the dynamics of Council bargaining and the complex calculations of rational political actors rather than structural conditioning.

In the case of neither the EMS nor EMU is there much evidence that national economic and financial elites inspired governmental initiative. For instance, central bankers played an essentially reactive role in the context of an agenda set by the European Council. Again the support of national employer organizations was mobilized, not least by UNICE on EMU; EMU was not driven by their pressure on national governments to proceed with EMU. Also, the questionable nature of the assumption of a permissive consensus was highlighted by the ratification difficulties of the Treaty on European Union.

The neo-federalist explanation

By contrast, the *neo-federalist approach* attributes key importance to the role of political vision and of a supportive and convincing economic doctrine.[17] It concedes

---

17. See e.g. J. Pinder, *European Community: The Building of a Union* (Oxford: Oxford University Press, 1991). On 'cooperative' federalism see E. Kirchner, *Decision Making in the European Community* (Manchester: Manchester University Press, 1992).

the importance of the general background of growth and interdependence and the increased potency of internal linkages in the integration process. But the emphasis of the neo-federalist approach is on the momentum imparted to EMU by EC elites who are federally minded and seek to engage the self-interests of national actors in benefiting from further integration. Of critical importance is the role of political leadership in pursuing a long-term view of the integration process and in maintaining a constitutional perspective on how to deal with the fundamental problems in integration. It is argued that the integration process has been regularly propelled forward by policy actors whose outlook was shaped by a critique of the nation state as the most appropriate vehicle to deal with economic and security problems that transcend borders.

In another variant, the EMS and EMU policy process is viewed as in a process of transition to a system of *'cooperative' federalism*: a process of engaging in joint tasks by pooling and mixing national sovereignty with Community powers and by a shift to majority voting. That transition is completed with the establishment of the European Central Bank. Meanwhile, the EMI is a prototype of cooperative federalism, with its EC-appointed and independent president and with – according to Article 8 of the Protocol establishing it – the provision that its Council members (central bank governors) 'may not seek or take any instructions from Community institutions or bodies or governments of member states'. Here was a body whose nature might be supposed to be different from that of the Committee of Central Bank Governors that it replaced.

In relation to European monetary integration the interest and engagement of federally minded officials like Jean Monnet went back at least to the period 1959–61 when Robert Triffin, his monetary policy adviser, was advocating a single currency and a European monetary authority with a European reserve fund. Triffin was later to be an influential voice in the context of the EMS debate of 1978–9. Also, before backing the launch of the EMS, Chancellor Schmidt had just written the German introduction to Monnet's *Memoirs*, in which he noted the importance attached by Monnet's Action Committee for the United States of Europe to monetary integration. Again, the German Foreign Minister, Hans-Dietrich Genscher, a pronounced federalist, played an important role in the relaunch of EMU at the Hanover Council in 1988. Thereafter, the momentum imparted by Jacques Delors as Commission president and the federalist ambitions of Chancellor Helmut Kohl ensured that the key actor in monetary integration, Germany, was kept on board, in the face of the reservations and reluctance of the Bundesbank.

But the impact of ideas about the proper relationship between European integration and the nation-state is more complex and contradictory than the neo-federalist approach allows. At one level, there is the existence of an ideology of 'union' among a core group of actors (principally the Christian Democratic governments). The behaviour of Chancellor Helmut Kohl at the Maastricht Council is not really explicable except by reference to profound ideological commitment to union, one deeply rooted in his own political background. On the other hand, beliefs about the value of sovereignty and of national identity are also powerful influences: witness, for instance, the arguments behind the separate Protocols in the Treaty on European Union for the UK and for Denmark and the anti-Maastricht arguments deployed during the

Danish and French referenda on this treaty in 1992. The ideological characters of British Toryism or French Gaullism are not readily malleable to a federalist vocation for the EC, and they represent powerful political forces in two of the three main EC states. Hence the neo-federal approach tends to exaggerate the control of 'federal' political leaders in the face of counter-ideologies, as well as (as we shall see) in the face of the self-interests of very powerful actors.

The neo-federalist explanation rests on a premise that federal (as opposed to other) ideas capture interest politics at the EC level. Though such a process might be in part discernible, the relationship between ideas and interests is in practice more complex. The nature and scope of EMU as defined in the Treaty on European Union reflected above all the interests and power of the national central bankers. European monetary integration depended on a key bargain between EC institutions and central bankers, hammered out in complex exchange relations. Ultimately, EMU had to be legitimized by reference to their interests and expertise. The process by which the central bankers captured EMU for their own priorities was at least as important as their own capture, which was in any case far from perfect. Some central bank governors remained unenthusiastic and uncommitted to EMU. But all were committed to price stability and central bank independence in using monetary policy instruments and to using EMU as a means of securing that objective. The self-interest of central bankers and their will to promote it was unlikely to be substantially altered by the creation of EMI for stage two. The EMI was hardly constituted in a way that would promote a new era of cooperative federalism in stage two.

The transaction costs explanation

In contrast to the essentially political explanations offered above, it is possible to identify a powerful structural logic of economic efficiency at the heart of the European integration process. Specifically, following the literature on institutional economics, European integration can be seen as offering to policy actors an opportunity to *economize on transaction costs*, on the costs of doing business in an increasingly integrated EC trading area.[18] Calculations of the inefficiencies induced by transaction costs in the even more integrated United States market are very high: for instance, that in 1970 more than 45 per cent of US national income was devoted to transacting.[19] In the context of the EC, especially before the single market programme, the 'costs of non-Europe' were bound to be much higher.[20] In the language of transaction cost analysis, new unified regulatory structures at the EC level potentially enable business actors to overcome the costs to transactions of 'bounded' rationality (of information

18. O. Williamson, *The Economic Institutions of Capitalism: Firms, Markets, Relational Contracting* (New York: The Free Press, 1985).
19. J. Wallis and D. North, 'Measuring the Transaction Sector in the American Economy, 1870–1970', in S.L. Engerman and R.E. Gallman (eds) *Long-Term Factors in American Economic Growth* (Chicago: University of Chicago Press, 1986).
20. P. Cecchini, *The European Challenge 1992: The Benefits of a Single Market* (Aldershot: Wildwood House, 1988). Based on Commission of the EC, 'The Economics of 1992: An Assessment of the Potential Economic Effects of Completing the Internal Market of the European Community', *European Economy* 35, March 1988.

costs, for example) and to safeguard against the hazards of opportunism (for instance, enforcement costs as regulators in other member states collude with their competitors).

In this context, the history of the new-found dynamism of the EC during the 1980s can be written in terms of the spread of a new technocratic ideology, centred on the EC Commission, but incorporating business and trade associations, major companies and national government officials. These 'Eurocrats' identified for themselves a new role as 'transaction cost engineers'; European integration became synonymous with the task of reducing the costs of doing business. This ideological renewal and role transformation can be seen as beginning with EC research and development policies, reaching its full flowering with the single market programme, and being extended to European monetary integration after 1987.

Transaction cost analysis has a powerful attraction, and its significance is not necessarily limited to the 1980s. One can, for instance, note the role that high transaction costs played in creating an incentive to the earliest postwar effort at European monetary integration, in the form of the European Payments Union, 1950–8. These transaction costs resulted from the fragmentation of the European economy consequent on the bilateralism of trade and payments and the lack of transferability of the bilateral balances. In the face of such powerful external constraints the EPU evolved into an efficient policy coordinator, using tight rules to correct external imbalances.[21]

With the extraordinary increase in intra-EC trade since 1960 it can be argued that the constraints posed by transaction costs and the incentives to reduce them have mounted. Transaction costs are a more powerful factor for the EC member states given that they are more open to international trade than the USA or Japan. The era of violent currency fluctuations, which set in with the end of the Bretton Woods system in 1971, coincided with the worsening of the EC's relative economic performance during that decade. For the US and Japan the fluctuations were external; for the EC they were internal, with the French franc and the D-Mark diverging from each other as much as either had done from the USA dollar or the yen. In this context the case for improving economic efficiency via exchange-rate stabilization through the EMS was more obviously pressing. The later shift towards EMU can be explained by the new hazards created by the enormous increase in international capital flows consequent on the liberalization of capital movement in EC (note the direct link to the Basle-Nyborg Agreement of 1987), as well as by the transaction costs incurred by multiple currencies and realignment risks in a single market. Hence, in the EC context, transaction costs created a notable bias in favour of putting exchange-rate stabilization at the forefront of EC integration and monetary integration before economic convergence. In other words, transaction cost analysis helps to explain why EMU evolved in the form of a qualititative leap towards monetary integration leading up the process rather than economic convergence and monetary integration moving in close tandem.

This approach is undoubtedly helpful in identifying the role of economic factors in creating new incentives for integration and in providing new arguments to support it. The strength of transaction cost arguments rests indeed on their ostensible objectivity,

21. J. Kaplan and G. Schleiminger, *The European Payments Union* (Oxford: Clarendon Press, 1989).

along with the appeal of economic efficiency as a criterion of government action. It can be persuasively argued that the new dynamism of European integration as a bargaining process since the mid-1980s rests solidly on the technocratic appeal of economic efficiency to EC Commission officials, national administrative elites and managers in trade associations, employer organizations and firms. This new dynamism seemed to rest on the intellectual confidence imparted by a breed of technocrats acting as in effect 'transaction cost engineers'. The transaction cost engineering approach to European integration was a unifying theme in 'The Costs of Non-Europe' research legitimizing the single market and in the 'One Market, One Money' report on EMU. Arguments about greater efficiency by economizing on transaction costs were also applicable at the political level: whether the new scope for qualified majority voting in the Single European Act (to ensure efficient implementation of the single market) or the Maastricht Treaty provisions expediting the transition from stage two to stage three of EMU.

The great problem with the transaction cost approach is that it rests on over-simple assumptions about the motives of the policy actors involved in the integration process. Even if one assumes the centrality of economic motivation, it does not follow that actors will necessarily accord priority to the gains from transaction cost reduction. Such gains may, in their view, be more than offset by the costs implicit in creating a monetary union in a non-optimal currency area: more directly by losses of output and employment from the monetary and fiscal policies consequent on pursuing tough convergence criteria, or the erosion of sovereignty.

Transaction cost analysis does not identify the will and the capability of the policy actors involved in European monetary integration as problematic. Indeed, the central questions may revolve around explaining the absence or failure of a will to economize on transaction costs or the inability to effect reductions of transaction costs. It may be that actors are motivated by non-instrumental motives, like a concern to retain sovereignty in monetary policy. The attitudes of the British Treasury towards EMU seem to be better explained in the latter way. Additionally, a whole series of economic, political and institutional factors can conspire to affect the implementation capacity of transaction cost engineers. In the framework of an approach that centres on bargaining relations issues of will and capability are central and draw attention, among other things, to the role of institutional incentives and constraints and political factors. The cases of France and Italy demonstrate, for instance, that the political motives of wresting monetary power from the Bundesbank and establishing respect *vis-à-vis* Germany were far more potent than economic calculations of transaction cost economizing in shaping policy on EMU.

The 'path dependency' explanation

Drawing on recent work in US economic history, it is possible to envisage European integration as a '*self-reinforcing mechanism*', driven by '*path dependence*'.[22] Adapting

---

22. W. Arthur, 'Self-Reinforcing Mechanisms in Economics', in P. Anderson, K. Arrow and D. Pines (eds) *The Economy as an Evolving Complex System* (Reading, Mass.: Addison-Wesley, 1988). Also D. North, *Institutions, Institutional Change and Economic Performance*, pp. 93 ff.

this theoretical argument, specific historical events can be interpreted as leading one route to EMU to triumph over another: in this case monetary integration over economic convergence, propelled initially by the the events of the falling US dollar in 1978 and later of the currency crises of 1983 and 1987.

A given path to EMU involves large set-up costs (see Ludlow on the EMS, notably on Schmidt spending some 200 hours in 1978 persuading people of its desirability); learning effects which improve its functioning (as after 1983 and 1987); habits of cooperation with particular actors (in the ECOFIN technical committees); and adaptive expectations in which increased importance of a given integration mechanism encourages beliefs of further development (i.e. of the transition from EMS to EMU). Together, these four 'self-reinforcing mechanisms' lead to 'lock-in' and 'path dependence' in European monetary integration, even though the path adopted may prove to be, in the long run, more inefficient than an abandoned alternative. The path is adhered to because of the massive increasing returns for the policy actors involved. They opt for incremental change within the chosen path. From this perspective, the Maastricht Treaty provisions on EMU can be seen as a case of 'path dependence', going back in a clear historical line to the perceptions and actions of Jenkins, Schmidt and Giscard d'Estaing in 1978–9 and even further to the 1960s.

Whilst again this approach has a seductive power, there is a need to recognize that European monetary integration takes place in an institutional setting within which the will and capability of specific actors remains critical. The capacity of actors to follow a particular path of integration, and the way in which they proceed down that path, is ultimately dependent on their will and capability. The great question is whether, in the context of the economic and political problems of the 1990s (with the prospect that protracted recession and unemployment will produce new challenging events, delivered not least via the financial markets), EMU's path as so precisely laid out in the Maastricht Treaty will prove adaptively efficient. A risk of 'lock-in' to economic inefficiency remains; so does the possibility of a redefinition of the policy goals and instruments of EMU. One should never discount the extent to which European monetary integration will be shaped by experience of the outcomes of existing commitments.

In essence, the structural theories outlined above share a common focus on external factors that constrain actors within the EMU policy process to behave in certain ways: whether change at the level of the world economy, the pressures of economic efficiency, historically conditioned path dependence, the dictates of federal ideology, internal linkage, a convergence of interests and policy preferences through policy learning or the imperative of extending and securing the power of the state. It can be said in their defence that they are complementary; each reveals a different facet of European monetary integration. But, their limitation is that, collectively as well as individually, they offer too limited and sometimes too static a picture of the evolving bargaining relationships underpinning the EMU policy process.

Inherent in an acceptance of them is the elusive search for a single theory of European integration. Structural theories offer the main advantage of parsimony in identifying key conditions that have affected the functioning of the EMS and EMU policy process. But they remain weak in explaining the actual dynamics of the process: namely, why given policy actors at a particular time activate, resist or exit from European monetary integration. In approaching the EMS and EMU as a dynamic policy process it remains possible to show how the insights of structural theories can be incorporated into modelling the functioning of the EMS and EMU. But such an approach does not involve a general pre-commitment or over-commitment to a single explanatory theory. It implies that the search for an all-embracing theory of European monetary integration is a will-o'-the-wisp, and that what is required is a method of analysis that leaves theoretical choices open.

The EMS and EMU as a dynamic policy process

In viewing the EMS and EMU as a dynamic policy process we are emphasizing that monetary integration is a complex process of political bargaining, in which the different relationships among the key policy actors are deeply affected by the extent to which they are voluntarist and contingent, as well as interdependent. Three assumptions are made about the EMS and EMU policy process: first, that the nature and development of these bargaining relationships is founded on the interests of the different actors involved and the extent to which those interests are interlocking; second, that the underlying basis of these relationships is conflictual as well as cooperative; and third, that the way in which the bargaining relationships evolve is shaped by the actual policy outcomes that are attributed to the EMS and EMU.[23]

In contrast to the structural approaches outlined above, greater stress is placed on the fragile and fluid character of European monetary integration and of the EMS and EMU policy process. More attention is given to the degree of mutual suspicion within Council bargaining, Franco-German bargaining and in EC–central bank bargaining; and to the potential for policy uncertainty and disarray (for instance over ERM realignments) in a context where governments are ultimately free to withhold their consent, even to veto change. These characteristics of the EMS policy process have been all too apparent, for instance in the failure of governments to agree planned realignments of currencies in the face of speculative onslaught against the ERM in 1992 and 1993.

An analysis of the EMS and EMU as a dynamic process of bargaining relations is consistent with the assumptions of rational choice theory. But it remains sensitive to the institutional setting – the two-level policy process – in which, and through which, Council bargaining takes place. Policy actors in the policy process are assumed to be intendly, albeit limitedly rational (the assumption of bounded rationality). They are also understood to be embedded in institutional contexts that provide a normative dimension to the policy process. As Herbert Simon emphasized, the incentive for actors to cooperate via institutional structures lies in their potential to reduce the problems of bounded rationality.[24] Institutional structures are, consequently, an important dimension in the analysis of behaviour by actors.

23. L. Parri, 'Political Exchange in the Italian Debate', *EUI Working Papers* 85: 174 (Florence: European University Institute, 1985). Also M. Bull, 'The Corporatist Ideal-Type and Political Exchange', *Political Studies* XL:2 (1992), pp. 255–72.
24. For the earliest formulation see H. Simon, *Administrative Behaviour* (New York: The Free Press, 1945). More recently, the 'new institutionalism' has redirected attention back to institutions. See e.g. J.G. March and J.P. Olsen, *Rediscovering Institutions* (New Haven, Conn.: Yale University Press, 1989).

In the case of EC integration that institutional context is very complex, involving in particular a two-level policy process in which the problems of rational choice include how to balance the different normative requirements at each level. At the level of EC institutions premium attaches to one's reputation as a reliable negotiator and 'good' European. At the national level requirements of party unity, political support and electoral advantage loom large. In this context there are difficult choices to be made between pursuing short-term and long-term interests in the integration process. Is it most rational to play a constructive role in managing the orderly development of the integration process: or should one exploit one's role in the integration process for one's own particular interest? In an analysis of the EMS and EMU as a dynamic policy process we are capturing the point that policy actors can change their minds about how to use their position in the integration process.

Central to the EMS and EMU as a dynamic policy process is the *willingness* and *capability* of the key actors involved to pursue monetary integration, in other words their strategic view and their implementation capacity.[25] These two factors are in turn interdependent. For the will to pursue European monetary integration may grow when the capacity to do so effectively is demonstrated; whilst, in the face of severe obstacles to implementation, the will to integrate may diminish.

The will for collective action

The *willingness* to enter into and develop the bargaining relationships that constitute the EMS and EMU policy process is likely to be strongly influenced by the ideological and institutional factors outlined in earlier chapters. We have seen (in particular in chapter 7) how important economic and political beliefs have been in providing reasons why key actors embraced the EMS and EMU policy process with such enthusiasm. Equally, we noted how brittle such beliefs could be in the face of changing economic and political circumstances in 1992–3. Beliefs are clearly of importance in engendering and sustaining the will to pursue EMU, and it is worth briefly summarizing the key beliefs that underpinned the rebirth of EMU in the late 1980s:

1   the economic belief that the long-term costs of devaluation to competitiveness (via heightened expectations of inflation) outweigh the benefits
2   the economic belief in the significance of the efficiency gains from eliminating the transaction costs of a multiple-currency policy regime
3   the economic belief in the superior benefits of economic policy coordination
4   the economic belief in the advantages of tying the hands of national monetary policy to a hard currency
5   the political belief that EMU provided an essential means of controlling the economic power of Germany, especially post-unification.

---

25.   E. Grande and V. Schneider, 'Reformstrategien und staatliche Handlungskapazitäten. Eine vergleichende Analyse institutionellen Wandels in der Telekommunikation in Westeuropa', *Politische Vierteljahresschrift* 32:3 (1991), pp. 452–77. Also Bull, 'The Corporatist Ideal-Type and Political Exchange', pp. 269–71.

But the political will and calculation to pursue European monetary integration cannot be fully explained in terms of such beliefs. For, by and large, actors will choose and ultimately be moved to act by more practical calculations of the specific losses and gains offered by integration. European monetary integration is then the story of how key actors weigh the losses and gains from specific proposals to develop the system and of the bargains that are struck on that basis.

The *losses* from entering into and persisting in the EMS and EMU policy process are pretty clear at the level of the member states. Governments are losing autonomy of action in that they agree to pursue policies, like maintaining high interest rates, that they might not otherwise have done had they not entered into such a relationship. Unwillingness to bear this cost played a critical role in the British government's exit from the ERM in 1992. Caution may stem from an uncertainty about the implications of monetary integration. Thus, in the case of the EMS, Prime Minister James Callaghan expressed his fear that choice of what turned out to be too high a rate for the pound could make unemployment much worse, the central fear of his government. Within months his successor Margaret Thatcher was stressing that choice of what proved to be too low a rate would undermine the priority to bearing down on inflation.[26]

The losses from entering into or developing European monetary integration may be substantive. Thus, following restrictive monetary policies in Germany consequent on the inflationary effects of unification, the prospect of higher interest rates and higher unemployment as the price of the EMS and EMU bore down ever more heavily on states with weaker economies and with greater problems in meeting the strict convergence criteria embodied in the Maastricht Treaty. By September 1992 these costs proved too great for Britain's and Italy's continued participation in the ERM. Concern about how economies actually perform within the EMS and EMU has clearly been a powerful factor in influencing the attitudes of national actors to, and their role in, the policy process.

The losses may also be symbolic, in the form of the loss of sovereignty and national identity. This cost figured prominently in the difficulties that the Labour government had in 1978–9 with the EMS and that the Conservative governments had before, during (1990–2) and after membership of the ERM.[27] British and Danish opt-outs from stage three of EMU were negotiated against this background.

In addition, losses may be defined in strongly institutional terms. Thus EMU clearly implied the ultimate erosion of the *de facto* policy leadership of the Bundesbank in European monetary integration. Germany was being asked to sacrifice one of its most successful and prestigious institutions. Indeed, the EMU provisions in the Maastricht Treaty were based on the tacit premise that the Bundesbank would be willing to preside over its own demise. This perceived high cost to Germany did at least enhance its negotiating power: over such issues as the design, siting and policies of the future European central bank; and with the added proviso, welcomed by the

---

26. R. Jenkins, *European Diary 1977–81* (London: Collins, 1989), p. 353.
27. Callaghan was faced by a House of Commons resolution, signed by 120 Labour MPs, rejecting 'any attempt by the EEC, its institutions or its member states to assume control of domestic policies through a new monetary system for the Community'.

Federal Constitutional Court in its judgment on the Maastricht Treaty in October 1993, that the Bundestag should be given the chance to vote on the fulfilment of the convergence criteria before the German government agreed to stage three.

The *gains* from entering or being in the EMS and EMU policy process can be classified into two types: direct and indirect.[28]

Direct gains

Direct gains relate to the actual content of the bargains concluded in the EMS and EMU policy process and centre on public-interest arguments. There are four main points.

First, there is an increased ability of key actors to affect monetary policy outcomes. Thus, for the German and French governments, the EMS offered a superior collective means to counter the 'irresponsibility' of the US Administration in monetary policy. The role of the EMS as a 'shock absorber' mechanism was particularly important to German actors. External shocks could be better absorbed by distributing their impact among the countries participating in the EMS and achieving a measure of coordination in national monetary policy responses that inevitably have spillover effects on other countries.

For the French, Italian and most other EC governments the transition from the EMS to EMU offered a means of correcting the asymmetry in the functioning of the EMS by Europeanizing monetary policy. In effect, the ERM's functioning was centrally affected by the domestic policy objectives of Germany. With EMU the policy objectives would relate to the EC economy as a whole, in the process taking more account of the interests of other EC states.

Second, the EMS and EMU policy process promised gains for central bankers and for EC officials in so far as it enhanced their status as policy makers and their capacity to secure their interests in policy. The Delors Committee symbolized the central role accorded to central bankers in giving a precise shape to EMU: whilst the Maastricht Treaty involved a stage two in which a new role would fall to the European Monetary Institute as in effect the revamped Committee of Central Bank Governors. Price stability and independence, two dominant interests of central bankers, were written into the Maastricht Treaty.

Third, participation in the EMS and EMU policy process promised increased effectiveness in policy implementation, notably in overcoming the costs for trade and monetary policy of floating exchange rates. In the course of the 1980s the ERM was increasingly valued as an external disciplinary mechanism for domestic policy via a stable exchange rate with the D-Mark (with effects via expectations about inflation). Thus the conversion of the British Chancellor of the Exchequer, Nigel Lawson, to membership of the ERM was based on the argument that a stable exchange rate would provide a more effective rule to govern monetary policy than past and failed efforts to give effect to domestic monetary targets. For French Finance Ministry policy makers the 'strong' franc (*franc fort*) within the ERM was indispensable to restore France's economic competitiveness.

In the case of EC governments with greater problems of economic convergence,

---

28. For the distinction between direct and indirect gains from political exchange see Bull, 'The Corporatist Ideal-Type and Political Exchange', p. 269.

like Italy and Spain, the disciplines of the ERM and of the convergence criteria for EMU offered a useful external crutch to legitimize the implementation of tough domestic fiscal reforms. Exit of the Italian lira from the ERM in September 1992 was a catalyst for more far-reaching fiscal retrenchment and political reform as a price of re-entry.

Fourth, for EC actors in particular European monetary integration was a central means of giving greater legitimacy to the cause of European union and the emergence of a new constitutional order for Europe. For central bankers it was a means of greater legitimacy for the objective of price stability. In both cases enhanced legitimacy for strongly held beliefs constituted a direct gain from European monetary integration. EC Commission officials could also identify the potential to legitimate the development of the EC's redistributive role (and therefore budget) as a means of offsetting some of the losses from EMU.

Indirect gains

Indirect gains from participation in the EMS and EMU policy process relate to corporate self-interests of the actors involved. Essentially the private face of bargaining, they include five main points.

First, for some actors there is an opportunity to expand their own power, prestige and patronage. Thus the management of the EMS offered an enhanced role for EC finance ministry and central bank officials, via their collaboration in the EC Monetary Committee, whilst the creation of the EMI in stage two of EMU involved the further prospect of an upgrading of the power and prestige of the central bank governors. EMU provided the French Inspectorate of Finance with new career opportunities and a prospect that diminished power at the national level could be retrieved at the EC level; the hard ERM had given it an alibi to impose long-held views about monetary rectitude on domestic politicians.

Second, there is an opportunity to gain greater political support. The EMU policy process offered the EC Commission a means of developing 'selective incentives' to encourage support for European integration: for instance by offering employer organizations, organized at the EC-level in UNICE, the prospect of reduced transaction costs.[29] More widely, in the 1980s national governmental actors identified the possibility of improving domestic political support by realizing the direct gains of the hard ERM. Foremost among these gains was increased competitiveness through 'competitive disinflation' as membership of the ERM forced downward adjustment of money costs.

Third, there is the benefit to EC institutions from the creation of 'insider groups', giving actors from these groups new influence over policy in exchange for support. By coopting central bankers ever more closely into an EC framework, their authority would add greater prestige to EC policy. A similar benefit was expected from the incorporation of networks of professional economists in the policy process. These insider groups could help to proselytize on behalf of the aims and interests of EC institutions.

---

29. On 'selective incentives' see M. Olson, *The Logic of Collective Action: Public Goods and the Theory of Groups* (New York: Schocken, 1968), pp. 51 *passim*.

Fourth, there is a more stable and supportive framework for policy actors with whom one's interests are interdependent but who are threatened by domestic problems, for instance southern European states like Italy. The value of the review of convergence programmes by ECOFIN for these states was recognized by other states in the EMS and EMU policy process.

Fifth, there is the enhancement of the reputation for effectiveness of the Council presidency. In taking on board the EMU issue at the Hanover Council of 1988 both Genscher and Kohl were keen to demonstrate the will of the German presidency to achieve a qualitative leap forward towards European union. More prosaically, Council bargaining is supported by a collective desire to help the presidency achieve results. As the presidency rotates, so each state has a self-interest in supporting this informal norm. The effects were visible in the conduct of the two IGCs of 1991, under successively the Luxembourg and Dutch governments. There was a manifest will to help the two governments to broker a deal.

The capability for collective action

The *capability* for collective action in the EMS and EMU policy process is indispensable; actors have to believe that they and their partners are capable of delivering on their commitment to the bargains negotiated and thus feel confident that the gains from monetary integration will in fact exceed the losses. In short, perceptions of capability, and the lessons of experience about the realities of capability, deeply affect the dynamics of the EMS and EMU policy process. This dimension of analysis draws our attention to the importance of institutional and organizational factors in the development and persistence of bargaining relationships within the policy process. Essentially two sets of conditions affect the capability of policy actors to enter into and sustain the development of the EMS and EMU policy process:

The institutional context
The first of the conditions is the *institutional parameters within which the policy actors operate* and the extent to which they facilitate unified and coherent action within the policy process (chapter 6). A basic question is whether the general institutional characteristics of the EC inhibit efforts to establish and develop bargaining relationships in monetary policy. Another is the degree to which the organization of the conduct of monetary policy at the national level retards the EMS and EMU policy process.

As far as the institutional character of EC integration is concerned, the two-level policy process is critical. At the level of the EC institutions the policy process fuses in a unique manner intergovernmental action, represented by the European Council and the Council of Ministers, with supranationalism, represented notably by the European Commission. The debate about the relative importance of the two (usually resolved in favour of intergovernmentalism) misses a key point that has been established in 'games theory'. The main transformation induced by institutional factors at the EC level is the premium placed on reputation as an honest and reliable negotiator. Reputation assumes a critical role in actors' calculations of interest in an institutional context that requires continuous rather than one-off bargaining, and in which gains achieved by an uncooperative stance in one area can be quickly paid for, at an excessive price, by losses in various other areas.[30] This informal constraint is both internalized and reinforced by peer-group pressure and the role of the Commission as the conscience of the Community. In the context of EMU it has been observable both in the new sense of corporate identity within, and more visible profile of, ECOFIN, especially with stage one from July 1990, and in the Committee of Central Bank Governors in the wake of the resurfacing of EMU on the agenda. The move towards tighter procedures for voluntary cooperation in economic policy with the ECOFIN decisions of March 1990 reflected this development.

At the same time, the fact that ultimate responsibility for monetary policy remained in national hands acted as a major constraint on voluntary coordination, at least in the case of the larger countries. The institutional factor that in most states the central banks did not have independence of their governments in the conduct of monetary policy created major limits on the capacity of central bankers to develop voluntary coordination. In the key case of Germany, the complex decision-making structure within the Bundesbank meant that in Council bargaining other negotiators could not assume that its president possessed delegated responsibility, a factor that led to serious misunderstandings and conflict at the informal ECOFIN meeting in Bath in September 1992. Against this institutional background the Committee of Central Bank Governors was inhibited by caution in confronting national policy makers. Perhaps even more decisively, implementation of the convergence criteria for EMU assumed a capacity for domestic budget leadership that was very variable.

In addition, the two-level policy process concentrated the main mechanisms of democratic accountability for governmental action at the national level. Domestic political factors of party and electoral management acted as key constraints, as the Maastricht Treaty ratification process painfully demonstrated both to governments and to the EC Commission. Party political and electoral accountability represented domestic trigger mechanisms that could inflict severe punishment on the political actors involved: the absolute and possibly enduring loss of office. A strategy that eased the political problems of reconciling the requirements of two different audiences within the two-level policy process was to keep a low-profile for EC business and to trust in the passivity of public opinion. With EMU and the Treaty on European Union, however, that strategy was more difficult to operate successfully.

Political, economic and cultural conditions
The *wider environment within which institutional actors have to operate* deeply affects the functioning of the EMS and EMU policy process; there are four main factors:

1 political conditions
2 ideological and cultural conditions
3 economic conditions
4 the nature and outcomes of EMS and EMU policies.

Political conditions notably the state of relations between government and legislature, the climate within the governing party or coalition, and electoral prospects

---

30. R. Axelrod, *The Evolution of Cooperation* (New York: Basic Books, 1984).

and outcomes. The political dynamics of the ratification process for the Maastricht Treaty encouraged a revision of views about EMU. The Danish referendum of summer 1992 suggested a crisis of popular legitimacy; the close 'yes' vote in the French referendum of September did little to dispel this sense of crisis, particularly as it occurred in the country that had been pivotal in the process of political initiative on EMU; whilst the difficulties of parliamentary ratification in Britain, revealing a pronounced cleavage on European union within the governing party, undermined its leadership role of the Council presidency at a critical juncture. The resultant and sudden crisis of political confidence in EMU served in turn to undermine the personal prestige and influence of Delors as Commission president and as a past agenda-setter in this sector. As, again, his personal commitment and drive for EMU had been so important, a central political support was undermined. Against this altered background it was noticeably difficult for Delors to shift the agenda after summer 1992 towards the idea of an EC initiative to promote concerted action for growth, in order to restore dynamism and legitimacy to the EMU process.

Another powerful political influence on the integration process comes from the underlying philosophy of consensus that underpins the functioning of EC institutions. Policy style at the EC level is essentially one of accommodation. But again, the outcomes of European monetary integration cannot be predicted simply by reference to this policy style. Of central importance is the way in which the consensus style operates in particular circumstances. How it operates is shaped significantly by the will and capability of the different actors involved. Thus, British reservations and hostility to the launch of the EMS and later EMU were not allowed to derail the process of agreement to proceed in either case. The will displayed by Britain's partners was too strong for them to be prevented from proceeding. On the other hand, the central bankers proved able to exert a veto on the development of the European Monetary Cooperation Fund after 1973 and to block the establishment of the European Monetary Fund provided for in the Brussels Resolution of 1978. Their veto was based on the protection of powerful self-interests.

Ideological and cultural conditions notably the degree of ideological commitment to European monetary integration, the extent of consensus about European union and the nature of the professional cultural worlds that have influenced policy on EMU. In many countries widespread commitment to European union helped to facilitate a process of European monetary integration that otherwise, on the basis of other perceptions of self-interest, might have been more difficult to support. In Italy, for instance, EMU implied deep fiscal retrenchment, including huge cuts in public expenditure and tax increases. In Germany it offered the prospect that the achievement of price stability might be endangered by an institution that might prove to be less rigorous and single-minded than the Bundesbank.

As we emphasized in chapter 8, the cultural context profoundly conditions the functioning of institutions; institutions have their own effect on economic efficiency and performance; and institutional convergence – with the exception of central bank independence – is subordinate to nominal convergence in the Treaty on European Union. Two characteristics of the functioning of the EMS and EMU policy process are clear: that different cultural contexts will mean that imported institutional arrangements, like central bank independence in France and Spain, will function differently – remember the integrative role of the Inspectorate of Finance and the absence of the same historically conditioned cultural aversion to inflation that supports the Bundesbank's effectiveness; and that culture will limit the very process of institutional convergence. Cultural and institutional diversity will impact, via continuing differences in economic performance, on the EMS and EMU policy process.

At a more policy-specific level, consistency between the goals of EMU and the commitment and priority of the Committee of Central Bank Governors to price stability was crucial. The compatibility of EMU with central banking culture and ideology was indispensable to its development. Also, the dependence of EMU on treaty revision drew the EMU policy process into the conventions of diplomacy in the IGC. EMU was, in other words, caught up in the powerful cultural cross-currents of the professional worlds of diplomacy and central banking (chapter 5).

Additionally, the impact of professional economists on the 'climate of ideas' about European monetary integration is not to be underestimated (chapter 7). The economic beliefs that they propagated not only were important in inspiring the will of key actors to develop the EMS and EMU policy process, but also prepared the ground for the wider acceptability of EMS and EMU initiatives. But, of course, the beliefs of economists and central bank governors did not amount to a generalized culture of economic stability in the EC.

Economic conditions notably the performance of macro-economic indicators relating to growth, employment and inflation and the behaviour of financial markets (chapter 8). Crucially (as we noted in chapter 5) the neogotiations about EMU from 1987 to 1991 took place against the background of the up-side of the economic cycle. In turn, this period of expansion correlated with the adoption of the single European market programme, to which EMU was presented as internally linked. In this respect economic conditions were crucially important in facilitating the early momentum of the EMU policy process.

By 1992, when via the Maastricht Treaty EMU was beginning to enter the wider public realm of debate, the economic cycle was moving firmly into the down-side. Most important of all, German unification had by summer 1992 ceased to act as a locomotor of growth for the German and European economies. Inflationary pressures, consequent on the escalating federal budget deficit produced by the costs of financing the reconstruction of the east, had prompted the Bundesbank to hike interests rates to a record high. Via the locking of exchange rates to the D-Mark (the 'new' EMS) and the commitment to convergence, and via the premium that had to be paid to encourage dealers to hold currencies that did not have the credibility of the D-Mark, other EC economies were forced to raise interest rates above the German level. Consequently, the ERM became an instrument of deflation. As Keynes emphasized, international currency regimes will tend to break down if they become instruments of deflation.[31]

In this respect the experience of Britain in the ERM between 1990 and 1992 is

31. R. Skidelsky, *John Maynard Keynes, Volume 2: The Economist as Saviour, 1920–37* (London: Macmillan, 1992).

instructive. ERM membership coincided with the most protracted recession since the interwar period; humiliating exit from the mechanism in 1992, combined with guilt by association with domestic recession, raised the political costs of later re-entry. The fundamental error of monetary mismanagement in British membership of the ERM was the initial choice (in October 1990) of an exchange rate for the prime purpose of bearing down on costs, in particular inflated real wages, rather than an exchange rate that reflected the competitive power of the national economy (whose weakness was apparent in the huge balance of trade deficit in the midst of recession). As British experience clearly reveals, protracted economic recession is a serious enemy of European monetary integration, unless European integration can somehow find an active fiscal dimension. In a report of summer 1992 the IMF outlined the costs in terms of output and jobs that would follow from the attempt to implement the convergence criteria contained in the Treaty on European Union. Later economic developments, notably the shift to estimates of below zero growth in the German economy in 1993, seemed to confirm that the costs of EMU had to be revised upwards or some collective policy adopted to reduce these costs via a coordinated growth strategy.

The behaviour of the financial markets had its most dramatic effects in speculative runs, seen for instance in 1986–7 and in most spectacular form in September 1992 when the British pound and the Italian lira were 'forced' to leave the ERM and in July/August 1993 when the EMS reacted by adopting very wide bands. These attacks reflected situations in which market operators had lost confidence in the will and capability of EMS policy makers to maintain parities in the face of a mismatch between their commitments and action to tackle economic fundamentals that were inconsistent with those commitments. They were deflected by realignment/exit of currencies; by sufficiently strong concerted action by central banks, as in the case of the French franc in September 1992, to reassert the determination of the authorities; or by a change of the rules of the game, as in August 1993. What emerged clearly from these cases was the degree of sensitivity of the EMS and EMU policy process to market pressures. Markets could inflict huge costs on the policy actors involved in managing the ERM, as in 1992 and 1993. These costs in turn generated policy reappraisal.

The nature and outcomes of EMS and EMU policies The stability and durability of the EMS and EMU policy process will depend on the 'quality' of its policies and their expected and actual outcomes. EMU proved to be a very different issue from that of the single market, its great and related predecessor issue. In the case of the single market, integration promised a wide range of technical improvements in the environment of business and trade within the Community, bound together by the positive symbolism of freedom of movement. With EMU, the symbolic dimension was more ambiguous. A single European currency meant a manifest, direct assault on a central symbol of sovereignty; money has (as we noted in the introduction) a cultural as well as technical dimension. Also, the economic and political outcomes attributed to the EMS have (as we have seen immediately above) decisively shaped attitudes towards European monetary integration. By 1992 the ERM and EMU had become linked to a policy strategy of competitive deflation, a type of linkage that never affected the single market. To the extent that the functioning of the EMS and EMU policy process is shaped by the nature and outcomes of its policies, structural explanations are of limited assistance.

Conclusion

As one reviews the complexity of the calculations that actors in the EMS policy process can make, and how interdependent and dynamic that policy process is, one might be forgiven for expecting its functioning to be chaotic and random. But, though some actors have been inconsistent in attitude and approach, and the attitude and approach of others has changed, the policy process has displayed a remarkable degree of coherence. Over the EMS the British government has been generally negative, usually in a reactive manner – ignoring the system – and sometimes, as on occasion in 1978 and after 'Black Wednesday' in 1992, actively hostile. Even so, from October 1990 to September 1992, it was positive in attitude. In short, the British government has adopted a variety of positions on the EMS. The Bundesbank's position on the EMS has, by contrast, evolved: from a negative view and a reactive approach in 1978–9 to a positive view and an activist approach. In doing so, it has joined a stable cluster of powerful actors at the heart of the EMS policy process. The German federal government, the French government (notably the Trésor), the Italian government (again particularly the Treasury) and the European Commission represent an inner core of actors who consistently take an activist approach to developing the EMS and are positive about it. The ejection of the Italian lira from the ERM in 1992 shows that a government, however positive, may be cast by events into a reactive role outside this core cluster. But clearly some actors are more important than others. The critical linchpin remains the Bundesbank which has joined its perception of public interest and its corporate interests to the EMS. That identification of interests by so powerful an actor matters more than anything else to the stability and development of the EMS policy process. The lesson of the analysis in this section is that, whilst this role of the Bundesbank could well endure, it remains potentially vulnerable and fragile: contingent on changing economic conditions and policy outcomes.

When one turns to EMU, the picture of coherence is again striking. The French Trésor, the Italian Treasury and the European Commission have taken a consistently positive view and an activist approach. Their perceptions of public interest and corporate interests have been married together in support of EMU. But, once the policy process focuses on the issue of EMU, a key difference emerges. Over the EMS Germany is, or rather has become, a relatively unified actor; the bargaining relations between the German federal government and the Bundesbank have operated relatively smoothly. Though Germany is understood to be the most powerful actor in EMU, it appears divided: with the federal government positive in view, though largely reactive in approach, and the Bundesbank both reactive and negative. The negative effects on Germany's capacity to play its leadership role are more apparent than real. In reality, the German federal government has acquired the key linchpin role: between Council bargaining at the EC level and the bargaining relations between itself and the Bundesbank. And, in turn, as the main gatekeeper to the foreign exchange markets, the Bundesbank has its own linchpin role to play: a role that involves the tail wagging the dog.

Where power lies: the nature of the EMS and EMU policy process

The dynamic nature of the EMS and EMU policy process is evident once one focuses on the calculative behaviour of key actors as they reassess their positions in the light of changing losses and gains from their engagement. But (as we have argued) this dynamics is structured in a deeper sense. The leading actors – heads of government, finance ministers and their officials, central bankers and EC officials – are embedded within structural features of the policy process. This deeper structure requires examination, not least if we are to gain some insight into where power lies in European monetary integration.

Who has bargaining power?

In seeking to answer the question of where power lies it is all too easy to jump to conclusions based on particular incidents, like ERM crises, which expose a particular facet of power (the financial markets), give prominence to a particular bargaining relation (between the EC and the foreign exchange operators), and reveal in its starkest form the policy leadership role of the anchor currency (the Bundesbank). Looked at over time and across policy issues and events, however, there is no easy answer to the question. We have seen how structural power has different sources. Different structures interact, but none is reducible to another: though external to the policy process, each shapes how the policy actors interact with each other and who has the greater power in the internal bargaining relations. The chief beneficiaries have been German policy actors, above all the Bundesbank – from the anchor currency role of the D-Mark; central bankers – from the ascendancy of sound money policy ideas; and foreign exchange market operators – with their 'wall of money'. Power has a tendency to gravitate in their direction, most of all towards the Bundesbank. But, overall, the picture is of an EMU policy process that possesses a hollow core; there is no single policy-brokering centre.

The internal dynamics of the EMS and EMU policy process and the essentially hollow core in EMU derive from the fact that, though very small and exclusive in nature, its leading actors are involved in a complex network of overlapping bargains. These bargains reflect interlocking and often conflicting interests and engender different policy networks. The key bargains on which we have focused in this book are:

- between the member state governments in the framework of the EC institutions
- between the French and German governments
- between the central bank governors and the EC
- between individual EC governments and their own central banks
- between the EC monetary authorities and the foreign exchange markets.

As we saw in chapter 8, the bargain between the monetary authorities and the foreign exchange markets is central to the functioning of the EMS and EMU policy process. The dynamics of this bargaining are rooted in a series of factors that impinge on this relationship, such as market structure, economic fundamentals and the nature and outcome of EMS and EMU policies. At the core of the bargain with the foreign exchange markets have been two considerations: to steer market expectations and provide exchange-rate stability via rules of the game in order that producers and consumers can exploit fully the advantages of international specialization; and, by means of abandoning the policy instrument of exchange controls in favour of freedom of movement of capital, to give incentives to, and reward those operating in, financial markets in order to maximize the availability of credit. Freedom of capital movement offered new opportunities to buyers and sellers in financial markets, not least to governments themselves. In turn, successive speculative runs have led the EMS to revise its rules on intervention, credit and realignment as signals to the market of resolve and confidence.

At the level of interstate bargaining the Franco-German relationship has remained central: from the role of the friendship of President Giscard d'Estaing and Chancellor Schmidt in helping to launch the EMS in 1978–9, via the initiatives of 1987–8, to the intense collaboration to ward off the speculative runs on the franc in September and November 1992. Here was an inner core within a privileged policy community, but an inner core characterized by an asymmetry of monetary power between the two states. Following the moment of truth for French policy in 1983, and despite the new tensions introduced by the effects of German unification, the striking characteristic was the will and capability of the monetary authorities of both countries to subordinate national policies to the achievement of two hard currencies at the heart of the system. For France that meant the pursuit of a macro-economic strategy of competitiveness through disinflation, with high attendant costs.[32]

Another characteristic of the EMS and EMU policy process is the ever tighter binding of the national central banks into the EC framework, a binding that is symbolized by the transformation of the Committee of Central Bank Governors into the European Monetary Institute with stage two. The Delors Committee represented a tacit acceptance of the primacy of bargaining with the central bankers by coopting them into the policy process for EMU. Technical expertise was a powerful bargaining resource for the central banks; they could claim to be the central repository of knowledge about how financial markets work. Equally, the central banks needed governments to define, legitimize and offer support to the rules of the game of the system. On this basis a close interdependence of interests was established, but with sound money dominating the policy process.

Meanwhile, at the heart of the EMS and EMU policy process, German policy leadership rested on a further, largely tacit bargain between federal fiscal and foreign policies and the monetary policy of the Bundesbank. Strains in this key relationship after 1990 had increasingly serious implications for the EMS and EMU policy process. Ultimately, the health and vitality of the EMS and EMU policy process derives from the continuous realignment of these powerful interests: the federal government, in which the foreign ministry is an influential voice, stressing the importance of security considerations and of retaining Germany's external reputation as a reliable and supportive partner in Council bargaining about the EMS and EMU; and the Bundesbank emphasizing the importance of domestic price stability for the continuing

---

32. O. Blanchard and P.-A. Muet, 'Competitiveness through Disinflation: An Assessment of the French Macro-Economic Strategy', *Economic Policy* 16 (1993), p. 12.

capability of the D-Mark to act as the credible anchor of the ERM. Intra-German bargaining was clearly vital to the functioning of the EMS and EMU policy process; other bargaining relations, like the Franco-German relationship, were highly dependent on its outcomes.

But, though cast into a policy leadership role, Germany remained one of twelve systems of domestic bargaining between governments and central banks. From the perspective of Council bargaining – which formally lay at the centre of the EMS and EMU policy process – each one of these bargains was of importance. The key traditional feature of finance ministry–central bank bargaining, at least outside Germany, was its hierarchical context. Governments were sensitive to monetary policy decisions because of their perceived macro-economic and therefore political importance; hence they liked to reserve decisions on interest rates to themselves. This hierarchical character of domestic bargaining deeply affected the functioning of the EMS and EMU policy process.

Equally, the forces undermining that traditionally hierarchical bargaining promised to transform the functioning of the EMS and EMU policy process in the 1990s. The capture of national economic policy by sound money ideas in the 1980s made governments more susceptible to critiques of the politicization of monetary policy as a cause of inflation. In short, changes in the climate of economic ideas helped to strengthen the case for central bank independence, thus disrupting the hierarchical pattern of bargaining. With the Treaty on European Union the capture of economic policy by sound money had its second level of victory – at the EC level. By the end of 1993 Belgium, France and Spain had acted to grant independence to their central banks, consistent with their treaty obligations: whilst in 1992 the Treasury passed sole responsibility for interest rates to the Bank of Italy.

The character of the policy process

In the language of political science, what kind of 'governance structure' does the EMS and EMU policy process possess? *Market* and *hierarchy* are clearly influential structural characteristics: with market in ascendancy as capital liberalization takes effect, and hierarchy in some retreat as central bank independence comes on to the policy agenda. The consequences of this change in the relative weight of different structural characteristics for the functioning of the EMS and EMU policy process are profound. The prospect of more autonomy of functioning is complemented by the threat of much greater difficulties in managing relations with the foreign exchange markets.

These changes have consequences for another structural feature of the EMS and EMU policy process: the nature of the policy *networks*. Hierarchy at the national level has supported the positions of governments as they bargained with each other about the rules of the game: in the IGC, in the EC Monetary Committee and in ECOFIN and the European Council. It has served the purpose of domestic solidarity to strengthen bargaining capability. The effect was to inject a powerful dimension of *pluralism* into Council bargaining. Its functioning was characterized by an intense competition for influence.

The interesting question was how pluralism operated in Council bargaining. Did it involve intergovernmental bargaining, or was a supranational style evident? We have seen in chapter 5 how a norm of intergovernmental bargaining may have operated but that, in the EMS and EMU policy process, in the aftermath of the Single European Act, a supranational style was visible. Pluralism may have dominated the EMS and EMU policy process via Council bargaining but, harnessed to a supranational policy style of upgrading common interests, it could take on an innovative character. We have also seen that the maintenance of such a policy style was deeply affected by underlying structural developments in the EC economy. The shift from the 'up-side' to the 'down-side' of the economic cycle was paralleled by the reassertion of an intergovernmental policy style.

But it does not follow that pluralism dominated all the policy networks on which the EMS and EMU are founded. The bargaining between the central banks, organized in the Committee of Central Bank Governors, and the EC monetary authorities displayed *corporatist* tendencies. Here was a monopoly representative organization that gained privileged incorporation into the EMS and EMU policy process: not least on the basis that it had the best prospect of reconciling the financial market operators to EMU. Essentially (as we saw in chapter 8) the central banks occupied a gatekeeper role between the financial markets and the EC, a 'brokerage' role that gave them institutionalized influence. They brought not only their interests to bear on the formulation and operation of policy but also (as chapter 6 noted) a central banking culture in which norms of solidarity were historically longer developed than those between governments. This corporatist network within the EMS and EMU policy process facilitated its relatively smooth functioning. Again, the dynamics of corporatism were affected by structural changes in the economic cycle and their effects in national economies. But they were not wholly dependent on this single factor.

Conclusions: a hollow core?

An analysis of the EMS and EMU policy process in terms of interlocking bargains and overlapping and contrasting policy networks has important implications for our conclusions about where power lies. The economic literature on the EMS harbours a contentious debate about whether the EMS is essentially an enlarged 'D-Mark-zone', characterized by German dominance. In the words of Gros and Thygesen: 'The EMS has thus become a hierarchic and asymmetric system'.[33] Certainly, the assertion of Giavazzi and Giovannini that 'Germany is the centre country and runs monetary policy for the whole system' found wide acceptance.[34] The key evidence relates to the important interface between the EMS and the foreign exchange markets. Here much evidence points to Germany's special position as policy-broker in the management of

33. D. Gros and N. Thygesen, *The EMS: Achievements, Current Issues and Directions for the Future*, CEPS Paper no. 35 (Brussels: Centre for European Policy Studies, 1988), p. 62.
34. F. Giavazzi and A. Giovannini, 'Models of the EMS: Is Europe a Greater Deutschmark Area?', in R. Bryant and R. Portes (eds) *Global Macroeconomics* (New York: St Martin's Press, 1987), p. 237. For a radical critique of the German dominance thesis see M. Fratianni and J. von Hagen, 'Asymmetries and Realignments in the EMS', in P. De Grauwe and L. Papademos (eds) *The European Monetary System in the 1990s* (London: Longman, 1990), pp. 86–111.

the EMS, promoting compromise or imposing settlements: notably, *de facto* German responsibility for setting the US dollar policy of the EC, in the process giving primacy to its own interests; asymmetry in foreign exchange market interventions, where Bundesbank interventions in the markets for EMS currencies are not only small compared to other EC central banks but also small relative to its interventions in the US dollar market; and asymmetry in the greater capacity of the Bundesbank to sterilize the impact of interventions through domestic open market operations, thus more effectively reducing the impact of the EMS in German monetary policy. This asymmetry in the burdens of monetary adjustment suggests German policy leadership in the EMS; that, at least with respect to the ERM, the EC's policy process has a solid core in the form of the central position of the Bundesbank.

But the evidence does not support the idea of German dominance in the sense of a will and capability to impose settlements. Other central banks and finance ministries are not simply forced to adjust passively to the policy actions and views of the Bundesbank. In the case of money supply and interest rate policies there is more evidence of an interactive relationship, with countries – including the Bundesbank – taking account of each other's behaviour and what is happening in the rest of the system.[35] Perhaps even more strikingly, between 1990 and 1993 the views of the Bundesbank on the need for realignment within the ERM were ignored. It took the crises of 1992 and 1993 to force realignments. Possession of structural power in some of its forms, and consequent capacity for policy leadership, do not amount to dominance of the policy process or even to an effective role in promoting compromise within the ERM.

We are reminded that central to the management of the EMS is the informal rule that the D-Mark is the anchor currency. This rule alone, never mind pressure from the Bonn government to take a cooperative line, invests the Bundesbank with a structural power that translates into *de facto* managerial responsibility within the ERM and permeates the bargaining relations in which it is involved and gives them added significance within the policy process. The result appears to be a special leadership role within the EMS. But the performance of that role is hedged by two restrictions: that its effective and responsible exercise requires some account to be taken of the powerful interests and sensibilities of other actors; and that the Bundesbank cannot control all the bargaining relations that comprise the EMS and EMU policy process. Looked at more closely, the Bundesbank's leadership and policy-brokering role in some dimensions of ERM management (like US dollar policy) does not translate to all dimensions (like realignments), let alone to the EMU policy process as a whole. In the case of realignments within the ERM the hollow core is most visibly revealed.

The limitation of economic views on the location of power in the EMS and EMU is their failure to note that the policy process rests on a set of interlocking bargains. Power in one, the bargaining relationship with foreign exchange markets, can undoubtedly spill over into leverage in other bargaining relationships, like that between central banks and the EC institutions – as this book has illustrated. But Council bargaining has its own dynamics, as has the Franco-German relationship,

---

35. This evidence is usefully summarized in D. Gros and N. Thygesen, *European Monetary Integration* (London: Longman, 1992), pp. 136–50.

imparting a broader interactive character to the policy process. In these bargaining relations historical and cultural factors are at work, inhibiting the over-assertive demonstration of German national interests and favouring the pursuit of French and other interests. Also, the norm of solidarity within the Committee of Central Bank Governors means that the full potential power of the Bundesbank, based on its market power, is not asserted. Here its leadership is intellectual and framed within a norm of reciprocity. It is facilitated by a disposition of national central bankers to admire a culture of economic stability and to imitate its characteristics. Overall, the cumulative effect of the pluralist and corporatist bargaining within the EMS and EMU policy process is to diffuse power, and to underline the essential uncontrollability of policy by any one actor, even those with structural power. Bargaining relations and rules of the game matter; economists tend to neglect both bargaining and institutions as policy phenomena.

It is not the purpose of this book to compare the EMS and EMU policy process with other policy processes at the EC level. What is clear is that pluralism is likely to be a general characteristic. The more interesting question is how it combines with other structural characteristics at the sectoral level. An examination of EC telecommunications policies reveals, for instance, a combination of pluralist with clientelist structures, with clientelism reflecting the efforts of governments and the EC Commission to promote specific producers.[36] What appears striking about the EMS and EMU policy process is its corporatism and interface with the foreign exchange markets. It is the specific combination of different structural features that gives the sector its *sui generis* character.

In summary, the EMS and EMU policy process does have discernible structural characteristics: of the market, hierarchy and of pluralist and corporatist networks. These characteristics reflect the weight of different organized interests: of the operators in foreign exchange markets, of governments and of central bankers. Among these elements corporatism has proved to be of growing importance. The element of corporatism was very much contingent on the representational monopoly of the central banks in relation to the financial markets, their associated technical expertise (not least in steering the markets), and their tradition of solidarity. As far as governments and the EC institutions were concerned, the crucial means of achieving the support that was needed to give momentum to the EMS and EMU policy process was cooption of the central bank governors. As EMU came on to the agenda and central bank independence took root in more countries, so the weight of corporatism as a structural characteristic of the policy process grew: with long-term political consequences for the future of European integration in general. Internally, at least, the policy process was better geared to surmount the problems of 'elusive' union: but at what cost in terms of wider public support for union?

To conclude, there is little evidence that a single actor – whether the Commission, ECOFIN or the Bundesbank – occupies the central policy-brokering role within the EMU policy process in any continuous sense, capable in a more or less autonomous

---

36. On the EC telecommunications and broadcasting policy sectors see K. Dyson and P. Humphreys (eds) *The Political Economy of Communications: International and European Dimensions* (London: Routledge, 1990).

way of promoting compromise or imposing settlements. In this sense, the EMU policy process has a 'hollow core'.[37] This conclusion may seem reassuring to those who distrust Brussels bureaucrats or German central bankers. But, on the negative side, the picture emerges of a policy process at the heart of European integration that is beset by enduring uncertainty and complex turbulence, disposed to pursue a scale of policy steps that fails to match the challenges, fiscal, monetary and political, that confront it. The poor management of the ERM crises of 1992 and 1993 was testimony to the implications of the hollow core in the policy process: and stage two of EMU, with its new European Monetary Institute and broad guidelines for economic policies as the basis for multilateral surveillance by ECOFIN, seemed scarcely well-designed to adequately fill this gap.

37. J. Heinz, E. Laumann, R. Nelson and R. Salisbury, *The Hollow Core: Private Interests in National Policy Making* (Cambridge, Mass.: Harvard University Press, 1993).

Chapter 10

ELUSIVE UNION
Problems and prospects

The higher one ascends, the poorer the visibility becomes.

(R.S. Thomas)

The drunkenness of things being various.

(Louis MacNeice)

When the history of European integration comes to be written from the perspective of the twenty-first century, the Treaty on European Union of 1993 will stand as a milestone. It will do so because of the remarkable way in which it 'constitutionalized' EMU and set out the path to a supranational policy process in a sector that had always been conceived of as at the heart of state sovereignty. Just how important a milestone it will be can be better seen from some future vantage point, when historians will be able to consider what in practice happened to this extraordinary project.

In chapter 9 we argued that the relaunch of EMU challenges existing explanatory theories and finds them individually and collectively wanting. The solution has not been to erect a new theory but to advocate an approach that is at once more encompassing and yet rigorous in specifying the key relationships that comprise and underpin the EMS and EMU policy process. This chapter addresses the problems and prospects for EMU in the 1990s. The aim is not to predict the future. It is to shed light on the EMS and EMU policy process by identifying the key problems that it faces and their implications for the policy process; and to tentatively sketch the main scenarios for its development.

The central question is whether the EMS and EMU policy process is confronting the key forces at work in the EC economy, and whether it is robust enough to affect how these forces operate. We are returning to the problem that we identified at the beginning of this book: is the enforcement mechanism for putting EMU into practice sufficiently strong and adjustable to deal with the main problems that the policy process is likely to face? Well before the Treaty on European Union was ratified, as early as autumn 1992, the EMS and EMU was an embattled, defensive policy process in an increasingly hostile world: very different in character from the self-confident, activist policy process of 1988–91. This transition raised questions not only about the EC's capacity to implement the treaty but also about the adequacy of the treaty as the basis for EMU.

Before we ask in more detail what has changed, it is worth reminding ourselves that the focus on the dynamics of change in this volume has brought out the underlying fragility of the EMS and EMU policy process and its essentially hollow core. This fragility has several sources:

1   a two-level policy process that, in the absence of political union, continues to mean that the EC lacks a robust institutional structure capable of providing an independent policy leadership on EMU
2   the vulnerability of policies, notably the ERM, to decline of the leadership role by the anchor of the system, Germany
3   the problem of the compatibility between the domestic political interests of the leader (Germany) and the calculation of the balance of costs and benefits of cooperation on the part of other countries with weaker currencies
4   the prospect of conflict between the goals of internal and external stability
5   the volatility of foreign exchange markets that operate according to their own rules.

The problems of the EMS and EMU in the 1990s

The EMS and EMU policy process was always likely to be sensitive to changes in the initial conditions that gave rise to it, for in a crucial sense it remains dependent on those initial conditions. These initial conditions refer to specific events and emerging forces that shaped the early character of the policy process, even if they are lost in the memories of the policy actors. They were the subject of chapters 4 and 5. But, as a historical process, the EMS and EMU are also time-dependent: the passage of time brings new events and forces, colluding either to reinforce the direction of change in the policy process or to establish, perhaps with a time lag, new trends and a new direction, whether a 'renationalization' of policies or a new path of evolution within the framework of the treaty.

   Initially, eight conditions influenced the development of the EMS and EMU policy process from 1987 onwards: some structural, others relating to the bargaining relations internal to the policy process. They were

1   a politically insulated policy process, in which scope was given for technical expertise to shape policy development, notably in the forms of the EC central bankers and the European Commission
2   the capacity of Franco-German relations to provide initiative and momentum on the EMS and EMU and a uniquely close inner channel of cooperation within the policy process
3   the up-side of the economic cycle, which engendered optimism, reduced the potential for policy conflicts and made a grand initiative appear sustainable (between 1984 and 1990 the EC's annual growth of GDP was 2.5 per cent or more)
4   substantial progress in achieving 'nominal' economic convergence
5   an ideological consensus that integrated the policy process around sound money policy ideas
6   a dominant economy with an unsullied reputation for economic and monetary virtue, in the shape of *Modell Deutschland*
7   a capacity of the monetary authorities to steer foreign exchange markets, based on sustaining the confidence of market operators that currency rates and economic fundamentals were consistent or could and would be made consistent by resolute action

8   the external dimension of stability in world currency relationships, notably in the US dollar/D-Mark and US dollar/yen rates.

To varying degrees, new events and forces have upset these initial conditions, eroding the foundations of the policy process and hedging it with uncertainty and doubt. To what extent have the eight favourable conditions given way to problems; and with what implications for EMU?

The problems of the politics of the policy process

In three senses the autonomy of the EMS and EMU policy process has been undermined since 1990: a legitimacy crisis, 'knock-on' effects from problems in other policy sectors, and the assertion of national agendas.

Legitimacy crisis

In the period 1987–91 the EMS and EMU policy process was able to gain an internal momentum based on the will and capability of EC political leaders to insulate it from political 'interference'. This insulation was possible because of the sense of solidarity that had been engendered by the successful process of implementing the single market programme; the consequent prestige of the Commission as policy leader; progress in attaining nominal economic convergence; the respect for the technical expertise of the central banks and for their role in managing the EMS; a convergence of economic policies around sound money ideas; and the climate of economic expansion. Together, these factors provided well-defined channels within which EMU could develop.

There were two underlying problems with the spirit of technocratic rationalism that came to dominate the policy process. In the first place, some of these conditions for insulating the policy process from politics were not sustainable. Sound money policy ideas and respect for the expertise of central banks were. But the momentum imparted by the single market was, post-1992, qualified by the policy discords unleashed by mounting economic recession. The European Commission's role as an orchestrator of agreement around new initiatives proved more difficult to play. More fundamentally, new political events and forces revealed the dangers of gambling on a technocratic approach. Money is, after all (as we emphasized in chapter 1), more than just a technical arrangement to promote economic efficiency. The EMU project constituted a huge political gamble on public perception of the technical superiority of a single currency. The dangers of such a gamble became evident in the Danish referendum of June 1992 and, most potently, in consistent opinion poll evidence that German citizens rejected a single currency by a large majority. This evidence underscored the continuing critiques from the Bundesbank and the high risk for the federal coalition parties from extreme right-wing parties gaining profile and electoral gains by presenting themselves as 'parties of the D-Mark'. In the German case it was difficult to persuade public opinion that the single currency could be technically superior to the D-Mark. More generally, there was the problem that money had cultural significance. It was an object of pride and identity, based not simply on its performance but also on historic associations and identities.

The most fundamental problem was that the EMS and EMU policy process had operated with an inadequate and misleading conception of the politics of EMU. EMU would be technically superior, at least outside Germany, in that it would 'depoliticize' the conduct of monetary policy. In an important sense depoliticization as the dominant theme on the policy agenda could be justified: namely, that democratic politicians, in the search to maximize short-term electoral advantage and to buy off the support of powerful groups, are all too disposed to debauch the currency. Inflation can be seen as a fraud on the body politic, a form of taxation by stealth that should be banned by taking monetary policy decisions (à la Bundesbank) out of the reach of partisan politics. In this sense depoliticization is about a self-imposed constraint on democratic politics to eliminate the moral hazards that can flow from 'low', competitive interest, politics.

But the grave error was to fail to recognize that, even with a depoliticized ESCB, monetary policy – and the currency in which it deals – remains in a more fundamental sense political. The activities of the ESCB in an EMU remain political in the 'high politics' sense that they rest upon the support of an EC political order that is able to coordinate monetary policy with fiscal and other policies and to mobilize consent: in effect, an EC government accountable to a European Parliament and, through that, to the people. In the absence of a European political order that promotes an affective identification with a single currency, by means of a range of common political symbols and channels for popular participation and influence, a depoliticized EC monetary policy lacks essential legitimacy.

The strategy of using EMU as a device to depoliticize monetary policy was incomplete: at best politically naive, at worst disingenuous. As the Bundesbank repeatedly argued, albeit for reasons of corporate self-interest as much as public interest, EMU and political union could not and should not be separated. The core political failure of the EMS and EMU policy process was that 'high' politics and 'low' politics did not march in tandem. The fault did not lie primarily with the central bankers, finance ministers and economists that populated the policy process. They could be expected to promote their professional interest in their autonomy. It lay with EC political leaders who, in providing insulation for the policy process, failed to put in place the political foundations for an effective EMU. Paradoxically, without those broader foundations, the depoliticized ESCB was likely to find itself dangerously politically exposed.

The prospect of a legitimacy crisis in the EC derived from a central paradox of the two-level policy process: that the integration of administrative and political elites in EC policy had not been matched by a process of relating this elite-driven process to democratic habits. Policy flowed increasingly in EC channels, but democracy continued to flow in national channels. New policy habits were not complemented by the evolution of new democratic habits. There was, in short, a failure of political reform; and, in its absence, minimal public understanding of the EC's purposes and procedures. The problems of ratification of the Treaty on European Union revealed this problem as the fundamental 'fault line' in the integration process. Suddenly each was in danger of doing serious damage to the other: policy integration to democratic habits, and democratic habits to policy integration.

But the political failure was also of another order. EMU represented a supranational leap that had to be negotiated and ratified through national political systems. At this level there was a demonstrable failure of political leadership. All too few leaders had the courage to justify EMU as an indispensable response to the diminishing power of individual EC states to deal with global economic challenges.

Knock-on effects from problems in other policy sectors

The EMS and EMU became bound up in a critical conjunction of events that raised new questions about the will and capability of member state governments to sustain the broad momentum to union. Ultimately, EMU could not isolate itself from that broader momentum, or rather in this case from a loss of general momentum. The Gulf War of 1990 did not show the EC at its best in defining a distinctive role for itself in international crisis management; the protracted and fast-changing Yugoslav crisis after December 1990 cast doubts on the EC's capacity to develop an effective foreign and security policy consistent with the ambitions of the Treaty on European Union; whilst the speed of disintegration of the former Soviet Union, and the acute problems of adjustment in the east central European states of Hungary, Poland and the Czech and Slovak republics, raised further questions not only about foreign and security policy but also about the adequacy of the economic response of the EC, notably in terms of opening its markets. Add to these unfolding events the turmoil of the ERM in autumn 1992 and summer 1993 and the picture emerges of an EC that had fallen victim to policy inertia. EMU was troubled not only by its own internal problems but also by increasing cross-infection from other policy sectors; in other words, its mounting difficulties of policy leadership were caught up in wider problems.

In 1993 EC priorities shifted to an expeditious approach to enlargement: initially to embrace applicants from EFTA (European Free Trade Area), notably Austria, Finland, Norway and Sweden; and then the east central European states. The implications of this agenda change, itself unleashed by the 'post-Cold-War' Europe ushered in by the breach of the Berlin Wall on 9 November 1989, were potentially enormous for EMU. They were also paradoxical. On the one hand, accession of the EFTA states promised to add strong economies to the EC, economies that were better able to fulfil the convergence criteria than many existing members. Indeed, an argument for their speedy entry was that the capacity to build a substantial coalition to move ahead with EMU was improved.

On the other hand, too fast a move to EMU could be seen as incompatible with the need to speed integration of the east central European states into the EC economy. The large-scale circulation of D-Marks there suggests, at least to influential members of the Bundesbank, that priority should be given to extending and improving the EMS in its present Germany-oriented form: and, if there must be union, then by making the D-Mark the single European currency, with the Bundesbank becoming the European central bank.[1] The political controversy that such a proposal would awaken if put formally on the agenda, notably with the French government, indicates the new

1. On this problem, seen from a Bundesbank perspective, see W. Nölling, *Abschied von der D-Mark* (Hamburg: W. Nölling, 1992). On the idea of the Bundesbank as the EC central bank and the D-Mark as the single currency, see the former Bundesbank director responsible for international affairs in L. Gieske, 'Institutionelle Aspekte einer Europäischen Wirtschafts- und Währungsunion' (Frankfurt: Deutsche Bundesbank, 1990).

difficulties about EMU that are thrown up by enlargement eastwards. In that altered context fundamental questions arise about the political centre of gravity of the EMU policy process. The Treaty on European Union was premised on the notion that the political centre of gravity would not change, other than to wrest power from Germany. But, with the new saliency to east central Europe and beyond after the events of 1989, German policy actors must naturally reconsider the implications for the EMS and EMU of the EC's interest (and its own) in integrating these states into the EC economy. The result is new complications and problems for the policy process.

Assertion of national agendas

It became clear that the EMS and EMU policy process was not being viewed simply in its own terms by the key policy actors involved; they were not prepared just to pursue its own logic and dynamics. Consistent with the nature of the two-level policy process, they looked at the EMS and EMU in terms of their own agendas. For French policy actors that was to defend the *franc fort* policy and to gain influence and preferably control over German interest rates: for German policy actors it was to manage German unification and to protect the stability and credibility of the D-Mark. In the case of British policy actors the increasingly pressing domestic agenda of getting out of recession came into sharp conflict with the requirements of ERM membership in the form of a veritable crisis of the policy process. This dimension of national interest gave an in-built potential for centrifugal pressure in the EMS and EMU policy process, a potential that was manifested in the technically poor management of the autumn 1992 ERM crisis, particularly in the informal ECOFIN at Bath.

In fact, once the ERM crisis broke, it became clear that the problem of the policy process had been hidden by the agenda of the previous five years. The EMS policy process had revealed itself at its most effective when key actors had shown how they could use leverage to move the integration process forward (as chapter 5 documented). But, when faced with the slippery slope from mounting doubts to turmoil in the foreign exchange markets, the policy process had shown itself to be technically very poor at pre-emptive realignments. The technical skill was demonstrated to lie in the Bundesbank, which had for long been arguing for the engineering of a D-Mark revaluation in the ERM and that the British pound was overvalued. In their reports on the ERM crisis the EC Monetary Committee and the Committee of Central Bank Governors were taking up positions long after they would have been useful. The nostrums of more flexible exchange rates and tighter surveillance of them were undoubtedly sensible in principle. But they raised the question of why they had not been put into effect earlier. There were two answers: the technical committees had been so preoccupied with the mechanism of the hard ERM and transition to EMU that they had lost sight of the underlying problems (a case of a self-reinforcing institutional mechanism); more seriously, national definitions of interest continued to inhibit the kind of full and frank communication and effective surveillance for which they called.

The ERM crises of 1992 and 1993 had demonstrated that, with the approaches of governments so locked into domestic agendas and problems, the policy process could easily degenerate into mutual recriminations. After a prolonged period of growing solidarity in ECOFIN, the revelation of the destructive potential of national interest came as something of a cathartic shock. In the face of powerful national interests, the reassertion of solidarity was at least a remarkable monument to the effects of repeated bargains at the EC level on the values, attitudes and concerns of the actors in the process (as chapter 6 demonstrated).

New problems in Franco-German bargaining relations?

Described as bound by 'cords of steel', Franco-German bargaining relations have been seen as the indispensable bedrock of the EC's stability and its capacity to seize and retain initiative. As we saw in chapters 4 and 5, this observation has been confirmed by the launch of the EMS and the relaunch of EMU, as well as by the public stress on the special close cooperation between the two central banks during the currency crises of autumn 1992 and summer 1993. In November 1993 the Franco-German Economic Council sought to inject more momentum into EMU by specially coordinating their convergence programmes to prepare for EMU. But, regularly in the history of the EC, domestic political problems have spilled over to infect Franco-German relations: in monetary integration most notably in 1968–9, 1987 and 1993. It is a mark of the significance that both sides attach to the relationship that there is such sensitivity and nervousness about the risks of breakdown.

In fact, tensions and conflicts in Franco-German relations have been a feature in the background to the launch of new initiatives: as after 1968–9 (the Hague summit of 1970), 1987 (the EMU initiative) and after the disagreement about German unification (the joint declaration on European political union of Kohl and Mitterrand before the Dublin summit of 1990). It was notable, for instance, that the dispute about German unification did not threaten to derail the negotiations on EMU but rather intensified them.

But the big question for the 1990s was whether the long-term effects of German unification would corrode 'the cords of steel'. The traditional nature of the Franco-German bargaining relation had been formed by a strange, historically conditioned brew of interests. On the one hand, there was a widespread French fear of German power and a perceived national interest in controlling that power; on the other, a German preference for a passive role and a perceived national interest in being a good and reliable European neighbour. These traditional perceptions of interest were readily apparent in the EMS and EMU policy process. French fear of Germany, conditioned by memories of 1871, 1914–18 and 1940, promised to endure. According to a survey after the French referendum on the Maastricht Treaty in September 1992, 21 per cent of Yes voters and 40 per cent of No voters said that fear of Germany's domination of Europe had determined their voting stance. It certainly played a large part in both the Yes and No campaigns. In electoral and party political terms assertion of French national interests was most strident when the French Gaullist party was in the ascendant, as in 1987 and 1993. But the degree of allergy to events and developments in Germany was in fact just as manifest with a Socialist-led government in 1989 over German unification.

The prospect for a more deep-seated change in this bargaining relationship over the EMS and EMU arose from the compound effects of German unification. On the one hand, the French policy elites watched anxiously as their German counterparts became more inwardly obsessed with domestic problems consequent on unification. At the same time they came to expect a more assertive demonstration of German national interests in the wake of becoming a fully sovereign state in 1990, and even more so once the problems of unification had been overcome and Germany had re-emerged as an even more dominant economy over Europe. The result was not only heightened nervousness in Paris but also a sense that France was confronted with a closing 'window of opportunity' to lock Germany, not least via EMU, into Europe before its reinforced economic strength would make it too powerful and confident a bargaining partner. The anti-EMU rhetoric of the German Republican Party, the rejection of a federal Europe by the Bavarian prime minister and party ally of Kohl in 1993, and the imminence of 'super election' year in Germany in 1994, conspired to raise French fears. This nervousness within the French policy elites was compounded by mounting domestic criticism of the *franc fort* policy in the face of a strait-jacket of high real interest rates and deepening recession, both of which could be attributed to German policy errors. The plain fact was that the hard ERM and EMU were imposing high output and job costs on France but not on Germany. For many this was the economic fundamental that mattered most.

A new French assertiveness in 1993 followed the election of a Gaullist-dominated government. Effectively exploiting the stronger nominal economic fundamentals of France than Germany, interest rates were cut below the German level, followed by the attempt to press the German Finance Minister and Bundesbank president to attend a meeting of the Franco-German Economic Council for talks on 'concerted interest rate cuts'. The French pressure reflected nervousness about the failure of the French economy to respond to eight interest rate cuts between the March elections and the end of June. It also displayed a double lack of sophistication: in revealing to the foreign exchange markets French nervousness about the compatibility of domestic policy requirements to tackle recession and the requirements of the ERM (leading to the weakening of the franc); and in directly challenging the independence of the Bundesbank. Unwilling to be a co-conspirator, Theo Waigel cancelled the meeting.

Probably the most significant change in 1993 was in the context of the bargaining relations between the two countries. There appeared to be a shift in the relative strength of the French and German bargaining positions. The French economy's stronger fundamentals with respect to inflation, the current account and the budget deficit helped to legitimize a greater French assertiveness. But in another sense the fundamentals of the French economy were not strong: reflected in the contrast between persistently higher levels of unemployment and mounting lost output, on the one hand, and interest rates that could still not escape from the heavy shadow of the Bundesbank, on the other. Also, the temporary weakening of the D-Mark within the ERM could be seen as not so much reflecting a decisive shift of monetary power in favour of France but as a normal process of the D-Mark easing in the ERM as the US dollar strengthened. A more accurate characterization of the Franco-German bargaining relationship was in terms of a balance of weakness. Neither economy was in good shape. In any case, relative weakening was unlikely to make the Bundesbank any more pliable, as the ERM crisis of July 1993 demonstrated. Its commitment to preserving a stable D-Mark meant that it would continue to pursue domestic disinflation with rigour. The EMS and EMU policy process was undergoing a slow motion clash between an irresistible force – the assertion of French national interests – and an immovable object – the Bundesbank's commitment to a stable D-Mark, a clash fuelled by the long-drawn-out consequences of German unification. When that clash came to a head in the special ECOFIN meeting of August 1993 in the context of the unmanageable assault on the French franc, the message that policy leadership in the monetary sphere rested with Germany was unmistakable. German strength determined the reform of the ERM; and it was clear that German interests – fortified by the conditions on 'opt-in' and 'opt-out' articulated by the Federal Constitutional Court – would determine the process of EMU.

Again the condition of the Franco-German bargaining relationship over the EMS and EMU could not be isolated from other issues and events affecting other relations between the two countries. In late 1989 and early 1990 one big and difficult issue had dominated the agenda: French hostility to German unification. By 1993 the problem was different: that conflicts had become so numerous, making them harder to manage. The conflicts ranged over monetary policy, the Uruguay round of trade talks under the General Agreement on Tariffs and Trade (GATT), Bosnia, telecommunications, waste recycling and bananas. Over GATT (especially the proposed farm trade reform) and bananas (the latter having a higher per capita consumption in Germany than anywhere else in the world) French preference for trade protectionism offended German policy makers; over telecommunications German official arguments that its trade treaty of 1954 with the United States prevented it implementing EC trade sanctions against American companies irritated their French counterparts. The impression was of Franco-German bargaining relations in a state of general stress, with real differences of philosophy characterizing trade policy.

But the big question was whether mounting stress would be capable, or would be allowed, to affect the 'high' politics of the Franco-German bargaining relations. Stresses and strains of this type are not new in the history of the EC. The technique of dealing with them has been to identify them as matters of 'low' politics and to keep them separate from 'high' politics. By generational background and ideology the political leadership under Kohl, Mitterrand and Balladur remained staunchly committed to European union and Franco-German relations as its core. As long as such a leadership remained in place, the stresses of low politics would not be allowed to infect the high politics of the bargaining relationship. And yet there was always the possibility of the straw that breaks the camel's back: of the one conflict too many, perhaps in itself not important but, piled on others, tipping the balance of judgement.

The problems of the down-side of the economic cycle and of structural crisis

Far more immediately serious for the EMS and EMU policy process was the deteriorating condition of the EC economies in the 1990s and the implications for EC and national policies. Policies are judged by the outcomes that are attributed to them. In the case of the EMS and EMU lost output and lost employment have been associated with the macro-economic policy strategies that they have spawned: competitive disinflation as an instrument under the hard ERM to enhance economic

341

competitiveness, and tough convergence criteria (notably on excessive deficits) as a precondition of EMU. Implementation of these EC-based policies would have been difficult enough in a context of economic expansion, the context within which EMU had been devised. But, with the 1990s, the EMS and EMU policy process had to deal with three deep-seated challenges:

1 the 'shock' of German unification, which unleashed inflationary pressures via soaring budget deficits and pressure for wage parity between east and west – with consequent tough restrictive monetary policy action by the Bundesbank
2 the pressure from east European economies seeking open access to the EC market for their products like food, textiles, chemicals, coal, steel and basic consumer goods and offering often skilled and well-educated labour forces whose wages were less than one-tenth of those in the heartlands of the EC
3 the relatively poor performance of the EC economy on the global stage, with falling share of international export markets for many manufactured goods, principally more sophisticated products; a failure to create jobs on the scale of the American and Japanese economies; and a rising and apparently intractable problem of long-term unemployment.

These ingredients combined to create a potent brew of cyclical 'down-turn' with structural crisis.

In an important respect, neither cyclical down-turn nor structural crisis was new. By definition, cyclical down-turns were recurrent, though differing in duration and intensity; and the idea of structural crisis formed the basis of the debate earlier in the 1980s about 'Euro-sclerosis', predating the wave of optimism associated with the single market programme.[2] What was distinctive was the combination of events and factors that underpinned the new down-turn and the nature of the debate about structural crisis in the 1990s.

Cyclical down-turn
The EC reached the top of an economic cycle in mid-1990. Initially, German unification served as a counterweight to the down-turn, as it unleashed a rapid expansion of the German market. But, by 1992, the Bundesbank's tough corrective action served to deepen recessionary forces: with negative growth forecast for the EC economy in 1993. The effects on the capacity of member state governments to meet the convergence criteria were dramatic. With falling tax revenues and accelerating public expenditure in recession, budget deficits soared. By 1993 only Luxembourg could meet all the convergence criteria. Germany, the anchor of the EMS, looked highly unlikely to qualify in 1996 or possibly beyond. More immediately, as recession ravaged output and employment, doubts arose – led by the foreign exchange markets – about the will and capability of some governments to square domestic economic and political pressures with the policy requirements of the ERM: a resolve that was tested in September 1992 and beyond. No factor was more potent in putting the EMS and

2. The term 'Euro-sclerosis' was first used by the German economist Herbert Giersch to refer to labour market rigidities and the prevalence of regulatory and tax barriers to competitiveness in EC industries.

EMU policy process on the defensive: no longer focused on planning the route to EMU but on crisis management.

Structural crisis

The combination of global competition with the end of the Cold War underlined the scale of the structural change in international competitiveness with which the EC had to deal. The indicators were clear: the EC's share of world trade had slipped from 21 per cent in 1981 to 16 per cent in 1991; an EC trade deficit of $90 billion with the rest of the world in 1992, roughly three times its 1985–90 average; a poor rate of job-creation (8.8 million new jobs in the EC between 1970 and 1990 compared with 20 million and 11 million respectively in the United States and Japan); only 60 per cent of the EC population of working age had a job in 1991, compared to 70 per cent in the United States and 75 per cent in Japan; and unemployment was perniciously higher than in the United States and Japan and increasing from one economic cycle to the next (with, in 1991, 45 per cent of unemployed people being long-term unemployed).

The focus of a mounting critique from industry and commerce was on high unit labour costs in manufacturing compared to the United States, the new industrial economies of south-east Asia and now eastern Europe. Two factors were seen as contributing to these high costs: the non-wage component of labour costs, which averages 24 per cent of total labour costs in the EC, compared to 20 per cent in the United States and 13 per cent in Japan; and rigidity in labour markets, in for instance labour mobility, pay determination and employment and working conditions. Their message of agenda-change – of cutting the social costs borne by businesses and of making labour markets more flexible – was difficult for the EMS and EMU policy process to resist. Without structural measures to promote recovery the EMS would remain locked in crisis management and diminishing credibility and EMU emptied of meaning; recovery depended on giving new confidence to the business sector.

Equally serious was the evidence of an unwillingness to embrace industrial restructuring provided by restrictive EC trade policies and industrial subsidies. Protective barriers surrounded such sectors as motor vehicles, consumer electronics and office machinery; the inward-looking protective bias of the trade agreements with central and east European states, notably for 'sensitive' products like steel and chemicals, subverted their role in stimulating economic activity in this region; whilst a rising proportion of EC GDP was devoted to industrial subsidies, causing significant income loss to EC consumers. Over the previous 30 years the EC's member states had succeeded in stimulating their growth rates to an unprecedented degree by increasing intra-EC trade: with a succession of measures from the creation of the customs union to the single European market. As this process of 'internal' stimulation reached its limits, the EC needed to look outwards to develop its trade with other world regions as the source of future stimulus to growth. In order to revive growth the EC needed to prepare a new trade policy agenda, designed to reverse the decline in export market shares of leading EC economies.

But, whereas labour market reforms, reforms of the welfare state to cut the social costs of businesses, cuts in industrial subsidies and less restrictive trade policies required action beyond the confines of the EMS and EMU policy process, and in this respect the fate of the EMS and EMU was outside the hands of its key policy actors, one crisis fell firmly into its lap: the public deficit crisis. It became clear that the public deficit crisis was in part a cyclical crisis, attributable to the effects of the recession on public finances, but to a much greater extent a structural one. In other words, it would not simply melt away with recovery.

By 1993 the public deficit crisis had come to the forefront of the agenda in the policy process. Two factors made it central: first, the need to put the Maastricht timetable back on track in the context of the shock of the speed of the deterioration in public finances; and second, the recognition in the policy process, notably by the EC central banks, that real interest rates had risen in the 1980s, that their reduction was crucial to sustained recovery and that very high and now growing levels of government borrowing were a crucial factor in contributing to the long-term upward march in real interest rates. Priority to a reduction of interest rates not only stemmed from the desire to stimulate private-sector investment (which had shown a worrying drop), but also would reduce the huge budgetary burden of interest-rate payments.

In tackling the deficit crisis the EC member states faced acute constraints. The scope to raise taxes appeared very limited in a highly competitive international market-place of mobile capital. Accordingly, tax increases were likely to fall on immobile or less mobile factors of production like labour and property. But here again there was the constraint that taxes on factors like labour still raise production costs. On the reverse side of the account public expenditure was being swollen by the effects of high unemployment (which itself was far from just cyclical) and of the demographic trend towards an ageing population. Faced with these constraints in the 1980s, EC governments had allowed fiscal problems to accumulate. They had been prepared, quite rightly, to allow the automatic budgetary stabilizers to work during recession, so that budget deficits rose. But, with recovery, they failed to act to pay off the debt taken on during the recession. Taxes rates were lowered, and public spending allowed to increase. The result was a secular trend to rising government debt. In short, even without the convergence criteria, the EMS and EMU policy process was focused on the need for a prolonged period of budgetary retrenchment to bring public debt ratios under control and break the long upward march in real interest rates.

In this respect at least there was an important consistency between the Maastricht Treaty's stipulations on nominal convergence and what the EMS and EMU policy makers would have chosen to do in any case. But the key question was whether EC governments, individually and collectively, had the will and capability to master the deficit crisis. Ideologically, from both Christian Democratic parties and Social Democratic parties there was an in-built hostility to radical reforms of the welfare state; politically, there were fears about social unrest and the potential for extremist parties to exploit that unrest, with consequent instability. Few who embraced the move to EMU in 1987–91 can have gleaned what the full implications were likely to be, and the enormity of the scale of the problems of domestic political adjustment that would follow.

Problems of convergence

As we have seen in previous chapters, problems of convergence have been at the heart of the debate about European monetary integration and union from the very outset, in the Werner Report and earlier. On the one hand, there were the advocates of the monetarist approach, who argued that monetary integration would drive forward economic convergence; on the other, those who belonged to the economist approach and stressed a slow process of economic convergence as the basis for EMU. The history of European monetary integration and union is a story of repeated attempts to find compromises between these two views.

Whatever one's views on the merits of these two approaches, the attainment of convergence has remained central to the functioning of two bargaining relationships: between the EC and the central banks, and between the EC monetary authorities and the foreign exchange markets. The EC central banks and the foreign exchange market operators have seen nominal convergence as decisive to the exchange-rate stability of the EMS and to the capacity of member states to make the necessary adjustments to belong to an EMU. Of particular importance to them were inflation rates, long-term interest rates, budget deficits and public debt, and indicators of cumulative competitiveness changes as illustration of strain within the EMS. The two key questions were how to define the convergence criteria and how restrictively to do so. In the Treaty on European Union (as we saw in chapters 5 and 7) a central bankers' definition prevailed, and the definitions were very restrictive. By 1993 the cumulative effects of German unification, of the down-side of the economic cycle and of structural crisis highlighted to central banks, notably the Bundesbank, the long-term nature of the convergence objectives and the priority to domestic action to re-establish credibility.

The context of the birth of the hard ERM and of EMU was a period of substantial progress towards nominal convergence, progress that increased the optimism of both EMS policy makers and foreign exchange market operators about the prospects for EMU. Among indicators of convergence, inflation had pride of place, for historical reasons.[3] For the original ERM 'narrow band' countries dispersion around average inflation, as measured by standard deviation, fell from some 5 per cent in 1979 to 2 per cent in 1987, whilst the inflation rate itself tumbled from some 9 per cent to well under 2 per cent. Though the inflation rate then picked up to 3 per cent in 1990, the standard deviation declined further to 0.4. The standard deviation continued to be well under 1 per cent in 1992 and 1993. Though this narrowing was assisted by the increase of German inflation post-unification, it reflected a continuing impressive performance by the narrow band countries in nominal convergence.

A similar impressive performance of the narrow band countries was apparent in both short-term and long-term interest rate convergence, which narrowed appreciably between 1987 and 1991. Long-term interest rates were an important indicator of the expectations of market operators about which countries were likely to form an EMU. The Danish and French referenda and the ERM crisis of 1992 forced these rates apart even for the narrow band countries, with large increases in short-term rates required in Ireland, Denmark and France. Yet, by summer 1993 convergence had been re-established, with Dutch and then Belgian and French rates managing to edge

---

3. For the figures in this and the succeeding paragraphs see Committee of Governors of the Central Banks of the Member States of the European Economic Community, *Annual Report 1992* (Basle: BIS, April 1993).

beneath German rates. These fluctuations of 1992–3 were a measure of the new degree of uncertainty in the foreign exchange markets about the prospects for convergence among even the ERM narrow band countries.

With respect to inflation and interest rates, once Britain, Greece, Italy, Portugal and Spain are added to the analysis of convergence, the prospects look even less promising. Once they are incorporated, the standard deviation in inflation climbs to 2.5 per cent in 1987–9, to 3.4 per cent in 1990 and then declines to 2 per cent in 1992. Long-term interest rates in these countries (and Denmark) showed little positive expectation of convergence in short-term rates. Britain, Italy and Spain were, unsurprisingly, to be the principal targets of the foreign exchange market operators in 1992. Along with Portugal they had recorded the largest losses of intra-ERM competitiveness, expressed in unit labour costs, between 1987 and August 1992.

Although inflation and interest rates do at least allow us to differentiate two main groupings of EC countries with respect to convergence, fiscal deficits and public debt offered less consolation. By 1992 the budget deficit in the EC as a whole had increased to 5.3 per cent (3.6 for the narrow band countries). On the positive side, the dispersion in the scale of these deficits, as measured by standard deviation, was falling, from 3.9 in 1987–9 to 2.5 in 1992: and again it was much smaller for the narrow band countries (0.9 per cent in 1992). But prospects were ominous. Not only Italy but also Belgium and the Netherlands already had substantial debt ratio problems. With rising real interest rates and falling growth of GDP their debt positions, and everyone else's, threatened to deteriorate. As we have seen, the problem was not only a cyclical deterioration in fiscal deficits but also a large structural component in these deficits.

The perception that major structural reforms were required raised a further question about the will and capability of the EC member states to take the requisite fiscal measures to promote convergence to meet the Maastricht criteria. The effect was twofold: to raise the profile (though not necessarily the effectiveness) of the ECOFIN's surveillance of convergence programmes (the critique of the British convergence programme of July 1993 was an indicator of a tougher approach); and to raise a new debate in the EC and at national level about structural reforms to public spending programmes. Fiscal convergence had moved to the centre ground of the EMS and EMU policy process. The scale of the fiscal convergence problem was not, however, matched by new increments of authority and power for the EC to act resolutely in this area. The solution to this problem lay in domestic policy processes and in the capacity for budgetary and policy leadership and innovation at the national level. That capacity was not uniformly high.

But the question mark was not only about structural reforms to public spending programmes, but also about structural reforms to the EC economies to facilitate convergence via an increased capacity of economies to adapt to change and to reduce cost pressures. One new target singled out in the Delors's White Paper of 1993 was the stringency of labour market regulation which varies considerably: at its least restrictive in Britain, Denmark and Ireland, and its toughest in Greece, Italy, the Netherlands and Spain. Another was inefficiencies in the non-traded goods and service sectors where competitive pressures are generally less powerful and thus inflationary pressures at their greatest. Here the Committee of Central Bank Governors played an important agenda-setting role within the EMS and EMU policy process.[4] Nominal convergence seemed to require a great deal more 'institutional' convergence than had been provided for in the Treaty on European Union.

In at least one respect, however, institutional convergence was in evidence: towards the Bundesbank model of central bank independence. In 1993 the initiative was taken by Belgium, France and Spain. The intent was to demonstrate the will of the governments concerned both to ensure that inflation was beaten and to be prepared for EMU. In effect, they were tying themselves to the mast. Benign effects were anticipated in accelerating nominal convergence and in making stage two of EMU a significant step forward. The European Monetary Institute was likely to be a more influential and effective institution, the more of its constituent central banks were independent. With institutional convergence around central bank independence, and a consequent increase in the capability of the EMI, there was a prospect that in stage two of EMU the EMS and EMU policy process could gain greater authority *vis-à-vis* the foreign exchange markets.

Sound money policy ideas: new problems of economic consensus?

A question that arises is what, if anything, will be the combined effects of cyclical down-turn and structural crisis on the climate of economic ideas that has come to underpin the EMS and EMU policy process. Under their effects will consensus around sound money policies erode? In attempting to answer this large question, the answers to two smaller questions will be critical. Are the policy values and interests promoted by sound money likely to be on the political retreat? And are economic events and developments sustaining or undermining the basic theoretical argument at the heart of priority to sound money: that, in the long term, there is no trade-off between inflation and unemployment?

As we argued in chapter 7, the strength and durability of sound money ideas derives from the fact that they promote and protect the interests of savers: electorally, savers have a dominant position. Their interest in protecting the value of hard-gained assets gives powerful support to low inflation as a policy goal. In this respect, the dominance of sound money ideas seems secure. Its capture of the policy process at national levels has been linked to a secular decline in the rate of inflation from economic cycle to economic cycle since the mid-1970s. But the costs have been considerable, in terms of the interests of certain social groups and in terms of some definitions of public interest. Pay differentials and income disparities have widened; unemployment has been pushed to high levels; poverty and long-term unemployment have grown; and deep-seated problems of crime and juvenile delinquency have bred in a context of deprivation and alienation. They may not be the inevitable consequence of a 'properly functioning' economy; but they are linked to the reality of sound money policies in economies whose markets tend to adjust much more slowly and painfully than theory suggests.

In practice, the EMS and EMU policy process has been able to leave issues of equity and cohesion to other policy sectors and to continue its overriding commitment

---

4. On these issues see Committee of Governors, *Annual Report 1992*.

to economic stability. More directly challenging to it has been the question of whether the economic argument about output and employment has been sustained in practice. Here no definitive answer is possible. In one sense, the sound money argument seems to have been undermined: for, with successive economic cycles since the 1970s, unemployment has continued to rise as inflation has fallen. This development is unquestionably serious and in the long term not sustainable. But the proponents of sound money policies can still claim that their argument that there is no long-term trade-off between inflation and unemployment holds. Unemployment is rising because governments have failed, with the possible exception of the British, to implement the kind of 'supply-side' measures needed to increase employment. Indeed, the structural crisis of the early 1990s was attributed by sound money economists to structural rigidities, notably in labour markets; their agenda for supply-side reform was strengthened, not weakened.

Here at least was one initial condition of EMU that remained well intact. As we have seen, economic events had not succeeded in disproving the sound money argument about unemployment, and the domestic political interests supporting disinflation were powerful. To these factors must be added the impact of the foreign exchange markets. The market operators 'represented' the interests of savers, acting on their behalf, and were able to reward or penalize monetary authorities by redeploying their highly mobile assets. In so doing they were making a statement about the sound money credentials of those authorities. There was, in short, no easy escape from sound money policy ideas in a world of internationally mobile capital. The EMS and EMU policy process remained bound to the mast of sound money.

The problem of fading virtue: the German economy at the crossroads

The EMS and EMU policy process had been given strength of purpose and cohesion by a mutual recognition by the policy actors, shared with the foreign exchange markets, that it possessed an 'internal' model of virtue: Germany. It was crucial to the stability of the EMS and to the prospects for EMU that the dominant economy of the EC was also the most virtuous. This virtue was enshrined in a consistent record of below average inflation (from 1980/81 to 1985/86 price inflation was cut down to virtually zero); a long-standing current account surplus (which had been rising as a percentage of GDP since the 1950s); and the fact that the D-Mark was the only currency never to be devalued in either the ERM or the 'snake'. No currency in the EC was considered safer: as it was the statutory responsibility of the Bundesbank to 'safeguard the currency', it was the main institutional beneficiary. The Bundesbank emerged as the most reputable and credible actor in European monetary policy: linked to that reputation, the German model of central bank independence served as the model for other EC states that wished to achieve a similar reputation and credibility with the foreign exchange markets. Economists might point to 'the fading miracle' in Germany, with its relative growth performance in decline since 1960, but its external surplus and price stability attested to great reserves of strength.[5]

5. H. Giersch, K.-H. Paque and H. Schmieding, *The Fading Miracle: Four Decades of Market Economy in Germany* (Cambridge: Cambridge University Press, 1992).

Central to the strength and cohesion of the EMS and EMU policy process had always been the smooth operation and effective performance of the bargaining relationship between the German federal government and the Bundesbank. At the heart of that relationship had always been norms of mutual respect and reciprocity. The federal government was expected to respect the independence of the Bundesbank in fulfilling its statutory obligation to 'safeguard the currency'; the Bundesbank to respect the primacy of the federal government in international monetary issues and over exchange rates. Reciprocity meant that each would seek to avoid by its actions outcomes that would make it more difficult for the other to discharge its responsibilities. Within this framework the Bundesbank's policy making was governed by a clear set of criteria that related to its mission: money supply, inflation, long yields, the D-Mark's level against the dollar, the D-Mark's level against ERM currencies, and the Bonn budget deficit. In 1990 these norms were undermined, with serious adverse consequences not only for economic and monetary policy management in Germany but also for the EMS and EMU policy process. Economic considerations were subordinated to political exigencies.

The strength and cohesion of the EMS and EMU policy process was one of the great casualties of the mismanagement of German unification post-1989. In this respect the great 'watershed' event was not 9 November 1989, when the Berlin Wall was breached, but 6 February 1990, when Chancellor Helmut Kohl decided to offer 'immediate' German monetary union (in fact it took place on 1 July). This event took place in an atmosphere of mounting confrontation between the federal government and the Bundesbank: in effect, a rupture of the normal bargaining relation between the two, with long-lasting consequences. In January the president of the Bundesbank, Karl-Otto Pöhl, had described the idea of German monetary union as 'fantastic' and 'very unrealistic'.[6]

In what followed, the Bundesbank stuck to its priority: to uphold the stability of the D-Mark; the federal government responded to fears of mass migration westwards and calculated the best means of maximizing electoral advantage for its parties. The objectives of the federal government prevailed; the Bundesbank was faced with the daunting task of limiting the ensuing damage to the stability of the D-Mark; by summer 1993, the D-Mark was being dethroned from its *primus inter pares* position in the ERM.

After the federal government's unilateral decision to pursue German monetary union, the Bundesbank suffered further setbacks. Its advice on the conversion rate of East Marks into D-Marks (it proposed 2 to 1) was overruled in favour of 1 to 1 for smaller savings deposits and 1.8 to 1 for other financial assets. Two negative results followed: first, a huge revaluation of the East Mark took place, with a devastating effect on the competitiveness of east German firms and thus on unemployment (industrial production in eastern Germany fell by 50 per cent in 12 months), and second, German money supply was immediately increased by 15 per cent. The second setback came when, without full consultation with the Bundesbank, the federal government created the German Unity Fund to shift the huge borrowing requirement

---

6. D. Marsh, *The Bundesbank: The Bank that Rules Europe* (London: Heinemann, 1992), p. 208.

for east Germany outside the normal budgetary procedures. This event inaugurated an acceleration of the budget deficit that was to further compound the troubles of the Bundesbank. The decision to borrow to cover most of the initial costs of the huge transfers from west to east was seen as irresponsible by the Bundesbank. This was followed, in the view of the Bundesbank, by a third mistake. With the 1991 agreement among wage negotiators that they would pursue wage equalization between east and west by 1994, the competitiveness of east German companies was further undermined. The Bundesbank's sense of being beleaguered in its efforts to uphold the stability of the D-Mark increased.

The reality of German virtue was that it had never simply depended on the independence of the Bundesbank. German virtue was a 'three-legged' stool: the exercise of budgetary discipline by federal and state governments, not least to take pressure off interest rates; a sense of macro-economic responsibility in the system of collective bargaining, with particular regard to unit labour costs; and the independence of the Bundesbank in managing monetary policy. With German unification the first two of these legs ceased to be virtuous, and the Bundesbank was forced to shoulder an increasingly unmanageable burden. By June 1993 foreign exchange market operators, like George Soros, were looking to the prospect that, despite its valiant efforts, the Bundesbank might be defeated by the force of German unification.

The signs of loss of virtue had been apparent for some time, but, as is characteristic of foreign exchange markets, it took some time for new information – particularly when it challenges a strongly entrenched image – to be identified as a a new trend. Germany's trade surplus had disappeared; its inflation rate was the fifth highest in the EC; its deficit/GDP ratio was, at 7.5 per cent, one of the highest in the EC; its hourly labour costs were the highest in the world; and its true level of unemployment (incorporating those on short-time working and make-work schemes) was more than 13 per cent of the workforce. The prospects for an economic miracle seemed dim in eastern Germany, where labour cost more than in the United States and Japan and was more than ten times more expensive than in neighbouring east central European states. In other words, the traditional anchor currency of the ERM had accumulated deep-seated problems. With its competitiveness eroded, German economic fundamentals could no longer be judged sound. For the first time in the history of the ERM the question of a depreciation of the D-Mark came on to the agenda.

The combination of the loss of virtue with intensifying domestic recession put the Bundesbank in acute difficulties. Though happy to share the anchor role with other currencies, it feared that the inflationary effects of a depreciation of the D-Mark would undermine its pursuit of a stable D-Mark and, in the long-term, domestic compet-itiveness. The Bundesbank had, in other words, no intention of sacrificing its role as an anchor currency. A serious risk to that role could be translated into an appalling problem for the Bundesbank, which was conscious that D-Mark assets held by foreigners had increased threefold between 1980 and 1991: to more than DM1 trillion. In turn, if the D-Mark ceased to share in the anchor role, the effects on the ERM would be likely to be disastrous: no other EC economy had the international strength as a trading economy and no currency (or combination of them) the world status or liquidity to perform this role adequately. The deepening recession suggested a need to speed up the reduction of interest rates, a move that would ease pressures elsewhere in the EMS. But, with a stubbornly high growth of money supply, the Bundesbank feared that such a move would do more to stoke up inflation, still at more than 4 per cent, than create a sustained recovery.

In the wake of German unification a new factor of uncertainty had emerged at the centre of the EMS and EMU policy process. The focus of attention was not simply the Bundesbank's decisions but the capacity of the German economic policy establishment to put the three-legged stool of virtue back in place. In short, the onus for stabilizing the EMS and keeping EMU on track was as much on the federal government's budget process and the collective bargaining process as the Bundesbank council. By summer 1993 the prospects for the restitution of this three-legged stool were at best uncertain. There were some grounds for moderate optimism. The outcome of the IG Metall strike in May had reflected a more conciliatory and realistic spirit in collective bargaining; whilst the combined effect of new federal tax and spending measures was equivalent to 2 per cent of GDP in 1994 and an extra 1.2 per cent in 1995. But the question remained of whether these changes were too little, too late, and whether they could be implemented. Ominously, the guru of the foreign exchange markets, George Soros, was by June 1993 predicting that the Bundesbank was heading for defeat. The stability of the EMS and any remaining coherence of purpose about EMU was in danger of being severely tested in the foreign exchange markets. By summer 1993 the new problem was that the Bundesbank was having to prove itself to the foreign exchange markets.

But the mistakes consequent on German unification were not just domestic German mistakes with implications for the other bargaining relations in the EMS and EMU policy process. There were also mistakes within that policy process. Adjustment to the effects of German unification could have been facilitated by a revaluation of the D-Mark or its temporary flotation instead of, as occurred, by deflation throughout the EC, via higher interest rates. EC policy makers decided to 'harden' the ERM, despite German unification, without doing anything to make the system better able to bear the strain. The results were seen in the ERM crisis of 1992.

The problem of the foreign exchange markets

In the period of the design of EMU, from 1988 to 1991, the foreign exchange markets did not present the EMS and EMU policy process with any destabilizing crises. But a crucial part of the rationale of EMU was the recognition that a decisive shift was underway in the relative power of the EC monetary authorities and the foreign exchange markets; that the EC's own actions in pursuing the single market initiative had played a major role in bringing about that shift; and that EMU offered a means of reasserting power over these markets. Without EMU the possibilities for unmanageable and destabilizing speculation were larger than ever before.

The first watershed event was the EC agreement of 1988 to abolish exchange controls. With this decision the EC monetary authorities were pledged to abandon one of their traditional, central policy instruments for dealing with the markets. They were also subjecting themselves to the full force of huge financial flows. The second set of watershed events involved the economic mismanagement of German unification, the consequent need for drastic remedial action by the Bundesbank and the unsustainable effects of that action on many ERM members, notably Britain and Italy. Once the effects of German unification revealed serious problems of economic fundamentals in members of the ERM, the policy process began to be faced with avalanches of money that far exceeded the intervention mechanisms of the EMS.

The exits from the ERM and successive parity changes that were forced by the foreign exchange markets in 1992–3 had a decisive effect on the EMS and EMU process. It demarcated a group of inner-core countries, with hard currencies; a group of outer-core countries, with soft currencies (those who had been forced into devaluations); and a group, led by Britain, that was ejected from the heart of the process. In turn, this distinction threw into prominence the idea of a 'fast-track' to EMU for the inner core. As we saw in chapter 5, this proposal raised many problems, but its very presence conveyed the sense of an altered post-Maastricht agenda, rooted in the new conditions established by the crisis of September 1992. The idea of a long timescale for EMU in the context of a hard ERM regime was always deeply suspect; against the background of the spreading effects of German unification, an unfavourable economic background and liberalized international capital movements, it seemed untenable. After the September 1992 crisis, the repeated commitment by ECOFIN to the Maastricht timetable and conditions carried little conviction, in the foreign exchange markets or elsewhere. Stage two would require much greater institutional authority for the EMI to act in managing the EMS than the treaty had provided.

The problem of world currency relationships

The EMS and EMU policy process has always operated within the constraints that the EC currencies that fall within its fold are but a part of a wider international set of currency relationships; that these world currency relationships are subject to significant and sometimes spectacular changes, after the collapse of the Bretton Woods system; that US dollar movements in particular have large and asymmetrical effects on prices and output in ERM countries; and that, accordingly, the decisions of the EC monetary authorities are far from being the only ones that affect the functioning of the EMS and the prospects for EMU. The US Federal Reserve Bank and the Japanese Finance Ministry and the Bank of Japan are formidable actors in the global financial markets, whilst (as we saw in chapter 8) the US dollar remains the key currency in foreign exchange transactions. By contrast, the ECU lacks significance as a world currency.

Indeed (as we saw in chapters 4 and 5) the birth of the EMS and the relaunch of EMU were substantially motivated by internal EC perceptions of the vulnerability of 'small' currencies in world currency markets in which the dominant currency was being managed irresponsibly. In this respect the collapse of the dollar in 1977–8 and the ERM crisis of 1987 were watershed events for European monetary integration.

Given this continuing vulnerability of the EMS and EMU policy process, currency and monetary coordination in G-7 has been seen as crucial to the achievement of a world currency stabilization that would relieve external pressures on the EMS and EMU policy process and crucially underpin the stability of the EMS and the pursuit of EMU. In practice, however, the complex interdependence that characterizes economic and monetary policies and the management of world currency relationships has complex effects. It makes for a high level of sensitivity and vulnerability to each other's actions. But the sensitivity and vulnerability remains asymmetric, favouring the United States, and the result is as likely to be discord as cooperation.

As an expression of cooperation, the Louvre Accord of February 1987 was in this respect a useful part of the background to the securing of a hard ERM and to the launch of the EMU project. Its key operative part was that the US dollar, yen and D-mark should be held in unpublished bands. In this way G-7 succeeded in dampening swings in the dollar: in turn, more international currency stability reduced speculation in realignments of the ERM.

But, after 1990, the monetary policies of the United States, Japan and Germany diverged. The United States eased monetary policy, a process that reached its limit in the months preceding the ERM crisis of September 1992. Japan started to ease policy a year and a half after the United States and did so more lightly. In sharp contrast, however, the Bundesbank began a process of tightening monetary policy to rid Germany of the inflationary effects of German unification. This asymmetry of monetary policy measures had, by 1992, drastic effects on world currency relationships: with the dollar falling and the D-Mark rising. With their currencies tied to the D-Mark, the members of the ERM found that they were losing competitiveness to the United States and that their currencies were threatened by the general surge into the D-Mark. The result of divergence between American and German monetary policy was months of chaos in the ERM and an undermining of the competitiveness of the EC economy as a whole, a process that could be attributed to the EMS.

By the early 1990s G-7 monetary policy was still in disarray. This disarray reflected the fact that the interests of the main actors did not appear to coincide. After being mired in prolonged recession, the US Federal Reserve was determined to hold on to a policy of low interest rates. The Bundesbank was, by contrast, caught between fast-deepening recession and obdurately high inflation; its preference was, accordingly, for carefully measured reductions in interest rates. In the case of Japan, the continuing obsession with the security offered by a huge current account surplus made for monetary policy easing that was too late and too modest. The logjam was unlikely to be broken until the German federal government let the Bundesbank off the hook by large reductions in the budget deficit and the Japanese government reappraised the value of its external surplus. This process was also not helped by the difficulties that G-7 was having in helping to broker a GATT agreement under the Uruguay round.

G-7 was in effect another arena, outside the EMS policy process, in which pressure could be brought on the Bundesbank to ease interest rates. Such pressure was no more likely to be successful there than in the European Council, ECOFIN or the Franco-German Economic Council. The crucial problem was (as we indicated above) the other two legs of the German three-legged stool. But, in the absence of a domestic solution to this problem the EMS and EMU policy process could expect to continue to suffer from the absence of world currency stabilization.

This survey of the problems of the EMS and EMU policy process in the 1990s has pinpointed two watershed events that have helped to reshape its development, opening up new potential outcomes, possibly within and possibly outside the Maastricht framework. They are German unification in 1990 and the ERM crises of 1992 and 1993. In one sense the Maastricht solution appears secure. Ideologically, the consensus provided by sound money ideas seems likely to endure, supported by the political strength of savers and reinforced by structural crisis, in particular the deficit crisis. But in other senses the Maastricht solution is challenged: by the down-side of the economic cycle, compounded by the effects of structural crisis; by the loss of German virtue; by the increased power of the foreign exchange markets; by the lack of stability in world currency relationships; and by a sense of a legitimacy crisis about European union at the heart of the EC, not least in relation to EMU itself. In drawing up the balance sheet it is more than tempting to conclude that EMU is doomed and the EMS highly fragile.

But such a conclusion would be both premature and partial. In assessing the prospects for the EMS and EMU one needs to focus not only on the problems that confront the policy process but also on the robustness of the policy process itself. For, in investigating the conditions for a transition to EMU, we need to recognize that the quality of the policy process is a vital condition. The crucial difference between earlier international monetary regimes and the EMS lies not in specific rules and policy instruments but in the qualitatively more sophisticated institutional context of the EC and of the EMS and EMU policy process. At the heart of the gold standard regimes and of the Bretton Woods system was nothing remotely equivalent: no element of supranationalism, no such scale of 'flanking' sectoral policy integration and not the same intensity of repetitive bargaining. There was no real equivalence to the complex set of interdependent bargaining relations on which the EMS and EMU policy process rested, and with which we have been concerned in this book. In assessing the prospects for the EMS and EMU it is important to retain a respect for the importance of institutional rules of the game and for the self-reinforcing character that they give to change. It is a particular fault of analyses by academic economists of the robustness of the EMS and of the prospects for EMU that they tend to overlook or underestimate this point.

Prospects for the EMS and EMU in the 1990s

In moving on to consider prospects we are necessarily forced to be tentative. There are various scenarios, each plausible if certain assumptions hold. But, as we shall argue here, some scenarios are more plausible than others: and what might happen may very well be shaped by events and conditions that we cannot now predict and therefore fall outside these scenarios. Three main scenarios will be considered, two of which do not lead to EMU: a 'renationalization' of policies; a process of *de facto* integration in an extended D-Mark zone; and a process of completing EMU.

A 'renationalization' of policies

One scenario involves the unwinding of the EMS and EMU policy process under the pressure of unsustainable conditions and accumulating adverse events and crises. Renationalization means one or both of two things: reclaiming domestic control of exchange rates, and thus the capacity to use the exchange rate as a policy instrument for economic adjustment; and reneging on the commitment to denationalize economic and monetary policies in an EMU.

In this scenario the costs of sticking to the disciplines of the ERM become too great in the vortex of pressures created by German unification, the loss of German virtue, the down-side of the economic cycle and structural crisis. The will to sustain monetary integration and union cannot be sustained as the capability to abide by the disciplines is eroded. The agents of destruction are the foreign exchange markets, which come to judge the mismatch between economic fundamentals and the ERM's requirements as unsustainable, or domestic party revolt and electoral threat: or a combination of the two. The exit of the British pound from the ERM is seen as a precedent for this process: for renationalizing exchange-rate policy. Obversely, the British and Danish 'opt-outs' from stage three of EMU, and the German adoption of an 'opt-in', reflect a desire to retain control over the process of the denationalization of monetary policy in general.

In certain circumstances there are strong short-term grounds for renationalizing policy. These circumstances are captured in the so-called Walters effect, namely, that when exchange rates are pegged among economies that are behaving differently (say, one with an inflation problem and another without), interest rate changes will not bear a clear relation to domestic economic needs.[7] By allowing the exchange rate to cushion some of the costs of adjustment, it is possible to tailor interest rates to these domestic needs. The argument that one is fulfilling one's international responsibilities by first putting one's own house in order has an obvious appeal and truth to it.

The problem with the scenario of renationalization when applied within the EC is that it ignores some elementary economic and political realities. In the first place, arguments for renationalization have to be set against the potentially high price to be paid for uncoordinated exchange rates in a highly interdependent trading and financial system like the EC. The use of devaluation as part of a package of measures to restore lost competitiveness may be desirable. But its virtues are restricted once the perception takes root that 'competitive' devaluation is being attempted; that a country is using exchange rate adjustment to create a competitive advantage. In so interdependent and open a trading and financial area as the EC a country is simply too sensitive and vulnerable to retaliatory action for such a policy measure to make sense. The consequence of competitive devaluation would also be to send risky signals to labour markets and to foreign exchange markets, and to erode the stable framework that is needed to underpin domestic structural reform. There are two possibilities for a renationalized exchange rate policy: that it begins to 'shadow' the ERM, staying within carefully defined limits and therefore not having so wide a scope for domestic policy action; or that it floats and is exposed to the greater vulnerability of 'floating' currencies to speculative runs, with consequent serious disruptions to its external trade.[8] By 1993 the British government had shown no sign of opting for a strategy of competitive devaluation.

Politically, advocacy of renationalization of economic and monetary policies, other than as a short-term measure of expediency, ignores the institutional realities of the European Community. This institution commits its members to the single market and

7. A. Walters, *Sterling in Danger: The Economic Consequences of Pegged Exchange Rates* (London: Collins with the Institute of Economic Affairs, 1990).
8. On the point that the impact of speculation increases, the more that currencies fluctuate, see the guru of the foreign exchange markets, G. Soros, *The Alchemy of Finance* (New York: Simon & Schuster, 1987).

to union: to fostering a pattern of trade interdependency and economic convergence that leads to 'ever closer union'. Here is a set of purposes that provide a standard by which the behaviour of national political actors can be evaluated. Informally, the institutional realities of repetitive bargaining in the two-level decision process of the EC reinforce this standard: in a context in which reputation and reliability with EC colleagues come to be highly valued by national policy actors.

In one scenario, other EC states might well take advantage of renationalization of economic and monetary policies as a short-term expediency, as Britain and Italy did in 1992. But institutional realities and economic realities of trade interdependence and shared vulnerability in global financial markets are likely to sustain their ambition for union, at least outside Britain and Denmark. According to another scenario, two factors will determine the fate of EC economic and monetary policies during the 1990s: a continuing mismatch between economic fundamentals and the requirements of the ERM, with foreign exchange markets forcing states to exit from the system, perhaps repeatedly (as earlier with the 'snake'); and a superior economic performance by those states that have exited, with Britain perhaps creating a counter-model to the ERM and EMU.

What happens will be influenced in part by institutional realities and the realities of trade interdependence and vulnerability in global currency markets, and in part by the perceived outcomes of economic policies and how these are evaluated in financial markets and in the political market-place. Policy is caught up in this vortex of pressures, capable of spinning on towards union or back to national self-determination.

An extended D-Mark zone

As we have seen, the EMS evolved *de facto* as a D-Mark zone, in the sense that the D-Mark became the anchor of the ERM; we have examined the reasons why this occurred and what it meant for the special role of the Bundesbank in the EMS and EMU policy process. One obvious scenario is continuity: with the role of the D-Mark extended as the EC extends eastwards, and with the Bundesbank consolidating its power as the central actor within the EMS and EMU policy process. In this scenario, EMU would not in fact be seriously on the agenda: if it were, then its politics would be determined by the preference of the Bundesbank that a single European currency should be the D-Mark.

The central question hanging over the scenario of an extended D-Mark zone is the likely fate of the German economy as it seeks to grapple with the huge problems of unification. We have noted how Germany's unification problems were exacerbated by policy errors in Bonn, principally the government's underestimation of the hurdles facing economic recovery in the east and its consequent failure to prepare in a timely way the people of western Germany to share the burdens of unification. In the short term, the effects on prospects for EMU were negative. As former Chancellor Helmut Schmidt predicted, EMU was not going to happen until German unification had been brought to a successful conclusion.[9] Germany was too unsettled a country to play a

9. H. Schmidt, *Handeln für Deutschland* (Berlin: Rowohlt, 1993).

leadership role in this process: in any case, by default of the federal government, any leadership role had passed to a Bundesbank that was unsympathetic to EMU.

In the medium to long term, the question of the fate of the German economy was more difficult to answer. One scenario involves Germany's economic fundamentals becoming incompatible with the continuance of its anchor role in the ERM. In that case the EMS has no real future as an extended D-Mark zone; a crisis-prone Germany would not be able to meet the convergence criteria of Maastricht, and the EC's member states would be faced with the option of either renationalizing economic and monetary policies or launching a new initiative.

Another scenario foresees several years of difficulties for the German economy but of difficulties that are manageable. How this scenario unfolds depends on how the difficulties are managed. If they are made manageable by the decisive action of the Bundesbank, its capacity to evolve the EMS into an extended D-Mark zone and to block EMU except on its own stringent terms will be almost unassailable. The reputation of the Bundesbank would if anything be enhanced, at the expense of the federal government, and the German economy's role in the EC and the wider Europe would be even more considerable. But, if the federal government proves capable of seizing the initiative in tackling the problems of the German economy, the outcome could be different. Then the impact of the Chancellor and of the Foreign Ministry in the German federal government–Bundesbank bargaining relationship could be more considerable, and, of course, they are part of the Council bargaining relationship with its capacity to take on issues of 'high' politics, like European union. So how a successful management of German unification affects the EMS and EMU policy process depends on *whose* reputation benefits most from this process. By mid-1993, despite the announcement of new huge measures to tackle the German budget deficit, it remained unclear whether the federal government would be able to restore its credibility in this fashion.

The realization of EMU

Beleaguered as the EMS and EMU policy process was after June 1992, the institutional commitment and even momentum towards EMU remained. A succession of political and economic reversals showed that this commitment was not paper-thin and that the momentum represented more than the good wind of fortune playing on the EC. The EMS and EMU policy process was revealed to be institutionally robust to continue steering its course.

With ratification of the Treaty on European Union, the EC was in effect 'constitutionalizing' EMU: such a process and outcome was bound to be influential in its own right in structuring policy choices. But the question remained of just how flexible in strategy and tactics the EMS and EMU policy process would be in accommodating the political and economic difficulties ahead. There were three possible scenarios, in ascending order of flexibility. The first involved completion of EMU on the terms, and according to the timetable, outlined in the Treaty on European Union. This scenario is the one to which the EC and the European Commission is committed. If the assumption holds that EC policy actors believe that treaties and legal texts matter, the Treaty on European Union will retain a firm hold on the minds of those involved in the EMS and EMU policy process: a hold reinforced by the repetitive bargaining at the heart of the policy process.

Should the economic and political difficulties mount, the EMS and EMU policy process could reconstruct the process of realizing EMU by developing stage two and the role of the EMI in a new manner but within the letter and spirit of the Treaty on European Union. One possibility is that the EMI could evolve as a much more authoritative institution as the number of independent and semi-independent central banks grows. Another is an agreement among a group of core ERM states to coordinate monetary policy even more closely: in effect, it would be to monetary union what the Schengen Agreement is to the free movement of people.[10]

A more radical step would involve a new fast-track to EMU, agreed as an alternative to a Treaty on European Union that was perceived as too flawed to serve as an adequate guide to action. The rationale is provided by the argument that the treaty's stage two is too long, impossible to operationalize (e.g. in relationship to no realignments) and an invitation to embarrassing failure. Political authority *vis-à-vis* the foreign exchange markets could be re-established only by decisive action by a small group of the hard currency countries at the core of the ERM. Its problem as a scenario is that it would require French acceptance of a German-led approach to EMU, for such a grouping would comprise a group of small states interlocked very closely with the German economy and France. It would also require a very bold act of federal political leadership and defiance of the Bundesbank.

Elusive union: a policy process caught between a 'self-reinforcing' institutional mechanism and political and market uncertainties

Since 1990 new events and new conditions have intervened to influence the nature and development of the EMS and EMU policy process and to cast serious doubt on its capacity to confront and influence the main forces at work: the abolition of exchange controls, German unification, cyclical down-turn and structural crisis, destabilization of world currency relationships and the ERM crises of 1992 and 1993. New stresses and conflicts have, as a consequence, been generated in the bargaining relationships that comprise the policy process: it is tempting to conclude that the EMS and EMU are so plagued by randomness that the prospects of the first for survival and of the second for realization are close to nil. The EMS and EMU policy process appears to be locked into the economic policy outcomes associated with its policies: vulnerable to mounting criticisms of the costs of competitive disinflation and to countries that have exited from the ERM emerging as economic counter-models.

But, in correctly identifying the EMS and EMU policy process as dynamic rather than structurally determined, we should not lose sight of the crucial fact that in dynamic policy processes randomness and order are merged. The element of underlying order needs to be retrieved from the flux of events and changes of conditions. That order is provided, first and foremost, by institutional rules of the game, as chapter 6 emphasized: by the quality of the policy process itself. In the case

10. See the Commissariat Général du Plan, *A French Perspective on EMU* (Paris: Centre d'Etudes Prospectives et d'Informations Internationales, February 1993); G. Bishop, *Is There a Rapid Route to an EMU of the Few?* (London: Salomon Brothers, May 1993).

of the EMS and EMU policy process those rules have depth: they are the elaborate rules and interactions special to the policy process itself, and that structure the bargaining relations involved; and they are the underlying features of the EC as an institution, on which it rests and from which it springs. The EC has itself rested on initial conditions, and reinforced those conditions, in ways that give an underlying momentum to the EMS and EMU: in particular, increasing trade interdependence, the idea of a single market and the idea of a decision-making process that irons out asymmetries of national power and enhances not only prosperity but also security. These conditions, and the rules of the game that they have generated, serve to sustain the EMS and EMU, even in the face of a harsher political and economic climate. They mean that the EMS and EMU has the attributes of a self-reinforcing mechanism, to a far greater extent than was ever true of the gold standard regimes and of the Bretton Woods system.

An underlying theme of this book has been that institutions have, pre-eminently, a political rationale: moreover, one that evolves over time. Consistent with this theme stress has been placed on the limitations of economic explanations of the EMS and EMU policy process and, in this chapter, of the capacity of economists to use economic analysis to clarify the prospects for EMU. Though the capture of the EMS and EMU policy process by sound money ideas was important in binding its actors together into a policy community, economic beliefs and arguments were always secondary to political beliefs and arguments: both in 1978–9 at its birth and in 1987–91. Arguments about the ineffectiveness and weakness of EC states in world currency markets and about national interest and power within the EC were always more decisive: with economic arguments being deployed to serve political purposes rather than driving forward the EMS and EMU. In the 1990s political beliefs are likely to continue to be the most potent factor: to the extent that they are locked into enduring external pressures and historically conditioned learning likely to prove resilient, even to the dynamics of economic policy performance.

But the most potent threats to EMU come from political and market uncertainties. They give union its elusive quality: summed up in its lack of effective control over the effects of German unification and internal developments in Germany, the down-side of the economic cycle, structural crisis, world currency relationships and foreign exchange market operators. We have noted, as a central characteristic of the two-level policy process, and reflecting the hollow core in the EMU policy process, that key policy actors tend to see the EMS and EMU in terms of their own agendas rather than as issues in their own right, and the technical weaknesses that result, for instance in conducting realignments. To the political problem of domestic agendas must be added a core political problem of the Maastricht process: that its implementation depends on the cooperation of an institution, the Bundesbank, that cannot have a corporate self-interest in ceding its pre-eminent position. Here is a central political paradox that casts a deep shadow over the prospects for EMU.

But, among the political uncertainties, the crisis of legitimacy is not to be underestimated. With all its institutional resilience, the EMS and EMU policy process is vulnerable to its failure to grasp that money is far more than a technical commodity. It is infused with cultural and political symbolism. As the ratification difficulties of the Treaty on European Union underlined, the EC had not as yet acquired such symbolism in the hearts and minds of the new citizens of the Union. For reasons of superior economic logic they were being presented with a radical rather than an evolutionary approach to EMU. There was no process by which citizens could gain some practical experience of the benefits of a common currency, an approach better adapted to overcoming political problems. Here, to a greater extent than anywhere else, was the Achilles' heel of EMU after treaty ratification. Its damage could be inflicted through national party, parliamentary and electoral channels, and was likely to feature in the history of EMU in the 1990s.

The threat of market uncertainty remains potent because of the seepage of power from the EC monetary authorities to the foreign exchange markets, a seepage that was analysed and evaluated in chapter 8. How this threat materializes depends on the will and capability of EC governments and monetary authorities to match economic fundamentals to the requirements of the ERM and EMU. German unification, the cyclical down-turn and structural crisis will combine to test this will and capability much more severely in the 1990s, with effects that are impossible to predict. As the consequent stresses, strains and policy conflicts in the EMS and EMU policy process mount, the most likely effect will be a new flexibility about the route to EMU: flexibility in adapting stage two, perhaps even in agreeing a 'monetary Schengen' or even a new fast-track initiative. A more short-term effect could well be a renationalization of policy, but most likely on a temporary basis for the large majority of states. It is much more likely that the EMS and EMU policy process will be sustained by the recognition of national policy actors that collective action, and eventual union, offered a superior means of reasserting control over foreign exchange markets and world currency relationships than a return to national action.

Caught between political and market uncertainties and self-reinforcing institutional mechanisms, and characterized by the hollow core at its heart, EMU looked likely to retain an elusive, even tragic quality: firmly, indeed irrevocably, on the agenda, but trapped in deep-seated strategic and tactical difficulties. With the EC's authority in fiscal coordination limited to exhortation and persuasion, and its miniscule role as a fiscal transfer mechanism, the capacity of the EMU policy process to deal with structural problems of adjustment was minimal. Devaluation and labour mobility provided two other classic instruments of adjustment, but (as we saw in chapter 7) they too offer little, if anything – competitive devaluation is ruled out, and cultural and linguistic barriers to labour mobility are high. The institutional centre of gravity in the EMS and EMU policy process is provided by monetary policy coordination and a central bankers' culture. Here was in effect the line of least resistance in economic and monetary policy coordination. Consequently, consistent with the sound money ethos of this culture, emphasis is placed on downward adjustment of costs and on structural reform of labour markets and of the 'non-traded' goods and service sectors for this purpose. The result is the prospect of a radical general change in the political and policy culture of the EC, in part signalled by the shift towards labour market deregulation in the Delors's White Paper on Competitiveness, Growth and Employment of December 1993.

When and if it comes, EMU will be a watershed event for the EC; meanwhile, it represented a watershed process, challenging inherited policy agendas and political ideologies across the EC. With it sound money and structural reform had come fully into their own at the level of the EC, their consequences radiating outwards across EC policy sectors and reshaping national policy debates in countries like Belgium and Spain. More fundamentally still, the resolve to pursue EMU brought forth a new debate on the constitutional and political basis of the new European Union. The 1990s are likely to further underline the point that constitutional and political debate about the EU and EMU stand in a mutually stimulating relation to each other: that technical arguments about EMU can give momentum to constitutional and political arguments, but will in turn find themselves circumscribed and channelled by constitutional and political arguments.

Index